MOSHE DAYAN

In this major reevaluation of Moshe Dayan's life and career, Eitan Shamir examines one of the most influential individuals in the history of modern Israel. As Israeli Defense Forces Chief of Staff, theater commander during the Sinai campaign, and defense minister during the Six-Day and Yom Kippur Wars, Dayan shaped Israeli history as well as the principles of Israel's security and foreign affairs. Eitan Shamir explores the basis and justification for Dayan's reputation as a strategist and what made his command and leadership unique. He reveals the ways in which Moshe Dayan led and planned his campaigns, how he made his decisions, and his style as a general and a strategist. His findings shed important new light on broader issues of military command and culture, political–military relations, insurgency and counterinsurgency, and the relations between small states and large powers, drawing lasting lessons for strategy today.

EITAN SHAMIR is a professor in the Political Studies Department at Bar-Ilan University and serves as the Managing Director of the Begin Sadat Center for Strategic Studies (BESA Center). He is the author, with Edward Luttwak, of *The Art of Military Innovation: Lessons from the Israel Defense Forces*.

Cambridge Military Histories

Edited by

GREGORY A. DADDIS, USS Midway Chair in Modern US Military History and Director of the Center for War and Society, San Diego State University

HEW STRACHAN, Professor of International Relations, University of St Andrews and Emeritus Fellow of All Souls College, Oxford

GEOFFREY WAWRO, Professor of Military History and Director of the Military History Center, University of North Texas

The aim of this series is to publish outstanding works of research on warfare throughout the ages and throughout the world. Books in the series take a broad approach to military history, examining war in all its military, strategic, political and economic aspects. The series complements *Studies in the Social and Cultural History of Modern Warfare* by focusing on the 'hard' military history of armies, tactics, strategy and warfare. Books in the series consist mainly of single author works – academically rigorous and groundbreaking – which are accessible to both academics and the interested general reader.

A full list of titles in the series can be found at:

www.cambridge.org/militaryhistories

MOSHE DAYAN

The Making of a Strategist

EITAN SHAMIR
Bar-Ilan University

Shaftesbury Road, Cambridge CB2 8EA, United Kingdom

One Liberty Plaza, 20th Floor, New York, NY 10006, USA

477 Williamstown Road, Port Melbourne, VIC 3207, Australia

314–321, 3rd Floor, Plot 3, Splendor Forum, Jasola District Centre,
New Delhi – 110025, India

103 Penang Road, #05–06/07, Visioncrest Commercial, Singapore 238467

Cambridge University Press is part of Cambridge University Press & Assessment,
a department of the University of Cambridge.

We share the University's mission to contribute to society through the pursuit of
education, learning and research at the highest international levels of excellence.

www.cambridge.org
Information on this title: www.cambridge.org/9781316515822

DOI: 10.1017/9781009026697

© Eitan Shamir 2025

This publication is in copyright. Subject to statutory exception and to the provisions
of relevant collective licensing agreements, no reproduction of any part may take
place without the written permission of Cambridge University Press & Assessment.

When citing this work, please include a reference to the DOI 10.1017/9781009026697

First published 2025

A catalogue record for this publication is available from the British Library

A Cataloging-in-Publication data record for this book is available from the Library of Congress

ISBN 978-1-316-51582-2 Hardback
ISBN 978-1-009-01173-0 Paperback

Cambridge University Press & Assessment has no responsibility for the persistence
or accuracy of URLs for external or third-party internet websites referred to in this
publication and does not guarantee that any content on such websites is, or will remain,
accurate or appropriate.

CONTENTS

List of Figures   *page* vi
List of Maps   vii
Acknowledgments   viii

Introduction   1

1   The Education of a Strategist   21

2   From Tactical Command to Political Negotiator: The War of Independence   48

3   Generalship   90

4   Theater Commander: The Sinai Campaign   136

5   "The Minister of Victory": The Six-Day War   194

6   Minister of the Palestinian Territories   237

7   The War of Attrition: Fighting Egyptians and Soviets   260

8   The God Who Failed   296

9   The Turning Point   339

10   The Dealmaker: Peace with Egypt   376

11   The Development of a Strategist   419

Index   441

FIGURES

1.1 Moshe Dayan (left) in Kibbutz Hanita with Yitzhak Sadeh and Yigal Allon, 1938. *page* 32
2.1 Dayan with members of the Israeli–Egyptian mixed Armistice commission, 1950. 88
3.1 Chief of Staff Moshe Dayan with Major Ariel Sharon (standing left of Dayan), Major General Assaf Simhoni (standing last on Dayan's left), and paratroopers' officers, 1955. 118
3.2 Dayan receives the National Order of the Legion of Honor, 1954. 124
4.1 Dayan's Sinai campaign plan on a pack of cigarettes, 1956. 156
4.2 Sinai Campaign 1956, General Moshe Dayan with Colonel Ariel Sharon. 170
5.1 Israeli Minister of Defense Moshe Dayan marching toward the captured wailing wall with IDF Chief of Staff Yitzhak Rabin (right), and General Uzi Narkiss, Commander of Central Command. 195
5.2 July 6, 1967, UN General Bull meeting Moshe Dayan to discuss posting UN observers along the Suez Canal. 230
6.1 Moshe Dayan in Vietnam with a US Army patrol, 1966. 242
6.2 Minister of Defense Moshe Dayan in conversation with a Palestinian in Hebron. 251
7.1 Minister of Defense Moshe Dayan, Suez Canal, War of Attrition, June 1970. 275
8.1 Minister of Defense Moshe Dayan with General Haim Barlev (center) and General Avraham Adan and General Ariel Sharon (head bandaged): Consultation near the Egyptian front. 322
9.1 Minister of Defense Moshe Dayan and General Ariel Sharon next to the Suez Canal, October 1973. 347
9.2 Minister of Defense Moshe Dayan with US Secretary of State Henry Kissinger, January 1974. 360
10.1 US President Jimmy Carter tours Gettysburg battlefield with leaders of Israel and Egypt. 394
10.2 Israeli Foreign Minister Moshe Dayan (left) and Egyptian President Anwar Al Sadat at Camp David, September 1978. 399
10.3 Israel's Foreign Minister Moshe Dayan, US President Jimmy Carter, and Israel's Prime Minister Menachem Begin. 405

MAPS

2.1 War of Independence (1948): "Dani Operation."   *page 62*
4.1 Sinai Campaign (1956).   173
5.1 The Six-Day War (1967): The Sinai Peninsula region.   217
5.2 The Six-Day War (1967): Judea and Samaria (West Bank) and the Golan Heights region.   231
7.1 The Bar-Lev Line.   269
8.1 Yom Kippur War (Oct. 1973): The peak of the Syrian attack on the Golan Heights.   324
8.2 Yom Kippur War (Oct. 1973): The IDF enclave in Syrian territory.   337
9.1 Yom Kippur War (Oct. 1973): Encirclement of the Egyptian Third Army.   352

ACKNOWLEDGMENTS

This book could not have been written without the generous help of many who played important roles in completing it.

I had just completed an article about Moshe Dayan when, by a twist of fate, I met Professor Uzi Rabi, the director of the Dayan Center, who mentioned an interesting-sounding Center project – a large-scale, up-to-date study of Dayan. In light of the many new studies and archival materials related to Dayan's work, released only over the last decade, the members of the Center's Executive Committee, led by Dr. Zalman Shoval, Dr. Yosef Chechanover, and Professor Rabi, wanted to pursue such a study, focusing particularly on Dayan's generalship and statesmanship. I want to extend my deepest gratitude to them for their trust and support throughout the long, arduous journey of researching and writing this book.

In particular, I would like to thank Dr. Zalman Shoval, who always made himself available to answer questions and assist with requests. He shared many important insights from the time he worked side by side with Dayan. Likewise, thanks are extended to Professor Rabi, who, in addition to giving me wonderful advice, always provided words of encouragement and guidance in crises. The dedicated staff members of the Dayan Center were invaluable in always being willing and able to lend me a helping hand.

Profound gratitude goes to fellow military historians Dr. Yagil Henkin and Dr. Zeev Elron from the Israeli Defense Force (IDF) History Department, who helped me greatly in writing about Dayan as Chief of Staff in the 1950s. The chapters about the Yom Kippur War were the most complex to compose, but I was most fortunate to enjoy the assistance of the best scholars of that time in Israel and abroad: Dr. Eado Hecht of the IDF Staff and Command College spent many hours explaining the IDF's military plans on the eve of the 1973 war; Dr. Shimon Golan helped me tremendously with long conversations that attempted to understand the order of events and the relationships within the High Command and between the military and political echelons; Professor Uri Bar-Yosef gave generously of his time to provide a detailed explanation of the background to the war and the intelligence failure; and Dr. Hagai Tzoref of the State Archive completed the picture with regard to the civilian leadership and the talks with Egypt before the war.

I was also fortunate to benefit from the many insights of Professor Martin van Creveld, who wrote an excellent study about Moshe Dayan about fifteen years ago, which unfortunately was published only in English. Strategy expert Dr. Edward Luttwak, with whom I worked on a different project, shared with me many observations as well as the content of several conversations he had with Dayan himself.

My uncle, Professor Shimon Shamir, is also a renowned historian of Egypt who had the opportunity to meet with important leaders from both sides of the conflict. From conversations with him, I learned a great deal about the spirit of the times and the personalities of the various leaders, especially Anwar al-Sadat, the leader of Egypt, who was first Dayan's adversary in 1973 and later the person with whom he conducted peace talks.

In addition to the assistance I received from scholars and researchers in academia, I was also helped by many people who knew Dayan personally and worked with him. Justice Elyakim Rubinstein, who was Dayan's legal advisor when he served as foreign minister and played an important role at Camp David, was kind enough to meet with me several times. The contribution of Neora Barnoach-Matalon, Dayan's secretary when he was Chief of Staff and a family friend for many years, was invaluable, as she shared many personal stories, anecdotes, and insights. Her door was always open to me; I was never made to feel I was imposing on her. She was available at all times for all matters, and I only hope I've made the best of the knowledge she so graciously lent.

Members of Dayan's family met with me to shed light on his life from a personal perspective and to share family materials. I would like to thank the late Ruth Dayan, Yael Dayan, and Lior Dayan for opening a window onto Dayan's personal life.

Documentary filmmaker Anat Goren produced an outstanding series about the Dayan family. Ms. Goren very generously shared knowledge and materials she collected while making the series that she felt could benefit this book.

My colleagues in the Political Science Department at Bar-Ilan University were a source of great strength and encouragement, especially Professor Rami Ginat, who was then Department Chair, himself a historian of modern Egypt. Our talks were another important source of knowledge, and he referred me to several contemporary research findings on the subject of Egypt and Soviet involvement in Egypt.

The writing of this book was preceded by several publications in peer-reviewed journals, including the *Journal of Strategic Studies* and *Intelligence and National Security*. While the content of this book differs from those previous articles, as the material has been updated and restructured in various ways, I wish to express my gratitude to these journals for publishing earlier versions of my ideas on the topic.[1]

In producing this book, several people worked tirelessly behind the scenes. Without their contribution, the final outcome would not have been possible. I was most fortunate to have had Revital Yerushalmi as research assistant; for her, no task was to difficult to fulfill. She devoted all her energy to ensuring the progress of this work. With unfailing patience, she located materials in archives and libraries and took meticulous notes. Above all, she was an incredible companion and true friend on this long journey.

The manuscript of this book was written in Hebrew. I was fortunate to have had the first-rate help of Susann Codish, translator, and Susan Doron, editor, of Academic Language Experts. With exemplary teamwork, they made my work available to the English-reading audience. I am most grateful to the Israel Science Foundation for its support in making the translating and editing work possible. My editor at Cambridge University Press, Michael Watson, offered invaluable professional support and advice, which played a crucial role in ensuring the successful completion of the book.

My beloved family was always there to cheer me on with unflagging optimism and support. My wife, Carmela Shamir, read the manuscript and provided valuable feedback. She and our children – Ella, Ido, and Yael – were a source of motivation and comfort, helping me to overcome even the biggest challenges. This book is lovingly dedicated to them.

---

[1] For Chapters 7 and 8: Portions of these chapters expand upon Eitan Shamir, "Moshe Dayan in the Yom Kippur War: a Reassessment", Intelligence and National Security, 36:7 (July 2021), pp. 1035–1052. https://doi.org/10.1080/02684527.2021.1946954.

For Chapter 11 (pp. 423–434): This section incorporates ideas and selected excerpts from Eitan Shamir, "How Leaders Exercise Emergent Strategy? Lessons from Moshe Dayan" Journal of Strategic Studies, 46:2 (August 2021) pp. 269–292. https://doi.org/10.1080/01402390.2021.1960163.

With thanks to Taylor & Francis for kind permission (https://www.tandfonline.com).

Introduction

A few years ago, Professor Uzi Rabi, the director of the Dayan Center at Tel Aviv University, invited me to join him at a meeting with a senior British political figure. Although this was during the Arab Spring, the guest had a request unrelated to current affairs: He wanted to hear a lecture about Moshe Dayan from an Israeli scholar. Rabi, knowing I had spent time researching Moshe Dayan, asked me to brief the guest. At the end of a short lecture and brief question-and-answer period, I was bold enough to ask our guest, surrounded by a large entourage, why he was so interested in Dayan. "Granted, he's a historic figure," I said, "but your itinerary is busy and surely you have more burning issues to deal with during your visit to Israel."

He answered:

> Long ago, when I was a young student in a seminar at Oxford, we were asked to select a military leader we considered one of the best of the twentieth century, present that leader in class, and justify our selection. I picked Moshe Dayan, a choice that aroused heated debate among the students. I therefore wanted to take advantage of this opportunity to hear the opinion of an Israeli scholar familiar with Dayan, who, from the time I was young, has always fascinated me.

This anecdote is but one example of the extent to which Moshe Dayan has aroused the interest of scholars and politicians and fired their imaginations to this day. Although many years have passed since his death, this fascination continues, not only in Israel, but throughout the world.

This book explores various aspects of Moshe Dayan, one of the most influential individuals in the history of Israel's first decades of existence as a modern state. At the same time, Dayan is also one of Israel's most controversial historic figures, although even his fiercest critics would not deny his profound impact on Israel's development. In fact, Dayan's story is the story of the state of Israel and of Zionism. To a large extent, his personal achievements, along with his lowest points, correspond to Israel's accomplishments and failures during the state's first three decades. While never prime minister, as chief of staff, defense minister, and foreign minister, Dayan shaped the principles of Israel's security and foreign affairs policies on an array of key issues, most still relevant to this day.

This work is not just another biography of Moshe Dayan. The many biographies about him can fill several shelves.[1] Dayan himself wrote much, including a detailed autobiography and other books.[2] Family members and long-time close associates also wrote about him, adding further dimensions to our understanding of his personality and personal philosophy.[3] One work even attempts to psychoanalyze Dayan, in order to fathom the secret of his charm and the motivations for his actions.[4]

What distinguishes this book is its focus on Dayan as a strategist, seeking to understand his way of thinking through the prism of theory and practice. Because Dayan dealt with strategy for most of his life and operated on the strategic level as both a military leader and a statesman, examining his decisions and actions through the strategic dimension and the corresponding theory can demystify the man and provide insight into his character and his actions.

Dayan's public image changed considerably over the years, due chiefly to the Yom Kippur War, in which Dayan played a central role, and the criticism of Israel's leadership and conduct during it. But, above all, the change in public perception about Dayan reflects the changes in Israeli society's values. Dayan wasn't merely another soldier or politician: He was the very embodiment of the sabra – the new Jew emerging in his own land, self-made, holding a hoe in one hand and a rifle in the other. A no-nonsense man lacking conventional

---

[1] Some biographies written about Moshe Dayan include Yehuda Harel, *Hamatzbi vehamedinai: Moshe Dayan* (Hebrew), Tel Aviv: Moked, 1968; Naphtali Lau-Lavie, *Moshe Dayan: A Biography*, London: Valentine Mitchell, 1968; Aryeh Hashaviya, *Ayin ahat lemars: Moshe Dayan – korot hayav* (Hebrew), Tel Aviv: Ahiasaf, 1969; Shabtai Teveth, *Moshe Dayan: Biografia* (Hebrew), Tel Aviv: Schoken, 1971; Avner Falk, *Moshe Dayan: Ha'ish veha'agada – biografia psikho'analitit* (Hebrew), Jerusalem: Kaneh Publishing, 1985; Robert Slater, *The Life of Moshe Dayan*, New York: St. Martin's Press, 1991; Ehud Ben-Ezer, *Omets: Sipuro shel Moshe Dayan* (Hebrew), Tel Aviv: Defense Ministry Publishers, 1997; Martin van Creveld, *Moshe Dayan*, London: Weidenfeld & Nicholson, 2004; Mordechai Bar-On, *Moshe Dayan: Korot hayav 1915–1981* (Hebrew), Tel Aviv: Am Oved, 2014.

[2] Dayan's autobiographies: Moshe Dayan, *Avnei derekh: Autobiografia* (Hebrew), Jerusalem: Idanim, 1976. The book was published also in English as Moshe Dayan, *Story of My Life*, New York: Da Capo Press, 1976; Moshe Dayan, *Yoman maarekhet Sinai* (Hebrew), Tel Aviv: Dvir, 1977; Mordechai Naor (ed.), *Moshe Dayan: Mikh'tvei ahava* (Hebrew), Tel Aviv: Yedioth Ahronoth Publishers, 2016.

[3] Books and other works his relatives and close associates have written include Ruth Dayan and Helga Dudman, *Ve'oulay ... Sipura shel Ruth Dayan* (Hebrew), Jerusalem: Weidenfeld & Nicholson, 1973; Yael Dayan, *Avi, bito* (Hebrew), Jerusalem: Idanim, 1986; Neora Barnoah-Matalon, *Makom tov batsad* (Hebrew), Tel Aviv: Kotarim Publishers, 2009; in the autobiographical series by Assi Dayan, "Hahayim kishmu'a" ("Life as a Rumor") (Hebrew) (trilogy), the first chapter deals with the relationship between Assi and his father, Moshe Dayan.

[4] Falk, *Moshe Dayan*.

etiquette, Dayan was known to be gruff, even outrageous, caring nothing for the limits of authority, hierarchies, and regulations. This attitude, however, often led to great achievements. And he had personal charm to spare, along with a sharp sense of humor. Always in touch with everything happening on the ground, Dayan's approach was highly practical while always looking to the future. Although deeply rooted in the past and the history of the Jewish people, his life's work was building his renewed homeland, aspiring to help ensure the successful future of the state. He became an ideal and an Israeli hero, as well as a well-known international brand.

However, in recent decades, many of Dayan's traits, once considered emblematic of a man of his time and highly praised, became negative symbols. His self-confidence was suddenly reinterpreted as arrogance, a sense of superiority that led to a traumatic national disaster. Dayan's long-time political camp, having lost power and its national hegemony, became subject to harsh criticism. Moreover, the Israeli sabra figure, which he represented more than anyone else, became a negative symbol, a legitimate target for censure by groups promoting a new national agenda. These groups rejected the Ashkenazi, secular, chauvinist, bellicose, and boastful Israeli who controlled everything and saw himself as above the law – everything that Dayan seemed to stand for. Although Dayan later joined the rival political camp and played an important part in achieving peace with Egypt, Israel's greatest foe, the dramatic reversal of his once-glowing political image remained unchanged, quite possibly because of profound changes in Israeli society.

Nonetheless, even after the passage of time, Dayan still deserves to belong to the pantheon of Israel's great leaders. Prime Minister Benjamin Netanyahu recalled the words of the late President Shimon Peres:

> Late at night at one of our many meetings at the President's House, I asked him, "Tell me, Shimon: from the heights of your lofty age, which of Israel's leader do you admire [the most]?" . . . In that conversation, he mentioned Rabin, Begin, and others, with, I must say, real appreciation for the unique contribution each of them made. But he surprised me a bit when he mentioned another man: Moshe Dayan. Shimon spoke of his courage in battle, his originality, and other traits. "Moshe," he said, "didn't give a hoot what anyone thought of him. Dayan completely ignored political considerations. He was what he wanted to be."[5]

Indeed, in complete contrast to his controversial public image in Israel, experts in Israel and throughout the world continue to consider Dayan one of the twentieth century's greatest military leaders. Richard Simpkin, for example, one of the most important post-World War II British military

---

[5] Full text of Benjamin Netanyahu's eulogy for Shimon Peres, *Times of Israel*, September 30, 2016. At: www.timesofisrael.com/full-text-of-benjamin-netanyahus-eulogy-for-shimon-peres.

thinkers, describes him as a "great military leader, head and shoulders above all his contemporaries."[6] Experienced and renowned military leaders and experts have echoed this opinion.[7] Books of military history citing the greatest military leaders of all time include Moshe Dayan as Israel's only representative.[8] Thus, several questions arise. First, what about Dayan makes so many military experts consider him the most important military leader in modern Israel's history? On what is his reputation as a military leader based, and is this reputation justified? Arguably, the gaps between public opinion and expert assessments of Dayan's historic contribution stem from Israelis' resentment about the Yom Kippur War and their difficulty in forgiving the colossal blunders surrounding it. Public criticism also included the entire generation of state founders, of which Dayan was a prominent representative. Foreign experts in leadership and strategy possibly examine Dayan from a different perspective and thus see him in the broader historical context of military leaders.

"Politics is the art of the possible," said Otto von Bismarck, the chancellor who united Germany. This can also apply to strategy, in which the components of planning and acting are rooted in the tension between the goals and the possible means of attaining them. The art of strategy, then, involves the ability to realize ambitious yet realistic ends, as every plan must weigh the limits of both the means and few methods of action available. Thus, the art lies in the greatest maximization possible. This aptly reflects Dayan as a military leader and as a statesman who operated in the world of strategy for most of his adult life. The compass that steered him was clear: ensuring the State of Israel's existence, security, and well-being. Attaining this objective demanded constant effort marked by adaptiveness, flexibility, and creativity to provide a response to a changing and emerging reality. For Dayan, there was no one single ideological or metatheoretical model, only an ever-changing reality posing new challenges to be addressed.

This book, then, is not a conventional biography covering all aspects of Dayan's life in chronological order. Rather, it focuses on Dayan's development as a military leader and statesman, seeking to understand the "Dayanesque" modus operandi and role as a historic figure, asking the following questions: How was his worldview shaped? How did he change over the years? What remained constant and what was in flux? How did he make decisions? How did he learn? It also explores political security challenges and fields in which he was involved, many still relevant today, including counterterrorism; military

---

[6] Richard Simpkin, *Race to the Swift: Thoughts on Twenty-First Century Warfare*, London: Brassey's, 1985, p. 305.
[7] Cf. Julian Thompson, "Foreword," in Martin van Creveld, *Moshe Dayan*, London: Weidenfeld & Nicholson, 2004, pp. 11, 14.
[8] E.g. Nigel Cawthorne, *100 Great Military Leaders: History's Greatest Masters of Warfare*, London: Arcturus Publishing, 2003.

innovation; building military forces; military morale and values; political–military relations and planning military campaigns; Israel's relationship with its neighbors; ruling occupied territories; and Israel as a small state facing large powers. In this sense, understanding Dayan's strategic approach can contribute to our ability to tackle today's challenges.

Dayan is considered the most enigmatic and most difficult to decipher among his generation's leaders, whose ideological and political considerations were clear to all. This makes the many debates about him more understandable. The historian Michael Oren described it well:

> When I research distinguished historical leaders, I get to know them fairly intimately ... But Dayan is an exception ... the more I learned about him, the less I felt I knew about him. He was a man of polar opposites – stirred and cold, creative and narrow-minded, fearless and cowardly, whose mind was capable of holding much more than two contrary opinions simultaneously ... With historic decisions, such as whether or not to conquer the Old City or the Golan Heights, he went from fierce opposition to unconditional support in a matter of hours, literally ... Moshe Dayan left behind a controversial legacy ... He was a leader of a stature not found anywhere in today's Middle East: the architect of Israel's most brilliant victory and of the later peace accords with Egypt, but also an expert at political intrigues and brazen shows of force. Behind his trademark, the black patch over his eye, hid an inaccessible mystery.[9]

This book's use of the strategic prism sheds light on hidden areas of Dayan's thoughts, enhancing our understanding of his character against the background of the challenges of his time. Unfortunately, as noted, many of the issues he grappled with continue to plague us to this day. Learning more about his strategies and coping mechanisms for facing them may help contemporary policymakers and strategists in meeting the challenges of the modern era.

What Is Strategy?

The word strategy has become increasingly prevalent in recent decades in multiple disciplines, including business, the media, public relations, and, of course, politics. Advisors in these fields call themselves strategic consultants, seeking to project prestige and respectability with the word "strategic." A senior government advisor once handed me his business card, identifying himself as a "Tactical Consultant." He explained that in a marketplace saturated with strategic consultants, he felt it was necessary to set himself apart.

One way to understand strategy is through the triangular concept of ends, means, and ways, and their interrelation, or as a process whose objective is

---

[9] Michael Oren, *Six Days of War: June 1967 and the Making of the Modern Middle East* (in Hebrew translation), Or Yehuda: Dvir, 2004, pp. 393–394.

attaining a relative advantage over rivals and preventing them from making any gains. A zero-sum game.

The term strategy developed in the context of war and its relationship with statesmanship and has been used in various ways in different cultures.[10] Carl von Clausewitz (1780–1831), considered the most important philosopher of war, analogized warfare and commerce as two human activities involving clashing interests. He viewed war as part of politics, which he considered a type of commerce, writing, "Politics is the womb in which war develops."[11] The Chinese leader Mao Tse-Tung (1893–1976) later echoed this sentiment: "War is politics with bloodshed while politics is war without bloodshed."[12] Clausewitz may have said it best: "War is merely the continuation of policy by other means," an adage familiar to every military officer and student of diplomacy and security. Clausewitz also defined strategy in a more limited way as "the use of battles to win the war."[13] Thus, his main contribution was not his use of the term strategy, but clarifying the relationship between war and politics and emphasizing that the goal of war is imposing one's will on the enemy.[14]

The narrow definition of strategy began expanding in the mid nineteenth century, due to political, technological, and social changes then unfolding in the West that transformed the nature of war. As the scope of military confrontation grew, the term strategy expanded and came to include a political rationale, mirroring Clausewitz's explanation that war was driven by policy

---

[10] The etymology of the word is the ancient Greek *strategos*, meaning army commander. A related word is *strategemon* (stratagem in English), meaning trick. The distinction between strategy – the way a military leader defends his homeland and defeats the enemy – and tactics – the total of principles facilitating the organization of a mass of armed men and moving them in certain directions, was first made during the reign of Justinian I (483–565 CE). However, many texts continued to use strategy for tactical and technical descriptions, and the distinction remained unclear. Until the French Revolution, few distinguished between strategy and tactics, referring simply to "military matters." In fact, texts in this field were primarily instructional materials for military leaders – collections of principles on managing a campaign. The French philosopher Jacques-Antoine-Hippolyte, Comte de Guibert (1743–1790) was one of the first who distinguished between tactics and "grand tactics." Shortly thereafter, Byzantine texts were translated into French and the word strategy came into use as part of the hierarchic distinction between tactics and strategy. Beatrice Heuser, *The Evolution of Strategy: Thinking War from Antiquity to the Present*, Cambridge: Cambridge University Press, 2010, pp. 4–5.

[11] Carl von Clausewitz, *On War*, edited and translated by Michael Howard and Peter Paret, Princeton, NJ: Princeton University Press, 1984, p. 149.

[12] Mao Tse-Tung, *Mao's Selected Works*, Vol. II, Section 64, Peking: Foreign Languages Press, 1967, p. 153.

[13] Clausewitz, *On War*, p. 6.

[14] Ibid., p. 6. "Politics" and "policy" are close cognates, as politics is the means to implement policies.

and was, in fact, integral to it. Early twentieth-century military thinkers further pursued the connection between military force and political achievement in the wake of dramatic changes in the nature of war. The British military theorist B. H. Liddell Hart (1895–1970) defined strategy as "the art of distributing and *applying military means* to fulfil the ends of policy,"[15] which, in its various forms, is the most commonly used definition in military literature.

Historically, countless figures, such as Alexander the Great and Napoleon, held military and political roles simultaneously. Such leaders had a political vision, dictated the strategy to fulfill that vision, and led military campaigns and the battles, some of them – Alexander comes to mind – actively fighting alongside their soldiers. However, some modern developments have led to the separation between the civilian echelon, which sets the political objectives, and the military echelon, which translates these into military objectives. Other changes include the creation of much larger armies together with increased specializations and technologies, and, in terms of knowledge and expertise, the distinction between those who manage the battle, the campaign, the theater of operations, and finally the political outcome. This has resulted in the differentiated levels of strategy accepted in contemporary military doctrine.

Levels of Strategy

Liddell Hart coined the phrase "grand strategy" to describe the level superseding strategy.[16] Grand strategy integrates all of a nation's components of power to attain political goals.[17] Literature further divides this into levels of war or levels of strategy referring to hierarchic layers of action. All these levels are part of the phenomenon of war, and the division between them reflects each one's unique characteristics and emphases. The highest level, then, is grand strategy, involving broad issues of war and peace for which the political echelon, aided by the professional echelon, is responsible. Historian Hal Brands defined grand strategy as:

> The intellectual architecture that gives form and structure to foreign policy ... a purposeful and coherent set of ideas about what a nation seeks to accomplish, and how it should go about it ... It requires a clear understanding of the nature of the international environment, a country's highest goals and interests within that environment, the primary threats

---

[15] In Heuser, *The Evolution of Strategy*, p. 8 (my emphasis).
[16] This section is based on a textbook written by Dr. Eado Hecht called *Musagei yesod bemilhama uvetsava* (Fundamental Concepts in War and the Military) (Hebrew), IDF Staff & Command College Press, 2010, which is used in various IDF courses. The author would like to thank Dr. Hecht for his permission to use the material.
[17] Ibid., p. 9. Earlier, the nineteenth-century Swiss military thinker Antoine Henri de Jomini used the phrase "military policy" – "la politique militaire" – to distinguish between this level and others.

to those goals and interests, and the ways that finite resources can be used for the competing challenges and opportunities.[18]

To manage a conflict, decision-makers have a range of means at their disposal: overt and covert diplomacy, which operates through compromise or force (threat to harm an opponent by one of these means); overt and covert propaganda (psychological warfare); economic policy (providing economic benefits or imposing boycotts); and the use of violence (war) or the threat of using it. Decision-makers may use multiples means, often simultaneously, and changing methods as needed.

The (military) strategy level focuses on the connection between force utilization (means) and political achievements (goals). Strategy theorist Colin Gray compared strategy to a bridge between policy (and politics) and war.[19] War-related issues determined at the national political level include: Against whom will the war be waged? What are the war's objectives? What is the scope of resources needed? What is the timing, and who will dictate it? Who are possible allies? What are the constraints (international, moral, legal)?

Ideally, the senior military echelon refers to the political echelon's decisions on these questions, clarifying the military achievement needed to realize the political goal. The military echelon then recommends to the political echelon military goals intended to persuade the enemy to submit to political demands to avoid paying a military price. Military goals can include damaging enemy capabilities, taking territorial control, eliciting certain enemy responses, or deterrence from certain actions (for example, on April 7, 2017, two US Navy ships fired Tomahawk missiles from an air-force base in Homs, Syria, to deter Assad's regime from continuing to use chemical weapons). Often, a combination of these alternatives is applied.

The military strategic echelon also determines the location of the military action and the sequence of operations in different theaters, such as where the main effort will initially be applied and where thereafter (graduated efforts). Alternatively, they may decide to apply equal efforts simultaneously in more than one theater (parallel efforts). These decisions about the order of importance of theaters and timing affect resource allocation in each theater at every stage of the war (thus, in the Yom Kippur War, because the Syrian front was initially determined to be more important than the Egyptian front, the main efforts and reserve forces were directed there on the second day of the war). Other strategic decisions of the military echelon may include the order of importance of the strategic goals in each geographical theater (which can change during fighting); the sequence of attaining them (serially or

---

[18] Hal Brands, *What Good Is Grand Strategy: Power and Purpose in American Statecraft from Harry S. Truman to George W. Bush*, Ithaca, NY: Cornell University Press, 2014, p. 3.

[19] Colin Gray, *The Strategy Bridge: Theory for Practice*, New York: Oxford University Press, 2010, p. 29.

simultaneously); and matching military resources to each front or theater commander based on the strategic goals and the operational circumstances (constraints dictated to the commander, the preferred manner of fighting, the scope and type of forces available, and more). The level – operational – refers to strategic operation, involving all operational and administrative activities associated with achieving the defined strategic goal in a given theater. When there are multiple strategic goals for a theater, several parallel operations may be conducted to attain them. In the IDF, the regional commands, Southern, Central and Northern commands, are responsible for the operational level.[20]

The last level is the art of managing the battle – tactics.[21] A battle is the actual fighting, conducted by the force encountering enemy forces, and including force actions at the edges of the battlefield. The typical mission of a tactical commander is to destroy or repel a defined enemy force.

The grand strategy is therefore the upper level, targeting all the other levels, deciding if the gamut of actions at the other levels will in fact improve the nation's political and security situation.[22]

Levels of success are not always closely related. Successive tactical victories do not guarantee operational success. For example, Rommel's tactical successes in the Western Desert in 1942 did not defeat of the British at the operational level because of his poor logistics. With every tactical advance lengthening his supply lines, each step forward actually led inexorably to his defeat. The relationships between the tactical, operational, and grand strategy levels are complex, especially when military results are intertwined with other factors, including diplomacy, the economy, the media, and public opinion. This is particularly evident in the context of a small nation dependent on the interests of the world's great powers. For example, while Israel had a clear military advantage at the end of the Yom Kippur War, it had to agree to ceasefire concessions because of US pressure.

Every military leader's most significant challenge is ensuring that one level of success contributes to success of the next: Tactical success must translate into operational success, and so on. The difficulty in linking the levels arises in part from strategy's paradoxical and fickle nature.

While common sense guides most social activities, strategic considerations are paramount in conflict situations, the operative logic differing from, perhaps even completely defying, conventional logic. Strategy, then, is characterized by "paradox, contradiction, and irony,"[23] its singular logic driven by the existence

---

[20] *Torat hamivtsa'im hameshutafim* (General Headquarters) (Hebrew), November 2006, p. 28.
[21] Military doctrine refers to another, lower level: the technotactical. It includes the military techniques and team drills of the soldiers and a few weapons systems.
[22] Edward N. Luttwak, *Strategy: The Logic of War and Peace*, Cambridge, MA: Harvard University Press, 2001, p. 208.
[23] Ibid., p. xii.

of the enemy seeking to disrupt each of your moves and prevent you from attaining your goals, thereby enabling the enemy to achieve their goals, which are contrary to yours and could even involve your obliteration. As Martin van Creveld has observed: "That opponent is allowed not just to try to achieve his objective but to actively prevent you from doing the same ... it a question of trying to detect, predict, interfere with and obstruct the opponent."[24]

The ancient Roman saying, "Si vis pacem, para bellum" – "If you want peace, prepare for war" – well reflects the paradoxical dimension aspects of strategic thinking. While conventional logic views the straight, paved, short, and illuminated road as the best route between Points A and B, strategic logic often finds the long, twisting, difficult, and dark road preferable, simply because the enemy may not be expecting you there. The military thinker Edward Luttwak argues that creating a surprise can provide an advantage but may weaken your overall power by splitting forces. Advancing into the enemy's territory while winning victories necessarily leads to longer supply lines, which weaken the winner while strengthening the defeated side (Nazi Germany in World War II and, Napoleon in 1812, both in Russia, being prime examples).[25] The defeated side often learns better, thus improving its chances in the future.[26]

Strategy represents multiple opposing options with differing advantages and disadvantages, much like the children's game Rock, Paper, Scissors: The uncertainty of your enemy's choice makes your choice so difficult. Van Creveld identifies such dilemmas at the campaign and tactical levels, including adhering to the goal versus flexibility, reserving forces versus pitching them into battle, concentrating forces versus dispersing them, the indirect versus the direct approach, advance versus retreat.[27] Colin Gray adds dilemmas in the field of strategy, such as attrition versus decision, conquest versus raid, using force versus enforcement by other means (e.g., economic sanctions), offense versus defense.[28] The essence of the art of strategy is deciding on the strategy while adapting it to a given reality or strategic context.

The Phenomenon of Friction and Its Effect on the Strategic Act

The second factor affecting the execution of the strategy is friction, a term used by Clausewitz to explain why he characterized war as the realm of uncertainty; this concept is among Clausewitz's most important contributions to military theory.[29] According to Clausewitz, friction explains why situations in war

---

[24] Martin van Creveld, *Wargames: From Gladiators to Gigabytes*, Cambridge: Cambridge University Press, 2013, p. 3.
[25] Luttwak, *Strategy*, pp. 17–18.
[26] Ibid., p. 57.
[27] Martin van Creveld, *More on War*, Oxford: Oxford University Press, 2017, pp. 101–109.
[28] Gray, *The Strategy Bridge*, p. 66.
[29] Clausewitz, *On War*, p. 101.

rarely develop according to plan. Friction seems to operate like Murphy's Law – anything that can go wrong will.[30] Nor is friction random; rather, it is a structural phenomenon inherent in the situation. Indeed, "everything in war is very simple, but the simplest thing is difficult. The difficulties accumulate and end by producing a kind of friction that is inconceivable unless one has experienced war."[31] Clausewitz concluded that friction "is the only concept that more or less corresponds to factors that distinguish real war from war on paper."[32] Even small, seemingly trivial disruptions could disrupt the best plan.

Clausewitz understood war as an unpredictable phenomenon that cannot be controlled in the conventional meaning of the word. Never complete or perfect in battle, war always generates unpredictable mistakes and gaps of information and understanding. Some claim that improved capabilities based on innovative technologies of information gathering and analysis may potentially help clear the fog of war by reducing friction's effects.[33] However, the human mind's ability to process information is limited, and this ability diminishes even more when people are under pressure. Moreover, the capabilities of digital information technologies may very well be offset by their inherent complexity. Even when new technologies generate the hoped-for achievements, these then require more resources and attention to their maintenance, thereby creating yet another source of friction.[34] Consequently, even in this age of information, friction will continue to be a disruptive factor.[35]

Overcoming Friction: Strategy as a System of Exploiting Opportunities

Helmuth Karl Bernhard Graf von Moltke (the Elder)[36] was a Prussian field marshal, serving for thirty-one years in the Prussian and then German army (following Germany's 1871 unification) (1857–1888). He shaped the German Army, which, under his leadership, became the foremost military force in the world at the time and led the army to decisive victories in three important campaigns.[37]

---

[30] Ibid., p. 119.
[31] Ibid.
[32] Ibid.
[33] Bill Owens, *Lifting the Fog of War*, New York: Farrar, Straus and Giroux, 2000, p. 15.
[34] Jacob W. Kipp and Lester W. Grau, "The Fog and Friction of Technology," *Military Review* 81:5 (September–October 2001), pp. 88–97 (p. 89).
[35] David Betz, "The More You Know the Less You Understand," *Journal of Strategic Studies* 29:3 (June 2006), pp. 505–533.
[36] To distinguish him from his nephew Helmuth Johann Ludwig von Moltke, called "the Younger," who also served as chief of staff of the German army from 1906 until 1914.
[37] The wars of unification, also known as the wars of German unification: the campaign against Denmark in 1864, the campaign against the Austrian Empire in 1866, and, most importantly, the campaign against Napoleon III's French Empire in 1870–1871. Among Moltke's achievements was the refining and development of the general staff into its

Like Clausewitz, whom he admired, Moltke believed in the effect of friction on war.[38] Perceiving war as a fluid, elusive phenomenon, and viewing the sphere of strategy as involving more art than science, Moltke wrote:

> Strategy affords tactics the means for fighting and the probability of winning by the direction of armies and their meetings at the place of combat. The demands of strategy grow silent in the face of a tactical victory and adapt themselves to the newly created situation. Strategy is a system of expedients. It is ... the continued development of the original leading thought in accordance with the constantly changing circumstance.[39]

Moltke concluded that there is no plan that can be guaranteed to survive its first encounter with the enemy's main force.[40]

Therefore, a military leader must rely on commanders' initiative to identify and exploit opportunities in the chaos of battle. For Moltke:

> The tactical result of an engagement forms the base for the strategic decisions ... because victory or defeat in battle changes the situation to such a degree that no human acumen is able to see beyond the first battle ... Prearranged designs (schema) collapse and only a proper estimate of the situation shows the commander the correct way. The advantage of the situation will never be fully utilized if the subordinate commander waits for orders. It will be generally more advisable to proceed actively and keep the initiative than to wait to [for] the opponent.[41]

Moltke handled the uncertain nature of the battlefield based on his understanding of command, termed *Auftragstaktik* – command informed by general instructions. This made flexibility possible, at the campaign and strategy levels. Overcoming the loss of control involves not imposing order on chaos through a centralized system, but decentralizing command instead.[42] The principles of initiative and independent decision-making were critical for him, and he would tell his officers that, as officers, they not only had to obey commands,

---

modern format, which exists to this day in most advanced armies in the world in various versions. He also developed and improved military education and applied a mission-command approach in his own army that encouraged initiative and exploited opportunities at all echelons. Hajo Holborn, "The Prussian-German School: Moltke and the Rise of the General Staff," in Peter Paret (ed.), *Makers of Modern Strategy: From Machiavelli to the Nuclear Age*, Princeton, NJ: Princeton University Press, 1986, pp. 281–295.

[38] Martin Samuels, *Command or Control: Command, Training and Tactics in the British and German Armies, 1888–1918*, London: Frank Cass, 1995, p. 11.

[39] Daniel J. Hughes (edited and translated), *Moltke on the Art of War: Selected Writings*, Novato, CA: Presidio, 1993, p. 47.

[40] Ibid., p. 92.

[41] Hughes, *Moltke on the Art of War*, p. 133.

[42] Van Creveld, *Command in War*, p. 122.

but also know when not to obey them.[43] For generations, the IDF, too, has adopted this approach to command and military leadership, terming it "mission command."[44] And it was Moshe Dayan as chief of staff who shaped the IDF and his commanders based on this approach.

Clausewitz's and Moltke's insights into the nature of war and the optimal command approach have remained relevant despite all the changes in the past century and a half. The Chairman of the Joint Chiefs of Staff, US General Mark Milley, appointed to his post in 2019, echoed Moltke's words of 150 years earlier:

> Subordinates need to understand that they have the freedom, and they are empowered to disobey a specific order, a specified task, in order to accomplish a purpose. Now, that takes a lot of judgment ... it can't just be willy-nilly disobedience. This has got to be disciplined disobedience to achieve the higher purpose.[45]

According to Colin Gray, many analysts err in their tendency to view Moltke's valuable approach to strategy as one emphasizing tactics at the expense of strategy.[46] Gray submits that Moltke's understanding of strategy is a response to uncertainty on the battlefield and the corresponding need to allow commanders maximal flexibility, with the uncertainty reflecting an essential truth about the nature of warfare and strategy for Moltke.[47] Events at the tactical level create a constantly changing reality, requiring adjustments from strategists that must match what Moltke terms "the original idea" – the strategic concept that includes the objective and the general principle of action for attaining it.[48] To realize the original strategic idea, the strategist must be attentive to tactical developments that may present unanticipated opportunities that could help realize the strategy. "This is learning through specific events," Gray wrote.[49]

A more traditional view considers strategy to be essentially a one-way process: An idea and plan are generated at the top of the organizational pyramid and trickle down to the most junior levels through plans and instructions. The junior levels' influence is not on strategy formation, but on the execution of the precise instructions each individual receives.

---

[43] Trevor N. Dupuy, *A Genius for War: The German Army and General Staff, 1807–1945*, Englewood Cliffs, NJ: Prentice-Hall, 1977, p. 116.
[44] See Eitan Shamir, *Pikud mesima* (Hebrew), Ben Shemen: Modan and Maarakhot, 2014, pp. 93–104.
[45] David Barno and Nora Bensahel, "Three Things the Army Chief of Staff Wants You to Know," *War on the Rocks*, May 23, 2017, https://warontherocks.com/2017/05/three-things-the-army-chief-of-staff-wants-you-to-know.
[46] Gray, *The Strategy Bridge*, pp. 124, 248.
[47] Ibid., p. 125.
[48] Ibid., pp. 124–125, 186.
[49] Ibid., p. 125.

The organizational management researcher Henry Mintzberg is a leading critic of the classical approach to strategy centered on the distinction between planning and execution.[50] He focuses instead on the leader's place and function in the strategic process, which are especially vital for a better understanding of Dayan's decision-making processes. According to Mintzberg, at the center of the strategic process is the solitary leader, equipped with singular mental abilities, wisdom, experience, and insights,[51] and providing a perspective and vision that bridge the present and the future.[52] Because the vision is more a general picture of the future organization than a detailed plan of action, it allows for flexibility, enabling the leader to make adjustments based on changing circumstances. Arguably, this interpretation envisages direction from the top together with room for evolving processes, reflecting a general direction and ideal picture of the future but nonetheless adaptable to changing conditions.[53]

Who is that leader? Mintzberg describes them as an "entrepreneur" – someone who loves independence, has a need to achieve, and tends to take calculated, not undue risks. Unlike the bureaucratic leader's first question when given a task – "What resources will I be given to complete the task?" – the entrepreneur immediately asks, "Where is the opportunity here?" The research describes the entrepreneur-leader as someone highly attentive to the environment and alert for the changes indicating an opportunity that can be exploited to an advantage. In contrast, the bureaucratic manager is mostly engaged with preserving resources and maintaining the status quo. Entrepreneurs, says Mintzberg, quickly transition from identifying an opportunity to taking action to realize it, and their actions tend to be revolutionary.[54] In general, entrepreneurial strategy therefore entails the constant search for new opportunities. Entrepreneurial leaders also tend to have difficulty accepting authority. The entrepreneur-leaders are less concerned with an orderly organizational structure or detailed working plans, instead harnessing the organization's commitment to work in the direction that they have set, according with their motivating vision and theory of underlying factors.[55] Entrepreneurs also take dramatic leaps forward in the face of great uncertainty by making major decisions that entail risk but also offer great opportunity and promise.[56]

Also helpful in understanding Dayan's patterns of leadership is Mintzberg's model of the "strategic learning school," further emphasizing that reality is

---

[50] Henry Mintzberg, Bruce Ahlsrand, and Joseph Lampel, *Strategy Safari: The Complete Guide through the Wilds of Strategic Management*, Englewood Cliffs, NJ: Prentice-Hall, 1998.
[51] Ibid., p. 124.
[52] Ibid., p. 137.
[53] Ibid., p. 125.
[54] Ibid., p. 133.
[55] Ibid., pp. 135–136.
[56] Ibid., p. 136.

constantly changing and unpredictable, making prior calculated control and highly detailed strategy impossible. Instead, strategy is the product of a process of learning in which its design and implementation are two interrelated processes. The leader is the main character whose learning is focused and then enables the entire system to learn, resulting in systemic learning. This approach allows for strategic initiatives to arise from all areas of the organization.[57]

Management researchers C. K. Prahalad and Gary Hamel introduced the key concept of "strategic intent" into the literature of management. Unlike a detailed master plan, applying strategic intent helps the organization decide on a clear, consistent, and uniform general, long-term direction that is intuitively accessible to everyone in the organization.[58] The leader's role is to define the strategic intent, provide a clear direction, inspire motivation to explore new areas, and create a sense of shared destiny and mission among all organization members.[59]

Strategy: Between Art and Science

The story goes that, once, a researcher in the field of decision-making was offered important positions by several elite universities after he developed a decision-making model for which he was awarded a very prestigious prize. In response to his difficulty in deciding between them, one colleague suggested, "Why don't you use your model, the one that got you the prize, to help you decide?" The researcher astounded answer: "What?! Are you crazy? This is a serious decision!"

Strategy is more art than science. But, unlike art, it does not exist in an abstract world of ideas; instead, it must translate the abstract and theoretical into an array of actions that affect reality. While multiple decision-making methodologies and methods help statesmen and military leaders analyze their surroundings better, make better decisions, organize the information, and create alternatives and prioritize them, ultimately, they are facing weighty, multivariable decisions involving many considerations, and leaders must decide on their own. According to Mintzberg, strategic decision-makers eventually face "the black box of strategy" about which there are no clear guidelines, and which requires them to use intuition and creativity.[60] The strategist weighs many variables, including probabilities and opportunities, political and economic considerations, and values and ideology, at times considering how

---

[57] Ibid., p. 208.
[58] Ibid., p. 219.
[59] Summary of Strategic Intent, *Value Based Management*, www.valuebasedmanagement.net/methods_hamel_prahalad_strategic_intent.html.
[60] Henry Mintzberg, "The Fall and Rise of Strategic Planning," *Harvard Business Review*, January–February 1994.

a decision will affect their legacy. Sometimes these considerations lead to decisions involving great risk, ones that the people around the leader find difficult to understand or justify in the moment; but the leader sees further and deeper and is guided by different considerations that may be hard to grasp in conventional rational terms. Thus, during the War of Independence, Israel's first prime minister, David Ben-Gurion, did not hesitate to confront his military commanders. Contravening narrow military logic, he assigned forces to break the siege of Jerusalem and open the road to the city – Operation Nachshon in April 1948, an operation that would prove to be a turning point in the war.[61] Another example is British prime minister Winston Churchill, who, despite the defeat of France and of the British expeditionary force against Germany, and despite Great Britain's isolated and hopeless position in May 1940, and notwithstanding his cabinet's opposition, remained determined not to enter into negotiations with the Germans and to continue to fight relentlessly.[62]

A strategist is born as an artist with a certain talent, a certain tendency to engage in this field. The strategist needs a combination of talent and motivation to reach any sort of leadership position. The Germans called this innate strategic ability *Fingerspitzengefühl*, literally "sensitivity in the fingertips," and the French *coup d'œil* – "a sharp eye," a somewhat ironic term in Dayan's case. The greatest military leaders wrote about having that *coup d'œil*. Frederick the Great (Friedrich II) wrote of it in his book *Military Instructions from the King of Prussia to His Generals*, as did Clausewitz in *On War*. All were agreed that the *coup d'œil* was a gift from God, an innate trait that develops over time.[63] The essence of the *coup d'œil* is the ability to see all the different possibilities at once and decide which is the best. Clausewitz wrote that it was the only way a commander could control events rather than be controlled by them.[64] Various circles all refer to the speed with which understanding is reached, not the result of long, exhausting discussions or of teamwork at headquarters, as is customary today, but rather a swift insight and decision of the solitary leader.

The concept of the *coup d'œil* relates mostly to the tactical battlefield, where events unfold dynamically and swiftly, with relatively clear and visible variables – the ground, the enemy, our forces – in military language, "situation assessment." However, this ability arguably exists at the strategic level as well, Soviet leader Joseph Stalin being an example. Historian Marc Ferro writes:

[61] David Tal, "Milhemet tashah: Milhamto shel Ben-Gurion" (Hebrew), *Iyunim bit'kumat yisrael* 13 (2003), pp. 115–138 (p. 123); Operation Nachshon, p. 124.
[62] Ian Kershaw, *Fateful Choices: Ten Decisions That Changed the World* (in Hebrew translation), Tel Aviv: Am Oved, 2007.
[63] Clausewitz, *On War*, p. 578; B. H. Liddell Hart, *Thoughts on War*, London: Faber & Faber, 1944.
[64] Clausewitz, *On War*, p. 578.

In August 1942, when Churchill informed Stalin of Operation Torch, the Allied invasion of French North Africa, he was stunned by the acuity of his interlocutor's strategic understanding. Stalin instantaneously realized the strategic advantages of Operation Torch and proceeded to enumerate the four major reasons to embark on it: attacking Rommel from the rear, ending the dependence on Spain, sparking a conflict between the French and Germans in France, and placing Italy in the line of fire.[65]

Ferro quoted Churchill's diary about Stalin: "I was most impressed by this precise analysis . . . Few people would have been able to follow, within minutes, the considerations to which we had given long and hard thought. He understood it all in the blink of an eye."[66] Stalin, who never received any formal military education or academic education in policy or strategy, was, according to Churchill's testimony, gifted with an almost instinctual grasp of these fields, which is not at all self-evident.

In recent decades, there have been comprehensive studies on the phenomenon of the instant or intuitive decision. These studies have, to an extent, lifted the fog about the mechanism of an ability considered to be innate rather than acquired. Still, what we do not know far exceeds what we do know. Malcolm Gladwell, in his popular book *Blink: The Power of Thinking without Thinking*, summarizes the scientific studies of the phenomenon. The scientific concept he uses is "adaptive unconscious," which he describes as an enormous computer quickly processing a great deal of the information one needs to function.[67] The brain does something that scientists call "thin slicing" because it identifies patterns in different situations and behaviors on the basis of very thin slices of experience.[68] This does not mean that this type of decision is free of errors of bias or judgment, but it does indicate that some people, in addition to their talent, have undergone certain kinds of experience and have become accustomed to training their minds in certain contexts, eventually becoming able to immediately identify a problem and suggest an alternative mode of action. Sometimes they find it difficult to explain, even in hindsight, how the answer leapt to their mind and why they were so certain they were right. They just knew and called it intuition.

In face of the chaotic nature of the strategic process, the strategist requires a high degree of sophistication and an inner sense or confidence leading them to try possible feasible actions, and, better yet, encourage others to do the same. Furthermore, the strategist must know something good when they see it.[69]

---

[65] Marc Ferro, *Ils étaient sept hommes en guerre: 1918-1945: histoire parallèle*, Paris: Robert Laffont, 2007, p. 266 (in Hebrew translation, *Shiva'a Gvarim Be'milchama*: Kinneret-Zmora-Bitan, Or Yehuda: Dvir, 2010).

[66] Ferro, *Ils étaient sept hommes en guerre*, p. 266.

[67] Malcolm Gladwell, *Blink: The Power of Thinking Without Thinking* (in Hebrew translation), Keter, Jerusalem, 2005, p. 13.

[68] Ibid., p. 21.

[69] Mintzberg et al., *Strategy Safari*, pp. 194-195.

"Only a Mule Never Changes Its Mind"

Dayan was known for changing his mind on various issues with some regularity. Some viewed this trait as inconsistency and criticized him for it, insisting that leaders should subscribe to a single big idea. Dayan's response to this was another of his famous quips: "Only a mule never changes its mind." As already noted by Michael Oren, Dayan's could hold more than just two contradictory positions simultaneously, and Dayan could shift from strenuous objection to unconditional support of a fateful decision in literally a matter of hours.[70] Dayan's ability to decide one way, and then change his decision – sometimes by 180 degrees – is important to understanding the unique way in which he developed and operated as a strategist.

Historian and philosopher Isaiah Berlin famously distinguished between hedgehogs and foxes. Hedgehogs are in-depth experts on a certain topic and their vision is narrow, whereas foxes dabble in many topics but take a broad view. According to the Greek proverb on which Berlin based his thoughts, "The fox knows many things, but the hedgehog knows one big thing." Historian John Gaddis claims that the successful strategist must be part-hedgehog and part-fox, citing F. Scott Fitzgerald who wrote that: "The test of a first-rate intelligence is the ability to hold two opposing ideas in mind at the same time and still be able to act." The strategist, says Gaddis, must be capable of having a clear direction, like the hedgehog, and sensitivity to a changing environment, like the fox.[71]

Dayan was an autodidact. Like most Israeli leaders, he felt that his military career was the result of necessity rather than choice. His study of war was driven not by from any professional interest or intellectual passion to understand war as a phenomenon, but from the practical need to solve concrete political problems by military means. He never felt he had to apologize for this direction, even describing wars as "the most exciting events in life."[72]

Dayan's intellectual abilities were manifested mainly in the spheres of strategy and statesmanship. His curiosity about people and places, his ability to change his mind, his critical thinking, his vivid imagination, and the fact that he never took anything for granted were all important components of his success. And, most importantly, his views on strategic matters never stopped developing. These traits led him to travel to Vietnam, where he was able to study a different type of war and develop a perspective on fighting different from what he had known in the Middle East. Dayan did not necessarily like to study in the rigid, sterile setting of the classroom, but it would be a mistake to think that Dayan was opposed to learning or the accumulation of knowledge.

---

[70] Oren, *Six Days of War*.
[71] John Lewis Gaddis, *On Grand Strategy*, New York: Allen Lane, 2018, pp. 19–20.
[72] In a 1972 interview Dayan gave to British journalist Llew Gardner. www.youtube.com/watch?v=FzVrRStVo9k.

He did detest learning in bureaucratic settings, seeing himself first and foremost as a man of action and experience.

Dayan's natural curiosity developed and shaped his strategic learning and new ideas. He therefore learned from every situation and experience. This resulted in a never-ending cycle of experiences from which he could articulate a frame of reference for understanding a new situation and finding solutions and ideas that, at that stage, represented an experiment aimed at testing the waters.

Thus, the central claim of this book is that Dayan's manner of learning and decision-making was dependent on the particular circumstances of every event. Nonetheless, over the years, Dayan's strategic approach evolved and matured. Dayan, who began his career as a junior tactical commander, became a military leader as well as a statesman whose major undertaking was in the realm of grand strategy.

About a decade has passed since the last biography of Moshe Dayan was published.[73] In this decade, various archives have made public many documents related to the decades in which Dayan was active.[74] These documents have made possible several in-depth studies of various periods, from the establishment of the state until the end of the 1970s.[75] The IDF's history department has published a host of studies on the IDF and the wars it fought during the period in which Dayan was chief of staff and defense minister, penned by its scholars and based on archival sources of the IDF that had mostly been closed to university researchers.[76] The book made use of these

---

[73] Mordechai Bar-On, *Moshe Dayan: Koron hayav 1915–1981*, Tel Aviv: Am Oved, 2014. The book was previously published in English in July 2012 as *Moshe Dayan: Israel's Controversial Hero* (New Haven, CT: Yale University Press), so the book is based on information that was available until that year.

[74] Especially the State Archive, which released many documents related to cabinet meetings between the Six-Day War and the Yom Kippur War.

[75] Some prominent examples: Yoav Gelber, *Haz'man hapalestini: Israel, yarden, vehapalestinim 1967–1970* (Hebrew), Hevel Modiin: Dvir, 2018; Yoav Gelber, *Hatasha: Hamilhama shenish'kek'ha* (Hebrew), Kinneret Zmora: Bitan, 2017; Boris Dolin, *Homat Suez Sipura shel hamilhama hasodit bein medinat yisrael livrit hamo'atzot* (Hebrew), Kinneret Zmora: Hevel Modiin, 2020; Amos Gilboa, *Mar modiin: Ahareleh, aluf Aharon Yariv, rosh aman*, Rishon Letsion: Miskal Publishing, 2013; Mordechai Bar-On, *K'shehatsava hehelif madav: Prakim behitpat'hut tsahal bashanim harishonot le'ahar milhemet ha'atsmaut 1949–1953* (Hebrew), Jerusalem: Yad Ben-Zvi, 2017; Yagil Henkin, *The 1956 Suez War and the New World Order in the Middle East: Exodus in Reverse*, Lanham, MD: Lexington Books, 2015; Meir Boymfeld, *Kfitsa lamayim hakarim: Hamaga'im hamedini'im bein yisrael, mitsrayim, ve'artsot habrit bashanim shekadmou lemilhemet yom hakippurim 1970–1973* (Hebrew), Reut: Effi Meltser, 2017; Israel Tal and Yair Tal, *Prakim lemilhemet yom hakippurim* (Hebrew), Rishon Letsion: Miskal Publishing (Yedioth Ahronoth and Hemed Books), 2019; Herzl Shapir, *Milhemet yom hakippurim: Mabat shoneh* (Hebrew), Ben Shemen: Modan and Maarakhot, 2020.

[76] In these publications, the series of book by Shimon Golan about decision-making in the uppermost command echelon stands out: Shimon Golan, *Hamilhama lehafsakat hahatasha: Kabalat hahahlatot barama haestrategit bemilhemet hahatasha bahazit hamitsrit*

publications to arrive at a more comprehensive and accurate historical assessment. But historical facts are one thing and interpretation another. Dayan is at the center of many debates and controversies among historians, and this book attempts to present to the reader both the debates about the various events and the author's own reading of them.

Structured chronologically, the chapters present the arc of Dayan's development as a strategist during a long career, focusing on security and geopolitical topics. The concluding chapter analyzes Dayan as a leader and strategist, examining both his strengths and his weaknesses.

(Hebrew), Ben Shemen: Modan and Maarakhot, 2018; Shimon Golan, *Milhama beyom hakippurim: Kabalat hahahlatot bapikud haelyon bemilhamat yom hakippurim* (Hebrew), Ben Shemen: Maarakhot and Modan, 2013; Shimon Golan, *Hafradat kohot betsel hahatasha: Kabalat hahahlatot badereg haestrategi bamasa umatann al heskemey hafradat hakohot aharey milhemet yom hakippurim* (Hebrew), Ben Shemen: Maarakhot and Modan, 2019; as well as other scholars in the history department: Zeev Elron, *Likrat hasivuv hasheni: Hat'murot betsahal vehashinuy shelo haya bitfisat habitahon 1952–1955* (Hebrew), Ben Shemen: Maarakhot and Modan, 2016; Eli Michelson, "Tahalikh halemida shel tsahal mimilhemet Sinai, November 1956–May 1957" (Hebrew), PhD dissertation, Hebrew University in Jerusalem, January 2019.

1

The Education of a Strategist

Moshe Dayan was born on May 20, 1915, in Kibbutz Degania Alef, the first child of Shmuel Dayan and Devorah, Second Aliyah immigrants to Israel.[1] Born in Ukraine, Shmuel joined the Zionist movement at a very young age, immigrating to Palestine in 1908. After working for several years as an itinerant farmhand to prepare himself for agricultural labor, in 1911 he joined Kibbutz Degania Alef in northern Israel, which had been established a year earlier as the first socialist communal settlement (kibbutz). Devorah, also from Ukraine, was a young idealist from a wealthy family. Disappointed by the failure of the 1905 revolution, she immigrated to the Land of Israel, where she worked as a laborer to fulfill her socialist vision.

Devorah met Shmuel after arriving in Degania in 1913, and they married in 1914, shortly after the outbreak of World War I. Not only were living conditions in Degania difficult, but the couple and their infant Moshe suffered from ill health. Their dissatisfaction was fueled by Shmuel's ideological objections to the kibbutz's totally communal life. He and others, claiming that the kibbutz structure limited their personal freedom, proposed a new form of settlement – the moshav – that they considered best for the nation and the individual. They formed a group to leave the kibbutz and found a communal settlement that maintained the traditional nuclear family and household.[2] Nahalal's first settlers, including Shmuel and Devorah, arrived there in September 1921 via a convoy of wagons and began the work of building the settlement, home to Moshe Dayan throughout his childhood and adolescence.[3]

There, Dayan learned from a young age that Zionism must be realized by "conquering" the soil.[4] The 1917 Balfour Declaration was a victory for political Zionism, but Shmuel still emphasized the importance of the actual land: "And here, my son, is where we began to conquer the land, not by war but by the

---

[1] The Second Aliyah was the wave of immigration of Jews to Palestine between 1904 and 1914, when the Ottoman Empire still ruled. This immigration wave was ended by the outbreak of World War I. During the Second Aliyah, some 35,000 Jews, mostly from Eastern European countries, came to the Land of Israel.
[2] Shabtai Teveth, *Moshe Dayan: Biografia* (Hebrew), Tel Aviv: Schoken, 1971, p. 33.
[3] Ibid., pp. 40–42.
[4] Moshe Dayan, *Avnei derekh: Autobiografia* (Hebrew), Jerusalem: Idanim, 1976, p. 16.

plow and by labor. Thus, the land will stay ours and we will never leave it."[5] His father also viewed his Arab neighbors negatively, as Dayan recalled: "that was the doctrine I grew up with and believed in – that Arabs are inferior, robbers, murderers, and prone to rioting."[6]

As a child, Moshe was close to his mother, who read him Russian literature, which he came to love,[7] and he became familiar with the works of the great Russian writers.[8] While he was a sensitive child,[9] he also showed a great deal of independence, roaming alone between Degania and Nahalal from a young age.

He considered his mother wise and intelligent and respected her much more than he did his father. While he felt he could discuss ideas with his mother, his father would issue categorical declarations that could not be questioned. Dayan felt his mother was more open, describing her as being "on the verge of liberalism." This attitude was manifested also toward Arabs: While Dayan's father was suspicious and kept his distance, his mother hosted them in their home.[10]

From an early age, Dayan began identifying with independent, nonconformist ideas that challenged the status quo. Rejecting the prevalent attitude in Nahalal that an academic education was less important than training for agricultural labor, and his father's vision that he become a farmer, Dayan wanted to continue studying.

In addition to Russian literature, Dayan read the Hebrew writings of Avraham Shlonksy and Natan Alterman and a wide range of classical literature in Hebrew translation. As a result, Dayan broadened his cultural horizons beyond those of his cohort in Nahalal, developing a level of sophistication unusual among his friends and acquaintances. According to Shabtai Teveth, who wrote a seminal biography of Dayan, this sophistication led to a complex view of the world, with room for shades of gray, unlike the black-and-white world of many of his contemporaries.[11] As a youth, Dayan loved ideological arguments and was active in a group called "The Hut," for which he organized debates and invited guest speakers. Even then, he tended to organize lectures on security and invited speakers on issues of Arab politics and culture.[12]

Dayan's Evolving Attitudes toward the Arab Enemy

Throughout his life as a soldier, military leader, and statesman, Dayan stood at the forefront of the Jewish people's struggle against the Arabs: Palestinian city

---

[5] Ibid., p. 28.
[6] Ibid., p. 32.
[7] Teveth, *Moshe Dayan*, p. 79.
[8] Naphtali Lau-Lavie, *Moshe Dayan*, London: Valentine Mitchell, 1968, p. 21.
[9] Teveth, *Moshe Dayan*, p. 79.
[10] Ibid., p. 99.
[11] Ibid., pp. 85–87.
[12] Ibid., pp. 123–124.

dwellers and rural *fellahin*, nomadic Bedouins, Arab inhabitants of neighboring Lebanon, Syria, Jordan, Iraq, and Egypt – they were all part of the Arab *ummah* (nation), speakers of Arabic, with a shared religion and ethos. Having grown up close to Arabs, and having been in contact with them during his adolescence, his attitudes toward them developed directly from his experiences and human contact with them in various contexts. Thus, when his worldview was being shaped, Dayan developed an understanding of the Arab perspective on the conflict along with empathy for them. Unlike many Jews of his day, who viewed Arabs as uncivilized barbarians, Dayan respected their connection to the land, even seeing in them a contemporary version of how the Jewish people must have lived in biblical times.

As a child, Dayan came into contact with the Arabs his mother hosted and those he met when his father would take him along as he traveled to the Arab village of Majdal on the Sea of Galilee to grind his wheat. For the child, this was a magical journey, during which his father would explain that the Arabs were hired farm laborers who had not evolved for hundreds of years, that their villages had no services or infrastructure, and that everybody was dirt poor, adding that they were largely responsible for their sorry state because they were lazy. But his harangues fell on deaf ears. Dayan was captivated by the Arabs he met and impressed by their ability to survive in this poverty and to make do with little.[13]

Even when running after his father's plow in the fields, Dayan met Arabs and Bedouins. One child, Wahash Hanhana from the Arab al-Mazarib tribe, became Dayan's friend, and they would plow the field and spend time together.[14] When the young Dayan went hiking with his classmates, they would encounter local Arabs in orchards and at springs. His friends recalled, "Moshe socialized with Arab kids more than the other Jewish kids. In particular, he liked the *fellahin*, the Arabs who labor and sweat. All of us were full of love for the laborers, but Moshe had a special attitude to them."[15]

Dayan read literature romanticizing the life of Arabs in the desert, including Moshe Smilansky's *Sons of Arabia*.[16] He even published a short story he wrote in the Nahalal newsletter with the heroes Ali and Mustafa, whom he and his friends joined on desert adventures, riding mares, wearing Bedouin clothing, and adopting Bedouin customs.

In his memoirs, Dayan noted that, while living in Degania, relations with the Arab neighbors were generally good, despite a few brief violent incidents:

---

[13] Ibid., p. 51.
[14] Ibid., pp. 51–52.
[15] Ibid., p. 67.
[16] Ibid., p. 67.

> A bond was forged between those who worked the land. Group members shared knowledge with their neighbors, there were courtesy visits back and forth, two families even made close friendships. The attacks, robberies, and murders of Jewish laborers were not driven by national motivation. The Arab gangs robbed and stole also from the Arab *fellahin* (peasants).[17]

But the violence between Jews and Arabs escalated on December 22, 1932, after a bomb was thrown into the shed of a Nahalal resident, Yaakobi, killing him and his eight-year-old son. The murder marked a turning point in Jewish–Arab relations because the motive was nationalistic: the perpetrators, from the Galilean town of Sfuriya, belonged to the *Qassamiya* nationalist movement.

The ever-curious Dayan, unable to accept his father's assertions at face value, wanted to investigate what was happening with the Arabs close-up, so he went to Sfuriya to interview the movement's members. "They are humble idealists; they pray often and operate on the basis of profound religious and national feeling," he wrote.[18] Recognizing their strength of belief and reflecting his optimism about the possibility of coexistence, he was deeply concerned: "The *Qassamiya* phenomenon shed light on the national, religious, and emotional chasm between those living to realize the Zionist vision and the Arabs; this chasm separates them even when it is concealed from the eye."[19]

The visits to Sfuriya typified Dayan's lifelong conduct. His great curiosity and extreme audacity led him to repeatedly risk his life; some considered his conduct reckless and foolhardy. Another aspect of his character, expressed in his visits to Sfuriya and throughout his career, was that he was never satisfied with secondhand reports and accounts; he always sought to come as close as possible to the scene and see things for himself.[20]

An unbridgeable gap opened up between Dayan and his father in their views of the Arabs. The father saw the Arabs who had murdered Yaakobi as nothing but "despicable murderers," arguing that "we are bringing them progress, and they murder us in return." The younger Dayan's view was more complex, believing that the Arabs' actions were motivated not by robbery but by nationalism.[21] The *Qassamiya* movement's members saw their actions as idealistic, reflecting the well-known adage that, "one person's terrorist is another's freedom fighter."

Relations with the Bedouin tribes living near Nahalal were also complex, sometimes friendly, at other times, conflict-ridden. Their confrontations indeed resembled ancient quarrels described in the Bible between farmers and nomadic herders.

---

[17] Dayan, *Avnei derekh*, p. 23.
[18] Ibid., p. 33.
[19] Ibid.
[20] Teveth, *Moshe Dayan*, p. 120.
[21] Ibid., p. 120.

The realization that the conflict was primal, premodern, with each side convinced of its righteousness, accompanied Dayan in the December 20, 1934, altercation with the neighboring al-Mazarib Bedouin tribe. This was one of many quarrels between Nahalal's inhabitants and the tribe's herders, who allowed their flocks to roam the expanding moshav's fields. That the settlers had purchased the land meant very little to the Bedouins, accustomed to using the fields around the moshav. On this day, a particularly violent brawl broke out between the Bedouins and some Nahalal members; a Bedouin clubbed Dayan over the head, wounding him badly. Nonetheless, Dayan continued what he had been doing – sowing the field – until he fell to the ground. That he continued sowing the field even when surrounded by Bedouins throwing rocks and clubbing him until he collapsed made a powerful impression on everyone there.[22] The story even made it into the newspaper, probably the first time Dayan became the focus of a news item. Certainly, the incident made him a local Nahalal hero.

Eyewitnesses claimed that Wahash, Dayan's childhood friend, had struck him from behind, while others accused a different tribesman.[23] Dayan understood the tribe's feelings and motives:

> I did not bear Wahash or the al-Mazarib tribe any ill will. Generations have been accustomed to herding in the *wadis* of Shimron and watering their flocks at the springs that have now become our possession. From my perspective, the Jewish National Fund is redeeming the land, but for Wahash and Abd al-Majid, these activities look and feel different. They've been told to get their tents out of the *wadi* where they and their ancestors have always lived. Six months later, I invited them to my wedding celebration. My invitation was gladly accepted; the Mazarib came in throngs.[24]

Indeed, al-Mazarib tribe members were among the guests at Dayan's wedding soon thereafter.[25]

The Arabs' closeness to nature and simplicity of life in that part of the land charmed Dayan. At this time, he still believed the two nations could coexist peacefully:

> My feelings about our Arab neighbors were positive. I liked their way of life and I respected them for their hard work, connection to the land, and immersion in the landscape around me. I had no doubt that it was possible to live with them in peace – they in their settlements and with their way of life and we in ours.[26]

---

[22] Ibid., pp. 137–138.
[23] Ibid., p. 139.
[24] Dayan, *Avnei derekh*, p. 34.
[25] Nowadays, the members of this tribe live in Zarzir near Nahalal, and many of them serve in the armed forces.
[26] Dayan, *Avnei derekh*, p. 32.

This tolerant attitude was strengthened by a hiking trip he took in the Beit She'an region during which Bedouins hosted him and his friends at their encampment – not the first time Dayan had been graciously hosted and protected by village elders – and it made a powerful impression on him. Dayan and his friends had their picture taken with the local emir who had extended his protection to them. Years later, Dayan made a point of locating him and sending him copies of the photos from the visit.[27]

On October 5, 1939, Dayan was apprehended by the British along with forty-two others, all Haganah (the underground Jewish Defense Organization) members, for illegal firearms possession. The forty-three were locked up in the Acre jail, which also housed Arabs with whom Dayan felt a kinship of destiny. In a letter to his siblings, he wrote:

> In practice, most of the Arab inmates are prisoners of the events, i.e., they represent the Arabs' current attitude to us. And every day, this parade goes around and around as a British officer and sergeant "supervise" it. The personal relations between us and the Revisionists,[28] on the one hand, and the Arabs on the other are very good ... Most of the gang members are idealists and religious believers, not mercenaries. And the personal suffering unifies us.[29]

At first, relations between the Arab and Jewish inmates were very tense, but over time, the two sides came to respect one another. Dayan saw this as an opportunity to learn more about the Arab perspective and deepen his understanding of their motives. He wrote:

> What goes on in the mind of the Arab who suddenly riots in Jaffa? I don't think I have reached a conclusion, but I have begun to understand them. Something's going on here, and it's not the bad guy versus the good guy. I've expressed this in my everyday life, in which I felt no antagonism towards Arabs as individuals.[30]

Evidence of the personal bonds Dayan forged came in 1942, after his release from jail, when he was invited as the guest of honor to the wedding of Abed Abeidat, a member of one of the gangs. After the War of Independence broke out, Dayan recruited Abeidat as his intelligence agent.[31]

---

[27] Teveth, *Moshe Dayan*, p. 133.
[28] Revisionists: The followers of the radical group Zeev Jabotinsky supported the creation of a Jewish state in the entire area of the British Mandate, including Transjordan. They formed two splinter groups – Etzel and Lehi – called the "Irgun" and "Stern Gang" by the British and considered terrorists.
[29] Teveth, *Moshe Dayan*, p. 196.
[30] Ibid., p. 197.
[31] Ibid., p. 248.

THE EDUCATION OF A STRATEGIST

Another of Dayan's connections was with Rashid Tahar, a Bedouin tracker, who had previously been a gang leader. Tahar, reputed to be a brave fighter, was well acquainted with the Syrian and Lebanese countryside. Later, despite his colleagues' concerns about Tahar's trustworthiness, Dayan decided to take him as a tracker on the operation to Lebanon in which Dayan lost his eye; ultimately, Rashid fought effectively and bravely on the front line and stayed by Dayan's side during the long evacuation to the Hadassah Hospital in Haifa.[32] Tahar proved his loyalty to his brothers in arms, quite the contrast to the popular notion that Arabs were treacherous.

The Young Fighter

Already as a young child, Dayan had learned to handle weapons, regularly participating in defense and guard duty as a matter of course.

> From as far back as I can remember myself, I remember there being a loaded rifle in the house. [My] familiarity with weapons was no different than my familiarity with the farm. Just as I don't remember when I started milking, I don't remember when I started caring for Father's carbine.[33]

At first, Dayan got permission to watch as his father cleaned his German carbine and its bullets. Later, he was allowed to clean it himself, and then to load it. At the age of ten, he practiced target shooting on bottles and such, but he received his own gun only when he was older. From the age of fourteen, when the men of Nahalal were called out, which would happen whenever someone in the settlement was threatened, Dayan would always be among the first to arrive on the scene, despite his young age.[34]

Following the 1929 pogroms against Jews, Nahalal's residents joined the Haganah, which provided training and weapons.[35] A group of adolescents, including Dayan, also joined. Their mission was to guard the training grounds and warn of approaching British troops. The youth also underwent self-defense and hand-to-hand combat training, an early form of Krav Maga, and weapons training.[36] In 1931, Dayan was one of a group of youths on horseback who patrolled Nahalal's fields. The youths were trained to ride like Cossacks by Nahum Habinsky and Yosef Dromi, former Russian army soldiers. Dayan was enchanted by their stories, imagining himself as a horseback-riding Cossack.[37] Years later, this image came to haunt him, as his political rival, then-Prime

---

[32] Dayan, *Avnei derekh*, p. 52.
[33] Teveth, *Moshe Dayan*, p. 104.
[34] Ibid., p. 108.
[35] Mordechai Bar-On, *Moshe Dayan: Koron hayav 1915–1981* (Hebrew), Tel Aviv: Am Oved, 2014, p. 31.
[36] Teveth, *Moshe Dayan*, p. 104.
[37] Ibid., p. 108.

Minister Levi Eshkol, sneeringly referred to him as a Cossack.[38] The riders would charge and scatter Bedouins who were herding their flocks on the settlement's fields. Dayan demonstrated courage and a fighting spirit, and his comrades testified to his gift for "battlefield leadership." While neither the strongest nor the fastest, he still stood out and set the tone.[39]

Enlisting in the Notrim

On July 12, 1935, Moshe Dayan married Ruth. The young couple then traveled to London, staying for six months to learn about the world beyond Nahalal.[40] Unlike his wife, Dayan deeply missed Palestine and felt uncomfortable in London. They returned in February 1936 and joined a group from Nahalal that was getting ready to settle Shimron, a new moshav in the north of the country.

In April 1936, the Arab Revolt erupted. This coincided with a new chapter in Dayan's military education as he enlisted in the Notrim (in Hebrew, "guard"), a British armed-police force manned by Jews. In his diary, Dayan noted that these were his first steps in military activity. The Notrim were recruited as an auxiliary force to help the British police, but one unit of the Notrim was unofficially subordinate to the Haganah, which recruited its members, while the salaries, weapons, and uniforms were all British.[41] The first Notrim enlisted in May 1936 and were sent to defend the rural settlements and fields around the Jordan Valley. In 1937, as guerrilla warfare intensified, the British recruited more men. The nearly 15,000 men were divided into 10 regional regiments. Dayan was recruited to the regiment responsible for Nahalal.

The units, equipped with pickup trucks, were meant to patrol and provide rapid responses to security problems. The British, needing local guides, chose Dayan as one, as he was familiar with the valley and its surroundings. The company's main mission was to prevent sabotage to the British-owned oil pipeline running from Kirkuk in northern Iraq to Haifa. The Arab fighters would puncture the pipeline, let the oil flow out, and then set fire to it, causing prolonged fires. This caused tremendous financial losses and disrupted oil supplies to Britain.

To protect the pipeline, the British also deployed the Royal Scots and the Yorkshire Rifleman Regiments, and Dayan used the English he had learned at school and during his recent stay in London to communicate with them. For Dayan, raised as a farmer-fighter who had brawled with local Arabs, this was his first encounter with a professional, hierarchical, disciplined army operating according to drills and procedures and maintaining a routine of formations and duty rosters. Dayan was not very impressed by the British ability

---

[38] Ibid.
[39] Ibid., p. 110.
[40] Bar-On, *Moshe Dayan*, p. 37.
[41] Ibid., p. 39.

to confront Arab saboteurs, telling friends that the British were untrained in field skills and unfit for such missions. He found them apathetic, loud, and clumsy, mostly relying simply on their presence to maintain order.[42] Dayan learned clear tactical lessons in irregular guerrilla warfare, noting in his diary:

> In the eight months of operating with His Royal Highness's army, I've seen the impotence of a regular army operating on the basis of established plans and procedures in confronting saboteurs who know the area, move on foot, are assimilated and involved with the local population, and choose the place and time that are convenient for them to strike. It was clear that the way to fight the gangs was by seizing the initiative. It is necessary to strike first and attack them in their bases and ambush them as they move.[43]

These were Dayan's first experiences in dealing with irregular warfare, a major and very palpable issue he had to confront throughout his career and his life.

In 1937, Dayan attended a British Army sergeants' course taught in English at the Tzrifin Camp by the 2nd Battalion Black Watch Regiment. He quickly realized that the shoe polishing and parade drills aspects of the military were not for him. His rebellious, individualistic free spirit was badly suited to the routine. Nonetheless, he understood the need of the British Empire's army for "this bullshit," as he called it, because no large entity can be managed without uniformity, discipline, and order.[44] But this particular course contributed nothing to helping him better confront the military challenges in the valley.

In the spring of 1937, Dayan was appointed commander of the mobile guard of Nahalal's Notrim unit. Here, he was noted for seizing the initiative and going on the offensive. Although this approach was not coordinated among them, it was shared by other prominent commanders, including Yitzhak Sadeh and Yaakov Dori.[45] Later, this approach, most closely identified with Sadeh, was dubbed "operating beyond the fence."[46]

---

[42] Teveth, *Moshe Dayan*, p. 157.
[43] Dayan, *Avnei derekh*, p. 36.
[44] Dayan, *Avnei derekh*, p. 37. This is how psychologist and military historian Dixon described military rituals in his book: Norman Dixon, *Hapsikhologiya shel hashmlumi'e-liyut batsava* (in Hebrew translation), Tel Aviv: Maarakhot, 2003. Dixon claimed that these rituals become the military's be-all and end-all, controlling it, and damaging the creativity and originality needed to confront new battlefield challenges.
[45] Yaakov Dori (1899–1973), the IDF's first chief of staff. Having immigrated to Palestine with his family in 1906, he enlisted in the British Army toward the end of World War I, serving in the Jewish Battalions. In 1939, he was appointed the Haganah's chief of staff and was responsible for preparing it for war in 1947. After the state's establishment, he was appointed the IDF commander, a position he held until 1949 when ill health forced him to resign.
[46] Teveth, *Moshe Dayan*, p. 159.

During his Notrim service, Dayan wrote a booklet, "Fieldcraft," addressing various aspects of the subject, such as knowing the terrain and exploiting it for guerrilla warfare, setting up ambushes, sneaking into enemy territory, and patrolling. Dayan sent the booklet, which was used as lesson plans, to Dori, then the Haganah commander of the northern sector and head of the Haganah's training headquarters. Dori was highly impressed, and while it was never published as an official handbook, it certainly influenced Haganah training.

The handbook criticized regular armies' rigidity, offering instead knowledge and skills required in situations that change on the ground, an approach Dayan applied throughout his long career. Dayan himself ran drills with his men using his methods, raiding protected Haganah compounds. In one exercise, he infiltrated the Haganah's Jo'ara base where most of the organization's courses were taught. The base guards argued that this penetration was not a real achievement because it was accomplished by breaking the rules. Dayan dismissively retorted that there were no rules of warfare in reality; fighters had to operate according to conditions on the ground and only the outcome mattered.[47]

Commanders' Course and Introduction to Yitzhak Sadeh

The next stage in Dayan's military development was taking the Haganah's six-week-long platoon commanders' course, the first to be explicitly defined as such.[48] Dayan considered it superior to the British Army course he had undergone; indeed, many of the participants would eventually form the IDF command backbone.[49] Most of the training consisted of daytime and nighttime field exercises. The course was unique in being entirely devoted to combat exercises, focusing on training units and mobile troops following the Haganah's field platoons' experiences during the Arab Revolt. Drills focused mainly on platoon and infantry squad structures. Sometimes, several platoons operated simultaneously, representing an innovation for the Haganah. Special emphasis was placed on the indirect approach, such as exploiting the enemy's weaknesses and attacking from the flank. Moreover, the course stressed the platoon commander's character and role. The trainees studied the doctrines of the classical thinkers, including Carl von Clausewitz, and influential contemporaries, such as John Frederick Fuller and Basil Henry Liddell Hart. They also took a course on the German army's tactics and structure after World War I.[50]

---

[47] Ibid., p. 164.
[48] Yigal Sheffy, *Sikat mem-mem: Hamahshava hats'va'it bakursim l'k'tsinim bahaganah* (Hebrew), Tel Aviv: Ministry of Defense Publishing, 1991, p. 61.
[49] Bar-On, *Moshe Dayan*, p. 41.
[50] Sheffy, *Sikat mem-mem*, pp. 63–66.

Here, Moshe Dayan first met Yitzhak Sadeh, who would go on to build the Palmach, the Haganah's elite fighting unit.[51] Dayan was profoundly impressed by the "old man" (his nickname), his courage, élan, and originality. Dayan also met Yigal Allon, one of the promising young leaders, for the first time during the course. With their very different personalities, Allon and Dayan were to become lifelong rivals.[52]

The next significant milestone in Dayan's development was his move to Hanita on the Lebanese border on March 21, 1938. Against the background of the Arab Revolt, some fifty "wall and tower" settlements were constructed, employing modular prefabricated structures on the ground so that a completely new settlement could be built overnight. The settlements were surrounded by a wall with an observation and communications tower, with tents for accommodation and a communal mess hall. Armed Haganah members and Notrim, stationed in different areas around Mandatory Palestine, would defend the "wall and tower" settlements. Dori led the settlement of Hanita, while Sadeh and his deputies Dayan and Allon commanded the defense force. They came under fierce attack already on their first night there, immediately after setting up the settlement; this was probably Dayan's first significant baptism by fire.

The attack on Hanita began at midnight. A large Arab force approached, getting within thirty meters of the new settlement. The defenders had 120 rifles and succeeded in fending off the Arabs at the cost of two dead. Dayan reported that Sadeh was not satisfied with simply defending Hanita and wanted to order a unit to go out on an offensive action, but Dori would not authorize what he considered too dangerous an action.[53] Another violent incident occurred four days later when an Arab gang attacked a group of laborers who were paving a road to the settlement. A platoon commanded by Sadeh overwhelmed them and drove them away. Sadeh praised Dayan and Allon for their performance.[54]

Hanita's founding was commemorated in a famous photograph of Yitzhak Sadeh embracing the two young, uniformed Notrim sergeants – Moshe Dayan on his right and Yigal Allon on his left (Figure 1.1). On the back of the photograph, Israel's future first president, Haim Weizmann, then president of the Zionist Federation and the Jewish Agency, inscribed the prescient words: "The General Staff."[55]

---

[51] Yitzhak Sadeh (1890–1952), an IDF general, commander, strategist, educator, and writer. He immigrated to Mandatory Palestine in 1920 and cofounded the Yosef Trumpeldor Labor and Defense Battalion (colloquially known as Gdud Ha'avoda). Sadeh served in the Haganah and founded the Field Platoons and the Special Operations Units. In 1941, he founded the Palmach (Strike Forces), which he commanded until 1945.
[52] Bar-On, *Moshe Dayan*, p. 40.
[53] Dayan, *Avnei derekh*, p. 38.
[54] Teveth, *Moshe Dayan*, p. 167.
[55] Yigal Allon (1918–1980), Israeli military man and politician, commander of the Palmach, an IDF commander in the War of Independence, a Member of Knesset (MK), and an

Figure 1.1 Moshe Dayan (left) in Kibbutz Hanita with Yitzhak Sadeh and Yigal Allon, 1938. Source: Universal History Archive/Contributor/Universal Images Group/Getty Images.

Orde Charles Wingate and His Influence

Dov Yermiya, a Haganah commander, recalled the arrival of Captain Orde Charles Wingate (1903–1944) to Hanita: "One night, a taxicab came to Hanita and a very strange figure emerged. He carried two rifles, a dictionary, and a few Hebrew newspapers. We looked at him with astonishment. We wondered how he had dared come here alone at night. This made a tremendous impression on us."[56]

In fact, Wingate was a British army officer who specialized in guerrilla warfare. He arrived in Mandatory Palestine in 1936 after having served in Sudan and Ethiopia, where he developed new methods for ambushes and raids. His unconventional military approach matched his uninhibited personality, which at times made him seem extremely eccentric. Coming from a Scottish family belonging to the Plymouth Brethren Church, which viewed the Jews as the chosen people and believed in the prophecy of the Day of Judgment, Wingate supported the Zionist enterprise for religious reasons, believing that

---

Israeli government minister. Allon and Dayan, two promising, native-born Israelis who followed a similar trajectory from the army to politics, long competed with one another, whether overtly or covertly.

[56] Teveth, *Moshe Dayan*, p. 168.

the war of the day of judgment would take place in Megiddo, and that the Jewish people had to prepare for it.

Wingate arrived in Mandatory Palestine in September 1936, serving first as an intelligence officer. In 1937, Wingate's recommendations on how to confront the Arab enemy in the land of Israel were finally accepted by the British military leadership. Following a comprehensive study Wingate had made of the modus operandi of the Arab gangs, a study that included discussions with the Haganah's leaders, on June 5, 1938, Wingate submitted a report recommending the formation of special night squads that he would lead, whose purpose would be to crush terrorism in the Land of Israel's northern region using unprecedented methods of warfare.

Dayan met Wingate in 1938 near Nahalal just when Wingate was undertaking his study of the Arab gangs. In fractured Hebrew, Wingate explained his ambush methods to the Shimron group, of which Dayan was then a member. Wingate reproached the settlement's defenders for not going beyond the wall and not initiating attacks on the enemy.[57]

Wingate's mastery of navigation and fieldcraft deeply impressed Dayan. He said that Wingate "is a groundbreaking military genius rebelling against conventions."[58] Wingate became a role model, and he and Dayan formed a relatively close relationship. For Dayan, the way Wingate led, such as eating and drinking in the field only after ensuring that his soldiers had eaten and drunk, or his insistence on being at the head of a raid formation rather than sending scouts before the forward line, demonstrated combat leadership at its best. Wingate combined the professional authority of an experienced British officer with extraordinary personal charisma and left a lasting impression on Dayan.

His Jewish unit included Dayan and many of the fighters who had secured Hanita.[59] The squad's base, commanded by Wingate, was located in Ein Harod; its objective was protecting the oil pipeline – the same mission that the Royal Scots and the Yorkshire Riflemen, whom Dayan had joined two years earlier, had carried out with little success. Wingate's immediate task was to have his unit take control of nighttime activities, which was a condition for securing the region. Until that time, only the Arab gangs operated at night.

Wingate's doctrine was based on maximal mobility, initiative and offense, intelligence, ruses, secrecy (deflection, misleading the enemy, infiltration, and surprise)[60] – principles that suited a small army with few resources and which

---

[57] Ibid., p. 168.
[58] Teveth, *Moshe Dayan*, p. 179.
[59] Wingate's squad in Ein Harod consisted of eighteen British men and twenty-four Jewish men, mostly from Hanita. Teveth, *Moshe Dayan*, p. 169.
[60] Shlomi Shetrit, "Plagot halayla hameyuhadot (SNS) bamered ha'aravi: Me'afyenim shel hayehidot vetorat halehima shela bemivhan hape'ilut hatsva'it" (Hebrew), MA thesis, Bar-Ilan University, Ramat Gan, 2013, p. 100.

were therefore enthusiastically adopted by the founders of the IDF. The Special Night Squads quickly seized control of the night and succeeded in stopping the attacks on the pipeline.

Wingate impressed his Jewish partners, including Dayan, with his familiarity with the terrain, daring, and great resourcefulness. Unlike other British officers, and similar to Dayan, he abhorred formations, criticism, salutes, and parades – all the hallmarks of a regular army. But he was meticulous about his weapons' cleanliness and carefully plotted his operations.

Among Wingate's best-known successful operations was one his unit carried out with Dayan and the Mobile Defense unit, attacking a Bedouin encampment near the village of al-Awadin. This was a transit station for delivering weapons to the Samaria region and a jumping-off point for the Arab gangs' assault and robbery raids. Wingate's plan was based on a ruse: A truck stopped about one kilometer before the village, near the railroad tracks, and men disguised as railroad workers disembarked. In reality, this was a squad of Dayan's men, who served as bait. Still inside the truck were Wingate's men, armed with two Lewis machine guns. The Arabs, who considered the laborers easy prey, hurried to attack them, but were then cut down by fire from the guns hidden in the truck. Panic overtook the Arabs, who scattered in all directions, but they then fell into the ambushes Wingate had placed all along the intersections to the village.

The ruse of camouflaging the men as railroad workers was actually Dayan's idea. Wingate's appreciation of and respect for Dayan was greatly enhanced following this operation. He identified in Dayan qualities he particularly appreciated, such as daring and creativity. As for the daring, Dayan had been one of the men disguised as a railroad worker, exposing him to considerable danger.[61]

Wingate profoundly influenced Dayan, paving the way for organizing units specially trained for guerrilla and counterinsurgency warfare. Wingate also influenced Dayan regarding retaliatory acts. Even then, it was clear that it would not always be possible to prevent the next Arab attack. This was true of the dreadful massacre in Tiberias on October 2, 1938. While Wingate and his men were concentrated elsewhere because of misleading information, the Arabs managed to attack and kill nineteen Jews in the city, eleven of them children. In response, Wingate carried out retaliatory operations in neighboring Arab villages. Dayan, too, initiated several retaliations: In one, he and his fellow fighters dressed as British soldiers, entered the heart of a village, and detonated a bomb in the house of the Mukhtar (village leader). Dayan would later initiate actions on his own without getting prior approval from his Haganah superiors.[62] In later years, Dayan would show understanding of

[61] Teveth, *Moshe Dayan*, p. 172.
[62] Bar-On, *Moshe Dayan*, p. 44.

subordinates who took local initiative and did not always ask for their commanders' authorization.

Wingate spent only about two and a half years in Palestine, leaving in May 1939, but he left a strong imprint on the Jewish settlement in general and the Haganah – who nicknamed him "The Friend" – in particular. As a military man, he was original, daring, and visionary. His methods of action and way of thinking about military matters served as an important foundation for constructing a Hebrew defense force, which would become the Israel Defense Force about a decade later. His military approach included collecting accurate intelligence before an operation, seizing the initiative, going on the offense, exploiting the advantage of night, using small, selected units, and shifting the fighting as rapidly as possible to enemy ground. These rules became fundamental components of the IDF's early doctrine of warfare. This approach was radically different from the preceding approach of passive defense of the settlements. To this day, the IDF considers him one of the people who had the most influence on its doctrine and philosophy.

In British Prison

The period between October 1939 and June 1941 was crucial in shaping Dayan's personality and worldview.[63] During this time, he was imprisoned for illegal possession of arms and sentenced to a ten-year term. While in prison, Dayan and his fellow Haganah members experienced a dramatic role reversal: During the riots, he had been a member of a legal force that fought the Arab subversion. Now, overnight, he and his comrades had themselves become a subversive force. The hunter had become the hunted. Dayan now experienced the same sense of persecution and need to hide that until then had been the enemy's – the Arabs, along with members of the splinter Jewish groups, Etzel and Lehi.

The background to all this was the outbreak of World War II in 1939. Although fought far from Mandatory Palestine, the war made its mark there too. The British had to focus on the tremendous challenge of winning the war and on May 19, 1939, they issued the White Paper, limiting Jewish immigration to Mandatory Palestine and forbidding Jews from buying land from Arabs in many parts of the region. Enmity and suspicion replaced cooperation between the Haganah and the British security forces, as the British began arresting Haganah members for illegal arms possession.

As a result of these developments and based on the fear that the British would raid the training camp where illegal arms were kept, the Haganah moved its commanders' courses from Jo'ara to Yavne'el, renaming the course a "Commanding Officers' Course." This was the first time an officers' course

---

[63] Teveth, *Moshe Dayan*, p. 175.

was given in a large-scale format, and it covered many subjects, including artillery, which until then had not been taught. The course was led by Dr. Raphael Lev, who had earlier served in the Austrian army. Among the first six course instructors, very carefully handpicked by Dori, were the perennial rivals Dayan and Allon.[64]

The courses in Yavne'el,[65] developed gradually based on the Haganah's original command course, are considered the first Haganah courses and were fully adapted to platoon commanders, like comparable courses in other advanced armies.[66] The objective was not just to train officers for platoon commander positions, but also to cultivate the commanders' independent thinking, stressing in-depth independent thought. The instructors encouraged students to acquire military education, gather information, plan, and seize the initiative.[67]

Lev, a World War I veteran, incorporated materials customarily studied in regular armies, making an important impact on the students and instructors. However, the materials were not suited to the unique circumstances of the Land of Israel, and therefore it was critical to balance his approach with that of other instructors. Among other things, they stressed that warfare had no single established solution. "Every act is based on the situation; use your head, guys, your head," exhorted Yosef Avidar.[68] The instructors from Wingate's Special Night Squads, with their combat experience, made a unique contribution to the course.

After the British inspected the course site in Yavne'el, where illegal weapons were discovered, the Haganah decided not to take any risks and moved the course to Ein Hashofet. The students and commanders were divided into several groups. The main mission of the core group, commanded by Lev and Moshe Carmel, was to carry unlicensed weapons to Ein Hashofet on foot at night. Dayan was among these forty-three men, the group known as the "Mem-Gimmel" (two Hebrew letters whose alphanumeric coding equals forty-three). En route, the group was discovered by a patrol of the Trans-Jordan Frontier Force, and its members were arrested and sent to the British prison in Acre.

In Acre Prison, the detainees were interrogated and beaten. The British reminded their subjects that bearing illegal weapons was punishable by death. At first, Dayan – unlike the other detainees – cooperated with his interrogators, but when they continued to beat him, he threatened vengeance from his comrades on the outside. The beatings stopped. Dayan decided to provide

---

[64] Teveth, *Moshe Dayan*, p. 176.
[65] Two courses were given twice. The second came to an earlier end than planned because of the arrest of the forty-three men.
[66] Sheffy, *Sikat mem-mem*, pp. 75–76.
[67] Ibid., p. 81.
[68] Ibid., p. 77.

certain innocuous information, such as their membership in the Haganah, while trying to explain to the British that the Haganah was not their enemy.

Dayan, used to the open vistas of the rural areas and fields of the Jezre'el Valley, found the experience of a narrow, locked cell difficult. In his diary, he wrote, "Our state of mind changed when the iron gates of the prison clanged shut behind us."[69]

The detainees became pawns between the British, who demanded that the Haganah fully relinquish their arms, and the Jewish Agency, which played the innocent, claiming that there was no such thing as a national armed organization such as the Haganah. It was the detainees' bad luck that the new British military leader in Mandatory Palestine, General Evelyn Hugh Barker, would later be revealed as a virulent anti-Semite. The men's trial lasted a few days, and British officers who had served with Dayan testified as character witnesses for him. However, the verdict was brutal: one life sentence and ten years' imprisonment for all the rest.

This was a harsh blow to the detainees' morale. After the verdict, they were moved to an Ottoman-era prison that had undergone only minor repairs during the British Mandate, where they were held under severe restrictions. There, the group organized and elected its officers. Dayan, chosen to maintain external contact with the prison authorities, submitted the group members' demands to them. His letters from that period show that he maintained his equanimity and did not sink into depression. He even managed to find some positive points in his situation, especially regarding relationships he formed with Arab gang members enduring the same fate as he. "Usually, life here is interesting," he wrote, "and we celebrated and enjoyed the three days of the holiday (the Eid al-Fitr marking the end of the month of Ramadan). The Arabs' attitude towards us is very good, even though most of them are gang members."[70] Close relationships even burgeoned between the Haganah members and the imprisoned Revisionists, their Jewish rivals.[71]

Unlike the other inmates, Dayan was indifferent to the prison's physical conditions and food, attributing his steeliness to his mother's character and how she had raised him.[72] Nonetheless, after his release, Dayan worried about returning to prison, and for the duration of the British Mandate, he did everything possible not to be caught in a situation threatening possible imprisonment. There is no doubt that his stay there left its scars. He emerged a different man than the one who had entered.[73]

---

[69] Dayan, *Avnei derekh*, p. 40.
[70] Teveth, *Moshe Dayan*, p. 192.
[71] Ibid., p. 195.
[72] Ibid., p. 202.
[73] Mordechai Naor (ed.), *Moshe Dayan: Mikh'tvei ahava* (Hebrew), Tel Aviv: Yedioth Ahronoth Publishers, 2016, p. 135.

The Injury

Dayan and his fellow fighters were released early from prison because of another strategic global shift – the threat from General Erwin Rommel, commander of the Afrika Korps, to Egypt and the Middle East, along with the Vichy regime's seizure of control of Syria and Lebanon in early 1941. Now feeling besieged, the British felt that they needed the cooperation of Palestine's Jews. This reversal led to the release of the Mem-Gimmel almost overnight after eighteen months in prison.

In response to security events, the Haganah decided to establish a national force to be on high alert to defend the Yishuv. The first two companies were commanded by Sadeh.[74] The men considered the most audacious and promising were appointed company commanders, including Dayan and Allon. The British approached the Haganah for scouts and sappers to help the British force invading Lebanon, which was under Vichy control. Dayan and some thirty of his men were sent together with an Australian force to Lebanon's western sector. Most of the men were unfamiliar with the terrain and inexperienced in war. Some, in fact, had never even had basic weapons training.

Dayan crossed deep into territory held by the Vichy soldiers to scout it out. Because he was unfamiliar with it, these incursions – usually initiated by Dayan, not the British – produced several useful reports on the conditions of the terrain, axes, and location of the French forces.

About these incursions, Dayan wrote:

> None of us knew Syria, the terrain where we were supposed to be the guides. Only one of us was highly proficient in Arabic,[75] yet according to the plan, we were supposed to impersonate and act like Arabs. Among the guys were some who had had no experience ever shooting with live ammunition. Most had no experience operating a machine or sub-machine gun, we'd been given no maps, and within a few days, we had to get these people ready to function as scouts familiar with the terrain. As for the problem of trust – we overcame that with the help of two experienced commanders. Illegal weapons – those came from the Haganah's storage. The most important question remained: knowing the terrain.[76]

The British invasion of Vichy-controlled Lebanon began on June 8, 1942. The night before, Dayan entered enemy territory with a spearheading force of

---

[74] On May 15, 1941, two companies were set up under the command of Sadeh, following a decision to establish a national force to protect the Yishuv and to serve as reserves for cooperation with the British Army. This force was the core from which the Palmach developed, although it took on its name only later. Although he adopted its notable social and political features, this made it possible for Dayan to claim, for the sake of political struggles later on, that he never served in the Palmach.

[75] Dayan's knowledge of the language was limited to basic conversational Arabic.

[76] Dayan, *Avnei derekh*, p. 49.

sixteen – ten Australians, five Israelis, and Tahar, their Arab guide. Their missions were to cut the communications line located near the coastal road and to block the road about 5 km north of the border. Both were successfully completed. The third mission was to seize control of two bridges next to Iskanderon village, which crossed the Lebanese coastal road.

The Israeli column was led by Dayan, Tahar, and Dayan's friend Zalman Mart, a commander in the Notrim who would later be Dayan's subordinate as battalion commander in the Jerusalem sector during the War of Independence.[77] The force's mission was to prevent the bridges from being demolished so that the invading British could use them. Arriving at the bridges, the men found that they were not rigged with explosives, and all they had to do was to wait for the main British invading force. When that failed to arrive – due to a delay at the border crossings where the French had laid mines, unknown to Dayan, Dayan and the Australian officers decided to move southwards and situate themselves near the bridges in a building that served as a local police station, unaware that the building served as the forward headquarters of the French force.

The French identified the advancing force, and a firefight erupted. According to testimonies, Dayan threw a grenade from a distance of about 25 m, stopping the machine gun on the building's roof. Then he and Mart rushed ahead and captured the structure. Four French soldiers died in the battle and ten or so surrendered. In Dayan's force, one Australian died, and several were wounded. Their main problem was that the unit was cut off, surrounded by the enemy and under enemy fire. Dayan organized the building's defense, and his fellow fighters operated the machine gun and mortar they seized from the French.[78] While Dayan was observing events with binoculars he had taken from a French officer, a bullet hit the binocular lens, shattering his left eye. He lay there wounded for about six hours, never losing consciousness, but without the ability to see, only hear. Dayan was wounded at 7 am; the British forces reached the building only at 1 pm. Dayan was evacuated by a British truck to Hadassah Hospital in Haifa. Before being taken in for treatment, he told Mart, "Never mind. I lived with two eyes for 26 years. It's not so bad – one can live with just one eye too." The story of Dayan's injury was covered by the Hebrew press, lauding him as a hero. The Australian officers also expressed deep admiration for his performance in battle.[79]

In this action, Dayan's future command qualities had already come to the fore: courage, risking his life while seizing the lead, coolheadedness

---

[77] Bar-On, *Moshe Dayan*, pp. 50–51.
[78] The Australians and the Israelis told somewhat different versions about who seized command of the unit, but there is no doubt that Dayan and Mart led the fighting and the rush. Teveth, *Moshe Dayan*, p. 213.
[79] Bar-On, *Moshe Dayan*, p. 53.

combined with an instinct for adventure, a desire for audacious action, and improvisational abilities.[80]

Dayan was optimistic and thought he would recover quickly, but his injury was actually quite severe. Dayan and Ruth moved in with Ruth's parents in Jerusalem so that he could get daily treatment at Hadassah Hospital. He suffered intensely from embedded shards, causing him headaches. His arm, full of shrapnel, became partly paralyzed. Some of these medical issues plagued him throughout his life. Attempts to reconstruct the eye socket so that he could be fitted with a glass eye failed, and Dayan was forced to wear a patch, which would become his trademark.

Soon, all this began to cloud his mood. He wrote, "I didn't think I'd be able to get back to military fitness, and sank into sad thoughts about the future – the life of cripple without a profession or financial foundation."[81]

Indeed, while his friends were rising through ranks and positions, Dayan felt that he was left behind because of his injury. Would he have joined the Palmach had he not been wounded? While the question remains open, it is doubtful that he would have found his place in the newly founded organization. The reason, according to Teveth, is that the Palmach reflected the ethos of the kibbutz movement, whereas Dayan was a "moshavnik," the owner of an independent farm in Nahalal. Furthermore, his individualism was ill suited to the ideological conformity the Palmach demanded.[82] Moreover, Allon, Dayan's prominent and constant rival, was appointed the Palmach's deputy commander and then its commander. It is unlikely the two would have found a place together at the top of so small an organization. Most Palmach members were from the kibbutz movement and were totally loyal to Allon. In fact, the only one who championed and supported Dayan was Sadeh.

Intelligence, Negotiations, Party Politics, and Political-Security Issues

Because of his injury, Dayan was sidelined from operational command activity, which is key in every military endeavor. However, what seemed at the time a disaster would later prove to be a blessing, as he acquired experience in areas that would serve him well in the future. First, he joined the Political Department of the Jewish Agency with the help of Reuven Shilo'ah, who was close to Ruth Dayan's parents and knew Dayan from the time he had worked on behalf of the Mem-Gimmel in Acre Prison. The Jewish Agency then had contacts with British intelligence as it prepared for the possibility of a German conquest of Palestine. In the middle of 1941, Dayan proposed establishing an espionage network – the Moshe Dayan Network. The plan included building

---

[80] Teveth, *Moshe Dayan*, p. 208.
[81] Dayan, *Avnei derekh*, p. 52.
[82] Teveth, *Moshe Dayan*, p. 227.

a network of radio stations to broadcast news about events in the conquered areas to the British. In September, a course was held for station operators, and Dayan set up six stations with the help of its graduates.[83]

Dayan devised other ideas he proposed to the British: setting up an undercover department with Jews impersonating Arabs, and a German department with German-speaking Jews who would impersonate Germans if Mandatory Palestine was occupied by the Nazis. The British accepted the proposals, but, in the end, it was left to the Palmach to execute them. The German department project was halted after the threat to Mandatory Palestine was removed following Rommel's defeat at El Alamein in the fall of 1942.

Before leaving Jerusalem to return to Nahalal, expecting to lead a quiet farmer's life, Dayan got caught up in another adventure. On Haganah instructions, Dayan embarked on a trip to Baghdad in August 1942 as part of a convoy of British trucks driven by Jews from the Yishuv. Dayan was asked to smuggle suitcases full of weapons meant for the self-defense of the Jews of Baghdad who had, a year previously, been the targets of the *Farhoud* – anti-Semitic riots against the Jewish community. To elude the British police, Dayan removed his eyepatch to avoid identification. He joined up with Enzo Sereni, the Jewish Agency's emissary there, contacted the local Haganah activists, and delivered the weapons to them. On the way back, he smuggled in two Jews who had fled Poland, one of them David Azrieli, who would become a renowned architect, developer, designer, philanthropist, and major real estate tycoon.

For several years, Dayan lived with his family developing the farm he had bought in Nahalal. He also spent time with his children, his sons Udi and Assaf, born in 1942 and 1945, respectively, joining his eldest, Yael. However, because of the turbulent events of the time, in 1944 he was again called on to undertake missions for the Haganah.

On February 1, 1944, Menachem Begin, Etzel's leader, declared a revolt against the British. This completely contravened the Jewish Agency's policy of Yishuv cooperation with the British effort, including recruiting an independent Jewish Brigade as part of the British Army (known as the Brigade, founded in July 1944). After two Lehi fighters killed Lord Moyne, the senior British representative to the Middle East, the Haganah leadership decided to eliminate these more radical organizations. A Haganah unit began actions against them named the Saison, French for "season" and an abbreviation for "saison de chasse" – hunting season. Dayan was recruited to the task by the Haganah, even though – or perhaps because – he had shown a positive attitude toward the Revisionists in Acre Prison and did not resent them for their ideology, as did many Palmach members.[84] For obvious reasons, Dayan spoke little about his part in this affair, but we do know that he met and spoke

---

[83] Bar-On, *Moshe Dayan*, p. 55.
[84] Teveth, *Moshe Dayan*, p. 234.

with the leaders of the various organizations. Begin wrote in his memoirs: "Dayan spoke warm words of encouragement ... [saying] that he respected our actions."[85] Dayan earned Begin's trust, and Begin never bore Dayan any ill will. Indeed, many years later, Begin appointed Dayan foreign minister in his government.

Dayan succeeded in establishing relations and building trust even with Lehi, a more militant organization than Etzel. One senior Lehi member who was held captive by the Palmach wrote to Dayan urging his presence at a meeting between Lehi and the Haganah: "You have already gained a reasonable degree of trust already ... You do understand that one of the guarantees of success for any negotiations is that spirit of personal sacrifice that creates a background for deep mutual understanding."[86] This was Dayan's first experience with negotiations between stubborn rivals, and he soon proved his talent. Comparing Allon's and Dayan's approaches to these organizations, Teveth noted that Allon detested the path chosen by Etzel fighters and felt they caused considerable damage. But due to conscientious objections, he resigned his position as commander of the Saison. In contrast, Dayan did not hesitate to fulfill the mission entrusted to him, even though he felt no animosity toward the splinter organizations and even showed a certain amount of respect for their activities. In this, he hewed to Ben-Gurion's approach that the best interests of *mamlachtiut* – the common values of a Jewish state outweighed all partisan politics.

Over the next few years, the dominant factions of the Palmach – made up of kibbutz members and members of the United Labor Movement (a splinter of Mapai, the Workers' Party of the Land of Israel, a democratic socialist party dominant in Israeli politics for many years) – kept Dayan at arm's length from operational activity. A vacuum was created when the Labor Unity Movement, known as Faction 2, broke off from Mapai and was filled by young people, including Dayan, who had already participated in the forum established by Israel Galili in 1939 nicknamed "the Young Turks" (adopting the name of the Ottoman reform movement forty years earlier). That forum was designed for open debate of various issues in a free atmosphere, where the participants' established ranks and hierarchies were of little importance. The forum discussed the establishment of a national General Staff and changes in the Haganah's structure.[87]

Dayan first became involved with party politics in the fall of 1944, focusing primarily on his own election, during which time he became acquainted with another young, ambitious politician, Shimon Persky, later known as Shimon

---

[85] Menachem Begin, *Hamered: Zikhronotav shel mefaked ha'irgun hatsva'I haleumi be'erets yisrael* (Hebrew), Jerusalem: Ahi'asasf, 1950, p. 391.
[86] Teveth, *Moshe Dayan*, p. 235.
[87] Yehuda Harel, *Halohem: Hayav ve'alilotav shel Moshe Dayan* (Hebrew), Tel Aviv: Moked, 1967, p. 58.

Peres.[88] In the winter of 1946, after being embroiled in the young party members' struggle with its elders at the sixth Mapai convention held September 5, 1946, where Dayan was a delegate, he and Peres traveled to Basel as observers at the 22nd World Zionist Congress, the core issue of which was the struggle between the leaders of the Zionist movement: David Ben-Gurion and Haim Weizmann. This was both a personal struggle and a struggle over what path the country should take. Weizmann was conciliatory toward the British, while Ben-Gurion, already courting the Americans, was more combative toward the British and their policies. Dayan was more activist than even Ben-Gurion and demanded decisive action against the British – more action and less talk, especially on the question of illegal immigration of Jews to Mandatory Palestine.[89] Dayan got up to speak, declaring: "I don't understand this argument, because this land is ours. And if someone tries to harm it, we will have to strike ... This is a war."[90]

At the Zionist General Council meeting after the Congress, Ben-Gurion – having given the gloomy forecast that, almost certainly, an all-out war with the Arabs would begin very soon – declared that he was assuming the security portfolio on the Jewish Agency Executive Board. He also summoned Dori, who had resigned as the Haganah's chief of staff, to Basel and convinced him to resume the position. Dori met with Dayan in Basel and told Dayan that he considered him one of the most senior leadership members, who would lead the nation into the future and confront the enormous security challenges facing it.[91]

The Yishuv's struggle against the British resumed in the summer of 1945, after the end of World War II. That fall, the Haganah started to coordinate its activities with Etzel and Lehi. The umbrella organization of the Jewish underground, the Rebel Movement, focused its activities on illegal immigration and attacking British targets. In October 1945, the Atlit detention camp was attacked; in November, the Palmach sabotaged trains and blew up British coastguard ships in the Gulf of Haifa; on June 17, 1946, the Palmach blew up eleven bridges linking Israel with its neighbors, thus cutting its land mass off temporarily. All these actions were led by Allon, who had since become the Palmach's commander, as well as other colleagues of Dayan who participated.

However, in the first part of the War of Independence, which started in November 1947, Dayan found himself at the rank of a mere major whereas his cohort – Yigal Allon, Shimon Avidan, and Yigal Yadin – and even those younger than he, including Yitzhak Rabin, had much higher ranks. The fact that he had not been clearly identified with the IDF's constituent groups – neither former

---

[88] Shimon Peres (1923–2016), politician and public figure who served as MK, minister, prime minister, and president of the State of Israel.
[89] Teveth, *Moshe Dayan*, p. 242.
[90] Ibid., p. 242.
[91] Ibid., p. 243.

British Army and Jewish Brigade members nor Palmach members with their fealty to the kibbutz movement – came to haunt him. Dayan belonged to the group loyal to Ben-Gurion, but even there, he was not part of the inner circle.[92] When the battles erupted, he made do with a staff position as an Arab affairs officer assigned to recruit agents to infiltrate the enemy's ranks and bring back intelligence,[93] a field in which he had experience. Nonetheless, this position ultimately had important, perhaps critical benefits for Dayan's future.

Now, Dayan was in constant touch with Chief of Staff Dori and Israel Galili, the head of the Haganah National Command Center, and above all with Ben-Gurion, who had assumed the security portfolio as of December 1946. On January 1, Ben-Gurion gathered the army and intelligence heads for a consultation on policy toward the Palestinian Arabs, a meeting to which Dayan was invited. He was appointed to a position on a small committee that consisted of the heads of intelligence and the Jewish Agency's political department, whose function was to coordinate policy on the Arabs in the Land of Israel. Dayan consequently accumulated considerable experience working with the top political and security cadres and was able to view their concerns and actions from up close. No less importantly, he became a familiar figure and established his status. In particular, he built a relationship of mutual trust and respect with Ben-Gurion – the most important leader of the state-building years.

On November 29, 1947, the General Assembly of the United Nations voted to end the British Mandate and partition the Land of Israel. Arab attacks against the Yishuv escalated the next day, opening the first part of the War of Independence. This involved a brutal, uncompromising struggle over control of the land at a time when the British were still nominally in charge. The struggle was led by the Haganah, supported by Etzel and Lehi. The fighting consisted mostly of guerrilla and terrorist acts and military operations of limited scope designed to achieve control of the central cities, strategic roads, and the rural region. Until April 1948, the Yishuv focused on defense, but at that point, it transitioned to an organized, widespread offensive. It completely vanquished the Palestinian-Arab forces creating a territorial and demographic continuum of Jewish settlements.[94]

On April 22, 1948, the Carmeli Brigade seized control of Haifa, and Ben-Gurion appointed Dayan to regulate abandoned Arab property. This was his first experience with a military government. Dayan ordered food and other goods moved to IDF storage to prevent looting and the transfer of wheat seeds to Jewish agricultural settlements. Some felt that this was

---

[92] Bar-On, *Moshe Dayan*, p. 61.
[93] Dayan recruited his agents primarily from the al-Mazarib tribe with whom he had grown up. At least one of them, Abd Abeidat, had been a gang member during the Arab Revolt. Teveth, *Moshe Dayan*, p. 248.
[94] Benny Morris, *1948: Toldot hamilhama ha'aravit-yisraelit harishona* (Hebrew), Tel Aviv: Am Oved, 2010.

a justified move given the damage the war had done to the settlements; others considered this act immoral.[95]

At this time, Dayan suffered a severe personal loss. In April 1948, his younger brother Zohar (Zorik) fell in battle in Ramat Yohanan against a Druze battalion fighting alongside the Arabs. Shortly thereafter, Giora Zaid[96] conducted negotiations with the Druze to get them to switch their allegiance to the Israeli side. He worried about Dayan's reactions, but when he raised the issue with him, Dayan almost instantaneously responded with support, a testament to his pragmatic nature. Zaid recalled that after broaching the topic with him, Dayan thought about it for a second and then said, "*Yallah* – let's do it."[97] At a meeting between the Druze leader Ismail Kabalan, Giora Zaid, and Dayan in Kiryat Amal, Dayan displayed an extraordinary personal ability to influence his interlocutor. He succeeded in convincing Kabalan that there was no conflict between the Druze and the Jews, and, in any case, the Jews were going to win the war.[98] This was the start of the alliance with the Druze in Israel, as a result of which they began serving in the IDF and in other state entities.

The second part of the war began with the invasion of the Arab state armies on May 15, 1948, the day following the official departure of the British and the establishment of the State of Israel. Dayan was thirty-two years old. After the establishment of the state, Dayan's position as Arab affairs officer lost all meaning. Although he wanted a combat position, he wasn't offered one. A frustrated Dayan wrote of this period:

> I wandered around underfoot. I had no work and I felt bad. I wanted to join one of the units. The emphasis then was on fighting the war, not managing or planning it. I wanted to be in a fighting unit, and it didn't matter to me if it was as a brigade or platoon commander.[99]

The Education of a Strategist: Summary

The literature dealing with the characteristics of strategic leaders and their training points to several important dimensions of effective leadership.[100] The first, charisma – meaning "the gift of God" – is innate. It is a talent,

---

[95] Teveth, *Moshe Dayan*, p. 251.
[96] Giora Zaid (1914–2005), the son of Hashomer members Zipporah and Alexander Zaid. The father was murdered in 1938 by a Bedouin. Giora grew up surrounded by Bedouin neighbors, spoke fluent Arabic, and was closely familiar with the customs of the Arab world.
[97] Teveth, *Moshe Dayan*, p. 249.
[98] "A Druze officer in Israel's service: The story of Ismail Kabalan" (Hebrew), *Davar*, December 8, 1960.
[99] Teveth, *Moshe Dayan*, p, 125.
[100] Yakov Ben Haim, "What Strategic Planners Need to Know," Workshop on Strategic Uncertainty in National Security Samuel Neaman Institute, Technion Haifa, June 26, 2018.

a personality-based ability to lead and affect people in various ways, which cannot be learned or simulated. Leaders should be equipped with knowledge and skills early in their development that can prepare them for diverse challenges, have professional knowledge of their fields of endeavor, and, at the same time, have extensive knowledge of world affairs. Leaders who experience and know the difficulties on the ground and the challenges faced by simple soldiers in the trenches have a clear advantage, because they know the practical significance of their fateful decisions on the people assigned to execute them. The optimal method of learning should combine academic studies with diverse practical experiences and trials. Personal mentoring by significant figures is key to the success of a strategic leader.

Dayan had all of this. All his experiences and life events were instructive because of his curiosity, his ability to adapt to different situations, and his unique capacity to hold complex, sometimes even contradictory opinions and yet continue to function effectively.

He was only a child when he got to know Arabs and their culture and religion up close. He viewed them not as one monolithic enemy, but as a stubborn and diversified rival fighting for what was right in their eyes. He was involved in conflicts between herders and farmers, echoing the most ancient struggle since the dawn of human civilization; and despite the complexity of international diplomacy, he never forgot that the fight over land was the source of everything else. Beyond this, Dayan considered Arabs an inseparable part of the landscape. Just as he accepted the land's sometimes brutal climate, he saw the Arabs – for good and for ill – as part of the package called the Land of Israel.

When incarcerated, Dayan developed some empathy toward the Arab side, which was using various means, including terrorism, to fight a foreign rule. He shared prison space with Arabs and with Jews from the splinter groups, which were then considered beyond the pale by most Haganah personnel, and he developed a liking for both. While their goals differed from his, they shared the path of struggle and sacrifice. Later, these realizations would deeply affect him.

Dayan learned to handle weapons and fight at an early age. He was blessed with outstanding instructors and mentors who taught him guerrilla tactics but mostly leadership. Wingate and Sadeh were the most prominent, but there were others. Other Haganah commanders, including Lev and Dori, helped him along his path. Furthermore, Dayan received formal military education through the British Army sergeants' course and the Haganah's platoon commanders' course in Yavne'el, which taught him how a formal army conducts itself. He led ambushes and patrols and, until his injury, participated in many guerrilla actions in which he proved his coolheadedness. For Dayan, the shattered eye was a curse, as it ended his operational promotions. However, the curse came with a blessing, because as a result of the injury, Dayan gained a different set of experiences, enabling him to develop the skills required of a leader at the strategic level. The first time Dayan conducted negotiations was when he represented the Mem-Gimmel before the Acre Prison authorities. After his injury, his negotiating skills were used when the Haganah reached out to the rival underground splinter groups, Etzel and Lehi. He also gained experience with the field of intelligence when he planned and set up an intelligence-gathering network and trained its personnel.

Just as important was the political experience he gained due to the relationship with Ben-Gurion and various Mapai politicos. Finally, he gained experience with political and security issues when he participated in the Young Turks forum and conversed with senior personnel, including Haganah Chief of Staff Dori. The special relationship that started to form with Ben-Gurion paved Dayan's future path. All of these constituted an excellent preparation for the challenges of the future and the key positions he would come to hold.

2

From Tactical Command to Political Negotiator
The War of Independence

The War of Independence broke out on November 30, 1947, and ended on July 20, 1949. It was Israel's longest and most grueling war. Throughout it, Moshe Dayan continued to evolve as a military leader and as a statesman. Like his comrades of the Palmach generation, he led several operations, demonstrating bravery, originality, and daring. After his years away from operational activities because of his wounded eye, his self-confidence returned, and his unique style of command and leadership began to take shape. Dayan gained experience in tactical warfare against the main opposing armies in the conflict – Syrian, Jordanian, and Egyptian – and encountered many forms of fighting: defensive battles, raids, and mobile offensive operations. In founding the 89th Battalion, he also gained experience in force building. While Dayan's actions were not always successful, he nonetheless acquired a reputation as a commander with a unique style, attracting both admirers and detractors.

Despite his renown as a commander, his operational record was unimpressive compared to some of his well-known Palmach colleagues (now officers in the Israel Defense Forces (IDF), Palmach forces having already been integrated into the IDF) – Yigal Allon, Yitzhak Rabin, and other frontline and brigade commanders. However, it was Ben-Gurion who held the key to Dayan's advancement, and following Dayan's wholehearted commitment and aggressive conduct during the *Altalena* affair, Ben-Gurion came to view Dayan as someone he could count on. Toward the end of the war, Dayan underwent his first real political test, becoming involved in political negotiations with Jordan, first with Abdullah al-Tal, Jordan's Jerusalem commander, then in direct talks with King Abdullah, and later in the Armistice Talks during the first half of 1949. Dayan proved his ability in the diplomatic-political sphere as well, achieving significant results. The political experience, coupled with the trust forged with Ben-Gurion, greatly contributed to Dayan's career in public life, far more than any operational experience his Palmach counterparts had earned, no matter how extensive.

Defending Degania Alef and Degania Bet

By April 1948, at the end of the period considered the first stage of the War of Independence, the Jewish side had bested the local Arabs in the fight over the Land of Israel. The second stage of the war began on May 15, 1948, when the regular armies of several Arab nations invaded the territory of the Hebrew state, intending to obliterate it. With these armies boasting organized forces with a structured chain of command and modern means of warfare, including tanks, planes, and artillery, this stage of the war became a campaign of high-intensity regular warfare between the sides.

Dayan was initially frustrated at being sidelined while his Palmach contemporaries Moshe Carmel, Yigal Allon, and Yitzhak Rabin became respected brigade commanders in the war's early days. However, he was soon called into action by Yitzhak Sadeh, Dayan's mentor and friend who greatly respected his capabilities. Sadeh had established a new brigade to receive armored vehicles purchased in Europe, and he offered Dayan the opportunity to establish a commando unit, the 89th Battalion, specializing in raids, within it. Dayan wrote in his diary: "When Yitzhak Sadeh offered me the 89th [Battalion], it was a gift from heaven."[1] Yigal Yadin, head of the General Staff Branch and the de facto Chief of Staff (Dori having fallen ill), also felt that Dayan, who had led a complex raid in 1941, was best suited to command such a unit. But while Dayan was gearing up to organize the unit, the situation changed yet again, as the Arab armies invaded Israel on May 15. On May 17 and 18, due to the escalation on the northern front, mostly around Degania Alef and Degania Bet, Dayan was sent to reinforce the defenders and stop the Syrian army, now on the verge of conquering the Jewish settlements. Dayan, born in Degania in 1910, now returned to defend his birthplace.

On paper, the Syrian army had 10,000 men, but the effective force included only one brigade (the 1st Brigade) of 2,000, divided into infantry battalions and an armored battalion equipped with light (11-ton) French tanks – Renault models 35 and 39 – with 37 mm cannons and armored vehicles with smaller cannons. The brigade also had four to six batteries of 75 mm and 105 mm artillery. Syria's 2nd Brigade was far less battle-ready, and the Syrian air force, with twenty training planes retrofitted as combat planes and ill-trained pilots, was no readier.[2]

The Syrians' campaign objectives were not clear. Their forces advanced on Israel through the Golan Heights and the southern banks of the Sea of Galilee, apparently heading for Afula, where they were to meet the Iraqi invasion force and then advance together to Haifa. On May 15, the Syrians attacked Kibbutz

---

[1] Shabtai Teveth, *Moshe Dayan: Biografia* (Hebrew), Tel Aviv: Schoken, 1971, p. 256.
[2] Benny Morris, *1948: Toldot hamilhama ha'aravit-yisraelit harishona* (Hebrew), Tel Aviv: Am Oved, 2010, p. 277.

Ein Gev in the Jordan Valley to divert attention from the main effort aimed at the Jordan Valley settlements.

The Golani Brigade's Barak Battalion and local Haganah fighters deployed in the Jordan Valley received reinforcements in the days after the attack. On May 18, the Syrians attacked the kibbutzim near Ein Gev and the village of Tsemah, which it conquered after several assaults, causing severe losses among the defenders. A Yiftach Brigade company tried to retake the town but was repelled. Tsemah's conquest was a serious blow to the morale of the Hebrew defending forces. In his diary, Ben-Gurion wrote, "There is a kind of panic in the Jordan Valley."[3] On May 19, nearby Masada and Shaar Hagolan were abandoned by their Jewish residents and looted by the region's Arabs.

This was the state of affairs when Dayan arrived. While Dayan's precise authority remained unclear, he soon took charge.[4] Dayan almost immediately toured the area and ordered the men to improve the trenches and defenses. He also decided to take up positions in Bet Yerah directly against the Syrian flank to defend Degania, even though that meant thinning out the defending line.[5]

With the situation in the Jordan Valley serious, four newly arrived 65 mm cannons (nicknamed Napoleonchiks), meant for the defense of Jerusalem, were diverted to this sector,[6] ultimately playing a decisive role in the battle. The Syrian attack began on May 20 at dawn. Although fearful, his confidence about being able to lead in battle having eroded after the years of not participating in operational missions, Dayan projected confidence to those around him. Haim Levkov (1916–1998), a Palmach commander who arrived with reinforcements, recalled that on the day of battle, the fighters were thirsty after their water had run out; Dayan encouraged them: "You're here, in the trenches, under the trees, in the shade. If you're thirsty, just image how thirsty the Syrians, running around across you in the field and under the sun, must be!" Levkov also recalled that when a worried mortarman with only eight mortar rounds left asked Dayan for instructions, Dayan retorted, "Shoot the first, then the second, the third, and so on. When you've shot off the eighth, come back and we'll see what else you can do."[7]

The Syrian infantry attack was preceded by an artillery barrage. By 8 a.m., the defenders succeeded in stopping the Syrian tanks using Molotov cocktails

---

[3] Ibid., p. 281.
[4] Teveth, *Moshe Dayan*, p. 259.
[5] Ibid., p. 260.
[6] The Napoleonchik ("Canon de 65 Montagne modele 1906") was a French-made mountain gun dating to the early twentieth century. Its main function was to fire at infantry forces. Smuggled into Israel one day before the British Mandate ended, the first cannons were barely functional and were missing sights. The Haganah fighters nicknamed them Napoleonchiks because they were small, old-looking, and French.
[7] Teveth, *Moshe Dayan*, p. 60.

and PIATs (Projector Infantry Anti-Tank Mk I) that Dayan had acquired,[8] and the battle became a static fight of attrition until around 1:30 p.m., when the Napoleonchiks were repositioned to defend Degania. That morning, Dayan and the gunnery and brigade commanders had argued about when to operate the cannons, Dayan wanting to wait and use them only the next day when it would be possible to crush the enemy's spirit. However, after learning that the defenders' situation was desperate, Dayan realized that immediate action was needed. The Napoleonchiks began bombarding the Syrian headquarters in Tsemah. The bombardment did the trick – mostly because of the noise and the surprise – and the Syrian forces retreated helter-skelter in a panic. Degania was saved, and the battle became part of the war's ethos.

While Degania's residents were reorganizing after the Syrian retreat, Dayan took aside Levi Eshkol, then the defense minister's aide and a member of Degania Bet, and rebuked him that the trenches had not been prepared properly by Degania Bet's residents. Dayan demanded that the trenches be improved immediately. Eshkol complied, but the incident might have undermined their relationship in later years.

Dayan decided to inspect the Tsemah police station, which had been briefly occupied by the Syrians. Upon entering Tsemah and finding it empty, Dayan realized that the Syrian force had simply left, apparently immediately after the bombardment. From this, he drew sweeping conclusions about the Arab enemy:

> This left an indelible impression on me. ... after three or four shells, they got up and fled, in total chaos ... Their flight without being attacked – after all, no one had approached Tsemah – and by night, they were gone. It occurred to me then that if you bang once on a can, they all flee, like birds.[9]

This was Dayan's first combat encounter with regular units of an Arab army and would affect his perception of how to fight the Arabs, especially his assessment that Arab military units tended to break under pressure. He would later learn that this wasn't always the case, a lesson that came at a heavy cost.

The harsh sights of war had a strong impact on Dayan; his previous experiences with fighting and killing had been less gruesome. The sight of dead bodies abandoned in Tsemah's fields and the many unevacuated wounded affected him deeply. He wrote: "A difficult, tragic, and depressing battle. A lot of young blood was spilled here. Not the blood of battle-tested soldiers. The blood of youngsters meeting death with their eyes wide open. The wounded, groaning, abandoned by the side of the road."[10]

The battle for Degania over, Dayan was summoned to Tel Aviv, where Sadeh charged him with commanding the 89th Battalion.

---

[8] Mordechai Bar-On, *Moshe Dayan: Koron hayav 1915–1981* (Hebrew), Tel Aviv: Am Oved, 2014, p. 63.
[9] Teveth, *Moshe Dayan*, p. 264.
[10] Moshe Dayan, *Avnei derekh: Autobiografia* (Hebrew), Jerusalem: Idanim, 1976, p. 61.

Establishing the 89th Raiding Battalion

The features of the 89th Motorized Raiding Battalion, the commando unit specializing in raids, were very similar to those that would later characterize small special units of the IDF, such as Unit 101 under Ariel Sharon and Sayeret Matkal and the General Staff Reconnaissance Unit commanded by Avraham Arnan. The original model was the Palmach – its spirit, relationships, style of leadership, and culture – in a post-Palmach era.

Sadeh's inspiration for the 89th Battalion came from the World War II British raiding units and their commanders, all the subject of legend.[11] These units, equipped with desert terrain vehicles, raided deep into the German rear, destroying important logistical installations, such as fuel depots and air fields, and creating significant psychological pressure on the Germans.

It was Dayan's job to transform Sadeh's idea into reality. Dayan, his self-confidence restored after receiving some of the credit for having stopped the Syrian army in Tsemah, wrote: "What I saw in Tsemah that night remade the warrior in me."[12] He told Sadeh that the Arab army could be challenged with relative ease, and that he understood now how such "mechanized cavalry" would be particularly effective.

In fact, he set up the unit out of thin air. Recruitment was selective, using the "bring-a-friend" method. Its atmosphere was unique, somewhat wild, challenging the hierarchy, discipline, and rigid rules of a military organization. Such units tend to take outsized risks at times and operate unconventionally, the culture and spirit of such units to a large extent inspired by and reflecting the charismatic nature of their founders and commanders.

Dayan described the battalion's establishment:

> When I returned from the Jordan Valley, I started work on the Motorized Raiding Battalion. The number I was given was 89 ... part of Yitzhak Sadeh's armored brigade. The brigade ... in my time, never functioned as a single unit, and the battalion's operations were independent. I was very happy with this job – it was exactly what I'd wanted. Yitzhak explained to me that the battalion was to resemble the raiding units the British had operated in World War II ... and Popski's Private Army. Obviously, on a small, local scope, without the means and expanses of the world powers in their war, but with the same spirit of audacity and originality. ... Its function would be to penetrate deep into enemy territory and operate behind the lines ... The weapons and people arrived by dribs and drabs, but the most important requirements were there from day one: the battle

---

[11] Vladimir Peniakoff, *Tsva'o hapratee shel Popski* (Hebrew translation of *Popski's Private Army*), Tel Aviv: Maarkhot, 1985.
[12] Teveth, *Moshe Dayan*, p. 265.

spirit, the desire to seek action and strike at the enemy, and the belief in ourselves and our might.[13]

The first step in creating a special or elite unit is to select the men with care. Dayan recruited his candidates from four sources: his friends from Nahalal and the other Jezre'el Valley settlements; veterans of the disbanded Lehi paramilitary organization (known pejoratively as the Stern Gang, considered extreme radicals and terrorists by the British and many Jews), evidence of Dayan's openness and lack of enmity toward previous rivals, unlike the resentment harbored by many of his Palmach friends; veterans of the Haganah's special operations unit from Tel Aviv who had participated in the battles over Jaffa; and Jewish volunteers from abroad.[14] Yohanan Peltz,[15] Dayan's deputy, hand-picked by Sadeh and known as a particularly audacious fighter, assumed he would command the unit, but Sadeh explained, "If the battalion commander is the person I'm considering, it'll be to your advantage to be his deputy, because he is important and has quite a future in store."[16]

Peltz and Dayan enjoined mutual admiration, even though one looked and behaved like a rigid British officer and the other like a guerrilla fighter; later, this contrast would lead to tension between them. Dayan asked Peltz to concentrate on the organization of the force, thus initiating a pattern that continued, even when he was the Chief of Staff: leaving his trusted deputy to handle organizational and logistical details, understanding the importance of the minutiae as well as the limits of his own personality in dealing with them.[17]

Peltz and Dayan faced two critical problems: manpower and means. Most of the good fighters were already serving elsewhere, thereby forcing them to tap an unused resource – former Lehi members. Most Haganah commanders wanted nothing to do with ex-Lehi fighters, but Peltz's impression was that Dayan wasn't keen on Palmach veterans because he needed to prove that he was better than they were. Peltz explained to Dayan that because the commando forces were volunteers, the army had to allow those interested to leave their units and transfer to the 89th Battalion. Peltz even persuaded the members of his own previous company, the Kiryati Brigade's 43rd Battalion, to join the new battalion. Upon learning that Dayan had poached his entire company, the commander, Amos Ben-Gurion, the prime minister's son, complained to his father, "What kind of an army are you building here,

---

[13] Dayan, *Avnei derekh*, p. 61.
[14] Bar-On, *Moshe Dayan*, p. 64.
[15] Yohanan Peltz immigrated to Mandatory Palestine in 1935 and joined the British Army on behalf of the Haganah, fighting in the Jewish Brigade. After World War II, he was a member of The Avengers, a group of Jews who tracked down and assassinated Nazi war criminals.
[16] Teveth, *Moshe Dayan*, p. 266.
[17] Ibid., p. 268.

where commanders steal people from one another?"[18] The "defectors" returned to the Kiryati Brigade. Dayan, however, continued to put pressure on the prime minister and, ultimately, reached a compromise, with both sides pretending there had simply been a misunderstanding – and some of the men were allowed to join Dayan's new battalion.

Nonetheless, the battalion-to-be still lacked soldiers. Dayan's men approached Tsvi Tsur, the commander of the 54th Battalion in the (5th) Givati Brigade, for help. Tsur had no people to spare but was willing to part with the eighteen men sitting in the brigade lockup, accused of, among other things, petty theft, looting, and being AWOL (Absent without leave). Dayan promised them he would cancel their trials and any punishment if they joined the new battalion. Dayan's men returned to the battalion with eighteen additional fighters.[19]

Although many brigade commanders banned recruiters from the 89th from entering their bases, many fighters showed up. A group of fiercely loyal Jezre'el Valley men who had known Dayan since childhood also joined the battalion.[20]

The 89th Battalion soon established a reputation for being wild, undisciplined, and eccentric. When Dayan was told the unit was short of jeeps, his answer was, "So go get some."[21] Men fresh from the brig because of petty theft needed no stronger hint, and soon enough, civilian jeeps were "lifted" and brought to the unit. Most importantly, the battalion was infused with Dayan's own spirit, projecting a strong feeling of camaraderie, which encouraged initiative – and practical jokes. Dayan, for example, would speed past the military police at the base's main gate upon entering, stopping 30 meters past the inspection point, forcing the guard to come to him. One day, an MP refused to walk over to Dayan and threatened to shoot Dayan unless he reversed the jeep to the inspection point. Dayan accelerated and fled.[22]

The soldiers of this nascent unit accepted this type of prankishness, which was natural for Dayan. It gave his men a sense of being unique and battle-ready, and they admired him more as a result.[23] Like other commando groups, the 89th Battalion enjoyed an atmosphere of freedom. As Dayan described: "Discipline in our battalion ... is unlike that in other battalions. ... men are free to come and go as they please. But no one leaves, because they didn't end up here by chance."[24]

---

[18] Ibid., p. 269.
[19] Ibid., p. 269.
[20] Such a loyal group gives a commander peace of mind and support but might be more prone to groupthink than a more heterogeneous one.
[21] Teveth, *Moshe Dayan*, p. 270.
[22] Ibid., p. 271.
[23] Ibid.
[24] Mordechai Naor (ed.), *Moshe Dayan: Mikh'tvei ahava* (Hebrew), Tel Aviv: Yedioth Ahronoth Publishers, 2016, p. 163.

The 89th Battalion recruits underwent expedited weapons training. Within a month, all preparations were complete. In the meantime, a fourth company had been formed that included volunteers from abroad. The question of commando operations arose when Peltz asked how and for what missions the battalion should be trained. Receiving only vague answers from Dayan and Sadeh, Peltz insisted that the battalion couldn't possibly sustain itself logistically behind enemy lines. In the end, the 89th Battalion operated like a mechanized raiding force, as did the 9th Battalion of the Negev Brigade, but because of Dayan, the 89th became the best known.

Fighting the Irgun

The 89th's first mission was aimed not against the Arabs but against the Irgun and its leader Menachem Begin.[25] Being surrounded by close loyalists enabled Dayan to meet the difficult challenge from Ben-Gurion: arresting Irgun members from the *Altalena* affair. Dayan explained: "The conflict between the government and the Irgun was political. Its military echo – at least the clash on the beach of Kfar Vitkin – lacked the ring of truth: ... this was not the enemy."[26]

The *Altalena* affair began in early 1947, when the Irgun sailed its own loyal fighters and their weapons to Israel on the *Altalena*. The ship arrived in Israel in June 1948 during the first truce of the War of Independence, with 940 passengers, including 120 women, and many weapons. The government and the Irgun agreed that the ship would unload at Kfar Vitkin. However, serious disagreements arose between the sides over the weapons, the government demanding them all for the IDF and the Irgun wanting to maintain some control.

Menachem Begin, who was on the ship, received an ultimatum to cede the unloaded weapons but didn't respond. The deadline passed, and the sides started firing, killing six Irgun members and two IDF soldiers. The ship fled south to Tel Aviv, with Begin hoping to reach a compromise with the government. But a large IDF force massed in Tel Aviv, and on the night of June 22, another battle erupted between them and Irgun fighters. Ben-Gurion ordered the IDF forces to shell the *Altalena*, causing the munitions still on board to explode. The ship was abandoned and ran aground, the battle continuing on shore; one IDF soldier and ten Irgun members died. The IDF ultimately received some of the weapons, but sixteen Irgun members and three IDF soldiers had been killed. This event, the nadir in the relationship between the Irgun and what had essentially

---

[25] The Irgun was a right-wing Zionist paramilitary organization that broke off from the Haganah in 1931 for ideological reasons.
[26] Dayan, *Avnei derekh*, p. 62.

been the Haganah, is also considered the end of the transition to one state and one army.

Originally, the Alexandroni Brigade had been ordered to prevent the *Altalena* unloading off Kfar Vitkin, but Dayan's 89th Brigade, located near Kfar Vitkin, was deemed more suitable. Dayan could have refused, but he opted to execute Sadeh's directive, enabling him to prove his loyalty to Ben-Gurion. Dayan chose the men he felt he could trust, those closest to him and Sa'ar. Some members of the battalion's Company A had been Irgun or Lehi members. Dayan could not be certain of their behavior in this situation. On the pretext of a spot weapons inspection, Dayan collected their rifles and removed the firing pins before proceeding to Kfar Vitkin with the two other companies and another company from the 82nd Armored Battalion.[27]

His mission was to surround the ship, prevent its men from breaking through with the weapons they had unloaded, and stop any outside forces from joining them. The brigade surrounded Kfar Vitkin and used jeeps and half-tracks to break through the Irgun's defensive line, pinning them into a narrow strip of beach. The sides exchanged fire; Dayan claimed that his men opened direct fire only after one of his men had been killed and several others injured.[28] At a certain point, Dayan left the area, handing command to Uri Bar-On (1925–1985), telling Bar-On that he had been instructed to accompany the coffin of US Army Colonel David (Mickey) Marcus to the United States. Bar-On represented the 89th Battalion at the June 22 meeting in which the Irgun agreed to terms of surrender, ending the tragic affair.

Several questions remain about Dayan's absence from the scene. Perhaps he was trying to avoid an uncomfortable situation. Nonetheless, Dayan had accepted this mission, which he could have turned down. Eyewitnesses described his behavior throughout as tenacious and "vigorous, aggressive, and propulsive."[29] Teveth suggests the possibility that:

> He'd brought the mission to the point where he could pass the baton to someone he trusted, making it possible for him to leave; this too was very much in character. When he considered an issue resolved, he felt free to hand off the finishing touches to a deputy. It may also be that he did not want to be overly drawn into the affair, which he knew was problematic and would, politically, haunt everyone involved.[30]

Whatever the reason, on June 21, bullets still whizzing, Dayan left the area to see his wife and children before traveling to the United States.

[27] Teveth, *Moshe Dayan*, p. 274.
[28] Ibid., p. 275.
[29] Ibid.
[30] Ibid., p. 276.

Captain Abraham (Abe) Baum

US Army Colonel David Daniel (Mickey) Marcus was an American Jewish officer who had fought in World War II and who volunteered to help the inexperienced IDF, which was in dire need of officers from Western armies with senior command knowledge and experience. Marcus served the IDF well by providing advice and training, writing reports requested for Ben-Gurion. On May 28, 1948, Marcus was given the command of the Jerusalem front and the three sector brigades – Harel, Etzioni, and the 7th. Marcus's end was tragic. On June 11, 1948, at 3:40 a.m., Marcus left camp, announcing his exit to the sentry. When he returned, a different sentry, who didn't know Marcus, was on duty. The sentry asked Marcus to identify himself, and Marcus answered in English. Unable to understand Marcus, the sentry shot and killed him.

Marcus's body was flown from Israel to be interred at the cemetery at his alma mater West Point. It was decided that Dayan and Yosef Harel (1918–2008; he had commanded Aliyah Bet ships, including the *Exodus*, and was a senior Israeli intelligence leader) would constitute the honor guard and fly the coffin home. Dayan, then a major, was given a temporary promotion to lieutenant colonel. After the interment ceremony, which took place on June 30, Dayan remained in New York for another week.

The most significant event of Dayan's US visit was his apparently accidental meeting with Abraham J. Baum, then a US Army captain and World War II veteran, who was in contact with Teddy Kollek,[31] who had traveled to the United States with a special Haganah mission. Baum, who ran his family-owned garment workshop in New York City, was charged with interviewing and selecting Americans volunteering for the Haganah and, later, the IDF. Dayan met Baum over cocktails at the bar of New York City's "Hotel 14," where Kollek and Harel were staying along with other Haganah mission members. Dayan's impression of Baum was quite positive: "Abe Baum was one of the most daring, decorated, and scarred fighters of the U.S. Army in World War II. The commander of the 4th Armored Division, Gen. John S. Wood, called him 'the bravest soldier of the Second World War.'"[32]

Baum was famous for a mission he led into German territory in which he displayed outstanding courage and leadership. Baum had enlisted in the US Army immediately after the Japanese attack on Pearl Harbor on December 7, 1941. Having climbed the ranks during the war, he was ordered to lead a motorized unit to carry out General George S. Patton's secret order to liberate the Hammelburg prisoner-of-war (POW) camp inside Germany territory, behind two German army divisions. Baum and his forces embarked on the mission on March 26,

---

[31] Teddy Kollek, Jerusalem's long-time mayor (1965–1993). In his youth, he was active in the Zionist movement Hehalutz. He served in several key Haganah positions (especially its intelligence division) and in the Jewish Agency's political department.
[32] Teveth, *Moshe Dayan*, p. 278.

1945. Despite strong enemy resistance and heavy casualties, they surged forward and managed to free some 1,200 Allied soldiers, before pushing forward to the camp, despite suffering even more losses. Leaving the camp with as many prisoners as he could, Baum and his forces were trapped by the Germans, with Baum and the few other survivors captured.[33] Baum was awarded the Distinguished Service Cross for his role in the mission.[34]

Despite the mission's flaws, Baum's execution of it was considered among the most valiant of the US Army and stirred the imagination of many. Dayan, who had been appointed commander of a motorized raiding unit, completely lacked experience in this type of fighting. In fact, Dayan was familiar only with infantry warfare – defensive, offensive, or in raids. Cavalry charges might have been suited to fighting Bedouin tribes near Nahalal or have played a role in adolescent fantasies, but they had no place in modern warfare. Dayan lacked any concept of how such a unit should fight and achieve its mission as a raiding force. It was no surprise, then, that he hung on Baum's every word as Baum explained the major principles of the motorized armored raiding doctrine:

1. Exploit every opportunity.
2. Use a large force to attack a target that can be taken by a smaller force. Make every effort to create the impression that the force is much larger than it really it.
3. Charge in narrow formations, preferably in a single column.
4. Use firepower as a psychological factor more than a lethal weapon. The only thing better than a dead enemy is a scared enemy.
5. If you have only a tiny force, you must constantly be on the move. The moment you stop moving, you've lost your advantage as an armored force.
6. Do not keep reserve units. Use them so that the enemy will think you have more.
7. Use infantry to occupy a target.
8. Reserve armored troops for counterattacks.[35]

In his memoirs, Dayan added notes – the most important, the need to move quickly in battle. He noted that the features characterizing the German theater of operations in World War II in which Baum had fought differed from those of the wars fought in Israel, yet there were some enlightening similarities. The most important were that the commander must be at the point of contact with the enemy on the front, remain in constant motion, study the situation with his own eyes, and direct the action accordingly.[36]

---

[33] There are several books and essays about the Baum Task Force. The description here is based on http://taskforcebaum.de/index1.html.
[34] Patton wanted to award Baum the Medal of Honor, the most prestigious military decoration, but because that would have required an investigation into the events, which Patton wanted to avoid, the Distinguished Service Cross was the highest honor possible under the circumstances.
[35] Teveth, *Moshe Dayan*, pp. 279–280.
[36] Dayan, *Avnei derekh*, p. 63.

One point missing from Dayan's memoir, which Dayan presumably realized: There was a difference between the Wehrmacht's war-fighting skill and that of the Arab enemy the IDF was facing. While the Wehrmacht quickly recovered from the shock of Baum's raid and reorganized effectively, Dayan's experience in Tsemah led him to conclude that rapid raids with movement and fire would destabilize the Arab force and cause it to withdraw.

The 89th Battalion: The Raid on Lod-Ramla

On March 20, 2003, US forces invaded Iraq in Operation Iraqi Freedom – the Second Iraq War – to end Saddam Hussein's dictatorship. On April 5, the 3rd Infantry Division and Marines reached the outskirts of Baghdad. Concerned that Baghdad was well fortified and that its defenders intended to turn the fight for the city into a kind of Battle of Stalingrad,[37] the initial US plans called for a gradual conquest. But Secretary of Defense Donald Rumsfeld demanded quick results. Unlike the senior generals, Rumsfeld felt that the enemy lacked resolve.[38] The commander of the 2nd Brigade decided to execute a "thunder run," that is, an armored raid.[39] On April 5, a Brigade task force, with Abrams tanks and Bradley Infantry Fighting Vehicles, sped through the streets of Baghdad, a city of some eight million, spewing fire in every direction. The force lost one tank and suffered a few light injuries, but it wreaked havoc and destruction as it crossed the city, reaching the international airport before leaving.

Two days later, on April 7, the 2nd Brigade carried out a second "thunder run" to seize control of the airport and weaken the Iraqi defenders, who this time, were waiting for the Americans along the route, causing the US troops to change their path at the last second. By combat's end, US forces controlled an area of Baghdad, later referred to as "the green zone," which led to the city falling much earlier and with far fewer casualties than initially predicted.[40]

---

[37] The Battle of Stalingrad, lasting from July 1942 through February 1943, was the bloodiest and among the most decisive battles the USSR fought against Nazi Germany in World War II. Lasting more than six months, both sides together suffered some two million dead, wounded, missing in action, and prisoners of war. The battle ended with the Red Army's decisive victory.

[38] Private email from US Army Col. Douglas Macgregor dated August 2, 2018. Macgregor was one of the architects of the 2003 US invasion into Iraq.

[39] The concept and practice of a "thunder run" – a rapid surge toward enemy lines with continuous fire – existed already in World War II and Vietnam.

[40] Globalsecurity.org: "On Point: The United States Army in Operation Iraqi Freedom," chapter 6: Regime Collapse, www.globalsecurity.org/military/library/report/2004/onpoint/ch-6.htm#thunder5; David Zucchino, *Thunder Run: Three Days in the Battle for Baghdad*, New York: Atlantic Books, 2005.

Over half a century earlier, in July 1948, Dayan had led a similar raid on Lod, albeit with a small battalion force in a much smaller city.[41] The 89th Battalion's raid was an electrifying operation that fired the imagination of many. As in a Hollywood Western, the battle scene featured a band of wild cavalrymen speeding across the city while shooting every which way. The only difference was that the men rode jeeps, not horses, and fired machine guns, not rifles. The leader was a commander with one eye covered by a prominent black patch, a detail that undoubtedly added a heroic layer to Dayan's myth, then already under construction.

Dayan returned from the United States after the first truce of the war had ended. Now, the IDF, better equipped and organized, was on the offensive, with priority given to the central front. The IDF carried out Operation Dani (named for Dani Mass, the commander of a convoy of thirty-five Haganah fighters killed while resupplying the besieged Gush Etzion). The Jordanian Legion was deployed in the central Lod–Ramla region, an excellent position from which to cut the nascent state in half and isolate Jerusalem. To meet this threat, the IDF gathered four brigades commanded by Dayan's Haganah and Palmach comrades. Yigal Allon, formerly the charismatic leader of the Palmach who had proven his battlefield skills in previous successful fights in the Upper Galilee, led the overall operation. Dayan was just a battalion commander, one of at least a dozen, subordinate to the brigade commanders. Operation Dani's purpose was to liberate Jerusalem and the road leading to the city from the Jordanian stranglehold by conquering the enemy forces in the bases of Lod, Ramla, Latroun, and Ramallah. The conquest would lift the threat against Tel Aviv and provide the IDF with an easily defended line in the Jerusalem foothills and with control of the railway junctions and international airport in Lod (Map 2.1).[42]

The IDF's concern that the Legion could use Lod and Ramla as starting points for conquering the land and cutting it in half was reasonable, but the Israelis had no idea of the Legion's manpower problem and munitions scarcity (resulting from the British embargo) or of King Abdullah's decision, made in consultation with the Legion's commander Glubb Pasha (Sir John Bagot Glubb), not to overstretch his forces and instead to try to preserve the gains Jordan had made to date, namely, the conquest of the West Bank.[43] Consequently, there was only a relatively small force stationed in Lod and

---

[41] Toward the end of the British Mandate of Palestine, the city of Lod had about 19,000 residents. See Allon Kadish, Avraham Sela, and Arnon Golan, *Kibush Lod, juli 1948* (Hebrew) (*The Conquest of Lod, July 1948*), Tel Aviv: Defense Ministry Publishers, 2000, p. 15. Ramla had about 18,000 residents. The total population of the two cities and adjacent villages was about 40,000.

[42] Netanel Lorch, *Korot milhemet ha'atsma'ut* (Hebrew), Ramat Gan: Masada, 1966, p. 323.

[43] Benny Morris, *Haderekh li'yerushalayim, Glubb Pasha, erets yisrael veha'yehudim* (Hebrew), Tel Aviv: Oved, 2006, pp. 182–183; Morris, *1948*, pp. 314–315.

Ramla; the city's defense relied primarily on local militias. Rather than the estimated 1,500 Jordanian legionnaires there were no more than 150 together with a few hundred irregulars. On July 10, the Arab Legion sent in another battalion with forty armored cars, significantly boosting the Legion's ability to fight Dayan's battalion. The Legion's function was essentially defensive, its main objective to deny the IDF any successes in these areas.[44]

The IDF's battle plan included a pincer attack with northern and southern arms. Yitzhak Sadeh's 8th Brigade, to which Dayan's 89th Battalion belonged, constituted part of the northern arm. The northern arm, including the Yiftach and Harel Brigades, two battalions from the Alexandroni and Kiryati Brigades, and some other auxiliary units, including engineers and reconnaissance, were to seize the Lod airport, link up with the moshav Ben Shemen, then under siege, and conquer the villages north of Lod. At the same time, the plan called for the southern arm to outflank Ramla and Lod and go through territory held by the enemy to cut them off. The two arms were meant to join in Ben Shemen.[45]

The operation began on the night between July 9 and 10. By then, Dayan was on his way back to Israel. While still in New York, he had been summoned by Ben-Gurion – now Israel's prime minister and defense minister – to attend an urgent meeting. Dayan, typically, ignored the request, instead rushing to meet up with his battalion, now preparing for the operation in Kiryat Aryeh (east of Tel Aviv). In Dayan's absence, his deputy, Peltz, had taken temporary command, preparing the battalion's battle plan. Teveth wrote that, according to battalion members, the men heaved a sigh of relief when they saw Dayan emerge from the vehicle, still in his dress uniform. "We felt ever so much better,"[46] recalled Teddy Eytan (the Hebrew name of Thadée Diffre), a Catholic French volunteer. Eytan recalled that spirits were very high thanks to Dayan's leadership, describing him as "very affable ... courageous, and level-headed. Humane, with psychological insight, interested in the fate and comfort of his men, able to win their affection and admiration and arouse in them awe and obedience without ever raising his voice."[47] In contrast, he described Peltz as someone who had stepped directly out of a British officers' club. It isn't difficult to imagine the popularity Dayan enjoyed and the closeness his men felt with him, unlike their reaction to Peltz's British-style distance and stiffness.[48]

---

[44] Yoav Gelber, *Komemiyot venakba: Israel, hafalestini, umedinot arav 1948* (Hebrew), Or Yehuda: Dvir, 2004.

[45] IDF, *Toldot milhemet hakomemiyut – sipur hama'arakha* (Hebrew), Tel Aviv: Ma'arakhot, 1970 (first printing 1958), p. 255.

[46] Teveth, *Moshe Dayan*, p. 280.

[47] Ibid.

[48] Ibid., p. 272; Teddy Eytan, *Negev: Volontaire français à la tête des commandos de la Haganha*, Geneva: La Baconnière, 1950.

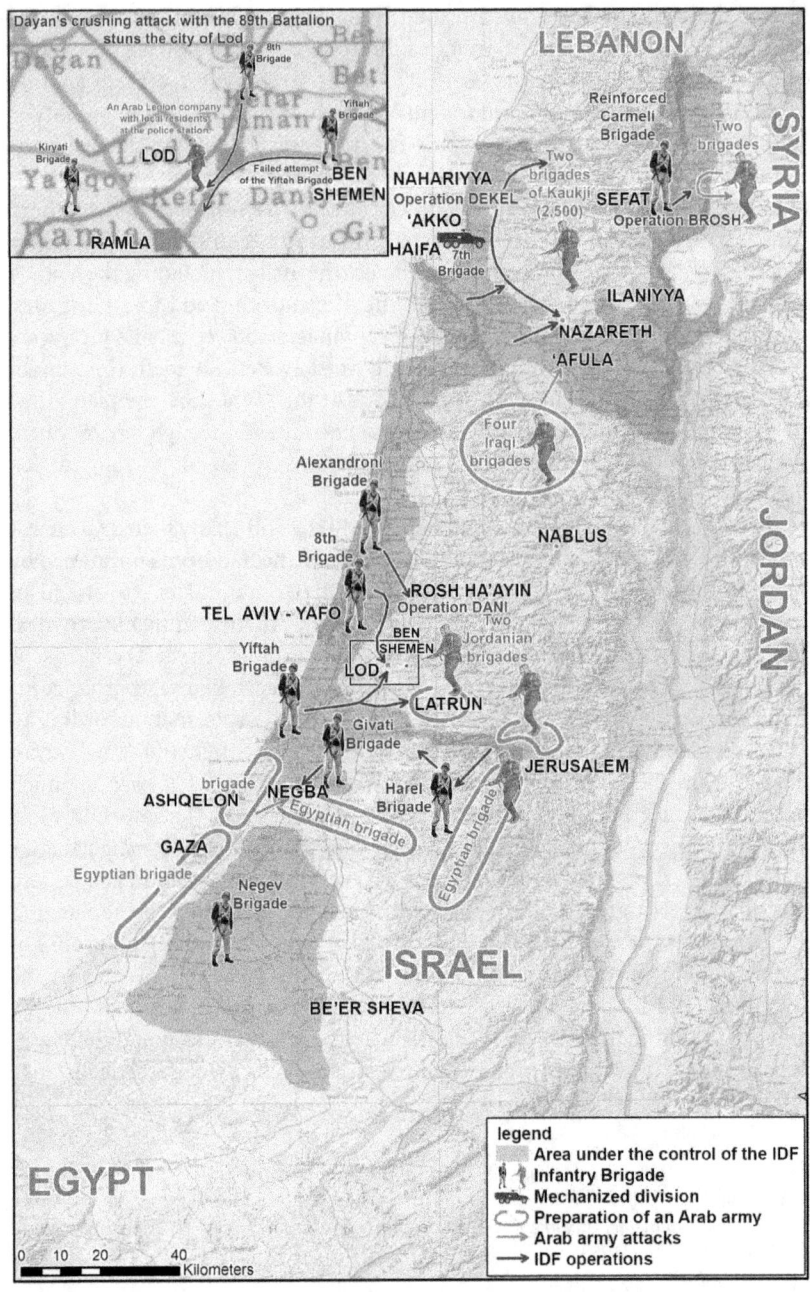

Map 2.1 War of Independence (1948): "Dani Operation."

The battalion's first objective was to conquer the village of Qula. In Dayan's absence, Peltz had trained and equipped the battalion and prepared a detailed plan to take the village. Peltz showed the plan to Dayan upon his return; at that point, he did not express any criticism or reservations. Peltz asked Dayan to resume command, but Dayan was hesitant, saying he wasn't familiar with the plan, and there was no time to make changes. Peltz then announced he was going to sleep and asked to be wakened at 3 a.m. before the operation. At this point, Dayan, having gone to change clothes, concluded that it was time to implement what Baum had taught him. He returned to the battalion, summoned the company commanders – although not Peltz, who was sleeping – and shared with them Baum's main principles:

> You know that I don't know a thing about mechanized warfare, so I asked. And that American commander told me that when it comes to armored forces there are no hard and fast rules except for one: travel on fire and wheels and never stop moving. If advancing – great. If not – retreat. But never, ever stop. Either forwards or back. I want you to do just that … we have to move as far ahead as possible.[49]

Dayan galvanized his men's enthusiasm with the confidence and optimism he projected, promising them they would reach Jerusalem. Sa'ar recalled how Dayan's appearance on the eve of the battle instilled a renewed fighting spirit in the men: "People treated him like sunlight. He possessed a kind of magical power that is difficult to describe. We were enchanted with him."[50] Dayan scrapped Peltz's detailed battle plan, which reflected Peltz's cautious British character: slow advance with both covering fire and an artillery barrage before surging ahead. Instead, Dayan decided that the force would move forward in single file and then spread out for a quick and brutal surge, similar to a cavalry charge.

Peltz was awakened at 2 a.m., about an hour before embarking on the operation, and was asked to come to a commanders' meeting. When he arrived, he saw that the commanders had already received new orders. Dayan told Peltz he had scrapped his plan, saying that it was fine for fighting a regular army, "but we aren't fighting the Germans, but Arabs."[51] Dayan hoped that the enemy would scatter before an extended battle developed, as had happened at Tsemah, and was certain that Peltz's plan required discipline and coordination better suited to a more experienced, professional unit than the 89th Battalion. Peltz, feeling frustrated and deceived, criticized Dayan's plan, claiming it reflected Dayan's lack of professional experience, an assessment that was probably accurate. However, the leadership and confidence that Dayan projected compensated for his gaps in professional knowledge. At

---

[49] Teveth, *Moshe Dayan*, p. 281.
[50] Ibid.
[51] Ibid.

times, such a gap between a leader's professional knowledge and his ability to sweep his subordinates along in his wake can lead to disaster on the battlefield. But Dayan's natural talent for reading battle conditions, combined with his quite astounding courage, meant that many of the operations he commanded were successful.

The 89th Battalion, with Dayan in the lead, stormed Qula after easily conquering some smaller villages around it. However, contrary to Dayan's expectation that the Arabs would scatter the way they had in Tsemah, the defenders of Qula fought back, the IDF official history reading, "A difficult battle raged in Qula."[52]

And thus, on a Saturday – Shabbat – at dawn, with the men moving in single file, Dayan in the lead and Peltz and a mortar bomb platoon on two armored vehicles bringing up the rear, the 89th Battalion began its attack on Qula. Unfortunately, the July 10 battle did not unfold as Dayan had anticipated. It was no longer sufficient to "bang on a tin can" to set the Arabs fleeing. Dayan needed Peltz, who had been right in assuming that the mortar bombs would be necessary, to set up and operate the mortars to allow Company B, commanded by Akiva Sa'ar, to surge toward the village under covering fire. Peltz did this under fire and difficult physical conditions and did it well.

The main file, led by Dayan, was pinned down by fire from the village. Dayan exited his vehicle and walked the length of the file issuing orders. During the fight, he changed his original plan and ordered his men to seize an objective that had not initially been included, to allow conquest from the flank. At this point, he left the battlefield – before the end of the battle but apparently after the outcome was already clear. He had again been called to report to Ben-Gurion in Tel Aviv. Dayan handed off command to Peltz, who continued the volley of mortar bombs, which was followed by Company B's final charge to conclude Qula's conquest, with only a few wounded. The Arabs, their resistance broken, fled in retreat.[53] The battalion set up camp in Tira, some 5 km north of Ben Shemen, and waited for new orders.

Overall, Dayan succeeded, and events proceeded more or less the way he had anticipated, despite fierce Arab resistance. But Peltz's assessment that the village needed to be weakened by artillery before being stormed also proved correct. Dayan demonstrated his ability to admit mistakes and change the battle plan during the fighting based on the situation on the ground, an attribute that would manifest itself over and over again.

Dayan, having ignored the original telegram he had received in New York summoning him to meet with Ben-Gurion in order to join first with his battalion, could no longer avoid meeting his supreme leader. Arriving in Tel Aviv, he learned that the subject for discussion was Jerusalem. Ben-Gurion was

---

[52] IDF, *Toldot milhemet hakomemiyut*, p. 254.
[53] Teveth, *Moshe Dayan*, p. 283.

worried the city might fall, which he believed would spell the end of the dream of a Jewish state. Dayan's success in Degania and his having gained Ben-Gurion's personal trust made him the most suitable candidate for the task of defending the city – in Ben-Gurion's view. He offered Dayan the position of commander of Jerusalem, replacing Major General David Shaltiel. Dayan demurred, preferring to stay with his battalion. Ben-Gurion agreed to a brief postponement of the appointment.[54]

On July 11, the 89th Battalion – without Dayan – entered the fighting in the Dir Tarif region, its forces deployed around Dir Tarif, Tira, and Qula. Peltz conducted the nighttime battle, his jeep-borne company stopping an armored Jordanian unit. Before returning to the battalion's staff quarters in nearby Tira from Dir Tarif, Peltz promised his men that he would return with reinforcements at dawn. After asking to be awakened at 4:30 a.m., he fell asleep under a tree around 1:00 a.m. But at 3:30 Dayan shook him awake, demanding an update. Peltz, exhausted by the last days' immense effort and responsibility, asked to sleep another hour. Dayan said, "Fine." When Peltz awakened, it was already 7 o'clock, and the battalion was nowhere to be seen. According to one version, Dayan told the fighters, "Let him sleep."[55] This was the nadir in the relationship between the guerrilla fighter and the professional officer. Years later, Peltz wrote scathing criticism of Dayan – about his military ignorance, his irresponsibility, and his savage, capricious nature. Peltz's criticism was not unfounded, but ultimately, it was Dayan, not Peltz, who captivated the men thanks to his charisma and courage.[56]

Dayan would later write that upon seeing the battalion scattered among the villages – some men fighting, some resting – he grew livid. He couldn't make sense of Peltz's complicated explanations and remained convinced that the battalion's force must be used only as one armored fist, and that scattering the men would impede their ability to execute the mission. On the spot, he decided to concentrate the entire battalion in Dir Tarif.[57]

Dayan left Tira at dawn and headed for Dir Tarif. As usual, he scanned the battlefield and saw a Jordanian armored vehicle, apparently in good repair, lying in a ditch across from the company's position. The force, under Jordanian fire, still dominating the other side of the hill, extricated the vehicle, dubbing it the "Terrible Tiger." The captured cannon-bearing Marmon-Herrington armored car added mechanized firepower and real protection, something the battalion – equipped with only half-tracks and jeeps – desperately needed.

[54] Ibid.
[55] Ibid., p. 284.
[56] Martin van Creveld, *Moshe Dayan*, London: Weidenfeld & Nicolson, 2004, p. 62.
[57] Dayan, *Avnei derekh*, p. 64.

At this point, there are differing versions as to how it was decided that Dayan's force would enter Lod and Ramla. Teveth's biography and Dayan's autobiography agree that Dayan was looking for his battalion's next mission. From his elevated observation point, he could see Lod in his unit's eastern sector and realized the city was sparsely defended. There were no defensive units stationed in the region, which constituted a corridor connecting the Legion forces deployed through the Lod–Beit-Naballah–Ramallah line.[58] Dayan gathered all the company commanders and announced that the battalion was leaving for Lod.[59] His declaration must have been met with astonishment, but the intensity of the admiration for Dayan and the authority he projected inspired the sense that the battalion could reach the ends of the earth if only the commander gave the order. About the battalion's reaction, Teveth wrote, "Merriment spread through the unit. For now, the exhaustion faded and enthusiastic eyes focused on the valley, on Lod."[60] Besides, after the baptism by fire in Qula, the battalion's confidence and feeling it could operate with coordinated units had gotten a boost.[61]

While he was pondering the idea, Dayan was speaking with Mula Cohen, the commander of the Yiftach Brigade, possibly originally designated to take Lod with the help of the 82nd Armored Battalion. The Yiftach Brigade had started to operate on the outskirts of Lod but had run into trouble and halted operations, and Cohen had been trying to reach the commander of the 82nd Armored Battalion, which was to have helped the Brigade, seeking assistance. Dayan showed up and learned that Cohen couldn't reach the right commander; Dayan volunteered for the mission.

The war's official history books relate the events somewhat differently, saying that Cohen decided to change the battle plan and use Dayan's 89th Commando Battalion instead of the 82nd Armored Battalion. This version ignores how the 89th came to this place to begin with and fails to explain how Allon, who had overall command of the operation, saw the situation.[62] According to historian Martin van Creveld, Dayan asked Allon to approve the change,[63] so that the initiative was Dayan's, and Allon agreed. In his memoirs, however, Dayan presented the decision as his alone. In an essay published in the periodical *Maarakhot*, Dayan wrote: "Indeed, the decision for the attack on Lod originated with the commander of the commando unit

---

[58] Teveth, *Moshe Dayan*, p. 287.
[59] Dayan, *Avnei derekh*, p. 65.
[60] Teveth, *Moshe Dayan*, p. 288.
[61] Dayan, *Avnei derekh*, p. 65.
[62] Teveth, *Moshe Dayan*, p. 289. Lau-Lavie, too, wrote (Naphtali Lau-Lavie, *Moshe Dayan*, London: Valentine Mitchell, 1968, p. 65) that Dayan made the decision unilaterally, and his book predates Teveth's (1968 and 1971 respectively).
[63] Van Creveld, *Moshe Dayan*, p. 63.

(albeit in coordination with the commander of the nearby infantry brigade) [Mula Cohen of the Yiftach Brigade]."[64] Historian Anita Shapira's version conflicts with that of Dayan, reporting that Allon came to the captured village of Daniel, where he found the raiding battalion instead of the 82nd Battalion after Cohen and Dayan had already formulated their plan. There was nothing for Allon to do but approve it.[65] Cohen, in his own memoirs, neither supports nor contradicts Dayan. He merely notes, drily, that contact with the tank company had broken down, and instead, "they succeeded in contacting Dayan's jeep battalion."[66] Yeruham Cohen, an intelligence officer with the 8th Brigade and close associate of Allon, wrote that Mula Cohen was very surprised by the arrival of Dayan's battalion, and his assessment corresponds with Dayan's.[67]

Another central issue was determining the battalion's mission. According to Allon, it was to seize a key location in the city, such as the police station, and wait for the Yiftach Brigade's infantry to join forces. It was also decided that in case the resistance proved too strong, the battalion would retreat from the city, but the confusion of the defenders would be exploited by Yiftach's forces to execute a raid.[68] In fact, it was the second scenario that unfolded. After the operation, some criticized the battalion for not holding on to the city, although there was no doubt that resistance was fierce and that the high number of casualties justified the retreat. Teveth implicitly criticizes Dayan for omitting from his memoir the fact that the order had been to hold on to the city. Perhaps Dayan dismissed that option right from the start. Yeruham Cohen corroborated that Allon had instructed Dayan to seize a key position until the arrival of Yiftach's fighters, but Dayan had explained that in light of the attrition of his force (in particular vehicles), he had been forced to retreat. According to Cohen, Allon accepted his decision, saying, "If a commander like Dayan seeks to retreat, apparently there is no other option."[69] In any event, Dayan probably thought that a mechanized battalion was not built to hold territory; that was a mission best carried out by the infantry.

Dayan's premission briefing reflected his original intentions:

> What was clear from the outset was that our job was not to exit the vehicles and not to hold positions outside the vehicles. We would drive back and forth while shooting; the Arabs would flee; and we'd be left with

[64] Moshe Dayan, "The Commando Battalion Ascends Lod" (Hebrew), *Maarakhot*, 62–63 (July 1950), p. 34.
[65] Anita Shapira, *Yigal Allon: Aviv holdo, biogreafia* (Hebrew), Bnei Brak: United Kibbutz, 2004, p. 368.
[66] Mula Cohen, *Latet ulekabel: Pirkei zikhronot ishi'im* (Hebrew), Bnei Brak: United Kibbutz, 2000, p. 140.
[67] Yeruham Cohen, *l'or hayom ubmacshach* (Hebrew), Tel Aviv: Miskal, 1969, p. 153.
[68] Teveth, *Moshe Dayan*, p. 289.
[69] Yeruham Cohen, 1969, p. 156.

a fire-free corridor of passage for Yiftach's men, who were holding the outskirts of the city but could not penetrate it.[70]

Dayan had left one company behind in Qula and gone to Lod without informing the brigade, exposing the flank in this region to counterattacks by the Arab Legion and angering Sadeh, his commander.[71] Nonetheless, en route to the target, Dayan briefed his men according to the principles he had learned from Baum in New York:

> You don't stop just because you encounter an obstacle ... The leading jeeps scatter aside and the [previously Jordanian] armored vehicle and the half-tracks surge ahead. If one of our vehicles is hit, one doesn't stop to fix it and one doesn't allow it to slow down the rest of the line. One passes it and continues onward. No one except for me is allowed to delay the convoy. We progress no matter what. We shoot, we trample, and we move forward.[72]

Dayan's plan involved driving fast across the first line of positions and then splitting the battalion into two axes, a good tactical move that would increase the enemy's confusion.[73] One axis would move north and the other south. The plan then called for the companies to reconnect at the junction, to "cause total bedlam, followed by surrender."[74] The battalion force, missing those still in Dir Tarif, numbered only 271 soldiers and officers, among whom 150 participated in the actual charge. The battalion had all of eight half-tracks, nine light armored vehicles, the Terrible Tiger armored car that they had to learn to operate, and twenty jeeps mounted with machine guns.

On the morning of July 11, Yiftach Brigade units engaged in battle on Lod's southeastern outskirts. At 6:20 p.m., the 89th Battalion started a raid that lasted forty-seven minutes, The battalion was arranged in single file and headed by Dayan. After heavy fire was aimed at the force, the Terrible Tiger took the lead and fired its cannon, clearing the way for the line to move ahead. Dayan issued commands, having the force spread out. At a certain point, he exited his vehicle, ran among the jeeps, and issued orders face-to-face. Throughout his years of military service, it was important to Dayan, especially at critical junctures, to be physically present among his subordinates and for them to hear the orders in his actual voice. The battalion advanced in its new, spread-out formation, while spraying fire in every direction and increasing its speed. The entire drive to the town was done under heavy fire, which grew more intense as the battalion entered the town and neared the police building at its

---

[70] Teveth, *Moshe Dayan*, p. 290.
[71] Yeruham Cohen, 1969, p. 158.
[72] Teveth, *Moshe Dayan*, p. 288.
[73] The US Army was criticized for traveling in a single convoy in the 2003 raid on Baghdad, but they succeeded.
[74] Teveth, *Moshe Dayan*, p. 290.

center. But then the plan went awry. The Terrible Tiger turned right, but instead of following it, the rest of the vehicles – the half-tracks and jeeps – turned left, because, according to Dayan's instructions, they were supposed to deploy in the courtyards of the buildings and take cover behind the stone walls. The Terrible Tiger continued on its own until it reached the town center, where it stood exchanging fire with the Jordanians inside the police building.

Meanwhile, the half-track now leading the column continued speeding past the town on a road through its outskirts, followed by the rest of the force. Later, it was discovered that a technical malfunction had prevented it from stopping. The force exited Lod and drove at speed past the Tegart Fort between it and Ramla. The surprised Legionnaires holding the fort let the first vehicles pass but then recovered and opened fire, hitting in particular the unarmored jeeps and their exposed riders. At this point, Dayan's radio ceased to function, and he temporarily lost the ability to command his force. Finally, the entire force stopped in Ramla. All the vehicles were peppered with bullet holes and steam billowed from the radiators.

The Jordanians having identified the force and firing artillery, Dayan decided to drive back to Ben Shemen, going again through Lod. Charging through Arab fire again, picking up casualties who had been left behind in the initial charge, they reached the Terrible Tiger, still in Lod, and then drove to Ben Shemen. Other than the Terrible Tiger and a couple of half-tracks, all of the remaining thirty-five vehicles were either towing other vehicles or being towed themselves. The battalion stopped only once upon reaching Ben Shemen, where it became clear that the losses had been greater than first thought: nine dead and seventeen wounded. On the Arab side, there were dozens of casualties.

Dayan's original plan went wrong. The line of vehicles did not enter the city where he had wanted it to; it had not split as planned and had taken a wrong turn, so that only the Terrible Tiger had actually entered the town proper. Still, despite the mishaps, Dayan continued to lead the assault, demonstrating initiative and determination in battle. In retrospect, this mistake actually assisted the Israeli attack – many of the Arab defenders, deployed against the stalled Yiftach attack, rushed to confront what seemed to them to be an outflanking move. The exposed column attracted most of the defenders' attention, especially as it passed by the Tegart Fort, south of the town. This enabled the Yiftach force to resume its attack.[75]

In the end, the action achieved its aim: the conquest of the two towns. At 8 p.m., Yigal Allon wrote a summary of the action. In it, he noted that while the forces defending Lod were temporarily stunned by the daring raid, tenacious fighting was still necessary to defeat it. That night, the Legion's soldiers left the town. Early on Monday, July 12, Lod and Ramla surrendered.

---

[75] Author's phone interview with Professor Kadish, Head of IDF History Department, May 15, 2021.

The Debate about the Raid

The IDF's official history describes the raid as follows:

> The raid on Lod, one of the most daring actions of the War of Independence, is typical of the inherent achievements of which light armored units are capable. No outpost was captured; no target of military value was destroyed. But the psychological impact – the shock, surprise, uncertainty about the enemy's whereabouts in the present and its plans for the future – was decisive.[76]

Anita Shapira summarized the battle and its effects on the central heroes of the affair:

> The story of Dayan and the raiding battalion is the story of the glory and romance of the conquest of Lod. The bold, charismatic but disobedient battalion commander gathered desperate, adventurous men around him ... and went to storm Lod ... Dayan's audacity captured the imagination and the headlines ... However, the ones who conquered Lod were the men of Yiftach who fought with caution and advanced step-by-step, without the glory of the brave act that caught people's imagination.[77]

As always, Dayan managed to leverage this into maximum public relations impact and notoriety. On September 24, 1948, about two and a half months after the battles for Lod and its environs, the popular newspaper *Davar* published an article about the 89th Battalion and its derring-do. And at the heart of the article was battalion commander Moshe Dayan.[78]

The raid on Lod was the first of many controversial affairs in Dayan's long career, offering a mere foretaste of some of Dayan's traits that would later manifest themselves in other contentious events. Dayan possessed charismatic leadership coupled with rare courage and daring, but he was also dismissive – some would say contemptuous – of the normal chain of command and of coherent military doctrines. If, at a given moment, an action seemed to him the right thing to do, he was willing to go all the way.

Dayan's lack of caution, seen by many as irresponsible or even disrespectful, angered some colleagues, especially his superiors and fellow commanders. Among them was his deputy Peltz. Peltz never adjusted to Dayan's style of command; to him, Dayan constantly seemed to be making amateurish, spur-of-the-moment moves.[79] Yiftach commander Mula Cohen, too, and the Dani

---

[76] IDF, *Toldot milhemet hakomemiyut*, p. 258.
[77] Shapira, *Yigal Allon*, pp. 369–370.
[78] Article cited by Naor (ed.), *Moshe Dayan*, pp. 161–166. It can be read on the Israel National Library website at http://jpress.org.il/Olive/APA/NLI_heb/sharedpages/SharedView.Page.aspx?sk=5C76C274&href=DAV/1948/09/24&page=3.
[79] Years later, Peltz wrote his memoirs in which he settled his account with Dayan. See van Creveld, *Moshe Dayan*, p. 62.

Operation commander Yigal Allon found it difficult to swallow that Dayan got most of the credit for subduing Ramla and Lod even though the Palmach units did most of the fighting. Even Yitzhak Sadeh, the revered teacher and commander of the 8th Brigade (to which Dayan's battalion belonged), was distressed because Dayan failed to update him on his moves, which in Sadeh's view could have affected the entire brigade.

In the War of Independence, undoubtedly Israel's longest and most difficult war, the army was based on the infantry, and much of its first stage was characterized by static defensive battles. In the second stage of the war, too, most IDF offensives were carried out by infantrymen advancing slowly and fighting long, exhausting battles over every inch. Given this, one can understand the great enthusiasm that the mechanized blitz charge aroused.

Dayan's approach in Lod reflected the Prusso-German *Auftragstaktik* tradition – a command method of issuing general orders, or, to use the IDF's official name, "mission command." Dayan intuitively picked up this principle from Orde Wingate, one of his instructors in the Haganah's platoon commanders' course.[80] This form of command favors the independence of junior commanders and encourages considerations of changing conditions. It is especially well suited to mechanized warfare and maneuvering, enabling commanders to quickly exploit sudden opportunities and reduce the long waiting times for receiving approval typical of military hierarchies. Generations of German generals were trained in this, notably tank commanders Erwin Rommel and Heinz Wilhelm Guderian, and in the US Army, General George Patton. Furthermore, Dayan's personally leading his battalion was also a rarity in the War of Independence, when most Israeli battalion commanders commanded from a static post behind the forces. Dayan's style of leadership was of a piece with the "command from the saddle" and "forward command" command approach, concepts that were to become firmly rooted norms in the IDF when Dayan became Chief of Staff.[81]

But at this stage of the war, the incident was extraordinary, and other IDF commanders realized that the raid reflected a different, innovative way of operating. Elhanan Oren, the war's official historian, wrote, "Operation Danny witnessed the birth of the mechanized formation."[82] Major General Israel Tal, later considered the father of Israel's armored corps and the architect of the Merkava tank, declared that, "the raid on Lod became part of the myth of the IDF's armored troops and made the story of the battle part of the Corps' battle heritage."[83] According to Haim Laskov, another future Chief of

---

[80] Ibid., pp. 19–20.
[81] Ibid., p. 100.
[82] Elhanan Oren, *Baderekh el ha'ir: Mivtsa dani, juli 1948* (Hebrew), Tel Aviv: Maarakhot, 1976, p. 107.
[83] Teveth, *Moshe Dayan*, p. 289.

Staff, the raid tipped the scales of the war.[84] Taking a more balanced approach, Yitzhak Rabin wrote that the raid did not topple Lod, "but it shook the [Arabs'] willingness to resist,"[85] and added that the Yiftach Brigade exploited the shock and captured the city with relentless fighting.[86]

Enemy testimony also appears to bolster the claim attributing the operation's success to the raid. In 1952, Dayan met Major Adib al-Qassam from the Arab-Jordanian Legion in a senior command course in Great Britain. Discussing 1948, al-Qassam told Dayan of the adventures of a certain Israeli commando unit that had raided Lod and Ramla. The Legionnaires, he said, tried to stop the raiders but failed and escaped to Latrun. Al-Qassam, expressing his amazement at the brave assault, had no idea he was speaking with the commander of the raid.[87]

Ironically, the response of Ben-Gurion, Dayan's patron, was cooler, perhaps because he wanted the IDF to be an orderly institution like the British Army. He was not enthusiastic about Dayan's rash methods, although he was undoubtedly impressed by his courage. In the July 10 meeting with Dayan, Ben-Gurion remonstrated, "This is not how you conduct a war,"[88] insisting that this action was nothing but a "trick": An assault must be launched "like a steamroller operating in a planned, systematic manner, step by step."[89] Dayan, unconvinced, left the meeting feeling they would just have to agree to disagree and wrote: "In his opinion, I'm a brave commander but a maverick, and in my opinion, he's a wise and inspired political leader who has learned and heard much about Arabs and warfare, but we don't know one another well. He may know *about* a thing but doesn't know *the* thing itself [emphasis added]"[90] – a good reflection of Dayan's general approach to strategy and military leadership. Despite his criticism of the charge on Lod, Ben-Gurion did not change his mind about Dayan being the right choice for commander of Jerusalem, perhaps that period's most sensitive appointment.

Immediately after the operation, Dayan and Allon wrote their summarizing reports. While Dayan stressed that "shock and awe" were the primary factor in Lod's surrender, Allon submitted a more balanced description of the significance of the action in the overall scheme of things, noting that the fall of the city was a consequence of the sum of the actions of the Yiftach Brigade and the

---

[84] Ibid., p. 294.
[85] Oren, *Baderekh el ha'ir*, p. 107.
[86] Yitzhak Rabin, *Pinkas sherut* (Hebrew) (published in English as *The Rabin Memoirs*), Tel Aviv: Maariv, 1979, vol. 1, p. 60.
[87] Naphtali Lau Lavie, *Moshe Dayan: A Biography*, Hartford, CT: Hartmore House, 1969, p. 66.
[88] Teveth, *Moshe Dayan*, p. 296.
[89] Dayan, *Avnei derekh*, p. 72. To a large extent, this was the operational method of Bernard Montgomery, the British general and hero of World War II, whom Ben-Gurion greatly admired.
[90] Ibid., p. 72.

89th Battalion.[91] The description of the raid in the literature of the war is based on an essay Dayan wrote and published in 1950 in *Maarakhot*,[92] the military lessons distilled as follows:

> The charge of the commando units to Lod was an action typical of fast-moving forces: a unit carrying light weapons – even if armored – is only good against light weapons.
>
> The number of jeeps in the commando unit ... more than half the unit's vehicles, gave it characteristics typical of the cavalry: mobility ... and inability to act without a vehicle ... There was also the powerful addition of massive firepower, maintainable while attacking on the move ...
>
> Such a unit must seize the initiative and exploit opportunities as they emerge during the rapidly-developing action. Indeed, the decision to attack Lod came from a commando unit commander ... a mission had not been included in the initial plan ...
>
> Speed is typical not only of the planning but also of the action ... The speed of motion ... shocks the enemy, destroys its formation, prevents it from reorganizing later on, and breaks its spirit.[93]

Dayan responded to criticism, insisting: "Such a unit cannot take time out to seize enemy positions." He also referred to the controversy over credit for the fall of Lod, apparently agreeing with Allon's battle summary:

> The unit's charge at the enemy's center – once it succeeds, it shocks and awes the enemy for a time. This is when the infantry can enter and do what it pleases ... Had the infantry unit not come to Lod to execute the actual conquest of the city and dig into it, had there been no one to pluck the fruit of the assault and exploit the enemy's panic, the city of Lod and its fighters might have stirred themselves into action and regrouped before long ...
>
> Another note is necessary: in practice ... this action was unusual. In this war, many units excelled in their men's courage, self-sacrifice, and audacity. What set this action apart was its daytime execution and the dynamism and speed of the chain of events at the hands of a unit after almost 36 hours of nonstop fighting.[94]

Dayan, thus, two years after the battle, agreed with Allon and, to an extent, with Ben-Gurion, that the action was unusual. Nonetheless, he maintained, and rightly so, that the raid led to Lod's rapid surrender. The unit's spirit became Dayan's greatest contribution to the transformation of the IDF in his term as Chief of Staff. The extent to which the *esprit de corps* in a campaign is a force multiplier is something Dayan learned on different occasions, but

---

[91] Teveth, *Moshe Dayan*, p. 295.
[92] Dayan, "The Commando Battalion."
[93] Ibid., p. 34.
[94] Ibid., p. 36.

undoubtedly the raid on Lod was the most prominent example, demonstrating what a fearless unit can accomplish.

Still, debates about the raid continued for decades. Despite what Dayan wrote in *Maarakhot*, the argument over the raid did not end there. In 2002, Lieutenant Colonel Boaz Zalmanovitch, while deputy commander of the Givati Brigade, wrote an essay on the conquest of Lod and its effect on the IDF,[95] arguing that the IDF learned the wrong lessons from the battle, which came to so influence the IDF for years, only because of Dayan's notoriety. Zalmanovitch argued that the "armored shock" approach was essentially superficial and became popular only because it had succeeded in peculiar circumstances,[96] and he linked it to the failure of the armored corps in the first stage of the Yom Kippur War.

Others too considered it the harbinger of the IDF's later shift to tank-based warfare, which some historians dubbed the "Israeli blitzkrieg."[97]

However, while the raid, which reflected Dayan's style of command, clearly inspired the IDF and demonstrated how a speedy mechanized raid can shock an enemy, it is hard to conclude that it directly affected the principles of building the ground forces in the IDF over the next twenty-five years.[98]

The raid on Lod highlighted much of what contributed to creating the great myth of Dayan, but it also planted in colleagues the seeds of resentment that would emerge later – anger, frustration, jealousy – leading to fierce criticism. It is interesting to compare Dayan at Lod with Dayan in the Six-Day War: In both cases – returning to his battalion from the United States in 1948 and being appointed defense minister in 1967 – his mere presence instilled high spirits and confidence in the troops. Both times, the critics claimed, Dayan showed up at the last minute, long after others had already worked hard on the preparation, only to pluck most of the glory.

The Yiftach Brigade had been stuck fighting in Lod before the 89th Battalion appeared and continued fighting after the 89th left. Mula Cohen wrote that Allon and Rabin both tried to persuade Dayan to camp with his battalion in Ben Shemen, but Dayan declared: "'I'm going to see Ben-Gurion in Tel Aviv to tell him I conquered Lod.' And that was the story in a nutshell – 'I conquered Lod' – when Lod had not been conquered in any way … He took off and went to report … not to his brigade commander … No, directly to Ben-Gurion."[99]

---

[95] Boaz Zalmanovitch, "The Conquest of Lod and Its Effect on the IDF" (Hebrew), *Maarakhot* 383 (May 2002), pp. 92–97.
[96] Ibid., p. 96.
[97] Eitan Shamir, *Pikud mesima* (Hebrew), Ben Shemen: Modan and Maarakhot, 2014, p. 99.
[98] It should be noted that Zalmanovitch himself hedged his statement, stating that his claims were hypotheses only and needed proof obtainable only by more research. See: Zalmanovitch, "Conquest of Lod," p. 96.
[99] Cohen, *Latet ulekabel*, pp. 140–141.

Cohen did concede that "after the fire storm, the Arabs of Lod were struck by terrible panic. It would therefore be wrong to say that what the 89th Battalion made no difference. It made a tremendous difference."[100] Given the assessment that the Yiftach Brigade had completed the seizure and occupation, while Dayan got the glory and an open door to Ben-Gurion, the frustration and jealousy Dayan aroused is easy to understand.

With Lod, Dayan clearly gambled boldly, took a risk, and succeeded. No doubt, Dayan both saved the day after the Yiftach's brigade was stopped and paved the way for the brigade's ultimate capture of the town.

Yigal Allon's many Palmach admirers likely had reason for resenting the maverick Dayan's preferential treatment from Ben-Gurion compared to the prime minister's unforgiving attitude to Allon. Perhaps Ben-Gurion had already found that, while Dayan was disobedient militarily, he was obedient politically, as proven during the Saison and the *Altalena* affair, while Allon had other ideological loyalties.[101] Therefore, Ben-Gurion, feeling he could trust Dayan, had asked him to take command of Jerusalem despite his unpredictability in battle. After hearing from Dayan on July 15, Ben-Gurion, impressed by the audacity if not by the method, again offered Dayan the Jerusalem command, which Dayan ultimately accepted.[102]

Operation Death to the Invader

Following the Lod battle, Dayan wanted time for the battalion to regain its strength, but the IDF Chief of Operations Yadin decided, after some hesitation, that the battalion must take part in the fighting in the south.

Operation Death to the Invader, led by the Givtai Brigade commander Lieutenant Colonel Shimon Avidan[103] called for the capture of two Egyptian army bases north of Plugot (then Majdal-Fallujah) and joining up with the forces besieged in the Negev. The Negev Brigade was supposed to arrive from the south and capture Kawkaba, while the 89th Battalion was meant to take the more distant Tel Karatiyya, behind the Egyptian lines, in a nighttime action. A Givati infantry company joined the battalion.

On July 15, the battalion of 220 men, 130 of them combat soldiers, and its spearhead, the Terrible Tiger armored car, moved south, terrain relatively

---

[100] Ibid., p. 141.
[101] Teveth, *Moshe Dayan*, p. 340.
[102] Ibid., p. 296.
[103] Shimon Avidan, the commander of the Givati Brigade during the War of Independence. After independence was declared, the national staff of the Haganah ordered Avidan to set up a brigade of field units. "Givati" had been Avidan's prestatehood alias. In the War of Independence, the brigade defended Tel Aviv and participated in opening the road to Jerusalem.

unfamiliar to Dayan. He wrote, "I did not know the Negev. I'd made a few trips there, but it always remained alien to me."[104]

Zero-hour was set for 10 p.m. In the afternoon, Dayan gathered his men to brief them on the plan, based on rapid movement while laying down fire. They were to reach the Egyptian-held Fallujah airfield, cross the nearby road from the southwest, and then cross Wadi Mufarar, thus reaching Tel Karatiyya from an unexpected direction and beginning the assault. To confuse the enemy, they were to drive through the Egyptian lines along a barely passable 5–6 km route.

Avidan, described as "grim-looking" and "rigid" and known to be risk-averse, was Dayan's opposite, which affected the men accordingly. For Avidan, the security of the force was paramount, making it difficult to prod him into an offensive.[105]

Dayan had two reservations. First, he found the culture in Haganah and Palmach units pretentious and self-righteous, imitating the Palmach's greatly admired – but in Dayan's opinion irrelevant – Red Army.[106] Dayan also disagreed with battalion commanders conducting the battle from the rear with remote management and troop control. Dayan preferred emphasizing leadership from the front, with control less important than helping drive the troops forward to reach their goals. He noted: "Via the wireless, you can get news and transmit instructions, but taking the battalion into battle can only be done by fighting together, not by remote control ... with the battalion commander ensconced in safety while he commands his men to surge ahead."[107] This approach would continue to characterize Dayan's leadership style even in his most senior positions.

Indeed, when the battalion started moving toward the Fallujah airfield, Dayan was in the third vehicle. En route, the convoy took heavy fire that killed the Terrible Tiger's cannoneer. When the force reached the *wadi* (a riverbed usually dry in the nonrainy season), the vehicles got stuck and a path had to be cleared for the convoy. Despite the tumult, Dayan, feeling faint, stepped aside for a short nap. At 4 a.m., the battalion started ascending from the *wadi* and stormed the village with the vehicles in front followed by a Givati Brigade infantry unit, encountering little resistance. By 6 a.m., the battalion had completed its mission, losing one man and more than half of its vehicles.

---

[104] Dayan, *Avnei derekh*, p. 72.
[105] Shapira, *Yigal Allon*, p. 387.
[106] Interestingly, at that time, the most widely read book by Palmach commanders was Alexandr Bek's novel (written in Russian and published in 1944) in its Hebrew translation, *Anshei Panapilov* (official English title, *Volokolamsk Highway*), United Kibbutz Publications, 1946, which tells the story of a Soviet battalion fighting the battle of Moscow in 1941 in World War II. See Yuval Shahal, "Isaac Babel: A War Correspondent," in *Kesher: Journal of Media and Communications History in Israel and the Jewish World* 35 (Winter 2007), pp. 5–7 (p. 5).
[107] Dayan, *Avnei derekh*, p. 73.

But, the operation, ostensibly successful, did not achieve its ultimate objective of breaking the Egyptians.

A few hours after the battled had ended, the Egyptians started bombarding Karatiyya with mortars and cannons. Dayan had already withdrawn his battalion, leaving Givati to hold the ground during the Egyptian counteroffensive, fighting heroically until the truce.[108] Avidan, believing the 89th Battalion had breached orders by leaving the battlefield, complained to Yadin, who ordered Dayan's court-martial. Dayan successfully justified his departure, arguing that a raiding battalion with nonarmored vehicles was not meant to seize and hold ground. The continuing controversies surrounding Dayan and many commanders' disapproval of his style led to opposition to his appointment as commander of Jerusalem.

After the battle, Dayan visited the wounded men from his unit, some of whom had lost eyes. To encourage them, he, with his typical cynicism, said, "Guys, there's nothing to see in this shitty world. You'll see well enough with one eye, too."[109] This would be the last battle in which Dayan led men in an attack, although in all future positions he continued to try to be on the front lines.

The second truce went into effect on July 19, and Dayan was appointed commander of the Jerusalem front on July 23.

Commander of the Jerusalem Sector

Dayan's time in Jerusalem can be divided into two periods: the first, assuming combat command of the Etzioni brigade, responsible for the sector, during the fighting; and the second, conducting the negotiations with the enemy and playing the role of officer-diplomat after the fighting had ended.[110]

In Jerusalem, Dayan was appointed brigade commander, a rank that entailed command and control of forces through intermediaries – battalion and company commanders – who, ideally, would have the same freedom of action Dayan had enjoyed as battalion commander – as well as a staff to formulate situation assessments, make decisions, and oversee all activity. This required a high degree of skill, especially training, and experience. When Dayan arrived in Jerusalem, he lacked both these things, and this was reflected in how the military operations in the city were executed. Until this point, Dayan's conduct had combined audacity, leadership – and luck

---

[108] Teveth, *Moshe Dayan*, p. 301.
[109] Dayan, *Avnei derekh*, p. 75.
[110] Military officers engaging in diplomacy is a common historical phenomenon. Despite the long-standing division between the political and military echelons, many officers are active in negotiating with the enemy. Examples can be found among officers from the colonial powers, including France and the United States, and among famous generals, such as Dwight D. Eisenhower and Douglas MacArthur in World War II.

(Napoleon is reported to have quipped, "I'd rather have lucky generals than good ones," echoed by General Dwight D. Eisenhower: "I would rather have a lucky general than a smart general ... They win battles"). But in Jerusalem, he had to command a large system, something for which he had no training. Worse still, luck eluded him. While there were some extenuating circumstances, they alone cannot explain the absence of military successes in Jerusalem.

Behind the appointment lay a bitter struggle between Ben-Gurion and Yadin along with the rest of the General Staff. In considering the reorganization and command of the four fronts, Yadin had proposed Eliyahu Ben-Hur (Cohen) to replace David Shaltiel as the Jerusalem commander. Ben-Gurion, however, suggested Dayan, whose candidacy was strongly opposed by the General Staff, which considered him uncontrollable. The conflicts peaked with letters of resignation from General Staff members submitted to Ben-Gurion on July 1 followed by a letter of resignation from Ben-Gurion himself. Ben-Gurion won this particular round of "chicken." After reaching a compromise giving Allon command of the southern front and Dayan command of the Jerusalem front,[111] everyone withdrew their resignations. Before concluding the appointments, Ben-Gurion met a delegation of 89th Battalion fighters headed by Yaakov Granek,[112] who urged him to leave Dayan in his current position as their commander. The battalion even threatened to strike. Ben-Gurion explained that the security of Jerusalem took precedence over their battalion.[113]

Dayan was appointed on July 23 and, surrounded by 89th Battalion and Nahalal stalwarts, assumed his new position in Jerusalem on August 1.[114] He arrived in a city cut in half, besieged, and under heavy shelling. City residents were reduced to drinking rainwater and making food from wild plants in their neighborhoods. The Etzioni Brigade suffered from poor training and low morale. The only sort of fighting they knew was positional warfare from fixed positions, aimed at wearing down and exhausting the enemy, much like the trench warfare of World War I. The brigade's only achievement lay in maintaining its position and not surrendering. Dayan toured the units, trying to raise the men's morale and urge their commanders to action, but it seemed to be too little, too late.

---

[111] Teveth, *Moshe Dayan*, pp. 303–304.
[112] Yaakov Granek, known by his underground nickname "Blond Dov," had been a Lehi commander and led 89th Battalion under Moshe Dayan's command in the War of Independence. During his service in Lehi, he planned and participated in many actions against the British.
[113] Teveth, *Moshe Dayan*, p. 304.
[114] Among others, Zalman Mart, Nahman Betser, Alex Broyde, Israel Gefen, Uri Bar-On, and Akiva Sa'ar. Teveth, *Moshe Dayan*, p. 304.

Beyond the low level of fighting fitness, which limited Dayan's sphere of action, there was another, no less significant constraint – the political one. At this stage, the question of Jerusalem was being discussed at the United Nations (UN) General Assembly and the Security Council, and international observers in the city prevented any kind of unilateral offensive initiative. Nonetheless, Dayan pushed Ben-Gurion and the General Staff to order action. He managed to get approval for two operations, but both, aimed at simply improving Israel's position before permanent agreements took effect, failed.

The first action was meant to drive a wedge between the Jordanian Legion, positioned east of Armon Hanatsiv (the Governor's Palace, named for the British High Commissioner's headquarters located on the hilltop), and the Egyptian army, deployed on the city's southern edges. The action, approved for the night between August 17 and 18, was to be carried out with some unequivocal, politically dictated caveats: It had to be completed within twenty-four hours, and the building, manned by UN personnel, could not be entered. After touring the area, the 62nd Battalion commander Meir Zorea and the Etzioni Brigade's operations officer Hillel Fefferman – both experienced officers – concluded that they had to seize the Governor's Palace in order to take the hill. Zorea explained this to Dayan, noting that the building was the hill's "vital ground,"[115] but Dayan seemed unfamiliar with the professional concept and was unwilling to breach the political restriction or defy Ben-Gurion. Even as a relatively junior officer, Dayan had shown sensitivity to the political aspect of military action, something that would characterize his military leadership in the future as well. Unfortunately, Dayan also tended to draw too heavily on the past and to underestimate the enemy based on past experience. Consequently, he authorized a limited Armon Hanatsiv action against the advice of his two officers.

The action ran into exactly the sort of trouble Zorea and Fefferman had anticipated. The forces found themselves stuck, exposed to fire on the hillside, and eventually had to withdraw to avoid exposure at daybreak. The force suffered a decisive defeat, and casualties were high: nine dead, five POWs, and twenty-one wounded.

The next day, Dayan gathered the men of the battalion for a dressing down. A stormy debate ensured, especially over the battalion commanders' having stayed behind to command, Zorea claiming that in a nighttime action of this type, it was better to lead from a command post in the rear to retain better control of the forces. (Today, despite impressive technological advances in command and control, the IDF's method remains closer to that of Dayan.[116])

---

[115] "Vital ground" is a professional military term. The IDF defines it as a piece of terrain without which the mission cannot be achieved. See Joint Operations, IDF GHQ Doctrine, November 2006, p. 112.

[116] According to IDF doctrine, in an offensive action, the battalion commander should be situated with the main attacking force immediately behind the first company leading the battalion. The doctrine differs regarding the location of a brigade commander, who is

Nonetheless, for the next mission, Dayan deferred to Zorea's knowledge and placed himself in the brigade command center, located higher up than the battlefield, where he could use his communications device to control the movements of the battalions.[117]

Fefferman also sharply criticized Dayan for acting unprofessionally and urged Dayan's removal. Instead, Fefferman was made battalion commander of the brigade's armored force, a step that soured the atmosphere in the brigade.[118] Over the next two months, Dayan devoted himself to rebuilding the brigade, his efforts even acknowledged by his two critics, Fefferman and Zorea. Dayan continued to demand missions, earning himself a reputation as an aggressive officer looking for action. But as the political process advanced, Ben-Gurion was increasingly unlikely to approve an operation.

Two months later, Dayan finally got what he wanted. With Operation "Yoav" starting on the southern front, Operation "To the Mountain" began on the central front to pin down the Egyptian army in the south Hebron Hills and keep it from intervening in the southern battles and to expand the Jerusalem corridor southwards.[119] On the last night of Operation "To the Mountain," October 15, Dayan was ordered to conduct Operation "Yekev," designed to enter Bethlehem from an unexpected direction: a high hill only lightly defended by the Egyptians. The idea was that if Israeli forces could overcome the topographical challenges, they could then easily overpower the enemy, thereby cutting the Egyptian forces off from the Jordanian troops on the Jerusalem–Bethlehem axis and possibly even taking Bethlehem.[120] Fefferman and the central front commander, Tsvi Ayalon, opposed the plan.

The main force was led by the Etzioni Brigade's Moriah Battalion, commanded by Zalman Mart, a longtime Dayan loyalist. Dayan, either believing it to be true or hoping to inspire the men, repeated his theory that "banging the tin can once" would send all the enemy forces into flight.

The force found climbing the cliffs more difficult than anticipated and became pinned down by enemy machine guns. One man was killed. Mart, concluding that there wasn't time left to complete the mission by morning, when the men would be sitting ducks, asked Dayan's permission to withdraw.

---

expected to place themselves where they think they have the most ability to affect the battle. Nonetheless, most brigade commanders tend to be in front of the troops, evidence of the victory of Dayan's school of thought. Email exchange with Lieutenant Colonel (res.) Boaz Zalmanovitz, previously head of the Doctrine Department in the IDF Operations Directorate.

[117] Teveth, *Moshe Dayan*, p. 314.
[118] Ibid., p. 310.
[119] History Division, General Staff, *Toldot milhemet hakomemiyut*, Tel Aviv: Maarakhot, 1970, first edition pub. 1959, p. 311.
[120] Morris, *1948*, p. 358.

Dayan, true to his principles of command, told Mart that as the commander in situ, only Mart could decide what to do. Mart decided to withdraw.[121]

These failures damaged Dayan's reputation and bolstered those who considered him an irresponsible military adventurer. Basing himself on past experiences, he had overestimated the capabilities of the undertrained, demoralized Israeli forces and underestimated the Egyptian soldiers' willingness to continue fighting when attacked. Luck did not favor him. But for Dayan, all these experiences, including failures, were important and instructive.

In his memoirs, Dayan made no attempt to whitewash the failure of Operation "Yekev." Dayan conceded they should have captured the Governor's Palace and its environs, as his officers had wanted, even referring to "vital ground": "Obviously, the directive forbidding the capture of the Governor's Palace and the immediate area around it from the outset precluded any possible use of the vital ground in the battlefield."[122] Summarizing the two failed actions, Dayan spoke of poor preparation, low battle fitness, and bad morale, factors he had not been able to change in any significant way during his command, citing the lack of any offensive action during this time and the front's static condition. In Jerusalem, Dayan met an army of "lazy bulls" rather than one of "noble stallions," as he famously recalled after the Sinai Campaign. He constantly faced this problem as a senior IDF commander, and while Chief of Staff he generated a revolution in this respect.

The principle that commanders should lead from the front was one of the most important that Dayan had learned from Wingate. After the battle of the Kastel (a strategic site near Jerusalem), a legend arose around a command issued by Shimon Alfasi: "Privates – fall back; commanders – stay and cover!" Israeli writer Yoram Kaniuk, who participated in the fighting, wrote: "Alfasi's command was to become a cornerstone for deciding that the place of commanders was in the forefront ... underpinning the call, 'Follow me!'"[123] But the reality during the War of Independence was that battalion and even company commanders did not lead their forces from the front, preferring to conduct the battle from their positions in the rear and rely on wireless communication to control the troops. Dayan was different. When the 89th Battalion delegation had approached Ben-Gurion to request that Dayan be allowed to remain with them, Ben-Gurion asked what was so special about him. They replied that he led the battalion's charge and was blunt and forthright with the

---

[121] Teveth, *Moshe Dayan*, p. 316. Teveth notes that even though Dayan was deeply disappointed by the failure of the action, he did not hound Mart as he had hounded Zorea and accepted his explanation for abandoning the mission. Although Dayan remained Mart's loyal friend, Dayan realized Mart's limitations as a commander and did not promote him through the ranks.

[122] Dayan, *Avnei derekh*, p. 76.

[123] From testimonies appearing on the Palmach website: http://info.palmach.org.il/show_item.asp?levelId=3503&itemId=6337&itemType=0&HI=19096&nofelId=3392.

soldiers.[124] Years later, when Dayan was appointed Chief of Staff, leading from the front would become a hallmark of IDF commanders.

As Dayan's days of fighting in the War of Independence ended, he became active in the armistice talks and was officially named commander of the Jerusalem front. The move to Jerusalem also led to an improved standard of living for Dayan and his family, who were housed in a large home (for that time) in the exclusive neighborhood of Rehaviya. Dayan's wife Ruth made the home a lively center for military personnel, diplomats, UN officials, and journalists, who could all converse with Dayan about professional issues and social matters. Dayan, who loved the open air of the outdoors, continued to tour the front lines and would return home to these gatherings dusty, his uniform caked in mud. He saw nothing wrong with this.[125] He kept on driving in a jeep, armed with a machine gun, which gave him a martial look at all times. Still, Dayan's way of life changed in his diplomatic position. Describing this time, he wrote, "There were many meetings … dinners, and cocktail parties. I gained weight and my name often appeared in newspaper headlines. In a few months, not only did my way of life change but also my way of thinking."[126]

During this period, Dayan developed a close relationship with the press. Indeed, Dayan was the only individual in uniform Ben-Gurion permitted to speak with the press, other than Chief of Staff Dori and Yadin. This made him a more familiar public figure than those senior to him in rank, including Allon. Dayan's personal charm also worked on journalists, who published his pronouncements in the domestic and international press. In addition, an officer at his headquarters, Alex Broida, who actually functioned as a press officer, marketed Dayan as an important future leader. Not surprising, then, that on July 18, 1949, *Life* magazine published an essay on Israel after the war, in which the caption of Dayan's photo referred to him as the heroic commander of Jerusalem and possible future prime minister.[127] Thus, the figure of Dayan was slowly but surely being fixed in the public mind, both in Israel and abroad, as a leader destined for greatness.

It was actually David Shaltiel who opened the talks with Jordan, meeting with Abdullah al-Tal, the Jordanian commander of the Jerusalem front, on July 21 after the second truce.[128] Dayan was appointed to his position two days later, but his diplomatic activity started only after the Governor's Palace defeat, on August 17, 1948, with the UN eager to prevent any renewal of the battle around the Governor's Palace and to finalize the sides' positions. On

---

[124] Dayan, *Avnei derekh*, p. 76.
[125] Ibid., p. 79.
[126] Ibid.
[127] "The New Israel," *Life*, 18 July, 1949.
[128] Ronen Yitzhak, *Abdullah Al-Tall: Arab Legion Officer*, Brighton: Sussex Academic Press, 2012, p. 56.

September 3, Dayan met for the first time with al-Tal. Despite mutual accusations of truce violations, the three promised to try to refrain from shouting, and Dayan conceded a small withdrawal.[129]

At the second meeting on September 5, Dayan suggested to al-Tal that they leave the table filled with the UN observers and speak privately. Dayan had developed a great deal of respect for al-Tal: "He stood head and shoulders above all the Arabs I met with during that time ... and he had great personal courage."[130] Dayan felt he could achieve more in a personal meeting at which the two warriors would find a common denominator than he could with numerous foreign mediators. The two soon notified the UN team that they were installing a direct telephone line between them and bypassing the UN headquarters. On November 28, the two met again, this time with UN mediation, and two days later, they signed a memorandum of understanding that Dayan described (somewhat naively, as veteran foreign ministry officials pointed out to him) as "a complete and sincere ceasefire" that included an agreement on the armistice lines to go into effect on December 1. Dayan and al-Tal met again before their direct phone line was installed on December 7. Their good relationship created calm and made it possible to resolve several local issues, such as a POW exchange, work permits for people to enter the Mount Scopus enclave, pilgrimages, and demilitarization.[131]

On December 12, the two men met again with UN observer Carlson, French Consul René Neville, US consular representative Biardet, and US military attaché Major Nicholas Andronowitz present. Dayan made the following surprising declaration: "My government instructed me to say that we are prepared to discuss an armistice and peace with the government of Transjordan, but we are not interested in continuing any talks on the basis of a truce. Of course, this does not apply to smaller issues ... which we can arrange between ourselves directly."[132]

Dayan and al-Tal's meetings following the ceasefire resolved some issues, such as ceasefire violations and the needs of the population Gradually, the men came to trust one another, making it possible to expand the November 30 truce to include southern Jerusalem at first, and, later, the area north of the city.

Al-Tal was a complex character. He presented himself as a nationalistic zealot safeguarding Arab interests. But there are many indications that this is the image he wanted to project publicly after the war, while privately expressing to his Israeli counterparts his support for the Israeli army's Jerusalem

---

[129] Ibid., p. 57.
[130] Dayan, *Avnei derekh*, p. 80.
[131] Yitzhak, *Abdullah Al-Tall*, p. 62.
[132] Shmuel Cohen Shani, "Between Beret and Top Hat: The Birth of 'Uniform Diplomacy' in the War of Independence" (Hebrew), *Bein haktavim*, The Dado Center for Interdisciplinary Military Studies, Vol. 24–25 (March 2020), pp. 103–124 (p. 115).

operations.[133] He also became popular among Israeli journalists mostly because he spoke of a possible peace, although he asked Dayan to try to arrange for *The Palestine Post* to publish a piece portraying him as a radical anti-Israel nationalist.[134]

From the beginning of their relationship, Dayan and al-Tal respected one another and their personal military accomplishments, even praising one another in their respective memoirs. The trust between them resulted in the strategically important agreement that included all of Jerusalem,[135] resulting in "absolute peace and quiet as a result of the truce agreement."[136] The central front was taken out of the cycle of fighting thanks to understandings and agreements between military commanders.

The commanders' secret channel of communication continued to operate throughout December, covering territorial arrangements included in the ceasefire agreement and the various elements of the subsequent peace agreement, including the division of Jerusalem and of the Dead Sea and mining arrangements there, train passage to Jerusalem, travel to Mount Scopus, and the fates of the Negev, the West Bank and Gaza Strip, and mixed Jewish–Arab cities. In practice, their meetings shaped the Armistice Agreements that would be publicly signed in Rhodes in July 1949, which reflected the secret arrangement that had already been pieced together on the ground while the Israeli army battled the Egyptian military in Operation "Horev," to which the Jordanian commander had given his clandestine imprimatur.[137]

Israel was also in contact with the Jordanians via European representatives: Eliyahu Sasson met in Paris with the Jordanian ambassador to Great Britain and Dayan and Reuven Shiloah from the Foreign Ministry met at Jaffa Gate on December 25 with Abdullah's envoy, his private physician. At this point, the local channel of talks over Jerusalem started to merge with the general political one, at the center of which was a comprehensive agreement with Jordan, where Dayan played a major role.

By the end of the war, the balance of power now favored Israel, not Jordan. While Abdullah's fear of an all-out Israeli attack now that the latter was stronger and held the upper hand brought him to the talks, he made demands Israeli could not possibly agree to, including withdrawing from Lod, Ramla, and Jerusalem's Arab neighborhoods and annexation of the Negev or at least the creation of a corridor under his control connecting the West Bank with the Gaza Strip and Israel's agreement that

---

[133] Yitzhak, *Abdullah Al-Tall*, p. 63.
[134] Ibid., p. 144.
[135] Cohen Shani, "Between Beret and Top Hat," p. 107.
[136] Ibid., p. 108.
[137] Ibid., p. 115.

Jordan absorb the West Bank. Israel wanted full peace with Jordan with minimal concessions on these issues.[138]

On January 1, 1949, King Abdullah appointed al-Tal as his representative to the negotiations; the next day, Dayan was appointed the Israeli representative in the talks with Jordan, together with Shiloah. The three met on January 3 at the Mandelbaum Gate in Jerusalem (an Israeli–Jordanian crossing). King Abdullah was demanding the Negev and an access road to the Gaza Strip, and Israel raised the 679 Israeli POWs held by Jordan. With the negotiations not making any real progress, King Abdullah instructed al-Tal to invite Dayan to a secret meeting at the royal palace.

On January 5, 1949, the two nations exchanged secret letters of authorization granting the military commanders the authority to discuss peace. Dayan and Sasson then met with King Abdullah in his palace on January 16, 1949, with Al-Tal included in the meeting. While the king hosted them with all due pomp and circumstance, Dayan and Sasson quickly grew impatient. But Abdullah insisted on first playing chess with them, and Sasson had to instruct Dayan not only to lose his game, but also to express amazement at the king's surprising moves.[139] Abdullah spoke of signing a peace treaty, but only if the other Arab nations signed armistice agreements in Rhodes, where talks had just gotten under way. This meeting ended without any resolution, and under pressure from the Israeli government and al-Tal, Dayan and Sasson arrived for the second meeting on January 30, hoping to secure the release of the Israeli POWs. This meeting, too, was mainly a social occasion with no visible results. Sasson instructed the impatient Dayan not to raise the issue of the POWs at any point. Before leaving the palace, it was, oddly, Sasson himself who broached the topic. He grabbed the king's sash – a nod to the ancient Bedouin practice allowing anyone holding the king's sash to make a request of him – and asked for the POWs' release. The king agreed, and arrangements for the captives' release were made that very night.[140] In his memoirs, Dayan noted that, in the end, "the talks produced no result, practically speaking," adding that the king impressed him as "a clever [ruler] who can be decisive."[141] The one clear achievement was the exchange of their POWs.

In February 1949, the UN appointed the American Ralph Bunche to mediate talks between the Arab states and Israel on the Greek island of Rhodes. Dayan was deputy to Reuven Shiloah, the head of Israel's delegation, but al-Tal remained in Jordan. Bunche took a liking to Dayan and Shiloah, with whom he spent a great deal of time in March. "Dayan and Shiloah are a much nicer

---

[138] Shimon Shamir, *Aliyatoo veshki'ato shel hashalom haham im yarden: Hamedina'ut hayisra'elit bi'ymei Hussein* (Hebrew), Tel Aviv: Kibbutz Mehuchad, 2012, p. 25.
[139] For more on the atmosphere of the talks, see Teveth, *Moshe Dayan*, pp. 326–327.
[140] Yitzhak, *Abdullah Al-Tall*, p. 67; Dayan, *Avnei derekh*, p. 85.
[141] Dayan, *Avnei derekh*, p. 85.

team than Eitan [Walter Eitan of the Foreign Ministry] and Yadin."[142] The negotiations began on March 4 and ended on April 3 with the signing of an agreement, and Jordan became the second nation after Egypt to sign an armistice agreement with Israel. Dayan enjoyed his trips around the island and the Jordanians' friendly attitude and was highly impressed by Bunche: "He inspired an atmosphere and trust and comfort ... He was one of those people whose wisdom you can enjoy not just when you agree with them, but also when you disagree with them and they've gotten the better of you."[143]

One stumbling block in the talks with the Jordanians was their demand to control the Negev. Israel decided to establish facts on the ground and, on March 5, embarked on Operation Uvda (Hebrew for "fact" but also a reference to Aavdat/Abdah, an ancient Nabatean city in the Negev Desert), taking five days to capture the entire Negev to Eilat. It was now clear that the power relations had reversed, and it was the strong Israel that was pressuring a weaker Jordan.

At this point, Yadin and Eitan were told to handle the talks, and Dayan returned to Israel,[144] continuing the talks with al-Tal and King Abdullah in late March. At a March 23 meeting with the king, Dayan, accompanied by Major Yehoshafat Harkavi,[145] demanded the strategic area of Wadi Ara that crosses the Triangle and issued a threat: Unless these demands were met, Israel would act against the Iraqi army encamped there. In short – war. In addition, Dayan demanded that the area of the old train tracks to Jerusalem be included as part of Israel.[146] In exchange, he offered concessions in the Mount Hebron region.

Abdullah, fearing another confrontation with the Israeli army, agreed to the terms. From Jordan's point of view, the agreement lifted the threat of further Israeli conquests. Most importantly, both sides saw the agreement as a preface to a future peace treaty, and the feeling was that such a peace was just around the corner.[147]

The Jordanians signed the maps Dayan had brought. When the king complained about the many concessions he was making, Dayan exclaimed that he and the two military men with him, Yadin and Harkabi, had all lost younger brothers in the war that the Arab nations, Jordan included, had

---

[142] Elad Ben-Dror, *Hametavekh: Ralph Bunche vehasikh'sukh ha'aravi-yisraeli* (Hebrew), Kiryat Sdeh Boker: The Ben-Gurion Research Institute for the Study of Israel and Zionism – Ben-Gurion University of the Negev, 2012, p. 227.
[143] Dayan, *Avnei derekh*, p. 86.
[144] Naor (ed.), *Moshe Dayan*, p. 174.
[145] Yehoshafat Harkavi enlisted in the British Army in 1943 and fought in World War II. In the War of Independence, he fought in the Jerusalem sector as a company commander in the Etzioni Brigade. He was a member of the Israeli delegation to Rhodes for the armistice agreement talks. He served as head of Military Intelligence from 1955 until 1959. Later, he was a professor of International Relations at the Hebrew University in Jerusalem. He was awarded the Israel Prize for political science in 1992.
[146] Teveth, *Moshe Dayan*, p. 336; Yitzhak, *Abdullah Al-Tall*, p. 71.
[147] Shamir, *Aliyatoo veshki'ato shel hashalom haham im yarden*, p. 24.

started. Now, Dayan said, the Arab nations would have to live with the outcome of that war.[148]

Shortly thereafter, on April 3, the Armistice Agreements were formally signed, Dayan signing on behalf of Israel. According to historian Avi Shlaim: "The agreement was a huge diplomatic victory for Israel ... providing Israel with significant territorial gains in the Negev and Wadi Ara (Figure 2.1)."[149]

On June 9, 1949, Dayan received an important appointment, taking charge of the armistice issues. He coordinated four committees – on Jordan, Egypt, Syria, and Lebanon – consisting of Israeli officers and UN mediators. Behind the scenes, Ben-Gurion preferred Dayan's advice to that of Moshe Sharett, his foreign minister, testimony to Dayan's growing influence.[150] Indeed, of all the officers, with the exception of Chief of Staff Allon, Dayan had the freest and most direct access to the prime minister. For example, after the Jordanians violated the Jerusalem agreements, Dayan and Ben-Gurion disagreed about applying military pressure. To discuss the issue, Dayan joined Ben-Gurion on August 28 for the long ride from the village of Shfaram in the north to Tel Aviv, during which the two could talk uninterruptedly and without outside pressure.[151]

From Tactical Commander to Political Negotiator

Dayan's progress can be described as no less than meteoric, a path that prepared him for the senior command and leadership positions he would hold in the future. His experiences in Degania, with the 89th Battalion, and in Jerusalem certainly helped him. But, as he said himself, the moment he became involved in the negotiations with the Jordanians, his thinking started to change, and he began studying geostrategic and geopolitical issues. He acknowledged that he was blessed with the very best teacher – David Ben-Gurion himself.

Dayan's contribution to the talks with Jordan was undoubtedly considerable:[152] from creating trust with Abdullah al-Tal, the Jordanian commander of the Jerusalem front and Dayan's direct enemy, reaching agreements with him on local issues, to conducting talks with Jordan over the arrangement overall. Harkabi, who was by Dayan's side at the end of the talks, noted that "Dayan was outstanding in conversation with the king; he floated a clever formula."[153] Teveth wrote that Dayan "proved diplomatic skill and tenacity," and that in bargaining with al-Tal he showed that "he was a brilliant, sophisticated bargainer

---

[148] Dayan, *Avnei derekh*, p. 88.
[149] Avi Shlaim, *Kir habarzel: Israel veha'olam ha'aravi* (Hebrew), Tel Aviv: Books in the Attic, 2005, p. 63 (published in English as *The Iron Wall: Israel and the Arab World*, London: Penguin, 2014).
[150] Ben-Dror, *Hametavekh*, p. 198.
[151] Dayan, *Avnei derekh*, p. 92.
[152] Yitzhak, *Abdullah Al-Tall*, p. 73.
[153] Teveth, *Moshe Dayan*, p. 337.

Figure 2.1 Dayan with members of the Israeli–Egyptian mixed Armistice commission, 1950. Source: Bettmann/Contributor/Bettmann/Getty Images.

for whom every foot of land mattered."[154] By contrast, Yadin was less kind about Dayan and maintained that Dayan's role "was very small, almost non-existent."[155] It may be that Yadin's assessment was a result of the jealousy he felt for the abilities Dayan displayed that overshadowed Yadin's role in Jordanian negotiations, which he had led before Dayan came aboard. Yadin felt that the talks with Jordan went well not because of Dayan's abilities but because they had been conducted by professional diplomats, including Sasson, and because the two nations had shared interests. Still, Yadin admitted that Dayan had a special knack for conducting negotiations with Arabs.[156]

In the end, only the opinion of one man mattered – that of Ben-Gurion. Only his reaction to Dayan counted, and Ben-Gurion was hugely impressed by Dayan's political and diplomatic finesse, leading him to attribute Israel's achievements in the talks with Jordan to Dayan. He felt that it was due to Dayan that Israel received the railway track to Jerusalem and Wadi Ara.[157]

[154] Ibid.
[155] Ibid., p. 335.
[156] Ibid.
[157] Ben-Gurion's letter of parting to the outgoing chief of staff in Dayan, *Avnei derekh*, p. 374.

Ben-Gurion learned to respect Dayan as an effective and courageous officer who could get the job done.

It was Ben-Gurion who asked Sasson to include Dayan in the meetings with the Jordanians. Dayan participated in those meetings more than any other Israeli representative. He carried out Ben-Gurion's instructions, steered the talks, reported to the prime minister, and advised him. Dayan was deeply impressed by Ben-Gurion and realized he had much to learn from such a towering politician and statesman. For example, Ben-Gurion taught Dayan always to ask about the ultimate goal – the "end state" in contemporary military terms – based on which one must define the central effort and from which one derives the methods of action.[158] On the other hand, Dayan was one of the few people in Ben-Gurion's surroundings who dared disagree and argue with him. In many cases, their divergence was the result of Dayan's preference for the concrete versus Ben-Gurion's penchant for abstraction, the breadth of history, and the conclusions drawn from the theories and theses in which he believed. Dayan once told Ben-Gurion:

> I look through the window and see the sun is setting. For me, this means that evening is starting. But you? The fact that the sun is setting now is unimportant, because you're seeing all the stars moving and the cosmos turning ... You're incapable of seeing a detail in isolation, as an episode.[159]

The trust and alliance between the two men greatly determined not only the personal fortunes of both but also the course that the developing state of Israel would take in the years to come.

Dayan's position as officer-diplomat in the talks with Jordan was very important in terms of his future professional path. Despite his successes in Degania and as commander of the 89th Battalion, Dayan had more than a few detractors in the IDF's elite command structure. Therefore, had he not led the talks with Jordan, he would have become just another commander in a long list of War of Independence commanders. His critics are prone to focus on his tactical failures. But as an officer-diplomat, Dayan's unique traits came to the fore.[160] Furthermore, it was actually after he had become an object of criticism and jealousy among former Palmach commanders that Ben-Gurion forged closer relations with him, as he felt Dayan, lacking supporters elsewhere, would be a loyal ally, someone he could trust. Thus was Dayan's future path paved.

---

[158] Teveth, *Moshe Dayan*, p. 331.
[159] Ibid., p. 334.
[160] Teveth, *Moshe Dayan*, p. 302.

3

Generalship

Before becoming Chief of Staff, Dayan had held two senior positions: commander of the Southern Command and commander of the Northern Command, in the course of which he was a member of the General Staff. He was not involved in any major military episodes in these positions, as Israel's main challenges following the War of Independence involved absorbing massive immigration and meeting economic challenges. In the security realm, the Armistice Agreements and the Arab nations' weakened economic and military condition made an imminent invasion appear unlikely; the security threat was "routine," not "basic,"[1] resulting from Arab refugees' ongoing infiltrations into Israel, most heading for central Israel, and attempts by the Arab states to make slight changes in the Armistice lines. Therefore, Dayan remained relatively untaxed as commander of these two Commands. This period of Dayan's life may be considered an interim stage dedicated mostly to learning and training before becoming Chief of Staff. As Ben-Gurion had promised, Dayan was able to improve his military training, taking a battalion commanders' course in Israel and a course at the British Army's Senior Officers' School in Devizes, England. He also participated in many IDF drills and exercises for testing its troops' fighting fitness. All this training was to play a major role in Dayan's understanding of military doctrine and the art of strategy.

The Chief of Staff in Israel is unmatched in scope and complexity anywhere else in the world. Officially, the Chief of Staff is the highest command rank in the IDF and is subject to the government's authority and subordinate to the defense minister. The Chief of Staff both heads the General Staff and commands all branches of the armed forces. As the IDF never developed distinct air-force or navy services, the General Staff is responsible for building and operating all air, sea, and ground forces. The Chief of Staff is subordinate to the government[2] due to this dual responsibility for all service branches in all

---

[1] Basic threats describe scenarios in which an Arab actor launches a major offensive (high-intensity war) with the intent of physically annihilating Israel. Routine threats involve scenarios in which Arabs conduct constant small-scale raids (low-intensity war) in order to wear down the Jewish population's resolve to remain in Israel.

[2] Following the findings of the Agranat Commission on the Yom Kippur War, the law was amended for the sake of clarification.

theaters.³ In fact, some scholars have claimed that the institution of Chief of Staff has "excess power."⁴

The position requires a broad regional and global strategic vision of the theater of war and an operational view of the various theaters and the functions of all the service branches in them. The major tasks involve deploying the armed forces to face current challenges, routine or basic, and building the military force to ensure the IDF's preparedness to face future ones, all while managing the great risks involved and maintaining public trust in the army.⁵

The 21st Chief of Staff, Lieutenant General Gadi Eizenkot, described the job as follows:

> The Chief of Staff has three unique functions in the IDF: seeing the comprehensive theater of war, which is a matter of strategy; taking a broad strategic view, which is a matter of meta-strategy; and taking an operational comprehensive service branch view. The Chief of Staff's major areas of work are the force building and deployment of the IDF. Israel's security reality is complex, requiring the Chief of Staff to engage in a continuous dialogue and ongoing process of clarification with the political echelon ... while developing mechanisms of learning and knowledge for the day-to-day operations, emergencies, and war.⁶

Recent Chiefs of Staff have faced many fundamental challenges similar to those Dayan faced in 1953: the relationship between the political and military echelons, public legitimacy, managing the Israeli public's expectations, the Chief of Staff's relationship with his subordinates, managing a strict budget, formulating multiyear force-construction plans, and maintaining a high level of alertness while concurrently building the military forces and updating the army's military doctrine.

As Lieutenant General Dan Halutz, Israel's 18th Chief of Staff between 2005 and 2007, described it: "The Chief of Staff's job is highly diverse, involving command and management of force-building and employment, understanding budgets, and a pinch of political insight. He [has] obligations not only to

---

³ Meir Finkel reports the Supreme Command's directives on the position: "The Chief of Staff [is] the high[est] commander in the army," and "The Chief of Staff commands and controls the use of force of the IDF and its construction by means of the chief commands and service branches." Meir Finkel, *Haramatkal* (Hebrew), Ben Shemen: Modan and Maarakhot, 2018, p. 17.
⁴ Emmanuel Waller, *Kil'lat hakelim hashvurim: Dimdumey ha'otsma hatsva'it vamedinit hayisraelit (1967–1982)* (Hebrew), Jerusalem: Schocken, 1987, pp. 164–167. On the excess power of the institution of the Chief of Staff, see also Avraham Rotem, *Bedek batyit batira* (Hebrew), Tel Aviv: Maarakhot, 2007, pp. 168–169.
⁵ Amos Yadlin, Itai Brun, and Udi Dekel, "The Ten Challenges Facing the Incoming Chief of Staff," *INSS Insight* 1130 (January 15, 2019), www.inss.org.il/wp-content/uploads/2019/01/No.-1130.pdf.
⁶ Lieutenant General Gadi Eizenkot in his introduction to Finkel, *Haramatkal*, p. 9.

those who appointed him but also to the public at large."⁷ Finkel aptly describes the uniqueness of Israel's Chief of Staff position compared to senior command positions in other Western nations:

> It is difficult to compare the IDF's Chief of Staff position to [its equivalent] in other armies. [Compared] to the U.S. Armed Forces, the Chief of Staff in the IDF to a large extent combines both the position of the Chairman of the Joint Chiefs of Staff, which ... would be parallel to the IDF Chief of Staff, and the position of the commander of the operational commands. [Essentially,] the IDF Chief of Staff combines the position of Gen. Dwight Eisenhower, who commanded the Allied Forces in Europe during World War II, and that of George Marshall, Chief of Staff of the U.S. Army, who created the force and sent it to fight.⁸

Southern Commander

The Armistice Agreements of July 22, 1949, ended a chapter Dayan's life; he now had to decide on his future.

For a short time after the War of Independence, a sense of normality prevailed in Israel. Many commanders and officers left the army for jobs in civilian life. Even Dayan, uncertain about the future and feeling he lacked a proper military education, which could impede his advancement, considered following suit. Moreover, as Teveth observed: "His desire to acquire military doctrine was not great, whereas his interest in policy was."⁹ Indeed, although Dayan would become Israel's most politically involved Chief of Staff, Ben-Gurion convinced Dayan to stay in the army and take over the Southern Command. Ironically, Ben-Gurion, who wanted a professional, orderly army loyal to the idea of "statehood," decided to appoint Dayan, the maverick (future prime minister Levi Eshkol would call Dayan "Abu Jildah"),¹⁰ to a senior IDF command position. Apparently, Dayan's unique combination of charisma as a leader, battlefield bravery, personal loyalty, and ability to turn Ben-Gurion's ideas into action appealed to "the Old Man." Dayan, realizing that Israel's struggle with its Arab enemies would not end soon and that his life was bound up in it, agreed.¹¹

In November 1949, Ben-Gurion appointed the thirty-two-year-old Yigal Yadin as Chief of Staff and the thirty-four-year-old Dayan commander of the Southern Command. At that time, Yitzhak Rabin, a Yigal Allon loyalist, was the Southern Command's Operational Division officer. Soon realizing it would

---

⁷ Yedioth Sefarim, *Begova Ha'enayim* (Hebrew), Tel Aviv: Chemed Books, 2010, p. 298.
⁸ Finkel, *Haramatkal*, pp. 18–19.
⁹ Shabtai Teveth, *Moshe Dayan: Biografia* (Hebrew), Tel Aviv: Schoken, 1971, p. 339.
¹⁰ The nickname, borrowed from the leader of a band of highway robbers active during the British Mandate, refers to someone wild and uncontrollable.
¹¹ Teveth, *Moshe Dayan*, p. 343.

be difficult for him to serve under Dayan, Rabin decided to leave his position, but not before writing a scathing criticism of Dayan to Allon: "Moshe Dayan shows up. I get him up to speed. The guy has no clue whatsoever ... he lacks even the most minimal military understanding beyond the company or battalion level. And he is utterly lacking in tact in his human relations."[12] Dayan did not replace any other staff officers who had worked with Allon, a sign of his great self-confidence.

Rabin accurately assessed Dayan's poor knowledge of military matters, as Dayan would have readily admitted, but not Dayan's interpersonal skills. While Dayan could be tactless, he was also adept at charming people and sweeping them up like a Pied Piper by creating an honest, easygoing, spirited atmosphere. Accompanied by his intelligence officer, Rehavam (Gandhi) Ze'evi, Dayan would often go out into the field to familiarize himself with the south, which he did not know well.[13] He paid little attention to order and procedures, placing his aide-de-camp, Tzvi Tzur, in charge of "all that military BS," as British psychologist Norman Dixon called it.[14] "Moshe wanted to put all he had into the main effort," Tzur related, "and viewed enforced order and discipline as manacles that had to be uncuffed."[15] Dayan, impatient with the military hierarchy's slow pace, would issue direct orders to any rank, ignoring the chain of command and without coordinating with others. While relations between the professional Tzur, attentive to procedure and discipline, and the unruly Dayan were difficult, albeit productive, Tzur continued working with Dayan in different capacities throughout Dayan's career. Ze'evi, who was the intelligence officer of the Southern Command, recalled Dayan's wild streak: Together they would "liberate" chickens from coops they spied and then roast them over open fires. Ze'evi also noted Dayan's more serious side: "Dayan would stick with a subject and dig deeply into it. At that time in the army, he focused almost exclusively on improving the operational capabilities."[16] According to Ze'evi, Dayan's command style enabled the people around him to express themselves and even voice criticism. "Dayan would test me and talk about his ideas before giving lectures so that I could critique them ... He wanted ... the pros and cons."[17]

Dayan's leadership of the Southern Command proved a period of relative calm in a turbulent career, but some of his unique patterns of command and

---

[12] Yemima Rosental (ed.), *Yitzhak Rabin, rosh memshelet yisrael, mivhar te'udot mipirkey hayav* (Hebrew), Vol. 1, Jerusalem: State Archives, 2005, p. 58.
[13] Michael Sheshar, *Sihot im Rehavam Zeevi (Gahndi)* (Hebrew), Tel Aviv: Yedioth Ahronoth, 1992, p. 155.
[14] Norman Dixon, *Hapsikhologiya shel hashlumi'eliyot batsava* (Hebrew), Tel Aviv: Defense Ministry Publishers, 2003, pp. 181–193.
[15] Teveth, *Moshe Dayan*, p. 347.
[16] Sheshar, *Sihot im Rehavam Zeevi*, p. 155.
[17] Ibid.

emphases were already in evidence: a lack of formality and many pranks, visiting the field for extended stays, unmediated relationships with soldiers, direct conduct, and an uncompromising insistence on maintaining a high operational level.

Advanced Command Courses

In 1950 and 1951, Dayan attended two advanced military training courses, one in Israel and the other in England. Israel's six-month battalion commanders' course had two parts: a battalion commanders' course first, followed by more advanced training for higher ranks. All the participants were senior ranking commanders, while the instructors, who had already taken the course, were lower in rank but relatively experienced in the subjects, such as Major Uzi Narkiss. The course, combining theory with planning exercises, imparted knowledge needed for senior staff and command work and provided a general military education. The study method combined theory with various planning exercises.[18]

Dayan, surrounded by former Palmach fighters who felt that his loyalty was with their ideological rival Mapai, did not gain universal adulation here. The course instructors found Dayan overly critical of the course material, but Narkiss saw Dayan, despite his criticism of the course, as someone who was there to learn.[19]

In his memoirs, Dayan wrote that he did not excel in technical knowledge and that the instructors thought he had a tactical mind but did not bother remembering details, such as the structure of the lead unit of a brigade on the move.[20] Dayan inveighed against the textbook solutions for the exercises, insisting that all solutions must be based on the immediate, concrete context. Contrary to the instructors' adherence to universal solutions transcending place, time, society, and culture, Dayan believed military action could be understood only in its specific political and social context.

Narkiss later wrote that "Dayan questioned these exercises from the outset. He excelled at tying the textbook solutions into knots firmly embedded in the land of Israel and disagreed with theoretical solutions to operational problems that did not take settlements on the ground into consideration."[21] In one exercise, the students had to deploy a brigade-level defense against an invasion by an Egyptian brigade. Military doctrine demanded that junctions be

---

[18] Sagi Turgan, *Mimeni ishit lo yetseh general: Hakh'sharat hapikud hak'ravi betsahal* (Hebrew), Jerusalem: Yad Ben Zvi, 2017, pp. 291–292.

[19] Uzi Narkiss, *Hayal shel yerushalayim* (Hebrew), Tel Aviv: Defense Ministry Publishers, 1991, 2nd ed., p. 139.

[20] Teveth, *Moshe Dayan*, p. 350; Moshe Dayan, *Avnei derekh: Autobiografia* (Hebrew), Jerusalem: Idanim, 1976, p. 103.

[21] Narkiss, *Hayal shel yerushalayim*, p. 139.

defended, thereby leaving some settlements outside the brigade's defense system. Dayan steadfastly refused to submit a plan of defense that abandoned a Jewish settlement. "Perhaps you could teach defense plans at West Point, but not in Israel," he argued.[22] The instructors asked him to ignore the context and relate only to the region, insisting these were military doctrine's binding principles for defending a region well. Dayan, unconvinced, insisted, "So give me a different location." The instructors had to change the solution to the exercise and include the settlements that had been omitted. Narkiss saw this insistence as crystallizing Dayan's IDF doctrine of regional defense, based on a combination of settlements that are static points of defense and mobile forces as part of brigade-level planning.[23]

To mark the end of the first course, Dayan drew a cartoon with him as the fox (the Southern Command symbol) and his instructors as an owl (the Doctrine Branch symbol). His accompanying rhyme pits the fox's "street smarts" against the owl's universal wisdom that fails to grasp reality, unable to digress from detached written law even when settlements fall into enemy hands. Dayan continued his rhyme when the course's second part ended, writing under the title "The Song of the Swan as Sung by the Fox,"[24] "I, personally, will never make a general." Teveth suggested that Dayan was torn between the strictures of his job and his love of freedom. Possibly Dayan, incapable of seeing himself as a general beyond a certain time and place in the land of Israel, the state of Israel, and the IDF, was disdainful of the technical, professional general possessing military technical, universal knowledge isolated from the context of place and culture.

Nonetheless, Dayan, whose weaknesses in military tactics were quite evident during his defense of Jerusalem, was well aware of his lack of interest and ability in instilling order, discipline, and procedures in subordinates. He therefore always made sure his staff included people like Tzur and Narkiss, telling Narkiss, "I want the best organized and most orderly command in the IDF."[25]

After concluding this course, Dayan was appointed to command the Northern Command before starting his second two-month senior commander course in Devizes, England in early 1952. Instructors here were British officers, experienced World War II veterans who understood what mattered and could balance doctrine and practicalities. Not surprisingly, then, Dayan found this course very helpful. Writing to Yadin and Ben-Gurion, he reported that: "[I came] to hear, see, and expand military horizons. The emphasis was on ... how to think and plan rather than on the outcome." With the British

---

[22] Teveth, *Moshe Dayan*, p. 350.
[23] Narkiss, *Hayal shel yerushalayim*, p. 139.
[24] Teveth, *Moshe Dayan*, pp. 351–352.
[25] Ibid., p. 354.

approach quite the opposite of the IDF's textbook solutions, Dayan had finally found a place where the methods were to his liking.[26]

Dayan received a highly positive assessment from the school's commander: "[Dayan] showed keen interest and worked hard ... He was intelligent and always contributed something to the debate. He possesses comprehensive knowledge of organization and tactics, and he is a very congenial fellow ... All in all, an outstanding exemplar of his army."[27]

Dayan returned to Israel in what was described as a state of high enthusiasm generated by the knowledge and tools from his recent studies. It may have been the only time in his life that Dayan was excited by any formal learning setting and did not criticize it harshly.[28] As the leader of an entire Command, he soon held a series of exercises applying the material he had learned.[29]

Exercise "Maneuver 2"

In August 1951, the IDF was in the midst of a series of large exercises led by Chief of Staff Yadin, intended to assess various aspects of the army. Its central maneuver, Maneuver 2, was designed to test "unit moves while fighting" and "the fighting methods of ground forces given enemy superiority in the air and armor."[30] The Southern Command, then under Dayan, played the enemy (the "greens"), fighting against the Central Command, led by Major General Tzvi Ayalon, playing the IDF (the "blues"). Taking ground, flanking, parachuting, and other fighting components were all drilled and tested in this exercise.

Narkiss was Dayan's operations officer, and the two formed a cohesive team. According to military staff doctrine, an operations officer serves as support for and an extension of the commander. Knowing the commander well, how they think, and their intentions, the operations officer is the commander's alter

---

[26] In Devizes, Dayan came into contact with experienced instructors who had planned and led large-scale operations, such as the invasion of German-occupied Normandy. Dayan learned the management of large systems and units, such as corps and divisions, knowledge then nonexistent in Israel.

[27] Report on Moshe Dayan at the end of the senior officers' course in Devizes, England, February 29, 1952. See Avner Falk, *Moshe Dayan, ha'ish veha'agada: Biografiya psikhologit* (Hebrew), Jerusalem: Cana Publishing House, 1985, p. 194.

[28] In addition to his criticism of Haganah courses, Dayan also found fault with his academic studies at the Hebrew University in Jerusalem, which he attended after leaving the military. In his memoirs, he likened his two years of university studies to a vacation, "and, like any vacation, they did not leave a very deep impression." Dayan, *Avnei derekh*, p. 377.

[29] Sheshar, *Sihot im Rehavam Zeevi*, p. 159.

[30] Mordechai Bar-On, *K'shehatsava hehelif madav: P'rakinm behitpat'hut tsahal bashanim harishinot le'ahar milhemet ha'atsmaut 1949–1953* (Hebrew), Jerusalem: Yad Ben Zvi, 2017, p. 97.

ego.³¹ Narkiss recounted that his room was next to Dayan's and that the two spent many hours together, discussing current issues while showering and shaving almost in the buff. They socialized with their families and developed a very close relationship.³²

In the first part of the Maneuver 2 exercise, the troop commanders, Dayan and Ayalon,³³ were to undertake a forty-eight-hour standard operating procedure, including intelligence gathering, troop preparation, and planning. In the previously structured exercise scenario, the "greens" would first invade Israeli soil and achieve partial successes. In the second stage, the "blues" would counterattack and oust the "greens" from their area. When Narkiss explained to Dayan the long, cumbersome standard operating procedures, Dayan ordered him to immediately shift to a shortened version and decided to run a combined planning and command group at the same time to facilitate a rapid transition to action. Major Uri Ben-Ari, then deputy commander of the 7th Brigade, on the "green" side, was eager to prove the armored corps' deep-penetration capabilities. Ben-Ari later recounted that Dayan "did not run the orders group according to the standard procedures formulated in the IDF's military school, but rather based on a different and unique rushed procedure, in this case applicable only to an armored force."³⁴ Dayan assigned the 7th Brigade the mission, which included breaking through the "blue" line and heading deep into "blue" territory – all the way to the "blue" command post in Ramla.

Ben-Ari was thrilled, but the rushed battle procedure and the mission he was given deviated from the exercise administration's instructions. The 7th Brigade surprised the "blue" force and conquered the command post as Dayan had instructed. Displeased with the 7th Brigade's Dayan-inspired stunt, the exercise administration ordered the brigade to remain in place for twenty-four hours to allow the "blue" force to regroup.³⁵

Dayan had essentially ordered a deep breach that completely ignored the enemy's pockets of resistance, bypassing them and aiming directly for the enemy's center of gravity: a small-scale blitzkrieg. The exercise administration rejected Dayan's approach, complaining he had not used the infantry, had moved across difficult terrain, and had not evacuated the settlements in his

---

[31] Spenser Wilkinson, *The Brain of an Army: A Popular Account of the German General Staff*, Westminster: Archibald Constable & Co., 1985, p. 142. Dayan was blessed with good operations officers who knew him well, complemented him, and, especially, compensated for his weaknesses.

[32] Narkiss, *Hayal shel yerushalayim*, pp. 141–142.

[33] In January 1948, Tzvi Ayalon, who had served in the Haganah, was appointed Deputy Chief of Staff until the end of the War of Independence.

[34] Uri Ben Ari, *No'a tanu'a! Sof: Hamaavak al derekh hashiryon* (Hebrew), Tel Aviv: Maarakhot, 1998, p. 128.

[35] Ibid., p. 177.

sector. "That doesn't take a genius," they told Dayan. Dayan's answer: "Actually, it does."[36] A fierce debate ensued between Dayan and the exercise administrators. Dayan rejected the claims against him outright, asserting that with nothing having been said to the contrary, he felt free to act as he had. In practice, the controversial move in the exercise was a preview of the move that the 7th Brigade would later make in the Sinai Campaign.

The most important result, however, was that Yadin came to realize the maneuvering capabilities of an armored brigade and the danger of an enemy possibly engaging in such a move. Ben-Ari felt that Dayan was correct in his unconventional approach to the exercise, and that the IDF benefited on two levels: it began recognizing its weakness in defense and learned about the potential of armor, which Ben-Ari would later prove in Sinai in 1956. In the meantime, the incident caused "a surge of real concern in the General Staff."[37]

Underlying Dayan's conduct in the maneuver was his fundamental rebellion against accepted rules and codes. For him, the exercise was not a fair sporting event governed by accepted rules, but a simulation of war, in which the sides exploit every situation and opportunity to achieve superiority. Dayan preferred shortening processes, commanding "from the saddle" while on the move, and creating the advantage of surprise, maneuvering faster than his enemy, as he demonstrated in real campaigns and operations he commanded in the future.

Dayan's approach to the exercise can be better clarified in terms of the distinction between finite and infinite games in game theory. Finite games, like group sports and chess, have clear rules, fixed players, and unchanging and clearly articulated goals. In contrast, in infinite games, the goal is not fixed but evolves constantly, as do the players and the rules. Though many view war as finite, with the sides fighting in a specified theater using similar methods until one side wins, war is actually infinite, with the goal, rules, and other components fluid, reflecting a chaotic political and military reality. This is how Dayan insisted on seeing the campaigns in which he participated.[38]

Northern Commander

In May 1952, Dayan was given command of the Northern Command after refusing Yadin's offer to become his deputy, feeling that his tendency to unequivocally express his own positions loud and clear made him ill suited to be anyone's deputy.[39] The head of the Northern Command Staff was Haim Bar-Lev, and its intelligence officer was Ariel Sharon. Sharon, then a young

---

[36] Teveth, *Moshe Dayan*, p. 357.
[37] Ibid.
[38] Simon Sinek, *The Infinite Games*, New York: Portfolio, 2019.
[39] Teveth, *Moshe Dayan*, p. 364.

command-level intelligence officer, was disappointed by the lack of action and was considering leaving the army to study. However, Sharon soon had an opportunity to prove to Dayan that he wasn't a run-of-the-mill officer at the end of 1952. Jordanian soldiers had abducted two Israeli soldiers during a routine patrol and would not release them. Israel was at a loss, but Dayan had an idea. He summoned Sharon and asked him if he could take some Jordanians hostage. Sharon rushed into action before Dayan had more time to think, immediately abducting two Jordanian soldiers on the al-Hasin Bridge border. Soon the Israeli POWs were exchanged for the Jordanian ones. Thus began a long-lasting Dayan–Sharon alliance, one marked by ups and downs, great appreciation along with great suspicion, and many joint achievements. For many years, Dayan was the army's master architect and Sharon the outstanding tactician who excelled at converting Dayan's ideas into successful ground actions. From commander of a small commando unit to corps commander, there was arguably no better military tactician than Arik Sharon. While leading the Northern Command, Dayan, who always considered the political angle, tried to advance negotiations with the Syrians on issues left unresolved by the Armistice Agreements, including Lake of Galilee fishing rights and the future of the demilitarized zones, both of which had led to violent clashes between the sides. He understood from his talks with Syrian officers that, at that stage, Syria had no intention of changing the status quo.[40]

Under Dayan, the Northern Command engaged in little operational activity. Nonetheless, Dayan frequently ran various exercises reflecting his way of thinking: a refusal to concede to routine and accepted conventions. He also routinely divided labor with his staff. Taking little interest in routine administration, he focused only on issues he deemed critical, what he called "strategic matters," his staff handling the rest, with each individual responsible for his specific area.

Chief of the General Staff Branch and Chief of Staff

As described on p. 90–92, the Chief of Staff is the supreme commander of the IDF, subordinate directly to the government and commanding all the services and operational forces.

Following sharp cuts to the IDF budget imposed by Ben-Gurion in 1952, Yadin resigned as Chief of Staff and was replaced by Mordechai Maklef on December 7. Dayan was appointed head of the General Staff Directorate and Acting Chief of Staff, refusing to accept the title "Deputy." A year later, on December 6, 1953, Dayan was officially appointed Chief of Staff. Years later, Dayan, too, would make no distinction between these two consecutive periods: "In terms of my memory, I don't draw a line between the time I headed the

---

[40] Dayan, *Avnei derekh*, p. 106.

General Staff Directorate and served as Chief of Staff."[41] Still, Neora Matalon, Dayan's secretary, described a change for the worse in Dayan's mood after being appointed Chief of Staff. The weight of the responsibility coupled with Ben-Gurion's absence after resigning from the government affected Dayan. Suddenly, he was subordinate to a defense minister (Pinchas Lavon) he didn't trust and a prime minister (Moshe Sharett) with whom he didn't agree.[42]

In these new positions, Dayan took over an army that was a mere shadow of the organization that had won the War of Independence. Most skilled commanders had already resigned, and the most talented young people preferred enlisting in administrative units and NAHAL, the IDF's paramilitary program combining military service and establishing agricultural settlements. The infantry, then the IDF's backbone, consisted of new immigrants undergoing the trials of moving to a new country and learning a new language. The army suffered from low-quality manpower with low potential, a lack of leadership, and low morale.[43] The challenge was immense. Maklef and then Dayan were charged with an enormous, two-pronged task: cutting back on the order of the battle and budgets while raising the IDF's fighting fitness for "the next round."[44] The IDF had multiple problems: limited resources, few and low-qualified enlistees, bloated command posts, and deteriorating fighting fitness and preparedness.[45] Dayan therefore had to address two major challenges in his work: fostering the IDF's fighting spirit, especially among the commanders, and changing the unbalanced structure of inflated commands at the expense of fighting units.[46]

Historian Yagil Henkin asked how the 1953 IDF, which had failed in half its routine security operations and lacked an armored command or a command and staff college; which could field only one battalion-sized armored task force deemed fit for service on short notice or for retaliation operations; whose own officers considered its armored forces "catastrophic"; and which was in deep crisis, lacking manpower, training, and equipment, could "transform itself in just three years and achieve a swift victory over the Egyptian army in 1956?"[47]

---

[41] Yaakov Erez and Ilan Kfir, *Sihot im Moshe Dayan* (Hebrew), Ramat Gan: Masada, 1981, p. 14.
[42] Author's interview with Neora Barnoach-Matalon, Herzliya, March 14, 2017.
[43] For more on the IDF's manpower crisis during the post-War of Independence period, see: Mordechai Bar-On, *When the Army Changed Its Uniform*, pp. 36–38. For more on the budget and cutbacks challenge, see ibid., pp. 275–276.
[44] Ze'ev Elron and Shaul Brunfeld, "The General Staff versus the Navy in a Gloomy Decade: 1953–1962" (Hebrew), *Yesodot*, The IDF History Department, Issue 1, 2019, pp. 195–255 (p. 168).
[45] Ibid., p. 170.
[46] Erez and Kfir, *Sihot im Moshe Dayan*, p. 15.
[47] Yagil Henkin, *The 1956 Suez War and the New World Order in the Middle East: Exodus in Reverse*, Lanham, MD: Lexington Books, 2015, p. 4.

Henkin's answer: it was the profound change both in spirit and in substance that Dayan created during his tenure as Chief of Staff that made the victory in the 1956 Sinai Campaign possible. Moreover, the change led to victory in the Six-Day War in 1967.

Many greeted Dayan's appointments with astonishment. Dayan's image was that of an undisciplined savage, and many saw his appointment to Chief of Staff as bordering on the irresponsible.[48] As head of the General Staff Directorate, he did not make Maklef's life easy, issuing contradictory instructions and never imposing discipline. He had never served as the chief of staff or as a deputy of a military commander, and, as usual, dealt only with topics that interested him, leaving matters of coordination and the details of staff work to his assistant, Meir Amit.

Of Dayan, Maklef related:

> He doesn't quarrel with others. He simply cuts them out ... Maj. Gen. Dayan cannot be tamed ... He possesses uncommon battle cunning ... He projects charismatic leadership to soldiers and people in general.[49]

While Dayan headed the General Staff Directorate, Israel faced two major challenges: fighting the ongoing threats of infiltrators and other ongoing security threats (immediate), and force building to prepare for another all-out war (fundamental). The first: Arabs crossing into Israel attacking Israeli villages and traffic, thereby transforming a strategic nuisance into a strategic threat. The second: building the IDF's capability to conduct a major war. Given the state of the army and Israel's economy, this complex challenge had both mental and material elements. The mental involved boosting fighting spirit, leadership, courage, and a belief in victory. The material entailed acquiring the weapons needed to conduct a modern war and developing a fighting doctrine responsive to the conditions the IDF was facing, including the unique terrains of the various theaters, and accounting for the IDF's and its enemies' strengths and weaknesses. Dayan's solution was to link the two challenges. Thus, reprisal operations had two goals: resolving the infiltration problem by setting a price tag for every Arab action against Israel while simultaneously training the army's units and commanders in all aspects of fighting – morale, leadership, and tactics.

The Reprisals and the Development of Israel's Security Concept

Israel's national security approach, developed over many years, has several elements, most set by Ben-Gurion. A few months before his first resignation from the government, Ben-Gurion presented an eighteen-point document

---

[48] Teveth, *Moshe Dayan*, p. 371.
[49] Ibid., p. 372.

emphasizing social, national, and moral resilience as essential national security elements and discussed national infrastructures and their capacity to raise resources.[50] Ben-Gurion's approach was expansive and far-sighted, yet practical and appropriate for the challenges of his time, befitting a visionary leader who took a broad view but was also practical and humane. Ben-Gurion considered an alliance with a strong international power critical for creating the diplomatic umbrella Israel needed so badly. Furthermore, from a very early stage, he pushed for developing a nuclear capability to ensure Israel's existence in the large, hostile expanse surrounding it. Ben-Gurion also identified an invasion by Arab armies and a rapid conquest of Israel as the most dangerous military threat of all. Since then, the national security doctrine has focused on that as the most fundamental threat. The response to that threat – *basic security* – was conceptualized over many decades in the cyclical triad of "deterrence"→ "early warning"→ "decision," the last defeating the imminent threat and recreating deterrence.

Dayan laid the groundwork for the second part of Israel's security concept – *routine security*. He developed a comprehensive approach designed to provide a response to the constant cross-border harassment raids by Arabs that, though deadly to the targeted individual Israelis living near the borders, were not as an immediate existential danger to the state as a full military invasion by Arab state armies.

From Dayan's perspective, routine security reprisals were also important for basic security.

> The War of Independence was, for the most part, a war fought on Israeli soil. The level of defense the IDF demonstrated was good, but this was not the case in offensives ... Then came the reprisals that kicked the level up. [The reprisals] led to two results: [The first was] the crystallization of the commander's role ... The other one was an articulation of standards for the army as a whole.[51]

Furthermore, "without two years of reprisal actions, the IDF would not have been capable of executing Operation Kadesh."[52] Even though they were small in scope and therefore limited in the sense of not reflecting many of the army's systems, the reprisal actions did test the IDF's fighting spirit and professionalism.

Dayan's clearest presentation of his routine security doctrine was given in a lecture to commanders. Its title, "Military Actions in Peacetime," was a typical Dayan oxymoron. In the lecture, he referred to "peacetime battles," explaining that the "tiny battles" mattered beyond routine security: They

[50] David Ben-Gurion, "Army and State" (Hebrew), *Maarakhot* 279–280 (June 1981).
[51] Moshe Dayan, "From One Stage to the Next" (Hebrew), *Maarakhot*, 118–119 (1959), pp. 52–54 (p. 52).
[52] Ibid., p. 53.

affected "the Arab assessment of Israel's strength and Israel's belief in its own power," thus strengthening deterrence.[53]

As Dayan explained, the rationale of the reprisals was complex, because military leadership in the region is complex. Noting the reluctance of the Jordanian and Egyptian regimes to stop Palestinian raids into Israel, Dayan argued that the reprisals provided Arab regimes with a reason to stop the raids lest Israel retaliate. "The motive forcing Arab governments and forces to [prevent raids] ... must be concrete, real, and certain: reprisals by the Israeli army and fear of them."[54] Rebutting criticism of the reprisals, Dayan noted that defensive measures were insufficient: "We did not have the means to safeguard every water pipe from being ruptured and every tree from being uprooted. We did not have the means to prevent the murders of farmers in their orchard and families in their beds. But we did have the power to set a steep price for our blood."[55]

Dayan also explained that the various diplomatic means that had been tried, including pressure on governments and appeals to the UN Security Council, had been useless.[56] Reprisals, Dayan insisted, were not acts of vengeance, but of punishment and deterrence. Dayan argued that even more important than their immediate effect – improving routine security – was that reprisals would force the Arabs to question whether the notion that Israel could be destroyed was even possible – improving basic security. Nonetheless, he said, it was necessary to remember that a test of war would require so much more: "Offensive missions our units will be charged with in wartime – to attack defended, fortified enemy strongpoints – will be much more serious, incomparable with these [reprisal] actions."[57] The ability to execute daring actions at a high level of performance must be instilled in the entire army, not just elite units, and "the battles in peacetime" were what would make it possible to nurture a fighting spirit and command training.[58]

On another occasion, Dayan clearly distinguished between routine and basic security, explaining that the army must confront two issues: "One is called 'routine security' and in practice it constitutes the maintenance of [everyday] life, the maintenance of what exists in a regime of the Armistice Agreements in the period between war and peace, or between one war and the next ... a period whose length no one knows but whose content is known." The other issue is "in a limited military area: ensuring victory if war breaks

---

[53] Moshe Dayan, "Military Actions in Peacetime: Moshe Dayan's Speech to Commanders" (Hebrew), *Maarakhot* 118–119 (1959), pp. 54–63 (p. 55).
[54] Ibid.
[55] Ibid., p. 56.
[56] Ibid.
[57] Ibid., p. 58.
[58] Ibid., p. 60.

out," relating to a threat scenario in which a regular state army invades the country.[59]

In the prestigious magazine *Foreign Affairs*, Dayan was able to present his political and security doctrine in the context of a public retort to British officer Lieutenant General Sir John Bagot Glubb's July 1, 1954, essay attacking Israel's policy and claiming that the Legion had never invaded Israeli soil. He accused Israel of conducting a violent campaign on Jordanian territory in response to innocent refugees crossing the Israeli border. Glubb further argued that the forces on the two sides were not symmetrical: On one side were innocent refugees crossing the border who should be referred to the police if they were causing damage, while on the other side were IDF forces intent on targeting Jordanian installations.[60]

Dayan's response to Glubb's analysis was published on January 1, 1955. Dayan explained the geostrategic challenge facing Israel, its international isolation, and Arab hostility to Israel's very existence. He detailed the real threat of terrorist and guerrilla attacks, followed by several suggestions for security arrangements on the Israel–Jordan border should Jordan agree to cooperate. Dayan detailed each Jordanian refusal individually, including Jordan's refusals to create long-term agreements from the Armistice Agreements and to conduct negotiations with Israel as required by Paragraph 8 of the Armistice Agreements, which could have paved a political path for reducing Middle East tensions. Dayan added that until tensions were indeed reduced, the IDF would confront essentially alone the difficult mission of safeguarding Israel's physical integrity. Jordan's refusal to cooperate was forcing Israel to use the military rather than the political alternative.[61]

Dayan also referred to peace and its centrality in Israel's security doctrine: "Peace is a condition for realizing Israel's mission and destiny," he declared.[62] However, it's unlikely that Dayan believed in the achievability of peace at this point. His outlook on peace can be found in the eulogy he gave at the funeral of Roi Rotberg, a twenty-one-year-old Nahal officer Dayan had visited in Nahal Oz just a few weeks before Rotberg's murder and mutilation by infiltrators on April 29, 1956. An enraged Dayan attended Rotberg's funeral and, according to Mordechai Bar-On,

---

[59] The Chief of Staff's address at a concluding event, Teachers' Camp, Negev, IDF Archive, file 1956-636-108, December 1954.

[60] John Bagot Glubb, (Glubb Pasha), "Violence on the Jordan–Israel Border: A Jordanian View," *Foreign Affairs* 32:4 (July 1954), pp. 552–562.

[61] Moshe Dayan, "Israel's Border and Security Problems," *Foreign Affairs* 33:2 (January 1955), pp. 250–267.

[62] Dayan, "Military Actions in Peacetime," p. 57.

shut himself up in a room for about half an hour and wrote a short, impassioned eulogy that would become a groundbreaking speech in the annals of Israel:[63]

> Early yesterday morning Roi was murdered. The quiet of the spring morning dazzled him and he did not see those waiting in ambush for him, at the edge of the furrow. Let us not cast the blame on the murderers today. Why should we declare their burning hatred for us? For eight years they have been sitting in the refugee camps in Gaza, and before their eyes we have been transforming the lands and the villages, where they and their fathers dwelt, into our estate.[64]

Dayan continued:

> It is not among the Arabs in Gaza, but in our own midst that we must seek Roi's blood. . . . Beyond the furrow of the border, a sea of hatred and desire for revenge is swelling, awaiting the day when serenity will dull our path, for the day when we will heed the ambassadors of malevolent hypocrisy who call upon us to lay down our arms. Roi's blood is crying out to us and only to us from his torn body . . . We will make our reckoning with ourselves today; we are a generation that settles the land but without the steel helmet and the cannon's muzzle, we will not be able to plant a tree and build a home. Let us not be deterred from seeing the loathing that is inflaming and filling the lives of the hundreds of thousands of Arabs who live around us. Let us not avert our eyes lest our arms weaken. This is the fate of our generation. This is our life's choice – to be prepared and armed, strong and determined, lest the sword be stricken from our fist and our lives cut down.[65]

The speech reflects Dayan's characteristic ambivalence: On the one hand, he could identify with the enemy's motives and even with their pain; on the other hand, he had an absolute belief in the necessity of an uncompromising armed conflict that would reinforce the imperative of settlement behind barricades with guns in hand, much like Ze'ev Jabotinsky's "iron wall" approach.[66] At this time, Dayan did not believe that a political process would be useful in calming the situation, and he harshly criticized the diplomatic effort in the eulogy.

Given the complexity of the message, two different political camps have exploited his words, with the Israeli left emphasizing the need to understand the other side, and the right warning that concessions would lead only to more

---

[63] Aluf Ben, "Militant and Post-Zionist" (Hebrew), *Haaretz*, May 12, 2011, www.haaretz.co.il/1.1173714.
[64] Benny Morris, *Milhemot hagvul shel yisrael 1949–1956: Hahistanenut ha'aravit, pe'ulot hag'mul vehas'fira le'ahor lemivtsa kadesh* (Hebrew), Tel Aviv: Am Oved, 1997, p. 396.
[65] Ibid.
[66] In the 1923 essay "Iron Wall," Zionist leader Ze'ev Jabotinsky argued that the Zionist endeavor would face stiff Arab resistance and could succeed only if the Jews had solid protection against Arab attacks, using the iron wall as a metaphor for such protection.

Arab aggression. In 2011, Aluf Ben, editor of the daily liberal-left *Haaretz*, wrote: "Today, Dayan would have been accused of being a post-Zionist, of identifying with terrorism, of violating the Nakba Law," but simultaneously, Ben argued, Dayan expresses Israeli belligerence in all its essence, quoting sociologist Baruch Kimmerling's view of the speech as "the most authentic expression of Israeli militarism."[67]

Israel carried out reprisals on its three major borders – with Egypt, Jordan, and Syria. Each border and nation had its own internal dynamics, but the three sectors were woven into a single system with interdependent components. After Ben-Gurion assumed the defense portfolio in 1955 in Moshe Sharett's government, Sharett's era of relative restraint ended, and audacious, aggressive reprisal actions resumed. Operation Gaza (February 28–March 1, 1955), launched in response to a Fedayeen raid that killed an Israeli, went awry, resulting in heavy losses to both sides.[68] It delivered a severe blow to Nasser, forcing him to bolster Egypt's presence in the Gaza Strip.[69] Some claim that this operation pushed Nasser into Soviet arms and led to the weapons deal signed between Egypt and Czechoslovakia.[70] Later studies showed that Nasser's decision to align with the USSR and receive military aid from the Eastern Bloc was made long before Operation Gaza.[71]

Shortly after the operation, the Egyptians once again began harassing Israel with live fire and land mines. The escalation became institutionalized when Egypt began organizing, training, and financing the Fedayeen guerrilla units, after which their raids became better organized and deadlier. In response, and after Dayan threatened to resign because the reprisal policy was not being implemented and Prime Minister Sharett was cancelling planned missions at the last minute, Israel raided Khan Yunis on August 31, 1955, killing more than seventy Egyptian soldiers and Fedayeen militia and injuring about sixty, and downing two Egyptian fighter jets the next day. Nasser suspended the Fedayeen raids but tightened the naval blockade on the Straits of Tiran and engaged in other hostile acts. The Egyptians had already placed artillery at Ras Nasrani to control the Straits

---

[67] Ben, "Militant and Post-Zionist"; Baruch Kimmerling, "Militarism in Israeli Society" (Hebrew), *Teoriya Vebikoret* 4 (Fall 1993), pp. 123–140.
[68] The Egyptians had thirty-seven dead and thirty-one wounded; Israel had eighteen dead and thirteen wounded.
[69] Morris, *Milhemot hagvul shel yisrael 1949–1956*, p. 382.
[70] See this claim in: Morris, *Milhemot hagvul shel yisrael 1949–1956*, p. 362.
[71] See Rami Ginat "Israel and Gaza Action and Egyptian–Czech Arms Deal: A Reassessment of Egypt's Policy on the Blocs" (Hebrew), in Michael M. Lasker and Ronen Yitzhak (eds.), *Etgarim bithoni'im umedini'im bemivhan hametsiut: Israel bein ha'olam ha'aravi vehazira habeinleumit* (Hebrew), Ramat Gan: Bar-Ilan University, 2013, pp. 313–341. This study demonstrates that Nasser decided to buy weapons from the Eastern Bloc before 1955, beginning in 1954. See, too, note 196 in Chapter 4.

in 1953, and in early 1955, they further restricted passage by closing the skies south of Israel to Israeli civilian air traffic.[72]

To prevent an Israeli response on its soil at an inconvenient time, Egypt ensured that the Fedayeen raids originated in Syria, Jordan, and Lebanon.[73] Sharett had managed to somewhat curb Ben-Gurion and Dayan's aggressive line. But when Ben-Gurion replaced Sharett as prime minister on November 2, 1955, he immediately restored an offensive policy against Egypt. That night, following a series of encroachments by Egyptian units into Israeli territory in the Nitsana region, including shooting at Israeli civilians and military there, in an attempt to move the armistice line, IDF paratroopers and the Golani and Nahal Brigades and reservist paratrooper companies launched Operation Volcano against Egypt, the largest IDF operation since 1948.

Weighing Moshe Sharett's moderate approach and Dayan and Ben-Gurion's more aggressive security approach, one can appreciate the many advantages Dayan and Ben-Gurion saw in reprisals. They viewed these actions as a proactive movement to shape reality, not just respond to it, especially given that Sharett's policy of restraint had failed to reduce the attacks or increase international support for Israel.[74] Above all, the atmosphere of that time must be understood. Israel – less than a decade after the Holocaust and the War of Independence – suffered from a profound sense of isolation. The country felt besieged in the face of frequent threats from Arab leaders and their propaganda machines, the blockade on Israeli shipping, the refusal of the international community and world powers to provide real aid, and the border incursions.

From September 1954 and for most of 1955, Jordanian authorities attempted to prevent raids across the Jordanian border, but during 1956 attacks from Jordan increased.[75] Israel at first adopted a policy of restraint, but after a series of killings of Israeli civilians, the government decided to respond, culminating with the Qalqilya action (Operation Samaria) on October 19, 1956. The goal of destroying a police fortification used by the Jordanian army was achieved, but not without a difficult fight against Jordanian Legion reinforcements, requiring IDF air-force (IAF) support and leaving eighteen Israeli paratroopers dead and sixty-eight wounded, along with eighty-eight Jordanian soldiers killed and fifteen wounded. The fact that Israeli plans had gone awry stunned Ben-Gurion and senior military commanders. At a debriefing session, Dayan harshly criticized Sharon, claiming Sharon's excessive zeal had needlessly endangered his men. Dayan also explained the

---

[72] Morris, *Milhemot hagvul shel yisrael 1949–1956*, p. 379.
[73] Ibid., p. 397.
[74] Ibid., p. 453.
[75] David Tal, *T'fisat habitahon hashotef shel yisrael: Mekoroteha vehitpathuta 1949–1956* (Hebrew), Be'er Sheva: Ben-Gurion University of the Negev, Ben-Gurion Heritage Institute, 1998, p. 222.

planning team's constraints and presented considerations that are familiar to any IDF officer to this day: avoiding collateral damage and civilian casualties[76] and preventing foreign (in 1956 – British) intervention.[77]

It should be noted that in contrast to the 1950s, when using the air force was considered escalatory and raised the risk of international intervention, today, using planes is more acceptable and, ironically, ground action now risks escalation and triggers an immediate international response.

Given the results, Dayan became firmly convinced that the era of reprisals was over. Meeting with journalists immediately after the action, Dayan questioned whether these actions were still necessary and what their purpose was.[78] Dayan spelled out the IDF's constraints: not seizing or holding any territory, avoiding harm to innocent bystanders, and not using certain weapons, such as planes.[79] A few days later, on October 17, Dayan answered his own questions at a conference with the operation commanders: "It seems we must completely change our operational formula."[80]

Speaking with Ben-Gurion, Dayan claimed that, "Were it possible to destroy entire villages; were it possible to deploy armored forces, artillery, and airplanes without limitation; were it possible to hold territory past dawn – things would be different."[81] However, the rationale of the reprisals was that they would be executed at a threshold lower than that of war – "actions of war during peacetime" as Dayan called them. He added that now that the enemy had developed an effective response and the risk of crossing the threshold had risen to unacceptable levels, the reprisals had lost their utility, and the strategy had run its course. For Dayan, the action in Qalqilya was what von Clausewitz had termed "the culminating point" of a particular strategy, that is, the point beyond which the cost begins to outweigh the benefit.[82]

Statements in various forums show his changed strategic assessment: The current situation "of neither war nor peace cannot go on," but "nothing absolute has been decided on as far as the future is concerned, it is clear to all of us that we have reached the end of the chapter of nighttime reprisal

---

[76] Morris, *Milhemot hagvul shel yisrael 1949–1956*, p. 426.
[77] Because of the defense treaty between Jordan and Great Britain, the Israeli concern was that using the IAF would lead to British intervention.
[78] Meeting between Chief of Staff Moshe Dayan and journalists after Qalqilya action, October 11, 1956, IDF Archive, 5/127/1973.
[79] Ibid.
[80] Document of debriefing of Operation Samaria, October 17, 1956, IDF Archive, 5/127/1973.
[81] Dayan, quoted by Bar-On in a conversation with Ben-Gurion. Mordechai Bar-On, *Sha'arey aza: Mediniyut habitahon vehahuts shel medinat yisrael 1955–1957* (Hebrew), Tel Aviv: Am Oved, 1992, p. 259.
[82] Carl von Clausewitz, *On War*, edited and translated by Michael Howard and Peter Paret, Princeton, NJ: Princeton University Press, 1984, p. 570.

actions."[83] "There will be an interregnum in which we will rethink our reprisal method."[84] Dayan considered the alternative to reprisals clear: Without any possibility of attaining peace, the only option was a preventive all-out war – a dramatic and risky step, but one that would immediately and profoundly change the strategic situation. He believed that such a war would result in calm borders and the lifting of restrictions on Israeli shipping in the Red Sea.[85]

The Qalqilya action, especially its tactics, faced strong criticism. Still, Dayan realized that the root of the problem was that the strategic conditions had changed:

> I do not disagree with the critical need of meticulous preparations and giving the soldiers a chance to rest beforehand. But . . . we must remember that a military action is not itself a goal [but] is undertaken to attain some political purpose; we, the army, must adapt to the conditions that the political setting dictates.[86]

The policy of reprisals is a source of disagreement for both ethical and utilitarian reasons. The debate over the reprisals – did they achieve their goal? – remains unresolved. Jonathan Shimshoni's systematic research into the reprisals concludes that the level of violence on the Jordanian border dropped because of increasingly effective action by the Jordanian Legion against the infiltrators in 1954 and 1955 and into 1956, itself the result of Israeli pressure.[87] His findings regarding the Egyptian front are less positive, showing only a short-term drop in violence following an action before it resumed again.[88] The escalation in violence and the failure of reprisals to stop Egyptian attacks were among the factors that led to the war in Sinai. In fact, at the time of the Qalqilya action, events were already moving toward war in Sinai.

The Reprisals as a Way to Raise Army Morale and Professionalism

The War of Independence over, Israel still lacked clearly defined or fenced borders. Palestinians therefore easily moved from outside Israel into the

---

[83] Dayan, *Avnei derekh*, pp. 250–251. Mordechai Bar-On, *Etgar vetigra: Haderekh lemivtsa Kadesh 1956* (Hebrew), Sde Boker Campus: Ben-Gurion Heritage Institute, 1991, pp. 232–233.
[84] Morris, *Milhemot hagvul shel yisrael 1949–1956*, p. 426. Quoted in the debriefing document of Operation Samaria, October 17, 1956, IDF Archive, 776/58/8.
[85] Teveth, *Moshe Dayan*, p. 440.
[86] Moshe Dayan, *Yoman ma'arkhet Sinai* (Hebrew), Tel Aviv: Am Hasefer, 1965, p. 43.
[87] Jonathan Shimshoni, *Israel and Conventional Deterrence: Border Warfare from 1953 to 1970*, Ithaca, NY: Cornell University Press, 1988, pp. 68–67. Brigadier General Yoni Shimshoni was Director of the Strategic Planning Division of the IDF.
[88] Ibid., p. 118.

country for a variety of reasons: some innocent, such going home; some criminal, such as theft and robbery; some nationalistic, seeking to harm Jews; and some combining the latter two. In addition to spontaneous infiltrations by individuals and small groups, a new phenomenon emerged: organized infiltration by armed groups to kill Israelis, destroy property, and gather intelligence.[89]

Under the guise of unorganized, nonviolent infiltration, Fedayeen units, supported mainly by Jordan and Egypt, began operating with the explicit aim of executing attacks on Israeli soil.[90] By 1956, some 300 civilians and 250 soldiers had been killed in these raids,[91] with considerable direct and indirect economic damage. The second major victim was the public sense of security, and people began abandoning settlements near the border.[92] These raids were the major security challenge in those years, becoming the focus of the Israeli security establishment's activity.[93]

Reprisals were not the only action taken by Israel. Other efforts included diplomatic talks, policing, and regional security.[94] But none stopped the phenomenon, which escalated. The idea of reprisals has existed since the start of documented military history. The ancient Romans engaged in reprisals against Germanic tribes raiding imperial soil, as did the British in response to raids by tribes on its empire's territory on what is now the Indian–Pakistani border.[95] Reprisals were part of the ethnocommunal nature of the Arab–Jewish conflict. Examples of reprisals in the history of the Yishuv include actions by Wingate during the Arab Revolt, which impressed Dayan, who had accompanied Wingate. The Haganah also engaged in reprisals, carrying out fourteen as early as December 1948.[96] When the war was regularized and fought against invading state armies, reprisals lost relevance, but after the war, the conflict resumed an

---

[89] Shimon Golan, *Gvul ham, milhama kara: Hitgabshut mediniyut habitahon shel yisrael 1949–1953* (Hebrew), Tel Aviv: Maarakhot, 2000, pp. 248–249; Zaki Shalom, *Mediniyut betsel mahloket: Mediniyut habitaho hashotef shel yisrael 1949–1956* (Hebrew), Tel Aviv: Maarakhot, 1996, pp. 11–14.

[90] For more on the infiltration problem, see Tal, *T'fisat habitahon hashotef shel yisrael*, pp. 23–41; and Morris, *Milhemot hagvul shel yisrael 1949–1956*, pp. 44–83.

[91] Zeev Drory, *Israel's Reprisal Policy, 1953–1956*, Abingdon: Routledge, 2004, p. 79.

[92] For details on the cost of infiltration, see: Morris, *Milhemot hagvul shel yisrael 1949–1956*, pp. 113–128.

[93] Drory, *Israel's Reprisal Policy*, p. 181.

[94] Tal, *T'fisat habitahon hashotef shel yisrael*, p. 26.

[95] For a historical survey, see Efraim Inbar and Eitan Shamir, "What after Counter-Insurgency? Raiding in Zones of Turmoil," *International Affairs* 92:6 (November 1, 2016), pp. 1427–1441; see also Jakub Grygiel, *Return of the Barbarians: Confronting Non-State Actors from Ancient Rome to the Present*, Cambridge: Cambridge University Press, 2019, pp. 65–72.

[96] Tal, *T'fisat habitahon hashotef shel yisrael*, p. 40.

ethnonational character marked by guerrilla warfare, terrorism, and vandalism. Consequently, the reprisals returned.[97]

Dayan already adopted the reprisal method in 1951. Responding to the arson of a granary in the Yatir region by infiltrators from the Hebron Hills, Dayan ordered the burning of two large granaries in the southern Hebron Hills. Teveth identified this as the first eye-for-an-eye operation, the foundation for the reprisal policy Dayan adopted as Chief of Staff.[98] Dayan conceded that, "Reprisals are the only method that has proven itself to be effective. Not justified, not moral. But effective." He felt that without reprisals, "The situation would have been many times worse and resulted in utter chaos."[99]

Dayan noted that low-quality soldiers were assigned to the infantry units bearing most of the burden of the reprisals and the defensive fighting on the border.[100] Indeed, the IDF's execution of these actions was abysmal, as seen in the battle at al-Mutila Hill in May 1951. Following a skirmish between an Israeli border patrol and Syrian cattle-herders crossing the border into Israel, a mixed force of Syrian army and villagers captured the hill inside Israel. Israel Defense Forces infantry spent five days trying to oust them – suffering forty-one killed and more than seventy wounded in a series of failed attacks. Success was finally achieved only after an Israeli aircraft strafed the exposed Syrians, compelling them to retreat.[101] In another incident, a force from the Givati Brigade failed in its attack on the village of Falama, a base for raids into Israel. After a furious Dayan sent the battalion to reattack the village, the force did a little better, but a lack of resolve and failure to complete the mission were still evident.[102]

Summarizing the period, historian Zeev Drory wrote: "Anyone who reads the reports of operations carried out in 1953 and early 1954 cannot fail to note the number of actions that that were not executed or failed in the initial stages

---

[97] In 1949, Ben-Gurion was already considering the possibility of reprisals, and since 1950, reprisals had been carried out with increasing frequency; see: Tal, *T'fisat habitahon hashotef shel yisrael*, p. 39; Morris, *Milhemot hagvul shel yisrael 1949–1956*, p. 210. Data on the exact number of reprisals is inconsistent, but at least one source notes that from 1950 to 1956 reprisals were carried out on Israel's borders with Egypt and with Jordan. In 1953 and 1954, most occurred on the Jordanian front, whereas in 1955, most were on the Egyptian front; see in Mordechai Bar-On (ed.), *Lenochach gvulot oyevim: tzava ubitachon ba'asor harishon shel medinat Yisrael* (Hebrew), Israel: Efy Meltzer, 2017.

[98] Teveth, *Moshe Dayan*, p. 348.

[99] For quotations from Dayan justifying the reprisals: Morris, *Milhemot hagvul shel yisrael 1949–1956*, pp. 204–205.

[100] See detailed data: Turgan, *Mimeni ishit lo yetseh general*, pp. 91–93. For example, 85 percent of men enlisted in Golani were new immigrants. Their rate in other infantry brigades was similar; ibid., p. 92.

[101] Zeev Drory, "Army and Society in 1950s Israel" (Hebrew), *Iyunim bit'kumat yisrael* 16 (2006), pp. 243–274 (pp. 262–264).

[102] Ibid., p. 264.

of attack or failed to attain any of the military goals dictated by the commanding echelon."[103] As head of the General Staff Directorate, Dayan presented data on the IDF failures: "Not only did the majority of the ambushes and pursuit of raiders fail. Only 13 of the 42 offensive missions conducted by the IDF succeeded."[104] Dayan was determined to effect a radical change in the situation and reform the IDF. First, he decided to improve the relationship between the "tail" – that is, support and logistical services – and the "teeth" – the fighting units. Dayan deemed improving the forces' fighting fitness urgent:

> I am absolutely determined to put an end of the shameful results of the battles between our units and the Arabs and the indifference of the IDF command, whose every rank accepts the disgraceful failures and lame excuses that "we just couldn't."
> The organizational changes are important, but ... the moment of truth is still war against the Arab armies. But how will we best the regular Arab armies if our soldiers retreat when facing the farmers in the National Guard?[105]

Dayan linked the reprisal policy with building the IDF's fitness for war. He saw reprisals not only as a deterrent but also a means for preparing the army and strengthening it for the fundamental test of security – a comprehensive war against the Arab armies. What bothered Dayan most was the phenomenon of commanders sitting together in command posts and conducting the battle through their communications devices, behavior he had harshly criticized in the War of Independence. He had three goals: improving the soldiers' willingness to sacrifice themselves; changing the function and location of the commanders; and changing the General Staff's fundamental approach to the issue of executing the mission.[106]

For Dayan, reprisals were equally important for proving the Israeli soldier to himself and to the enemy: "The clashes on the borders will determine how the Arab public and army view the image and force of the Israeli soldier."[107] Dayan's objective, then, was to reform the IDF's fighting spirit. He announced he would accept the explanation of a failed mission only if the unit commander had lost at least half of his forces during a skirmish.[108] Dayan also demanded, counterintuitively, that commanders stop looking for ruses and indirect approaches, because sometimes: "the way to complete an assignment is to

---

[103] Drory, "Army and Society," p. 265. Dayan noted the failed action in *Avnei derekh*, pp. 111–112.
[104] Tom Segev, *Medina bekhol mehir: Sipur hayav shel David Ben-Gurion* (Hebrew), Ben Shemen: Keter, 2018, p. 486.
[105] Dayan, *Avnei derekh*, p. 113.
[106] Ibid.
[107] Morris, *Milhemot hagvul shel yisrael 1949-1956*, p. 205.
[108] Dayan, *Avnei derekh*, p. 113.

Strafe break through, to breach, to conduct a real fight over the objective while paying with the coin of loss."[109]

However, no top-down orders or threats issued against commanders suffice to make them perform.[110] To achieve a cultural revolution in the ethos of fighting and self-sacrifice, it is necessary to create a leadership model that inspires and motivates people to action, a model people will strive to emulate.[111]

The Merger That Generated a Revolution

The solution to the profound crisis in the IDF's fighting spirit and command spontaneously emerged in the first half of 1953 from the bottom up, when Moshe Dayan was still head of the General Staff Directorate. There were many Palestinian raids in the sector of the reservist Jerusalem Brigade commanded by Colonel Mishael Shaham, who decided on a daring action to blow up the house of Samueli, the Arab leader responsible. Realizing no reservist or even regular army unit was capable of executing such a mission, Shaham suggested organizing a small, elite unit of outstanding volunteers capable of success in this task. Ariel Sharon, previously Dayan's daring Southern Command intelligence officer, and now a student at the Hebrew University and a reserve battalion commander in the Jerusalem Brigade, seemed to Shaham the ideal choice to command this dedicated unit. Sharon accepted Shaham's offer and then recruited seven friends. Disguised as civilians, they went to blow up Samueli's house. The unit accidentally dynamited a nearby building, and that, too, with only partial success and was forced to retreat under fire.

Nonetheless convinced they had hit on a solution, Shaham and Sharon came to see Chief of Staff Maklef and persuaded him to establish a special unit to carry out actions across the border. The unit, they said, would be able to carry out the government's reprisal policy, thereby allowing the rest of the army to devote its time to training for war against the Arab armies. Dayan opposed the idea, convinced that reprisals offered preparation for war for all IDF units, and it was wrong to exclude the regular military units.[112] He argued that it would only cause greater deterioration, leaving the army with no operational activity at all. Interestingly, Dayan's approach was similar to that of the US Marine Corps. For many years, the Marines opposed establishing special Marine units, viewing all the Marines as special and realizing that such forces channel the best soldiers and commanders to small units with a relatively small impact on war but a possible critical impact on regular units who lose the best. Given the

---

[109] Teveth, *Moshe Dayan*, p. 387.
[110] Dayan, *Avnei derekh*, p. 113.
[111] Teveth, *Moshe Dayan*, p. 388.
[112] Ibid., p. 22.

IDF's manpower crisis, Dayan's opposition to establishing a special unit was entirely understandable. Nonetheless, Maklef ordered the unit's establishment.[113] Dayan was soon on excellent terms with Unit 101 members Ariel Sharon and Meir Har-Zion, who personified the very traits Dayan wanted to instill in IDF commanders and soldiers.

The unit existed for less than six months before merging with the paratrooper brigade in January 1954.[114] It comprised just a few dozen fighters, lacking standard uniforms and standard weapons, and recruitment was based on the "bring a friend" system. The men engaged in chaotic guerrilla warfare, executing small, fairly insignificant raids. Still, they demonstrated extraordinary courage and resourcefulness. Word of the group spread far and wide, and Unit 101 became a legend that fired the imagination of every member of the IDF.

One Unit 101 innovation involved commanders leading from the front, both during an attack itself and en route to the objective. Before the state's establishment, trained unit trackers had exclusive expertise in navigation. Commanders saw no need to navigate themselves, instead following the trackers. In battle, battalion commanders and, sometimes, even company commanders, stayed hundreds of meters, sometimes a few kilometers, behind the forward forces, making it difficult for them to understand how the battle was going and forcing them to rely on reports from the front line. Given the limited means of communication available then, commanders clearly had trouble properly assessing the state of the battle and issuing appropriate orders.

Inspired by Unit 101, it became abundantly clear just how important it was that commanders of all ranks be able to navigate. This ability helped establish the norm that the commander's place was in the front, heading the force. In his quiet way, Unit 101's Meir Har-Zion had provided a personal example of the new style commander.[115] In that sense, the unit did have an impact on the army, an important goal for Dayan. On the other hand, its men thought they were above the law, as when the unit seized control of an IDF military police station in Tiberias and beat up the military policemen who had arrested a unit member in December 1953.[116] Sharon and Dayan swept this gross disciplinary

---

[113] "Order to Establish Unit 101," July 30, 1953, Procedure on Unit Deployment, IDF Archive 38/433/1956.
[114] "Order to Dismantle Unit 101," January 29, 1954, IDF Archive, 156/25/1955.
[115] Uzi Eilam, "Meir Har-Zion's Unique Contribution" (Hebrew), *Haaretz*, March 16, 2014.
[116] Uzi Eilam wrote that Sharon, apparently with Dayan's approval, ordered a reprisal against the MPs, which was led by Shlomo Baum. The action was carried out as a military operation in every way. See Uzi Eilam, *P'shita leylit: Pe'ulot hatagmul – mehagana le'yozma* (Hebrew), Rishon Lezion: Yedioth Ahronoth and Hemed Books, 2020, p. 82.

violation under the carpet, and the attackers were never charged.[117] But it was clear that the existence of so unruly a group within the IDF could not continue – it was merged into a regular army unit, the paratrooper battalion.

The change in Dayan's stance on the unit – from initial opposition to enthusiastic support, was related to an unintentional shift in its original designation. After merging with the paratrooper battalion, it ceased being a special operations unit and became an agent of change.[118] Its men turned into the spearhead of the paratroopers' transformation and ultimately the transformation of the IDF as a whole. At the time, the paratroopers were a cohesive group with a good reputation. But when carrying out operational missions, they didn't demonstrate any more courage or professionalism than any other unit.[119]

The shift in Unit 101's raison d'être began in mid October 1953, when the IDF conducted a reprisal that militarily was a success that proved the validity of the concept but politically and ethically was a disaster that compelled a major change in Israel's strategy against the Fedayeen attacks. A series of deadly attacks were conducted in central Israel by Fedayeen from Jordan. Finally, following the death of an Israeli mother and two children and the severe wounding of a third child, the government decided to retaliate by capturing the village of Qibya, evacuating the population, and exploding the houses. Some 130 soldiers – one-third of them Unit 101 members, the rest paratroopers – participated. A Jordanian army strongpoint and the village were captured successfully, with only one Israeli soldier being wounded. The population was ordered with megaphones to leave their homes, and most did; however, approximately seventy stayed hidden and were killed when the houses were exploded.

The political ramifications were disastrous – both inside Israel and abroad, the results generated angry criticism. Whatever the justification for retaliatory action per se, the killing of so many civilians was not an act Israelis could accept, nor would it be accepted internationally, even if it was unintentional. Dayan realized that Israel's strategy had to change. A pure defensive against the Palestinian raids had failed, and reprisals were still the only effective way to deter future attacks (following the Qibya reprisal, there was a sharp decrease in the number of attacks from Jordan that lasted months), but the targets of the reprisals had to be changed to ones more morally acceptable – military and governmental installations of the countries hosting the attackers of Israel. This

---

[117] Nir Hefetz and Gadi Blum, *Haro'eh: Sipur hayav shel Ariel Sharon* (Hebrew), Tel Aviv: Yedioth Books, 2005, pp. 102–103.

[118] According to the theory of organizational change, an agent of change is a member of an organization that leads and steers the change in it. See https://businessjargons.com/change-agent.html.

[119] Arik Sharon, *Warrior: An Autobiography*, Simon & Schuster Paperbacks, New York, 1989, p. 92.

entailed greater military risk – more Israeli casualties and the direct involvement of the Arab governments who might respond by escalating their support for the Palestinian raiders or escalating their own military actions against Israel – but would also require improving the professionalism of the Israeli forces. As concluded by the military strategist Edward Luttwak, strategy is the realm of "contradictions, irony, and paradox."[120]

Dayan became Chief of Staff six weeks after the Qibya raid. Two weeks later, Dayan decided to merge Unit 101 with the 890th Paratrooper battalion.[121] Whether the idea originated with Dayan[122] or someone in his circle,[123] Dayan had a profound grasp of the revolutionary advantages of the merger and did all he could to ensure its success. This merger was innovative, even groundbreaking. It was neither a top-to-bottom change from the top of the hierarchy aimed at the lower ranks, nor a bottom-to-top initiative from the ground and adopted by the command echelon, as military innovation is generally described in the literature.[124] Instead, the innovation was lateral, merging units so that one with a successful culture could transmit its values and codes of conduct to another – until this culture was instilled in all the units. Historian Mordechai Bar-On, then head of Dayan's bureau (1956–1957), wrote that the great process of change in the IDF would never have happened if the 101 had remained on its own.[125]

Dayan appointed Sharon to command the merged force. Yehuda Harari, who had commanded the paratroopers until then and had hoped to continue to hold that position, was so unceremoniously dumped by Dayan that even Sharon expressed regret about it in his autobiography.[126] This was not the last time Dayan would act heartlessly toward people he didn't respect. With Sharon, this was simply another point in a long and complicated relationship: "[The relationship] was complex and characterized by mutual appreciation

---

[120] Edward N. Luttwak, *Strategy: The Logic of War and Peace*, Cambridge, MA: Harvard University Press, 2001, p. 18.

[121] General Staff meeting, December 20, 1957, IDF Archive, in Turgan, *Mimeni ishit lo yetseh general*, p. 47.

[122] Teveth, *Moshe Dayan*, p. 397. Teveth wrote: "It came to him to inspire a single entity with the spirit of Unit 101 consequent to the action in Qibya in which two units operated together under Sharon's command. Despite the political fallout, for Dayan this was a successful military operation."

[123] Meir Amit, *Rosh berosh: Mabat ishi al eru'im gedolim ufarshiyot ne'elamot* (Hebrew), Or Yehuda: Maariv-Hed Arzi Publications, 1999, p. 39.

[124] Adam Grissom, "The Future of Military Innovation Studies," *Journal of Strategic Studies* 29:5 (2006), pp. 905–934.

[125] Bar-On (ed.), *Lenochach gvulot oyevim: tzava ubitachon ba'asor harishon shel medinat Yisrael*, p. 125.

[126] Ariel Sharon, *Warrior: An Autobiography*, New York: Simon & Schuster Paperbacks, 1989, p. 74.

and respect, but it was also charged with suspicions."[127] At times, there was real warmth and closeness, but also "alienation, sometimes simultaneously."[128] Even if tensions sometimes ran high, they both understood they needed one another's gifts: Dayan needed Sharon, a brilliant field commander and tactician, to put daring strategic plans into practice, while Sharon needed an unusual strategist like Dayan to focus his raging force during many difficult missions, limit it when necessary, and shield it from criticism whenever it crossed red lines.

In both units, there were men who opposed the merger. There was certainly a disparity between the unruly, disorganized Unit 101 and the relatively disciplined paratrooper unit. Aware of this, Dayan tried as much as possible to reduce any possible fallout, including a personnel exodus. Announcing the merger at a party for Unit 101, Dayan heaped lavish praise on its men and then dropped the bomb: The unit was to be merged with the paratrooper brigade, creating a single entity. He explained that the unit should raise the level of the entire army: "The unit has sketched out new ways of fighting. It is now time to share these ways with the whole IDF."[129] For two full years, until December 1955, Dayan accompanied the new merged unit on their missions, waited for them to return, went to see them in training, and celebrated their successes with them.[130] Ultimately, the paratroopers became an elite unit swathed in a glow of legendary heroism. Following Dayan's 1954 US visit with the Army Rangers, he decided that all IDF officers would have to jump from an airplane as a test of courage and a symbol of their status. Of course, Dayan himself took the course, and Sharon, too, wore the paratrooper wings emblem.

In Sharon, Dayan had finally found an aggressive, proactive commander. Sharon later related that he would call Dayan after Arab attacks to suggest plans and ideas he had already prepared and drilled.[131] Between 1953 and 1956, the paratroopers carried out some seventy reprisals, almost all of which were missions the paratroopers initiated and proposed.[132] Dayan was responsible for the open atmosphere in which field ranks were encouraged to make suggestions, an atmosphere that persists in the IDF to this day. For example, in 2002, at the height of the Second Intifada, infantry commanders – whether from paratroopers, Nahal, Givati, or Golani brigades – were the ones who pushed for the chasing of terrorists into West Bank cities in face of their hesitant senior superiors who feared mass casualties in the dense urban terrain.[133]

---

[127] Ibid., p. 74.
[128] Ibid., p. 112.
[129] Uri Even, *Arik: Darko shel lohem* (Hebrew), Tel Aviv: Bustan, 1974, p. 85.
[130] Sharon, *Warrior*, p. 111.
[131] Ibid., p. 98.
[132] Drory, *Israel's Reprisal Policy*, p. 198.
[133] Amos Harel and Avi Issacharoff, *Hamilhama hashvi'it: Eikh nitsahnu velama hifsadnu bamilhama im hafalestinim* (Hebrew), Tel Aviv: Yedioth Books, Tel Aviv, 2014.

Figure 3.1 Chief of Staff Moshe Dayan with Major Ariel Sharon (standing left of Dayan), Major General Assaf Simhoni (standing last on Dayan's left), and paratroopers' officers, 1955. Source: Universal History Archive/Contributor/Universal Images Group/Getty Images.

Dayan wrote:

> Instead of having units coming back and, as in the past, making excuses for why they didn't do what they had been tasked with, the paratroopers had to explain, after every action, why they had done more than what was expected. The veins and arteries of the IDF were coursing with self-confidence. The paratroopers were the spearhead, and other units followed in their footsteps.[134]

With the merger between Unit 101 and the 89th Battalion, Dayan finally got what he would some years later call his "Noble Stallions" (Figure 3.1).

The Reprisals: Escalation or Deterrence?

Beginning in the late 1980s, it became fashionable to claim that from a certain point the reprisal operations were no longer to deter Arab attacks but rather to deliberately escalate the situation so that Israel would have a pretext to initiate an all-out war. Typical is Benny Morris's assertion that:

---

[134] Dayan, *Avnei derekh*, p. 115.

Dayan wanted war. Time after time, he hoped that a reprisal raid would embarrass the Arab nation attacked or challenge it sufficiently to engage in a reprisal of its own, which would then provide Israel with a pretext to cause the exchanges of fire to deteriorate into a war in which Israel would be able to realize strategic goals of the highest importance, such as the conquest of the West Bank or Sinai, or the destruction of the Egyptian army.[135]

A debate among supporters of this thesis developed over the timing of the change: during 1954, during 1955, or only toward the end of 1955.

From the day Nasser became the de facto ruler of Egypt in early 1954, Ben-Gurion repeatedly asserted that he was Israel's most dangerous enemy, given that Nasser had the will and charisma to unite the Arab states in a combined war against Israel, was openly declaring the intention to do exactly that, and was actively operating to achieve it. Allegedly, according to the abovementioned historians, the increased aggressiveness of Israel's reprisal operations against Egypt from February 28, 1955, was not a response to Palestinian raids from Gaza supported by the Egyptians, but an attempt to provoke Egypt to war in order to humiliate Nasser. However, comparing the incidence of attacks from Egyptian territory into Israel and the number of Israeli reprisals does not support this claim – through 1955, there were 450 to 500 attacks from Egyptian territory into Israel, to which Israel responded with 6 reprisals; from January to October 1956, there were more than 300 attacks from Egyptian territory into Israel, to which Israel responded with 4 reprisals. Clearly, Israel did not need an ulterior motive for its continued reprisal policy.

A secondary assertion is that the February 28, 1955, Israeli raid into Gaza was so embarrassing for Nasser that it pushed him into the Soviet camp to acquire the large amounts and quality of armaments denied him by the West, and that this too would lead to Israel's looking for a pretext for war with Egypt in order to preempt the expected change in the balance of forces. However, Middle East expert Rami Ginat has clearly demonstrated that the weapons agreement was signed before the reprisal.[136] Nasser's public statement that the reprisal was the cause was untrue.

[135] Morris, *Milhemot hagvul shel yisrael 1949–1956* (Hebrew), p. 205. Other authors with a similar message include Yair Evron, *Hadilemma hagarinit shel yisrael* (Hebrew), Ramat Efal: Yad Tabenkin, 1987, p. 48; Moti Golani (ed.), *Hets shahor: Peulat aza umediniyut hagmul shel yisrael bishnot ha-50* (Hebrew), Tel Aviv: Maarakhot, 1994, p. 25; Moti Golani, *Tihyeh milhama bakayits: Haderekh lemilhemet Sinai 1955–1956* (Hebrew), Tel Aviv: Maarakhot, 1997, pp. 41–44, 87–90, 587; David Tal, "Israel's Road to the 1956 War," *International Journal of Middle East Studies* 28:1 (February 1996), pp. 59–81 (p. 75); Zeev Maoz, *Defending the Holy Land: A Critical Analysis of Israel's Security and Foreign Policy*, Ann Arbor: University of Michigan Press, 2008, pp. 57–58.

[136] See Rami Ginat, "Israel and Gaza Action and Egyptian–Czech Arms Deal: A Reassessment of Egypt's Policy on the Blocs" (Hebrew), in Michael M. Lasker and Ronen Yitzhak (eds.), *Etgarim bithoni'im umedini'im bemivhan hametsiut: Israel bein ha'olam ha'aravi vehazira habeinleumit* (Hebrew), Ramat Gan: Bar-Ilan University, 2013, 313–341. This study

Furthermore, historian Ze'ev Elron responded to these claims with a study based on primary documents from the IDF archive.[137] He found no evidence of preparations for an impending war, certainly not one initiated by Israel, before September–October 1955, the period at which the Czech arms deal began arriving in Egypt and Syria, more than doubling their heavy weapons arsenal and improving it qualitatively, thus dramatically changing in their favor the ratio of forces between them and the IDF. Furthermore, he found that the IDF did not see itself capable of conducting the required offensive operations should a war break out. Conducting these would require a dramatic change in the IDF's force composition – from an infantry-based army with some tanks and aircraft support, to an army based on a strike force composed of armored brigades, a more powerful air force, and paratroops. This understanding had been elucidated already by Ben-Gurion in his eighteen-point national security plan presented to the government in September 1953.[138] Given the poor performance of the existing infantry units in small-scale actions described on p. 121, and the long-term effort, still in progress, to improve that performance, initiating a war was in any case not a viable option even if the IDF decided to change its doctrine to an infantry-based offensive. In fact, until summer 1956, Israel had no source to provide the aircraft and tanks required by its offensive doctrine or the contingency plans it had prepared.

Throughout 1954 and 1955, the IDF was, Elron writes, in a state of "long-term force development at the expense of immediate readiness." In January 1954, a month after his appointment to Chief of Staff, Dayan told the assembled General Staff:

> I think ... *there will be no war for the next two years*. On the other hand, [eventually] there will be a war with the Arabs. I think that the last two months are a better indication of this than the three years since the [War of Independence].[139]

At the time Dayan was supposedly working to provoke a war, writes Elron, he was actually overseeing a reduction in IDF capabilities to conduct that war:

demonstrates that Nasser had already turned to the Soviets to buy weapons in 1954. See, too, note 196 in Chapter 4. Further evidence is provided by Navon, then serving in Military Intelligence: Yitzhak Navon, *Kol haderekh: Otobiografiya* (Hebrew), Jerusalem: Keter Books, 2015, p. 172. Navon recalls intelligence about Egyptian arms negotiations with the Soviets already in 1953.

[137] Ze'ev Elron, "Hatmurot betsahal vehashinuy shelo haya bitfisat habitahon, December 1952 to September 1955" (Hebrew), PhD diss., Hebrew University, Jerusalem, 2009.

[138] See summary of document in Dayan, *Avnei derekh*, p. 138; also Yitzhak Ben-Israel, *Tfisat habitahon shel yisrael* (Hebrew), Ben Shemen: Broadcast University, Ministry of Defense, Laor and Modan Publications, 2013, pp. 13–68.

[139] Dayan's address at the General Staff meeting of January 14, 1954, cited by Elron, "Hatmurot betsahal vehashinuy shelo haya bitfisat habitahon," p. 137. Emphasis added.

Because of this way of thinking [long-term preparations at the expense of readiness for immediate war], it was possible to reduce the regular army personnel, abandon buying older weaponry, and devote all efforts to building the army reserves and equipping them with advanced weapons systems. [Moreover,] in late 1954 and early 1955, Dayan went further.... regular army units were thinned out or disbanded, the Southern Command [facing Egypt] was abolished, and soldiers in their last six months of service were sent to receive agricultural training. In addition, training was limited and various opportunities to acquire weapons, ammunition, and other critical supplies were postponed.[140]

Elron concludes that "the reprisals and aggressive declarations by security establishment leaders were meant to strengthen Israeli deterrence and obscure the [IDF's] low state of readiness. Dayan and [Defense Minister] Lavon were barking because they knew the IDF was incapable of biting."[141]

From late summer 1955, the strategic situation began to change ominously. In response to Egyptian-instigated Palestinian Fedayeen raids in August, the IDF conducted two reprisals in Egypt, the first since February. Simultaneously, the Southern Command was reinstituted. In early September, the Egyptians advanced a division, including an armored brigade, into Sinai. The strengthened Egyptian forces in the peninsula and their deployment placement in the front line led to a critical change in Israel's strategic position, as the time needed for an early warning was now substantially reduced from what it had been since 1952 and 1953 when the Egyptians withdrew most of their forces from Sinai. Furthermore, in early September 1955 Egypt closed the Tiran Straits to all shipping to or from the Israeli port of Eilat, this in addition to the previous continuous denial of passage through the Suez Canal. Israel declared it would use all means available to open the straits (a contingency military plan had already been prepared) but in fact focused solely on diplomatic activity at the UN and envoys to the Western powers. The response was muted. Meanwhile, Britain and the United States initiated the Alpha Program for peace in the Middle East. Though the program's development began in 1954, it was publicized in August 1955. The essence of the program was a series of significant territorial concessions by Israel and acceptance of numerous Palestinians into its territory in return for peace with the Arab states. In total, Western criticism of Israel's policy with only limited criticism of Arab aggressiveness to Israel and the demand that Israel make significant concessions did not bode well for their caring for Israel's security. In late September began the arrival of the weapons from Czechoslovakia to Egypt and Syria. Following this development, Dayan did repeatedly discuss a preemptive war with Ben-Gurion before the weapons would be absorbed by the Egyptians and Syrians, but

---

[140] Elron, "Hatmurot betsahal vehashinuy shelo haya bitfisat habitahon," p. 389.
[141] Ibid., p. 392.

Ben-Gurion repeatedly refused, preferring to balance the Czech deal with a counterdeal between Israel and Western states, who would definitely not agree to an Israeli military initiative. On October 19, 1955, Egypt and Syria signed a military pact.[142]

On October 23, Ben-Gurion responded to the cumulative effects of the above by instructing Dayan to prepare operational plans for three possible scenarios: occupying the Gaza Strip to put an end to the Fedayeen attacks; attacking into northern Sinai to drive back the Egyptian forces; and occupying the Tiran Straits to ensure Israel's freedom of shipping in the Red Sea. Such contingency plans had been prepared before, and therefore the instruction was to update them, signaling an understanding that Israel's situation had changed – Dayan was to change the direction of IDF activity from long-term building of forces to readiness for an imminent war.

Dayan had already begun preparations for such a change – he had reconstituted the Southern Command and begun updating operational plans during the summer. The latter included Operation Yarkon, a daring reconnaissance operation in the depths of eastern Sinai to check the trafficability of terrain from Eilat to Sharm El Sheikh (the Egyptian shore of the Tiran Straits).

Operation Yarkon set out to map the route between June 9 and June 12, 1955. True to his goal of bringing the quality of other units up to the standard of the paratroopers, Dayan tasked the commander of the Givati Brigade, Colonel Haim Bar-Lev (a future Chief of Staff), with the daring operation.

Shortly before the start of Operation Yarkon, however, Ben-Gurion had doubts, and Dayan had to encourage him to implement the plan. A note Dayan wrote to Ben-Gurion and Ben-Gurion's answer during a debate in the parliamentary Security and Foreign Affairs Committee shed further light on their relationship. "I propose you approve the [unit] going on the patrol," Dayan wrote to Ben-Gurion. "Many complex preparations have already been done. In the coming days, we can avoid, to the extent possible, contact with the Egyptian guard troops in the Gaza Strip. Postponing the patrol by a month does not seem like an option. If you decide not to carry it out now, it would be best to call it off altogether." Ben-Gurion responded, "Fine. Responsibility for the underlined is yours."[143]

On Thursday, June 9, a team of six men were landed by boat at Dahab and walked north toward Eilat. On June 11, after intelligence revealed that the Egyptians were searching for the team, it was extracted from enemy territory in a daring mission executed by six Piper planes. Dayan awaited the men with bottles of cold juice in hand. A few weeks later, he hosted a party for them and top IDF

---

[142] Bar-On (ed.), *Lenochach gvulot oyevim: tzava ubitachon ba'asor harishon shel medinat Yisrael*, pp. 310–311.
[143] Merav Halperin, "25 Years since Operation Yarkon: Special Ops Pioneer" (Hebrew), *Biton heil ha'avir* 15:117 (June 1980), pp. 9–17 (p. 12).

officers at his house, where he awarded the six citations of merit for their tenacity and resolve. Furthermore, the information they gathered proved most useful during the Sinai War.[144] Operation Yarkon's historical importance lies in it being the first mission coordinated among the IDF's air, ground, and naval forces.[145]

Ben-Gurion and Dayan could discuss major operations, but, as both knew, the IDF at their disposal was still incapable of conducting them. It could defend, it could conduct limited offensive operations, but it could not conduct the deep, fast offensive required to achieve the objectives stated by Ben-Gurion. The fact remained that Israel did not have the arsenal and force composition to conduct these operations and would not unless it found a source willing to sell it the necessary equipment. Israel was not looking for a war, it was looking for a major ally.

Military Diplomacy: Relations with France

Ben-Gurion decided that Israel, a small nation in a large, hostile environment, should seek the patronage of a large military power to help it politically, militarily, and technologically based on shared values and interests. In the early 1950s, Israel lacked such a patron. It had distanced itself from the Soviets, whereas the British and the Americans were courting the Arabs to curb Soviet influence. Small and weak, Israel was not viewed as sufficiently important to become a significant strategic partner in British and US efforts.

This left France, whose social-democrat leaders were sympathetic to then-socialist Israel and were therefore considered ideologically compatible. Furthermore, France and Israel did not have a problematic past, as was the case with Great Britain. With the outbreak of the Algerian Revolution in 1954, actively aided by Egyptian President Gamal Abdul Nasser, relations between France and Israel went into higher gear, ushering in the Israeli–French honeymoon.

While changing historical circumstances led to the two nations' new bond, the personality of the leaders and each leader's individual contribution also played a role. The most important person in cementing relations with France was Shimon Peres, deftly maneuvering behind the scenes of the arms acquisition agreements, while working very closely with Dayan, with whom Peres was totally enchanted.[146] Dayan's intelligence, charm, and persuasiveness about

---

[144] See: "Operation Yarkon: By Fire and Water" (Hebrew), Armored Corps Memorial, Latroun Park, January 27, 2011. Available at https://rb.gy/7697sb; published on February 12, 2018.

[145] "Operation Yarkon," Israel Intelligence Heritage and Commemoration Center (IICC). Available at www.intelligence.org.il/?module=articles&item_id=16&article_id=34&art_category_id=7. See also: "Operation Yarkon: By Fire and Water" (Hebrew), Armored Corps Memorial, Latroun Park, January 27, 2011.

[146] Michael Bar-Zohar, *Ke'of hahol: Shimon Peres – habiografiya* (Hebrew), Tel Aviv: Miskal, 2006, p. 130.

Figure 3.2 Dayan receives the National Order of the Legion of Honor, 1954. Source: Bettmann/Contributor/Bettmann/Getty Images.

the IDF's strength proved critical to France's decision to gamble on a military and political partnership with Israel.

The figure of Dayan, with the black patch covering his left eye, burst into public consciousness in France in August 1954 when the French awarded him the National Order of the Legion of Honor (Figure 3.2). Dayan was suspicious of the French, doubting their military capabilities after their defeats in World War II and Vietnam. Nonetheless, during his 1954 visit, Dayan developed respect for France after learning it had much to offer in many fields, especially the military one.[147]

Dayan's great contribution to ties with France is well documented in the literature.[148] However, it is important to emphasize that it was the cooperation between Dayan and Peres that ultimately led to the arms deals with France. One task was Dayan's alone: persuading France that the IDF was an effective army that could best Egypt. With his personal charisma, Dayan succeeded. It is reported that after Dayan told the French delegation that the IDF could reach the Suez Canal within a week, Inspector General of the French Air Force

---

[147] Yitzhak Bar-On, *Mitriya beyom sagrir* ... : *Yehasim bithoni'im bein tsarfat leyisrael 1948–1956* (Hebrew), Maccabim: Effi Meltser Publishers, 2010, p. 106.

[148] Bar-On, *Mitriya beyom sagrir*; Bar-Zohar, *Ke'of hahol*.

General Maurice Challe asked Dayan, "So you've conquered [the Sinai Peninsula], you've reached [the Canal]. How long can you hold it?" Dayan's first answered that this was a political question. When Challe insisted, Dayan, trying to be a wise guy, scratched his head for a few seconds before answering, "350 years." The French first appeared offended by the arrogant answer, but after Challe noted the playful look in Dayan's eye, he became one of Dayan's ardent admirers.[149]

However, personal charisma is not enough to persuade professional officers. Dayan had to prove the IDF's capabilities to the high-ranking French military delegation that landed in Israel on October 2, 1956. The French were convinced, and Dayan noted to himself that, "The French saw an army whose organizational skill and technical command are beyond what they expected."[150] Dayan, confident in the army he was leading, knew how to transmit this to the French.

France's admiration for the IDF was an important component in its decision to forge closer relations with Israel and cooperate militarily. Every nation choosing a strategic partner is interested in one with a high level of military performance. This was true also in the case of France and Israel in the 1950s. The reprisals were critical, impressing the French with the IDF's ability, determination, and cumulative experience in conducting such operations. In the historical debate over the reprisals and their usefulness, this subject is barely mentioned.

Changing the Culture

While Chief of Staff, Dayan launched several meaningful reforms in the army that led to essential changes in the IDF's organizational culture, thereby leaving his imprint on the military for decades. Dayan's extraordinary leadership style was matched by his management style. Organizational psychologist Edgar Schein has noted the ability of leaders to change and reshape an organizational culture in several ways: selecting the issues to which they will devote most of their time and resources; their responses to critical events and organizational crises; articulating the standards for success; and deciding which individuals in the organization to reward and promote.[151] As Chief of Staff, Dayan used most of the tools available to him as leader so that his leadership messages were crystal clear.

---

[149] Gazit, in Bar-On (ed.), *Lenochach gvulot oyevim: tzava ubitachon ba'asor harishon shel medinat Yisrael*, p. 176.
[150] Bar-On, *Mitriya beyom sagrir*, pp. 450–451.
[151] Edgar E. Schein, *Organizational Culture and Leadership*, San Francisco: Jossey-Bass, 2004, p. 245.

Dayan preferred working with a small team. His personal staff included his bureau head Shlomo Gazit and secretary Neora Barnoach-Matalon. Until his appointment, the Chief of Staff's office looked like and operated like its British Army counterpart, with its etiquette and norms of crisply pressed uniforms, order, and discipline. With the maverick Dayan, things were different.[152] He turned the Chief of Staff's roomy, well-equipped, and, for its time, luxuriously appointed office into a conference room,[153] choosing for himself a much smaller space for routine appointments where he insisted on having a standard field desk covered with a military blanket, so that visiting field commanders wouldn't feel as if they'd landed on an alien planet, far removed from their life in the field.[154] Dayan also instructed that the air conditioner not be used – moves made to express solidarity with the soldiers in the field. Furthermore, he made a point of taking his meals in the regular mess where the junior officers ate, rather than in the senior officers' dining hall. When he toured the field, he always wore a field uniform and sat on the ground in the dirt and dust with the men. In addition to scheduled visits, Dayan often went into the field without notice to conduct spot checks of camps and bases.[155]

All of these activities were clear declarations that a spirit of change was in the air. Perhaps they were small and symbolic, but they were nonetheless significant.[156] The key message communicated was that of action: things must be put in motion and executed without delay.

In a concluding discussion with the second graduating cohort of the IDF Command and Staff College, Dayan, who abhorred military bureaucracy, warned:

> Too often, the IDF is unrealistic about warfare and doctrine. Staff officers are too invested in the daily work and too rarely do they lift their heads to see where they actually are in relation to real life. It seems to me that the IDF Command and Staff College is also going too much in that direction. The result is too little doing. There are many subjects and missions that, by their nature, aren't smooth: they have different jagged edges and can never be fully coordinated. Too often, the insistence on full coordination leads to concessions or compromises over the actual critical action.[157]

Dayan also had an extraordinary time-management style, which ensured him maximal flexibility and freedom of action. Quite unlike other senior figures, he would leave his schedule open and adaptable, refusing to block

---

[152] Neora Barnoach-Matalon, *Makom tov batsad* (Hebrew), Tel Aviv: Kotarim Publishers, 2009, p. 21.
[153] Gazit, in Bar-On (ed.), *Lenochach gvulot oyevim: tzava ubitachon ba'asor harishon shel medinat Yisrael*, p. 172.
[154] Barnoach-Matalon, *Makom tov batsad*, p. 30.
[155] Ibid., p. 35.
[156] Author's interview with Shlomo Gazit, Herzliya, February 2017.
[157] Dayan, *Avnei derekh*, p. 212.

out appointments, meetings, and visits weeks in advance. In fact, his calendar was blank, with a few recurring events, such as his weekly discussion with the defense minister or a cabinet meeting. His blank calendar afforded him the ability to respond to unexpected matters, and a lot of time to think.[158] This was undoubtedly the most obvious manifestation of Dayan's perception of reality as changing unceasingly and of the futility of rigid planning. On any given day, he could therefore decide to visit a military base without giving prior warning to see if the duty commanders were actually there and watch as the soldiers returned from an overnight exercise. He also made monthly planned visits together with senior officers to solve lateral problems. This way, he always had time to meet to discuss urgent issues on the spot.

As commander, he relied on his staff to the full extent possible, believing that the coordinating and the professional staff were capable of handling all the issues with which he was charged.[159] Dayan would identify a problem, make his position clear, and deal with it down to the last detail until he saw change in the right direction, at which point he would lose interest and hand the problem over to his staff to follow through.[160] This was his modus operandi as defense minister, too. He trusted that the officers on his staff were capable of providing solutions to diverse situations without his involvement; he would focus all his energy on one, at most two issues.[161] In general, he had a great deal of faith in the professionalism of many of the officers working under him. One such person was Lieutenant Colonel Aharon Yariv (later Director of Military Intelligence), whom Dayan wanted to become the new commander for the IDF Command and Staff College. Responding to Yariv's self-doubts about his suitability, Dayan stated, "If Ben-Zvi can be president, Maklef Chief of Staff, and I head of the General Staff Directorate, you can be Commander of the IDF Command and Staff College."[162]

Dayan didn't much care for how things looked. His uniform tended to be rumpled, and his close staff members were forced to argue with him about maintaining a minimally decent appearance. However, he cared deeply about the messages he communicated to the rank and file. He was extremely careful with every word he said that would be published in the press and every sentence that appeared in every speech he gave. He wrote his own speeches and coined phrases that became part of canonical Hebrew. He would practice

---

[158] From author's interview with Shlomo Gazit, September 18, 2016, Kfar Saba; Gazit, in Bar-On (ed.), *Lenochach gvulot oyevim: tzava ubitachon ba'asor harishon shel medinat Yisrael*, p. 173; see also: Barnoach-Matalon, *Makom tov batsad*, p. 25.
[159] In principle and in terms of doctrine, Dayan's approach was correct. See *Hatora habsisit lepikud uleshlita* (Hebrew), General Staff 6-sub-01, General Staff Directorate.
[160] Barnoach-Matalon, *Makom tov batsad*, p. 30.
[161] Author interview with Shlomo Gazit, Herzliya, October 12, 2018.
[162] Teveth, *Moshe Dayan*, p. 380.

his speeches in an empty room of his bureau and used his closest assistants, Matalon and Gazit, as his sounding boards.[163]

According to the people with whom he worked closely at this time, Dayan spent a lot of time poring over intelligence materials, unit condition reports, and even soldier complaints. He was particularly angered by acts of hazing and bullying and tended to deal with them personally.

Soon after becoming Chief of Staff at the end of 1953, Dayan began focusing on the major and most essential challenge: returning the fighting spirit to the army, and the ability to command and lead to the field commanders. This, as described on p. 117, was accomplished via the reprisals executed by Unit 101 and the paratroopers. His second objective was to reduce the gaps between the General Staff echelon and the field. Aware of the importance of symbolic actions by leaders, he made a point of having members of the General Staff show their presence in the field, with himself at the head, wearing their field uniforms just as the training units did, in order to improve relations between staff and field.

Dayan behaved in unusual ways to make a point. For example, he issued an invitation to Haim Levkov, then a major, to attend an IDF commanders' warfare drills conference; all the participants were senior to Levkov, who usually went above and beyond in executing commands. Dayan used Levkov as a living example to demonstrate to more superior officers, who were making excuses for their failures, how a commander should behave: initiate action and go beyond the limits of the official order.[164] Another incident related to imposing discipline on air-force pilots who performed stunts in the air. Dayan discharged a pilot who had performed the most egregious stunts from the military to serve as a warning to others. The pilot in question requested to be readmitted, and Dayan agreed, knowing he had achieved the intended effect.[165] The result was a major culture shift in the air force.

Another incident reflecting Dayan's unusual mode of conduct occurred on a visit to an army base soon after his appointment as Chief of Staff. Dayan stopped the car en route to pick some oranges in a grove. When he reached the base, he got out of the vehicle holding handfuls of oranges and threw them at the surprised base commander who was standing at tense attention and saluting him. By the next day, the whole army was talking about the impish, convention-defying Chief of Staff.

To shake the army out of its torpor, Dayan also paid surprise visits to bases. He'd travel alone, at night, and enter camps to check discipline, guard duty, and stand-by shifts. During these visits, he made sure to address soldier complaints, including about returning from patrol and having nothing to eat because the kitchen was closed. Dayan issued an order and made sure himself

---

[163] Barnoach-Matalon, *Makom tov batsad*, p. 28.
[164] Teveth, *Moshe Dayan*, p. 386.
[165] Ibid., p. 409.

that combat soldiers would be met with a hot meal, at whatever time of day or night, every time they returned from operational activities. These visits often led to Dayan issuing new guidelines to senior commanders about patrols, learning, and improving the current situation.[166] Dayan's interventions not only led to operational alertness and attention to procedure but also created the sense that someone was looking out for and listening to the men.

Another cultural/ethical code Dayan assimilated into the IDF was never to leave any wounded behind. This followed an incident in June 1954, when the force left behind Sergeant Yitzhak Jibli during a paratrooper action in Jordan. Jibli was captured and tortured. Dayan authorized the paratroopers to abduct Jordanian Legionnaires for a POW exchange. After Jibli was returned, it was made very clear that wounded men were never again to be left behind.[167]

One daring, controversial step Dayan took was his decision to force officers to retire around the age of forty to keep the army young and ostensibly allow them to begin a second civilian career. This plan was first met by shock, but an adamant Dayan forced his will on the system. The dual career path became a fact and changed the IDF and Israel's civilian life, into which many ex-army figures have since then integrated.[168] His ousting of many officers upon becoming Chief of Staff made him appear heartless, but it served his agenda. The overall size of the very expensive standing army was reduced, and the money saved was used to acquire weapons and other equipment the IDF sorely needed.

Another area in which Dayan made changes was the Nahal, which attracted some of the best and the brightest but whose contribution to combat was negligible. The kibbutz lobby, a powerful entity at the time, accused Dayan of being antikibbutz because he came from a moshav. Dayan persisted, successfully bridging the gap by establishing a Nahal paratrooper battalion, the 88th Battalion (renamed the 50th Battalion after the 1956 war), which became an outstanding elite airborne unit.[169]

Dayan was strict but fair regarding the IDF's promotions policy. Worried about the IDF turning into an army of many generals and few soldiers, he wanted to avoid inflating the upper ranks, a goal that did not help his popularity among officers who were expecting advancement. Nevertheless, Dayan fought to make sure that Yitzhak Rabin – not a great ally – was promoted to the rank of major general because he felt Rabin deserved it, and he had no problem arguing about it with Defense Minister Pinhas Lavon.[170]

---

[166] Ibid., p. 411.
[167] Ibid., p. 402.
[168] Ibid., p. 407.
[169] See Dayan's conversation with Ben-Gurion about the Nahal: Dayan, *Avnei derekh*, pp. 161, 170–171. About the fury of the kibbutzim, see Mordechai Bar-On, *Moshe Dayan: Korot hayav 1915–1981*, Tel Aviv: Am Oved, 2014, p. 125.
[170] Teveth, *Moshe Dayan*, p. 405.

Military Reforms and Force Buildup

Dayan is often portrayed as someone who did not deal with force development, leaving this to his staff officers. Prime Minister Sharett wrote that "[Dayan] has no clue or interest in running the military budget and its economy."[171] While Dayan indeed did not write many staff documents, he also probably did not read many of them either, because reading exacerbated his postinjury headaches.[172] Dayan carved out a unique role. As one of his bureau chiefs, Eli Zeira, recalls, Dayan told him that the General Staff was composed of three divisions – plus one: "I [i.e., Dayan] am the head of the fourth division. I do whatever the others aren't doing."[173]

An important organizational change was splitting the General Staff Directorate into several units: intelligence, training, and operations. First, realizing that intelligence is critical in Israel, Dayan separated intelligence, then a department, from the General Staff Directorate and elevated into an independent directorate.[174] This enabled the Intelligence Directorate to develop and become a major influence on Israel's security establishment. Dayan explained that because of the importance of intelligence and his own personal involvement in political realms, the IDF Intelligence unit must be subordinate only to the Chief of Staff and the defense minister.[175] In fact, he had three reasons: the importance of intelligence to the IDF; intelligence leaders' need to be in direct contact with the Chief of Staff and defense minister due to their frequent involvement with the interface between strategy and policy issues; and moving positions from the Chief of Staff's bureau to intelligence.[176]

Dayan also elevated the training department into a distinct directorate, reflecting the importance he attributed to it;[177] he appointed his rival Yitzhak Rabin as Director of the Training Directorate, acknowledging Rabin's talent and trusting Rabin could best collate the IDF's organizational knowledge and turn it

---

[171] Sharett, *Yoman ishi* (Hebrew), Maariv Library, Tel Aviv, 197, p. 202.

[172] Teveth, *Moshe Dayan*, p. 380.

[173] Nir Mann's interview with Eli Zeira. Appears as an appendix to Mann's book, *Toldot mahaneh hamatkal bashanim 1948-1955* (Hebrew) (*The History of the General Staff Camp 1948-1955*), cited by Elron, "Hatmurot betsahal vehashinuy shelo haya bitfisat habitahon," pp. 130, 132. According to Zeira, Dayan avoided dealing with logistical and organizational matters.

[174] Efraim Lapid, *Lohamei haseter: Hamodi'in hayisraeli – mabat mibifnim* (Hebrew), Rishon Letsion: Miskal Publishers (Yedioth Ahronoth and Sifrei Hemed), 2017, p. 37.

[175] Elron, "Hatmurot betsahal vehashinuy shelo haya bitfisat habitahon," p. 130, citing Dayan at a General Staff meeting on December 20, 1953 (p. 131).

[176] David Siman-Tov and Shai Horowitz, *Aman yotseh la'or: He'asor harishon le'agaf hamodi'in betsahal* (Hebrew), Tel Aviv: Maarakhot, 2013.

[177] In a December 20, 1953, General Staff meeting, Dayan declared, "Training is the most important matter." Cited by Elron, "Hatmurot betsahal vehashinuy shelo haya bitfisat habitahon," p. 131.

into a doctrine and training methods.[178] Rabin indeed translated Dayan's principles – placing the commander ahead of his men, keeping to the mission no matter what, and encouraging all ranks to take the initiative – into a military doctrine and a comprehensive training system. Some claimed that, beyond legitimate reasons for breaking up the General Staff Directorate, Dayan, who, having directed it, was aware of the organization's massive strength, wanted to weaken that locus of power and thereby increase his own as Chief of Staff.[179]

When Dayan became Director of the General Staff Directorate, the IDF widely assumed there was no immediate threat of overall war, but that the army should be built to handle such a scenario. The planning team of IDF force construction prepared a six-year master plan designed to allow the IDF to successfully confront an overall war, a scenario that was drilled in war games and planning exercises.

The major changes made in the IDF during Dayan's tenure as Director of the General Staff Directorate and Chief of Staff before the Sinai War included:

- Upgrading and expanding the reserves, especially infantry units; organizational change and improving combat support and logistics;
- Establishing three new infantry brigades in 1955;
- Establishing division-level task-force headquarters in February 1955;
- Adding five artillery battalions to the existing ten, and establishing four artillery group headquarters for multibattalion missions;
- Establishing combat engineer units in the regular army and reserves;
- Establishing an armored corps headquarters;
- Assimilating the "mission command" approach, an ethos whereby commanders seize the initiative, go on the offense, and lead the force.[180]

Because of the urgent need for cutbacks, Dayan believed that rather than maintaining a large and expensive standing army, he could train a functional reserve army able to deploy rapidly. Expanding the reserves and other organizational changes introduced by Dayan resulted in a decline in the IDF's immediate readiness for war, but force building was focused on the long-term future.[181]

Dayan's tenure as Chief of Staff witnessed two extremely dramatic developments regarding force building. First, the IDF shifted its reliance on piston-engine aircraft to jet-engine aircraft. Second, the IDF made the armored corps the backbone of the ground forces.

---

[178] For more on the appointment, see Yitzhak Rabin, *Pinkas sherut* (Hebrew), Tel Aviv: Maariv, 1979, vol. 1, p. 92.
[179] Elron, "Hatmurot betsahal vehashinuy shelo haya bitfisat habitahon," p. 132.
[180] For the "mission command" as a command approach in the IDF, see: *Tora besisit matkalit, pikud ushlita* (Hebrew), Ekked, General Staff Directorate, Doctrine and Training, November 2006, p. 33.
[181] Elron, "Hatmurot betsahal vehashinuy shelo haya bitfisat habitahon," pp. 185–186.

There was a heated discussion over the navy. It was obvious that the small Israeli navy was incapable of winning a campaign against the larger and better-equipped Egyptian one; thus, any investments in the navy came at the expense of critical investments in the air and ground forces, who were considered more important in Israel's strategic situation. Therefore, Dayan's decided not to neutralize the navy's capabilities altogether but chose not to allocate it large budgets that might weaken the air or armored forces, to which he wanted to give a relative advantage. For example, meeting the navy's demand for destroyers to defeat Egyptians in naval battles would have made it impossible for the IDF to acquire tanks and planes. Dayan's position was that the navy should be given "modest operational flexibility" so as not to give the Egyptians a completely free hand, even if by means of a relatively inferior force.[182] To this end, two old destroyers were purchased for Mediterranean operations but only some commando boats for the Red Sea. Elron and Shaul Bronfeld noted that:

> Dayan's decisions ... were the result of a logical, consistent strategic view implementing his security approach to the naval theater rather than of ignorance or hostility towards the navy. Just as he viewed the need for destroyers in the Mediterranean theater ... as early as 1955, he identified the great importance of establishing a small naval base in Eilat that would pose a threat to the Egyptian presence and give the IDF a certain freedom of action in the Gulf of Eilat and the Red Sea.[183]

Despite the common opinion that Dayan disdained armored fighting, he in fact strengthened the Armored Corps, even giving it its own headquarters, which helped bring about the armored revolution in the IDF regarding acquisitions, training, and operational doctrine.[184] The headquarters was designed as a dedicated professional headquarters rather than operative headquarters like the regional commands. This upgraded the Armored Corps's status, making it close to that of the air force and the navy, even though it continued to be part of the ground forces. Amiad Bresner, the Armored Corps's historian, has written that there is no doubt that establishing the headquarters was "a revolution affecting the organization and operation of the armored forces."[185] Dayan also eliminated the armored brigade headquarters, making armored battalions directly subordinate to the Armored Corps headquarters. This provided the force with greater operational flexibility and manpower savings.[186] All these moves were aimed at making the Armored Corps into

---

[182] Elron and Brunfeld, "The General Staff Versus the Navy" (Hebrew), p. 183.
[183] Ibid., p. 191.
[184] Amiad Bresner, *Susim abirim: Hitpat'hut utmurot bashiryon hayisraeli mitom milhemet ha'atsmaut ve'ad milhemet Sinai* (Hebrew), Tel Aviv: Maarakhot, 1999, p. 175.
[185] Ibid., p. 178.
[186] Ibid., p. 179.

"a mobile armored force that would serve as the key means for concentrating effort and General Staff reserves."[187]

Dayan also made some impulsive decisions, such as eliminating the Southern Command, merging it with the Central Command in order to reduce budgetary spending. The change proved highly problematic, especially because the Southern Command had been responsible for the sector where Israel's strongest enemy – Egypt – was located. Indeed, a year later, when the situation there deteriorated, Dayan unhesitatingly admitted his misjudgment and reversed the decision, appointing its former commander Meir Amit to reestablish the Southern Command and allowing Amit to take all the people he wanted for this task on condition he reconstituted the command within twenty-four hours.[188] Still, Dayan insisted that the shake-up he had generated benefited a body as unwieldy as the IDF.[189]

As Chief of Staff, Dayan was very cautious on strategic issues. He worried mostly about being criticized by Ben-Gurion, who focused on Israel's international standing, not operational matters. For example, in the Qalqilya reprisal operation, Dayan was reluctant to use the IAF or artillery without Ben-Gurion's approval as defense minister because of the strategic/political significance of their employment.[190] His reluctance may also have been personal, resulting from Dayan's awe of Ben-Gurion. Ben-Gurion returned the admiration, writing to Dayan:

> You've demonstrated two fundamental yet contradictory traits that have made you into one of the most outstanding soldiers of the Israel Defense Force: almost insane audacity balanced by profound tactical and strategic thinking.[191]

Regarding orderly staff work, requiring patience, order, discipline, and organizational skills, Dayan was able to compensate for his self-acknowledged deficiencies with his keen intuition about people. Still, when it came to fighting spirit and battle readiness, Dayan was meticulous down to the last platoon sergeant. Some said they preferred to die in battle rather than receive a tongue-lashing from Dayan. But he also personally greeted with juice those soldiers who returned from raids. Promotions were given only to the bravest, who had shown courage under fire. For staff and service units, Dayan

---

[187] Benny Michelson, "Why the Armored Corps Headquarters Was Established" (Hebrew), *59 shanim lehakamat mifkedet gyasot hashiryon* (*Fifty-Nine Years since the Establishment of the Armored Corps Headquarters*), July 2019, Armored Corps Museum, Latroun Park, https://rb.gy/cumyhw, published on July 22, 2013.
[188] Teveth, *Moshe Dayan*, p. 412.
[189] Ibid.
[190] For details of this operation, which marked the end of the period of reprisals, see Chapter 5.
[191] Letter of goodbye to outgoing Chief of Staff Moshe Dayan by David Ben-Gurion, January 27, 1958, in Dayan, *Avnei derekh*, p. 375.

would find the people who understood him and were capable of carrying out his wishes with minimal involvement on his part.

On the one hand, Dayan did not maintain a formal distance, as is customary between generals and the rank-and-file, and he created an atmosphere of familiarity and openness. On the other hand, the people around him were awestruck by him both because of his position and even more so because of the power his personality radiated. No one was really intimate with him, and therefore there was always a sense of mystery, of the unknown, about him. Moreover, Dayan's mood was mercurial, in part because of the headaches he suffered since his injury. These often made him impatient and prone to cut off his interlocutors for no apparent reason, causing offense. He apologized only rarely.[192]

His attitude to people was instrumental. Amit said of him:

> He neither loves nor hates. Rather, he either appreciates or doesn't. He appreciates the brave who fill him with inspiration; [he appreciates] the wise with who he enjoys talking about problems that preoccupy him and topics he likes, such as archeology. The stupid and the cowardly he simply ignores. For him, they don't exist.[193]

The combination of these traits – a distant, mysterious figure with mood swings, and his aura as an extraordinary military leader – created the larger-than-life character whom subordinates venerated and feared in equal measure.

As Chief of Staff, Dayan worked under the government and also under central figures with whom he came into contact and who affected his outlook. The first, obviously, was Ben-Gurion, who appointed him Chief of Staff. Dayan admired – some say idolized – Ben-Gurion, viewing reality much as the older man did. In many ways, the two complemented one another. Dayan's attitude to Sharett, who was appointed prime minister on December 7, 1953, after Ben-Gurion's resignation, was very different. Sharett held a much more appeasing political line than his predecessor's, and Dayan, who did not respect Sharett's opinion, continued to consult with Ben-Gurion, who had retired to Kibbutz Sde Boker in the Negev.

After Ben-Gurion was reappointed defense minister in February 1955, he looked into the state of the IDF. In April, he reported to the government that he had found "tremendous progress both in training the army and in army equipment." He added that "savings in manpower [that] did not reduce the army's fighting capacity, and very important work in acquisitions, as well as a new and important institution: the IDF Command and Staff College." Ben-Gurion attributed these improvements to the work of Defense Minister Lavon and Dayan, concluding "If the regular army was greatly reduced and the cohort

---

[192] Ibid., p. 414.
[193] Ibid., p. 415.

cut back in size . . . the force of the army has markedly increased." It seems that Ben-Gurion's impression resulted from him identifying the combative and confident spirit with which Dayan had managed to infuse the IDF. There is no doubt that Ben-Gurion gave Dayan most of the credit for the change he observed.

During Sharett's term as prime minister, Dayan and Peres were the principal figures in IDF force construction, with Dayan curbing Lavon's less hawkish influence in this field.[194] After Ben-Gurion assumed the Defense Ministry, the three principals were Ben-Gurion, Dayan, and Peres working in close coordination. Most major decisions were made in their weekly forum of three, which Ben-Gurion dubbed his "limited staff."[195] In November, Ben-Gurion was nominated again as prime minister. Now the trio, Ben-Gurion, Dayan, and Peres, were free to lead Israel to the Sinai Campaign on October 1956, sharing the mission of building and strengthening the IDF for that crucial campaign.

* * *

While Chief of Staff, Dayan continued processes initiated by his predecessors Yadin and Maklef regarding organization and force construction, but the army he was handed was suffering from a severe crisis of morale, which was reflected in poor performance. Dayan kindled a revolution in the IDF's fighting spirit, making it aggressive, audacious, and proactive. Dayan's second contribution lay in setting correct priorities in the organization and in force construction at a time of particularly poor resources. His third – albeit controversial – contribution was devising the reprisals policy and developing a doctrine of routine security in addition to the doctrine of fundamental security. Fourth, he truly revolutionized the figure of the commander. Dayan focused on the commanders, as he felt that they were key to determining the level of functionality of the system as a whole. When he left office, the command ranks were excellent, noted for seizing initiative and assuming responsibility. But the real test of every military leader is war, and this was still to come.

---

[194] Elron, "Hatmurot betsahal vehashinuy shelo haya bitfisat habitahon," p. 268.
[195] Bar-On, *Moshe Dayan*, p. 111.

4

Theater Commander

The Sinai Campaign

The Road to War: The Geostrategic Shift

The events leading to the Sinai Campaign resulted from political and geopolitical developments much broader than the Israeli–Egyptian conflict – the Cold War's start and colonialism's end. Great Britain and France, once great imperial powers, were struggling to retain their power and reposition themselves in the international system as former colonies became independent nations. These changes coincided with developments in Egypt–Israel relations, bringing these historic processes together to create "a perfect storm": When the interests of the two fading world powers and those of the tiny nascent nation corresponded, a tripartite Israeli–French–British collusion was born.[1]

Great Britain, the most important global power in the Middle East for the first half of the twentieth century, had interests in many locations throughout the region. In the early 1950s, Great Britain still had military forces in Egypt, wielded considerable influence in Iraq, and had British officers commanding

---

[1] Much has been written about the events leading to the Sinai Campaign. In this book, I have relied on the writings of Mordechai Bar-On, Moshe Dayan's bureau chief at that time, and on other studies published in recent years: Mordechai Bar-On, *Etgar vetigra: Haderekh lemivtsa Kadesh 1956* (Hebrew), Sde Boker Campus: Ben-Gurion Heritage Institute, 1991; Mordechai Bar-On, *Sha'arey aza: Mediniyut habitahon vehahuts shel medinat yisrael 1955–1957* (Hebrew), Tel Aviv: Am Oved, 1992; Haggai Golan and Shaul Shay (eds.), *Bir'om hamano'im: 50 shana lemilhemet Sinai* (Hebrew), Tel Aviv: Maarakhot, 2006; Yair Evron, *Hadilemma hagarinit shel yisrael* (Hebrew), Ramat Efal: Yad Tabenkin, 1987; Mordechai Bar-On (ed.), *Lenochach gvulot oyevim: tzava ubitachon ba'asor harishon shel medinat Yisrael*, Israel: Efy Meltzer, 2017; Moshe Shemesh and Ilan Troan (eds.), *Mivtsa Kadesh uma'arekhet Suez 1956: Iyun mehadash* (Hebrew), Sde Boker: The Ben-Gurion Heritage Institute, 1994; Moshe Dayan, *Yoman Ma'arekhet Sinai* (Hebrew), Tel Aviv: Am Hassefer, 1966; Michael Oren, *The Origins of the Second Arab–Israeli War*, Abingdon: Frank Cass, 1992; Yagil Henkin, *The 1956 Suez War and the New World Order in the Middle East: Exodus in Reverse*, Lanham, MD: Lexington Books, 2015; Zaki Shalom, *Mediniyut betsel mahloket: Mediniyut habitahon hashotef shel yisrael 1949–1956* (Hebrew), Tel Aviv: Maarakhot, 1996.

the Jordanian Legion.² After its troop withdrawal from Egypt in 1954, Great Britain found Jordan, with which it had signed a defense treaty in March 1948, more strategically important than ever before.

Following Nasser's seizure of power in Egypt, Great Britain, with the United States as mediator, was forced to withdraw its troops from Egypt and the Suez Canal region and thus became reliant on Egyptian goodwill in order to control the Canal, even though it was owned by a joint French and British company. Israel followed these developments with increasing anxiety, creating an atmosphere that proved fertile ground for the ill-fated "Lavon Affair," involving an attempt by Israel's intelligence services to disrupt Great Britain's departure from Egypt while Egypt was negotiating the future of the Suez Canal. The scheme failed, earning the affair the sobriquet *ha'esek habish* ("The Unfortunate Affair" or "The Bad Business"), which damaged Israel's image among the British, who already viewed the new state as an obstacle to their efforts to impose order in the Middle East and retain their influence there.

After granting independence to its protectorates – Lebanon in 1943 and Syria in 1946 – France followed Middle East developments and their impact on its North African colonies with concern. With their joint ownership of the Suez Canal, France and Great Britain had a common interest in the Middle East. Together with the United States, in 1950, they agreed to restrict weapons sales to Arab nations and Israel, trying to contain the Arab–Israeli confrontation. These Western nations, also concerned with the expansion of Soviet influence, saw Egypt, with its size, strategic location, and the Suez Canal, as the keystone of Middle East stability.³

However, cracks eventually appeared in their supposedly joint interests. Under Presidents Harry Truman and Dwight Eisenhower, the United State viewed Great Britain's presence and activity as a continuation of the old, now irrelevant imperialism. The Americans successfully mediated between the British and the Egyptians over Great Britain's military withdrawal, but their refusal to provide arms to Egypt made Egypt look to the Soviets, who had come to favor the Arabs after originally supporting Israel's establishment. Realizing that Great Britain was withdrawing from the region, Josef Stalin felt the time had come for Soviet domination. In 1951, when Egypt began blocking Israeli ships from the Suez Canal – in contravention of the Convention of Constantinople guaranteeing free passage⁴ – the USSR abstained in a UN vote to condemn Egypt.⁵ At the end of 1953, the Soviet Union, now viewing

---

² British officer Sir John Bagot Glubb (Glubb Pasha) headed the Legion from 1939 until 1956.
³ Henkin, *The 1956 Suez War*, p. 19.
⁴ Convention between Great Britain, Germany, Austria-Hungary, Spain, France, Italy, The Netherlands, Russia, and Turkey, respecting the free navigation of the Suez maritime canal signed at Constantinople, October 29, 1888.
⁵ Henkin, *The 1956 Suez War*, p. 24.

Israel as part of the Western bloc, began vetoing anti-Egyptian resolutions, followed by promises, starting from 1954, to supply Egypt with weapons and civilian aid.

Once the canal was nationalized, the Israeli–Egyptian trajectory intersected with the British/French–Egyptian one. Just as Israel's view of the Czech arms deal of September 1955 (called "Czech" to obscure the Soviet Union as the actual source) began the countdown to a clash with Egypt, the global powers' view of Egypt's July 26, 1956, declaration of the Suez Canal's nationalization began their countdown to action.

Having prevented Israeli ships from sailing through the Suez Canal since 1951, in 1953 Egypt also denied freedom of shipping to any known Israeli ship flying a foreign flag. That year, Egypt also blocked the Tiran Straits before extending its blockade to the airspace above the Straits in September 1955,[6] all in contravention of treaties and international law. Already in September 1954, Israel, under Moshe Sharett's leadership, tried to rouse the world to act against Egypt for its gross violation of international law, sending the merchant vessel *Bat Galim* to the Suez Canal. As expected, the Egyptian police raided the ship and arrested all aboard. To Israel's great disappointment, the international response was tepid. In addition, the three superpowers' restriction on weapons to the sides harmed Israel the most. The Western powers wanted a balance of arms between Israel and each Arab nation separately, whereas Israel felt it faced a coalition of Arab states.[7]

The crises between Israel and Egypt through 1954 and 1955 did not yet deteriorate into war because neither side was militarily prepared and the Western powers exerted their influence. Worried about the British response, in December 1955 Ben-Gurion rejected Dayan's Omer Plan to seize Sharm El Sheikh and open the Tiran Straits for shipping to and from Eilat, fearing it would provide Great Britain grounds for returning the Negev to Egypt and Jordan.[8] Similarly, Egypt could not allow itself to defy the Western powers at this point.

With the combustible Egypt–Israel situation worrying them, the Western powers tried to ameliorate Middle East tensions through various alliances and pacts, such as the Baghdad Pact, which so angered Nasser that he signed a defense treaty with Syria.[9] The United States and Great Britain sought to

---

[6] Mati Greenberg, "The Background to the War and Its Steps: An Overview" (Hebrew), in Haggai Golan and Shaul Shay (eds.), *Bir'om hamano'im: 50 shana lemilhemet Sinai* (Hebrew), Tel Aviv: Maarakhot, 2006, pp. 11–14.

[7] Henkin, *The 1956 Suez War*, p. 41.

[8] Moshe Dayan, *Avnei derekh: Autobiografia* (Hebrew), Jerusalem: Idanim, 1976, p. 174; Neora Barnoach-Matalon, *Makom tov batsad* (Hebrew), Tel Aviv: Kotarim Publishers, 2009, p. 93.

[9] The Baghdad Pact was a defense treaty signed in February 1955 by Iraq, Turkey, and Pakistan, which were joined about two months later by Great Britain and Iran. This geostrategic regional alliance was meant to create a physical barrier between the Soviet Union and the nations of the Middle East.

maintain stable patron–client relations to curb Soviet penetration and to ensure the supply of oil, freedom of shipping, and other economic and national interests. Hoping for stability, they proposed various initiatives, the most important being Operation Alpha, a joint US State Department and British Foreign Office initiative predicated on far-reaching Israeli concessions[10] coupled with compensation to Egypt for agreeing to the unpopular step of making peace with Israel. The British, intent on acquiring Egyptian goodwill at Israel's expense, tried appeasing the Arab nations. Any appearance of the Western nations' interests coinciding was superficial, as the British wanted to preserve the old order's advantages. The Americans, considering colonialism defunct, strove to impose a new American order instead, naively believing that their anticolonialism would win them favor from the nations of the region.

The US State Department and the British Foreign Office, believing that the Israeli–Arab conflict was the obstacle standing between the West and the Arabs, hoped Israel would make extensive territorial concessions in the Negev, in the north, and at the Sea of Galilee, agree to the internationalization of Jerusalem, and take in some Palestinian refugees from Israel's War of Independence in exchange for guaranteeing Israel's security, although without a full peace agreement.[11] The White House, concerned over the American Jewish vote, was somewhat more moderate.[12]

Both Egypt and Israel refused to accept the proposal. Israel was unwilling to trust promises and guarantees and demanded direct negotiations between the sides and arms from the Americans. Nasser refused any direct contact with Israel and worked to unite the Arab world under his leadership, relying on the Soviet Union for assistance and leading to an eventual severing of ties with the West.[13] Gradually, it became clear to all that Nasser was not interested in any settlement with Israel. Although Operation Alpha was buried in the winter of 1955–1956, the American refusal to supply arms to Israel to prevent the possibility of war only increased Israel's worry, paradoxically bringing it closer to the brink of war and intensifying its focus on acquiring weapons. In the spring of 1956, Israel, through the intensive efforts of Defense Ministry Director General Shimon Peres, assisted by Dayan, turned to France for salvation.

French interests in the Arab world were unambiguous: maintaining its influence in its former colonies of Syria and Lebanon and its partial ownership of the Suez Canal. But, above all, the main consideration for the French was its

---

[10] See Office of the Historian, Draft Memorandum from Francis H. Russell to the Secretary of State, Foreign Relations of The United States, 1955–1957, Arab–Israeli Dispute, 1955, Volume XIV, Washington, 24 May 1955. At https://history.state.gov/historicaldocuments/frus1955-57v14/d107.
[11] Bar-On, *Sha'arey aza*, p. 110.
[12] Ibid., p. 123.
[13] Ibid., p. 140.

colony Algeria, where a million French citizens lived in the throes of an uprising against the French regime. The French were convinced Nasser was providing the rebels with military and moral support.

For the French, Nasser was a strategic enemy; nor were the British pleased with him. He exerted his influence on the Arab nations to oppose the Baghdad Pact, signing a defense treaty with Syria and Saudi Arabia in October 1955. He provoked Britain primarily by pulling the strings of Jordan and Syria to isolate the pro-Western Iraq. For example, Nasser instigated anti-Baghdad Pact riots in Jordan that threatened the existence of the pro-British monarchy. Finally, in March 1956, to prove he was not a British puppet, King Hussein was compelled to dismiss Glubb Pasha and his British officers, purging the Jordanian Legion of foreigners. The British blamed Nasser and began trying to isolate and weaken, perhaps even topple, him. The Americans, having wearied of Nasser and his rejection of their peace initiatives, regretted the generous assistance they had offered to build the Aswan High Dam. In July 1956, the US Congress voted to end the financial aid earmarked for the project.

The pressure from the Western powers to induce Nasser to change his policy had the opposite effect. Nasser declared the Suez Canal nationalized on July 26, 1956,[14] a decision he had calculated carefully, it serving both his domestic and his external interests. He stationed forces near the Canal but assumed that Britain and France would not attack.

In terms of the array of forces and interests, the nationalization of the Suez Canal was a crystallizing moment. France, interested in ousting Nasser, provided Israel with weapons and training. Although its position was more complicated, only Great Britain was needed to complete the puzzle. Although diminished, Great Britain was still an important world power maintaining significant armed forces in the Middle East as well as an enormous navy.

The Treaty with France

In terms of relations with Israel, France filled the vacuum left by Great Britain and the United States. With similar views about the Middle East, the French and Israelis forged a closer relationship – "the beginning of a beautiful friendship."[15] Their close ties had actually coalesced long before the Suez Canal nationalization, which set both nations on a path of cooperation against Nasser. The sympathy of France's socialist leadership for Israel also played a role, with their official public disapproval of some Israeli actions sometimes accompanied by unofficial expressions of sympathy via bilateral diplomatic

---

[14] Henkin, *The 1956 Suez War*, p. 60.
[15] Spoken by Rick Blaine (played by Humphrey Bogart) at the end of *Casablanca* (1942), this is one of the iconic one-liners made famous by the film.

channels.[16] France's need to find new markets for its military industry's products and Israel's desperation to counter the 1955 Czech arms deal for Egypt and Syria also contributed to their burgeoning relationship. The Suez Canal nationalization in July 1956 simply accelerated all these processes, with France, having identified Nasser as a clear and present danger, eager to act immediately. The primary reason the two nations embraced each other was an age-old one: My enemy's enemy is my friend.

Having already promised to supply Israel with advanced planes in October 1955, in April 1956, France sent Israel three Mystère IVs, the first of twenty-four. But the crucial change came with the new French government – a coalition between the Popular Republican Movement and the Radical Socialists, who shared a sympathy for Israel. Prime Minister Guy Mollet and Defense Minister Maurice Bourgès-Maunoury were personally very supportive of Israel. Peres leveraged the opportunity to submit an extraordinary acquisitions request: Vautour bombers, sixty Mystères, and hundreds of tanks and artillery. On April 30, Peres reported to Dayan that Bourgès-Maunoury had hinted of the possibility of a meaningful change in France's policy toward Israel.

Another impetus for the Israeli–French bond came after Israel's intelligence managed to intercept messages exchanged among Egypt, Italy, and Switzerland. While unable to decipher them in full, Israel was certain they were connected to Algeria and would therefore interest the French. France's espionage services were excited to receive the material, and with the support of the prime minister and minister of Algerian affairs – again without informing French foreign ministry at the Quai d'Orsay – it was decided to hold a secret conference. On June 22, 1956, Shimon Peres, Military Intelligence Director Yehoshua Harkaby, and Moshe Dayan flew to Paris, their final destination being a chateau in the town of Vermars.

The Vermars conference lasted two days and resulted in two agreements. The first was to provide Israel with arms, including 72 Mystère aircraft, 200 AMX-13 light tanks, and upgraded Sherman tanks,[17] as well as ammunition and spare parts, for which Israel was desperate. The second agreement involved what Israel would provide France in return: intelligence, including Israeli help in gathering information on Egypt's role in the Algerian rebellion.

An understanding between the two nations quickly emerged: France would secretly arm Israel not only far from the prying eyes of the Americans and the British but also without the knowledge of the Quai d'Orsay. The IDF's force building was starting in earnest.

---

[16] Henkin, *The 1956 Suez War*, p. 54.
[17] These tanks were of significantly lower quality than the Soviet tanks the Egyptians had acquired through the Czech arms deal. Israel had hoped for tanks of equal quality but was forced to make do with what was on offer.

At the Vermars conference, Dayan explained to his French interlocutors that Nasser's objectives were unifying the whole Arab world, ousting the West from the Middle East, and entering into a treaty with the Soviets. Dayan noted that Nasser could not attain these goals without defeating Israel, which represented both a geographical and national obstacle. Therefore, the joint French–Israeli interests were obvious: ousting Nasser or at least thwarting his objectives. The French accepted Dayan's analysis but thought that toppling Nasser was a political decision to be made by higher-ranking officials.[18]

In his memoirs, Dayan noted that his self-confidence was bolstered in the wake of these talks. Although it was not his first experience participating in negotiations with international parties, it was the first time he led and chaired a delegation. "Ben-Gurion had instructed me, but that didn't bother me. There was no conflict between my opinions and the policy he set out. I accepted Ben-Gurion not just because of his formal authority, but because I saw him as a political and national mentor who stood head and shoulders above everyone around him."[19] Dayan took pride in the respect France showed for the experience Israel had gained in the reprisal operations: "When we discussed military actions, they looked up to us. I enjoyed seeing that."[20]

Upon his return from France, Dayan noted in an interview that the IDF was facing three different challenges: cutting routine operational budgets and using the money for acquisitions; integrating the equipment and training the troops to use it; and strengthening army discipline.

In early July 1956, weapons and ammunition started arriving from France via clandestine French flotillas. At Ben-Gurion's recommendation, Dayan appointed Haim Laskov – reputed to have good organizational skills – to spearhead establishing training programs for the fighters and the units, even though Dayan and the British-trained Laskov had been at loggerheads when Laskov commanded the armored corps. But Laskov also wanted an armored corps capable of fighting deep within enemy territory and able to breach fronts and advance quickly, the approach underpinning every Israeli move. For the first time, such moves were possible with the supply of French tanks.

The Israeli Air Force (IAF) was vastly improved by the receipt of the Mystères, but integrating them into the system was expensive, while training the pilots was time-consuming. When the war broke out, the IAI had forty-eight planes, but only one squadron operated by Israelis, with the rest flown by French airmen.

Ben-Gurion and Dayan began working on Israel's part of the deal. Having proven its expertise in reprisals, Israel promised to help the French plan various actions against Algerian rebel bases in Libya and Tunisia and offered

---

[18] Dayan, *Avnei derekh*, p. 205.
[19] Ibid., p. 207.
[20] Ibid.

to help with intelligence gathering.[21] However, events were to change Israel's planned course. After the weapons and munitions arrived from France, Dayan again decided to focus on integrating equipment and completing force building before undertaking any large-scale IDF operation. In fact, following the murder of two workers on the road to Eilat on July 9, 1956, a strange role reversal took place, with Dayan opposing Ben-Gurion's suggested reprisal response. Dayan had different priorities: "If we bombard a large police station or something like that, we jeopardize the acquisitions operation. The French can stick to the deal only if the situation in Israel is not too tense and the United States and Great Britain don't make any problems." Unlike in the past, Dayan now preferred to avoid actions liable to exacerbate the situation.[22]

Near-War with Great Britain

Several unplanned and uncontrollable events disrupted Dayan's plans. With the continuing deterioration along the Jordanian border in the spring of 1956, and Israeli retaliations to Jordanian-based terrorist attacks and Jordan responding in kind, Britain, Jordan's patron, became embroiled to the point of danger of a military clash with Israel. From this point until the start of the Sinai Campaign, a situation historian Edward Luttwak called "strategic confusion" prevailed. On the one hand, there were an ongoing escalating tensions on the Jordanian–Israeli border that almost led to an armed confrontation in October 1956 between Israel and Great Britain, while on the other hand, in mid October 1956 there was the emerging axis of cooperation among Israel, France, and Britain in establishing a military coalition to lead a major attack on Egypt. It seems that only figures such as Ben-Gurion and Dayan were capable of skillfully handling so deeply contradictory a strategic situation. Dayan, with typical brilliance, even managed to turn it to Israel's advantage.

During 1955, after a series of severe Israeli reprisals, there was a reduction of attacks from Jordan into Israel. However, after their command ranks, led by Lieutenant General Sir John Glubb, were expelled in March 1956, Legion discipline deteriorated, leading to increased tensions in July. During August and September, firefights, sabotage, and attacks on Israeli civilians escalated, now involving Jordanian soldiers as well. In response, Israeli paratroopers raided several Jordanian targets: On September 11, Israeli forces attacked the al-Rahwa strongpoint near Hebron. Legendary paratrooper Meir Har-Zion was wounded, and Dayan stood by his bedside in the hospital until Har-Zion regained consciousness.[23]

---

[21] Mordechai Bar-On, *Moshe Dayan: Korot hayav 1915–1981*, Tel Aviv: Am Oved, 2014, p. 137.
[22] Ibid., p. 138.
[23] Ibid., p. 140.

Two days later, the paratroopers attacked the Jordanian fortification of Arendel, and on September 25, during Operation Lulav, they raided Jordanian police and military positions near Hussan.

With the British officers expelled from Jordan, the British obligation to the kingdom might have been expected to diminish, but it actually intensified. Great Britain became even more eager to prove its commitment, hoping to keep Jordan from turning to Nasser for help. Thus, the Jordanians enjoyed the protection of British power, still considerable, without any reciprocal obligation.[24] In September 1956, following several Israeli raids, Whitehall warned Israel that it would activate its defense treaty with Jordan.

The British threat was real. Already by June 1955, the British General Staff had prepared a detailed plan for a military attack on Israel should the defense treaty with Jordan be implemented, including attacking airfields and other strategic installations as well as an aerial and naval blockade on Israel. Claude Pelly, commander of all Royal Air Force (RAF) units in the Middle East, wrote in a memo: "Damage to civilian installations and harm to civilians are inevitable." The RAF estimated that the IAF (most of whose fleet of planes still had piston-powered engines) would be a tough enemy but could be defeated within two weeks. The plan, named Cordage, was approved in February 1956.[25]

Conflict with the British was avoided thanks to cooperation with France. The British military's highest ranks pressured their government to decide whether to embark on Operation Musketeer with Israel against Nasser or to activate Operation Cordage, arguing that it was best to attack Israel first to prevent Israel from exploiting the chance to attack Jordan again once British troops were busy with Musketeer. Despite Israel's decision to maintain its cool in the weeks leading to the campaign, another case of murder of Israelis led to a reprisal near Qalqilya on October 10, 1956.

As the troops were fighting, a political drama was unfolding. King Hussein, worried that Israel was intent on total war with Jordan, called General Sir Charles Keightley, British Commander in Chief of Middle East Land Forces, to demand the activation of their defense treaty. The British informed the Israelis, advising that they were considering intervention. British Prime Minister Anthony Eden wrote in his memoir that, "We were called on to help and our planes were ready to take off."[26] On October 12, the British let Israel know that they intended to allow an Iraqi division to enter Jordan, a step that, for Israel, would cross a red line. The British legal representative told Ben-Gurion, "If Israel takes military action, Britain will side with Jordan." Ben-Gurion replied

---

[24] Henkin, *The 1956 Suez War*, p. 96.
[25] Yuval Shoham, "The Target: The Israeli Air Force" (Hebrew), *Biton heyl ha'avir* 193 (June 2010), www.iaf.org.il/5571-34955-he/IAF.aspx.
[26] Cited in Bar-On, *Sha'arey aza*, p. 255.

that Israel reserved its right to act freely.[27] Both in Israel and around the world, the strong impression was that war was imminent on Israel's Jordanian front,[28] but, for now, the Iraqi forces postponed their entry, instead positioning themselves near the Jordanian border.

The events on Israel's Jordanian border made Ben-Gurion suspect Great Britain's motivations more than ever, making cooperation with the two world powers against Egypt very difficult. These suspicions were heightened when it emerged on October 15 that the function the British had assigned to Israel in Musketeer was providing Britain with a pretext by playing the aggressor in starting the war against Egypt.

Before the October Qalqilya action, the IDF had already armed itself with a significant quantity of weapons from France. The treaty with the French was being cobbled together, and Dayan and the IDF General Staff were preparing the "Kadesh" plan to conquer the Sinai Peninsula. The only missing piece was Great Britain, which had to decide which side to take. In the end, it decided to join France and Israel after becoming convinced it might be able to regain control of the Suez Canal, a strategic asset of the highest order for Great Britain. To understand this decision, it is necessary to go back a few weeks to early September, when the Israeli–French connection was taking form.

Dayan Plans a Campaign

On September 1, Ben-Gurion attended an IDF General Staff meeting to discuss the doctrine of armored corps deployment. During the meeting, a telegram was delivered from the Israeli attaché in Paris containing information about the British and French intention to seize and occupy the Suez Canal in an operation, code-named Musketeer, to reverse the canal's nationalization. The telegram also asked Israel to join the campaign on D-day +7.

Immediately after Nasser announced the nationalization of the Suez Canal on July 26, 1956, France and Great Britain had begun planning a joint military operation against Egypt. Great Britain continued to try diplomatic and political means to resolve the situation, including a conference of nations that used the canal (Israel and Egypt boycotted the conference) and appeals to the UN. France was interested in military action but had to endure the British diplomatic efforts. On the military level, France needed Great Britain as a military ally, as the British RAF forces, with their superior high-capacity bombers, could bomb Egypt from their airbases in Cyprus; on the political level, France needed to support Great Britain as a fellow member of the UN Security Council.[29] And Great Britain, unlike France, was leery of involving Israel in any action.

---

[27] Dayan, *Yoman Ma'arekhet Sinai*, p. 49.
[28] Bar-On, *Sha'arey aza*, p. 255.
[29] Henkin, *The 1956 Suez War*, p. 81.

On September 18, Shimon Peres met with the French Defense Minister, who shared France's thoughts about the latest proposed operation's feasibility, possible partners, and timing. Before leaving for Paris, Peres consulted with Dayan, who outlined Israel's interests in any upcoming action: Israel would prefer that the Suez Canal return to being an international shipping route, but this issue had to be decided entirely by the global powers. Israel wanted to gain control of the Tiran Straits and the outskirts of Sinai but could not get involved with Great Britain on the Jordanian front while fighting in the south.[30] After Peres returned to Israel on September 25, Israel received a French missive inviting a senior delegation to examine a possible joint French–Israeli operation. That delegation, headed by Foreign Minister Golda Meir, departed on September 29 and included Dayan, Peres, and Transportation Minister Moshe Carmel. The French participants at what would become known as the St. Germain Conference were Foreign Minister Christian Pineau, Defense Minister Bourgès-Maunoury, and senior army officers.

The delegation returned to Israel on October 2 having achieved great success for Israel. General Maurice Challe, who had been sent earlier to Israel, submitted an enthusiastic report saying that the IDF was well trained, well equipped, and, in his opinion, capable of fighting the Egyptian army on its own.[31] The French agreed to the Israeli request for military acquisitions, heralding the first stirrings of a joint French–Israeli operation. Israel presented France with its policy principles: Israel would promise not to attack Jordan if the British did not intervene to help Jordan, and the United States would be so informed; the Sinai Peninsula would be demilitarized after the war; Israel would control the Tiran Straits to prevent Egypt from imposing a naval blockade; and Israel would start peace negotiations with the regime that would replace Nasser's.

The conference revealed disagreements in France's top security echelon about going it alone with Israel or joining with Britain in Operation Musketeer. From Israel's perspective, as Ben-Gurion recorded in his diary, the lack of British participation would be problematic, because France's own military and political capabilities in the region were limited and might expose Israel to Egyptian reprisals. But Great Britain was not interested in any overt joint action with Israel, claiming its damage to Britain's relations with the Arab world would outweigh any operational benefit.[32] France and Israel each had reasons for seeking a British obligation to act: France needed Britain's operational capability, Middle East bases, and additional diplomatic backing, while Israel wanted to ensure the British would not attack Israel while it was busy with an operation against Egypt.

During this period from the end of September and through October, at St. Germain and afterward, Dayan was the unquestioned leader on the Israeli

---

[30] Bar-On, *Moshe Dayan*, p. 142.
[31] Henkin, *The 1956 Suez War*, p. 93.
[32] Ibid., p. 95.

side,[33] coordinating the military aspect with France and equally active on the political front. While Ben-Gurion focused on difficulties and risks, Dayan proposed solutions. He appeared self-confident and assertive even with the authoritative "old man": "I told Ben-Gurion he was going overboard with his worries about the risk of being bombed ... I might have taken too sharp a tone, but I'm not sorry."[34] Ben-Gurion acceded to Dayan's lead and did not stop the continuation of the joint preparations; still, Dayan could not solve the central problem of Great Britain at this point.

Thus, even as the IDF was preparing military plans, the political situation remained uncertain. Israel, assuming that only France would participate, planned for the IDF to fight in all of Sinai east of the Suez Canal, defeat the Egyptian army, and seize control of the peninsula. The IDF would be operating alone, although on a schedule coordinated with the French, who would be operating on a different front. This made it possible to plan free of political constraints and focus on operational considerations alone.[35]

The Egyptian army had some 100,000 regular and standing men, with a similar number in its National Guard. The ground troops included three infantry divisions, an armored division, and a separate Palestinian division. By the start of the campaign, Egypt had received weapons from the Czech arms deal, including 500 armored vehicles, 230 T-34 medium tanks, 100 mobile cannons, 200 armored personnel carriers, 200 trailed cannon barrels, 200 jet planes (150 MiG-15s and 50 medium II-28s), and 70 cargo planes, as well as two destroyers and 12 torpedo ships. While these weapons dramatically tilted the balance of power in Egypt's favor, during the Sinai Campaign the Egyptians were not yet trained on the equipment or fully proficient in its use. Nor had the Egyptian army developed a military doctrine for using these weapons.[36] This situation was one factor in Israel's decision to fight a preemptive war.

Strategically, the joint French–British threat to the Suez Canal served Israel's interests. Following its declaration of nationalization, Egypt, fearing a French–British action to retake the canal, moved one division and two armored brigades out of the Sinai Peninsula, redeploying them along the canal. Only one division remained in Sinai to defend Egypt's front with Israel, the Palestinian division defending Gaza, and two battalions (one infantry and

---

[33] Moti Golani, *Tihyeh milhama bakayits: Haderekh lemilhemet Sinai 1955–1956* (Hebrew), Tel Aviv: Maarakhot, 1997, vol. 1, p. 279.
[34] Ibid., p. 278.
[35] Mordechai Bar-On, "The Impact of Political Considerations on Operational Planning," in Moshe Shemesh and Ilan Troan (eds.), *Mivtsa Kadesh uma'arekhet Suez 1956: Iyun mehadash* (Hebrew), Sde Boker: The Ben-Gurion Heritage Institute, 1994, pp. 182–202.
[36] Yona Bendman, "Egypt: The Egyptian Army in the Sinai Campaign" (Hebrew), in Moshe Shemesh and Ilan Troan (eds.), *Mivtsa Kadesh uma'arekhet Suez 1956: Iyun mehadash* (Hebrew), Sde Boker: The Ben-Gurion Heritage Institute, 1994, pp. 65–97 (p. 65); Henkin, *The 1956 Suez War*, p. 48.

one motorized) to defend the Gulf of Aqaba and southern Sinai, respectively.[37] The Egyptian defense plan – prepared by former Wehrmacht officers working as consultants to the Egyptians – focused on northern Sinai, where they had built a deep defensive system to prevent Israel from seizing control of vital targets in the Suez Canal zone.[38]

When Dayan returned from the St. Germain conference, he felt the moment of decision was approaching. He therefore initiated preparation of the "Kadesh" plan. Some claim Dayan's initiative was aimed at pressuring Ben-Gurion to begin a process whose outcome was already known.[39] In his instructions to the High Command staff, Dayan stressed the following: "The key is speed: we must end the campaign as fast as possible." To achieve this speed and avoid a head-on confrontation, he planned on parachuting forces deep inside enemy territory, along with landing from the sea, bypassing enemy systems, and breaking through enemy lines on land.[40] Already, Dayan was planning on capturing fortifications near the Suez Canal. The plan was audacious, reflecting the fighting ethos Dayan had instilled in the army when Chief of Staff. He described the senior officers' reactions: "The knowledge that it was time to prepare for battle acted like an electric current. In terms of their emotions, those present had already entered the campaign with heart and soul ... They knew full well the meaning of the get-ready order; nonetheless, not only were they not deterred, they rejoiced at the opportunity to meet the challenge."[41] The operational instructions were consolidated into a detailed campaign plan overseen by the IDF Military Intelligence (AMAN) Director Meir Amit. The last version was finalized and officially published on October 5, 1956.

The order's "Intent" section stated that "IDF forces will conquer the northern Sinai, establish a defensive line on the east bank of the Suez Canal, and defend the state's interests in the other sectors."[42] The plans were based on an attack on two axes. The first was an attack on el-Arish by two paratrooper battalions dropped from the air and a third battalion landed by sea in tandem with Laskov's division breaking through the Rafah sector. For the second axis, the Golani infantry brigade would capture the forward fortifications and the 27th Armored Brigade would bypass from the south and join up with the paratroopers in el-Arish. The division commanded by Colonel Yehuda Wallach, which included the 7th Armored Brigade and two infantry brigades, was placed in the central axis running the length of the Nitzana–Isma'iliya Road. The 7th Brigade was expected to launch an assault near Quseima and

[37] Bendman, "Egypt," p. 71.
[38] Ibid., p. 68.
[39] Golani, *Tihyeh milhama bakayits*, vol. 1, p. 314.
[40] Bar-On, Bar-On, "The Impact of Political Considerations on Operational Planning," p. 185.
[41] Dayan, *Avnei derekh*, p. 252.
[42] Dayan, *Yoman Ma'arekhet Sinai*, Appendix 2, p. 180.

execute a rapid flanking maneuver from the south. This way, the well-fortified zone of Abu Agheila–Um Qatef would be attacked from the west and the east simultaneously. The 9th Mechanized Brigade was to provide a diversion. According to the order, all of these were to occur on "D-day" itself and end the following day, lasting no more than forty-eight hours. According to the plan, the armored brigades would, in the next stage, continue moving toward the Suez Canal and complete the clearing of the northern half of the peninsula, whereas the paratroop brigade would land near Sharm El Sheikh. The order also called for parachuting smaller forces near the Suez Canal to confuse the enemy's rear and disrupt Egypt's supply and reinforcement lines into the peninsula. The General Staff assumed that the IDF would complete the occupation of the Sinai Peninsula within four or five days.[43]

The IAF's major role in the plan would be to help the ground troops, based on the assumption that the French would extend assistance by destroying the main force of the Egyptian air force. The navy was supposed to land troops and defend Israel's shores, corresponding to its limited capabilities at that time.

In practice, the plan adopted the demand of the armored forces commanders, especially Uri Ben-Ari, to concentrate the armored forces, using it as a closed fist to deliver a knockout punch, contrary to Dayan's opinion that it was preferable to scatter the armored troops and strengthen the less-trained infantry units with tanks.

The "Kadesh" plan,[44] prepared according to Dayan's general instructions and constraints, reflected many of the key principles of war that would later become the hallmark of the IDF's doctrine. The campaign plan employed an indirect approach strategy, as IDF troops did not attack the Egyptian fortifications but, instead, attempted to bypass them and advance as fast as they could to isolate them, assuming that once cut off, the Egyptians would collapse on their own.[45] Using the armored troops as an independent concentrated steel fist fulfilled another principle – speed – imposed due to the political constraint of achieving the objectives before superpower intervention halted the IDF. The Sinai Campaign also showcased the buildup of the reserves, an issue to which Dayan paid a great deal of attention during his term as Chief of Staff. Yet another principle realized was the unprecedented scope of cooperation among the IDF's services branches (air–sea–land) and

---

[43] Bar-On, "The Impact of Political Considerations on Operational Planning," p. 186.
[44] Dayan mentions "Kadesh 1" and "Kadesh 2" in his book *Diary of the Sinai Campaign*, pp. 185–187. "Kadesh 2" was the updated version of "Kadesh 1," taking into account the political dictates decided on during the Sèvres conference.
[45] The relationship between the IDF and Liddell Hart, who coined the phrase "indirect approach," was a close one. IDF officers frequently used the phrase, whose general meaning was the attempt to avoid places where the enemy was strong and, instead, attack those enemy weak spots that, if damaged, would cause the enemy to collapse; and use lots of ruses, surprises, and deceit.

corps (armored–engineering–infantry–artillery). Above all, the campaign used the principles of surprise and deception. Strategically, the deception was to exploit the tension with Jordan to create the impression that Israel was about to go to war against Jordan, when it actually intended to fight Egypt.

Just before the campaign, the IDF received more equipment from France. On October 20, it took possession of some 100 upgraded Sherman tanks (the "super-Sherman"), 200 APCs, 300 trucks, 20 tank carriers, and more, including recovery-tanks and mine-clearing engineering tanks. Unlike the Egyptian army, the IDF integrated the equipment within days, and many of the new items got their baptism by fire in the Sinai Campaign.[46]

The plan's key goals were to advance and pose a threat to Egypt at the Suez Canal, and to occupy the northern Sinai. Opening the Straits of Tiran was among the secondary objectives. When setting these priorities, Dayan was taking into account Israel's allies, who wanted the IDF to threaten Egypt at the canal. Dayan's thinking on this was set before the finalization of the agreements at the Sèvres conference on October 22. At this point, Dayan forbade a large call-up of reservists so as to preserve the element of surprise.[47]

France invited Israel and Great Britain to another conference reserved for the most senior levels to discuss the proposal of Maurice Challe, Inspector General of the French Air Force – the "Challe scenario." At the center of the plan – to which the British agreed on October 16 – was that Israel initiate a war with Egypt, whereafter Great Britain and France would issue an ultimatum to Israel and Egypt, demanding neither come closer than 10 miles (about 16 km) of the Suez Canal so that British and French forces could deploy around it and ensure freedom of shipping. Should Egypt refuse, after seventy-two hours the allies would begin an aerial bombardment and invade and seize the canal zone. This way, Great Britain would have a pretext to get involved that avoided the appearance of cooperation with Israel. Rather, it would play the role of the responsible adult entering the region to make order and preserve stability and international trade.

France thought it had found the magic formula, but Ben-Gurion was far from enthusiastic about Israel playing the role of aggressor. Moreover, given British military support for Jordan, Ben-Gurion distrusted their intentions. He worried that the British would allow the Iraqi army into Jordan and could betray Israel with various political initiatives, such as Operation Alpha, to gain the support of Egypt and the Arab world.

Despite his reservations, Ben-Gurion could not reject the invitation of Israel's most important – in fact, only – ally to come to Paris to debate the proposal, while Dayan felt that the possibility of Israel obtaining French and

---

[46] Bar-On, *Sha'arey aza*, p. 286.
[47] Ibid., p. 269.

British help was a golden opportunity. On the eve of his flight, Dayan told Ben-Gurion:

> We must consider what might happen if we refuse and what [may happen] if we agree [to the British and French request to embark on the campaign on their terms]. If we refuse, we will be missing out on a historic opportunity that will not come again and we will have to continue to go up against Nasser by ourselves, without the French and British armies and without getting French aid in the form of the equipment they're giving us as part of the joint campaign. Do we have the confidence that we will in fact be able, politically speaking, to begin the campaign by ourselves and seize Sharm al-Sheikh to ensure freedom of shipping to Eilat?[48]

Dayan, then, had no doubt that the IDF could overcome Egypt militarily. For him, the problem was lack of political support.

Dayan, aware that Ben-Gurion feared an Egyptian bombardment of Israeli cities (Ben-Gurion, in London during World War II, had never forgotten the London Blitz), asked IAF commander Dan Tolkovsky to provide Ben-Gurion with data on Israel's aerial defense needs. The French proposed an original idea: to station French squadrons, so-called volunteer forces, to be used only if the Israeli rear were attacked from the air. At this point, Dayan contemplated a solution that would satisfy both the British demand and Ben-Gurion's concerns: "We'll execute small-scope ground assaults near the canal that will not necessarily result in an Egyptian aerial response against Israeli cities but will allow Great Britain and France to view them as a cause for intervention."[49]

On October 21, Ben-Gurion told General Challe that he would not cooperate in a scenario in which Israel plays the role of the aggressor and the global powers that of the fair and impartial mediators. Challe's reassurances to Ben-Gurion were to no avail. Still, in discussions with his close advisors Peres, Dayan, and Meir just two days earlier, Ben-Gurion was optimistic, speaking about the campaign as one that would reorganize the whole of the Middle East.[50]

The conference opened on October 22 in a chateau in the elegant Paris suburb of Sèvres.[51] The first meeting was attended by French Prime Minister Mollet, Foreign Minister Pineau, Defense Minister Bourgès-Maunoury, and their aides. The Israeli side was represented by Ben-Gurion, Dayan, Peres, and their aides. The conversation focused on the upcoming talks with the British, and Ben-Gurion used the opportunity to speak of reshaping the Middle East along the lines Israel preferred. He felt that the United States, Great Britain, France, and Israel shared an interest in unseating Nasser and redrawing the

---

[48] Dayan, *Avnei derekh*, p. 253.
[49] Ibid., p. 255.
[50] Bar-On, *Sha'arey aza*, p. 274.
[51] For a detailed account in English of the conference, see Avi Shlaim, "The Protocol of Sèvres, 1956: Anatomy of a War Plot," *International Affairs* 73:3 (1997): 509–530.

region's borders to ensure greater stability.[52] This would mean postponing any action and politically preparing the ground. However, with the French adamant that Challe's military plan was the only option, the sole discussion to be had was about improving tactical matters, such as how close to the canal Israel would be allowed to go, or cutting the time for France and Great Britain to enter the operation after it was begun by Israel, or the scope of French military assistance to Israel. There certainly would be no postponement, France explained.

Dayan noticed that in contrast to the French the Israeli delegation was more like "a rabbi and his disciples," recounting that, "Our internal consultations are not arguments and decisions, but rather attempts – Shimon Peres's and my own – to persuade Ben-Gurion to accept our suggestions. And even then, we only do it if they're of any interest to him, if he hasn't made the final decision yet himself."[53] The French acted as intermediaries between the Israelis and the British delegation, represented by British Foreign Secretary Selwyn Lloyd and his secretary Donald Logan, who later arrived in Sèvres. Dayan vividly described the encounter with Lloyd: "Britain's foreign minister may well have been a friendly man, pleasant, charming, amiable. If so, he showed near-genius in concealing these virtues. His manner could not have been more antagonistic. His whole demeanor expressed distaste – for the place, the company and the topic."[54] Lloyd was not unaware of the Israelis' suspicions. In his memoirs, he noted, "It would seem that the Israelis have no reason to trust anything a British minister might have to say."[55]

At this point, when it seemed the talks were stuck between Israel's unwillingness to be painted as aggressor, as the plan called for, and Great Britain's unwillingness to cooperate with Israel in any scenario, Dayan devised a creative suggestion to bridge the gap and give both sides what they wanted. Mordechai Bar-On, then head of the Chief of Staff's bureau and present at the meeting, described the scene, adding his interpretation:

> Before the participants scattered, Moshe Dayan addressed Ben-Gurion in Hebrew and asked for permission to make a suggestion of his own that might, he thought, help them out of the impasse. Ben-Gurion gave him permission to speak but said he did not necessarily agree. Dayan switched to English and said he wanted to say something that was his idea, and his alone. He suggested that, on D-day/zero hour, Israel would begin an offensive in Sinai with a raid deep inside Egyptian territory that would place the Israeli forces close enough to the Suez Canal for the British and

---

[52] Bar-On, *Sha'arey aza*, p. 277.
[53] Dayan, 1976, p. 260.
[54] Cited in Shlaim, "Protocol of Sèvres," p. 516.
[55] Cited in Mordechai Bar-On, "Three Days in Sèvres, October 1956: Personal Testimony" (Hebrew), in Haggai Golan and Shaul Shay (eds.), *Bir'om hamano'im: 50 shana lemilhemet Sinai* (Hebrew), Tel Aviv: Maarakhot, 2006, pp. 15–42 (p. 25).

French to claim that shipping was at risk, whereupon they would, as in Challe's scenario, be able to demand that the sides withdraw their troops. Twenty-four hours later, the Allies would begin bombing the Egyptian bases according to their operational plans.[56]

The major change Dayan was proposing to Challe's plan was that instead of Israel starting the war with full force, the first stage would involve a limited attack – a raid similar to Israeli reprisals of the preceding two years – although this time, it would be deeper and more extensive and, most importantly, would seem to endanger shipping through the Suez Canal. While Dayan preferred to shorten the time between Israel's assault and the beginning of the French and British military intervention, unlike Ben-Gurion, who insisted that the allies launch military action simultaneously with Israel, Dayan fundamentally accepted the principle that Israel would start the war by itself and allow the British to play the ultimatum game.[57]

Dayan's proposal did not solve the problem of Israel playing the aggressor, but it did solve a different essential issue: Ben-Gurion's worry that the British would get cold feet at the last minute and leave Israel alone in the war. In such a case, Dayan's plan left room for withdrawal and denial.

On the one hand, under the cover of an action that would look like a reprisal, Dayan would be able to withdraw troops if necessary, without real escalation. On the other hand, the idea meant starting the action "in reverse" by parachuting troops close to the Suez Canal and creating the appearance of an actual threat to Suez Canal shipping, whereupon Great Britain and France would be able to enter the campaign immediately without Israel being left to fight the Egyptian army on its own for an extended period of time.

The idea was both original and creative, based on military force creating a reality that would provide the political pretexts to act, with the military action having no internal military rationale other than providing the political pretexts needed to undertake the campaign. Dayan was thinking about an operation that, for the first twenty-four hours, would have two simultaneous components: a campaign starting a war against Egypt and its concluding act; that is, a short, limited military action that also served as the opening salvo in a larger military campaign. Dayan's plan would make it possible for both scenarios to occur at the same time depending on how events developed: the withdrawal of the Israeli force from the canal should Great Britain and France at the last moment decide not to intervene; and the continuation of the Israeli assault to conquer Sinai should the two allies stick to the plan.

After Dayan first introduced the idea to the French in discussions, it was time for a recess, during which Dayan fleshed out the idea for Ben-Gurion. Two weeks earlier, while planning "Kadesh," Dayan had marked several

---

[56] Bar-On, "Three Days in Sèvres," p. 23.
[57] Ibid.

west-to-east passes that were closest to the canal where he intended to parachute small paratrooper units charged with disrupting Egypt's supply lines and reinforcement routes; one of the passes was known as the Mitla. Dayan wanted to exploit the location of the pass to satisfy the Allies' demand for an Israeli presence very near the Suez Canal.

Should things go badly, he said, he'd be able to rescue the force without trouble. Because the force was a commando unit trained for raids, the Egyptians would think this was a reprisal, not the start of a full-scale war. In consultation with Peres, Dayan presented his plan in detail. A paratrooper battalion would be dropped into the Mitla Pass. At the same time, two other paratrooper battalions would seize a few border fortifications and break into Sinai to join and reinforce the parachuted troop. If necessary, all troops would retreat to the border after joining up. Shortly after the landing, Israeli infantry, without tanks or aircraft, would attack the Egyptian forward positions – to convey again the impression of a reprisal action. Thirty-six hours later, the Allies – if they kept their word – would begin an aerial bombardment to destroy the Egyptian air force. Only then would the Israeli army launch an all-out assault.

Great Britain, Lloyd said, would participate only if Israel fulfilled the role spelled out for it in Challe's scenario, that is, a full-scale assault, the English expression being "a real act of war," and then face Egypt alone for the next seventy-two hours. The British and French would issue an identical ultimatum to Israel and Egypt, noting retroactively that Israel had committed an act of aggression. Great Britain would not intervene on behalf of Jordan should Jordan attack first but would intervene should it be attacked by Israel. Also, Lloyd added, Great Britain was still supporting the Iraqi army's entry into Jordan.[58]

Ben-Gurion, outraged by the British suggestions, issued an unequivocal "no." The sides seemed to have reached an impasse. After a few hours and some more talks with the French, who were eager to make progress, Ben-Gurion raised again Dayan's idea, adding a new demand: Israel would be issued not an ultimatum, but a request not to approach the canal from the east. In any event, he said, Israel had no intention of reaching the canal. The British agreed to reduce the time between Israel's opening salvo and the allies' intervention to thirty-six hours, but no less. Moreover, the British were willing to ignore that French pilots were manning Israeli squadrons to defend Israel's airspace.

Dayan, with Ben-Gurion's blessing, sat in a room off to the side to dictate the details of Israel's suggestions and conditions, which were ultimately the basis for the agreement signed the next day:

---

[58] From Israel's point of view, the possibility of the Iraqi army entering Jordan crossed a red line because the significance was a strong military coalition to the east threatening to split Israel at its narrow waist.

- Israel would not begin a full-scale war but, instead, would embark on an action that would be perceived as a threat to freedom of shipping in the Suez Canal.
- Instead of issuing an ultimatum to Israel, the allies would issue an "appeal," with language different from that in the ultimatum issued to Egypt.
- Great Britain and France would join the fighting no later than thirty-six hours after Israel's first strike.
- As part of the call to stop its act of war, Egypt would also be asked to stop its acts of aggression against Israel.
- Two French squadrons of Mystère fighter planes with French pilots would be stationed in Israel, and two French battleships would be anchored near Israel's shores.
- Great Britain would not help Jordan or Iraq should either or both attack Israel. Israel pledged not to attack Jordan.
- Israel's intention was to annex the territory east of the el-Arish/Sharm El Sheikh line; France and Great Britain would not oppose this annexation.

Lloyd noted Dayan's plan in his diary and, on the 23rd, left for London to report to the British Cabinet. Foreign Minister Pineau, lacking confidence that Lloyd had fully grasped Dayan's plan, followed him to London to report directly to British Prime Minister Eden. It would later emerge that Lloyd had indeed failed to fully understand the complexity of Dayan's "both this and that" plan and simply reported to the cabinet that Israel was refusing to meet the condition of starting a full-scale war.

While France and Israel awaited the British response in Sèvres, the former proposed staging an Egyptian bombing that would serve as a pretext for attacking Egypt. Dayan rejected the idea outright. "You can't stage reality," he said. "Reasons for attacking Egypt are strewn along the entire border like grains of sand." Ben-Gurion, clearly torn, continued debating the idea. While the representatives in Sèvres were still deliberating on how to cooperate, news came that an Egyptian cargo ship loaded with weapons destined for the Algerian rebels had just been intercepted off Oran. The French were stunned, and there was strong public pressure on France to act against Nasser.[59]

Meanwhile, with Pineau still in London, the Israeli leaders used the time for internal consultations. Ben-Gurion presented Dayan with twenty questions, about which Dayan would later write, "A weight was lifted from my heart": Based on the type of questions – all relating to "how" – he realized that "if" was no longer an issue. Ben-Gurion had decided in favor of action.[60]

---

[59] Paul Gaujac, "France and the Crises of Suez: An Appraisal Forty Years" in *The 1956 War: Collusion and Rivalry in the Middle East* (Abingdon: Routledge, 2014), pp. 47–64 (p. 56).
[60] Dayan, *Avnei derekh*, p. 262.

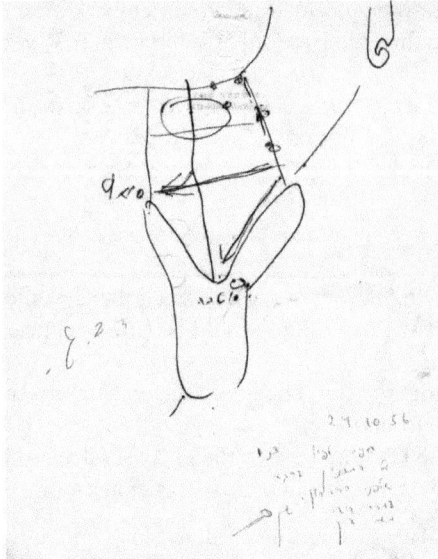

Figure 4.1 Dayan's Sinai campaign plan on a pack of cigarettes, 1956.

Wanting to add a graphic sketch to his verbal description, Dayan began looking around for a scrap of paper. Peres handed him a pack of cigarettes on which Dayan drew a map of the Sinai Peninsula and the anticipated troop movements. "I was happy we didn't have a [real] map of Sinai handy: on the white cigarette pack – without the mountains, dunes, and *wadis* – the plan looked not only clear but also simple and easy to execute."[61] Years later, Peres related in an interview that he asked both Dayan and Ben-Gurion to sign the packet, which then became an official state document (Figure 4.1). Every night, Peres recounted, he and Dayan would prepare answers to Ben-Gurion's list of questions.[62]

Dayan explained to Ben-Gurion that parachuting a paratrooper battalion and having two other paratrooper battalions, accompanied by tanks, joining up with the first would prevent the British from claiming that this was an insufficient pretext for the intervention the Israelis sought, as decided on in Sèvres. Dayan, with his typical wisecracking, said that on the maps the statesmen were using, where the ratios were much smaller than those of military maps, the paratroopers' drop would look very close to the canal.[63]

[61] Ibid., p. 263.
[62] Yossi Melman, "Sinai Campaign Plan on Cigarette Packet; IDF Archive Reveals Secret Files from the Sinai Campaign," *Haaretz*, October 7, 2006.
[63] Bar-On, "Three Days in Sèvres," p. 32.

In the meantime, back in London, Pineau had managed to persuade Eden that Dayan's plan satisfied British demands. He returned to Sèvres with a document that was essentially Britain's agreement to Israel's conditions.[64] The parties decided that the action would begin on October 29. Later, the British representatives also arrived back in Sèvres, whereupon the document of understandings was drawn up, in which Israel basically achieved the entire list of demands Dayan had presented to Pineau before the latter left for London. The agreement was signed that evening.[65] The telegram Dayan sent to Meir Amit read: "Chances for an imminent war in Sinai are high. Call up Zarro's units [Meir Zorea's armored troops]. Make sure the call-up remains secret; immediately, execute a deception in the direction of Jordan vis-à-vis Iraq's entrance."[66] Immediately after returning to Israel, Dayan made the necessary adaptation to the "Kadesh" plan renaming it "Kadesh 2."

During this time, there were developments on the opposing side as well. On October 25, talks began among the armies of Jordan, Egypt, and Syria, after which they announced the establishment of a joint command and full coordination among them. The Iraqi division again prepared to move. Four days before the Sinai Campaign, Israel seemed to be in a very difficult position – facing a new Arab coalition. Furthermore, Egypt was receiving weapons from the Soviet Union, and Jordan had its British military umbrella. But this situation actually served Dayan's ruse, because the call-up of IDF troops was perceived as being aimed at Jordan, where conflict was expected to erupt as the border heated up. And it was clear that, for Israel, the entrance of Iraqi troops into Jordan would be a *casus belli*.

The problem Dayan now faced was the secrecy in which the Sèvres agreements were shrouded, mostly because the British did not want to reveal their cooperation with Israel. Dayan, obligated by his promise to Ben-Gurion to do everything to fulfill Israel's part in the deal, shared what he knew only with Meir Amit and a few close officers and assistants, including Shlomo Gazit. Dayan gathered all senior IDF officers and, without revealing the essence of the Sèvres agreements, gave them instructions, including the principles for formulating the campaign plan:

- Separate the actions Israel would undertake on behalf of the Allies and those it would undertake for its own ends.
- The army would act alone for thirty-six hours, during which as little military action as possible would be taken.
- From the moment of the intervention, it was necessary to act quickly, especially with regard to seizing control of the Tiran Straits.

[64] Bar-On, *Sha'arey aza*, p. 285.
[65] For the document's fate, see Mordechai Bar-On, *Gvulot ashenim: Iyunim betoldot medinat yisrael 1948–1976* (Hebrew), Jerusalem: Yad Ben Zvi, 2001.
[66] Cited in Bar-On, *Sha'arey aza*, p. 288.

- At this stage, secrecy was of the essence, and consequently, some of the instructions given would seem bizarre and contrary to military rationale. Therefore, blind obedience was required.[67]

Even before the Sèvres conference, Ben-Gurion had told Dayan he was very worried about heavy losses in this war. Dayan promised there would be no more than 250 casualties. According to Gazit, who was present at this conversation, the army expected very few losses; this assessment, which Dayan pronounced with assurance, influenced Ben-Gurion's decision to support a campaign. When they left the meeting, Gazit asked Dayan how he could give such a promise with such certitude, Dayan answered, "If the decision is made to go to war and we win, no one will go back to check and argue about the number of casualties; but if, God forbid, we lose, we will all have much worse things to worry about."[68]

Still, Dayan took casualties – the IDF's and the enemy's – with utter seriousness, as reflected in his instructions on "defeating enemy forces" but "not destroying enemy forces." "Best that less blood be spilled," Dayan said, and therefore his goals of his instructions were "disrupting the Egyptian forces and making them collapse."[69]

The new plan, "Kadesh 2," differed in five major ways from the original "Kadesh 1" plan, all relating to the first stage – those thirty-six hours in which the IDF was in a state of full-scale war against Egypt disguised as a large reprisal until the allies' intervention:[70]

1. The IAF would limit itself to defending the nation's skies and would not attack Egyptian air-force bases.
2. The political constraints meant that the IDF's best brigade had to be deployed not to conquer el-Arish and Sharm El Sheikh but rather to satisfy the British pretext for a real act of war. On the other hand, only the paratroopers could jump far behind enemy lines and thus provide the pretext for the campaign in general.
3. Instead of breaking past the enemy lines immediately, engaging in flanking maneuvers deep into the enemy system, and exploiting speed and surprise to shock and collapse the enemy, the armored troops now had to wait at the starting line for thirty-six hours.
4. The mission of conquering Israel's major target, Sharm El Sheikh, intended to break the blockade on Eilat, was given to a mechanized reserves brigade that was supposed to make its way through the desert. This was far from

---

[67] Bar-On, "The Impact of Political Considerations on Operational Planning," p. 191.
[68] Shlomo Gazit, *Bitsmatim makhri'im: Mehapalmah lerashut aman* (Hebrew), Rishon Lezion: Miskal, 2016, p. 94.
[69] Dayan, *Avnei derekh*, p. 267.
[70] Bar-On, "The Impact of Political Considerations on Operational Planning," p. 192.

optimal, but because the paratroopers brigade had been tasked with a different mission, there was no force left to parachute in or land from the sea.

5. Regarding French military aid, despite the General Staff's assessment that the IDF did not need any external assistance whatsoever, Dayan and Ben-Gurion insisted – for political reasons – on accepting military aid directly from France. The French provided two squadrons to defend the nation's skies and warships sailing the Mediterranean near the coast of Gaza to provide artillery assistance. Ultimately, it emerged that the assistance was, militarily speaking, redundant but politically significant.

Dayan's Sèvres plan may have helped the parties resolve the impasse they had reached. However, its translation into operative terms meant that Israel's strike force – the armored troops and the air force – were on standby for thirty-six hours, in complete and utter contradiction of the approach Dayan, as Chief of Staff, had instilled in IDF commanders: forward assault, initiative, audacity, and speed. And because he could not share his reasons with the field command ranks, they felt intensely frustrated. This discontent threatened to unravel the fragile plan Dayan had so painstakingly woven together.

Commanding the Theater

Dayan's advancement through the army ranks had certainly been meteoric. Within a mere seven or eight years, he had risen from battalion commander to commander of all of Israel's armed forces. On October 29, 1956, he found himself leading them into battle, which made him commander of a theater of war. Of the uniqueness of command of a theater, Edward Luttwak wrote:

> Because the logic of strategy at the theater level relates military strength to territorial space, we can understand much of it in visual terms, examining forces and their movements in a bird's eye view, or perhaps one should say in a satellite overview. Of course, strategy has a spatial aspect at every level, but at the tactical level it is the detailed nature of the terrain that matters, while the combat encounters of the operational level could be much the same in any number of different geographical settings. At the theater level, however, some specific territory is the very object of the struggle. It may be as large as a continent or as small as an island; it can be a province, a region, an entire country, or a group of countries; but in any case, a "theater of war" must form a reasonably self-contained space rather than just one part of a larger whole.[71]

---

[71] Edward Luttwak, *Strategy: The Logic of War and Peace*, revised edition, Cambridge, MA: Harvard University Press, 2001, p. 138.

Dayan's theater, the Sinai Peninsula, was notable for some unique features: a desert expanse with many barely passable sections, and mountain ranges with a limited number of passes suited to a military force.

The first stage of the campaign was the call-up, which had to involve misdirection and secrecy about Israel's real intentions. Immediately after the Sèvres conference closed, Dayan told Meir Amit: "Trigger a ruse aimed at Jordan having to do with Iraq's entrance [into the theater] at once."[72] With Israel's ground troops depending mainly on its reservists, a call-up of reservists was liable to reveal the army's offensive intentions. This time, tensions with Jordan over the Qalqilya action and the news that Iraqi forces were about to cross into Jordan worked in Israel's favor. The deception aimed at both external and internal consumption, and erroneous reports that the Iraqi army was already in Jordan were leaked intentionally so that the called-up reservists would think they were on their way to fight Jordan.

The time left until the start of the campaign allowed for minimal training and force-deployment opportunities. All efforts were directed at calling up the troops, arming them, and hurriedly preparing them. Dayan closely followed the call-up in person.[73] The units got organized at their home bases, and because Israel is so small and enjoys the advantage of "interior lines,"[74] the troops could depart for the Egyptian border with just a few hours to spare before the start of the war. There was another helpful external development: These preparations took place while the eyes of the world were focused on an entirely different global crises – the Hungarian uprising against the USSR, which began on October 23. The British believed that Eisenhower, also facing reelection, would support a move leading to Nasser's ouster, an assessment that turned out to be completely wrong.

The campaign's second stage began with actions that today would be called special operations. On the night of October 28, an IAF [Gloster] Meteor NF-13 plane lifted off. It flew over the Mediterranean near the Lebanese–Syrian border, thus kicking off Operation Tarnegol (Rooster): the objective – downing an aircraft carrying the Egyptian Chief of Staff Abdul Hakim Amar and General Staff members back home from an official visit in Syria. According to intelligence, they had been drawing up joint plans to attack Israel.[75] The Israeli

---

[72] Cited in Golani, *Tihyeh milhama bakayits*, p. 425.
[73] Ibid., p. 428.
[74] A concept coined by Antoine-Henri Jomini, a nineteenth-century military thinker. It refers to a central position on one side that gives that side an advantage. Interior lines make it possible to quickly move from one front to another to stop an invading army or to preempt it by penetrating enemy lines as well as to speed up military moves and increase the chances of surprise, critical for a nation seeking a rapid victory.
[75] For a description of the operation, see Henkin, *The 1956 Suez War*, pp. 119–121; and Yoash Zidon-Chato, *Bayom, balayil ba'arafel* (Hebrew), Or Yehuda: Maariv Library, 1995, pp. 223–227.

Meteor night-fighter flew so close to the Ilyushin, the Soviet-made transport planes supplied to the Egyptians, that the pilots were able to look through the windows and ascertain that all the passengers were indeed military officers. After the plane's identification was absolutely certain, they were given the green light to fire. The Egyptian pilot did not have a chance to report the hit, and the plane plunged into the sea. Eighteen of Egypt's most senior officers perished, but not Amar, who was not on the plane, having decided to postpone his own return. In hindsight, Israel benefited from Amar's survival, because it emerged that he was poorly equipped to run the army; had he perished, he might have been replaced with someone better qualified. But the immediate significance was that Egypt entered the war missing half of its senior General Staff officers. For thirty-two years, the Egyptians believed that plane crash was an accident, learning the truth only after Israel published details of the operation.

After the pilots' return, Dayan toasted them at IDF headquarters. "When you downed the Egyptian General Staff, you won half the war," Dayan told them. "Now let's lift our glasses to [winning] the second half."[76]

Another component of the second part of the campaign would be defined today as an information operation. On October 29, at 2 p.m., six Mustang fighter planes lifted off from the air-force base in Ekron. They were equipped with a specially constructed device consisting of a rope and a weight at its end meant to cut the telephone lines from the Egyptian command centers in Sinai to the army's headquarters in Cairo, thereby cutting the Egyptian units in Sinai off from their commanders. The assumption was that the Egyptians would immediately switch to using wireless radio communications, which were relatively easy for Israel to intercept and decode. The improvised cutting devices failed, and the pilots resorted to cutting the phone lines with their planes' wings and propellers. They succeeded in cutting almost all communications lines; all planes returned safely to base. As they were flying home, sixteen Dakotas – in four waves of four – full of Israeli paratroopers and accompanied by Mystère and Ouragan planes were already headed for the Mitla Pass.[77]

The third stage was the first significant military action, whose entire rationale was to serve as a political pretext in accordance with the agreement reached in Sèvres. The force was supposed to land west of the Mitla Pass, but the photography sorties by the IAF had revealed a small tent encampment that could possibly be an Egyptian force stationed there. Not wanting to initiate a battle while the force was alone, the landing site was shifted to a site a few kilometers east of the Mitla. The new site was 60 kilometers east of the Suez Canal and could not really be seen as a threat to the Suez Canal by anyone

---

[76] Cited in Henkin, *The 1956 Suez War*, p. 120.
[77] Ibid., pp. 121–122.

familiar with the topography, but, as Dayan said, on a typical geographic map used by the media and politicians, the change would not be noticed.[78]

While waiting for the rest of the brigade to join them with trucks to carry them back to Israel if the war was aborted, the paradropped battalion was exposed to possible Egyptian counterattacks – especially since to provide the pretext the action had to be published in the media. Digging in, the battalion received assistance and supplies from the air, including from the French planes stationed in Cyprus. The battalion dug in and waited. Twelve Mystères circled the paratroopers two-by-two to provide them with aerial cover.

On October 29 at 5 p.m., the 890th Paratroop Battalion made the jump, hiked 7 kilometers to a location near the eastern entrance to the Mitla Pass, and dug in to wait. Meanwhile, the rest of the 202nd Paratrooper Brigade, reinforced by engineering tanks and smaller field artillery pieces, drove across the border to join up with the parachuted battalion. The trek was long, and en route they had to defeat small Egyptian forces. Advancing roughly 200 kilometers in approximately 30 hours, the brigade joined the 890th Battalion and enlarged the perimeter of its hastily prepared defensive position. For the most part, other than being on the eastern, rather than the western, end of the Pass, this stage unfolded according to the original plan.

Simultaneously with the central "pretext" move at the Mitla, the IDF continued to call up and assemble its forces and operate at other locations to prepare for the large-scale action. In case the 202 Paratrooper Brigade did not reach the paradropped battalion, the IDF planned two other routes to reach it: the 4th Infantry Brigade attacked through the fortified Egyptian defenses at Quseima and the 9th Infantry Brigade drove south from Eilat. In addition to preparing alternative routes to reach the paratroopers, these actions also were the first stage for preparing the advance through northern Sinai and the advance to Sharm El Sheikh.

At this point, Cairo began receiving reports from Egyptian patrols on Israeli troops movements in Sinai. That night, the Voice of Israel radio station reported on raids of Fedayeen targets near the border and the Suez Canal. The mention of the canal was critical in providing the Allies with the pretext they wanted. The Egyptians were confused. According to Egyptian journalist Muhammad Hassin Hakel, considered a close confidant of Nasser, the president called him and said, "Something very strange is happening. The Israelis are in Sinai and they seem to be fighting the sands, because they are occupying one empty position after the other!"[79]

On October 29, a few hours before the paratroopers' jump, Nasser sympathizers passed on information to the Egyptian military attaché in Paris that Israel, Great Britain, and France were planning to attack Egypt.

---

[78] Golani, *Tihyeh milhama bakayits*, p. 444.
[79] Henkin, *The 1956 Suez War*, p. 124.

Unconvinced,[80] Nasser and his staff hypothesized that the act might be the start of an all-out Israeli assault, but nothing more. Therefore, the Egyptians decided to reinforce their troops in Sinai and sent in two brigades held in reserve. The Egyptians intended to use bombers to blow up IAF bases, but the Egyptian air-force command soon discovered its planes had no fuel. It also became clear that the Egyptian General Staff had suffered a severe blow from the deaths of its eighteen senior officers; the skills of the remaining officers, Nasser political appointments, were subpar, and they were having difficulties putting together an effective response.

Until this point, events had gone more or less according to plan; but things soon began to go wrong. Although a desert, the Sinai Peninsula's topography limits free movement, with large zones of dunes, steep mountains, and *wadis* making vehicular passage nearly impossible. The war in Sinai was fought over control of the passable routes with which it was possible to control the whole peninsula. Israel's war plan focused on breaking through on two major routes in the northern Sinai to head for the Canal, and on a third route located farther south to head for Sharm El Sheikh on the shore of the Tiran Straits.

According to "Kadesh 2," after the Allies' intervention, thirty-six hours after the paradrop at the Mitla Pass, the 77th Division would enter via the northernmost axis, Rafah–el-Arish–Qantra. The 38th Division, the IDF's largest and strongest division, which included the 7th Brigade, the army's only armored brigade, was tasked with seizing control of the central and most convenient axis in Sinai, between Nitsana and Isma'iliya, thereby splitting the Sinai in two. The division's objective was to seize control also of secondary routes going through Quseima and Abu Agheila that allowed passage to Bir Gifgafa and to Bir Hasana in the depths of Sinai. The Egyptians, well aware of the importance of this central axis, had built a tight network of fortifications in the area, defended by 6,000 soldiers.

Thus, the Sinai theater was divided into two sectors:

- The central sector, where the 38th Division commanded by Colonel Yehuda Wallach was located. Colonel Assaf Simhoni, the Commander of the Southern Command, was the direct commander of the sector.
- The northern sector, the site of the 77th Division commanded by Major General Haim Laskov, under direct command of the General Staff.

The Chief of Staff also directly commanded the 9th Brigade, whose function was to move through the southernmost route from Eilat to Sharm El Sheikh, and the 202nd Paratrooper Brigade.

The 7th Armored Brigade was commanded by Colonel Uri Ben-Ari, who had already proven capable of executing a lightning maneuver with his

[80] Ibid.

armored force. It was under command of the Southern Command, but not to be used without General Staff approval.

This disorganized command structure created command and control difficulties.

The skilled and dynamic Southern Command commander Simhoni, well liked by Ben-Gurion, was now facing a difficult dilemma. Not having been entrusted with the secret of the political agreements and the Sèvres ploy, he could not fathom why the paratroopers had been taken from their original mission and sent to a totally unimportant location in the desert, nor why he was not allowed to use his tanks and was limited in the use of most of his force. As Dayan had anticipated, the campaign plan seemed bizarre, even irrational, to Simhoni. Simhoni was certain the Egyptians would respond with full force to the initial Israeli moves. Assessing that the IAF was not about to attack Egyptian air forces to prevent them from attacking Israeli ground forces, Simhoni thought it was time to act, because pace and speed are critical in operations such as this one. "The General Staff's gone crazy," he told his subordinates.[81] Therefore, he ignored Dayan's explicit orders to the General Staff demanding blind obedience even if the orders seemed irrational.[82]

There was also a personal aspect: Simhoni was embittered by Dayan's attitude to him and because he had not been promoted to major general when appointed to command the Southern Command. In addition, Simhoni's closeness with Ben-Gurion gave him confidence in defying Dayan. During the war, Simhoni's criticism and anger toward Dayan mounted; on one occasion, he went so far as to say, "Dayan has got to go ... Ben-Gurion promised me I'd be appointed Chief of Staff."[83]

The Prussian military philosopher Carl von Clausewitz spoke about the rules of military grammar, the internal set of rules that guides military moves and is liable to clash with the political rationale it serves. That was the situation in the Southern Command before October 29. Simhoni probably had some awareness of the political constraints but found it difficult to accept their ramifications for military planning.[84] Being sure that waiting would allow the enemy to be proactive, he ordered that the 38th Division and 7th Brigade troops prepare for immediate entry to Sinai. His justification was "intelligence reports" – later found to be wrong – regarding Egyptian troop movements from west of Abu Agela.[85]

---

[81] Amos Carmel (research: Tsila Rosenblit), *Aluf hanitsahon: Assaf Simhoni* (Hebrew), Tel Aviv: Miskal, 2009, p. 314.
[82] Cited in Golani, *Tihyeh milhama bakayits*, p. 482.
[83] Simhoni said this in a conversation with Uzi Narkiss, then assistant to the Director of Military Intelligence. Cited in Henkin, *The 1956 Suez War*, p. 138.
[84] See testimony of Yeshayahu Gavish, Director of Operations, General Staff, in Bar-On (ed.), *Lenochach gvulot oyevim: tzava ubitachon ba'asor harishon shel medinat Yisrael*, p. 330.
[85] Golani, *Tihyeh milhama bakayits*, p. 457.

On the night of October 29, the 38th Division sent a brigade each to attack Quseima and Um Qatef but ran into difficulty taking the Egyptian positions. The attack at Um Qatef failed completely, and the one at Quseima had only partial success. Simhoni decided not to wait – he ordered 7th Armored Brigade to attack through Quseima, turn north, and attack Um Qatef from its rear. The brigade commander also sent some of his force to advance deep into Sinai.

This decision would remain the heart of a deeply visceral, years-long fight between supporters of Dayan and Simhoni loyalists.[86] In Simhoni's defense was the claim that he operated in a gray area, that he applied a senior commander's scrutiny and deliberation on the ground exactly as Dayan would have expected of him, and, most importantly, that he made a point of reporting the entry of the 7th Brigade to the Sinai zone to the Supreme Command, thinking that if the move was problematic, he would be instructed to stop. But the answer he got made him think he had its authority to proceed.[87] Perhaps in the fog of war, the people in the Command did not fully comprehend the meaning of the move. Dayan himself was not told of Simhoni's decision till after it was implemented. Simhoni was convinced he had done what he was obligated to do as a commander, and therefore any allegations against him were unfounded and overstated.

Dayan left the Supreme Command outpost early in the campaign and, as was his wont, went to observe on-the-ground events in person. In the morning of the 30th, he received word about the 7th Brigade's advance. Although he was seething with rage that the brigade had entered deep into Egyptian territory, given the ramifications if the British and French did not join the war, he understood it was pointless to try to change the move now. He now had no choice but to try to exploit the brigade's military successes and hope they wouldn't damage the political plan. This decision is evidence of Dayan's flexible nature and sensitivity to changing reality and new opportunities. He wasn't wedded to any plan, not even his own. Dayan visited Simhoni's headquarters at noon. There, according to various testimonies, he dressed Simhoni down for ignoring his orders.[88] In his diary he wrote:

> Yesterday, I brutally clashed with the Commander of the Southern Command who, against the General Staff order, activated the 7th Armored Brigade before the designated time ... Despite the explicit instructions ... despite the explanations of the reasons for the order, the Southern Command Commander clung to his opinion that there was not a moment to lose and, immediately as the action began, it

---

[86] In Yechiam Weitz's review of *Aluf hanitsahon*, he wrote, "To a large extent, this book was written as a way for the Simhoni family to settle its account with Dayan himself and his supporters and loyalists"; "The Marshall's Baton in His Rucksack" (Hebrew), *Haaretz*, December 15, 2009.
[87] Carmel, *Aluf hanitsahon*, pp. 322–327.
[88] See, for example, Uzi Narkiss's testimony in Henkin, *The 1956 Suez War*, p. 138.

was necessary to seize the initiative, the element of surprise, to the extent possible. He therefore decided to deploy all the forces at his disposal already on D-day ... He views the General Staff instructions on the matter as a political and military blunder that we are destined to pay for dearly in the future ... I did not have a shadow of a doubt about the order now required, and I already saw in my mind's eye all the tanks turning around and returning to the staging area in Nahal Ruth as they had come. In terms of order and discipline, there is no doubt that this must be the order issued, but is it the right order in terms of the conduct of the campaign?[89]

Simhoni's move had placed Dayan in a quandary: to stop the brigade and even have it go back for the sake of sticking to the plan and his promise to Ben-Gurion, or to exploit the military success the brigade had attained to continue the momentum? Dayan chose the latter:

What's done cannot be undone. If the progress of the armored brigade into Sinai does in fact cause an increased Egyptian action (especially aerial) before the time we set, we cannot prevent it now, and it is therefore better to generate the maximal benefit possible from the armored brigade's entrance into the campaign.[90]

Dayan met in person with Ben-Ari and briefed him himself, cutting Simhoni – Ben-Ari's direct commander – out of the loop. Bar-On described the purpose of the advance as: "The brigade should advance westwards and penetrate everywhere it is easy to do so and without heavy losses. Everywhere the brigade encounters opposition, it must stop and direct the rest of the troops to new routes ... the forces must flow like a stream finding its way through many channels and choosing the most convenient passes for its waters to flow."[91] This was not the first time Dayan was accused of skipping over the chain of command. But this move may be viewed in several ways. Military doctrine distinguishes between skipping the ranks and shortening the chain of command. In practice, they appear the same, but the circumstances and justification to employ them are different. Skipping the chain of command refers to a commander issuing binding orders directly to a commander further down the chain of command, that is, a rank or two or more lower than the individual issuing the order. This is hardly ideal; bypassing ranks is detrimental and forbidden because it violates the principle of unity of command. In contrast, shortening the chain of command does not violate the unity of command and therefore is permitted by military doctrine only temporarily and only for the period of time necessary to exploit an opportunity or respond to a risk. In this case, where Dayan viewed intervention as necessary because of

---

[89] Dayan, *Yoman Ma'arekhet Sinai*, pp. 80–82.
[90] Ibid., p. 82.
[91] Ibid.

a fundamental change to the plan, and given the rapid rate of operations and movement, it is certainly arguable that he operated in accordance with the rules of shortening the chain of command.[92]

Dayan's words reflected the indirect approach, called the maneuverist approach by the US Army in the 1980s. This approach is based on deep penetration and avoidance of areas where the enemy is strong and depends on rapid movement that also destabilizes the enemy. The starting point of this approach is not finding the enemy's concentration of strength but staying far from it and exploiting superiority against the enemy's points of weakness. Success depends on a combination of surprise and lightning-speed execution so that the weakness is attacked before the enemy can respond.[93] Thus the orders given to the 7th Brigade to follow the paths of least resistance and disengage from engagements with major enemy forces.

Despite Dayan's anger at Simhoni and Ben-Ari, he knew that their conduct was a direct result of the military lessons and culture he had himself instilled in the IDF, with initiative and aggression the supreme values. He therefore concluded: "Despite all my displeasure both at the violation of discipline and at the deployment of the 7th Brigade ahead of time and without a suitable plan, I could not deny the sympathy I felt for the armored brigade going into action before permission was granted." In his diary, he wrote what would become the IDF's motto for decades: "better to be engaged in restraining the noble stallion than in prodding the reluctant ox."[94]

On the night of October 30–31, Ben-Ari – heeding Dayan's instructions to bypass hurdles – moved his brigade through the al-Deja Pass, enabling him to encircle Um Qatef northward and reach the western road to Isma'iliya and the Suez Canal.[95] While one battalion captured the rear positions of the Egyptian Um Qatef defensive system, the others continued west, defeating the Egyptian 1st Armored Brigade en route. On November 2, the first tanks of the 7th were stopped some 16 kilometers from the canal, just as the agreement with the Allies had stipulated. Speed of success also brought dangers – Israeli aircraft mistook the brigade units so far in the Egyptian rear for Egyptians and attacked them.

Meanwhile, the battle at Um Qatef was going badly for the Israelis. The 10th Reserve Infantry Brigade was ill prepared, and its commander, Shmuel Guder, made several major blunders in planning and conducting the battle.[96] Dayan

---

[92] Ekked, Operations Division, Doctrine and Training, *Tora b'sisit matkalit: Pikud ushlita* (Hebrew), November 2006, pp. 123–125.
[93] The approach is described in Luttwak, *Strategy*, pp. 126; discussion about attrition on pp. 126–130.
[94] Dayan, *Yoman Ma'arekhet Sinai*, p. 85.
[95] Uri Ben Ari, *No'a tanu'a! Sof: Hamaavak al derekh hashiryon* (Hebrew), Tel Aviv: Maarakhot, 1998, pp. 274–275.
[96] Henkin, *The 1956 Suez War*, p. 148.

passed a message along to Guder that unless he carried out the mission, he would be dismissed. By morning, it was clear the assault had failed. The brigade's battalions, after getting lost and realizing they were fighting peripheral positions only, retreated at dawn. Guder later gave Dayan a long list of excuses for the failed attack. An enraged Dayan dismissed him.

On the night of October 31, Dayan brought the 37th Brigade into the fight. This was supposedly an armored brigade, but in practice, it was in its initial stages of constitution and only partially trained and equipped. Dayan wanted to deploy the brigade to assist the 10th Brigade, now believing that tanks were the key to success in the desert. Intelligence reports on the anticipated approach of Egypt's 1st Armored Division reinforced his decision, and thus the 37th Brigade was sent into battle. However, with its commander, Shmuel Glinka, overeager to fight, it was inserted too quickly into battle.[97] From the entire brigade, only two battalions attacked, and these were conducted badly. The attack was stopped by heavy Egyptian fire, and the troops retreated with heavy losses: twenty dead and sixty-five wounded, including Glinka, who later died of his wounds.

Dayan assumed responsibility for the flawed assault, writing, "This mistake happened at the ranks above the fighting units. The disintegrating fighting – the command, the General Staff, and the Chief of Staff (me) are responsible for that."[98] In his judgment, the reasons for failure were the pressure he had exerted on the command to develop the axis and the command's mistaken assessment that the Egyptian resistance in Um Qatef was crumbling. Furthermore, there were significant command and control problems on the part of the forward command and the Supreme Command outposts, as well as errors in understanding where the forces were located due to confused reports.[99]

On the battlefield, the will of both sides is tested, and the question is who will break first. The party that delays its breaking point wins. And, indeed, despite the Israelis' blunders and failures, by November 1, the Egyptians in the fortified zone of Um Qatef, having endured poundings from the ground and air, were utterly spent. At 5 p.m., the Egyptian command, following the beginning of the Franco-British offensive on the Suez Canal, decided to concentrate its forces on defending Egypt proper and ordered them to retreat. Furthermore, the Egyptians had exhausted their supply and ammunition capabilities. The retreat, which began in an orderly fashion, turned into a frightened melee, and most of the Egyptian force fell into Israeli captivity.[100] The battle for Um Qatef was over, and Dayan – very unhappy with the Israeli forces' hesitancy and unwieldiness – laconically remarked, "The Egyptians fought well while we

---

[97] Golani, *Tihyeh milhama bakayits*, p. 500.
[98] Ibid., p. 501.
[99] Ibid.; Shabtai Teveth, *Moshe Dayan: Biografia* (Hebrew), Tel Aviv: Schoken, 1971, p. 465.
[100] Henkin, *The 1956 Suez War*, p. 154.

fought badly."[101] However, he leveled the most criticism at the Egyptian defensive concept demonstrated at Um Qatef:

> I don't know if the doctrine the Egyptians adopted is something they got from their British or German or Russian teachers. Whatever the case, according to the Egyptian General Staff approach, the Abu Agheila system was supposed to have served as a barrier to an assault on Sinai in the central sector of Qusayma–Nitsana. The Egyptian command decided that this defense, built on six major forts – Qusaym and Um Qatef, Um Sihan, Abu Agela, Sakhar Ruefa, and Ras Matamor – held by an infantry brigade with assisting elements – must stop an Israeli attempt to break through and destroy any enemy unit that managed to penetrate.[102]

Dayan added that the power of these forts to stop troops in the Sinai Desert was inadequate, noting that these were not the type of huge European fortifications that can control the length and breadth of entire regions.[103] From Dayan's perspective, Egypt's major failing was its concept of static warfare. His critique of Egypt's passive fighting is understandable; of greater interest is the comparison he drew between Europe and Sinai, just as he had done in his battalion commanders' course, when he was requested to plan his defense against an Egyptian invasion of Israel. Dayan again stressed the unique context and the fact that it is simply not possible to copy a certain model from one place to another.

On October 31, in the morning, Israel received a message that the Allies' entry would be delayed. Ben-Gurion's deep-seated worries about an Allied betrayal now seemed justified. It was only later that Israel realized the delay was due to operational circumstances: The Allies' militaries needed a longer staging time than planned because the political echelon's schedule had not taken into consideration the pace of military organization.

Meanwhile, a ferocious battle with many casualties on both sides had ensued at the Mitla Pass – a location chosen deliberately to avoid such a battle. Dayan learned the details of what happened when he returned to the command center in Ramla, having already heard highlights over the wireless. Because of the change in the parachute drop site, the force was deployed east of the Pass in open ground. The brigade commander, Ariel Sharon, was not privy to the reason his brigade had been sent to the Mitla Pass and that its mission, once the Allies joined the war, had been fulfilled. He knew only that the original objective had been west of the Pass and had been changed to prevent a lone battalion engaging with a possibly superior enemy. Furthermore, intelligence reports suggested an enemy armored force was advancing toward the Pass from the west. If that force attacked the brigade in its current position, with its

---

[101] Carmel, *Aluf hanitsahon*, p. 340.
[102] Dayan, *Yoman Ma'arekhet Sinai*, p. 112.
[103] Ibid., pp. 112–113.

Figure 4.2 Sinai Campaign 1956, General Moshe Dayan with Colonel Ariel Sharon. Source: Universal History Archive/Contributor/Universal Images Group/Getty Images.

very light complement of antitank weapons, it might be overwhelmed. Sharon wanted to enter the Pass, where enemy armor would be limited in its ability to maneuver and he would come closer to the original objective (Figure 4.2).

On the morning of October 31, Head of Central Command Rehavam Zeevi was sent to observe the situation. Zeevi forbade Sharon to enter the Pass with his whole force but permitted him to send a patrol. Sharon sent a large patrol to see if it would be possible to seize and hold the Pass and allow the rest of the brigade to deploy. What Sharon did not know was that five infantry companies from the Egyptian 2nd Brigade had arrived earlier and had already deployed on the steep slopes on either side of the Pass, armed with 57 mm antitank cannons and recoilless cannons, presenting a deadly ambush for any force entering the Pass. Sharon, waiting for Dayan to show up, stayed behind, leaving Deputy Brigade Commander Yitzhak (Haka) Hofi to lead the force. The force that entered the pass at noon was trapped by crossfire, and Sharon was forced to send further troops to rescue them by clearing the slopes. A fierce hand-to-hand fight ensued from crevice to crevice, similar to the battles the US Marines had fought with the Japanese at Iwo Jima. After a few hours, the paratroopers overcame the Egyptians, leaving behind 260 enemy dead, but at the cost of 38 dead and 120 wounded IDF men (20 percent of all IDF casualties in the war). It was a heroic fight, replete with outstanding acts of courage and sacrifice, becoming part of the IDF legend of heroism, comradeship, and determination.

Tactically, the battle inspired generations of commanders. However, strategically and operationally, it was meaningless – especially as it transpired that the intelligence that had triggered it was wrong – there were no Egyptian armored forces in this sector. The High Command's frustration and rage at Sharon were profound.[104]

Dayan summarized his evaluation of what had happened with the paratroopers: "Some on the General Staff were furious with me, saying I'm forgiving and lenient with the paratroopers ... There is no need to say how sorry we are." Dayan stressed that commanders sometimes had to deviate from an instruction for a local tactical reason that only he could appreciate on the spot, just as Dayan had done in 1948. On the other hand, he drew a critical distinction between errors and violations of orders. Dayan added that he was frustrated because he had not been able to make his commanders submit an honest report or create a situation of full trust with them. It was fairly obvious that he meant Sharon, even if he didn't mention him by name. Dayan repeated the principle he had formulated in response to Simhoni and Ben-Ari, reflecting his preference for "noble stallions": "The truth is that I view cases in which units do not fulfill their combat mission as a serious problem ... rather than the cases in which units exceed their remit and act beyond whatever they were tasked with."[105]

Dayan thus shaped the IDF's military culture for generations of commanders: its core – initiative and action, even if these sometimes take a steep toll. Ultimately, Dayan dismissed only one commander, Guder, and not for lack of discipline stemming from too much initiative but for the opposite – lack of initiative and resolve.

In the evening of the third day of the war, the Allies finally began the aerial bombardment Israel had been waiting for, and there was no longer any reason to hold back. Dayan gave the order to deploy all the forces as spelled out in "Kadesh 2." Simhoni had direct command of the 38th Division, and the campaign in the central sector was decided, so Dayan left for the northern sector where the campaign was starting. The goal: the conquest of Rafah and el-Arish.

As Dayan entered el-Arish on November 2, a barrage of fire whizzed past his head, killing a soldier standing nearby. By noon, Dayan received the report that el-Arish was captured. Dayan, worried about American and Soviet political pressure on the British and French – scheduled to begin their ground offensive only on November 5 – to halt their offensive, urged the troops to complete the conquest of Sinai, especially Sharm El Sheikh, to allow for the opening of the Tiran Straits. As always, he toured the units to learn firsthand about the situation on the ground. While driving around, indifferent to the danger, he

---

[104] Henkin, *The 1956 Suez War*, pp. 159–161; Golani, *Tihyeh milhama bakayits*, p. 517.
[105] Dayan, *Yoman Ma'arekhet Sinai*, p. 92.

passed columns of retreating Egyptian army units whose soldiers were still armed with their personal weapons. Dayan later wrote: "There was nothing stopping a group of men from taking cover and turning us into sieves with their machine guns."[106] However, the defeated Egyptian – exhausted and thirsty – did not recognize the Israeli leader and showed no interest in him. This would change dramatically by the end of the campaign, when the black eyepatch became Dayan's internationally recognized trademark.

Because the 9th Brigade had not yet been able to take Sharm El Sheikh, Dayan, competing against the diplomatic clock, sent the paratroopers there. By the time the paratroopers arrived, the 9th Brigade had managed to capture the fortifications around Sharm El Sheikh. This marked the end of the IDF's job: It now controlled half of the Sinai Peninsula, although its forces were stopped about 15 kilometers from the Suez Canal, as decided on in Sèvres. On November 5, the Sinai Campaign concluded after a mere eight days. Israel's losses: 172 dead, 817 wounded, and three missing in action (MIA). The war's military objectives were fully achieved. The victory was stunning (Map 4.1).

Dayan conducted a closing ceremony with the General Staff in Sharm El Sheikh together with the 9th Brigade. He did not inform Simhoni of the ceremony in time, and Simhoni was forced to find a light plane that would fly him to the ceremony so that he wouldn't miss it. Returning from the ceremony, the plane crashed; Simhoni and the flight crew – Lieutenant Colonel Asher Dromi and supervising pilot Binyamin Gordon – were all killed. Dayan allowed himself to be more generous about Simhoni in death than in life, writing, "There is a note of fateful tragedy to this death of the CO of the Southern Command after the end of the war rather than in battle."[107] In the Chief of Staff's order of the day, Dayan wrote, "With the fall of Assaf, the Israel Defense Force lost a great commander, a commander who in his 34 years of life did not miss a single campaign of his people's wars. A soldier who was in his spirit, his body, and his body a courageous, intelligent field battle commander."

At the closing ceremony, Dayan read Ben-Gurion's letter to the fighters: "You have brought the biggest and most glorious operation in the annals of our nation to a successful conclusion." Ben-Gurion, swept up by the general euphoria, decreed the "establishment of the third Israelite kingdom." Although the war was over, Dayan faced yet another battle: After meeting Ben-Gurion in Jerusalem, he was returning to Tel Aviv when his vehicle was caught in a Fedayeen ambush. Dayan and his small entourage jumped out of the car and sought cover. Dayan proposed an assault on the shooters, but Mordechai

---

[106] Bar-On, *Moshe Dayan*, p. 168.
[107] Ibid., p. 169. Many were upset by Dayan's treatment of Simhoni, and there were even some conspiracy theories according to which there had been something intentional about the death; after all, he had been en route to Ben-Gurion to explain why his conduct had been proper and how Dayan had failed.

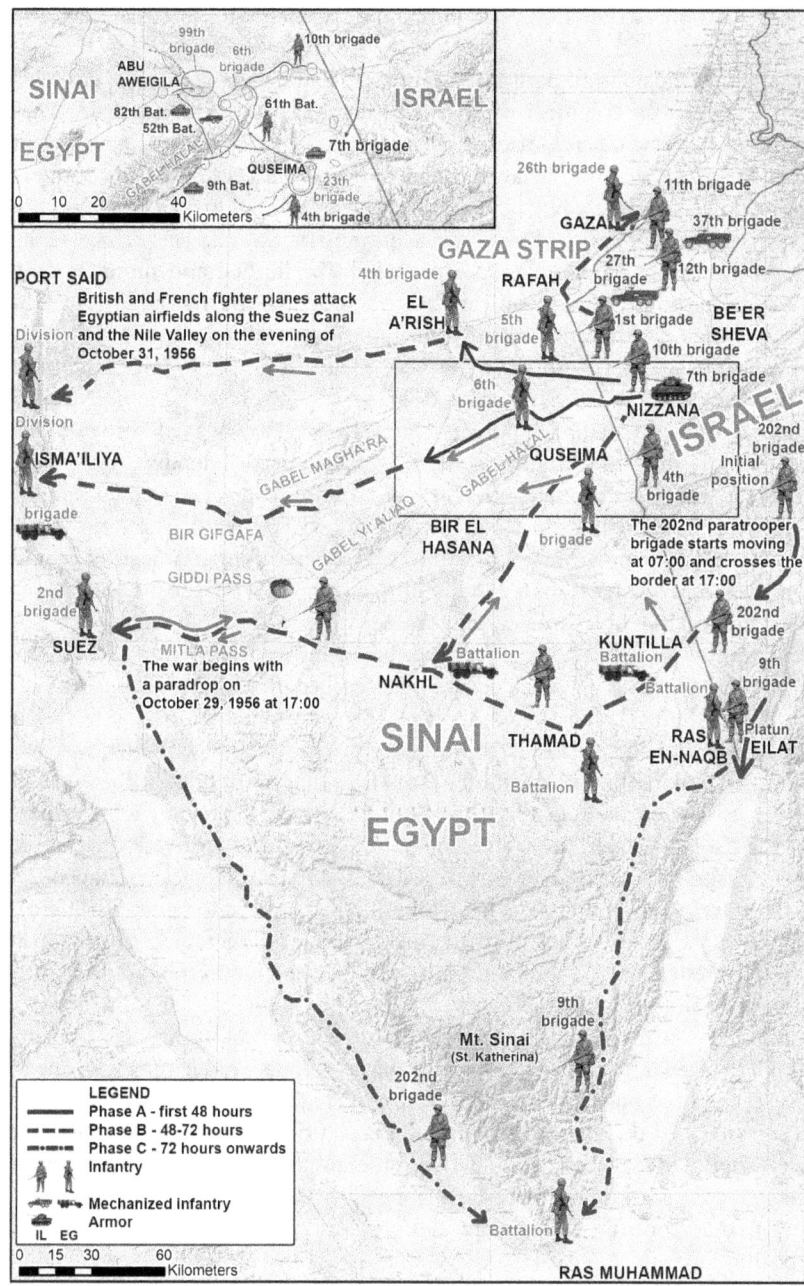

Map 4.1 Sinai Campaign (1956).

Bar-On, his bureau chief, stopped him. Reinforcements appeared on the scene within minutes.[108]

Now that the political part of the campaign had begun, Dayan hoped Israel would at least gain control of Sharm El Sheikh, Gaza, and a strip of land connecting the two. Ben-Gurion first approved Dayan's request to pave a road from Eilat to Sharm El Sheikh but had to backtrack because of heavy international pressure, including from the United States, that involved the threat of sanctions. Israel's major diplomatic achievement was the acceptance of its demand that Egyptian forces in Sinai would be limited and monitored by UN forces, who would also control a buffer zone between Israel and Egypt, and the opening of the Tiran Straits to Israeli maritime traffic. Convinced that the Israeli offensive was provoked by the Fedayeen attacks from Egyptian-controlled territory, Nasser ordered his army to prevent them. Nasser's example was emulated by King Hussein of Jordan. For the next ten years, the number of such attacks into Israel was reduced considerably. The high-intensity war therefore had positive repercussions on Israel's low-intensity security as well. Furthermore, the war convinced Nasser that the Arab world was completely unready to achieve its goal of eradicating Israel and would continue to be so unless united under him. For the next decade, he focused his attentions on the inter-Arab conflicts rather than on the Arab–Israeli conflict. Both routine security and basic security had improved.

The IDF withdrawal, which began in December after the British and French troops had left, was conducted in stages. Dayan ordered all usable Egyptian equipment transported to Israel and the destruction of whatever was left behind. Thinking that in the future the IDF would again fight in this terrain, Dayan instructed all units to free their officers to tour the region and familiarize themselves with it, as he was doing. Of course, one motivation for these tours was to indulge in his hobby of searching for archeological artefacts.

Ben-Gurion, under pressure from the Allies, was forced to return all of Sinai. On January 15, 1957, Israel returned el-Arish at a formal ceremony. A resentful Dayan, in attendance, told a journalist why he was there: "IDF commanders must taste all the dishes, the bitter as well as the sweet."[109] The United States continued pressuring Israel to complete a full withdrawal from all the territories it had taken or to face sanctions. Dayan was combative, deeming it wrong to give in without a fight for control of Gaza and Sharm El Sheikh, even at the cost of sanctions. At this point, Dayan's and Ben-Gurion's positions were diametrically opposed – a classic clash between the military man's narrower point of view and the statesman's broader perspective. Ben-Gurion made it clear to Dayan that control of Gaza did not necessarily offer any great benefits, a position Dayan would adopt years later, on the eve of the Six-Day War. On

---

[108] Ibid., p. 170.
[109] Ibid., p. 178.

March 8, after dragging its feet as long as possible, Israel completed its Sinai withdrawal, having controlled it for five months. When Dayan was asked why, given his disagreements with Ben-Gurion, he had not resigned, he answered: "I would take a very dim view of a Chief of Staff who'd throw his weight around to affect a government decision ... Anyone who accepts the role of soldier, including the Chief of Staff, must accept the government's security policy."[110]

This was, of course, Dayan playing the innocent. In a similar situation, when serving under Moshe Sharett, Dayan did tender his resignation. The truth lay not in the job or the rank but in the person. Dayan was deeply in awe of Ben-Gurion.

In any case, Dayan would not stay in his position for long. His retirement was imminent.

Evaluating Dayan as a Theater and Campaign Commander

Dayan chose to command the Sinai Campaign in his own unique way, which reflected his personality, for better and for worse. In this, too, as in many other aspects of his life, he provoked heated debate and conflicting charges. In the army, opinions about Dayan varied: Some were awed by his unique military leadership skills, while others harshly criticized his conduct as commander. He was censured for not issuing clear instructions, resulting in the 7th Brigade being sent into battle without authorization. He was also blamed for the losses at Um Qatef and the ill-advised deployment of the 10th and 37th Brigades.

The fact that Dayan was unavailable at key decision-making moments was partly responsible for these failures. Dayan's overall tendency remained as it had always been – to be as close as possible to the point of engagement. He did not invent a new method of command; it is common military doctrine that when a commander is not in the command post, a substitute designated by the commander is authorized to act in his stead. This second-in-command handles the routine management of a campaign, implementing the commander's orders as given; only the commander may change them through his substitute. This arrangement is designed "for situations in which the commander leaves the command post ... to issue commands closer to the front, tour the ground, conduct meetings, etc., but the command continues to function properly and his absence from the command center does not affect his functioning; on the contrary, his absence ensures and strengthens it."[111]

Dayan availed himself of this practice to the extreme. He was aware of the problematic situation his extended absences created at the command post and felt he had to justify himself:

---

[110] Ibid., p. 183.
[111] Ekked, Operations Division, Doctrine and Training, *Tora b'sisit matkalit: Pikud ushlita* (Hebrew), November 2006, p. 42.

> I am considering joining the units attacking Rafah until the conquest of el-Arish is concluded. For the first two days of the campaign, its routine management will be placed in the trustworthy hands of staff officers (General Staff Branch) who have outstanding knowledge and judgment. I spent most of the first two days of the campaign in the field. In the evening, I returned to the command post, and remained in constant radio communication with headquarters; the staff officers say this isn't enough and that my absence from the staff disrupts the proper operations of work. They may be right, but I am incapable – or unwilling – to behave otherwise.[112]

On another occasion, Dayan expressed his romantic longing "for the good old days of simple wars. When the time of war approached, the commander would mount his white steed and the trumpeter would sound the call to charge the enemy."[113]

Shlomo Gazit, who was by Dayan's side, described his conduct on the battlefield:

> I spent the four days of fighting closely following the campaign ... We did not see the Chief of Staff for those 96 hours. Dayan scurried from one force to another in the Sinai, while Meir Amit, the head of the General Staff Branch, stayed behind and ran the Central Command post and the war. Dayan behaved this way primarily because of his personality, and I am certain that he did not much care about military doctrinal protocol on the Chief of Staff's appropriate location during fighting.[114]

Rehavam Ze'evi, the chief staff officer of the Southern Command, would later describe Dayan's habit of conferring far-reaching authority on staff officers and the head of the Operations Division left behind in the Central Command post:

> Other than Moshe Dayan, I know no other Chief of Staff who would have allowed his deputy or the head of the Operations Division as much freedom of action as Meir Amit was given, for good and for bad, during the Sinai Campaign. Moshe got up and went down to the front and didn't come back for the next 72 hours until the battle was over. I was with him, as the chief staff officer of the Southern Command, until the conquest of el-Arish, and we didn't have the faintest idea of what was happening at the General Staff ... Now, in retrospect, when I ask myself how Dayan could have left the IDF main Command post in Ramleh in Meir's hands for him to do all the work, I have come to the conclusion that there was both good and bad in his conduct. No staff officer likes having the commander breathing down his neck, but every once in a while, every staff officer

---

[112] Dayan, *Avnei derekh*, p. 288.
[113] Dayan, *Yoman Ma'arekhet Sinai*, p. 37.
[114] Gazit, *Bitsmatim makhri'im*, p. 99.

wants to receive confirmation that he isn't straying from the commander's intentions and "getting off-track." ... Dayan moved as far ahead as he could, mostly out of curiosity – to see, have a say, get unscreened and unprocessed reports. He also knew that this projected confidence to the troops. Soldiers in the tanks and half-tracks driving past would stop and applaud him. It was impossible to keep him out of sight, which was something he didn't want in any case.[115]

Meir Amit, who had to bear much of the day-to-day command responsibility and who had earned Moshe Dayan's full trust and backing, complained that Dayan was always running around in the field and was generally unavailable. "No matter how much you plan, prepare, and coordinate ahead of time, the circumstances that develop on the ground dictate a different reality." Nevertheless, he also noted that "Dayan's spirit hovered over the ground."[116]

Indeed, in the headquarters, Amit made several important – although not, it is worth noting, critical – decisions on his own because Dayan was incommunicado. In his memoirs, Uzi Narkiss, Amit's assistant during the Sinai Campaign, described one such decision:

> My natural place during the campaign was in the Main Command post ... in an abandoned orchard near Kibbutz Na'an. This is where the Chief of Staff, too, should have been, at least in theory. But Moshe Dayan thought differently. He never even bothered to stay in regular contact with us. As a result, in those days, the burden of the overall management of the IDF fell on the shoulders of Meir Amit ... and, in his absence, on me. On more than one occasion, Amit or I had to make decisions on matters that would, under normal circumstances, have been outside our purview. And Dayan himself would eventually become angry about some of them. On those occasions, he would say, "Well, what can you, back there in Israel, understand already?" and then, in hindsight, he would learn to live with our decisions.[117]

Shlomo Gazit, too, had to look for Dayan during the fighting, but according to him, it was Dayan who personally directed the field officers. Gazit added:

> The change that Dayan instituted was that any operational plan made by the General Staff would not simply be imposed from the top down but would be followed by a stage of planning by the field officers, in planning groups and command groups. He would sit in the forward command room; he would be physically present, on the front line, during the implementation of the plan ... This custom was introduced in those

---

[115] Michael Shahar, *Sichot im Rehavam Ze'evi Ghandi*, Tel Aviv: Yedioth Ahronot, 1992, pp. 160–161.
[116] Meir Amit, *Rosh berosh: Mabat ishi al eru'im gedolim ufarshiyot ne'elamot* (Hebrew), Or Yehuda: Maariv-Hed Arzi Publications, 1999, p. 72.
[117] Uzi Narkiss, *Hayal shell Yeushalim*, Tel Aviv: Ministry of Defense Press, 1991, p. 182.

critical years. To my satisfaction, and the satisfaction of us all, this conduct is prevalent to this day in all army units.[118]

Dayan firmly believed that a commander, including the most senior, must be in the field. "You cannot know what war is from stories someone reports to you. If you really want to know, go into the field ... Even someone who understands or thinks he understands what war is, to know it, he must see it, feel it – through field glasses or any other method."[119] Dayan spent most of the campaign on the battlefield, lacking patience for conducting the campaign from a command post. Above all, he wanted to be on the spot at the locations where, by being present and gathering his own unfiltered impressions, he could have an impact on the outcome. Mordechai Bar-On explained that Dayan thought it right to be in the field both as a leader to rally the troops and as a military commander to make decisions at key moments. "In practice, in the field, in the battle, the outcome is determined by the combat troops who carry out the fighting."[120]

During the campaign, Dayan's daily schedule involved flying to the front in a light aircraft, staying on the ground for hours at a time, and maneuvering among positions with a small group of commanders in two command vehicles. Toward evening, he would return to the Central Command Post to provide updates and further instructions, after which he would go to visit Ben-Gurion to update him about the day's events.

Dayan was present at several important events on the battlefield. For example, when he met up with 38th Division and the 7th Brigade face to face during the critical hours of its early charge, which he had not managed to stop, he directed the brigade commander and the Southern Command commander on the battlefield. Later on, he joined the attack of 77th Division in Rafah. During the fighting, Dayan took personal risks, coming under fire five times. There were some who found this behavior irresponsible and unnecessary.

Dayan could engage in this style of command, referred to as "leading from the front" or forward command, because the campaign had been planned in a way that created the ideal conditions for the command style he preferred. Unlike most typical campaign objectives – such as destroying enemy forces and conquering territory – Dayan defined the campaign's objectives to support the political ones: the collapse of the Egyptian army in the Sinai Peninsula and reaching certain locations. To this end, the IDF was to reach the Suez Canal quickly while conquering some critical points, including Sharm El Sheikh, along the way, while also causing the Egyptian military forces to retreat in

---

[118] Gazit, in Bar-On (ed.), *Lenochach gvulot oyevim: tzava ubitachon ba'asor harishon shel medinat Yisrael*, p. 174.

[119] Yaakov Erez and Ilan Kfir, *Sihot eem Moshe Dayan: Ha'azinu vesha'alu* (Hebrew), Massada: Ramat Gan, Ma'ariv Library Editions, 1981, p. 96.

[120] Bar-On, *Moshe Dayan*, p. 159.

a panic. One notable element of the campaign was the absence of a specific destination where the forces were supposed to converge, as is customary in such campaigns. Instead, each force was supposed to advance independently of the others and reach its destination in the general vicinity of the Suez Canal.[121]

In 1956, brigades enjoyed considerable independence in battlefield decision-making, and the ranks above them only guided them to ensure that the brigades' actions would correspond with the goals set for them. The campaign Dayan planned required very little coordination, thus allowing the forces on the ground a high level of independence. Each tactical problem was handled separately, without regard for other sectors' challenges. Only in Sharm El Sheikh was there an attempt to coordinate the entry of two forces from different directions to seize control of the area. The campaign was planned so that Dayan would be able to command from the front, and the general tendency was to rapidly improvise war maneuvers while advancing.[122]

In his book *Diary of the Sinai Campaign*, Dayan explained:

> We can build our action on units that do not depend on one another and whose command posts, which must receive reports and give the required instructions, are found within the fighting units. Should we exploit this advantage, we will – after the initial breakthrough – be able to continue to fight the Egyptians before they have the chance to reorganize . . . I believe that we can conduct the fighting in a way that will not give them time to recoup after our attack and will not cause breaks in the battle . . . We will build separate forces for the main missions, and each force will have to reach its final destination with one battle, one breath – to fight and advance continuously from its breakthrough to the completion of its mission. I know that this approach is not suited to every campaign, but, in my opinion, it is correct under the current circumstances, with the arena being the Sinai Peninsula and the enemy being the Egyptian army. It is also suited to our army and the nature of our commanders. I can take an IDF unit commander and point out the Suez Canal for him and say, "This is your destination, and this is the route along which you should move. During the action, don't call me to ask for help with manpower, fire, or vehicles. You already have all that we were able to allocate to you and no more. Report on progress. You must be at the canal [within] 48 hours." I can give instructions like this to our unit commanders because I know they are ready and willing to accept such missions and are capable of carrying them out.[123]

But this command style came at a price. Laskov and Zore'a wrote: "If the spirit of the commander encourages noble stallions to surge forward, it

---

[121] Edward Luttwak and Dan Horowitz, *The Israeli Army*, London: Allen Lane, 1975, p. 146.
[122] Ibid., p. 163.
[123] Dayan, *Yoman Ma'arekhet Sinai*, p. 36.

sometimes happens that these horses will not only run, but also kick, which is what happened with the 7th Brigade and at the Mitla Pass."[124]

Shlomo Gazit, in contrast, assessed Dayan's command of the war positively:

> My own personal opinion is that Dayan's approach is correct and appropriate. In the short wars the IDF conducts, the General Staff's job is pretty much done by the time the first shot is fired. The General Staff has organized, equipped, and trained the units to fight, for better and for worse. It has also approved the battle plans. Control and decisions, if needed during the fighting, are best made in the field on the basis of unfiltered information about the real situation. There, on the ground, together with the commanders, the Chief of Staff can have an impact and decide the outcome.[125]

Historian Martin van Creveld, an expert in military command, had a similar assessment. He saw Dayan as an example of a commander who provides his staff with freedom of action to conduct routine command and control activities, while he focuses entirely on forward command on the battlefield. In Sinai, Dayan's presence helped push the forces forward. However, as noted on p. 185, this method can have a cost in terms of confusion and mistakes, which, in fact, occurred during the campaign. Nonetheless, van Creveld concluded, every campaign must be judged by its results.[126]

Dayan neither invented this approach nor was he the first to apply it. However, he took it to its extreme and thus enjoyed its full benefits. Yet he also suffered its full drawbacks. Forward-command style was applied by prominent armored-corps commanders in World War II, the most renowned being Erwin Rommel, Heinz Guderian, and George Patton. The method, first developed primarily by the Germans, favored a war of rapid movement that would cause the enemy lines to collapse within a short period of time.[127] The significant difference between Dayan and these commanders was that they served as field commanders answering to another echelon above them, often at a remove of several military command levels from the top echelon, whereas Dayan was the supreme military commander, answerable only to the political echelon.

The forward command approach in rapid maneuver warfare relies on the mission command approach (the original German term is *Auftragstaktik*).[128] The central tenet of this approach is that maximal decision-making authority

---

[124] General Haim Laskov and Major General Meir Zore'a, "Vehaya kee tetseh lemilhama" (Hebrew), *Maariv*, October 10, 1965, https://bit.ly/36eROm2.
[125] Gazit, *Bitsmatim makhri'im*, p. 99.
[126] Martin van Creveld, *Moshe Dayan*, London: Weidenfeld & Nicholson, 2004, pp. 92–95.
[127] Robert M. Citino, *The German Way of War: From the Thirty Years' War to the Third Reich*, La Vergne: University Press of Kansas, 2005.
[128] See explanation of this topic in Chapter 3.

should be granted to subordinates after the command echelon clarifies to them that their mission is part of a greater objective. In that context, the mission is always realized in light of the objective, and if the situation on the ground changes and the mission is no longer relevant, the commander on the ground is free to decide to change it or even abort it.[129]

Another aspect of this approach is the double command system of the chief of operations (or the chief of staff in some cases) together with the commander, whereby the two together form a unified team. The chief of operations, who remains in the command post for command-and-control purposes, coupled with a commander in the field, who is present to examine and assess the situation up close, have an impact at critical decision-making junctures, when timing is critical and there is a need to rally the fighting forces. Successfully achieving this type of command system requires profound understanding and absolute trust between the commander and his chief of operations. British historian Spencer Wilkinson described the relationship as so deep that the chief of operations could be considered "the alter ego of the commander."[130] Military history is familiar with several such pairs – General Herman Balck (Commander) and General Friedrich von Mellenthin (Chief of Staff), who commanded a German Panzer Corps on the eastern front in World War II, and the better-known General Paul von Hindenburg (Commander) and General Erich Ludendorff (Chief of Staff), who commanded the Russian front in World War I.

The famous German Chief of Staff Helmuth von Moltke the Elder, considered responsible for integrating the mission-command approach into the German army, believed that most preparations and decisions are actually made before war breaks out. Later, most decisions are made by the field commanders on the spot. Moltke led the Prussian army through three wars at the end of the nineteenth century and was victorious in them all. He rarely intervened in the course of a campaign, doing so only when he felt his input was critical. Even then, his instructions would sometimes arrive at the battlefield too late. Since the advent of modern communications technology, commanders have been able to stay in constant communication with their subordinates and have tended to get more involved in what happens on the battlefield.

It is imperative, though, that the commander maintains the authority to make the "fundamental decisions" – as defined in the doctrine – themselves and not delegate the authority to make them to others. These include "decisions related to the objective, mission, factors affecting [the campaign, such as political constraints], operational concept, methods of action of our forces and

---

[129] For more on mission command, see Eitan Shamir, Transforming Command: *The Pursuit of Mission Command in the US, British, and Israeli Armies,* Stanford CA: Stanford University Press, 2011.

[130] Spencer Wilkinson, *The Brain of an Army: A Popular Account of the German General Staff,* Westminster: Archibald Constable and Co., 1895, p. 56.

those of the enemy, operational outline, operational plan, and operation's order."[131] The commander is the only person authorized to make these fundamental decisions.

The fundamental decisions will differ depending on the particular geopolitical military context. In the case of Israel, where a war might be fought on a number of fronts simultaneously, the Chief of the General Staff of the IDF, who generally counsels and supervises the various commands and provides briefings to the government, is usually forced to make only a limited number of fundamental decisions during the fighting, such as to commit his reserves forces to a specific front at the expense of the other. In the case of a single front war, such as the Sinai Campaign, there were not many decisions that needed the General Staff's intervention. In a single-front war, there are very few critical decisions the Chief of Staff must make on the spot. Furthermore, a gifted Chief of Operations, such as Meir Amit, who was closely familiar with the situation in general and the spirit of his commander in particular, was perfectly capable of taking over, enabling Dayan to move to the front to assess the situation with his own eyes. The Chief of the General Staff's presence on the ground at critical junctures can be highly significant.

The most important military thinker of all time, Carl von Clausewitz, famously noted that war is the "kingdom of uncertainty." Today, there is not a single military officer anywhere who cannot quote this saying, but few understand it in depth, and even fewer are capable of operating in accordance with its ramifications. Today, the IDF's main headquarters, referred to as "The Pit," is located in the Kirya in the center of Tel Aviv. It is equipped with the most advanced telecommunications devices available, fed by the best forms of information-gathering satellites, unmanned aerial vehicles, and advanced tools for monitoring and transmitting communications. The Israeli Chief of Staff can sit in "The Pit," receive very accurate information about every arena in real time, and conduct the campaign from there.[132]

In Dayan's time, none of this existed. While wireless communication was used, the devices did not always work very well, and the situation assessment received from the battlefield was often fragmented, confused, and delayed.[133] Had Dayan stayed at the Command Center, it is safe to assume he would not have managed to get an accurate impression of the battle in real time; therefore, his presence on the ground was more beneficial than his presence at the Command Center would have been.

---

[131] Ekked, Operations Division, Doctrine and Training, *Tora b'sisit matkalit: Pikud ushlita* (Hebrew), November 2006, p. 40.

[132] Yoav Zeitun, "Biladi: Ts'fu behatsatsa nedira babor bakirya" ["Exclusive: A large glimpse of the pit in the Kirya"] (Hebrew), *Ynet*, April 22, 2015, www.ynet.co.il/articles/0,7340,L-4649195,00.html.

[133] Amit, *Rosh berosh*, p. 76.

Dayan's style of forward command, even if less suited to today's technological reality, is not without rationale or value. His style of command is rarely practiced these days because of fear of failures and errors and worries about possible committees of inquiry. Dayan, however, operated in an era in which he was free of the restrictive combination of modern technology and rigid bureaucratic norms in this regard.

The Campaign's Lessons for the IDF

Despite its errors and flaws, the Sinai Campaign was ultimately a great success. The unanticipated early entry of the 7th Brigade did not cause the political damage Dayan had feared and significantly contributed to the IDF's offensive momentum. The paratroopers' troubles in the unnecessary Mitla Pass battle caused heavy losses but had no impact on the campaign. The failed attempts of the 10th and 37th Brigades to conquer Um Qatef did not delay the campaign and essentially had no effect on it, as the positions finally fell after being abandoned by the exhausted, encircled Egyptian soldiers. There were other botched moves, which are to be expected in any large-scale military clash, but ultimately, all the objectives of the eight-day blitzkrieg were attained at the cost of 172 dead, 3 MIA, and 817 wounded – fewer than Dayan's original estimate of 250 dead he had given Ben-Gurion.

Postwar, Dayan spearheaded processes meant to ensure that the IDF learned valuable lessons from the campaign. Shlomo Gazit gave an account of one the debriefing sessions Dayan held. After listening to his commanders' complaints, Dayan said:

> I listened to the debates for two whole days; I heard the many comments and claims made by the disputants who appeared here about what was lacking, what was flawed, what was impaired. And then I asked myself, "Wait a minute ... Who actually won this war? The Egyptians or we? ... If we did, how do we explain the huge gap between this phenomenal victory and the endless list of all the things that are wrong with the army?" I can only draw but one clear, unequivocal conclusion: we won not despite everything we lacked but because of everything we lacked. We won because, in recent years, the IDF has been able to focus on what really matters – only on whatever can bring about a decision in war with the clear, unequivocal knowledge that we are wronging all other issues and discriminating against them, because they are not critical to achieving a decision. We did not spread our resources along all parts of the sector; we focused on what mattered.[134]

---

[134] Gazit, in Bar-On (ed.), *Lenochach gvulot oyevim: tzava ubitachon ba'asor harishon shel medinat Yisrael*, p. 178.

With these words, Dayan expressed what researcher Yitzhak Ben-Israel calls "the force-building approach of the relative advantage." As the people's army of a small nation, the IDF will always suffer from a certain disadvantage. As such, Israel has no choice but to take the route of focusing its effort on areas where it can create a relative advantage, making conscious decisions to neglect certain areas in order to create a relative advantage and wrest a decisive victory from the enemy.[135] In terms of having a relative advantage, certain clear lessons emerged from the war, first and foremost prioritizing building up the forces of the armored corps and the air force.[136] For the IDF, the most surprising discovery of the Sinai Campaign, however, was the tremendous power of the armored corps,[137] which led to a genuine revolution in the IDF. Uri Ben Ari, the 7th Brigade commander, who would one day become the Armored Corps commander, wrote: "The outcome of the Kadesh Campaign ... represents a revolution in the IDF's strategic military thinking in general and in that of the Armored Corps in particular."[138]

Haim Laskov, with the strict British Army approach, and Moshe Dayan, the "partisan," could not have been more dissimilar, yet Dayan admired Laskov's professionalism and his vast knowledge of military matters, while Laskov admired Dayan's creativity. Of Dayan, Laskov reflected: "It was said that administration was not his strong suit. Perhaps. But he passed the most important test of all: he produced bricks of force out of a minuscule amount of straw."[139] Dayan and Laskov had essential differences of opinion about the deployment of the armored corps in war. Generally, the disagreement between them is presented as follows: Dayan viewed the armored corps as serving a supporting role for the infantry. He did not know how to operate armored troops in the modern manner, as had the Germans in World War II and as have all other armies since then. Laskov, in contrast, promoted a program whereby armored troops would be organized in independent brigades. The war in Sinai proved Laskov right. To Dayan's credit, it must be said that he admitted his mistake, and after the war, he worked to transform the armored troops into a corps that would form the backbone of the IDF's ground forces.

However, reality was more complicated at the time. Dayan felt that the equipment available to the IDF – light French AMX tanks and decrepit American Sherman tanks – was inadequate. His opinion was reinforced by

---

[135] Yitzhak Ben-Israel, "Torat hayehasiut shel banyan ko'ah" (Hebrew), *Ma'arakhot* 352–353 (August 1997), pp. 33–42.

[136] Bar-On (ed.), *Lenochach gvulot oyevim: tzava ubitachon ba'asor harishon shel medinat Yisrael*, p. 178; the author's interview with Dan Tolkovsky, October 10, 2017, Tel Aviv.

[137] Amiad Bresner, *Susim abirim: Hitpat'hut umurot bashiryon hayisraeli mitom milhemet ha'atsmaut ve'ad milhemet Sinai* (Hebrew), Tel Aviv: Maarakhot, 1999, p. 408.

[138] Ibid., p. 422.

[139] Mordechai Naor, *Laskov: Lohem, adam, haver* (Hebrew), Tel Aviv: Ministry of Defense Publications, 1988, p. 325.

the fact that during the army maneuvers, many tanks developed mechanical problems, most never reaching their destination – the most extreme case being Exercise "Pelet" conducted merely six months before the war.[140]

> The only tangible result of this maneuver was the last gasp of readiness of the armored troops in term of the tanks' usability. One Sherman tank burned to a cinder and many broke down. But especially dire was the condition of the AMXs. Of 60, 40 are now out of commission ... Were it necessary to operate all of the armored troops at the same time, it is highly doubtful that [the IDF] would be capable of putting more than 50 tanks on the battlefield.[141]

Mordechai (Motta) Gur, citing a senior commander, apparently Dayan, observed: "One would have to be a genius to believe that tanks, especially those that were shipped to Israel, would be able to travel all the way to the canal."[142]

Because of the problems that came to light during the "Pelet" exercise, Laskov, who had outstanding organizational skills and, as already mentioned, was an enthusiastic supporter of making armored troops into a decisive corps on the ground, was appointed to rebuild the corps. As the war would show, he was extremely successful – the repaired and refurbished tanks did indeed reach the canal. On the doctrinal issue, his appointment prolonged and even exacerbated the conflict between his and Dayan's approaches. At the end of August 1956, Dayan decided to hold an extended debate in which General Staff officers could share their opinions. Dayan's position was articulated in a document he entitled "How Will the Armored Troops Fight?"[143] The basic idea, explained in great detail, was to distribute armored troops among the infantry formations. Laskov, in contrast, formulated a document calling for concentrating all the armored troops into a single division to serve as a strike force, surging ahead and destroying the enemy's armored troops.

The decisive debate, which took place on September 1, 1956, was chaired by Prime Minister and Defense Minister David Ben-Gurion and the Director General of the Defense Ministry Shimon Peres. After the sides presented their positions and the General Staff generals discussed the matter, Dayan summarized the meeting by saying that Laskov's approach had some good points, and Laskov, too, highlighted the aspects of Dayan's approach that he found acceptable, although he was still critical of it overall.[144]

---

[140] Ibid., p. 259.
[141] Logbook of the bureau of the Chief of Staff, quoted on the Yad Lashiryon website: https://yadlashiryon.com/armor_wars/sinai-war/.
[142] Bresner, *Susim abirim*, p. 409.
[143] Bresner, *Susim abirim*, p. 322.
[144] For more on the debate over doctrine and the discussion at the General Staff, see Bresner, *Susim abirim*, pp. 322–332.

In fact, before the war began, Dayan determined that the battle would be decided by mobile infantry reaching the targets, while tanks would be brought by tank carriers. Armored Corps historian Amiad Bresner wrote: "The execution differed radically from anything Dayan's doctrine foresaw." The armored forces led by tanks did well with the missions they were assigned. Bresner added:

> It would be right to say that Laskov's doctrine, which favored maximal concentration of armor within an armored division, was also not realized ... Armored brigades operated in brigade settings; the two armored brigades that were relatively ready for action were split – one along each axis of movement – with a third armored brigade far from the scene of action ... The action of the 7th Brigade represented a small-scale application of Laskov's doctrine.[145]

This leads to the question of why the IDF operated according to neither Dayan's nor Laskov's doctrines. The answer can be found in the enemy's conduct and the battlefield reality that developed, as well as in it being another manifestation of the flexibility in troop deployment and local freedom of action Dayan gave his commanders in the field. In fact, in this respect, although Laskov criticized Dayan, he admired "his audacity and broad strategic vision."[146]

Dayan's flexibility of thought proved itself again and left a deep impression. Meir Zore'a (Zaro) said of Dayan: "At the right moment, he understood that what those crazy people had said about armored troops was real and therefore ordered that it be implemented."[147] As early as November 2, as the key battles in Sinai were ending, Dayan realized that an armored revolution had occurred in the IDF, and, at a General Staff meeting, he said: "With all due respect to the 10th and 11th Brigades, it must be said that the armored troops did most of the work ... All actions to date were undertaken by means of armored troops and planes."[148]

Years later, Dayan recalled that time as follows:

> I can say that the question of how to operate the armored forces did come up. I, Moshe Dayan from Nahalal, didn't know about it. For me, the infantry was the "queen of battle" and the function of everyone else was to assist her ... The armored forces are an independent force and, instead of the armored assisting the infantry, an inverse situation was created. The armored forces are an independent force [that] needs some assistance, including artillery and to a certain extent, assistance from the infantry.[149]

---

[145] Bresner, *Susim abirim*, p. 410–411.
[146] Naor, *Laskov*, p. 259.
[147] Ibid., p. 260.
[148] Bresner, *Susim abirim*, p. 422.
[149] Cited in Erez and Kfir, *Sihot eem Moshe Dayan*, p. 42.

However, beyond any of this, the foremost lesson Dayan learned from the war in Sinai was the importance of speed. Again, he came to the realization that, in war, a commander must be personally present on the battlefield.[150] The Sinai Campaign also proved the advantages of taking a proactive stance, such as beginning a preventive war or landing a preliminary strike, an approach that was used a decade later in the Six-Day War. The conclusion was that in the future, too, wars would be short because of the political pressure exerted by the world powers. Another factor dictating the need for a short war was the use of the reserves, which had been deployed in large numbers for the first time at the cost of halting most productive economic activity. These constraints led to planning a campaign that would lead to a decisive and rapid collapse of the enemy. A year after the Sinai Campaign, Dayan spoke in favor of force building based on the relative advantage principle,[151] saying: "I'm for us building our force in the near future on offense and strong, rapid, execution capabilities rather than on defense ... We must focus our preference of one at the expense of the other. To satisfy all – that is not my objective."[152]

At a gathering of the senior command echelon that took place on December 27, 1956, shortly after the Sinai campaign, Dayan stressed the importance of speed in battle. Dayan felt that speed was the most significant advantage the IDF had over the Arab armies. He warned that superfluous planning could create unnecessary burdens and cause the army to focus on the marginal instead of on the central issues, thereby undermining the important element of speed. He repeatedly expressed concern that the lessons from the Sinai Campaign might result in overplanning. Dayan added a further warning: The Sinai Campaign was atypical, because it ran more or less according to plan.[153]

Dayan was afraid that the orderly procedures and logistical forces would stop the fighting forces, the "noble stallions" he so favored and nurtured. He feared too many procedures would be introduced that might limit the IDF commanders and force them to abide to the strict command and control chain, not allowing them to maneuver flexibly, as he was used to doing. He also worried about overplanning, which could undermine improvisation and initiative. In practice, in the Sinai Campaign, the maneuvering forces advanced rapidly, and the logistical forces had trouble keeping up. Dayan was afraid that the maneuvering forces would be subordinated to the pace of the logistical forces, rather than the other way around.[154]

---

[150] Bar-On (ed.), *Lenochach gvulot oyevim: tzava ubitachon ba'asor harishon shel medinat Yisrael*, p. 184.
[151] Ben-Israel, "Torat hayehasiut shel banyan ko'ah."
[152] Cited in Bresner, *Susim abirim*, p. 421.
[153] Ibid., p. 163.
[154] Eli Michelson, "Tahalikh halemida shel tsahal mimilhemet Sinai, november 1956 – mai 1957" (Hebrew), PhD diss., Hebrew University in Jerusalem, January 2019, pp. 208, 226.

On an ethical level, Dayan rebuked the commanders for poor treatment of prisoners of war, including shootings, considering such behavior damaging to both Jews and Arabs. It could damage the Arabs' opinion of Israel and the possibility that the peoples would be able to live side by side in peace in the future. He also felt it harmed Israeli society and could corrupt the country's youth. The issue of looting posed another ethical problem for Dayan, who emphasized that: "Anyone who brings [as much as] a watch home is like someone sticking a knife into the body of the IDF."[155]

As Chief of Staff, Dayan was mainly responsible for building up the army's forces and for its optimal operation in wartime. When he assumed the position, the IDF was at the lowest point in its history. After three years of building up the forces and training the IDF commanders, the IDF proved that it could take the Sinai Peninsula in eight days, parachute a paratrooper force deep into enemy territory, and operate armored units that crossed hundreds of kilometers of desert terrain. Moreover, the IDF proved itself capable of conducting joint air and ground battles and executing special operations based on intelligence. As Dayan said, the Sinai Campaign "gave the IDF its wings."[156] Dayan laid all the foundations for building the forces, which were continued and expanded during Haim Laskov's and Yitzhak Rabin's tenures as Chief of Staff, a fact that became amply evident in the Six-Day War. According to no less than Ezer Weitzman, the head of the Operations Division during the 1967 war: "In terms of the ground armies, there is no doubt that the action in 1956 contributed most of the knowledge and experience in attaining the lightning-speed victory in 1967."[157]

The Campaign's Achievements

In the study of history, there is a constant tension between two schools of thought. One, the structural school, stresses that geopolitical structures and inherent interests dictate action. According to the structuralists, the impact of any one leader is marginal, because events are determined by the very structure of the interests involved. In contrast, the personality school of thought stresses the importance of character and decisions of the leader in the shaping of world events.

France, Great Britain, and Israel were on a collision course with Egypt, each for its own reasons, regardless of any leader's character or personality. However, the personalities of the leaders played a significant role in the historical drama. Nasser was a clear example; it was his personal charisma and vision that brought the Arab world under his leadership. Other leaders'

---

[155] Ibid., p. 206.
[156] Erez and Kfir, *Sihot eem Moshe Dayan*, p. 41.
[157] Evron, *Hadilemma hagarinit shel yisrael*, p. 145.

characters in the crisis were crucial as well: Ben-Gurion, hesitant about embarking on a military venture, needed the confidence Dayan gave him. Dayan promised Ben-Gurion that Israel's losses would be low, and at the critical juncture, it was Dayan who came up with a creative solution that made it possible for Ben-Gurion to make the decision to take a risk. It is doubtful that Ben-Gurion would have given his approval to go to war without this.

The causes of the Sinai Campaign were not the constant harassment by the Palestinians from Gaza and Egypt, the blockade of the Tiran Straits, the rising threat of Nasser uniting the Arab world to attack Israel, or the Czech arms deal, though all these reasons existed in the minds and debates of the Israeli security leadership. They were in fact the outcome of a combination of several geostrategic events, only some of which were directly linked to Israel. In the background was the global "cold war" with the Soviets, working to destabilize Western relations with the Middle East, but the direct causes were of course the constant conflicts between Nasser and Britain over its residual presence in the Middle East (Sudan, Jordan, Iraq, and the canal zone) and his attempts to derail the anti-Soviet Baghdad Pact, the conflict with France over ownership of the Suez Canal, and Nasser's assistance to the Algerian rebellion. The nationalization of the Suez Canal brought all these conflicts to a head.

For all the reasons Israel might have wanted to defeat Egypt, if France had not decided to go to war and requested Israel join, Ben Gurion would not have initiated it on his own. The support of a major power, to provide political and military support for Israel, was one of the fundamental tenets of his security concept. It would remain so in the future too – Israel would not initiate the Six-Day War before the government understood there was American approval, it would risk not calling up the reserves prior to the Yom Kippur War to avoid being seen as escalating tensions, and more. The Czech arms deal with Egypt and Syria had completely unbalanced the military equilibrium against Israel – only a parallel deal with another power could restore it. France was the only state that had agreed to match the Czech arms deal, but in return it wanted Israeli involvement in France's war with Egypt. When Ben-Gurion asked Dayan "Remind me again: why are we going to war?" he knew the answer all too well: France. French Prime Minister Guy Mollet had made it clear to Ben-Gurion that cooperation in the nuclear field was tied to Israel's cooperation regarding Egypt.[158] France made Ben-Gurion an offer he couldn't refuse. The benefit – reducing the Egyptian threat (especially the threat of Nasser uniting the Arab world under him) and also making an ally of a global power – was simply too much to resist. Nevertheless, historian Avi Shlaim was correct to stress that the "reactor was an added bonus. His [Ben-Gurion's] overall aim at

---

[158] Yitzhak Bar-On, *Mitriya beyom sagrir ... : Yehasim bithoni'im bein tsarfat leyisrael 1948–1956* (Hebrew), Maccabim: Effi Meltser Publishers, 2010, p. 514.

this time was to consolidate the alliance with France."[159] It might also convert Britain from a hostile power to an ally. And yet, even after the French and British proposal to fight with them he was hesitant and agreed only after Dayan promised him a workable military solution to his political quandary – on the one hand was the fear of facing international disapproval and on the other the need for an ally capable of supplying Israel with weapons.

Neither France nor Britain achieved their objectives in the war. Worse for them, the campaign entrenched their status in the new world order as second-tier powers. Not only did Nasser's regime not fall, it grew stronger, an early example of the thinking that a nondefeat is no different than a victory, an idea that would, years later, be honed by Hezbollah and Hamas in their clashes with Israel. The essence of the idea is that surviving an encounter with much stronger forces ensures the struggle continues until victory is achieved.

Israel, however, undoubtedly benefited from the war. Ten years after the war, Dayan summarized Israel's achievements in an article in the Israeli daily newspaper *Ma'ariv*. He identified the gains attained – chief among them the removal of the blockade in the Tiran Straits, the end of the cross-border attacks from Egyptian territory, the defeat of the Egyptian army, thus achieving a radical change in the balance of military power in its favor and reducing the probability of a war also with the other Arab states, and the reduction (though not to zero) of cross-border attacks from Jordan and Syria too, the cementing of the alliance with France as Israel's prime weapons supplier, and the status of a major player in the Middle East rather than someone who could be ignored.[160] Israel's basic security and routine security were both enhanced considerably.

Dayan concluded his article with two interesting observations. The first was about Gaza. He wrote that he regretted relinquishing the Gaza Strip to Egypt, believing that if it had remained under Israeli control, it would have been possible to reach an arrangement with Jordan. Jordan would then have settled the Gaza Strip refugees on its soil and built a port in Gaza to link it with the Mediterranean Sea. His second observation concerned the UN observers stationed in Sinai. Dayan opposed having a foreign force serving as a barrier, believing that both sides would eventually have to get used to the presence of the other. He wrote, "I prefer a normalization of hostility to artificial arrangements ... The barrier of foreign forces only serves to create a fiction of neighborly relations and thus postpones peace."[161]

Various parties have criticized the war's achievements. Some have claimed the campaign delayed peace and entrenched Arab hostility, specifically Nasser's, to Israel. It has also been claimed that Israel "sullied itself" by

---

[159] Shlaim, "Protocol of Sèvres," p. 524.
[160] Moshe Dayan, "Sinai: Ten Years Later" (Hebrew), *Ma'ariv*, November 11, 1966.
[161] Ibid., pp. 62–63.

cooperating with European imperialism.[162] But, in hindsight, it is difficult to argue with the Sinai Campaign's political successes. Because of it, no one presented Israel with proposals that, like Plan Alpha, would break off portions of its territory. Israel's deterrence vis-à-vis the regional nations was enhanced, and Israel's global status improved. Thanks to the reputation it gained from the war, Israel signed diplomatic agreements with Iran, Turkey, and Ethiopia, as well as many African nations with which Israel would enjoy flourishing relations for over a decade. Israel's relations with France became even more friendly and generated the benefits Israel expected – until the Six-Day War, when France reversed its policy and became pro-Arab. After the withdrawal from Sinai was complete, Israel's relations with the United States also improved. In fact, this was when the United States started to see Israel as a nation with capabilities, an island of stability in a volatile region of a Cold War world. Historian Yagil Henkin summarized the benefits of the Sinai Campaign: "With the hindsight of 60 years, [we see that] Suez played a crucial role in transforming Israel in the eyes of the world from a fledgling state, a haven for Holocaust refugees and Jews who were forced to leave Arab countries, to a regional power."[163] Domestically, too, the ten years following the Sinai Campaign were among the calmest in the history of the state, allowing the assimilation of waves of immigrants and the peace and quiet so important for laying a socioeconomic infrastructure.

For Dayan personally, the Sinai Campaign was a high point in his career. It made him an international celebrity. Journalists flocked to his doorstep seeking interviews. Not only statesmen, but also movie stars, singers, and other celebrities wanted to meet him. About a year before his discharge from the army, in November 1957, he toured several nations, including Burma, Italy, France, and Great Britain to meet with colleagues. In Great Britain, famed historian and military thinker Sir Basil Henry Liddell Hart arranged for Dayan to meet legendary Field Marshal Bernard Law Montgomery, then serving as the Deputy Supreme Allied Commander Europe. While Montgomery treated Dayan like an equal with whom he could share ideas, he still did most of the talking. It is notable that, about a decade earlier, Montgomery, as Chief of the Imperial General Staff, had been in charge of putting down the rebellion of the Jewish underground organizations against British rule in Palestine. Liddell Hart noted that he had never before heard Monty speak so openly. Hart also told Dayan that when he walked the field marshal to his car, Monty told him, "Dayan is tough but I like him."[164]

---

[162] Shimon Shamir in an interview in Evron, *Hadilemma hagarinit shel yisrael*, p. 181. This opinion was unequivocally voiced also by others, such as journalist Uri Avnery and Moshe Sneh. See Sneh's statements at the end of the Sinai Campaign: https://rb.gy/8dr9pc; see also: Amit, *Rosh berosh*, p. 79.
[163] Henkin, *The 1956 Suez War*, p. 274.
[164] Bar-On, *Moshe Dayan*, p. 178.

Dayan's Retirement from Military Life

After the war, Dayan often lectured to officers about the war and its lessons. He also led debriefings to study military conclusions and participated in different forums dealing with the war. However, he focused his attention primarily on political developments in Israel and the world. The details of the military withdrawal and the administrative issues involved were handled by the staff divisions under Meir Amit's leadership. Dayan was not asked to deal with them, nor did he ask to do so. He concentrated on one subject: the difficult negotiations that Ben-Gurion, via Golda Meir and Abba Eban, was conducting with the US administration about Israel's withdrawal from Sinai.

Nonetheless, it was clear that Dayan's days in the IDF were numbered. In the last months of his tenure as Chief of Staff, he was mostly involved with political matters, especially international Middle East policy. He was pessimistic as usual. He worried about the closer ties being forged by the Soviet Union with the Arab nations, and although he didn't believe that the Arab nations would dare to start a war with Israel on their own in the near future, he realized that they were liable to do so with the help of the USSR.[165]

In November 1957, Ben-Gurion accepted Dayan's decision to leave the military, appointing Haim Laskov in his stead. Dayan was not thrilled with the choice, but accepted Ben-Gurion's pick and cooperated with his replacement. Laskov's recommendation to Ben-Gurion was to leave Dayan in the position: "Thanks to Moshe, there's a light in the army; not a light – lightning,"[166] he told him. But the matter was closed, and Dayan told Laskov that until he assumed office, he – Dayan – would not make any decisions Laskov disagreed with.

Laskov, and Yitzhak Rabin after him, continued the IDF's force buildup using Dayan's paradigm. Years later, when Laskov was asked about the differences between his and Dayan's tenures as Chief of Staff, he said, "I supported Dayan's approach, which encouraged a fighting spirit and combat values, an approach based on an austerity budget. I didn't disagree with Dayan about any of these and I continued his direction."[167] Laskov provided impetus for a post-1956 approach and built an army based on armor and an air force, capable of executing rapid, decisive maneuvering campaigns.

Despite certain differences in personalities between the two, a relationship of deep mutual admiration developed between them in the years to come. Dayan respected Laskov, saying of him that he was probably the only Haganah veteran "who appreciated his way of thinking and understood where he was going." He knew that Laskov had great qualities that a military organization

---

[165] Ibid., p. 184. This would not be their last meeting. Dayan saw Monty again before his trip to Vietnam in 1966.
[166] Naor, *Laskov*, p. 273.
[167] Ibid., p. 277.

could use and which he lacked himself. Laskov used to say, "From Moses [the biblical figure] to Moses [Moshe Dayan] there has been none like Moses,"[168] and despite being aware of Dayan's flaws and often criticizing him for them, Laskov was certain that they in no way detracted from Dayan's leadership or ability to think. He compared Dayan to British Vice-Admiral Horatio Nelson, adding, "A rare blend – a simultaneously rebellious and loyal commander." Above all, Dayan excelled as Chief of Staff thanks to his ability to take both a military and a political view simultaneously, a trait on full display in the planning of the Sinai Campaign. Later, Major General Rehavam (Gandhi) Zeevi would say of him, "We, as military men, are interested in the professional side of things: a better-informed use of the tank, this ammunition, that cannon, and so on. But Dayan, more than any other commander I've known, integrated the political side into the military. He did this even as far back as his time in the Southern Command."[169]

The changing of the guard – the ceremony in which the Chief of Staff baton was handed from Dayan to Laskov – took place on January 29, 1958. In his farewell to the soldiers of the IDF, Dayan congratulated them and thanked them for their dedication and self-sacrifice. He mentioned the names of some of those who had fallen on his watch – generals as well as rank-and-file soldiers.[170]

The period of generalship had ended. The next chapter – Dayan's life in politics and matters of state – was just beginning.

---

[168] Naor, *Laskov*, p. 325.
[169] Shahar, *Sichot im Rehavam Ze'evi Ghandi*, pp. 160–161.
[170] Ibid., p. 376.

5

"The Minister of Victory"

The Six-Day War

Two iconic images exemplify Dayan reputation as "the minister of victory." The first is Ilan Broner's famous photograph of Dayan, dressed in fatigues, with a helmet and holstered pistol, striding though Lions' Gate on June 7, 1967, with Chief of Staff Yitzhak Rabin on his right and commander of the Central Command Uzi Narkiss on his left (Figure 5.1). The second, an illustration adorning *Time* magazine's June 16, 1967, cover, depicts Dayan against a background of a burned-out military vehicle, with the headline, "How Did Israel Win the War?" Superimposed on Dayan appears the two-word answer: "General Dayan." Dayan's political rivals claimed he stole their glory,[1] that he appeared out of nowhere just a few weeks before the war, was appointed defense minister less than four days prior to the first battle, then swept up all the credit, acting as if he had single-handedly won the war.

For example, Ami Gluska cites a confrontation between Major General Ezer Weizman, Director of the General Staff Division, and Prime Minister and then Defense Minister Levi Eshkol on June 1, 1967, after Eshkol agreed to let Dayan run the Defense Ministry:

> "Give the order and the IDF will go to war! What do you need Moshe Dayan for?" Weizman yelled at Eshkol while trying to rip his major general stripes off one of his shirt sleeves. But it was too late; the die had been cast. Eshkol gave up the defense portfolio with a heavy heart. Dayan snapped up the victor's wreath and the hero's aura, and Eshkol never forgave himself.[2]

On the morning of June 7, when the news broke that the Old City of Jerusalem had been conquered, Eshkol wanted to go to the Western Wall but was told that the firefight was still ongoing. He arrived only in the evening and received very little media attention. Instead, the first pages of the next morning's newspapers prominently featured the photograph of Dayan, with Eshkol mentioned only briefly on the inside pages. Eshkol's military secretary, Brigadier General Israel Lior, furious, expressed Eshkol's thoughts, writing: "Dayan stole the glory." Lior

---

[1] Shlomo Nakdimon, "How Moshe Dayan elbowed Levi Eshkol into history's margins" (Hebrew), *Haaretz*, June 2, 2011.

[2] Ami Gluska, *Eshkol: Ten pekuda! Tsahal vememshelet yisrael baderekh lemilhemet sheshet hayamin 1963–1967* (Hebrew), Tel Aviv: Maarakhot, 2016, p. 1.

Figure 5.1 Israeli Minister of Defense Moshe Dayan marching toward the captured wailing wall with IDF Chief of Staff Yitzhak Rabin (right), and General Uzi Narkiss, Commander of Central Command. Source: Getty Images/Staff/Hulton Archive/Getty Images.

was likely speaking for Eshkol who, enraged after Dayan had ordered the Golan Heights conquest toward the war's end, branded Dayan "loathsome."[3]

---

[3] Eitan Haber, *Hayom tifrots milhama: Zikhronot shel tat aluf Yisrael Lior, hamazkir hatseva'i shel rosh hamemshala Levi Eshkol ve Golda Meir* (Hebrew), Tel Aviv: Idanim, 1987, pp. 233–234.

True, Dayan, a cunning politician, fully exploited the opportunity that had fallen into his lap, branding himself "the minister of victory." It is also true that the glory the charismatic Dayan reaped sometimes came at the expense of recognizing other key players' contributions. Dayan, adulated in Israel and internationally, was already considered Israel's savior before the war. The victory merely cemented his special status and strengthened him further. The change in Dayan's public image after the Yom Kippur War and contemporary historiography's emphasis on Eshkol and Rabin's roles then have increasingly led historians to stress others' contributions and reduce or even negate Dayan's part.[4] However, success and failure in large political and military campaigns are not part of a zero-sum game whereby Dayan's contribution necessarily detracts from others' importance. Significant contributors include Prime Minister Levi Eshkol, who led the nation with political wisdom, using his experience to maximize the political options and obtain American backing, and Chief of Staff Yitzhak Rabin, who prepared the army and the operational plans assisted by possibly Israel's best General Staff.

Nevertheless, Dayan's achievements were considerable. Although he assumed the position of defense minister just days before the war, his contribution was decisive, not only in terms of morale, as the common wisdom holds, but also in the war's planning, decision-making, and conduct.

Dayan's last-minute appointment as defense minister – getting "called from the bench" – suited his personality and style of action. Others might have found it difficult to take control with so little lead time. Dayan, however, immersed himself in a rapid learning process, visiting the fronts and units and speaking with commanders. His ability not to wed himself to one single way of acting to attain the defined objective enabled him to switch among several alternatives during the war and make decisions based on developments on the ground. His actions exemplified careful conduct on the one hand and exploitation of opportunities on the other. Not understanding Dayan's shifting positions, his rivals and critics accused him of inconsistency. For example, when Dayan suddenly changed his mind about conquering the Golan Heights, Rabin responded: "The unpredictable Moshe Dayan, whose moves are unseen, has surprised us yet again."[5] Yeshayahu Gavish, commander of the Southern

---

[4] See, e.g., Aryeh Naor, "The Ouster of Levi Eshkol from the Defense Minister's Position and the Results of the Six-Day War: Anatomy of a Savior Complex" (Hebrew), in Devora Cohen and Moshe Lisk (eds.), *Tsomtei hakhra'ot ufarshiyot mafte'ah beyisrael* (Hebrew), Be'er Sheva: The Ben-Gurion Institute for the Study of Israel and Zionism, Ben-Gurion University of the Negev, 2010, pp. 462–475; Yehiam Weiz, "'Not Hesitant': Levi Eshkol as Political Leader and Statesman" (Hebrew), lecture at the Israel Studies Department at Bar-Ilan University, "50 Years since the Six-Day War," May 15, 2017, www.youtube.com/watch?v=d2qPcH-RPOM.

[5] Yitzhak Rabin, *Pinkas sherut* (Hebrew) (published in English as *The Rabin Memoirs*), Tel Aviv: Maariv, 1979, Vol. 1, p. 238.

Command, wrote: "Dayan issues orders and that's the end of the matter ... I'm not exaggerating when I say that he has very often been wrong, shot from the hip, and enjoyed personal prestige that goes far beyond reason."[6] In practice, Dayan's decisions were far from "shots from the hip." A common thread ran through Dayan's deliberations, reflecting an internal rationale that corresponded with a dynamic reality that changed virtually every hour. He truly acted upon the idea that strategy was essentially "a system of expedients."[7]

Dayan 1958–1967

For Dayan, the period between 1958 and 1967 was filled with party politics and some state-level activities, but little military-political activity. Dayan devoted only 17 pages to that decade in his 520-page autobiography, and his biographer Shabtai Teveth gave it only 18.[8] Dayan had ended his tenure as Chief of Staff as the acknowledged hero of the Sinai Campaign. Enjoying an international reputation in Israel and abroad, he received the kind of acclaim, even adulation, usually reserved for rock stars.[9] No one failed to recognize the victor with the eyepatch. His image became identified with that of Israel.[10] After briefly studying at the Hebrew University, he, like many other former military men, entered the political arena. There, he naturally gravitated toward his patron David Ben-Gurion, linking his political destiny with that of the "old man." His career started to take off after the 1959 elections, when Ben-Gurion appointed Dayan Minister of Agriculture, a post he held for five years before resigning in 1964 in the wake of the power struggle between Ben-Gurion and Eshkol over the nature of the party and the establishment of the Labor Alignment.[11] After the Lavon Affair, Ben-Gurion left Mapai and founded the Rafi Party with Dayan and Shimon Peres. Rafi, having won only 10 (of 120) Knesset seats in the 1965 election and given the personal animosity between Ben-Gurion and Eshkol, was not a coalition partner. However, unlike Peres and Ben-Gurion,

---

[6] Yeshayahu Gavish, *Sadin adom – sippur hayay: Mehapalmah ve'ad leveit hapalmah* (Hebrew), Or Yehuda: Kinneret, Zmora-Bitan, Dvir, 2016, p. 203.
[7] Daniel J. Hughes (ed. and trans.), *Moltke on the Art of War: Selected Writings*, Novato, CA: Presidio, 1993, p. 47.
[8] Yael Dayan, *Avi, bito* (Hebrew), Jerusalem: Idanim, 1986, p. 110.
[9] Mark A. Raider, "Moshe Dayan: Israel's No. 1 Hero (in America)," *Journal of Israeli History* 37:1 (2019), pp. 21–59.
[10] Professor Yaakov Ben-Haim from the Technion, an expert on decision-making, told me that in those years he happened to be visiting Japan. A random stranger asked him where he was from, and he answered "Israel." The stranger looked at him and moved his head to indicate he didn't understand. Then Ben-Haim covered one eye and said "Dayan." The stranger's face lit up with a smile, and he nodded enthusiastically while also covering one eye and repeating, "Moshe Dayan, Moshe Dayan, Israel."
[11] The result of a union of two parties: Mapai and Ahdut HaAvoda.

Dayan was able to maintain a relatively professional relationship with Eshkol.[12]

Until his appointment as defense minister in June 1967, Dayan served as a regular Member of Knesset (MK), sitting on the Foreign Affairs and Security Committee. During 1966, a bored Dayan, always looking for excitement, traveled to Vietnam as a correspondent for the *Maariv* daily newspaper, afterward writing *Yoman Vietnam* [*Vietnam Diary*][13] about his experiences there (which are covered in the next chapter). His stay in Vietnam profoundly influenced his thinking and would shape his policy on the territories occupied after the Six-Day War. While in Vietnam, he also published pieces in several foreign newspapers, thereby remaining in the international public eye as a military expert.[14]

Before the crisis erupted in mid May 1967, Dayan shared the general consensus that Egypt, entangled in Yemen, was unlikely to embark on a war against Israel in the next few years. As Egypt, the biggest Arab nation with the largest and best-equipped army, was the main axis of the anti-Israel coalition, it was generally assumed that the rest of the Arab nations would not go to war without it.

Learning in a Crisis: May 14 to June 1, 1967

Many historians believe that the roots of the crisis ultimately leading to the Six-Day War can be found in a series of incidents in northern Israel. The Syrians were not satisfied with the Armistice Agreement signed between them and Israel in July 1949, especially as regards the location of the border and the regulation of activity in the demilitarized zones defined on the Israeli side of the border – the Israelis claimed these were demilitarized but allowed civilian activity, the Syrians claimed that no Israeli activity should be allowed in them. To these was added a disagreement over water rights – about a third of the water feeding the Sea of Galilee, Israel's most important source of fresh water, came from rivers and streams from Syria and Lebanon. Israel built a series of pipes to take water from that area to central and southern Israel, and the Syrians opposed this project. From 1949 till 1967, the Syrians initiated hundreds of small-scale fire attacks on Israeli farmers, water-project operators, and soldiers along the border, as well as some larger attacks that included artillery bombardment of Israeli villages near the border. Israel responded in kind, adding an occasional infantry raid when Syrian attacks escalated. In 1964, Syria initiated a project to divert the water flowing from its territory into Israel to Jordan, bypassing Israel and thus threatening its ability to maintain its

---

[12] Gluska, *Eshkol*, p. 421.
[13] Moshe Dayan, *Yoman Vietnam* (Hebrew), Tel Aviv: Dvir, 1977.
[14] Interview with Neora Barnoach-Matalon, Herzliya, July 15, 2017.

population, agriculture, and industrial water requirements. Israel responded by shooting up the Syrian mechanical digging equipment until, in 1966, the Syrians ceased their project.[15]

However, the Syrian harassment of Israeli farmers did not cease – and in early 1967, it even escalated. Early on April 7, 1967, two Israeli tractors were fired on by Syrian artillery immediately upon entering the demilitarized zone.[16] The Syrians then began shelling Kibbutz Gadot. Usually Israel responded only tit-for-tat, but this time, pressured by the civilians living under Syrian attacks, Prime Minister Eshkol authorized the IAF to silence the Syrian artillery. Syrian aircraft intervened to protect their artillery, and six were shot down.[17] Dayan harshly criticized the move in the Knesset. "Have you gone crazy? You're leading the nation to war!"[18] At this point, Dayan – in contrast to his having championed a preventive war against Egypt over a decade earlier – was not interested in hostilities.

For a few days, there was quiet; then the small-scale harassment by the Syrians was resumed. In early May, Israeli leaders threatened another large retaliation but did nothing. On May 10, the Soviets provided Syria and Egypt with intelligence that Israel was indeed massing forces on the Syrian border. Egyptian and Syrian reconnaissance flights over the Golan Heights proved this information false, but Gamal Abd al-Nasser, President of Egypt, saw an opportunity to improve his status in the constant political struggle between the Arab state leaders over the position of the supreme Arab leader. On May 14, 1967, he ordered his army into Sinai, in a direct breach of the 1957 accords in which Israel agreed to vacate the Sinai, recently captured in the Sinai War. His rationale – Israel did not intend to invade Syria, but Nasser could later claim that it was due to his threats and military mobilization that Israel was deterred and canceled its plans to attack the Syrians. Initially, Israeli intelligence assessed correctly Nasser's design, and Israel's response was muted. But Nasser lost control of the situation – his actions were received with growing acclaim across the Arab world, urging him to actually lead them to war with Israel. On May 16, Nasser demanded the UN remove its buffer force from eastern Sinai, fully expecting it to refuse and thus giving him an excuse for not attacking Israel. But on May 18, the UN forces withdrew. On May 22, Nasser closed the Tiran Straits, cutting Israel's commercial ties with Asia and East Africa again. The growing presence of forces in Sinai and the beginning of preparations for war in other Arab states compelled the Israeli

---

[15] Michael Oren, *Shisha yamim shel milhama: Hama'arakha sheshinta et pnei hamizrah hatikhon* (Hebrew) [originally published in English as *Six Days of War: June 1967 and the Making of the Modern Middle East*, New York: Oxford University Press, 2002], Or Yehuda: Dvir, 2004, p. 44.
[16] Ibid., p. 71.
[17] Ibid., p. 72.
[18] Gluska, *Eshkol*, p. 196.

government to mobilize its reserve forces, but it still sought a diplomatic solution.

Once the crisis began, after "the horses had already bolted from the stable," Dayan adapted to the new reality conceptually and emotionally, getting back into uniform to prepare for a war that now seemed inevitable. On May 20, Dayan asked Eshkol for permission to visit the Southern Command to check out the situation there, and to begin his reserve duty so that he could tour the south in uniform. After receiving a car, driver, and accompanying officer,[19] Dayan donned his uniform, bedecked with his lieutenant general insignia, determined to use this time to study the situation. For Dayan, learning and studying were an unmediated process, calling for gaining firsthand impressions. Just as he had done as Chief of Staff and again when studying the war in Vietnam, he insisted on being on the ground, speaking with soldiers and commanders, and assessing the army's morale and fighting fitness in person. In his diary, he wrote, "All those days, I toured IDF units in the south, the north, and the center. From time to time, I'd go home to Tel Aviv, hear what was happening, and respond to what I'd heard."[20] He toured the IDF much as he had toured in Vietnam: Systematically, he began with the senior commanders and command centers, followed by speaking with the next tier down, from the strategic to the tactical, where strategy is translated into action. Dayan noted, "I wanted to see what the IDF is really like. What it can and cannot do ... I found a much better IDF. My soul was truly revived."[21]

In keeping with his habits, during the prewar waiting period, Dayan avoided uttering any unequivocal position on what would be preferable – waiting for diplomatic efforts to bear fruit (the political echelon's position) or launching a preemptive assault (the military echelon's position). At this stage, he did not intervene in the army's operational planning. Until he joined the government, that aspect of the war had been entirely the IDF's domain, as the political echelon lacked the requisite professional knowledge of military issues.[22]

Dayan and Rabin met on May 22. Dayan noted that Rabin initiated the meeting, wanting to hear Dayan's opinion even though Dayan was "just a civilian." In the meeting, Dayan said that he assumed Nasser would close the Tiran Straits, which, in fact, Nasser did that day, and this would give Israel the opportunity to pulverize the Egyptian army in Sinai. But, as in the past, Dayan also expressed reservations about conquering the Gaza Strip. However,

---

[19] Moshe Dayan, *Avnei derekh: Autobiografia* (Hebrew), Jerusalem: Idanim, 1976, p. 399. See the letter of May 25 in which Dayan asks of Eshkol to be called up for reserve duty. It seems that Dayan acted informally and submitted his formal request to regularize his call-up duty only two days later (the letter appears in his book *Avnei derekh*, p. 408).

[20] Dayan, *Avnei derekh*, p. 398.

[21] Yaakov Erez and Ilan Kfir, *Sihot eem Moshe Dayan: Ha'azinu vesha'alu* (Hebrew), Massada: Ramat Gan, Ma'ariv Library Editions, 1981, p. 46.

[22] Gluska, *Eshkol*, pp. 422, 424.

two days earlier, Rabin had recommended conquering Gaza to use as a bargaining chip,[23] feeling that a preemptive strike was a condition for victory. Dayan doubted the government had the courage to order a first strike.[24] At the meeting, Dayan saw a fatigued, lethargic, and insecure Rabin. Dayan told Rabin that he, too, had erred in assessing Nasser's desire for a confrontation. In response to Rabin's remark that it may have been possible to avoid this situation by striking harder at Syria, Dayan disagreed, suggesting that the strikes against Syria had exposed Israel's impotence, which had directly led to Egypt's involvement. Dayan thought further escalation on the Syrian border would only make things worse.

The next day, the cabinet met after Nasser closed the Tiran Straits, cutting Israel's commerce with eastern Africa and Asia. The meeting was attended also by opposition MKs, including Dayan, who said that Israel should agree to the American request to give diplomacy a chance for the next forty-eight hours, despite believing that the diplomatic efforts were probably futile. He added that should diplomacy fail, Israel needed to strike at the Egyptian army and destroy it. Furthermore, he said, Israel had to assume that the other Arab states and Arabs living in Israel would join the campaign, emphasizing that it was imperative to win the very first battle in order to deter this.[25]

Given the high regard for Dayan's professional knowledge, his grim assessment on Israel's unfavorable situation troubled the ministers. Dayan asked to study the IDF's plans. He said that the war's objective was to destroy hundreds of enemy tanks and airplanes within two or three days. He argued that the destruction of enemy forces, not territorial gains, was critical and insisted that the first battles had to be decisive. "We're not Great Britain that can afford to lose the first few battles and then regroup."[26] Eshkol wavered, wanting to postpone action until the IDF completed mobilization and other preparations. Dayan responded, "I don't share that opinion,"[27] instead supporting a forty-eight-hour wait only.

Dayan continued touring bases and units, arriving on May 23 at the Southern Command, where he met with Southern Command commander Yeshayahu Gavish and other commanders. He studied the different contingency plans, concluding that they were "not cohesive, incapable of forcing Egypt to make a change."[28] For Dayan, the latter was crucial, because the IDF's advantages over the plodding, lumbering Egyptian army were its flexibility and improvisational ability. He felt that a plan that would force the Egyptian

---

[23] Shimon Golan, *Milhama beshalosh hazitot: Kabalat hah'latot bapikud ha'elyon bemilhemet sheshet hayamim* (Hebrew), Tel Aviv: Maarakhot, 2007, p. 75.
[24] Dayan, *Avnei derekh*, p. 399.
[25] Ibid., p. 400.
[26] Gluska, *Eshkol*, p. 273.
[27] Ibid.
[28] Dayan, *Avnei derekh*, p. 401.

military – trained in warfare according to fixed, preconceived scenarios – to shift course would damage its fighting ability. Nonetheless, Dayan reined himself in. "It may be too soon for me to comment. I've been disengaged from the IDF for 10 years, and first I have to study matters before I can reach the correct conclusions."[29]

Writing about that meeting, Gavish said that Dayan told him, "I can tell you that we'll win the campaign, but victory will mean the loss of our best youths … We will lose 20,000 young fighters, but I'll say it again: you will win the war." Dayan defined the objective as: "The destruction of the Egyptian army in Sinai and the conquest of Sharm El Sheikh to protect shipping through the Straits of Tiran." Gavish recalled that "Moshe gave me confidence and the clear knowledge of what to aim for."[30]

From the Southern Command, Dayan traveled to Major General Israel Tal's 84th Division and then to Colonel Shmuel Gonen's 7th Brigade. Finding them full of confidence and fighting spirit raised Dayan's spirits.[31] That evening, he met again with Gavish, who told him that the action currently approved included the conquest of the Gaza Strip and an aerial strike. This was in fact the Atzmon Plan, whose objectives were to destroy the Egyptian air force, conquer the Gaza Strip, and confine the enemy forces in the other sectors, all to serve as preliminary steps to a general assault to conquer Sinai.[32]

In the preceding General Staff debate, most of the generals had supported a more inclusive plan, codenamed Kardom, although they assumed the government would not approve it.[33] Dayan did not like Kardom for two reasons. The first was political: Gaza, with its massive population, was liable to turn from a bargaining chip to a bone that would stick in Israel's craw and become a perpetual burden. The second was military: It was, he felt, necessary to find a way to focus on the Egyptian army in the Sinai and generate a big clash between the IDF and the Egyptian army, leading to the latter's destruction. He explained that this was required not just to remove the military threat but also to meet Israel's need for a clear Israeli victory over the strongest Arab military without any allied assistance.[34] Until then, Egypt's narrative was that only the assistance of the UK and France to the IDF had led to Egypt's defeat in the Sinai Campaign.[35] Creating deterrence vis-à-vis the Arab world required Israel to prove it could win alone.

Dayan was planning on meeting with Chief of Staff Rabin on May 24 at night, but he received word that Rabin was ill (Rabin had collapsed, apparently

---

[29] Ibid.
[30] Gavish, *Sadin adom – sippur hayay*, pp. 132–134.
[31] Dayan, *Avnei derekh*, p. 402.
[32] For more about the plan, see Golan, *Milhama beshalosh hazitot*, pp. 80, 90–91.
[33] Ibid., p. 88.
[34] Dayan, *Avnei derekh*, pp. 402–403.
[35] From Nasser speech on May 22; Golan, *Milhama beshalosh hazitot*, p. 92.

from physical and mental exhaustion; the reason given at the time was nicotine poisoning). As a result, Dayan decided to meet with Ariel Sharon, commander of the 38th Division, and later with Colonel Yekutiel Adam, commander of the 99th Brigade, and Colonel Mordechai Zippori, commander of the 14th Brigade. Together, they went to visit the companies. Dayan recalled, "It is amazing how many commanders of all ranks who tell me, 'I was in the Sinai Campaign, I have memories and ambitions for this territory.' From their mouths to the depths of my heart."[36] Because Dayan was certain war would break out the next day, he got a quartermaster to issue him a uniform, helmet, and equipment.

In the meantime, the General Staff – without Rabin and responding to the news that the Egyptian 4th Division had reached the frontlines of Sinai – formulated Kardom 2, rendering Kardom 1, which had assumed that the 4th Division was not in Sinai, irrelevant. As instructed by the General Staff, despite opposition, the plan again shrank to conquering just the Gaza Strip and advancing to el-Arish with the aim of seizing it. The assumption was that the world powers would stop the IDF within forty-eight hours, which was not enough time for the army to complete the conquest.[37]

Dayan, eager to exercise real influence, sought to enlist, even as a private. On May 25, he wrote to Eshkol, asking to be called up for military service, but promising that if this was not possible, he would continue to visit the field, serving as the eyes and ears of the government on the ground. On May 26, Dayan toured the border with the Gaza Strip and the brigades and battalions stationed there. He met and spoke with commanders, visiting a number of brigade and division commanders. That afternoon, Dayan met with Ben-Gurion, who presented his ideas to Dayan, the core being an air strike on Sharm El Sheikh. Ben-Gurion explained that, in response, Nasser would go to war while Israel held the international advantage. Dayan appreciated Ben-Gurion's clear analysis, but completely rejected his conclusions, believing that Israel had to attack the border zone from the air and on the ground. Dayan believed that military considerations were primary, that Israel must not take any chances, and that concerns about gaining superpower support were less relevant because the war would be short. While Ben-Gurion insisted that political considerations came first, Dayan was not convinced.[38]

That day, Dayan also met with Meir Amit, Director of the national intelligence agency Mossad and former Director of Operations Branch in the Sinai Campaign, and laid out what he saw as the war's objective: to achieve a confrontation with the Egyptian force and destroy it in the eastern Sinai. Dayan did not agree that conquering territory would be a bargaining

---

[36] Dayan, *Avnei derekh*, p. 403.
[37] Golan, *Milhama beshalosh hazitot*, p. 101.
[38] Dayan, *Avnei derekh*, p. 411.

chip for attaining freedom of shipping, and he opposed conquering the Gaza Strip and reaching the Suez Canal.[39] All these meetings were held on the basis of personal relationships, because Dayan still had no official function.

Dayan continued touring. On May 27, he met with Major General Ezer Weizman, Director of the General Staff Division, who urged him to begin the offensive right away. Dayan wanted to see the materials from AMAN – the IDF Intelligence Directorate – because he was not yet sure of the Egyptians' intentions. Later, AMAN Deputy Director David Carmon informed Dayan of Egypt's preparations in Sinai and the options open to Israel.[40]

On May 28, responding to US President Lyndon B. Johnson's request to give diplomacy a chance to work, the government met and voted to wait. The army fumed, as did the Israeli public, feeling that the decision reflected a state of confusion. Public pressure for leadership changes mounted. That day, Eshkol gave his infamous "stuttering speech," triggering widespread disappointment within the army and among the public. Eshkol, finding it difficult to read the corrected version of his handwritten speech, stammered, sounding unsure at a time when he needed to project confidence and determination. The damage to morale was considerable. Israel Lior recalled that soldiers and their commanders at the front burst out crying after hearing the speech.[41] The day continued going badly for Eshkol when, at a General Staff forum meeting, he clashed with the "noble stallions" urging him to act.

Gavish wrote that the pressure to appoint a "security authority" – either Dayan or Allon – stemmed largely from the disconnect between the General Staff generals and Eshkol, and the former's disrespect for the latter. Gavish described a visit Eshkol paid to the command after the announcement that the UN observers had been expelled: "The prime minister demonstrated very little understanding of the military topics I presented. My impression was that he didn't have a clue about the army and that he didn't fully grasp the situation."[42]

Recounting the dramatic meeting between Eshkol and the General Staff, Gavish noted that the frustrated generals felt that they were not being understood and that no one was listening to them. He wrote: "Eshkol seems detached from the situation ... General Staff generals have started to realize that the prime minister isn't living in reality."[43] The sense of discomfort wasn't helped by a new command and new order, Rogel 4, to prepare for defense for two more weeks. The atmosphere was on the brink of exploding.[44] After that meeting, which made it clear that an attack would not be approved, the

---

[39] Ibid., p. 412.
[40] Ibid., pp. 412–413.
[41] Haber, *Hayom tifrots milhama*, p. 194.
[42] Gavish, *Sadin adom – sippur hayay*, p. 113.
[43] Ibid., pp. 126–128.
[44] Brigadier General Israel Tal quoted in: Golan, *Milhama beshalosh hazitot*, p. 125.

General Staff examined the option of sending the reserves back home. In fact, the IDF's plans were for transitioning from offense to defense.[45]

On May 30, Dayan continued to use his connections and personal status to keep abreast of planning, meeting in Eilat with Navy Commander Shlomo Erel, who presented the options for seizing Sharm El Sheikh from the sea. At the day's end, back in Tel Aviv, Dayan again met with Meir Amit, who was about to leave on a mission to the United States.

The key event that day was King Hussein's meeting with the Egyptian president, where they decided to subordinate the Jordanian army to the Egyptian military command and Hussein agreed to allow Iraqi troops onto Jordanian soil. With the IDF transitioning to deployment and a mental state of waiting and defense, the joint Jordanian–Egyptian decision triggered an important shift, making the Jordanian front suddenly more important, second only to the Egyptian one, with the Syrian front dropping to third place. The military importance stemmed from its location – the Jordanian West Bank, especially the Samaria region. Bulging into central Israel and leaving only 16 to 30 kilometers between it and the Mediterranean Sea, it also enjoyed a pronounced advantage of elevation – the hills of Samaria looking down on the coastal plain. The Jordanian army was highly professional but small, and the greater fear was that it would be reinforced by a large Iraqi expeditionary force. The IDF General Staff were now discussing the conquest of the West Bank in tandem with defending the Egyptian front, assuming a situation in which the Jordanian front would actually become Iraqi.[46]

Dayan had major reservations about these plans. On May 31, he met with Uzi Narkiss, Central Command commander, to review the Central Command plans. Dayan felt it was imperative to focus on beating the Egyptian army first, with minimal forces diverted to the other fronts – therefore, till the Egyptians were beaten, the strategy facing Jordan should be defensive.[47] Later that day, Dayan declined an appointment as deputy prime minister, because he was interested in commanding the southern front.[48] In the evening, the Chief of Staff and General Staff reviewed the plans and agreed with Dayan's conclusions that the main enemy was Egypt: "Let no [other] front divert the IDF from what's most important."[49]

Dayan met with Rabin to discuss being appointed commander of the southern front. Rabin asked Dayan if he would accept his authority. Dayan, maybe influenced by his visits to the US armed forces and his Vietnam experience, answered that their relationship should be similar to that between

---

[45] Golan, *Milhama beshalosh hazitot*, p. 131.
[46] Ibid., p. 135.
[47] Ibid., p. 138.
[48] Dayan, *Avnei derekh*, p. 416.
[49] Golan, *Milhama beshalosh hazitot*, p. 140.

the Chairman of the Joint Chiefs of Staff and the commander of the theater of operations. Rabin answered, justifiably, that the example wasn't relevant to Israel.[50] Dayan again stressed that Rabin was the Chief of Staff and that Dayan was not interested in replacing him.

On June 1, Dayan visited Central Command and joined Narkiss for an observation of the front. Dayan studied the Central Command plans and expressed approval.[51] In the afternoon, Dayan met with Deputy Director of AMAN David (Dudik) Carmon in the underground bunker housing the IDF Supreme Command in Tel Aviv (known as "the Pit"). At this point, Dayan assumed he would be appointed commander of the southern front.

Lieutenant Colonel Shaikeh Bareket, the Director of the IAF Intelligence Department, having heard Dayan was attending a highly secret briefing with AMAN's Deputy Director, burst into the room and told the stunned Dayan he had different intelligence assessments than AMAN did. Bareket, unlike AMAN, believed there was a high probability that the Egyptians would initiate a war and that the IDF must strike first. After recovering from the young lieutenant colonel's presumptuousness, Dayan listened. In general, Dayan respected opinions that differed from the consensus. Finally, Bareket said, "You're wasting time. Go and get yourself appointed defense minister, you'll be the victory minister."[52] Dayan followed Bareket's advice.

As this was happening, Rabin was meeting with Eshkol, who told Rabin about a telegram he'd received from Walt W. Rostow, US National Security Advisor.[53] The telegram, sent on behalf of President Lyndon B. Johnson, said that the United States could not help open the Tiran Straits. This was a blow to Israel: The diplomatic option had hit a dead end.

Appointment as Defense Minister: Instilling Confidence, June 1 to 5

On June 1, Prime Minister Eshkol surrendered to political pressure to form a national unity government with the leading opposition parties. At 4:15 p.m., Eshkol informed Dayan he was appointing him defense minister.[54] At 4:30 p.m., Dayan was sworn in, and his authority defined in very clear terms. Eshkol also appointed former Chief of Staff Yigael Yadin as his security advisor – and as a counterweight to Dayan. It was while Dayan was en route to the prime minister's bureau that Eshkol had the highly charged encounter with Ezer

---

[50] Rabin, *Pinkas sherut*, p. 176.
[51] Dayan, *Avnei derekh*, p. 417.
[52] Author's interview with Shaikeh Bareket, Ramat Hasharon, May 10, 2017. The story also appears in Amos Gilboa, *Mar modi'in: Ahreleh, aluf aharon yariv, rosh aman* (Hebrew), Tel Aviv: Miskal, 2013, p. 291.
[53] Haber, *Hayom tifrots milhama*.
[54] Ibid., p. 182.

Weizman described at the beginning of this chapter. Eshkol was stunned.[55] Weizman's outburst both stemmed from personal frustrations about other appointments and reflected a widespread feeling among the other General Staff generals. Clearly, the General Staff was under great pressure, which they in turn exerted on the political echelon, especially Eshkol, in the run-up to the war.

The public, unlike the generals, greeted Dayan's appointment with ecstasy. As he assumed office, it had become clear to all that the diplomatic option had failed; there was a sense that the noose was tightening around Israel's neck. Due to the Hussein–Nasser agreement and the approaching Iraqi military presence in Jordan, Dayan wholeheartedly shared the army's opinion that it was time to act, and that further delay was harmful. Dayan's focus was on the Egyptian army, the biggest threat – defeat it quickly and perhaps the others would back down; he hoped to maintain a low level of escalation on the other fronts.

Avner Falk described the atmosphere generated by Dayan's appointment:

> I was a student ... at Washington University in St. Louis. Every day before the war, we'd meet at the B'nai B'rith [Jewish organization) student center ... One of us ... came in and announced, with a tone of victory, "Guys, don't worry, Dayan has been made defense minister. We're going to win!" All the Israelis there heaved a sigh of relief and clapped and cheered. Moshe Dayan's name was magic.[56]

Similarly, Uri Even recorded the reaction to Dayan's appointment among soldiers: "The news [of Dayan's appointment] sped like a whirlwind through the camps scattered in the desert. Soldiers whooped and clasped hands. They saw the appointment not only as a way out of the exhausting, pointless waiting, but also as a chance for victory."[57]

On June 2, the government and the General Staff held another discussion, now with Dayan installed as defense minister. Gavish described the atmosphere in the room:

> The prime minister again spoke of the need for a political resolution, but Moshe Dayan and Menachem Begin changed the balance of power. We left the meeting with the feeling there was someone to trust. It wasn't just our feeling; it seemed as if we were swept along by a general sense in the nation. Moshe Dayan changed the mood and mindset from one extreme to the other. It was bizarre, but true.[58]

---

[55] Golan, *Milhama beshalosh hazitot*, p. 143.
[56] Avner Falk, *Moshe Dayan: Ha'ish veha'agada – biografia psikho'analitit* (Hebrew), Jerusalem: Kaneh Publishing, 1985, p. 254.
[57] Uri Even, *Arik: Darko shel lohem* (Hebrew), Tel Aviv: Bustan, 1974, p. 171.
[58] Gavish, *Sadin adom – sippur hayay*, pp. 146–147.

Even Ezer Weizman, who, only a few hours earlier was furious about Eshkol appointing Dayan wrote, "He came at exactly the right time, gave us strength, dissipated the doubts ... gave a tremendous push to [our] willingness to fight ... to the demand not to go for some limited action, but for the total destruction of the Egyptian army."[59]

In the discussion, Rabin reviewed the military buildup around Israel: "A military noose is tightening around us, one that I don't believe anyone else is going to loosen for us ... It is necessary to deal Nasser and the Egyptian army a blow while [defending] on the other fronts."[60] Dayan explained that further delay would mean many casualties. In addition, the IDF needed time to complete its main missions before the superpowers stopped Israel. Based on his experience in the Sinai Campaign, he estimated that it would be possible to conclude the mission in six days. Rabin wrote: "We found support and encouragement for our position in the words of the new defense minister, Moshe Dayan, in his debut performance in his new position."[61]

Dayan stressed the importance of time. With each passing day, the enemy was improving its fortifications, which had serious ramifications: more casualties when the attack came and slower progress through enemy territory. Also, the superpowers could force Israel to stop the campaign before all its goals were achieved. Because Dayan wanted first to annihilate the Egyptian army and then conquer Sharm El Sheikh to open the Tiran Straits, he worried that delayed progress would make it impossible to complete the second stage.[62]

After the meeting, the prime minister invited Dayan, Eban, and Allon, along with Rabin and the director general of the Prime Minister's Office, to the penultimate discussion before the final one that would determine whether or not Israel was going to war. Dayan opened, saying that Israel had to strike now. The objective was defeating the Egyptian army, to remove the immediate threat and renew deterrence, not capturing territory, though to do the former some territory must be taken. The campaign, he added, would last three to five days, during which time the IDF would destroy Egypt's air force and conquer important locations in Sinai. Allon proposed a plan for reaching the Suez Canal, but Dayan nixed it.

At 7:30 p.m. that day, the Southern Command's attack plans were presented to Rabin. They included two options: either occupying territory to be held as a political bargaining chip or destroying the Egyptian military force located in eastern Sinai and occupying a buffer zone there. Haim Bar-Lev, Ezer Weizman, and Israel Tal all supported the first option, which was not contingent on aerial

---

[59] Ezer Weizman, *Lekh shamayim, lekh erets* (Hebrew), Tel Aviv: Maariv Publications, 1975, p. 265.
[60] Golan, *Milhama beshalosh hazitot*, p. 149.
[61] Rabin, *Pinkas sherut*, p. 181.
[62] A special General Staff session with the Ministerial Committee on Security, June 2, 1967, State Archive, File No. EES0002.

superiority or calm on the Jordanian front. Major Generals Gavish, Yaffe, and Sharon favored the second option. Dayan arrived at 8:30 p.m. and heard both alternatives.

Based on his Sinai Campaign experience, Dayan stressed the importance of the limited time available to complete the operation, and that any territory taken would be returned after the war. He explained that it was essential to destroy the enemy's armored forces from the flanks and when it was on the move. The Egyptians would send armored troops to any focus of attack; that was when it had to be crushed. During the discussion, Dayan reiterated his opposition to occupying the Gaza Strip and reaching the Suez Canal. At this point, he forced the meeting to a decision: It was clear that the main mission was destroying the Egyptian army in Sinai. To make that happen, given the deployment of the Egyptian army, it was necessary to conquer most of the peninsula, but for political reasons, the army had to keep away from the Suez Canal.[63] By presenting an unequivocal position in favor of the large offensive plan to destroy the Egyptian military, Dayan once and for all buried the more limited plans the IDF had proposed.

From June 2 to June 4, Eshkol's position on delaying the action gradually weakened. The messages from the United States were ambiguous. In contrast, French President Charles de Gaulle warned Israel against going to war, and Soviet leader Leonid Brezhnev issued threats. It became clear that the United States was going to renege on its promise to send an international flotilla to break the naval blockade at the Tiran Straits.[64] "We have gotten all we could out of our political efforts,"[65] admitted Eshkol, whose confidence about taking military action had grown in light of the reports Meir Amit was sending from the United States, where he had met secretly with US Secretary of Defense Robert McNamara on June 1 with President Johnson's knowledge and blessing. The impression Amit got from McNamara was that the United States would not oppose an Israeli action – "a blinking yellow light" is how he later described it. A missive from the US president affirming the US commitment to Israel's security arrived at a meeting held on June 4. McNamara added, "We exchanged opinions with General Amit." Israel interpreted this to mean that the United States understood Israel's situation and accepted its position.[66]

On June 4 at 8:30 a.m., the Ministerial Committee on Security held a meeting that began with Foreign Minister Abba Eban reading a message from McNamara, which stated that, personally, McNamara greatly respected Dayan, who had brought back from Vietnam the most balanced report and assessment he had seen, and praised Israel's current defense minister's clarity

---

[63] Golan, *Milhama beshalosh hazitot*, pp. 159–160.
[64] Mordechai Bar-On, *Moshe Dayan: Korot hayav 1915–1981*, Tel Aviv: Am Oved, 2014, p. 219.
[65] Ibid., p. 220.
[66] Oren, *Shisha yamim shel milhama*, p. 197.

of thought.[67] Dayan was flattered, later noting McNamara's comment about him in his diary.[68]

It seems that at this point in the meeting, Dayan felt that his moment had come. He began presenting a very detailed review that included a situation assessment and considerations for making a decision. He started with a note of humor, perhaps inspired by McNamara's compliment, that he now wanted to speak about the security considerations in the Israeli theater rather than those in the Vietnamese one. He later noted that he was one of the few in the Israeli security establishment who had warned about closing the Straits and went on to explain that Nasser was trapping himself with his declarations because they were creating a situation to which he had now committed himself. "Before Nasser signs any promissory notes, he has to have them covered."[69] Dayan added that there had been a serious development in the last twenty-four hours, the subordination of the Jordanian army to the Egyptian military, which opened another front and directly threatened Jerusalem, and updates on Egyptian troop deployment, especially of the tanks, indicated offensive intentions. To underscore his point, he related that in the battles for el-Alamein and other locations in World War II, fewer than 1,000 tanks had been stationed; now, even more were in position. His conclusion: "If they take action first, we'll be busy defending ourselves and we won't be able to reach el-Arish or anyplace else. On the other hand, if we seize the initiative, we'll achieve something."[70]

Dayan then rebutted Abba Eban's two arguments against an Israeli offensive, the first relating to the commitment Israel had made to the US president to wait another week for the formation of an international flotilla, the second to firing the first shot, because the United States had asked, "Don't be those who shoot first." In this situation, said Dayan, "We'll be at the enemy's mercy for a whole week. The enemy will be free to initiate an attack at any time. And even if the ships come and they shoot at them and we respond with all our might, they will obviously be ready for our response." Israel's problem, Dayan explained, was that its qualitative advantage in some areas could not compensate for its severe numerical disadvantage. Therefore, taking the first shot had – in Dayan's terminology – "fatal" implications. He concluded, "We have a military ring that is closing in on us, and therefore the military must take precedence over the political consideration, no matter the political state of affairs. We'll begin a military campaign, but the political campaign will get started only three days later, assuming the Russians don't intervene during those first three days." Should that happen, warned Dayan, Israel would be in dire political straits, but, "We'll be alive; we'll survive militarily

---

[67] Meeting of the Ministerial Committee on Security, June 2, 1967, State Archive, File No. EES0002.
[68] Dayan, *Avnei derekh*, p. 427.
[69] Ministerial Committee on Security, June 4.
[70] Ibid.

and that's the right order of priorities at this time."⁷¹ Later in the discussion, Eshkol again raised the possibility that the US Sixth Fleet would arrive and serve as a deterrent, but this was more wishful thinking than a realistic scenario. Dayan's answer reflected his experience in Vietnam: He said that he preferred the IDF, because thousands of Marines couldn't do more than the IDF's tanks, noting that half a million US soldiers were incapable of defeating 200,000 Vietnamese. Eshkol had, of course, meant the Sixth Fleet as a symbolic deterrent from one of the world's two superpowers, sending a strong message beyond its mere presence. Presumably Dayan understood Eshkol's meaning, but he also judged that US power had been eroded and that the Vietnamese were showing that it was possible to challenge the Americans.

The expanded government met at noon, and Dayan updated the other ministers. Dayan found the reinforcing of Arab forces at the front in Sinai, in Jordan, and in Syria quite worrisome. Furthermore, an intercepted Egyptian message suggested that they were planning to initiate a simultaneous offensive within days, perhaps even the following day, on June 5. He added that losing the initiative would have severe repercussions. "We're not like the Americans," he said. "We have no strategic reserves or depth ... While we sit around and wait, they're building strength and digging in." If the Arabs attacked first, the war would be inside Israel instead of in their territory. A preemptive strike, he said, that destroyed 100 Egyptian airplanes would be "worth more than any added weapons we might get from the United States over the next six months." According to him, the fear of an arms embargo was insignificant compared to the advantage of a preemptive blow. The only chance of winning the war would be with a first strike. "Then we breach Sinai and hold the other fronts with few troops. The first blow is what will make it possible to dictate the direction of the entire war. There's a limit to our ability to win, and in a different scenario we're liable to lose."⁷²

When formulating the government decision, Abba Eban, for obvious reasons, asked to erase the word "preemptive." In response, Dayan offered the following wording:

1. The government has decided to take military action that will free Israel from the military noose closing around it and prevent an attack about to be launched against it by the United Arab Headquarters.
2. The government has authorized the prime minister and defense minister to authorize the General Staff to determine the timing of the action.
3. Cabinet members will receive information about our military actions as soon as possible.⁷³

---

⁷¹ Meeting of Ministerial Committee on Security, June 4, 1947, State Archive, File No. EES0002.
⁷² Expanded meeting of Ministerial Committee on Security, June 4, 1967, afternoon, State Archive, File No. 0012//9.
⁷³ Expanded session of Ministerial Committee.

Dayan's phrasing became the government's decision, with the addition of a paragraph about the foreign minister's diplomatic efforts. It was decided that zero hour would be 7:30 a.m. the next day. Dayan immediately left for the Northern Command to meet with David Elazar, stressing the importance of the Syrian front staying defensive. "We have no desire to open a third front," he said. Dayan shared his belief that the Jordanians would start fighting but that the Syrians might stay calm and make do with shelling nearby settlements.[74]

In the evening, Dayan hosted a discussion in his office. In attendance were Yigael Yadin, the prime minister's security advisor, Tsvi Tsur, the defense minister's assistant, and AMAN's Director Aharon Yariv, who was studying the possibility of staging an Egyptian aggression to serve as a pretext for an Israeli assault. Dayan rejected the idea, because he felt that all lies are eventually uncovered. "Morality and justice are on our side," he said, "and we don't need tricks like that."[75] Afterward, he went to the Pit to meet with representatives from the navy, instructing them, too, not to escalate the Syrian sector.

Similar to his ruse in the Sinai Campaign, Dayan again tried to deceive the enemy or, more accurately, lull them into a false sense of security. Since his appointment as defense minister, Dayan had actively been creating misdirection by giving the impression that Israel had no intention of launching an offensive but was waiting for a lifeline from the international community. At the end of a June 1 interview, *Times* journalist Winston Churchill (named for his grandfather, the British prime minister) asked Dayan for a not-for-attribution comment as to whether "something" could be expected to happen in the next few days that would make it worthwhile to stay in the country. Dayan replied that Churchill could freely fly back to London.[76] In his diary, Dayan rationalized the misleading answer he gave the young reporter, writing that because the young Churchill was a true friend of Israel, it was only right that he should help in leading the enemy astray. Similarly, Dayan gave other media outlets the impression that Israel was not headed to war. On June 3, at his first press conference as defense minister, he declared, "It is too late to respond to the blockade on the Straits of Tiran in the military realm and too soon to draw conclusions about the diplomatic path."[77] In any case, the actual decision was made only in the afternoon of June 4.

At around midnight between the 4th and the 5th, the prime minister met with senior ministers, who accepted Dayan's advice on how to handle the public announcement: issue a brief statement on the outbreak of hostilities between the IDF and the Egyptian army and later issue a more detailed

---

[74] Golan, *Milhama beshalosh hazitot*, p. 182.
[75] Dayan, *Avnei derekh*, p. 430.
[76] Ibid., p. 423.
[77] Bar-On, *Moshe Dayan*, p. 223.

announcement after information from the front starts coming in. In that meeting, Dayan added that the Jordanians had to know they mustn't attack.[78]

On June 4, the Operations Department issued the Nahshonim Order – the final plan for the campaign. In the south, the IDF's objective was to destroy the Egyptian army by advancing deep into Sinai and surrounding most of it by capturing key locations necessary for the Egyptians to withdraw their troops. They were also to prepare for the options of conquering the Gaza Strip and moving toward the Suez Canal and reaching Sharm El Sheikh – if it was decided to do so during the operation. On the other fronts, the order directed the IDF to assume a defensive position.[79] The plan included intelligence deception in the center of the sector in the Mitzpeh Ramon area to draw concentrations of Egyptian troops from the north to the south.

On June 5, at 7:30 a.m., Dayan arrived at the IAF "Pit." Fifteen minutes later, after the Israeli planes reached their first objectives and began to attack, air-raid sirens sounded throughout Israel. The war had begun.

The Conduct of the War: June 5 to 10

Day 1: Destroying the Arab Air Forces, Breaching Sinai, Dilemmas vis-à-vis Jordan

In the morning, nearly all the IAF's functioning aircraft were sent to attack the Egyptian airfields. Operation Moked (Focus) was under way. Flying at low altitude and with radio silence so as not to be picked up by Egypt's radar system, the planes dropped their first bombs on the Egyptian runways and airplane hangars at 7:45 a.m. Understanding that Operation Moked would determine the fate of the war, everyone awaited news of the outcome of the IAF's attack. Around 9:30 a.m., the first reports started coming in: They verified the success of the Israeli attack on the Egyptian airfields. The General Staff's Operations Division, responding to Egyptian shelling from Gaza of the adjacent Israeli villages, then ordered the Southern Command to conquer the Gaza Strip, in contravention of the defense minister's earlier instructions. Dayan, arriving at the Pit at about 10:40 a.m., asked that reporters be sent to Kibbutz Nahal Oz to report on the shelling in order to legitimize the IDF's action in the Gaza Strip.[80]

At 10:55, Dayan spoke with Rabin, and the two agreed to prioritize aerial assistance to the Egyptian sector after the attack on the airfields was completed. Dayan asked that the IDF's achievements not be published yet so that Egypt

---

[78] Haber, *Hayom tifrots milhama*, p. 222.
[79] Order for Operation Nahshonim, cited in Golan, *Milhama beshalosh hazitot*, p. 189. According to Gavish, Yitahk (Haka) Hofi, head of operations at the General Staff, added the words "be prepared to conquer the Canal": Gavish, *Sadin adom – sippur hayay*, p. 156.
[80] Golan, *Milhama beshalosh hazitot*, p. 203.

would be trapped by its own propaganda, already declaring tremendous victories against Israel. At 11 a.m., Dayan addressed the nation on the radio, exhorting listeners that, "They outnumber us, but we will overcome. We are a small but courageous people; we pursue peace but are willing to fight for our lives and land."[81]

On the war's first day, the major dilemma facing Israel's leaders was how to respond to Jordan joining the hostilities. The Foreign Ministry requested the UN commander in Jerusalem to send a message to King Hussein from Eshkol, that if Jordan did not attack, it would not be attacked. However, orders for the Jordanian army to join the fighting were intercepted by Israeli intelligence at about 9:00 a.m. In a discussion held at 10:40 a.m., Dayan said that he didn't care if Jordan attacked, apparently because the Sinai actions were going well. Yadin suggested informing Jordan that the Egyptian air force was destroyed to deter them, and Dayan agreed on condition the Jordanians did not interpret the move as an expression of Israeli distress. It is not clear if they knew of Eshkol's earlier message or if they hoped that a repetition would at least limit Jordan's participation and perhaps achieve an early ceasefire. At about 10:45 a.m., Jordanian troops fired into Jerusalem with small arms; at 11:31 a.m., Jordanian artillery opened fire, and Jordanian aircraft took off shortly afterward. At 11:50 a.m., Dayan ordered the IAF to attack Jordan's airfields and artillery batteries. Over the next hour, news of more extensive Jordanian shelling came in, as did reports on Jordanian preparations for a ground offensive to take Israeli Jerusalem.

The Jordanian actions raised dilemmas on how to respond: Should forces be diverted to face them from other fronts, even at the expense of weakening the main effort against Egypt? Should the response be only with air strikes and stand-off ground fire? Would this suffice to protect Israel's civilians from Jordanian artillery fire? How to respond to a threat of attack against the Israeli enclave on Mount Scopus? In deliberations between Dayan and the General Staff and between Dayan and the government, Dayan maintained that Israel's military objective was to decisively defeat the Egyptians, and therefore Israel should not complicate matters by fighting on two fronts. The IDF should prepare a ground offensive toward Mount Scopus and into Samaria to destroy Jordanian artillery, but initially it should make do with counterfire and air strikes.[82]

Shortly after 1:00 p.m., a Jordanian force advanced into the neutral zone of Armon HaNatziv, overlooking southern Jerusalem, taking over the UN regional command post located there. At 2:00 p.m., a Jordanian patrol advanced further toward Israel but was halted by Israeli fire. This was reported

---

[81] The speech appears in: Dayan, *Avnei derekh*, p. 435; Golan, *Milhama beshalosh hazitot*, p. 204.
[82] Golan, *Milhama beshalosh hazitot*, p. 208.

to the Israeli High Command at approximately 2:15 p.m. Dayan wished to order an immediate counterattack, but Rabin convinced him to wait.[83] At 2:25 p.m., the UN informed Israel that it was attempting to negotiate the withdrawal of the Jordanians. At 2:50 p.m., Rabin and Dayan each ordered Central Command to delay the counterattack.[84] However, relaying the order took time, and at 3:00 p.m., before the counterattacking unit received the order to halt, it had begun to attack, and by 4:00 p.m., the mountain was in Israeli hands.

Meanwhile, the fighting in Sinai was achieving better results than expected, requiring less attention from Dayan and Rabin than the Jordanian front. The Syrian front, except for exchanges of artillery fire and some air strikes, which ceased when the Syrian air force was destroyed in the late afternoon, also seemed to be static. Dayan had authorized the transfer to Jerusalem of a paratroop brigade whose mission in Sinai had been cancelled as no longer relevant. At 2:55 p.m., he ordered that if Jordan did not agree to a ceasefire by midnight, this brigade would attack through Sheikh Jarrakh, northern Jordanian Jerusalem, to Mount Scopus. A mechanized brigade was to attack toward Mount Scopus on a route bypassing Jerusalem from the north. Northern Command was also ordered to divert two brigades from the Syrian border to attack into Samaria from the north, and a Central Command brigade would attack into Samaria from the west. The focus was to be the destruction or expulsion of Jordanian artillery bombarding Israeli towns and villages and airfields. At approximately 5:00 p.m., the first of these forces began their attacks, and the others gradually joined in as they arrived each in its allotted sector. Meanwhile, the Israeli forces at Armon HaNatziv attacked into Judea, the southern West Bank. The last to arrive and attack were the paratroopers from Sinai.

Contrary to the previous planning and Dayan's preliminary intentions, the Jordanian front escalated sooner than expected, and the IDF was compelled to reinforce that front at the expense of the Egyptian and Syrian fronts and to transition from defensive to offensive operations.

At 9 p.m., Dayan and Rabin held a long consultation about Sinai. Two of the IDF's three divisions had advanced deep into the Egyptian forces during the day, one was to begin its attack at night. Dayan and Rabin suggested to Southern Command that the last division delay its attack to the morning to receive aerial support, now that the IAF had completely achieved aerial supremacy. The division commander, Sharon, preferred to attack at night without air support – his decision was accepted.[85]

---

[83] From the impressions of the Chief of Staff's Bureau Chief Colonel Rafi Efrat during the event, in Golan, *Milhama beshalosh hazitot*, p. 214.
[84] Ibid.
[85] Commander of Southern Command Gavish authorized Sharon's decision, and at 11 p.m., the division launched its assault. In Golan, *Milhama beshalosh hazitot*, p. 227.

Day 2, June 6: Breaching Sinai and Toppling the Egyptian Resistance

Eshkol, Rabin, and Dayan met during that night to discuss priorities for the coming days. Eshkol authorized Dayan's proposals: giving preference to destroying the Egyptian armored forces, continuing on to Sharm El Sheikh, and, finally, seizing the West Bank. Regarding the Syrian front, Rabin asked Dayan if anything else needed doing. Dayan answered: "This needs checking. Be prepared but don't execute."[86]

Fighting in Sinai continued throughout the night. By morning, a clearer picture emerged: The IDF had sped ahead into Sinai in every sector, the General Staff kept busy coordinating aerial support and opening logistical and other bottlenecks to expedite the troops' advance. Simultaneously, the IDF also advanced through the West Bank and Jordanian Jerusalem, defeating the defending Jordanian units. Jordanian reinforcements ascending from the Jordan Valley were delayed by air strikes on the narrow mountain road.[87]

In the morning of June 6, the General Staff met with Dayan. At the end of the discussion, Dayan determined their objectives and priorities at this stage.

The main effort was still Egypt – occupation of the Gaza Strip, begun to halt artillery fire on surrounding Israeli villages, was to be completed; Israeli forces were to advance along the Mediterranean coast to 10 kilometers from the Suez Canal – but not to reach it; and the final destruction of Egyptian forces in central Sinai was to begin (Map 5.1).

On the Jordanian front the forces were to complete the missions allotted the previous day.

The Syrian front was to remain defensive despite Syrian fire and ground raids.

In a meeting one hour later with Rabin, Dayan, worried that a ceasefire would be imposed on Israel before it had a chance to achieve its central goals, pressed for a rapid completion of the Sharm El Sheikh conquest. In his book, Rabin described Dayan's genuine fear of Soviet intervention and the need to reach Sharm El Sheikh before the war ended.[88]

The day before the discussion, Israeli military intelligence (Unit 8200) had intercepted a phone conversation between King Hussein and President Nasser in which the two had coordinated to issue a false statement that it was US and UK airplanes that had destroyed their respective air forces. After serious deliberation, Dayan decided to publicize the lie because of its propaganda value, which he viewed as having strategic value, this despite fierce opposition from AMAN, concerned that the move would expose its capabilities and impel the other side to take steps that would make it difficult to achieve such intelligence coups in the future.

---

[86] Ibid., p. 228.
[87] Ibid., p. 231.
[88] Rabin, *Pinkas sherut*, p. 191.

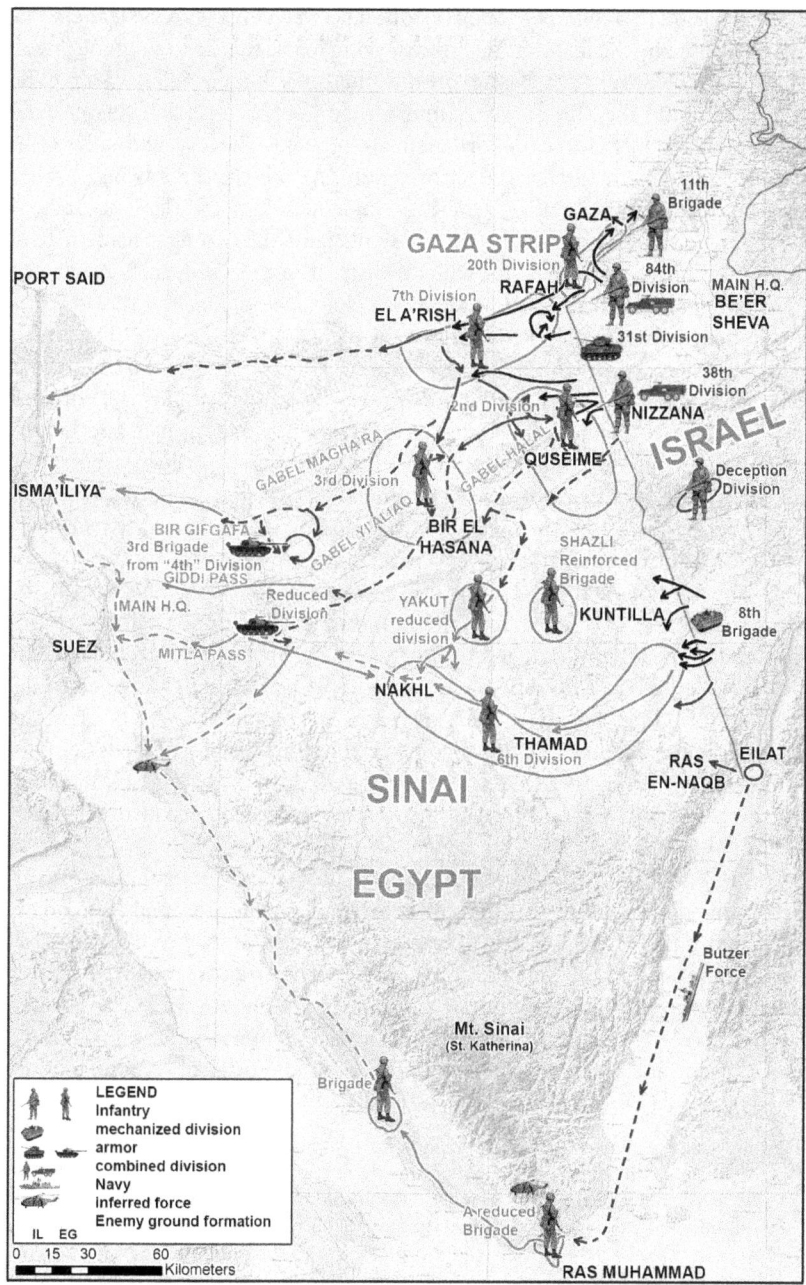

Map 5.1 The Six-Day War (1967): The Sinai Peninsula region.

The decision to publicize the conversation between the two Arab leaders was also motivated by the fear that Egypt was trying to use this lie to drag the Soviet Union into the war, in accordance with stipulations in their defense pact to be triggered should the United States intervene on behalf of Israel. Nasser even lied to his own ally to force the Jordanian air force into the fray, telling Hussein that the Egyptian air force was destroying the IAF. Nasser already had a fairly clear picture of the situation, whereas Hussein was in the dark because of Israel's radio silence imposed by Dayan. Publicizing the two Arab leaders' false announcement would thus sow mutual distrust and drive a wedge between them. The conversation was broadcast on Israeli radio, and the IDF spokesperson held a press conference at which the recording was played.[89] Dayan felt that the conversation would "expose Nasser. This is excellent for the implicated Americans and will help them disprove Nasser's lies, and it will enhance Israel's image."[90] Dayan was correct: The broadcast made waves and helped burnish the reputation of Israel's intelligence services as capable of penetrating the innermost chambers of the Arab rulers.[91] Although some damage was done and some sources burned from the disclosure, it seems that Dayan's strategic-political consideration was correct.

On the Jordanian front, Dayan ordered that a line to Mount Scopus be established by the day's end. He wanted to complete the conquest of the Mount Scopus–Mount of Olives ridge but directed the army not to descend into the Jordan Valley and to allow anyone wanting to flee east access to an open route. This had the added benefit of making it easier to complete the conquest of the West Bank. He also ordered the encirclement of the Old City of Jerusalem but not yet entry into it. In addition, he commanded the IAF to attack the Iraqi brigade advancing through Jordan and destroy it, to deter Iraq from sending additional troops.[92]

The IDF had the Old City surrounded by noon. Dayan visited the sector, met with the Central Command commander Narkiss, and personally instructed him on his next steps. Narkiss wanted to enter the Old City, but Dayan continued to refuse, thinking it best to first seize control of the road to Jericho to prevent the possibility of a Jordanian counterattack. Dayan wanted an action aimed at seizing control of the strategic mountain ridge and linking up with Central Command and Northern Command troops,[93] feeling that the

---

[89] Efraim Lapid, *Lohamei haseter: Hamodi'in hayisraeli – mabat mibifnim* (Hebrew), Tel Aviv: Miskal, 2017, pp. 70–73; Gilboa, *Mar modiin*, pp. 312–316, 318–319. These two books, which describe the affair, were written by senior members of the Israeli intelligence community who felt it was a mistake to have published the information because the sources were exposed.

[90] Gilboa, *Mar modiin*, p. 315.

[91] Ibid., p. 319.

[92] Golan, *Milhama beshalosh hazitot*, p. 237.

[93] Ibid., p. 241.

latter was tantamount to Israel having control of the entire region. Dayan argued that there was no point in risking street battles in the Old City, assessing that after it was encircled, it would fall of its own accord. He instructed Narkiss "to leave this Vatican [alone],"[94] meaning the Old City with its holy sites for the three main religions. His critics, especially on the extreme political right, took this phrase out of context to prove that the cynical Dayan had no respect for what is holy to the Jewish people.[95]

In the discussion held in the Ministerial Committee on Security, several ministers, galvanized by the good news streaming in from the front, pressed for the immediate conquest of Jerusalem's Old City. Dayan insisted on not entering it until after the conquest of Sharm El Sheikh had been completed. The government left the decision about entering the city to Dayan, who for now was content with encirclement alone.[96] Dayan said, "Militarily, we could enter the city, but I suggest we not do so ... I suggest and request that that army be given two more days to effect the most critical moves."[97]

The General Staff translated Dayan's instructions into the Nahshonim 2 order issued at 5:45 p.m.: The IDF was to reach Sharm El Sheikh, continue destroying the Egyptian troops, conquer the West Bank to the edge of the high ground, and hold the line on the Syrian front, with the option of grabbing some land in the north later on.[98] At night, despite differing reports on the encirclement of Jerusalem's Old City, Dayan still delayed entrance because, in his opinion, the encirclement was not yet complete. As he had instructed, the road to Jericho had been opened, but the 10th and 55th Brigades had still not finished setting up around the city. Nonetheless, Dayan had already instructed that a military governor be appointed for the Old City after its conquest and issued other administrative orders (including preventing Jews from entering, as there was still a risk of land mines and snipers). He also clarified instructions about not harming civilians anywhere in the West Bank.

AMAN passed information to Dayan at 9:10 p.m. indicating that the Jordanians, trying to buy time before a ceasefire and thus prevent Israel from occupying the city and the West Bank, had ordered their troops not to retreat and to get ready to defend. Dayan gave the order to conquer Jerusalem's Old City. He made the decision alone, based on the authority granted to him hours earlier at the Ministerial Committee on Security meeting.[99] Dayan instructed that absolute precedence be given to Jerusalem and ordered the army to

---

[94] Uzi Narkiss, *Ahat yerushalayim* (Hebrew), Tel Aviv: Am Oved, 1976, p. 214.
[95] See, e.g., Naor, "The Ouster of Levi Eshkol" (Hebrew), p. 477.
[96] Golan, *Milhama beshalosh hazitot*, p. 245.
[97] Minutes of meeting of the Ministerial Committee on Security, June 2, 1967, State Archive, File No. EES0002.
[98] Golan, *Milhama beshalosh hazitot*, p. 244.
[99] Gideon Avital-Epstein, *'67, yerushalayim, milhama* (Hebrew), Tel Aviv: Matar, 2017, p. 495.

complete the conquest of the Old City that night or the next day.[100] In reality, by the late afternoon of June 6, IDF forces had reached positions from which it was possible to encircle the city, the condition Dayan set for the conquest. The Old City was completely encircled physically by 9 a.m. on the 7th, after the conquest of the Mount of Olives (Augusta Victoria), whereupon the attack began. Also by midday on the 6th, the IDF had opened access to Mount Scopus, so that although the Old City was not yet fully encircled, by evening, the IDF, by means of fire and observation, controlled the entire city. At 6 a.m. on June 7, Rabin issued the directive to complete the encirclement, but about fifteen minutes later, Dayan issued another directive instructing the military to not only encircle the Old City, but also to enter it. Dayan asked Deputy Chief of Staff Haim Bar-Lev to come to Jerusalem to see for himself whether it made sense to seize control of the Old City while avoiding needless bloodshed or damage to holy sites. The written order to enter the city was formulated and sent to the Central Command at 9:30 that morning, but by the time the order reached the forces on the ground, the battle to breach the city was already in high gear.[101]

Day 3, June 7: Conquest of Old Jerusalem and the West Bank

At around 1 a.m. on June 7, word came that the Egyptians were retreating from Quseima and Sharm El Sheikh in Sinai. Because of this and because it was becoming increasingly likely that the UN Security Council would pass a ceasefire resolution, Dayan again impressed on Rabin the urgency of conquering the strategic location of Sharm El Sheikh; indeed, by 1:45 a.m. Israel time, the UN Security Council had decided on a ceasefire. Therefore, the General Staff focused on plans for the immediate conquest of Sharm El Sheikh, whether by air or sea.[102] In the morning, reports from the southern front stated that the Egyptians were withdrawing but remained organized, thus still representing a threat; in the Gaza Strip, fighting continued. At 8:30 a.m., Dayan's assessment was that the Egyptians would soon collapse and that the orderly retreat would turn into a panicked flight. He also expressed concern that Israeli troops would advance too far in their pursuit. His attention was focused primarily on Sharm El Sheikh. He decided that the 14th Brigade should rush in and demanded that an unambiguous order to that effect be issued.[103] Even before the order was given, at 11:01 a.m., word came in – that Israeli torpedo ships had reached Sharm El Sheikh and that the area seemed

---

[100] Boaz Zalmanovitch (ed.), *Likhbosh et hahar: Hamaarakha bazira hayardenit bemilhemet sheshet hayamim* (Hebrew), Ben Shemen: Operations Directorate. Doctrine and Training – History Department, Defense Ministry and Modan, 2017, p. 252.
[101] Ibid., pp. 252–253.
[102] Ibid., p. 251.
[103] Ibid., p. 253.

free of Egyptian troops. At 12:15 p.m., members of the Israeli navy disembarked and planted the Israeli flag on the shore.

The conduct of the war and prioritization during the fighting were mostly in Dayan's hands, but not without lengthy arguments with his fellow government ministers. Dayan recalled:

> When it came to planning the fighting in the West Bank, I had bitter arguments with the top political echelon – Levi Eshkol, Yigal Allon, and Menachem Begin. I'd decided that our fighting must first and foremost focus on controlling the mountain ridge. This had been obvious to all generals who had fought in the region, since the time of Joshua Bin-Nun until today... I didn't see any need for a frontal breach into Jerusalem or a house-to-house fight... I very much wanted the city to surrender without a fight... In any case, the international diplomatic activity that had already begun forced us to rush our moves, so that just before morning on June 7, I authorized entrance to the Old City. My assumption was validated. As we advanced, the Legion withdrew all its troops.[104]

Dayan decided "to close the city and enter"; he also directed Bar-Lev to come to Jerusalem to personally oversee the conquest of the Old City, ensure protection of the holy sites, and prevent looting. He also appointed Colonel Shlomo Lahat as governor of East Jerusalem.

At 7 a.m., Dayan spoke first with Eshkol and then with Begin, telling both that he had ordered entry into the Old City even though the encirclement was not yet completed. Half an hour later, Dayan told the assistant to the Director of General Staff Divison, Rehavam Ze'evi, that the speed of conquering the Old City was more important than anything else and that he was authorizing the use of artillery and planes, but only until the Old City was breached and not near the holy sites. Accordingly, the Operations Department sent out an order permitting the use of artillery and air cover within the Old City, "except for the al-Aqsa mosque, the Omar Mosque, and the Church of the Holy Sepulcher. These must not be damaged."[105]

At around 10 a.m., the 55th Paratroopers Brigade and Jerusalem Brigade entered the city and captured the Western Wall and the Temple Mount. Dayan wanted to go up to the Temple Mount with the Chief of Staff at 1 p.m. In accordance with his order, no troops approached the mosques on the Temple Mount.

At 10:50 a.m., it was suggested that a radio warning be broadcast to the Jordanians that, unless they stopped firing at Jerusalem, the IDF would bomb Amman. Arie Braun, Dayan's secretary, noted that it was Israel Lior, Eshkol's

---

[104] Arie Braun, *Hotam ishi: Moshe Dayan bemilhemet sheshet hayamim ve'ahareha* (Hebrew), Tel Aviv: Yedioth Ahronoth, 1997, p. 70.

[105] Golan, *Milhama beshalosh hazitot*, p. 257. Golan cites a telegram that the Operations Department sent to the Central Command.

military secretary, who had suggested the idea in the prime minister's name. Dayan rejected it, saying that making good on the threat was liable to topple King Hussein, which was not in Israel's best interests.

At 11:30 a.m., a pared-down Ministerial Committee met for a situation assessment. Eshkol repeated the war's objectives and priorities as Dayan had defined them, mentioned the UN Security Council's ceasefire resolution, and added that Israel had an interest in conquering Syrian territory to halt the Syrian attacks on Israel's border villages, but that Israel did not, at this point, want to open another front. Dayan submitted an update on the West Bank and said that within a few days, the government would have to decide whether to accept administrative responsibility for the newly occupied territories, and, if yes, to prepare. Later in the discussion, Dayan shared his own – minority – opinion about the Syrian front, opposing the conquest of the Golan Heights because of Syria's relationship with the Soviet Union and because Israel did not really want to conquer it. Afterward, he instructed the Northern Command to investigate ways of possibly seizing the areas of the Golan Heights belonging to Israel that had been taken by Syria since 1949 and authorized the transfer of two regional brigades from the southern to the northern front. Regarding the IDF reaching the Suez Canal, Dayan ordered the IDF not to do so, arguing that sitting on the Canal would create a clear locus of conflict for the Egyptians. Still, he authorized forces to advance as far as they needed to pursue the retreating Egyptian troops, thereby leaving the door open for violating his own instructions.[106]

In Jerusalem, at 1:45 p.m., Dayan entered the Old City through the Lions' Gate, Rabin to his left and Narkiss to his right. He made sure in advance that their entrance would be documented. The photograph of that moment became one of the most recognizable shots of the war and further glorified the myth surrounding Dayan as the man most identified with victory. After inserting a note into a crack in the Western Wall inscribed with the words "May peace descend upon the House of Israel,"[107] Dayan gave a short speech about the unification of Jerusalem, the divided city, the hand held out in peace to enemies, and the promise of free access to the sites holy to Muslims and Christians. "We have not come to Jerusalem to conquer the holy [sites] of others nor to hem in the activities of members of other religions, but to ensure its peace and to live in it with others in brotherhood."[108]

Eshkol arrived in the city only at 7 p.m. on a visit that received scant attention.

In the evening, the political locus moved to the Security Council's ceasefire resolution. The Soviets issued an ultimatum: Unless Israel stopped the fighting,

---

[106] Ibid., p. 261.
[107] From testimony of Colonel Efrat and Major General Narkiss, ibid., p. 259.
[108] Avital-Epstein, '67, yerushalayim, milhama, p. 273.

the USSR would sever relations and assist the Arabs. In the meantime, King Hussein and President Nasser both refused the ceasefire and declared they would continue to fight.

In the evening, Dayan instructed the General Staff to prepare plans for the government to implement during and after the battles. He also issued instructions on preparing logistical plans to deal with the new assets that had now fallen into Israel's hands.[109] He claimed it was necessary to block all axes and not allow the Egyptian forces to flee Sinai, unlike his instructions for the West Bank, where he allowed the Jordanians to retreat. Dayan now instructed the IDF to reach the banks of the Suez Canal. When Bar-Lev noted that this order contravened Dayan's previous orders, Dayan answered that the situation had changed. Dayan wrote:

> In practice, I had a choice: to strike the Egyptian army to the extent we could, to which end we had to get all the way to the Canal, or to stop somewhere in Sinai, whereupon not only would there be fewer Egyptian losses, but the Egyptian would be liable to take heart and not ask for a ceasefire ... Between these options, I chose to prefer the immediate operative consideration, to realize the national objective – without being sidetracked by a conflict that had nothing to do with us, i.e., fighting over control of the Suez Canal, [which] we will have to address after the battles are over.[110]

In hindsight, Dayan was not sidetracked from the central goal of destroying the Egyptian army, even at the price of the constraint he had imposed of not reaching the Suez Canal. The future would prove that he was deluding himself on this point and that his initial intuition had been correct. In the meantime, the IDF prepared to carry out his orders and capture Tiran Island.

On the night of June 7, Rabin briefed the Ministerial Committee. After reviewing the situation on the different fronts, Dayan said that, in principle, Israel, having already attained the war's objectives, could agree to a ceasefire. As for the Golan Heights, he said, it was possible to seize only Tel Azaziat before the ceasefire, not the entire Heights. It was therefore decided to embark on a limited action on the Syrian front.[111]

The approaching ceasefire, scheduled to go into effect at the end of the third day, pushed Dayan to reconsider his instructions and change some of them, the most important one being the order not to reach the Suez Canal. Until this point, Dayan had ordered that the bridges over the Jordan River not be destroyed, to allow the Jordanians to retreat; now, he instructed that they be blown up to isolate the West Bank from Jordan.

---

[109] Ibid., p. 273.
[110] Dayan, *Avnei derekh*, p. 443.
[111] Golan, *Milhama beshalosh hazitot*, p. 275.

Day 4, June 8: Egypt and Jordan Defeated

On the fourth day of the war, the fight against Jordan and Egypt had been exhausted, and attention turned to Syria. Here, Dayan faced pressure from both the ministers and the Northern Command to attack and occupy the Golan Heights. Meeting with Meir Amit and Aharon Yariv at 8 a.m., Dayan explained that he opposed an attack because it seemed likely Israel would not be able to stay in the Golan Heights due to international pressure, a conclusion he probably arrived at based on his Sinai Campaign experience, when the global powers would not let Israel hold on to the territories it had conquered. Dayan also raised his serious concern about a Soviet response, as Syria was the USSR's chief client state.[112] Late morning, there was another discussion about where the IDF should stop its advance in Sinai. Dayan again expressed his objection to the IDF reaching the Suez Canal and concluded: "The battles will continue until the time when the final decision on the final line of advance is made." This meant he had not decided on a clear line where the IDF would halt its advance. At noon, Major General Tal pressed Dayan for clarifications on his division's missions. Meanwhile, on the other fronts, Jordan had agreed to a ceasefire, while Syria had announced it was laying down its arms.[113]

Large tank battles still raged in central Sinai that afternoon. Dayan, now down in "the Pit," was advised of developments and gave instructions on the locations the IDF must reach, including the Ras Sudar Junction. Concerned about airplane reserves – given approximately 20 percent losses – Dayan asked his assistant, Tsvi Tsur, to handle new plane acquisitions. At the same time, he began to think about the future and instructed the Chief of Staff to look into the possibility of releasing the reservists, something the Israeli economy desperately needed after an almost month-long call-up duty of most of the nation's reservists during the mid-May waiting period. Consulting together at 6 p.m., Eshkol and Dayan decided that the IDF would not deploy along the Suez Canal. Indeed, the Operations Department ordered the IDF to halt at least 10 kilometers from the Canal.[114] But despite the order, at 5:45 a.m. the next morning, the commander of the Southern Command telegraphed Rabin that Israeli army forces were deployed on the bank of the Suez Canal.[115]

Earlier, at 10:30 p.m., Rabin and Dayan had held a discussion following the news that Egypt had announced its agreement to a ceasefire. About an hour later, Dayan summarized the outline of his policy for now: He directed that

---

[112] Golan, *Milhama beshalosh hazitot*, p. 259. This interest is evident even today, as manifested by Russia's presence in Syria.

[113] Ibid., p. 284.

[114] A telegram that the Operations Department issued after the consultation, in Golan, *Milhama beshalosh hazitot*, p. 289.

[115] Testimony of the Chief of Staff's Bureau Director Colonel Efrat, in Golan, *Milhama beshalosh hazitot*, p. 292.

Jerusalem be united and that the fighting in Sinai continue, changing his mind about reaching the Suez Canal in order to complete the destruction of Egypt's last units in Sinai.[116] He did not, however, change his mind about the Syrian front, where he decided that Israel would not initiate an assault. During the day, the Northern Command had applied constant pressure, demanding extensive action in the Golan Heights. Elazar objected to a limited action there, which meant, as he put it, "paying the price without getting anything in return."[117]

Earlier on the 8th, at noon, Elazar, Rabin, and Eshkol held a series of meetings without Dayan, who was in the Hebron Hills outside Jerusalem on a tour, like the many tours he had taken during the fighting, to see the ground for himself. The meetings addressed the possibility of an extensive action in the Golan Heights, the intention being to pressure Dayan to agree. Upon his return to Tel Aviv, Dayan expressed his objection to action in the north, insisting it was necessary to cool the sector down. He added that if the Syrians continued their aggression despite the IDF's restraint, he would suggest to the government to conquer all of the Golan Heights.[118]

At 7:10 p.m., the prime minister summoned the Ministerial Committee on Security to decide on what action to take against Syria. Representatives of northern settlements had been invited to the meeting. Opening the proceedings, Rabin explained why a limited action in the Golan Heights would not resolve the problem. Different ministers raised various pros and cons in the ensuing discussion. At this point, Dayan expressed his opposition to decisions about questions of how to conduct the war being made in the government or in the Ministerial Committee on Security. He said that the government must be kept abreast of developments, but it was not the appropriate forum for deciding on how many kilometers the army should advance. He reminded those present that just one day earlier, the government had authorized a forum, which included Rabin, Dayan, and Eshkol, to make decisions of precisely that nature.[119] It may be that Dayan knew that in the smaller forum he'd be able to steer things his way with greater ease, because neither Eshkol nor Rabin questioned his authority.

Militarily, too, Dayan claimed – unlike Elazar's previous assessment – that there weren't enough Israeli forces near the Golan Heights for it to be easily captured, and therefore heavy losses were to be expected. Finally, he expressed his concern about not only a possible Soviet intervention, but also the response from France – Israel's aircraft provider. If the settlements couldn't live with the

---

[116] Golan, *Milhama beshalosh hazitot*, p. 197.
[117] From Elazar's testimony, in Golan, *Milhama beshalosh hazitot*, p. 293.
[118] From testimony of the Chief of Staff's Bureau Director Colonel Efrat, in Golan, *Milhama beshalosh hazitot*, p. 295.
[119] Minutes of Ministerial Committee on Security, June 8, 1967, State Archive.

shelling, he suggested, it was necessary to move them.[120] This regrettable statement, which of course shocked all those in attendance, severely damaged Dayan for years to come, as his opponents loved to use it against him. Presumably, this provocative declaration came in response to the pressure being applied to him. For him, it was imperative to impress on everyone the primary considerations of the situation on the front and the pressure of the superpowers. These were of general national significance, as opposed to the state of affairs in one settlement or another. At the conclusion of the meeting, Dayan's position was accepted, and it was decided to defer action for a day or two, during which plans would be made and Israel would avoid provoking the Syrians.[121]

At 11:10 p.m., Dayan and Rabin spoke with Elazar and informed him of the Ministerial Committee's decision. Addressing Elazar, Dayan added that if conditions changed, Dayan was authorized to order the conquest of the Golan Heights.[122]

Elazar testified that in that phone conversation, Dayan presented him with three reasons against a northern campaign: one, he still wasn't certain if Egypt would honor the ceasefire; two, he was worried about repercussions from the Soviets; and, three, he was worried about heavy losses. Elazar answered that he was capable of executing the action, and were it not done now, later generations would regret the missed opportunity.[123] Later, testifying about these conversations, each stressed a different point: Dayan highlighted the possibility that the decision could still change; Elazar emphasized his arguments against Dayan's decision not to take action at that time. Various efforts were made to influence Dayan to change his mind. The last and most desperate attempt was sending Uzi Feinerman, the Moshav Movement secretary, Dayan's personal friend and fellow party member, to plead the case. The two met at 2 a.m. Feinerman, too, told Dayan that this was a historic opportunity and that if it weren't exploited, later generations would rue the decision. He spoke about the settlements' distress and made myriad other arguments. But Dayan stuck to his guns and his reasoning. When Feinerman left close to daybreak, his impression was there would be no assault on Syria.

Days 5 and 6, June 9–10

In his diary, Dayan wrote: "On June 9 at 7 a.m., I instructed the commander of the Northern Command to commence action. Things had changed overnight and in the morning. My reasons, especially the short-term ones, were no longer

---

[120] Ibid.
[121] Ibid.
[122] From Elazar's testimony, in Golan, *Milhama beshalosh hazitot*, pp. 298–299.
[123] Ibid., p. 299.

relevant."[124] Indeed, while a disappointed Feinerman was making his way home by car, he had no idea that Dayan had done an about-face.

Dayan would later point to three factors that had changed during those hours: The Egyptians had agreed to the ceasefire; the Soviets were no longer talking about intervening, and there were no signs to indicate any intervention; and intelligence reports were coming in saying that the Syrian front had collapsed. These developments made Dayan reverse course. The first two reports were correct, the last was wrong.

Shortly after 6 a.m., Dayan came to the Operations Department war room, where he was informed of a telegram Egyptian President Nasser had sent to Syrian President Nureddin al-Atassi warning him that Israel was about to concentrate its forces against Syria to destroy its military. He urged al-Attassi to agree to the ceasefire, concluding with, "We've lost the campaign. God will help us in the future."[125] The telegram had been delivered a little after 3 a.m. Various testimonies, also from Bar-Lev and officers present in the war room, attribute Dayan's decision to aerial photos constantly coming in that showed Syrian forces withdrawing.[126] In fact, intelligence personnel realized that the Syrian camps around Quneitra were empty. From this evidence, they allowed themselves to draw the somewhat far-reaching conclusion that the Syrian army was in retreat, perhaps, as suggested by historian Amos Gilboa, in order to prompt the echelons above them to execute an attack in the Golan Heights. AMAN Director Aharon Yariv was a bit suspicious about the interpretation of the photos, but Dayan told him, "My conclusion is – and I guarantee it – that the Syrian front is collapsing."[127] Now, shortly before arriving at the Operations Department at 5:45 a.m., Dayan had received a telegram from the Southern Command saying the IDF was at the Suez Canal and in control of the Sinai Peninsula, making it clear that battles in Sinai were over.[128] For Dayan, this meant that it was now possible to move brigades to reinforce the Northern Command; in fact, much of the 8th brigade had already begun moving north from Sinai, and now the 80th and the 45th Brigades were also ordered north. David Elazar, commander of the Northern Command, added that, nonetheless, the worry that "generations to come" would "rue the missed opportunity" affected Dayan. In the phone conversation with Elazar approving the action, Dayan backed his decision, explaining that the Egyptians had accepted the ceasefire and there were signs indicating the Syrian army's collapse.[129]

---

[124] Dayan, *Avnei derekh*, p. 643.
[125] Gilboa, *Mar modiin*, p. 322.
[126] Golan, *Milhama beshalosh hazitot*, pp. 302–303.
[127] Gilboa, *Mar modiin*, p. 323.
[128] Braun, *Hotam ishi*, p. 87.
[129] Elazar testimony in Golan, *Milhama beshalosh hazitot*, p. 304.

Once it was decided to act in the Golan Heights, it was a race against the clock – in which Dayan skipped over the chain of command. According to him, he did so because the opportunity had presented itself, and therefore doing so did not violate any principles of military doctrine. For this reason, he decided not to consult with or receive the approval of either Eshkol or Rabin, who were at home. Dayan insisted that he knew that they would support the move, because they had supported it up until then, while he had been opposing it. Furthermore, he argued, he assumed that should objections to the action arise, there would be enough time to cancel it, because it would take the forces several hours to get going. Dayan added that Rabin was sleeping at home that night and was inaccessible. Rabin, who immediately came to "the Pit," did not seem pleased by Dayan deciding above his head and wrote sarcastically, "For reasons I still do not understand, he instructed Dado to attack. There was no attention paid to the particulars of authority ... Who would deal with such petty details when the time had come for the Syrians to pay for their aggression?"[130] Eshkol came to "the Pit" before 9 a.m., whereupon Dayan explained to him the overnight developments and the circumstances that had led him to change his decision. Dayan estimated that by 3 or 4 p.m., the IDF would complete the conquest of the Golan Heights.[131]

At 9:30 a.m., Dayan updated the Ministerial Committee about the Golan Heights conquest and explained the background to his order. Minister Moshe Shapira voiced his objection, using Dayan's own arguments from the night before. Other ministers joined him in criticizing the about-face, although they, unlike Shapira, did not demand that the order be reversed. They did, however, demand explanations from Eshkol, who was now saying that once the attack was underway there was no way to stop it, which wasn't altogether accurate. Dayan interceded to explain the reasons for his new decision, stressing that decisions change depending on changing conditions, which had also been the case with the Jordanian front. The meeting came to an end without any formal decision.

The offensive began toward 11:30 a.m.

At 4:30 p.m., Dayan left for a tour of the north to examine the attack plan the Northern Command had formulated. Dayan suggested concentrating efforts on the Banias sector and holding the territory between Banias and Beit Hamekhes, but Elazar wanted to concentrate on conquering the Tawfiq compound in the Golan Heights above Tel Katzir, which had often been the source of fire toward the kibbutz. Dayan accepted on condition that the conquest not entail many losses.[132]

---

[130] Rabin, *Pinkas sherut*, p. 200.
[131] Haber, *Hayom tifrots milhama*, p. 253.
[132] Braun, *Hotam ishi*, p. 94.

In the evening, word came that the UN Security Council intended to declare a ceasefire within two hours. Therefore, at 7:35 p.m., Dayan ordered that the fighting be concluded by the early morning hours of Saturday, June 10. Based on this constraint, he now wanted to cancel the attack on the Tawfiq compound. Rabin instructed Elazar, but Elazar reported that the assault was already underway. Rabin suspected the answer wasn't entirely accurate; after the war, it became clear that his suspicion had been correct and that it still would have been possible to stop the 80th Brigade paratroopers. At 11:30 p.m., Rabin reported to Dayan that the paratroopers were delayed, whereupon Dayan realized that the previous report had been misleading. Referring to the incident in his book, Dayan wrote: "Not everything is smooth with Elazar. The information I'm getting isn't accurate ... I didn't say anything to the Chief of Staff, but inside I was fuming, but even more, so I was saddened."[133] Braun, Dayan's secretary, noted in his book that these were the first manifestations of a later relationship of mutual suspicion between Dayan and Elazar during the Yom Kippur War.[134]

At 9 p.m., Dayan informed Rabin that the government had decided to postpone the start of the ceasefire until midday of June 10, thereby giving the Northern Command another few hours to complete the conquest. At 10:45 p.m., Dayan broached Rabin's idea of bombing Damascus in response to heavy Syrian shelling of the Jordan Valley to Eshkol. Dayan persuaded Eshkol that the damage of such a move would far outweigh any benefit. At this point, Dayan told Rabin that the Ministerial Committee on Security would probably cave into pressure and agree to a ceasefire in the morning; therefore, the IDF had to complete the move that night.

At the Ministerial Committee on Security meeting early in the morning on June 10, Dayan asked for another twenty-four hours to deepen and expand the territory Israel controlled. His intention was to enter the Syrian Heights, but Abba Eban was pessimistic about the possibility of gaining that much time.[135]

At 8:45 a.m. on June 10, a message arrived from US Secretary of State Dean Rusk about the ceasefire, a clear sign that the pressure on Israel was mounting. Accordingly, Dayan ordered the ground offensive finished by 11 a.m. and the aerial assault by 2 p.m. At that moment, Dayan felt that US support was extremely important, both politically and for restocking the IDF with military acquisitions. However, it now emerged that the Syrian military in the Golan Heights had collapsed, and Dayan ordered the action be further accelerated to conclude it by 2 p.m., including the conquest of Quneitra.

---

[133] Dayan, *Avnei derekh*, p. 480.
[134] Braun, *Hotam ishi*, p. 96.
[135] Minutes of meeting of the Ministerial Committee on Security, June 10, 1967 (4:30 a.m.), State Archive, File # 0013qq9.

At 10:15 a.m., Dayan spoke with Eshkol, who asked Dayan to end the fighting by 2 p.m. Dayan suggested the issue be reexamined then: "If we can, we'll keep going. If not, we won't."[136] Over the next several hours, the pressure to implement the ceasefire increased exponentially, and at 12:05 p.m., Dayan allowed UN observers to tour the area to reduce that pressure.[137]

Meeting with Eshkol and Elazar at around the same time, Dayan asked for the opportunity to seize control of Quneitra by 2 p.m. and suggested a ruse to buy time. He had heard that the head of the UN observer staff, Norwegian General Odd Bull, was in Tiberias and was planning to drive to the Golan Heights to declare the ceasefire in effect. Dayan suggested inviting Bull to a 2 p.m. meeting at the Defense Ministry offices in Tel Aviv, which was at least a two-hour drive away. The purpose of the meeting – to inform Bull that Israel was willing to accept the ceasefire. Dayan added, "As far as I know the Norwegian mind, he will not offer a practical suggestion on the spot. We won't tell him how we suggest he end the fire. It's best to let him offer it to us."[138] Dayan was fairly sure that by the time Bull suggested the ceasefire, Israel would have gained several hours (Figure 5.2; Map 5.2).

Figure 5.2 July 6, 1967, UN General Bull meeting Moshe Dayan to discuss posting UN observers along the Suez Canal. Source: Santi Visalli/Contributor/Archive Photos/Getty Images.

---

[136] Braun, *Hotam ishi*, p. 98.
[137] Ibid.
[138] Ibid.

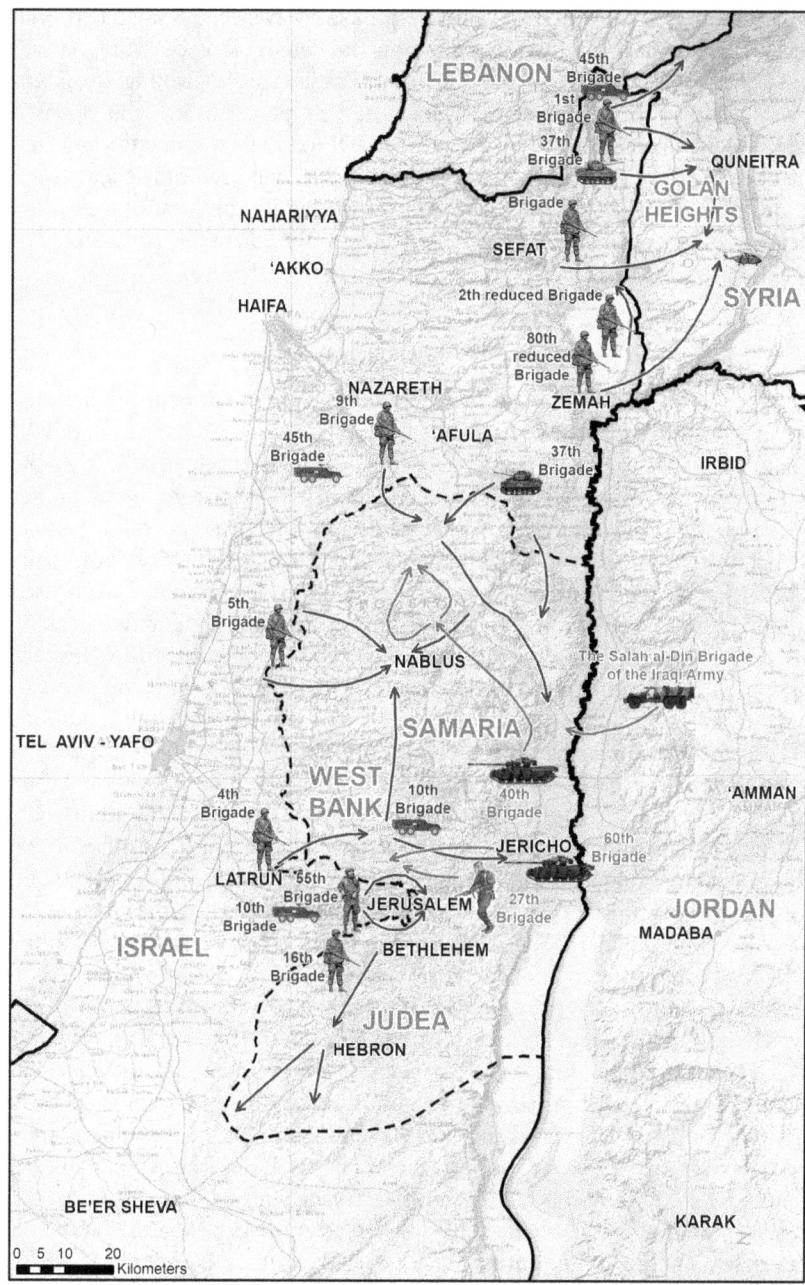

Map 5.2 The Six-Day War (1967): Judea and Samaria (West Bank) and the Golan Heights region.

The meeting with Bull was held at 3 p.m. As Dayan had anticipated, Bull needed time to figure out the coordination and details of the ceasefire. At 5:40 p.m., Bull called Dayan to tell him that Damascus was willing to accept a comprehensive ceasefire to take effect at 6:30 p.m. Dayan, who updated Eshkol, had already known at 4 p.m. that IDF had taken Quneitra and that the objectives of the fighting in the Golan Heights had been fully achieved.

On the morning of June 11, the IDF completed its conquest of the Golan Heights. In Jerusalem, the government declared "the end of the battles between Israel, Egypt, Jordan, and Syria."[139]

Minister of Victory: Did Dayan Earn It?

In the crisis leading to the Six-Day War and during the days of the fighting, Dayan's positions flip-flopped. At first, he thought Israel had painted itself into an unnecessary corner of intrigue and felt that war was avoidable. But when the skies darkened over Israel, he concluded that the nation must go to war – a war it would win even though it would be tough. He searched for a way to participate personally in the conflict. Lacking any real political power, he asked to serve as the commander of the Southern Command. Dayan used the time he had to study the army on the ground, visiting IDF units, speaking with commanders and soldiers of all ranks, and assessing the army's morale, equipment, readiness, and operational plans. Finally, a few days before the war, and helped by a tailwind of Israeli public opinion, the political conditions coalesced, and he was appointed defense minister, assuming the job at a time when the public regarded him as their savior. His new function greatly raised the morale of the army, which was mostly comprised of reservists, an inseparable part of Israeli society, and of civilians. Dayan empowered the officers who felt they had no one to speak for them in the political echelon in general and with the prime minister in particular. The Duke of Wellington, the victor of the Battle at Waterloo in 1815, used to say of Napoleon that "his presence on the field made the difference of forty thousand men."[140] Dayan's influence on national morale, imprinted on the collective memory, was so powerful that it overshadowed his actual performance and contributions to the war.

Dayan did not see himself as part of the government. The government members, as he said himself, likewise did not see him as one of their own. He was similarly distant from the General Staff, whose members were a cohesive group of former Palmach members (twelve of fifteen General Staff members), and because it had been a full decade since he had left the army. Furthermore, he was older than most and had more experience. Dayan was therefore alone, a separate entity, not connected to others. He felt the weight of

---

[139] Gilboa, *Mar modiin*, p. 327.
[140] www.wellingtoncollection.co.uk/wellington-stories/wellington-and-napoleon.

the responsibility and, for the first time in his life, that he was the supreme authority. He didn't consider Eshkol any kind of expert on security matters as he had considered Ben-Gurion; in fact, Dayan felt that even Ben-Gurion was "living in a long-gone world" and that his assessments weren't as sharp as they once were. Dayan realized that in this war, he would have to rely on himself.[141] Perhaps it was this insight that, at least partially, explains some of the decisions he made and his conduct in the war. "My personal impression," wrote Neora Barnoach-Matalon, his long-time personal assistant, "was that Moshe was completely on his own."[142]

Nonetheless, Dayan's assumption of the defense minister's position had an immediate impact on the timing of the war. On this matter, he was determined, even as some government ministers hesitated. For the IDF's senior command echelon, he had the authority of a military man with extensive knowledge and experience beyond his personal charisma and popular image. This affected both the public and the troops in the field. Dayan was the one who had conquered Sinai as Chief of Staff; it was Dayan who had prepared the 1956 plans and approved them; it was Dayan who had visited almost every single location in Sinai; and it was Dayan who, in the months before Israel's withdrawal, had toured the region almost obsessively. There wasn't a single officer who knew Sinai better than he did. The central campaign of the 1967 war again occurred in Sinai, and it was therefore obvious that Dayan's opinion mattered. He was also well acquainted with the Jordanian front from his command of the Jerusalem front during the War of Independence. Israeli Air Force commander Mordechai Hod was quite explicit in his assessment of Dayan's decision to go to war: "What Moshe Dayan gave the State of Israel was that, without him, it would not have been possible to decide to go to war. The government didn't have the guts to decide to go to war."[143]

The most significant subject on which Dayan exerted his influence was war objectives. He focused on the main goal – destroying the Egyptian army, which was the biggest threat to Israel, and on the opening of the Tiran Straits. He thereby created a clear list of priorities for the army and the political echelon. For Dayan, conquering territory was secondary; he felt that a limited action, as suggested in some of the General Staff plans, would not have achieved the goal of relieving Israel of the Egyptian threat. Later on, Ezer Weizman would say, "Dayan gave tremendous impetus to the willingness to fight, to the demand not to go for some partial or limited action, but to the complete and utter destruction of the Egyptian army."[144] Mordechai Hod, in the testimony he

[141] Dayan, *Avnei derekh*, p. 432.
[142] Neora Barnoach-Matalon, *Makom tov batsad* (Hebrew), Tel Aviv: Kotarim Publishers, 2009, p. 186.
[143] Testimony of Air Force Commander Major General Mordechai Hod, November 14, 1969, IDF and Security Establishment Archive, Delivery 192/1974, File 1156, p. 17.
[144] Weizman, *Lekh shamayim, lekh erets*, p. 265.

submitted after the war, referred to Dayan's influence on the operation's goals and plans:

> What we had before Moshe Dayan was a plan that was willing to make do and stop at the smallest problem ... What Moshe Dayan did, the moment he arrived to serve as defense minister, was to fixate on one fact ... He told us that, with this plan, we will not end the war ... He challenged the existing plan. [For him], it was necessary to strike the Egyptian army and take all of Sinai and not to anger the gods – not to touch the Suez Canal.[145]

Dayan defined the war's objectives and priorities before the General Staff on the second day of the war. Before that, during the waiting period, the IDF had begun updating its already prepared plans for defense and offense. Within a few days, five defense plans were prepared, followed by four offense plans for the Egyptian front alone, with offensive plans also made for the other fronts. Obviously, this affected the readiness of the forces, because every plan changed the composition of troops and their orders, and the commanders were forced to learn them anew and move troops from one place to another.

Dayan joined preparations in the midstream, and his ideas had some influence on the planning. The final Southern Command plan was concluded and issued as an order on June 3, only two days before its implementation, and the final General Staff plan was concluded and issued as an order only on June 4. Nonetheless, differences in emphasis are evident at every level: The Southern Command highlighted the conquest of certain territories, whereas the General Staff insisted on destruction of enemy forces. Arguably, Dayan's insistence on destroying the Egyptian army stemmed from his experience in the Sinai Campaign, when the territory conquered did not remain in Israel's hands. Dayan must have concluded that conquering land was only a means for destroying as many units of the Egyptian army as possible.

The question of the war's objectives caused disagreements between the political and military echelons. For the political rungs, the main problem was the blockade on the Tiran Straits, while for the military, the main problem was the concentration of forces in Sinai. Dayan settled the question, defining the concentration of the Egyptian forces in Sinai as the major threat; its destruction, of course, also meant opening the Straits.

Dayan used the term "annihilation" rather than "decision," the word currently favored by the IDF. "annihilation" was the word used by Carl von Clausewitz, which for years was imprecisely translated as "decision," becoming the source of confusion and argument to this day.[146] The meaning of "annihilation" was inflicting losses on the Egyptian force to the point it stopped

---

[145] Testimony of Air Force Commander Major General Mordechai Hod, November 14, 1969, IDF and Security Establishment Archive, Delivery 192/1974, File 1156, p. 17.

[146] For more on the Clausewitz's concept of destruction, see Beatrice Heuser, *The Evolution of Strategy*, Cambridge: Cambridge University Press, 2010, pp. 145–146.

existing as an organized, effective military power. Once the Egyptian army was destroyed, the threat from the other Arab armies became insignificant. Driven by this objective, Dayan took care to concentrate efforts on the Egyptian front and avoid the temptation to open other fronts in order to avoid unnecessary entanglements. Therefore, on the second day of the campaign, he defined the objectives as destroying the Egyptian armored force, conquering Sharm El Sheikh, and conquering the West Bank up to the edge of the mountain ridge, while also preventing engagement with the Syrians.[147] He imposed restrictions before and during the fighting, some of which were ignored: The IDF did reach the Suez Canal, conquer the Gaza Strip, and open a front against Jordan already on the second day of the war, albeit in response to Jordanian provocation. Dayan staved off the conquest of the Golan Heights until the last day.

Dayan, in his typical opportunistic fashion, adapted to the opportunities and successes, his favored modus operandi for campaigns of rapid movement and a tight sequence of events like the Six-Day War in which windows of opportunity quickly opened and closed. Dayan was involved in all major decisions about the war, although he tried not to intervene in its routine management.[148]

While steering military moves during the war, Dayan took international sensitivities into consideration. This was especially evident in his sensitivity to the Holy Basin, the Jerusalem region with a high concentration of historic holy sites. He personally instructed Narkiss of the Central Command to avoid collateral damage there. Damage to the Dome of the Rock, the third holiest site in Islam, could have united the entire Muslim world against Israel. In his deliberations about the Golan Heights conquest, he showed special sensitivity to the possible involvement of the Soviet Union.

In all of Israel's wars, decision-makers have always faced two clocks: the political and the military/operational. The latter has its own time constraints, especially on land. The movement of large numbers of troops takes a specific amount of time that cannot be shortened; the same is true for the seizure of a unit of land. Dayan was aware of both clocks and the necessity of keeping them synchronized. Thanks to deviousness, during the battles on the Golan Heights, he succeeded in buying precious political time from UN representatives, thus allowing the army to complete its mission of occupying the Golan Heights.

Dayan's appointment as defense minister on the eve of the war placed him in a particularly challenging situation. Under Israeli law, "The IDF is subordinate to the government, and the Chief of Staff is subject to the authority of the Government and is subordinate to the Minister of Defense."[149] But this law

---

[147] Bar-On, *Moshe Dayan*, p. 231.
[148] Ibid., p. 230.
[149] "Basic Law: The Military" (Hebrew), Knesset website, https://fs.knesset.gov.il//8/law/8_ls1_289725.PDF. English translation at https://m.knesset.gov.il/EN/activity/documents/BasicLawsPDF/BasicLawTheMilitary.pdf.

was passed only following the 1973 war and the Agranat Commission in 1976 and therefore was not in force when Dayan became defense minister. Consequently, he intervened in the military plans for the war taking place on three fronts but limited his instructions to those "fundamental decisions" and operational matters with clear political and international ramifications.

In the great victory of the Six-Day War, the immense expectations of Dayan were realized. In the eyes of the public in Israel and around the world, there was a clear link between Dayan and Israel's success; he seemed virtually invincible. He did not bother dispelling his omnipotent image. In fact, he helped cultivate it. In the end, Dayan fell captive to his own myth.

6

Minister of the Palestinian Territories

Following the Six-Day War, Moshe Dayan's reputation at home and abroad soared. In the late 1960s and early 1970s, Dayan became an icon, his black eyepatch making him the most recognized Israeli in the world. Describing the Dayan worship he encountered when visiting the United States in late 1967, Ezer Weizman related, "Moshe's name is on everyone's lips with total adoration, like a modern Genghis Khan, and it opens every door."[1]

Dayan was especially popular in the United States, beginning with his visit to Vietnam and continuing to rise after the Six-Day War.[2] In Israel and abroad, Dayan's image, usually in uniform, appeared on postcards, posters, and trinkets, a vivid representation of Israel and its might.[3] Throughout the world, "Israeli" meant Moshe Dayan and vice versa. For example, after hearing that his guest was from Israel, a host in Nepal covered one eye, exclaiming, "Israel!" A magazine survey in then-Rhodesia (now Zimbabwe) asked readers which general they thought best suited to head an army: Dayan surpassed Patton, Montgomery, and Rommel.

His black eyepatch became a fashion accessory,[4] and his image sold like hotcakes, whether in victory albums or reproduced on wood, commemorative metal plates, buttons, lapel pins, medals, commemorative coins, pens, pencils, watches, memo pads, or even men's perfume.[5]

However, neither this tremendous popularity nor the great victory attributed to him brought security or peace. Instead, new challenges faced Israel. Although its newly expanded borders made the country more defensible, it soon became clear that the Israeli–Arab conflict had not ended but had merely changed form. It was obvious that Egypt would reject Israel's presence on the Suez Canal and in the Sinai Peninsula, and, with the USSR's help in pursuit of

---

[1] Ezer Weizman, *Lekha shamayim, lekha arets* (Hebrew), Tel Aviv: Maariv Library, 1975, p. 303.
[2] Mark A. Raider, "Moshe Dayan: 'Israel's No. 1 Hero' (in America)," *Journal of Israeli History* 37: 1 (2019), pp. 21–59 – DOI: 10.1080/13531042.2019.1633790.
[3] Haim Grossman, "Commemorative Image of an Israeli Hero Reflected in the Applied Arts" (Hebrew), *Israel* 13, 2008, pp. 181–208 (p. 182).
[4] Robert Slater, *Warrior Statesman: The Life of Moshe Dayan*, New York: St Martin's Press, 1st ed., 1991, p. 282.
[5] Ibid., p. 196.

its Cold War interests, Egypt would be able to quickly rebuild its army. In the West Bank and Gaza Strip, the occupation meant ruling over a hostile Arab population with increased Palestinian guerrilla and terror activity.

Dayan was one of the first to face this new reality. Between the Six-Day War and the Yom Kippur War, he was preoccupied with managing and determining the territories' future and the War of Attrition on the Egyptian front. His visit to Vietnam before the Six-Day War taught him about the importance of controlling a hostile populace, guerrilla subversion, and terrorism, and how to try to avoid repeating the mistakes the United States had made.

Dayan Studies the Vietnam War

The sixth parliamentary election in 1965 disappointed Dayan; his party, garnering only 10 of the Knesset's 120 seats, was not invited to join the governing coalition. Now a mere MK lacking an executive position, Dayan became bored with routine parliamentary work. Fearing he was stagnating professionally, he accepted an offer to travel to Vietnam as a journalist and analyst for the *New York Times* and *Maariv*. Dayan explained his decision to travel to a foreign war zone:

> It's the only war currently being fought in the world. Hardly any one of us has ever seen or fought in a war of this scope with the most modern techniques. My main expertise is security. Just like a plant disease specialist travels to see plant diseases to see how to treat them, I want to see and study the war in Vietnam and its implications for war in our own region.[6]

To begin by learning the war's background, Dayan first flew to France and met with acquaintances from the 1950s who had fought in the First Indochina War (1946–1954). Most generals assessed the US approach of using massive force against an unseen enemy embedded in the population to be ineffective.[7] In the UK, he met with Field Marshal Bernard Law Montgomery, who believed that the United States' biggest problem in Vietnam was the lack of a clear goal.[8]

Dayan continued to the United States and was impressed by the nation's immense power and advanced technology. Arriving in July 1966, US Army morale was high, and the military was certain that its massive intervention would lead to a decisive victory. Although deluged by statistics of enemy casualties and other evidence of military success, Dayan quickly noticed that even basic questions posed to his Pentagon hosts revealed that matters were not as simple as they seemed. To the keen-sighted Dayan, the positive figures his hosts presented on the map did not reflect reality on the ground.

---

[6] Ibid., p. 550.
[7] Moshe Dayan, *Yoman Vietnam* (Hebrew), Tel Aviv: Dvir, 1977, pp. 7–17.
[8] Ibid., pp. 8–20.

Even where there was a significant US presence, it appeared that the enemy quickly reestablished control once American soldiers were not physically present.[9] Dayan's suspicions were confirmed when he met US Defense Secretary Robert McNamara, who admitted the Americans were having trouble ensuring the southern population's security.[10] Later, when already in Vietnam, Dayan learned that there wasn't a single traffic route in South Vietnam safe from the Vietcong, nor was there anything stopping the enemy from returning to places that had been "cleared" and "pacified."

Dayan also met with National Security Council Director Walt W. Rostow and President Johnson's special advisor Maxwell Taylor, former Chairman of the Joint Chiefs of Staff. Rostow, a Harvard economist, explained that the global desire for economic growth would drive the peoples of Asia into the US orbit. While Rostow would later be proven partially correct, Dayan remained unconvinced. Having experienced the Israeli–Arab conflict, he had seen the Arab determination to rid themselves of Western patrons despite the economic costs[11] and recognized the American lack of understanding about Vietnamese motives for fighting.

McNamara was deeply impressed with Dayan. Mossad Director Meir Amit recalled an encounter where McNamara was informed that Dayan had been appointed Israel's defense minister. McNamara, almost hugging Amit, exclaimed, "I admire him, give him my very best wishes."[12]

After visiting Washington, Dayan realized that no one in the Pentagon or White House could clearly explain how the Americans intended to win the war. He summarized the problem the United States faced, noting that they lacked a clear territorial path to victory, and that they were unable to cross the 17th parallel marking the border between North and South Vietnam and unable to bomb the civilian population. Dayan questioned: How would the war end? How would they reach a decisive position? And how would they measure progress?[13]

Landing in Saigon on July 25, 1966, Dayan received US Army fatigues and went into the field. Meeting local South Vietnamese leaders, he soon understood that the Vietcong were stronger than official US assessments indicated. In August, Dayan visited field units scattered around the country, first joining a Marines company commanded by 1st Lieutenant Charles C. Krulak. Later, as a much-decorated general, Krulak would develop a concept in which the military units would be split simultaneously between peacekeeping tasks, fighting off the enemy, and providing humanitarian aid to residents; he coined

---

[9] Ibid., pp. 26–29.
[10] Ibid., pp. 39–40.
[11] Ibid., pp. 29–34.
[12] Meir Amit, *Rosh berosh: Mabat ishi al eru'im gedolim ufarshiyot ne'elamot* (Hebrew), Or Yehuda: Maariv-Hed Arzi Publications, 1999, p. 241.
[13] Dayan, *Yoman Vietnam*, p. 40.

some fundamental military phrases, including the "strategic corporal" and "three-block war."[14]

Thirty-five years later, General Krulak told Israeli historian Martin van Creveld, "One evening ... Dayan asked us what we were doing there. Afterwards, he offered his opinion that the U.S. strategy was wrong. You have to be 'where the people are,' and not try in vain to chase the Vietcong in the mountains where they weren't."[15]

Dayan then visited a different Marines unit busy trying to establish calm. He noticed their excellent discipline but observed that civilians were doing most of the work. He also felt that the Marines, charged with ensuring security, were not trying to help the South Vietnamese farmers improve their standard of living by introducing more modern agricultural methods. General Westmoreland, the US Army commander in South Vietnam, felt that overemphasizing civilian pacification and Americanization programs only produced convenient targets for Vietcong guerrillas and preferred creating a situation in which the Vietcong were forced to fight the occupied population rather than the Americans.[16]

Dayan also visited the 1st Cavalry Division, which was entirely helicoptered. He found the helicopters' flexibility, used for rapid troop movement from one location to the next, phenomenal, with the division able to place an entire battalion anywhere with just four hours' notice. And yet, Dayan noted, that was four hours too late, as the enemy would be long gone. In his analysis, the biggest problem of this type of warfare was the lack of accurate tactical intelligence. Four decades later, fighting elusive enemies in Iraq, Afghanistan, Judea, Samaria, the Gaza Strip, and Lebanon, the United States and Israel would construct sophisticated tactical intelligence-gathering tools, the key for effectively confronting enemies merging seamlessly into the environment.

During his visit to this division, Dayan insisted on a frontline tour with the infantry. His host reluctantly agreed, attaching Dayan to a team unlikely to encounter trouble. However, the patrol came under fire and took cover, aiming artillery fire at the enemy with air support. Directing the counterfire while taking cover, the US commander noticed that Dayan had disappeared. The commander soon found Dayan sitting on small heap of earth, facing the fire. "Come down here," the terrified man called to Dayan. "Just the opposite," Dayan retorted, "come up here where you can really understand the battle."[17]

---

[14] Charles C. Krulak, *The Strategic Corporal: Leadership in the Three-Block War*, Fort Leavenworth, KS: Center for Army Lessons Learned Fort Leavenworth KS Virtual Research Library, 1999, pp. 11–23.
[15] Martin van Creveld, *Moshe Dayan*, London: Weidenefeld & Nicolson, 2004, p. 117.
[16] Dayan, *Yoman Vietnam*, p. 178.
[17] Creveld, *Moshe Dayan*, p. 118.

While touring villages, Dayan began understanding how the Americans should adapt.[18] In his diary, he wrote that to really "win the hearts and minds" of the Vietnamese, that is, to earn the population's support, so critical to victory, "they have to offer better long-term solutions for the villagers than the Vietcong can give. The Americans must create a functioning administration and set up model villages."[19] He believed that appealing to the Vietnamese nationalistic character and extended family values could help turn the tide against the Vietcong.[20]

Before leaving, Dayan wrote in his diary that the Americans, like the French before them, did not understand the problem they were facing. He found much of the statistical data published about the war's progress incorrect, and the idea that the Vietnamese people wanted to become Americanized false. Instead, Dayan saw the struggle for South Vietnamese support as being largely social, with the Communists offering an ideology that the Americans needed to counter with a better alternative.[21] "The Americans are winning everything," he concluded soberly, "except for the war."[22] The first lesson he learned about fighting in this type of warfare was as follows:

> The major operational problem that U.S. forces faced in Vietnam was lack of intelligence, the inability to distinguish the foe from material environments and the civilian population ... [With it], most of the blows they land miss their mark. The only effect is to drive the enemy into the civilian setting. Worse still, the lack of precise intelligence incessantly leads to the Americans mistakenly harming innocent bystanders, thus pushing massive population segments straight into the Vietcong's open arms. Nothing contributes more to hatred than seeing friends and relatives killed.[23]

Dayan believed that winning the hearts and minds of the locals could be achieved through social justice, addressing the refugee crisis, and offering an alternative ideology than Communism that better met their needs.[24]

Dayan's Vietnamese journey lasted about three months. Returning to Israel, he published several articles that were later collected and issued as *Vietnam Diary*. This visit and his writings positioned him as an international expert on the Vietnam War, enhancing his public image as an expert in security matters in the eyes of the public and of leaders in Israel and abroad. The Vietnam experience certainly played a role in Dayan becoming defense minister less than a year later, just before the beginning of the Six-Day War (Figure 6.1).

---

[18] Dayan, *Yoman Vietnam*, p. 149.
[19] Ibid., p. 148.
[20] Ibid., p. 148.
[21] Ibid., pp. 137, 142, 148, 151.
[22] Ibid., p. 111.
[23] Creveld, *Moshe Dayan*, pp. 120–121.
[24] Ibid., p. 150.

Figure 6.1 Moshe Dayan in Vietnam with a US Army patrol, 1966. Source: Keystone-France/Contributor/Gamma-Keystone/Getty Images.

Governing the Palestinian Territories

Jumping forward to September 29, 2019, Brigadier General Eran Niv, upon concluding his term as IDF commander of the Judea and Samaria Division, was interviewed by *Haaretz*. Discussing the issue of terror attacks, Niv commented that the West Bank was running almost peacefully, with fewer victims from terrorist attacks and fairly negligible political repercussions.[25]

Niv's guiding principles were rooted in policies defined by Dayan as defense minister. After two years in the West Bank, Niv claimed that only about 1 percent of Palestinians engage in violence, although a few more may want to but are deterred by the cost. He stressed the importance of keeping the other

[25] Amos Harel and Yaniv Kubovich, "Outgoing division commander pleased with coordination in West Bank but knows anything can happen" (Hebrew), *Haaretz*, September 29, 2019.

99 percent outside that circle.[26] He insisted that, "You may not apply a broad hand. You must act only against those engaged in violence. Collective punishment is problematic both morally and professionally. All you do is push more people into confronting you."[27] Niv's approach reflects the principles Dayan formulated for managing the occupied territories immediately after the Six-Day War.

In the Six-Day War, Israel had gained control of the West Bank and Gaza Strip, home to about one million Palestinians, many quite hostile to Israel. Dayan faced the question of how to govern noncitizen residents. This was part of a broader issue surrounding the future of the occupied territories and a final arrangement with the Palestinians and the larger Arab world. While somewhat sensitive to Palestinian ambitions, Dayan objected to ceding all the occupied territories. This contradiction – controlling the occupied land without ruling the people living on it – preoccupied him his entire life. Mordechai Bar-On wrote that the realistic Dayan saw little chance for peace, but the sensitive Dayan understood ties to the land. On this paradox, Teveth wrote, "Dayan was the first statesman who stressed the role played in war by a people's yearning for its historical heritage."[28]

However, the analytical Dayan knew that controlling a foreign population was not sustainable. He had reservations about ruling another nation and would often cite historical precedents illustrating the problems with trying to govern a different people:

> You do not just conquer areas; you also conquer populations, and it is not so simple to annex a population and to convert it into nationals of the conquering State. In this generation in particular, when it is the citizens who determine who will rule them and not the rulers who make subjects their nationals and tyrannize them, sooner or later it is the will of the people that decides.[29]

Dayan exhibited empathy for Palestinian aspirations, even stating that had he been a Palestinian he would have joined a terrorist organization if it helped establish a Palestinian state. Given these conflicting positions – security considerations, the perceived need to continue holding the territories, and a fear of, even revulsion about, playing the role of occupier – Dayan's policy inconsistencies are not surprising. While attempting to make new borders permanent, he also left options open for negotiations and avoiding a binational state and continuing to rule the population without the population feeling ruled.[30]

---

[26] Ibid.
[27] Ibid.
[28] Shabtai Teveth, *Moshe Dayan: Biografia* (Hebrew), Tel Aviv: Schoken, 1971, p. 585.
[29] Slater, *Warrior Statesman*, p. 290.
[30] Mordechai Bar-On, "Ruling Another People" (Hebrew), *Alakhson*, August 2014, p. 4.

Dayan felt it crucial to restore normal life to the Palestinians living in the occupied territories. After blowing up bridges over the Jordan River at the end of the Six-Day War, he ordered the construction of new ones to replace those he had demolished.[31] This was classic Dayan: changing his mind based on what he saw for himself in the field.

He viewed the annexation of a portion of the occupied territories as a long-term, desirable outcome but understood that in the absence of a fundamental political settlement, coexistence was possible only through liberalism and minimal intervention. Dayan favored integrating the Israeli and Palestinian economies through an "open bridges policy": real bridges that emphasized genuine connections between the peoples.[32] However, he faced challenges similar to those the Americans encountered in Vietnam and for which he had criticized them: the lack of a long-term goal. With the occupied territories' future uncertain, Dayan had to maintain calm and ensure a reasonable daily routine while keeping all possible political solutions open, especially given Israel's June 19, 1967, avowal of its willingness to return land in exchange for peace treaties.

Immediately after the war, Dayan began formulating a position for the territories as part of resolving the Israeli–Arab conflict, urging Eshkol to discuss it in a government forum. Dayan favored US involvement to mediate negotiations. While opposing total annexation, Dayan nonetheless considered returning to the 1967 borders a mistake. Options included creating autonomous areas or returning territories to Jordan after demilitarizing them. Dayan's concept focused on functional division: dividing the territory but not the practical authority and management. Israel would retain military control and make foreign affairs and security decisions.

On June 13, 1967, Eshkol began a debate to discuss Israel's position toward peace agreements with its neighbors, as the issue was going to be raised at the UN General Council at the behest of the Arab nations and Communist bloc.[33] During the government debate on the topic on June 18–19, Dayan proposed the following: Israel will suggest signing peace treaties with Egypt and Syria on the basis of the international borders; the border with the Jordanian kingdom will be the Jordan River. In the absence of a signed peace treaty, Israel will hold the territories in the Sinai Peninsula and Syrian Heights; the Gaza Strip will be included in Israel according to the international border.[34]

---

[31] Ibid., p. 1.

[32] Arie Braun, *Hotam ishi: Moshe Dayan bemilhemet sheshet hayamim ve'ahareha* (Hebrew), Tel Aviv: Yedioth Ahronoth, 1997, p. 114.

[33] From an essay by Yossi Goldstein, "Changes in Positions in the Eshkol, Rabin, and Golda Governments over the Future of Judea, Samaria, and the Gaza Sector, 1967–1977" (Hebrew), *Meh'karei Yehuda veshomron* (2011), pp. 300–330 (p. 304).

[34] Minutes of government meeting in which Israel's proposal for arranging the borders was decided according to this formulation: government meeting, June 18, 1967 (afternoon), (Moshe Dayan's proposal on p. 99), File No. 0002ees.

The government agreed about the future of the Sinai Peninsula and Golan Heights but disagreed on the West Bank and Gaza Strip. Dayan believed "Judea and Samaria are a part of our land and they should be settled, not abandoned." However, Dayan remained equivocal – "We're waiting for a call from Hussein," he said and did not join the Movement for a Whole Israel, whose raison d'être was to fight for annexing the occupied territories to Israel.[35]

In the June 19 government discussion, Dayan suggested annexing the West Bank and imposing military rule there until a solution was found; his preferred solution was self-government by the inhabitants, and foreign affairs and security government by Israel, without Israeli citizenship for the inhabitants but also with Jewish settlement in the territories.[36] While remaining very empathetic to the inhabitants, Dayan was hawkish on the subject of returning to the 1949 borders. "In 1949," he said, "we had untenable borders to which we must not return, because they are worse than war. Their significance is permanent warfare."[37]

Dayan wanted to maintain the status quo, not cutting the West Bank off from Jordan while also ensuring agreements to regulate the inhabitants' lives and secure their income.[38] By sheer force of personality, Dayan, officially responsible only for security, but personally committed to managing the inhabitants' daily lives, took charge of "the territories' portfolio," creating cooperation among various government offices even though no one entity coordinated the various bodies handling the territories.[39]

Dayan neutralized Eshkol, who headed the Ministerial Committee on the Territories, by not bringing issues to the committee for discussion, another source of tension between them.[40]

Dayan often spoke about Vietnam's lessons, emphasizing that Israel must not impose "Israelization" on the Palestinian population in any way whatsoever.[41] Vietnam had strengthened his belief that continuing to hold on to the territories meant forcing occupation on another people. Nonetheless, he felt that he had found a successful compromise: maximum liberty in everyday conduct, maintaining contact with the rest of the Arab world, open borders, and freedom of speech, but zero tolerance of terrorism.[42]

---

[35] Bar-On, "Ruling Another People," p. 3.
[36] Government Meeting, June 18, 1967, State Archive, "Peace Plan after Six-Day War," June 19, 1967, Document 3, File # 0002ees.
[37] Bar-On, "Ruling Another People," p. 3.
[38] Shlomo Gazit, *Hamakel vehagezer: Hamimshal hayisraeli bi'yehuda veshomron* (Hebrew), Tel Aviv: Zmora-Bitan, 1985, pp. 129–138.
[39] Ibid., p. 92.
[40] Yossi Goldstein, *Eshkol: Biography* (Hebrew), Jerusalem: Keter, 2003, pp. 585–586.
[41] Braun, *Hotam ishi*, p. 145.
[42] Ibid., p. 146.

In his many interviews about the territories, Dayan expressed ambivalence, sometimes suggesting autonomy for the Palestinians, sometimes emphasizing the Jewish people's deep historic connection to the conquered land. Skeptical that a full peace was possible, he was prepared to accept partial arrangements of nonviolence: "between worse lines with an arrangement close to peace and better lines with an arrangement that is less than peace – I favor the latter."[43]

Dayan's three major principles for controlling the territories were: minimal Israeli presence, maximal autonomy, and open bridges, including free movement between the territories and the Arab states.[44] On the second day of the Six-Day War, he explained his vision for how Israel should relate to the Palestinians: "We must treat the Arabs as equal to us in civilian and humanitarian terms. [Israel must] reduce as much as possible its intervention in their affairs and not relate to them as enemies unless they act against us."[45] In an earlier speech, he said, "I am not afraid of Fatah actions, but I do worry about a national uprising... I have hope we can prevent [an uprising] if we give them freedom of a kind that will make fighting against us pointless... and we must take care not to act like occupiers... Only then do we stand a chance."[46]

Believing that prosperity would reduce the chances of a feared national uprising, Dayan focused on improving public services for the Palestinian population. This policy proved effective in countering early efforts by armed members of Fatah attempting to mobilize rebellion.[47] Dayan had told Palestinian leaders that while he didn't expect them to fight the infiltrators or help him fight them, he would not tolerate any active cooperation by the local Palestinians.[48]

In the early years of Israeli occupation, Dayan's policy generated positive results because it was quickly implemented. He closely followed developments within the communities and was often the first to notice changes. He set up a group of private informants with extensive contacts with the Palestinians and direct access to him and was personally involved in selecting every Israeli administration governor and administrator. While he encouraged open discussions, once he made a decision, he made sure everyone backed it in full.[49]

---

[43] Citation from Dayan addressing a General Staff discussion, January 15, 1968, in Yoav Gelber, *Haz'man hafalestini: Shalosh hashanim shebahen yisrael hafkha knufiyot le'am: Yisreal, yarden vehafalestinim 1967–1979* (Hebrew), Hevel Modiin: Dvir, 2018, p. 97.

[44] Shlomo Gazit, *Meta'em bemalkodet: 30 shnot mediniyut yisraelir bashtahim* (Hebrew), Tel Aviv: Zmora-Bitan, 1999, p. 62.

[45] Braun, *Hotam ishi*, p. 149.

[46] Ibid., p. 160.

[47] Fatah is a Palestinian nationalist and social democratic political party that espoused armed resistance against Israel. Founded in 1959, today it is the largest faction of the confederated multiparty Palestine Liberation Organization (PLO).

[48] Ibid., p. 12.

[49] Gazit, *Meta'em bemalkodet*, pp. 74–75.

Dayan sought to avoid collective punishments and unnecessary fines and opposed demolishing homes unless they were directly connected with terrorists. Still, while defense minister, Dayan did not always withstand pressure and authorized – even initiated – actions viewed as collective punishment.[50]

Dayan could not entirely prevent revolts, such as the large one in Nablus in 1967, giving rise to intense public outcry among Israelis. The violence was quelled through a combination of carrot-and-stick approaches, imposing curfews, making arrests whenever there was unrest, but helping inhabitants during periods of calm. Dayan explained that it was unthinkable for the state to support those supporting terrorism against Israel and even receiving money from Jordan for doing so.[51] Meeting with mayors in the major West Bank cities, Dayan assumed personal responsibility and demanded an end to cooperation with terrorists and entering into a dialogue about complaints. In November, Dayan reported that the revolt was subdued and over, and life had returned to normal.[52] Dayan worried less about international reactions than about cracks in the Israeli consensus about the territories.

The Gaza Strip, which Dayan had originally opposed occupying, presented a unique challenge. In 1970, security there had deteriorated badly, and Israel had lost control in some areas. Ariel Sharon, the Southern Command commander, developed new tactical methods involving constantly pursuing the terrorists, forcing them to flee and hide. A diametric contrast to Dayan's policy of a low-profile military presence, Sharon's stronger presence improved intelligence and exposed the bunkers that had been dug underneath Gaza citrus groves. However, it failed to achieve the goal of gaining control of the crowded refugee camps. Dayan suggested dividing the Strip into smaller sectors by destroying a line of buildings along existing alleys. The new wider alleys could be patrolled and supervised and better expose the terrorists. Soon, rumors began spreading that Israel planned to use the guise of fighting terrorists to destroy all the camp and scatter the population to other cities. Sharon himself helped verify the rumor, destroying many more homes than Dayan had either planned or approved. The result was immediate: The community elders begged Israel to stop the home demolitions, promising to cooperate in action against the terrorists. The Gaza Strip finally entered a period of calm in July 1972.[53]

Dayan's approach to running the territories again reflected a strong presence in the field, as he engaged in numerous, often unscheduled visits and direct conversations with people of all backgrounds, sometimes issuing

---

[50] Ibid.
[51] From minutes of meeting of Foreign Affairs and Security Committee, September 26, 1967, in Gelber, *Haz'man hafalestini*, p. 247.
[52] Gelber, *Haz'man hafalestini*, pp. 248–249.
[53] Gazit, *Meta'em bemalkodet*, pp. 71–73.

instructions based on what he saw.[54] He often bypassed bureaucracy[55] and reversed army commanders' decisions to demolish houses and expel residents, helping inhabitants return and rebuild their lives.[56]

As defense minister, Dayan matured and acted with greater deliberation. Nevertheless, he continued operating as he had when Chief of Staff. Gazit wrote:

> If you were to look at his calendar when he was defense minister, you'd find a cabinet meeting every Sunday, a staff meeting every Friday, and another day for touring the IDF or the territories. The rest of the days and times were blank ... so, when he came to the office in the morning, he dealt with issues he'd been thinking and worrying about during the night or when fiddling with his collection of pottery and antiquities. He would summon people for impromptu meetings (and, who, really, would tell the defense minister, "Sorry, but I have previous plans"?) or he'd eliminate the problems troubling him with a phone call. Or – and this was often the case – he'd invite himself on an unplanned visit to check up on things and get an unmediated impression of what was happening.[57]

Dayan carefully and personally chose military governors for the occupied territories, seeking ethical, combat-tested officers capable of winning support. He expected them to act modestly and respectfully.[58] His policy included using extreme means against potential uprisings, but he promised fair and humane treatment of the population, safeguarding holy sites, and honoring the clergy. Respecting the local tribal structure was crucial, as was avoiding unnecessary contact between soldiers and civilians and providing welfare and medical services.[59] Yitzhak Eini Abadi, Governor of Khan Yunis, recalled Dayan instructing him:

> As governor, you will represent the inhabitants of Khan Yunis to us, not the other way around ... hence it is our duty to fight to get whatever they need. The condition for this is having the heart to do it. If you don't have the heart – there's no point in taking the job.[60]

A significant aspect of his policy involved forming personal connections and empowering local leaders to create a functional mechanism providing services without a national government.[61]

---

[54] Gazit, *Hamakel vehagezer*, p. 87.
[55] Braun, *Hotam ishi*, p. 143.
[56] The villages were Amusa, Huba, Dir Ayub, Yallou, and Beit Nuba: ibid., p. 153.
[57] Shlomo Gazit, *Bitsmatim makhri'im: Mehapalmah lerashut aman* (Hebrew), Rishon Lezion: Miskal, 2016, p. 165.
[58] Moshe Elad, *Im tirtsu – Zo hagada: Hamimshal hatsva'i bagada hamaaravit ba'asor harishon 1967-1977* (Hebrew), Haifa: Pardes, 2015, p. 60.
[59] Gazit, *Bitsmatim makhri'im*, pp. 162-163.
[60] Gazit, *Bitsmatim makhri'im*, pp. 170-171.
[61] Gazit, *Hamakel vehagezer*, p. 203.

Dayan invited Fadwa Tuqan, the "poet of Palestine," to his home to understand the Palestinians' perspective on nationalism. Dayan thought it important to know the mood among Palestinians and learn "what this public [Palestinian] thinks, what it will put up with, and for what it will fight, not just what its political leaders say."[62] Dayan also would get personally involved in disputes, showing up in person, summoning the parties, and making on-the-spot decisions.[63] The Arabs of Gaza treated Dayan with reverence. Abadi recalled:

> The reverence towards Dayan on the part of Gaza Strip Arabs stemmed primarily from his charisma. He knew how to act like a Bedouin, walk among them, clap them on the shoulder. The esteemed of Gaza felt adulation because of his behavior, his simplicity, his ability to go into a refugee camp and reach the last of the downtrodden and wretched and the children.[64]

Dayan's dominant, charismatic personality led to cooperation among most government ministries and the military, although his rivalries with some ministers, especially his problematic relationship with Prime Minister Eshkol, sometimes presented obstacles to implementing policies Dayan sought to advance.[65]

Dayan's policy also faced criticism, particularly concerning the Palestinians' lack of significant political rights, Dayan's desire to annex territories, and the problem of economic integration. Indeed, Dayan's policies led not to a strong, independent economy in the territories but to their economic dependence on Israel, leading his critics to brand his approach as neocolonialist.[66]

Economic peace and integration were not achieved overnight. Despite some 100,000 Palestinian laborers working in Israel in the 1970s, economic measures failed to prevent, and actually strengthened, the development of Palestinian nationalism. Finance Minister Pinchas Sapir had supported separate economies as a means of leading to future agreements,[67] as opposed to Dayan's use of cheap Arab labor that benefited the Israeli economy but impeded local Palestinian economic growth. However, antioccupation activist and scholar Niv Gordon observed that the most impressive characteristic of the early years of the occupation was Israel's attempt to improve the Palestinian population's standard of living and economic prosperity, even if this simultaneously undermined

---

[62] Mordechai Bar-On, *Moshe Dayan: Korot hayav 1915–1981*, Tel Aviv: Am Oved, 2014, p. 246.
[63] Gazit, *Bitsmatim makhri'im*, p. 168.
[64] Yizhar Be'er, "Moshe Dayan's Last Monologue: Antithesis to 'Dayan: The First Family'" (Hebrew), in the blog Sacred Cows – Israeli Myths, *Haaretz*, July 30, 2019, www.haaretz.co.il/blogs/israelimyths/BLOG-1.7581303
[65] Gazit, *Hamakel vehagezer*, p. 125.
[66] Shimon Shamir, "Integration and Its Cost" (Hebrew), *Haaretz*, December 25, 1968.
[67] Bar-On, *Moshe Dayan*, p. 248.

Palestinian attempts to create an independent economy. Anyone reading military reports will find lengthy discussions about ways to reduce unemployment and create economic growth, something the Military Government considered a means of preventing social unrest and resistance.[68]

Dayan's views were reflected in a plan presented to the government to establish Jewish settlements alongside Arab population centers, setting forth a rebuttal to Allon's plan to annex the Jordan Valley. Dayan wanted to build four urban centers along the watershed.[69] The division in Dayan's plan was functional: The territory itself would not be divided, but authority and management in practice would be.

Dayan believed Israel must engage in dialogue with the Palestinians but did not believe local West Bank dignitaries and mayors were the right interlocutors. He preferred to engage with Yasser Arafat, but attempts failed.[70] Regardless, Dayan preferred the Palestinian to the Jordanian route, because the Jordanians would not be able to make a separate peace treaty without the agreement of the rest of the Arab states. Dayan put forward five conditions for peace with Jordan: Jordanian forces not crossing the Jordan and Israel keeping bases along the mountain ridge and in the West Bank; Jordanian citizenship and administration west of the Jordan; Jews' right to live in the West Bank; resettling Gaza refugees in Jordan and Israeli reparations to help; Jerusalem's unification under Israel; and uniting Jerusalem under Israeli sovereignty with Jordan having special standing at the holy sites.[71] For critics, two states was the only solution, with Israel returning all or most of the territories to facilitate the establishment of a Palestinian state.[72]

Although Dayan did not consider civilian settlement of primary importance, neither did he oppose settlement initiatives, viewing them as evidence of the Israeli determination to continue to hold the territories. After a group of religious settlers, defying Dayan's wishes, took up residence in the heart of Arab Hebron in 1968, Dayan did not remove them, despite their provocation and the fact that he disapproved of Jewish settlement in the heart of Arab population centers. Instead, he moved them to the outskirts of Hebron, where the town of Kiryat Arba eventually developed.[73]

In the first years after the Six-Day War, the policy of the administration in the occupied territories succeeded thanks to painstaking implementation, with

---

[68] Niv Gordon, "Dowries and Brides: An Analysis of Israeli Structures of Occupation" (Hebrew), *Sotsiologiya yisraelit* 9:2 (2008), pp. 271–296 (p. 283).
[69] Gazit, *Meta'em bemalkodet*, p. 145.
[70] Ibid., p. 148.
[71] Dayan's statement as it appears in the minutes of a consultation with Eshkol and other ministers, May 29, 1968, State Archive; ibid., p. 199.
[72] For a critique of Israel's policy in the territories in these years, see Benny Morris, *Korbanot: Toldot hasikhsukh hatsiyoni-aravi 1881–2001* (Hebrew), Tel Aviv: Am Oved, 2003, pp. 320–323.
[73] Gazit, *Hamakel vehagezer*, p. 177.

Dayan involved in shaping and executing policy on the ground.[74] While defense minister, Dayan focused on preventing a popular uprising in the territories, which Fatah cells were constantly trying to organize, which would spiral out of control. Dayan, adopting a balanced policy and generally avoiding collective punishment, maintained a relatively effective separation between the subversive and violent Fatah and the mainly law-abiding population.[75] By the early 1970s, the popular uprising had petered out, and acts of terrorism all but stopped. According to Dayan, the war against terrorism and guerrillas had moved from the occupied territories to Israel's borders with Jordan and Syria.[76]

Paradoxically, one negative result of military government in the occupied territories was the sense of calm and convenience Israel now enjoyed. A new generation of Israelis was born and grew up within the reality of the occupation, never having known anything else. This was also true of the local Palestinian population (Figure 6.2). In 1999, some 80 percent of inhabitants of the territories were born after 1967.[77] The paradoxical result of Dayan's policy was a creation of a more educated, aware, and nationalistic generation – the one that in 1987 would be responsible for the outbreak of the First Intifada (Arabic, "Uprising").

Figure 6.2 Minister of Defense Moshe Dayan in conversation with a Palestinian in Hebron. Source: -/Stringer/AFP/Getty Images.

---

[74] Gazit, *Meta'em bemalkodet*, pp. 72–73.
[75] Gelber, *Haz'man hafalestini*, pp. 274–277.
[76] From minutes of meeting of Foreign Affairs and Security Committee, August 24, 1967, in: Gelber, *Haz'man hafalestini*, p. 308.
[77] Gazit, Meta'em bemalkodet, pp. 153.

Dayan and the Temple Mount

The conquest of the Temple Mount in 1967 immediately raised some important questions: What was the right policy for so sensitive a location? How could Jewish aspirations be realized for this holy site without arousing Muslim rage? Dayan wanted to prevent the national-territorial conflict from becoming a religious one. Many, especially in the religious right wing, accused Dayan of not having been deeply interested in conquering Jerusalem, claiming that the secular Dayan, lacking religious feeling or even real respect for the place, had ignored its importance and made excessive concessions to the Arabs.[78] This criticism was based on what many viewed as Dayan's opposition to the city's conquest, especially the infamous statement he reportedly made to Uzi Narkiss while gazing upon the Old City: "Who needs this whole Vatican anyway?"[79] But there are no hints in contemporaneous minutes of Dayan ever opposing East Jerusalem's conquest on principle. As for his reputed remark, Narkiss reported it as evidence of Dayan's ordering him not to damage any of the holy sites.[80]

In fact, as soon as the IDF seized control of the Temple Mount and the Western Wall, Dayan hurried there and gave an impassioned speech at the Western Wall:

> We have returned to the holiest of our sites never to be parted from it again. Israel extends its hand in peace to its Arab neighbors. Full freedom of religion and religious rights will be ensured to members of other religions. We have not come to conquer what is holy to others or reduce their religious rights but rather to ensure the unity of the city and live in it with others in brotherhood.[81]

Dayan also placed a note in the Western Wall, an act his critics interpreted cynically, claiming he did so for political gain, to cement himself in the public consciousness as the holy city's liberator.[82]

Undoubtedly, Dayan was a thoroughly political person, and political calculations were an inseparable part of his being. Still, it is likely that the man who wrote *Living with the Bible* and who fiercely loved the landscapes and history of his country experienced genuine excitement upon first touching the stones of

---

[78] Nurit Gringer, "Who Stole the Temple Mount from the Jewish People" (Hebrew), *Mahlaka Rishona*, March 19, 2012.

[79] See, e.g., Arieh Naor, "The Ouster of Levi Eshkol from the Defense Minister's Position and the Results of the Six-Day War: Anatomy of a Savior Complex" (Hebrew), in Devora Cohen and Moshe Lisk (eds.), *Tsomtei hakhra'ot ufarshiyot mafte'ah beyisrael* (Hebrew), Be'er Sheva: The Ben-Gurion Institute for the Study of Israel and Zionism, Ben-Gurion University of the Negev, 2010, p. 477.

[80] Uzi Narkiss, *Ahat yerushalayim* (Hebrew), Tel Aviv: Am Oved, 1975, p. 214.

[81] Ibid., p. 254.

[82] See, e.g., the staging of the photo of entering the city: Arik Bender, "Missed the Moment: The Story of the Photograph from the Six Days" (Hebrew), *NRG*, June 6, 2022, www.nrg.co.il/online/1/ART2/247/979.html.

the Western Wall and climbing the steps of the Temple Mount. He, like the rest of the Jewish people, was certain to have been swept up by this unique historic occasion. However, despite the elation, he was the first to realize that intense work was needed to regulate the extremely complex situation and preempt any possible conflicts.[83]

His comprehensive approach to the fate and management of the holy sites considered the religious aspirations and dreams of both sides as much as possible but imposed certain restrictions. Thus, each could live in peace with the solution without receiving all it wanted. Immediately after arriving at the Temple Mount, Dayan trying speaking with its administrators: "At first, they refused, but when I sat down on the carpets and crossed my legs the way Arabs do, they too were forced to do so and entered the discussion. . . . I said to them, 'The war is over and life should go back to normal.'"[84]

Regarding the location's status, Dayan was unequivocal: "Israel's soldiers will vacate the grounds and place themselves beyond the compound. The Israeli administration is responsible for general security, but will not intervene in internal guarding or supervision . . . We have not come to seize control of their holy sites or interfere with their religious life."[85] He also ensured the Jewish side's interests.[86]

His orders given in the first days after the war became the mainstays of Israel's Temple Mount policy: Guarding the Temple Mount would remain the responsibility of the Waqf, the Jordanian-appointed entity tasked with controlling and managing Islamic sites on the Temple Mount; the IDF would leave the compound, and Israel would be generally responsible for maintaining order; and security establishment units would be stationed at Mughrabi Gate. Dayan, fearing a religious war while also favoring freedom of religion and ritual, supported banning Jewish prayers on the Temple Mount while ending the Jordanian practice of censoring the Friday sermon (the *khutba*). However, he made it clear that the *imam* (preacher) would be punished if he incited the crowd to violence. Dayan also opened the gates of the Temple Mount to Muslim pilgrims from all over the world, despite some officers' concerns.

Dayan's Temple Mount policy was based on his profound historical, religious, and political awareness of the location's explosive potential. Dayan felt Israel, as victor, could afford to behave with dignity and keep the delicate balance. "I have no doubt that *because* we are in control, we must be tolerant and conciliatory."[87] Dayan's principles remain in force even today and are referred to as the Temple Mount "status quo."

---

[83] Moshe Dayan, *Avnei derekh: Autobiografia* (Hebrew), Jerusalem: Idanim, 1976, p. 497.
[84] Ibid., pp. 497–498.
[85] Ibid., p. 498.
[86] Ibid.
[87] Ibid.

The War on Palestinian Terrorism and Guerrilla Operations

After the Six-Day War, aided and encouraged by Arab states, the various Palestinian liberation organizations – especially Fatah and the Palestine Liberation Organization (PLO, led by Yasser Arafat from 1969) – began launching terrorist attacks and guerilla operations against Israel. They were inspired by national decolonization liberation struggles, especially that of Algeria, which seemed to the Palestinians to so resemble their own. Hassanein Heikal, of the Egyptian daily *Al-Ahram*, wrote that guerrilla combat would best Israel, as it had bested France and the United States in Algeria and Vietnam.[88] Consequently, until the War of Attrition intensified in March 1969, the Jordanian border was Israel's most active front for about eighteen months, and most of the IDF's elite forces were deployed there to defend against the indiscriminate terrorist and guerrilla acts the PLO turned to after failing to foment a civil uprising in the West Bank.[89]

In the fall of 1967, the Palestinian organizations, backed by generous support from Arab states, started focusing on attacking settlements and IDF units close to the border, with numerous incidents there during 1968.[90] This was an exhausting, frustrating, usually defensive struggle for the IDF, with no decisive outcome. "The army is not built – organizationally or mentally – for situations in which there is no 'one-fell-swoop' solution," said Dayan, adding, "This is a different circumstance and it requires a different response and policy."[91]

The major dilemma Dayan and Israel's other leaders faced, like the one faced in the 1950s when confronting the Fedayeen in Gaza (and, even more so, as they would face many years later in the struggle against Hezbollah), involved a strong terrorist organization embedded in a weak state in which the terrorists had managed to create a ministate. After the organization attacks Israel, the host state, Jordan in the past and Lebanon today, claims any attacks on it are pointless, as they have no control over the attacker. Israel faced either attacking the host state and forcing it to act against the organization or exercising restraint, as an attack would create tension with the host state and worsen the situation.

As in the 1950s, when the borders were wide open, Palestinian terrorist cells, mostly Fatah-affiliated, infiltrated Israel from Jordan to carry out attacks and to incite rebellion among the West Bank population. Thus, Dayan and the IDF had to confront incursions, mainly from Jordan, but also from Syria, along

---

[88] Gelber, *Haz'man hafalestini*, p. 418.
[89] Dayan's overview at Knesset Foreign Affairs and Security Committee meeting, December 24, 1968, State Archive, pp. 5–9.
[90] Gelber, *Haz'man hafalestini*, p. 352.
[91] Dayan, minutes of Knesset Foreign Affairs and Security Committee meeting, April 30, 1969, in Gelber, *Haz'man hafalestini*, p. 385.

with managing daily activity and establishing good relations between the locals and the military government. In response to the threat from these terrorist cells, the IDF set up special units and fortified the region, thereby successfully eliminating most of the terrorist threat with patrols and ambushes. Dayan personally participated in an ambush that caught and killed three infiltrators. Dayan, who was armed and got off several shots, appreciated the break in his routine and the opportunity to join the action.[92]

In October 1967, Dayan proposed direct coordination between the IDF and Jordanian commanders to stop the incursions, but King Hussein declined, claiming he was already doing everything he could, and probably fearing to be seen as a collaborator of Israel.[93] Dayan tried again in December 1967, sending a message to the king via Nablus mayor Hamadi Cna'an, but this effort also failed, and King Hussein continued to be evasive.[94] Some on the Israeli side felt that Hussein was ignoring the incursions and that some of his officers were, in fact, cooperating with the terrorists.[95]

In addition to the incursions, there were attacks and provocations, including mortar bomb and rocket fire on Israeli Jordan Valley towns and villages. Dayan ordered a strong response and investment in bomb shelters and other forms of passive protection. Along the border, artillery exchanges between the Jordanian army and the IDF were common, climaxing with Operation Shibboleth on February 15, 1968. Although Dayan preferred focusing on military targets, the entire Jordanian front suffered damage and many inhabitants left and fled to Amman.[96]

In March 1968, the IDF embarked on a large operation, Operation Karameh, to end the terrorist attacks. Karameh, a Jordanian village, had become the base of operations for the Fatah and Popular Front for the Liberation of Palestine (PFLP). After debating whether or not to target Jordan, the IDF decided to launch the operation on March 21 to inflict serious, long-lasting damage on the organizations, rendering them unable to harm Israel. The night before, Dayan suffered near-fatal injuries at an archeological dig and remained hospitalized for the next three weeks.

Although the operation caused substantial Palestinian and Jordanian casualties, the IDF, after sustaining heavy losses and being forced to abandon armored vehicles and considerable matériel on Jordanian soil, faced criticism for poor planning and flawed command and control. The Palestinians appropriated the Jordanian army's relative success against the Israelis as their own. This purported "victory" became a foundational Palestinian heroic myth,

[92] Dayan, *Avnei derekh*, p. 536.
[93] Gelber, *Haz'man hafalestini*, p. 311.
[94] Dayan, minutes of Cabinet security affairs meeting, December 14, 1967, in Gelber, *Haz'man hafalestini*, p. 312.
[95] Ibid., p. 326.
[96] Ibid., pp. 328–330.

thereby increasing Fatah's ranks and strengthening their status. However, relations between the Jordanian army and the terrorist organizations deteriorated considerably after the Palestinians took credit for the army's success.[97]

In spring 1968, the IDF built a complex system of barriers along the Jordanian border in the Jordan Valley to prevent terrorist teams from crossing into Israel. Pursuit operations by the IDF often led to infiltrators' deaths, but also IDF losses, including senior officers.

Senior officers continued to view their role as leading pursuits, a practice for which the IDF continued to pay dearly. Dayan, who for years had stayed true to the ethos of a field commander literally leading his troops, changed his mind over time, now stressing that a company or battalion commander should not issue radio orders from a protected office but should also not be at the forefront of the assault force. Rather, Dayan explained, the commander was to be "in the second or third vehicle ... so they can ask him without the radio, so they can hear from those who are at the front what's happening and what they can see."[98] In government debates, Dayan defended the senior commanders leading rather than following their troops but ordered the Chief of Staff to issue instructions preventing any officer above the rank of company commander (captain) from physically leading assaults.[99]

The IDF command, frustrated by the protracted hostilities, demanded the end of the distinction between the Jordanian army and the terrorist organizations. The terrorist bases were located adjacent to military bases, making it difficult to pinpoint action against the terrorists. Dayan made it clear that caution was needed not just to avoid harming Jordan but also due to the American request to protect the king and his kingdom.[100] Later, Dayan would rule out actions like the one in Karameh, citing the risks of high losses and alienating international public opinion.

Furthermore, Dayan expected the center of action to soon move to the Egyptian front, now starting to heat up.[101] In the spring and summer of 1968, terrorist groups – with Egypt's backing – began stepping up their activities on the southern front.[102] A May 1969 coordinated attack on an IDF outpost in the Jordan Valley caused casualties to the Israeli side, leading

---

[97] Ibid., p. 354.
[98] Yaakov Erez and Ilan Kfir, *Sihot im Moshe Dayan* (Hebrew), Ramat Gan: Massada, 1981, p. 67.
[99] Foreign Affairs and Security Committee meeting, September 27, 1968, in Gelber, *Haz'man hafalestini*, p. 370.
[100] Dayan, minutes of General Staff meeting, January 13, 1969, pp. 24–26, in Gelber, *Haz'man hafalestini*, p. 377. In 2006, in the Second Lebanon War, Israel faced similar pressure from the United States, which asked Israel not to damage Lebanon or the regime of Prime Minister Fouad Siniora, whom the United States viewed as an ally.
[101] Ibid., p. 378.
[102] Ibid., p. 384.

Dayan to note that the terrorists' military skills had improved. "This was an exemplary unit with an exemplary commander," he said.[103] Still, throughout 1969, the IDF chalked up good results, either capturing or intercepting most infiltrating terrorist teams, with low IDF losses.[104]

From late June 1967 until May 20, 1970, the terrorists lost 1,621 men, most on the Jordanian border. Nonetheless, the fighting never stopped, and Israel was stymied. The IDF stopped most incursions, but Israeli border towns and villages were subject to artillery fire.[105] Despite ceasefire agreements, terrorists continued operating from Jordan and Lebanon while Israel's response ability remained limited.

In February 1969, Fatah seized control of the Palestinian National Council and the PLO, electing Yasser Arafat as its chairman and effective head of the PLO. Arafat soon positioned himself as the Palestinians' representative. Dayan, unlike most Israeli leaders, viewed the developing battle between King Hussein and Arafat as a fight over the right to represent the Palestinian people. Ultimately, the king was forced to recognize Arafat's leadership over the Palestinians in order to save his kingdom.

Israel's successful prevention of Palestinian terrorist incursions exacerbated tensions with the Jordanian army, culminating in clashes between them toward the end of 1969. Tensions worsened the next year, when Iraqi forces, more likely to help the terrorists, arrived in Jordan. Dayan sought US support for a joint Jordanian–Israeli effort against the terrorists and the Iraqis. The Jordanians privately requested that Dayan approve IAF help against the Iraqis; Israel agreed to help Hussein should a confrontation erupt with the Palestinian groups.[106]

Very worried about the situation in Jordan, Dayan raised his concerns about what he saw as an imminent and major clash between Hussein and the Palestinians with US Secretary of State Joseph Sisco during his visit to Israel in April 1970. Israel, Dayan added, was the only regional entity that could save Jordan.[107] Contrary to assessments by AMAN and senior IDF officers that the terrorists would defeat Hussein, Dayan thought that the king's power was greater than it seemed and that he could best the terrorist organizations.[108] Still, various US sources felt that Hussein's chances of survival were slim.[109]

---

[103] Dayan's overview, minutes of Knesset Foreign Affairs and Security Committee meeting, May 6, 1969, in Gelber, *Haz'man hafalestini*, p. 389.
[104] Ibid., p. 396.
[105] Ibid., p. 415.
[106] From political-security consultation, April 9, 1970, State Archive, in Gelber, *Haz'man hafalestini*, pp. 433–434.
[107] Minutes of Dayan's conservation with Sisco, April 15, 1970, in Gelber, *Haz'man hafalestini*, p. 436.
[108] Dayan at General Staff meeting, May 4, 1970, in Gelber, *Haz'man hafalestini*, p. 438.
[109] Ibid., p. 437.

The proverbial straw that broke the camel's – Jordan's – back was the PFLP's skyjacking of three civilian planes belonging to Western airline companies (a fourth was skyjacked a few days later). The terrorists forced the planes to land in Jordan, the passengers were held hostage, and on September 6, 1970, the terrorists blew up the planes. In response, on September 17, the Jordanian army launched an offensive against terrorist enclaves. Syria exhorted Jordanian troops to rebel and warned it would intervene on behalf of the terrorists.[110] The following day, Syria made good on its threat: Two armored brigades and one mechanized brigade attacked Jordan. Jordan pressured the United States, which turned to Israel. Golda Meir and Moshe Dayan ordered photographic sorties and transmitted the resulting intelligence to the United States,[111] which asked Israel to intervene militarily on Jordan's behalf on September 20. Dayan criticized the United States for wasting time before asking Israel to act,[112] seeing it as further evidence of US ambivalence in its Israel policy. While acknowledging Israel's capabilities and willingness to help, the United States hesitated to fully cooperate, fearing to anger Arab allies, especially the Saudis.

Dayan prepared to attack Syria, drawing up a combined air and ground offensive. But Prime Minister Meir and Dayan worried about the possible outcome of massive Israeli intervention, which could drag the entire region into an all-out war. Dayan, as usual, was concerned about Soviet interference and did not trust that the United States would support Israel politically or militarily if the USSR intervened.[113]

From September 20 to 22, the IDF fired artillery at Syrian positions in Irbid, and IAF planes carried out warning sorties above the Syrian troops, while Jordan managed to repel the Syrian attack. On September 23, Syria started its retreat, leaving the Jordanian army clearly in control. Thousands of terrorists had been killed, and the rest fled. The king thanked Meir and Dayan for their help. A ceasefire was declared on September 25.

For Israel, what came to be known as Black September had several positive outcomes. For one, it ended the incessant harassment on the Jordanian border, which became almost completely peaceful. A second and more strategic benefit was that the United States learned it had a firm anchor in the Middle East, although the changed perception was mostly Kissinger's personally and in the

---

[110] From a report to US Deputy National Security Advisor Alexander Haig, and from Haig to Kissinger, September 17, in Gelber, *Haz'man hafalestini*, p. 464.

[111] Transcription of telephone call between Kissinger and Rabin, September 20, 1970, in Gelber, *Haz'man hafalestini*, p. 472.

[112] Telegram sent by Evan Zoharlan, a US State Department official working at the US Embassy in Tel Aviv to the State Department, September 21, 1970, about his conversation with Dayan at the airport, waiting for Golda Meir's return from abroad, in Gelber, *Haz'man hafalestini*, p. 474.

[113] Ibid., p. 481.

Department of Defense rather than within the State Department.[114] Despite distrusting the United States, Dayan viewed the crisis as an opportunity for Israel to strengthen its ties with the superpower. He later noted that he was meticulous in ensuring that every report to the Americans was completely reliable to make them feel they could trust Israel.[115] Indeed, President Richard Nixon wrote to Meir that he would never forget Israel's part in propping up Jordan and stopping efforts to overturn the regime. He thought the United States was fortunate to have an ally such as Israel in the Middle East, and this would be taken into consideration in all future developments.[116]

However, following the Jordanian episode, there were also some regional developments less favorable to Israel, including regime change in Syria, with the ascent of Hafez al-Assad, who was no less hostile to Israel than the previous leader – and possibly more daring. In addition, terrorists were now entrenching themselves into a new host nation, Lebanon, thus opening up another front against Israel. This development ended only with Israel's invasion of Lebanon in 1982, causing Hezbollah's rise to prominence, which continues to challenge Israel to this day.

Unlike on the Egyptian front, where Dayan had escalated the situation to reach a ceasefire, with Jordan, he avoided escalation. First, the nature of the enemy differed, as Jordan, while unstable, was favorably inclined toward Israel. Second, civilian settlements on the Jordanian border were more vulnerable, unlike the Sinai, where there were no civilian settlements. Dayan had to consider these factors in balancing on the tightrope between restraint and military response.

Dayan, summarizing the events, attributed the eradication of terrorism from Israel and the occupied West Bank to three factors: his stick-and-carrot policy; military and intelligence activities; and the sequence of events in Jordan that resulted in Black September.[117]

---

[114] Aharon Yariv at General Staff debate on October 12, 1970, in Gelber, *Haz'man hafalestini*, p. 492.
[115] Erez and Kfir, *Sihot im Moshe Dayan*, p. 67.
[116] Amos Gilboa, *Mar modi'in: Ahreleh, aluf aharon yariv, rosh aman* (Hebrew), Tel Aviv: Miskal, 2013, p. 543.
[117] Dayan, *Avnei derekh*, p. 541.

7

The War of Attrition

Fighting Egyptians and Soviets

The War of Attrition exposed cracks in the national consensus and triggered political and social processes that intensified after the Yom Kippur War.[1] It led to significant Soviet involvement on the Arab side and increased US aid to Israel, marking the beginning of the United States becoming Israel's primary arms provider and diplomatic supporter. Its conclusion was essentially, and significantly, the opening act of the Yom Kippur War.

Recently, renewed interest in the War of Attrition has sparked new publications examining it,[2] focusing mainly on two key features of the war. First, although large in scope, the war was fundamentally limited; each side aimed not for the other's defeat, but rather exhaustion. Egypt sought to force Israel to retreat from the Suez Canal, while Israel wanted to prevent Egypt from gaining anything through violence. To stop Egypt's violence, Israel's strategy involved escalating the situation to deescalate it; that is, increasing the violence to a level that would deter Egypt and restrain its actions. This strategy, known as escalation dominance, requires one side to out-escalate the other at any given moment to demonstrate superiority and force a concession.

The challenge with this strategy is accurately assessing appropriate force levels. Excessive escalation may push the opponent to respond forcefully, potentially snowballing into an unintended all-out war. The strategy demands balancing between escalation and predicting the other side's reaction.

The War of Attrition has gained renewed interest also due to the Soviet Union's involvement in the conflict, in which Israel fought Egypt, a Soviet client state. While the Soviets did not appear to have aggressive intentions toward Israel, they intervened directly against Israel to avoid another humiliation of their client state. Russia's current Middle East presence and its interests in the region resemble the situation in the 1970s, particularly regarding Israel's attacks in Syria, where the regime is supported by Russia, as Egypt had been. There are, of course, differences, such as Russia's and Israel's

---

[1] Yoav Gelber, *Hatasha: Hamilhama shenish'k'ha* (Hebrew), Hevel Modiin: Kinneret, Zmora Bitan, Dvir, 2017, p. 651.

[2] Boris Dolin, *Homat Suez: Sipura shel hamilhama hasodit bein medinat yisrael livrit hamo'etsot* (Hebrew), Hevel Modiin: Kinneret Zmora, 2020.

diplomatic relations and military coordination today, reflecting their shared regional interests and Israel's increased regional strength.

Egypt renewed the fighting along the Canal on July 1, 1967, merely three weeks after the end of the Six-Day War. Fighting was sporadic until Egypt formally declared the War of Attrition on March 8, 1968, and then became a daily event. Egypt's declared goal was to force Israel to retreat from the Canal. Although unsuccessful, it did generate other benefits for Egypt and brought it closer to its goal. The war ended with a ceasefire agreement on August 8, 1970. A period of calm followed until the outbreak of the Yom Kippur War on October 6, 1973.

Dayan had been against the IDF reaching the Suez Canal during the Six-Day War, concerned about long-term conflict and knowing Egypt would not accept Israel's presence. While he was proved correct, once the army was at the Canal, he worked to ensure Israel would not retreat in the face of Egyptian force. For Egypt, the Suez Canal was of cardinal strategic importance and symbolized renewed Egyptian nationalism. While understanding these feelings, Dayan now had to deal with the situation at hand and not fold under pressure, lest it set a precedent. A partial retreat was discussed during the War of Attrition, but Dayan's minority position did not prevail against his veteran political rivals; ultimately, Israel's presence on the Suez Canal may have led to the grim 1973 war, although arguably, without that war, the sides would not have reached the full peace agreement of 1979.

Golda Meir was Israel's prime minister for most of the War of Attrition, replacing Levi Eshkol. While Dayan's relationship with Eshkol was contentious, Dayan maintained effective relations with Meir, despite his earlier reservations about her. Meir respected Dayan's defense and security expertise, on which she depended, and he remained loyal and transparent in return. Dayan accepted Meir's authority, as he had Ben-Gurion's, but felt more equal to Meir due to his age and experience, as well as her lacking Ben-Gurion's unique status.

Dayan believed that the Arab armies' 1967 defeat would not necessarily lead to peace, as the Arab states had not admitted defeat; and, with time, signs emerged that another round of fighting was imminent. He emphasized that Israel's presence at the Suez Canal was reason enough for another war. Having gone to war twice in Sinai, he favored Israel's presence in Sharm El Sheikh, preferring it to an unreliable peace treaty.[3] This explains the context of his famous statement, "Better Sharm [El Sheikh] without peace than peace without Sharm [El Sheikh]."[4] Dayan was pessimistic about the possibility of an

---

[3] Dayan's statements in the minutes of a General Staff meeting, January 15, 1968, in Yoav Gelber, *Hatasha: Hamilhama shenish'kek'ha* (Hebrew), Kinneret Zmora: Bitan, 2017, p. 22.

[4] "Dayan: Better Sharm without peace than peace without Sharm" (Hebrew), *Maariv*, March 10, 1971.

agreement and believed Israel could last within its new borders even while preparing for war, managing the occupied territories, and fighting Fatah.[5] He spoke about the Arabs' deep-seated hatred for Israel and inability to accept its existence. In fact, Dayan felt the Arabs would prefer to fight another war than take steps toward peace.[6] About six weeks before a major artillery bombardment fired on the Suez Canal on September 8, 1968, Dayan said that the Egyptians "would recognize Israel's strength."[7] Predicting that the Arabs were preparing to renew the war,[8] he emphasized that Israel would not retreat from the Canal even if faced with extended hostilities.

Dayan and the General Staff were greatly preoccupied with the question of the next war, even discussing conquering the capital cities of Arab states as a way to achieve peace. Dayan, apprehensive about this course of action, had more reservations than others.[9] He agreed with assessments that Egyptians could cross the Canal and hold it but that they would not try to occupy Sinai; he concluded that no threat of an Egyptian invasion of Sinai was imminent.[10]

On June 13, 1967, Dayan declared: "We're waiting for a telephone from the Arabs."[11] However, Egypt rejected Israel's government offer of a peace treaty conditioned on freedom of shipping and demilitarization of the Sinai; Egypt demanded an unconditional withdrawal instead. Despite the financial loss incurred, it preferred a closed canal to allowing transit to Israeli ships. The gap remained, and only after two bloody wars did the sides arrive at a compromise, essentially based on the original Israeli offer.[12] Dayan summarized Israel's position in the years to come as "Peace or we stay where we are."[13]

The War of Attrition: Main Actions

The War of Attrition marked the first time Egypt, Israel's most powerful adversary, employed an all-out strategy of attrition against Israel rather than one of decisive maneuver or harassment to force it to withdraw from the Suez Canal or to seek political negotiations from a position of weakness. This new strategy also dictated Israel's response, mainly due to political constraints

---

[5] Cited in *Maariv*, May 24, 1968, in Gelber, *Hatasha*, p. 23.
[6] Ibid., p. 312.
[7] Dayan's review in minutes of Foreign Affairs and Security Committee meeting, July 23, 1968, State Archive, File. No. 0013qtm, p. 6.
[8] Dayan's review in minutes of Foreign Affairs and Security Committee meeting, July 27, 1968, State Archive, File. No. 0013qtm, pp. 2–4.
[9] Gelber, *Hatasha*, p. 329.
[10] Carmit Guy, *Bar-Lev: Biografia* (Hebrew), Tel Aviv: Am Oved, 1998, p. 174.
[11] *Maariv*, June 13, 1967.
[12] Shimon Golan, *Hamilhama lehafsakat hahatasha: Kabalat hahahlatot barama haestrategit bemilhemet hahatasha bahazit hamitsrit* (Hebrew), Ben Shemen: Maarakhot and Modan, 2018, p. 18.
[13] Gelber, *Hatasha*, p. 34.

preventing it from launching a full-scale assault across the Suez Canal to destroy Egyptian forces. Israel could justify an all-out attack on Egyptian territory only in response to a similar threat from Egypt. In this situation, Israel had to operate within a set of rules imposed by its enemies, engaging in a counterwar of attrition. In response to the Egyptians, who aimed to demoralize Israel through mounting losses, Israel conducted targeted attacks and continuously sought the Egyptians' breaking point.

Gaining an upper hand in these conditions hinged on the ability to exploit the enemy's weaknesses, maintain a superior position, and escalate until the other side conceded. Political constraints made it difficult for Israel to fully benefit from decisive military moves. Egypt was backed by a global superpower – the Soviet Union nearly unconditionally committed to Egyptian military success. In comparison, Israel was supported by the United States, a more hesitant superpower, which, at best, created uncertainty and, in practice, imposed limitations on Israel. Additionally, Egypt understood that it could pressure Israel by threatening regional stability, considered a United States interest; this would result in US efforts to restrain Israel and pressure it into making concessions. Dayan recognized the problematic nature of the United States as Israel's primary ally.

Following the Six-Day War, Nasser rebuilt the Egyptian army with Soviet help. With a reconstructed army, in March 1969, Nasser began the seventeen-month-long War of Attrition that cost hundreds of Israeli and thousands of Egyptian lives. Egypt deployed two armies totaling some 100,000 soldiers along 100 miles of the Canal, and the Soviets provided reinforcement with 15,000 aerial defense troops and advisors. Due to firefights along the Canal, around 700,000 Egyptians living nearby became internal refugees.[14]

The IDF prepared for two main scenarios: an Egyptian attempt to cross the Suez Canal and establish a presence east of it, or an artillery campaign and raids. Chief of Staff Bar-Lev defined the army's mission as "denying the enemy any achievement by means of a tough defense of the water line." This definition had significant implications for the Yom Kippur War.[15] Israel's objective was to maintain the status quo. The goal was to achieve a ceasefire without relinquishing the IDF's deployment along the Canal. The key question for Dayan and Bar-Lev was how to make Egypt agree to a ceasefire. Israel's artillery was numerically inferior to that of Egypt, so in July 1969 the government authorized mass involvement of the air force – an act that a decade before would have been regarded as escalatory.

In January 1970, to add political pressure on Nasser, Israel conducted air raids on military installations in and around Cairo. It was not the targets that were important, but their location – publicly embarrassing Nasser because of his failure to prevent Israeli aircraft flying where they willed.

---

[14] Benny Morris, *Korbanot: Toldot hasikhsukh hatsiyoni-aravi 1881–2001* (Hebrew), Tel Aviv: Am Oved, 2003, p. 328.
[15] Golan, *Hamilhama lehafsakat hahatasha*, p. 257.

A month earlier, on December 9, 1969, as Egypt's casualties soared and it failed to contend with the IAF, it requested Soviet participation in the war. The Soviets concurred and sent aircraft and surface-to-air missile units to assist the Egyptians; these began arriving in March 1970 and deployed around Cairo. Not willing to directly confront the Soviet superpower, Israel stopped its air raids near Cairo but continued attacking forward Egyptian units.

Gradually the Soviets clandestinely pushed units forward toward the Canal. Israel began striking these units but publicly stated it was attacking Egyptian units. The Soviets maintained this fiction. Both sides suffered casualties. When Soviet aircraft began crossing the Canal, Israel's government initially ordered evasion by Israeli aircraft then authorized an ambush in which the Soviets lost five aircraft – again both sides maintained the fiction that the Soviet casualties were actually Egyptian.

The escalation was reaching dangerous levels, and both sides decided the time had come to stop. A ceasefire was arranged by the Soviets and the United States, and the war officially ended at midnight August 7–8, 1970.

Dayan and the Concern over Soviet Involvement

With Soviet help, already by October 1967, Egypt had replaced two-thirds of its losses in tanks, four-fifths of its planes, and a majority of its artillery. Soviet technicians, engineers, and consultants helped install and operate weapons systems and instruct the Egyptians on their use.[16] Dayan, deeply concerned by Egypt's progress and the failure to reach a settlement, nevertheless did not predict war in 1968.[17] He was worried about war in the longer term, believing[18] that Soviet support for Syria and Egypt was an attempt to establish footholds[19] and that the USSR's reaction would depend on the United States' actions as long as neither Israel nor the Soviets crossed the Canal.

Mossad intelligence in 1968 supported Dayan's view that the USSR was concerned about conflicts with the United States over Egypt.[20] Dayan dismissed claims that the USSR aimed to destroy Israel,[21] but, despite AMAN's and others' optimistic assessments, he worried about possible

---

[16] Gelber, *Hatasha*, p. 299.
[17] Dayan's statements in minutes of Foreign Affairs and Security Committee meeting, October 3, 1967, State Archive, File. No. 0013qtm, p. 4.
[18] From minutes of meeting between Joseph J. Sisco, Assistant Secretary of State for International Organization Affairs, and Dayan and General Staff officers on July 16, 1968, in Gelber, *Hatasha*, p. 301.
[19] Minutes of Alignment Faction meeting in the Knesset, January 30, 1968, in Gelber, *Hatasha*, p. 306.
[20] Ibid., p. 310.
[21] Dayan's statements in minutes of Foreign Affairs and Security Committee meeting, June 23, 1970, State Archive, File. No. 001460S, pp. 3–11.

military entanglements with the Soviets defending their client state, a concern later validated.

In June 1967, Dayan requested an overview of Soviet involvement in the Middle East from AMAN,[22] and by July, he had begun discussing the likelihood of Soviet military intervention against Israel. He argued that if Israel discussed this internally, it wouldn't "faint" but would be mentally prepared.[23] While convinced that Israel needed to prepare for a possible confrontation with the Soviets, he was not fearful. At a gathering of the senior command staff on June 29, Dayan explained his general skepticism of AMAN's assessments: "I'm not always convinced that AMAN has thought it through correctly ... and I consider for myself what AMAN has considered."[24] Dayan warned of Soviet involvement and of Egypt's opposition to Israel's presence at the Suez Canal, adding that Israel's decision would not change even if Soviet pilots and tank crews participated in the campaign.[25] On July 5, Dayan led a General Staff discussion about the USSR's involvement in the region and the possibility of increased Soviet pressure and aid to Arab nations. Addressing the extent of possible Soviet involvement, Dayan concluded by saying it was too early to tell – the real question was: "What exactly do the Russians really want in the Middle East?"[26]

Dayan believed that the USSR would not let Egypt fall, while Allon thought Soviet technological inferiority would keep it out. Dayan disagreed, believing that the Soviets' political calculations would outweigh any technological limitations.[27] Dayan emphasized the need for US support, believing that the Americans could neutralize the USSR to help Israel, which could not face the Soviets on its own.[28]

Prewar Incidents

Between July 1967 and March 1968, skirmishes occurred on the banks of the Suez Canal, initiated by Egypt. Israel's attempts to sail through the Canal in mid July were met with fierce resistance, leading to an escalation in fire and de facto paralysis of shipping. Despite Dayan's initial objection to Israel's

---

[22] Amos Gilboa, *Mar modi'in: Ahreleh, aluf aharon yariv, rosh aman* (Hebrew), Tel Aviv: Miskal, 2013, p. 333.
[23] Ibid., p. 336.
[24] Ibid., p. 338.
[25] Ibid., p. 339.
[26] Golan, *Hamilhama lehafsakat hahatasha*, pp. 19-21.
[27] It is worth noting that this remains true today, as Russia has found ways to compensate for its inferiority compared to the United States by using proxies and by the determined application of its available power.
[28] Dima Adamsky, *Mivtsa Kavkaz: Hahitarvut hasovyetit vehahafta'a hayisraelit bemilhemet hahatasha* (Hebrew), Tel Aviv: Maarakhot, 2006, pp. 72-74, 162-164.

presence on the Canal, once the IDF was there, he adopted an uncompromising position: if Israel could not use the Canal, neither could Egypt. As was characteristic for him, Dayan explained that, despite his previous objection to approaching the Canal, once it was decided to take up positions there, it was necessary to safeguard Israel's rights.[29]

The attempt to establish facts on the ground at the Suez Canal was Dayan's idea, and Eshkol agreed without government approval.[30] Eshkol's military secretary, often critical of Dayan, wrote that Dayan was proved correct: The Egyptians accepted Israel's presence on the Suez Canal, and calm was soon restored.[31] In addition, Egyptian civilians were evacuated from along the Canal, and shipping through it stopped on September 26, 1967.[32]

Once the initial incidents ended, the IDF established rules of response and escalation and began setting up its pattern of deployment along the Suez. Dayan asked Rabin about tank deployment, reflecting his penchant for learning and understanding the tactical details and considerations before saying anything.[33]

Meanwhile, the superpowers pressured Israel. With France turning its back on Israel, including de Gaulle's arms embargo, Israel became increasingly reliant on the United States for weapons and diplomatic support. Dayan handed off research and acquisitions to his deputy, Tsvi Tsur, but contacts with the French defense establishment proved fruitless. Dayan sought alternatives, and these would reshape the character of Israel's security establishment and fix fundamental principles that are in place to this day. The decision was made to transition to US systems, marking the beginning of the special strategic relationship between the United States and Israel. Unlike the Soviet Union, which gave almost unlimited aid to its client states, the United States used its assistance to apply political pressure on Israel either to wrest political concessions from it or to rein in Israeli military actions, while always casting sidelong glances at the Arab nations in which it had clear interests. During the second half of 1967, the United States delayed its delivery of Phantoms and Skyhawks, a deal that had already been signed. Having learned a lesson from the French embargo, Israel decided to diversify its sources and, in particular, enlist local industry to develop and manufacture arms right at home. Various enterprises were launched, including the Merkava tank, the Gabriel missiles, and the Nesher and Kfir aircraft for the IAF.[34]

---

[29] Gelber, *Hatasha*, p. 332.
[30] Eitan Haber, *Hayom tifrots milhama: Zikhronot shel tat aluf Yisrael Lior, hamazkir hatseva'i shel rosh hamemshala Levi Eshkol ve Golda Meir* (Hebrew), Tel Aviv: Idanim, 1987, p. 286; Gelber, *Hatasha*, p. 332.
[31] Haber, *Hayom tifrots milhama*, p. 288.
[32] Gelber, *Hatasha*, p. 334.
[33] Golan, *Hamilhama lehafsakat hahatasha*, p. 23.
[34] From: *Rav-aluf Moshe Dayan: Rosh hamateh haclali harevi'i, sidrat haramatkalim, hativat TOHAD* (Hebrew), Doctrine and Training Directorate, April 2018, p. 64.

The most notable incident of the time was the sinking of the Israeli Z class destroyer INS Eilat by Egyptian missiles in October 1967, which led to the IDF attacking refineries and fertilizer plants in Suez. The escalation likely deterred Nasser, who was not prepared for a large-scale conflict with Israel. Despite criticism of the action, Dayan prevented the establishment of an inquiry commission. In any event, Israel was transitioning to missile boats, although the navy had not yet taken possession of them.[35] Indeed, the navy gained a lot of momentum during Dayan's tenure.

The sinking of the INS Eilat prompted the Israeli navy, the neglected stepsibling to the ground forces and the air force, to rethink its force construction and direction. The decision to transition to missile boats had already been made in the early 1960s.[36] Shlomo Erell, the navy's commander from 1966 to 1969, credited Dayan for developing a strategic vision for the navy. Unlike the IDF General Staff, Dayan understood the geostrategic ramifications for the naval theater of operations created by the Six-Day War. Erell wrote: "While the General Staff ... wanted us ... to prepare for defending the long shores of northern Sinai and the Suez Gulf against infiltrations ... Dayan went much further and developed his own approach."[37]

Dayan's vision included Israel securing its own shipping lane in the Suez Canal and Bab al-Mandab Straits, rather than relying on ineffectual international treaties. Understanding that Israel would need to defend any path to shipping rights, Dayan determined that Israel must develop sufficient naval force to allow for a naval presence along every shipping route. In today's terminology, he wanted the navy to project power across great distances.[38]

Dayan ordered patrols to show a naval presence in the Mediterranean and the Red Sea. The first Saar boats were neither large nor powerful enough for this task, leading the navy to develop the larger Saar 4. While recognizing the gap between the goal and the means, Dayan exhorted the navy to "Find solutions!" spurring the navy to find interim fixes. Over the objections of IDF generals, already in 1968, Dayan ordered the IDF to procure vessels capable of controlling Israel's commercial sea-lanes. In the Yom Kippur War, the first missile-boat war in history, the much-strengthened Israeli navy handily defeated those of Egypt and Syria. As Erell concluded: "Were it not for the opportunity that presented itself to the navy thanks to Moshe Dayan's vision about the Red Sea theater – a vision [not] shared by Haim Bar-Lev, the new Chief of Staff – the navy's size

---

[35] Gelber, *Hatasha*, p. 336.
[36] Shaul Bronfeld, "The Naval Revolution: The Missile Boat Flotilla" (Hebrew), *Bein Haktavim* (December 2017), pp. 33–57 (p. 37).
[37] Shlomo Erell, *Lefanekha hayam: Sipuro shel yamai, mefaked velohem* (Hebrew), Tel Aviv: Defense Ministry Publishers, 1998, pp. 281–282.
[38] Ibid.

and progress since the 1980s and onwards would have been much more modest."[39]

During this period, the government and the General Staff debated Israel's borders. Although the current borders were considered optimal for defense, they understood that in the event of a peace agreement, territorial concessions would be necessary. Dayan believed that despite the operational advantages of the Suez Canal, it could not be a peacetime border. Additionally, potential war scenarios with Egypt were discussed, including the possibility of a limited war to dislodge the IDF from the canal zone,[40] envisioning the strategic concept adopted by Egyptian President Sadat in 1973.

From January to August 1968, several small skirmishes occurred along the Suez Canal. In September, Egyptian artillery bombarded the entire length of the canal, intending to cause heavy Israeli losses and force a retreat. In response to a question from Yitzhak Rabin, Israel's ambassador to Washington, Dayan explained that Israel needed to control the Canal but wanted to avoid escalation. If Egypt continued, the IDF would react severely to make the enemy understand "that it's not worth [their] while to play with fire."[41] In October 1968, as Egypt continued, Dayan authorized Operation Shock of November 1, designed to damage electricity lines to Cairo. However, Israel's main response was defensive, including upgrading fortifications, constructing the Bar-Lev Line – a system of fortifications along the Suez Canal – and making plans to defend Sinai against Egyptian attacks (Map 7.1).

In November 1968, Dayan concluded that Egypt had no intention of signing a peace agreement with Israel and was rebuilding its military. He believed that Egypt wanted to conquer the region between the Suez Canal and Sharm El Sheikh, prioritizing seizing the canal zone. The IDF would have to prepare for this scenario, which, with Soviet backing, could happen as early as 1969.

When the War of Attrition officially began on March 8, 1968, Dayan, thinking it could last two to three years, supported a policy of preserving forces, minimal mobilization of reservists, and minimizing Israeli losses by reducing ground-force involvement and using the IAF. Dayan disagreed with the rest of the General Staff that this was the first phase of an all-out Egyptian offensive, believing that Egypt wasn't prepared and that the eastern front was calm, adding a caveat: "There are other opinions as well, and one must remember that our logic is not theirs."[42] However, he ordered preparation for a possible Egyptian attack in March 1969 intended to push the IDF back to the mountain passes – some 40 kilometers from the canal. The plans focused

---

[39] Ibid., p. 288.
[40] Golan, *Hamilhama lehafsakat hahatasha*, pp. 35–37.
[41] From General Staff debate on September 9, 1968, in ibid., p. 52.
[42] Dayan's statements; minutes of Foreign Affairs and Security Committee meeting of May 6, 1969, State Archive, in in Gelber, *Hatasha*, p. 366.

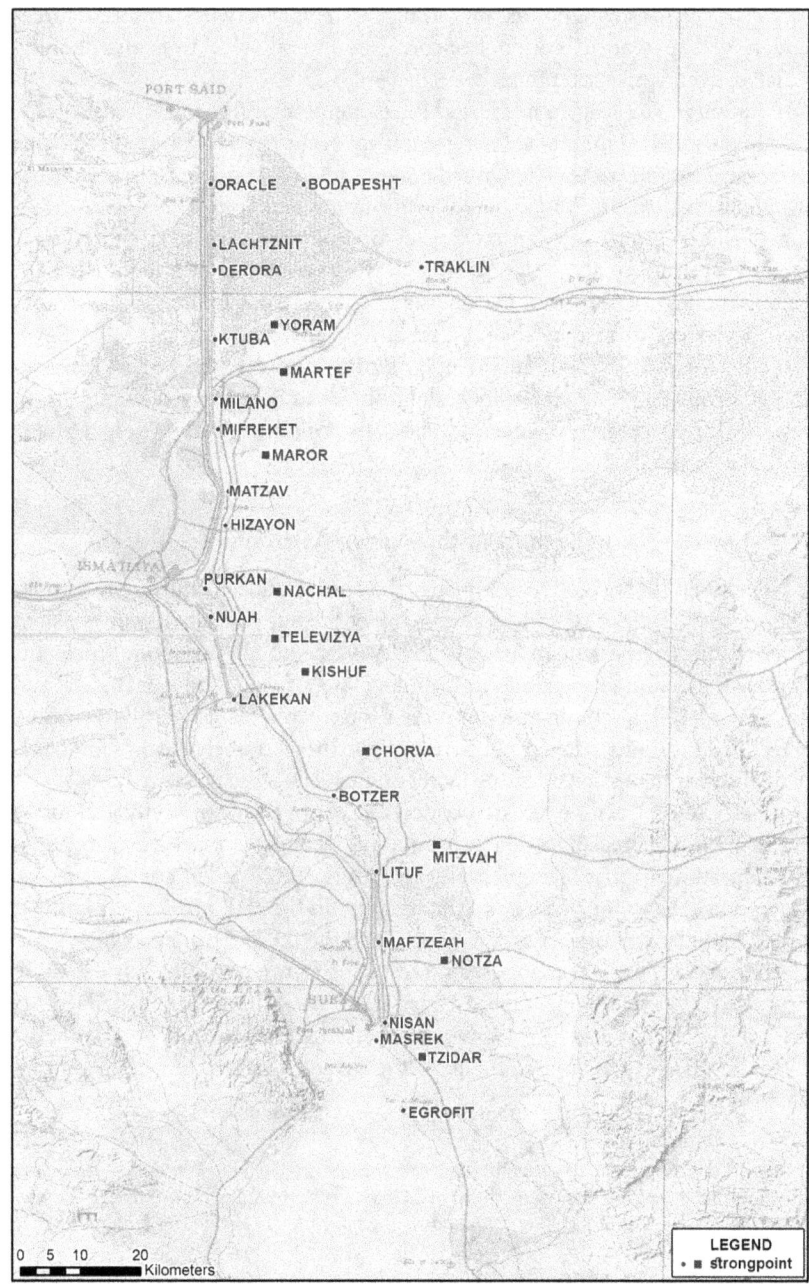

Map 7.1 The Bar-Lev Line.

on the forward strongpoints providing surveillance, with armored forces hidden in the rear to conduct surprise counterattacks, thus maintaining initiative even while defending.[43]

In January 1969, Dayan addressed the General Staff forum about the political pressures Israel might face to retreat from occupied territories in exchange for nonaggression pacts. The United States could exert pressure by withholding Phantoms, while France could continue its embargo. Dayan also mentioned the nuclear issue and US pressure on Israel to join the nuclear nonproliferation treaty. It was difficult to assess new president Richard Nixon's policy at the time. Dayan suggested that the United States would push Egypt to switch allegiance, as the Soviets could not provide what Egypt wanted – this would eventually happen during Anwar Sadat's regime. Dayan warned against a political deadlock that might lead Egypt to escalate to all-out war. While believing the chances were low, he nonetheless urged preparedness for that eventuality.[44]

The Start of the War of Attrition

In November 1968, the IDF completed the construction of thirty-two strongpoints and obstacles along the eastern bank of the Suez Canal, despite constant interruptions from Egyptian fire. In early 1969, the number of serious incidents increased, including the killing of Egyptian Chief of Staff Abdul Manam Riyad and several senior commanders by an experimental Israeli artillery rocket. Israel's fortifications proved effective against the extremely heavy bombardments fired at them, considerably increasing Israel's sense of security.[45]

In early May, Dayan expressed concerns about Israel's passivity and losses and proposed increasing raids and targeting economic assets. Dayan posed three questions to the General Staff: Politically, could Israel continue facing Arab and superpower pressure? Militarily, could the IDF prevent the conflict spreading to Israel's other borders? And could the IDF deescalate any Egyptian or Arab acts of war (Dayan focused on restoring calm not completely defeating the enemy)?[46] The IDF generals all answered "yes." Dayan acknowledged the IDF's resilience but also Egypt's increasing strength and means. To Dayan, the IDF's presence at the Suez Canal had "the dynamic nature of a collision that would only worsen."[47]

---

[43] Maoz Plan, Southern Command, December 1968, in Golan, *Hamilhama lehafsakat hahatasha*, p. 69; repetition of these principles in Meir Finkel, *Haramatkal: Mehkar hashva'ati shel shisha hebetim betifkudo shel mefaked hatsava* (Hebrew), Ben Shemen: Maarakhot and Modan, 2018, p. 74.
[44] Golan, *Hamilhama lehafsakat hahatasha*, p. 81.
[45] Ibid., p. 84.
[46] From General Staff debate on April 28, 1969, ibid., p. 96.
[47] From General Staff debate on May 5, 1969, ibid., p. 98.

In April 1969, Golda Meir and Dayan discussed the Arabs' perception of not having lost the Six-Day War and their continued rejection of Israel's right to exist. In May 1969, Dayan and the General Staff discussed the possibility that the Arabs would engage in a large-scale war. Dayan posed the dilemmas of Israel's decision-makers in a conflict before the General Staff: When would Egypt engage in a large-scale war? What should be done to stop the shooting at the canal? Should the IAF be employed to damage the Egyptian economy?[48] AMAN believed that escalation was needed to stop the fire.[49]

In June 1969, Dayan proposed attacking Egyptian power stations and authorized the IDF to use the IAF deep within Egypt to draw Egyptians into aerial fights.[50] On July 14, Dayan authorized the raid on Green Island but, concerned about harming the Soviet advisors, held off on attacking Port Said. That July, Dayan summarized this war's constraints. First, Israel's dependence on American diplomatic help and matériel demanded that they not harm relations with the United States. Second was avoiding dragging the Soviets into a direct confrontation with Israel. Lastly, the other Arab states must be kept out of the fray. For Dayan, the objective was a new Suez ceasefire,[51] as he hoped the supply of Hawk missiles and Phantom airplanes would tip the balance of power in Israel's favor.[52]

Deploying the Israel Air Force to Attack the Canal

On July 14, 1969, Dayan received government authorization for significant IAF deployment in the campaign, despite concern over the danger of the Egyptian surface-to-air missile systems. Six days later, a new stage of the fighting began[53] with Operation Boxer, which destroyed SA-2 batteries and downed six Egyptian planes. Addressing the General Staff on July 27, Dayan, said that the IDF's activity had not achieved the hoped-for ceasefire but had made conditions for the frontline forces a little easier. He felt that if Egypt wanted war, it was better sooner rather than later. He also found the passive presence at the Canal not good for the army and its men. People never get used to shelling, he said, they merely "take losses and have their strength sapped."[54] Thus, Dayan actually sought an escalation that would result in either war or

---

[48] Gilboa, *Mar modi'in*, p. 421.
[49] Ibid., p. 447.
[50] Dayan in the defense minister's bureau, June 17, 1969; Golan, *Hamilhama lehafsakat hahatasha*, p. 105.
[51] Gelber, *Hatasha*, p. 374.
[52] Ibid., p. 373.
[53] Golan, *Hamilhama lehafsakat hahatasha*, p. 112; Mustafa Kbha, *Harb al-istanzaf: Milhemet hahatasha bire'i hamekorot hamitsri'im* (Hebrew), Efal: Yad Tabenkin, The Israel Institute for the Study of Settlement, Security, and Foreign Affairs Policy, Efal and Tel Aviv University, 1995, p. 87.
[54] Weekly meeting, defense minister's bureau, the Kirya, Tel Aviv, July 27, 1969, in Golan, *Hamilhama lehafsakat hahatasha*, p. 117.

calm and requested authorization for strikes on infrastructure, even suggesting "bringing fire closer to the Russian ships in Port Said."[55]

Shooting at the Suez Canal continued, and in September, the IDF conducted several raids in Egypt, including the successful Operation Raviv, an audacious action – like those of Dayan in the past – of Israeli armored forces disguised as Egyptian troops, which advanced 25 kilometers into Egypt and destroyed many installations, causing high Egyptian casualties, with Israel downing eleven aircraft in ensuing battles immediately thereafter.[56] Following the operation, Dayan spoke about US–Israeli relations. Dayan's questioning of AMAN Director Aharon Yariv about toppling Nasser led to an argument whose central dilemma still arises today regarding possible regime change in Gaza or Syria: Is the devil you know better than his replacement whom you don't?

Despite everything, the Egyptians continued firing at the IDF forces near the Canal throughout October. Dayan's discussions with the Chief of Staff late in December about the possibility of striking several Egyptian infrastructure targets demonstrate Dayan's wide-ranging, cohesive strategic thinking. He had clear priorities for the army: First, mitigate conditions for the soldiers stationed on the Canal; then, prevent new surface-to-air missile batteries being stationed near the Canal; and third, shake up Cairo by, for example, blacking it out by interfering with the electricity supply. Dayan also warned of the limitations: no harm to the Soviets, no harm to economic targets, no harm to Cairo itself (meaning direct physical damage).

He also worried about political constraints that might be imposed on Israel due to talks with the Americans and the Egyptians.[57] Earlier, on December 9, US Secretary of State William P. Rogers had publicly proposed an agreement, later called the Rogers Plan: Israel would withdraw from Sinai, after which negotiations on a peace agreement would be conducted. Now, Dayan was worried that the United States would impose an arms embargo to force Israel to accept the plan.[58] None of this came to pass, because in mid February, the Arabs rejected the Rogers Plan,[59] as it meant acquiescing to Israel's existence.

Deep Strikes and the Anti-Soviet Campaign until the Ceasefire: January–August 1970

Strikes deep within Egyptian territory were another stage of escalation. Already in September 1969, Israel had begun to receive US Phantom airplanes, capable of carrying large payloads and with a greater range of travel than previous aircraft,

[55] Ibid., p. 118.
[56] Ibid., p. 121.
[57] Weekly meeting, defense minister's bureau, the Kirya, Tel Aviv, November 7, 1969, Golan, *Hamilhama lehafsakat hahatasha*, p. 131.
[58] General Staff discussion on July 6, 1970, in ibid., p. 456.
[59] Dayan's statements in minutes of General Staff discussion, March 11, 1970, ibid., p. 170.

giving the IAF a new competitive edge. Attacks by the IAF in December and January near the Canal and even deeper inland had only a limited effect.[60] The war had three main theaters: the Suez Canal front line, the shore of the Suez Gulf where most special operations were carried out, and deep in Egyptian territory, that is, the Cairo region, which came under bombardment starting in January.[61] In the discussions in early January about these bombing runs, Dayan was cautious, whereas Rabin, Allon, and Weizman were all pushing for them, with Rabin insisting that the Americans would not object.[62] Unlike most of the other ministers, Dayan was not certain of US support for bombing near Cairo. He considered Allon's approach to risk even more Soviet aid to Egypt, which was already massive.[63] For Dayan, the bombings near Cairo were meant solely to take the pressure off the Canal and warn the Egyptians against further escalation.[64]

In January 1970, Israel initiated Operation Priha (Blossom), involving air and commando raids on Egyptian military forces along the Canal and deep in Egypt, trying to pressure Egypt into a ceasefire. Operations mostly affected morale, and Dayan and the General Staff were still looking for Egypt's Achilles' heel to make it stop its fire. Dayan asked AMAN to prepare a staff paper on the question: "What is the straw that will break Gamal [Arabic for 'camel'] Abdul Nasser's back?" Bombings near Cairo? Bombings deeper still? Heli-borne commando raids?[65]

Dayan's talks with the General Staff show that Israel faced uncertainty about America's support and the arrival of more Phantom fighter jets and that Israel was preoccupied about a potential Soviet response. Israel expected the USSR to export advanced aerial defense systems to Egypt but did not believe that Soviet pilots would protect Egypt's skies.[66]

In February, Israel continued its policy of bombing Egypt's heartland, sometimes accidentally causing civilian casualties. On February 13, Dayan rejected a proposal to strike at civilian water installations, fearing it could be seen as a violation of Israel's commitment to the United States to strike only military targets.[67] The United States criticized Israel harshly for civilian casualties and even threatened to stop supplying Phantoms.

In mid February, AMAN reports indicated the presence of surface-to-air missiles near the Suez Canal, raising concerns that Egypt planned to deploy

---

[60] From minutes of General Staff discussion on March 2, 1970, ibid., p. 414.
[61] Ibid., p. 415.
[62] From minutes of Foreign Ministry directors' meeting on November 11, 1969, ibid., p. 420.
[63] Ibid., p. 422.
[64] Ibid., p. 429.
[65] From General Staff discussion on February 4, 1970, Golan, *Hamilhama lehafsakat hahatasha*, p. 153.
[66] Ibid., p. 154.
[67] Weekly meeting, defense minister's bureau, the Kirya, Tel Aviv, February 13. 1970, ibid., p. 156.

these weapons along the entire front line, which would severely affect Israel's military capabilities in the region. Dayan became convinced of the immediate need to attack the missile locations. AMAN also indicated that Egypt was preparing for large numbers of Soviet advisors and technicians at these sites and their integration into the Egyptian effort.[68]

A common misperception is that the Soviet intervention, beginning in March, was a response to Israel's deep-strike raids beginning in January. In fact, the decision on Soviet intervention was made in December 1969, following which forces were deployed.[69] Therefore, it was not the deep raids that caused Soviet intervention (Operation Caucasus), but rather the successes of the Israeli air force along the canal. However, initially the Soviets stressed that these forces were to defend the Egyptian rear, not the Suez Canal front line.[70] During March and April, the Soviets deployed three squadrons, integrated into Egypt's aerial defense, around Cairo, Alexandria, and the Aswan Dam area.

Back in January, Dayan, still hoping the Soviets would not intervene, repeated that Israel was being careful not to strike at civilian targets. Regarding the possibility of downing Soviet planes, Dayan remarked, "The Soviets aren't Jews: they don't get depressed when a plane falls or a pilot is killed ... Only we, the Israelis, think it's possible to prosecute a war without anyone getting hurt."[71]

Dayan felt that if the Americans supported a ceasefire policy, Israel should cooperate and support US policy. Dayan had two objectives for the front: first, to prevent and disrupt Egypt's preparations for a full-scale war, and, second, to achieve a ceasefire.[72] He worried that the United States was more concerned with appeasing the Arabs than with conceding to the USSR and would therefore keep Israel from "breaking" Egypt to score points in the Arab world.[73] However, though US support seemed reluctant, it continued, with the Americans agreeing to provide Israel with airplanes to replace those that had been damaged, but not to reinforce the IAF with additional planes.

In February and March 1970, Dayan held talks with General Staff generals to assess the situation. Responding to Sharon's claim that the Egyptian army had

---

[68] Consultation on activity in Egypt, defense minister's bureau, the Kirya, February 16, 1970, ibid., p. 158.
[69] Shmuel Gordon, *30 sha'ot be'oktober: Hahlatot goraliyot – heil ha'avir bit'hilat milhemet yom kippur* (Hebrew), Tel Aviv: Maariv Library, 2008, p. 103.
[70] Muhammad al-Ghani al-Gamasi, *Milhemet oktober 1973: Zikhronot marshal al-gamasi* (Hebrew translation from Arabic), Tel Aviv: Intelligence Corps, 1996, pp. 116–117.
[71] Security overview, Dayan at a Foreign Affairs and Security Committee meeting, January 23, 1970, pp. 3–6.
[72] Dayan's statements in minutes of General Staff discussion, March 11, 1970, in Gelber, *Hatasha*, p. 482.
[73] Ibid., p. 490.

not been sufficiently damaged, Dayan, agreeing, did note that Egypt's physical condition and morale had suffered, particularly as the fact that the IDF was sitting right along the Suez Canal undermined Egypt's claim of being the leader of the Arab world.[74] Dayan decided to continue pressure on the Canal to force Egypt into a defensive posture, while taking care not to arouse the ire of the United States, then under Soviet pressure not to provide Israel with more Phantoms, although the Soviets were continuing to send Egypt advanced SA-3 missiles on the pretext that they were defensive.[75] In March, Dayan feared that the War of Attrition might escalate to the point that the USSR would dispatch Soviet pilots against Israel if the Soviet ground-based antiair systems could not stop the IAF (Figure 7.1).[76]

The presence of Soviet soldiers manning Egyptian surface-to-air missile batteries posed a dilemma for Israel, leading to mixed messages from the United States. Dayan instructed the IDF to prepare a document on the operative ramifications of the US position.[77] Ultimately, the Americans supported Israel's activities on the Canal but opposed deep strikes. By April 1970, Soviet

Figure 7.1 Minister of Defense Moshe Dayan, Suez Canal, War of Attrition, June 1970.
Source: Central Press/Stringer/Hulton Archive/Getty Images.

---

[74] Dayan's statements in General Staff discussion on March 9, 1970, Golan, *Hamilhama lehafsakat hahatasha*, p. 162.
[75] Ibid., pp. 167–169.
[76] Meeting with newspaper editors, defense minister's bureau, the Kirya, Tel Aviv, March 20, 1970, ibid., p. 172.
[77] Weekly meeting, defense minister's bureau, the Kirya, ibid., p. 182.

pilots began flying over Egypt, creating potential for a direct clash between Israel and the USSR, as Dayan foresaw the inevitability of the IDF having to face Soviet flyers directly.[78] Already in June, Dayan said that should Israel's presence on the Canal lead to clashes with Soviet pilots, it would not change Israel's decision to maintain its presence there.[79] Dayan also thought the USSR would avoid a comprehensive confrontation, believing they were committed to preventing an Egyptian defeat and to reconstructing the Egyptian army.[80]

Mid April saw an increase in the USSR's involvement, including Soviet pilots flying MiG-21s, resulting in Dayan pressing the Americans for more resources and accelerating Israeli military manufacturing.[81]

Ending Deep Air Strikes, Continuing Canal Attacks to Stop Antiaircraft Missile Deployment

Throughout April, fire was exchanged between Egyptian and Israeli forces. On May 1, Dayan held a discussion with the General Staff about reducing IDF losses. Regarding technical strategic issues, Dayan presented six considerations and constraints to guide Israel's decisions: the impact of the Rogers Plan; not providing the Americans with a pretext to stop supplying aircraft; not providing the Soviets with a pretext to increase military involvement; reducing IDF losses; impact on other fronts; and making appropriate/necessary deep strikes as long as they did not have an effect on the other considerations.[82]

Ultimately, Dayan concluded that operating primarily against artillery fire, the major cause of Israeli losses, was necessary, but deep strikes were off the table. He noted the need to avoid clashes with the Soviets, although such could be expected to happen over the coming month. He added, "If we clash, we clash."[83] Rejecting the proposal of Sharon, then commanding the Southern Command, to occupy territory temporarily, and the suggestions of other officers pushing for a more aggressive approach, fearing this could threaten American support, Dayan repeated his assessment that the Soviet presence in Egypt meant that eventually Soviet forces would clash with the IDF.[84]

He considered three possible scenarios for Soviet intervention: more of the same; an expansion of the defensive sector up to the ceasefire line at the Suez Canal; or full integration into Egyptian military activity. As for a possible

---

[78] Gelber, *Hatasha*, p. 434.
[79] Gilboa, *Mar modi'in*, p. 339.
[80] From Dayan's statements at the Foreign Affairs and Security Committee, April 28, 1970, in: Golan, *Hamilhama lehafsakat hahatasha*, p. 186.
[81] From operational discussion, defense minister's bureau, the Kirya, April 20, 1970, in Golan, *Hamilhama lehafsakat hahatasha*, p. 184.
[82] Ibid., p. 190.
[83] Ibid., p. 191.
[84] Ibid., p. 192.

settlement, Dayan said that the important question was whether there were territories that should not be conceded even in exchange for a settlement: "If I have to return Sharm El-Sheikh, I prefer not to make peace."[85]

In April 1970, Dayan informed the US diplomat Joseph John Sisco that Egypt was crucial for peace in the Arab world, that Nasser chose the War of Attrition due to a lack of alternatives, and that the Soviets had their reasons for participating. Dayan assured Sisco that Israel did not want any escalation but wanted to understand why the Americans had not informed Israel about potential Soviet involvement.[86] Dayan aimed to influence the United States to end the war, although he realized that the Egyptians might exploit any calm to improve their operative capabilities. Still, he thought it possible that a ceasefire would put the sides on the road to a peace settlement.[87] Should a war break out, Dayan preferred a full-scale war in which Israel could act decisively, without American constraints.

By the end of May, Dayan had repeatedly suggested withdrawing 30 kilometers from the Canal's northern part, seeing no tactical advantage to remaining there. He questioned the wisdom of continuing deep air force raids. Bar-Lev countered that pulling back would enable Egypt to build military bridges for crossing the Canal. Paradoxically, Dayan worried that Egyptian failures would increase Soviet involvement.[88]

In June 1970, Dayan felt that the country's leadership was facing critical challenges: Rising deaths from Egyptian attacks created lower public trust in the government, uncertainty about future of Soviet intervention, and doubts over the continued US supply of Phantom fighter jets. He concluded: "[The IDF] must prepare a plan for withdrawing from the front line in case the Soviets turn more aggressive. In the meantime, the government will maximize the IDF's power to deal harsh blows to Egypt."[89] Dayan was increasingly concerned that, supported by Soviet forces,[90] Egypt would try to seize control of the airspace above the Suez Canal, creating a difficult operational problem for the IAF. Dayan's analysis acknowledged that Israel could try to escalate and push for a decision, but this risked US opposition and even sanctions as well as increased Soviet involvement. He advised that maintaining a low level of intensity was advisable, given that there was no choice but to keep going.[91]

---

[85] Ibid., p. 197.
[86] From meeting between Dayan and Sisco, April 15, 1970, in Gelber, *Hatasha*, p. 508.
[87] Ibid., p. 510.
[88] Dayan, minutes of Foreign Affairs and Security Committee meeting, May 26, 1970, State Archive, File No. 001460s, pp. 2–11.
[89] From operational discussion, defense minister's bureau, the Kirya, May 31, 1970, in Golan, *Hamilhama lehafsakat hahatasha*, p. 212.
[90] Gelber, *Hatasha*, p. 446.
[91] Dayan's statements in Foreign Affairs and Security Committee meeting, June 23, 1970, State Archive, File No. 001460s, pp. 3–18.

The leadership of the IAF did not fear confrontation with the Soviets; the "word on the street" was that only Dayan was worried.[92] But the young pilots and officers failed to grasp that Dayan wasn't concerned about the outcome of a particular dogfight, but about the ramifications of a direct conflict with a world superpower. Ironically, this difference of approach had existed years before between him – then young and invincible – and Ben-Gurion.

His first plan rejected, Rogers proposed another on June 19, 1970, one involving Israel–Egypt negotiations under the aegis of the Swedish UN representative Gunnar Jarring. On July 23, the Egyptians announced they would accept the new plan on condition that Israel first withdraw to the 1967 lines and admit Arab refugees. Israel refused, leading to increased political pressure from the United States, which demanded that any meeting between the Israeli premier and the US president was contingent on Israel accepting the new Rogers Plan.[93] Dayan did not trust the Americans, saying, "What [more] can you expect of them?"[94]

From February 1970, the IAF had struggled against Soviet aerial defense missile systems at the Suez Canal, escalating its efforts throughout the spring and summer. On June 30, Israel suffered its first aerial losses to Soviet surface-to-air missile units, losing two Phantom jets. It lacked the solution to defeat these technologically more advanced and better-trained units.[95] On July 18, the IAF used new American antielectronic equipment in an attack, but it turned out to be useless in disrupting the Soviet missile system.

Despite US mediation efforts, Egypt, with Soviet support, continued reinforcing its antiaircraft systems at the Canal. Israel decided to attack the missiles; Dayan advised not to do so right away, but to study the issue in depth, prepare the equipment, and wait for a better opportunity. Once again, and in contrast to his image, Dayan represented the more moderate voice. He asked the army to prepare for the eventuality that Egypt would, with Soviet help, launch a canal-crossing offensive,[96] emphasizing the need for continued discussions with the United States.

On July 27, after a month of continuing IDF attacks on the surface-to-air missile batteries, the Israelis, sighting Soviet planes covering for Egyptian aircraft up to 50 kilometers from the Suez Canal, decided on a preemptive attack. Dayan, recognizing that the IAF and Soviet pilots would inevitably clash, found it preferable to take the initiative and make it happen. The entrapment plan worked, and the Israelis shot down four Soviet MiG-21s, badly damaged the fifth, and killed some of the pilots.[97] However, the Soviet

---

[92] Gordon, *30 sha'ot be'oktober*, p. 73.
[93] Gelber, *Hatasha*, p. 466.
[94] Ibid., pp. 514, 515.
[95] Gordon, *30 sha'ot be'oktober*, p. 75.
[96] Golan, *Hamilhama lehafsakat hahatasha*, p. 231; Gilboa, *Mar modi'in*, p. 510.
[97] For more on the aerial fight, see Gordon, *30 sha'ot be'oktober*, pp. 78–79.

response was swift: Egypt shifted more missiles over to the Canal and parked more planes at its most easterly airfield.[98] The United States pressed Israel to avoid escalation; Dayan expressed deep concern about the situation.[99]

By now, Israel had no choice: Israel losses were too high, and, as Dayan had learned, there was no way to overcome the densely arrayed missile batteries.[100]

The Egyptians, too, were exhausted and accepted the Rogers Plan in principle, hoping Israel would "freeze" the situation at the Canal. On August 2, Israel also announced it was accepting the Rogers Plan. On August 8, the ceasefire agreement went into effect. Dayan authorized a last strike on August 7, only hours before the ceasefire began.

In the talks preceding the agreement, Dayan insisted on: ending the state of warfare on the basis of UN Security Council Resolution 242; Israel's withdrawal from the territories to borders to be determined by peace agreements; and Israel neither setting nor accepting any preconditions.[101] The agreement stipulated that Egypt would not change the military status quo 50 kilometers east and west of the ceasefire line. Dayan also insisted on including a paragraph in the agreement on upholding the Geneva Convention on POWs.[102]

However, within hours of the ceasefire, the Egyptians began moving their surface-to-air missile batteries closer to the Canal. Dayan aggressively demanded an attack. However, the United States demanded that Israel not act, and the government decided not to attack due to the need for a ground maneuver, fear over a large-scale confrontation with the Soviets, and generous US promises of security assistance.[103] In September, after the United States finally agreed to confirm Israel's claims that Egypt had moved the missiles in violation of the agreement, Dayan demanded an immediate aerial attack, threatening to resign if his demand was rejected.[104] Despite his belligerent declarations, he backtracked from this proposal, accepting Prime Minister Meir's position that an attack was not politically possible.

Simultaneously, while demanding an attack on the missile sites, even threatening to resign, Dayan nevertheless proposed a partial settlement along the Canal, suggesting a separation of forces (meaning an Israeli withdrawal of 30 kilometers) and mutual demilitarization of the area to enable renewal of transit.

---

[98] Gelber, *Hatasha*, p. 464.
[99] Moshe Dayan, *Avnei derekh: Autobiografia* (Hebrew), Jerusalem: Idanim, 1976, p. 518.
[100] Gordon, *30 sha'ot be'oktober*, p. 81.
[101] Gelber, *Hatasha*, p. 553.
[102] From the formula of the US proposal with Dayan's emendations, in ibid., p. 575.
[103] Adamsky, *Mivtsa Kavkaz*, p. 175.
[104] Meir Boymfeld, *Kfitsa lamayim hakarim: Hamaga'im hamedini'im bein yisrael, mitsrayim ve'artshot habrit bashanim shekadmu lemilhemet yom hakipurim 1970–1973* (Hebrew), Reut: Effi Meltser Ltd., 2017; Gad Yaacobi, *Kehut hase'ara: Eikh huhmats hesder bein yisrael lemitsrayim velo nimne'a milhemet yom hakipurim* (Hebrew), Tel Aviv: Yedioth Books, 1989, p. 32.

The War: Conclusion, Outcomes, and Implications

Israel attained its immediate objective: It stood firm and did not move from its Suez Canal positions. Its demand for direct negotiations without preconditions remained. Nasser's announcements early in the war about "what was taken by force will be restored by force" were revealed as empty bluster. Egypt's economy was badly damaged; the cities along the Suez Canal were destroyed, and shipping did not resume. Some 3,000 Egyptians died and about 10,000 were wounded. Israel suffered 259 deaths and more than 1,000 injured. The price Egypt paid was steep. On the other hand, it also made some gains: The USSR, whose involvement grew throughout, strengthened and rebuilt the Egyptian army to so significant an extent that Egypt could plan its next war against Israel. As for moving the surface-to-air missile systems to the canal line after the ceasefire, an argument can be made that even without the War of Attrition, had Egypt decided to build missile systems near the Suez, Israel was politically constrained from embarking on a unilateral military campaign to destroy them.[105]

In hindsight, Dayan explained the war's objectives and outcomes:

> The Egyptian approach was as follows: we're a nation of 40 million residents [to Israel's 3 million then] and can take losses. The power relations in war were based on the gap in our population ratio. Israel, they thought, wouldn't be able to handle the pressure, would not be able to extend reserve duty or lose many men, whereas Egypt could. ... the Egyptian assumption ... turned out to be false.[106]

Dayan explained his preference for employing airpower, a preference widely shared by today's political decision-makers because of the development of precision weapons and because of greater political sensitivities: "I'd rather dispatch a plane to bomb and blow up five buildings where the pilot will come back to the base 30 minutes or an hour later and drink a cup of tea than send out a battalion of men overnight and know that some will be killed ... and there is always the chance of something going wrong."[107] Dayan had expressed similar views when he was Chief of Staff.[108]

An argument can be made that Egypt had successes in the War of Attrition: Inter alia, the Egyptian army restored its self-confidence by engaging in proactive operations against the IDF, building its force with Soviet matériel, and proving to itself the effectiveness of its antiaircraft defense against the IAF.

---

[105] Golan, *Hamilhama lehafsakat hahatasha*, p. 273.
[106] Yaakov Erez and Ilan Kfir, *Sihot im Moshe Dayan* (Hebrew), Ramat Gan: Massada, 1981, pp. 72–73.
[107] Ibid., pp. 72–73.
[108] Lieutenant General Dayan in meeting with the press after the Qalqiliya action, October 11, 1956, IDF Archive, File 1973-127-5, and internal investigation about Operation Samaria (Qalqiliya), October 17, 1956, IDF Archive, File 1973-127-5.

On the Egyptian side, too, opinions differ as to the war's success. Some feel the War of Attrition was a mistake, causing economic devastation to Egypt. Others highlight that Egypt did not emerge as the loser and was thus not humiliated, and it enjoyed an opportunity to train and toughen the army, even if at heavy cost to Egypt's people and infrastructure.[109] In practice, both sides were exhausted, both nations paid a steep toll in human life, and Egypt also paid exorbitantly in resources.[110]

What sets the War of Attrition apart from other Israeli–Arab confrontations is the constraints both sides experienced.[111] For Egypt, its limitations were mainly military, while for Israel they were primarily political, making it impossible to reach a decision. Dayan was very clear-eyed on this difference, even if some of his generals did not understand why Israel's military advantage could not be maximized.[112]

Israel's policy of escalation was ultimately problematic, as it invited Soviet intervention. And, to a large extent, Dayan had anticipated this, even if Israeli intelligence had assessed that the chances of this occurring was low. Israel's objective had been to escalate to the point where Egypt could not bear any more loses, when it was clear to all that Egypt would turn to the USSR for help. Thus, as long as Israel insisted on staying at the Suez Canal and acted to stop Egyptian fire by escalating to Egypt's point of intolerability, the inevitable conclusion was Soviet involvement. The only way to change the situation would have been to reverse Israel's policy on remaining at the Canal, and this was something that the Israeli government – Dayan included – refused to do, certainly not under the threat of force.[113] The Soviet Union's involvement became a challenge for the United States and led to American involvement on behalf of Israel, making Israel a junior US ally against the Soviets, completely unintentionally.[114] This increasing dependence on the United States in turn resulted in Israel losing more than a little of its autonomy.[115] Thus, Egypt made three critical gains: It learned that the IAF did not have a suitable response to Egypt's antiaircraft missile system; its deployment of the antiaircraft missile system along the Canal proved sufficient protection for forces crossing to the east; and Israel grew more dependent on the United States, which would prevent it from carrying out a preemptive strike on the eve of the Yom Kippur War.

---

[109] Mustafa Kabha, *Milhemet ha'hatashah b'rei ha'mekorot ha'mitzriyim* (Hebrew), Efal: Yad Tabenkin, University of Tel Aviv Press, 1995, pp. 135–136.

[110] Golan, *Hamilhama lehafsakat hahatasha*, p. 265; Yaacov Bar-Siman-Tov, *The Israeli-Egyptian War of Attrition, 1969–1970*, New York: Columbia University Press, 1st ed., 1980, p. 189.

[111] Dan Shiftan, *Hatasha: Ha'estrategiya hamedinit shel mitsrayim hanatserit be'ikvot milhemet 1967* (Hebrew), Tel Aviv: Maarakhot, 1989, p. 395.

[112] Ezer Weizman, *Lekha shamayim, lekha arets* (Hebrew), Tel Aviv: Maariv Library, 1975, pp. 310, 313; Gelber, *Hatasha*, pp. 415, 593.

[113] Shiftan, *Hatasha*, p. 403.

[114] Ibid., p. 407.

[115] Bar-Siman-Tov, 1980, p. 191.

Dayan's Leadership in the War of Attrition

In the War of Attrition, Dayan was the link between the political and military echelons. Highly familiar with the Sinai Peninsula and the Egyptian enemy, he often expressed his opinion on tactical matters but was careful not to impose his view on the Chief of Staff and the army. Drawing a clear line between the political and the military, Dayan kept the political echelon up-to-date at weekly government meetings. Dayan's considerations at these meetings were matter of fact regarding the authority he assumed and decisions he passed on. Sometimes, when he disagreed with the Chief of Staff, he would present both opinions to the prime minister or the ministerial committee and let them decide.[116]

As defense minister, Dayan continued touring the country and leading numerous General Staff discussions, in which he often debated questions straddling military action and political outcomes. Dictating an open, free debate, he would first update the General Staff on political developments before hearing military updates. Then, he would present the day's core dilemmas, always clearly and pointedly articulated as a series of questions related in particular to the emerging political situation with direct implications for the manner of military action. Sometimes these were political constraints on the army's manner of operation, such as the selection of means and targets, and sometimes these were the possible political ramifications of certain military actions. Dayan made a point of listening closely to the generals before summarizing the military actions he thought should be taken and their political impact, sometimes followed by a request that the army prepare a suitable plan in response to a political scenario. Thus, Dayan functioned as a bridge, to use Colin Gray's metaphor for strategy,[117] connecting political insights and considerations with the possible military modus operandi in the face of the constraints he never failed to mention. Likely aware that he, more than anyone else, was capable of carefully calibrating the effects of a specified use of force within the context of broader political visions, Dayan generally made sure to get involved in issues for which he felt that military action would have political or policy significance.[118]

Throughout this period, Moshe Dayan's creative mind continued to churn away. Weizman described two of Dayan's initiatives he considered prescient. At the beginning of 1968, Dayan sent Chief Engineering Officer Elhanan Klein to purchase equipment for crossing the Suez Canal. According to Weizman, Dayan's other idea – of building a military airfield at Sharm El Sheikh for

---

[116] Ibid., p. 263.
[117] Colin S. Gray, *The Strategy Bridge: Theory for Practice*, New York: Oxford University Press, 2010.
[118] Gelber, *Hatasha*, pp. 460–461.

extending the IAF's reach inside Egypt, made Moti Hod and Weizman feel embarrassed for not having thought of it themselves.[119]

The War of Attrition was the first conflict to reveal cracks in the national consensus. The fact that it was forced on the nation, was long-lasting and distant, and resulted in heavy losses aroused discontent and criticism. These feelings were manifested in various ways and at different levels, from prominent intellectual and cultural figures to even high-school students voicing disillusionment. For example, a letter sent to the prime minister in April 1970 from a graduating high-school class even went so far as to call for a refusal to serve in the army (though all of the signatories enlisted when their time came and some became officers). Dayan understood the nation's resentment at a relatively early stage, exhorting a kibbutz youth about to be drafted to: "Be neither spoiled nor tired. Do not grow fatigued, nor fold up the flag."[120]

Dayan pointed out that this was the cost of war; it was necessary to be resolute and remember that the objectives of the War of Attrition were highly important. He expressed confidence in the ability of Israelis to adapt to the situation and withstand the challenges.[121]

It isn't difficult to find contradictions in Dayan's statements and decisions, for there were many. While he spoke early on about the need to prepare mentally for a clash with the Soviets and authorized an attack on Soviet planes and other targets that would cause losses to the Soviets, at the same time, he was careful not to cross any Rubicons and constantly warned of direct conflict with the USSR, telling his confidant Gad Yaacobi that, "To the extent possible, we have to avoid a confrontation with the Red Army."[122] Arguably, this reflected a profound inner tension between his insistence on pursuing Israel's objectives and his desire to avoid a clash with a superpower, aware as he was of the costs involved.

Another difficulty Dayan faced was the Americans' hesitant backing. Throughout the conflict, Dayan repeatedly expressed his distrust of American support at the moment of truth, given US inconsistency. He was always aware of the fundamental asymmetry to the Middle East: While Egypt and Syria enjoyed unconditional Soviet loyalty, the United States and other Western nations had interests on both the Israeli and Arab sides. Thus, while the Arab nations enjoyed access to and influence on Western nations, Israel had no access whatsoever to the Soviet Union.

---

[119] Weizman, *Lekha shamayim, lekha arets*, p. 305.
[120] Dayan speaking at a youth convention of the kibbutz movement Hever Hakvutsot Vehakibbutzim at el-Hama, in Gelber, *Hatasha*, p. 593.
[121] Ibid., p. 598.
[122] Gad Yaacobi, *Kehut hase'ara: Eikh huhmats hesder bein yisrael lemitsrayim velo nimne'a milhemet yom hakippurim* (Hebrew), Tel Aviv: Yedioth Books, 1989, p. 40.

Dayan's Proposal for an Israeli Withdrawal from the Suez Canal

Scholars continue to debate whether the Israeli government let the opportunity for peace slip by before the Yom Kippur War.[124] Furthermore, today Dayan is seen in the Israeli collective consciousness as the representative of the rigid, blind, arrogant stance of the Israeli government, which refused to show flexibility toward Egypt. Some public statements of Dayan, such as "Better Sharm [El Sheikh] without peace than peace without Sharm [El Sheikh],"[125] were indelibly inscribed in the public mind as supporting his hawkish image. But historical study shows the gap between this image and reality.

When analyzing the Israeli government's positions, we must try to ignore that which we know only in hindsight: the terrible cost of the 1973 war and the stable peace agreement achieved after it. We must also remember that an important factor for the state's leaders was their profound distrust of Egypt and its intentions to abide by agreements, a distrust based on past experience: Egypt's violation of the separation of forces agreement at the end of the War of Attrition in August and September of 1970, when Egypt moved its antiaircraft missiles up to the Suez Canal despite having committed itself to not doing so. While Sadat had replaced Nasser, Sadat was seen as a Nasser's heir with respect to hostility toward Israel. Moreover, the government was constrained by a security establishment that insisted that the lines Israel was occupying were the best defense for the nation and preferable to any number of international guarantees, shown by history to be useless. In addition, the fundamental outlines of the policy of Golda Meir's policy were based on a decision of

---

[123] Jonathan Shimshoni, *Israel and Conventional Deterrence: Border Warfare from 1953 to 1970*, Ithaca, NY: Cornell University Press, 1988, p. 220.

[124] Among the scholars who argue that Israel missed the opportunity for peace: Eli Podeh, *Chances for Peace: Missed Opportunities in the Israeli Palestinian Conflict*, Austin: University of Texas Press, 2015; Boaz Vanetik and Zaki Shalom, *Milhemet yom hakippurim: Hamilhama she'efshar haya limno'a* (Hebrew), Tel Aviv: Resling Publishing, 2012; Uri Bar-Yosef, *Hatsofeh shenirdam: Hafta'at yom hakippurim umekoroteha* (Hebrew), Shoham: Zmora Bitan, 2001; Yigal Kipnis, *1973: Haderekh lemilhama* (Hebrew), Or Yehuda: Dvir, 2012. More recent studies disagree: see Meir Boymfeld, *Kfitsa lamayim hakarim: Hamaga'im hamedini'im bein yisrael, mitsrayim ve'artshot habrit bashanim shekadmu lemilhemet yom hakippurim 1970–1973* (Hebrew), Reut: Effi Meltser Ltd., 2017; and Yoav Gelber's study, published in the course of the writing of this book, Yoav Gelber, *Rahav: Darka shel yisraell el milhemet yom hakippurim* (Hebrew), Hevel Modiin: Dvir, 2021.

[125] *Maariv*, March 10, 1971.

Eshkol's government that until peace agreements were signed, Israel would continue to occupy the territories it held as of June 10.[126]

The talks between the states between 1970 and 1973 were conducted through mediators, unlike the direct negotiations in 1979 that led to a peace agreement. A key player then was the United States, represented by William Rogers from the State Department and National Security Advisor Henry Kissinger. Other major mediators were the USSR and the UN, via Gunnar Jarring.

At the start of the talks with Egypt, still during the War of Attrition, two possible outlines of agreements were presented, Israel's and Egypt's. Egypt sought a comprehensive settlement in exchange for an a priori Israeli commitment to retreat from all occupied land and to restore Palestinian rights (essentially a barbed requirement calling for Israel's dissolution). Israel proposed first a partial interim agreement for the Canal without further commitments and, should this succeed, continued talks to discuss Israeli territorial concessions in return for full peace. In the first half of 1972, US policymakers accepted Israel's plan – presented at the end of 1971 – a gradual agreement that would begin with an interim agreement linked to future agreements, not a stand-alone settlement.[127] In February 1973, Egypt offered its Ismail initiative, which differed little from its opening position. Sadat continued preparing for war, initially setting mid-May as the date for its initiation.

Dayan was the conciliator of the government, working ceaselessly to find some sort of formula that would satisfy Israel's security requirements while also making significant enough concessions to Egypt to generate sufficient mutual trust and interests to preserve a state of nonaggression and even start down the road to full peace. Henry Kissinger wrote that the suggestion of an interim withdrawal from the Suez Canal as an alternative to a comprehensive settlement was the product of "Dayan's fertile mind" in the summer of 1970.[128] By contrast, Yaacobi claimed that Colonel Yaakov Nevo, the Hatzor base commander, had first mentioned the notion of Israel initiating the opening of the Suez Canal to shipping in the context of a ceasefire already in June 1970 and that Yaacobi brought the idea to Dayan's attention. At first, Dayan opposed it, but he changed his mind, thinking there was a chance for a partial settlement due to changed circumstances.[129] At the end of 1970, Dayan felt the time was right because of the immense economic cost Egypt

---

[126] Cabinet meeting, June 18, 1967, Paragraph 558, State Archive 8164/7-a.
[127] Haggai Tsoref, "Golda Meir's Government before the Yom Kippur War: Response to Yigal Kipnis" (Hebrew), *Iyunim bit'kumat yisrael*, The Ben-Gurion Institute for the Study of Israel and Zionism, Ben-Gurion University of the Negev, Sdeh Boker Campus, Vol. 28 (2017), pp. 7–43 (p. 38).
[128] Henry Kissinger, *White House Years*, Tel Aviv: Yediot Achronot, 1980, vol. 3, p. 1316.
[129] Yaacobi, *Kehut hase'ara*, p. 22; Gad Yaacobi, *Hesed haz'man: Pirkey otobi'ografiya* (Hebrew), Tel Aviv: Miskal, Yedioth Achronoth, and Hemed Books, 2002, p. 88.

had suffered during the war. The opening and reconstruction of the Canal and adjacent industries and settlements were, he thought, prime Egyptian interests that could possibly generate positive dynamics for promoting peace.[130]

Dayan was dissatisfied that the August 1970 US-initiated ceasefire agreement ending the fighting at the Canal (and in practice ending the War of Attrition) was limited to three months. The duration of the agreement was in fact a critical issue throughout the talks. Therefore, on August 4, 1970, he suggested a three-stage separation of forces plan: withdrawing heavy weapons from both sides of the Canal to a distance of 30 kilometers; later, withdrawing forces with light weapons; and, finally, embarking on permanent settlement talks. Dayan was convinced that opening the Suez Canal to shipping would serve as the best guarantor that both sides, especially Egypt, would maintain the peace.[131]

Earlier, in June, Dayan told Yaacobi that he had reservations about the government's official policy over three fundamental issues: He thought direct talks were not necessary; he felt that peace would come only after a gradual series of negotiations; and he was interested in increased US involvement on the Middle East to counterbalance Soviet meddling. Israel began promoting Dayan's proposals in September.[132] Prime Minister Golda Meir was not enthusiastic about Dayan's suggestions, but she did not reject their utility in the future, and she therefore authorized him to speak of his idea during his scheduled visit to the United States in December 1970; at this stage, she preferred a comprehensive agreement to be achieved by Jarring, and she adopted the gradual settlement approach only the following year. But before Meir's visit, Israel's US ambassador Yitzhak Rabin made it clear that Dayan's position was not the government's. Indeed, during Meir's September visit, the idea was not discussed, perhaps because Dayan himself had not yet fully articulated it, having planned on raising it during his visit to the United States.[133] However, in an October 3 interview, Dayan did discuss the separation of forces settlement.[134]

Dayan continued to champion a line different from that of the government. On November 7, 1970, he gave his "Cold Water Speech" in response to the government's agreement to accept UN Resolution 242 as the basis for talks (according to the Israeli interpretation, Resolution 242's emphasis was on

---

[130] Arie Braun, *Moshe Dayan bemilhemet yom hakippurim* (Hebrew), Tel Aviv: Idanim Publishing, 1993, pp. 11–13.

[131] Boymfeld, *Kfitsa lamayim hakarim*, p. 24.

[132] Ibid., p. 46.

[133] Foreign Ministry documents on Golda Meir's main topics of conversation with the president and secretary of state during her visit to Washington, State Archive, in Boymfeld, *Kfitsa lamayim hakarim*, p. 48.

[134] Yehoshua Raviv, "Early Attempts at Interim Arrangement between Israel and Egypt (1971–1972)" (Hebrew), *Maarakhot* 243–244 (April–May 1975), pp. 2–17 (p. 6).

retreating from "territories" rather than "*the* territories," meaning withdrawing only from some of the land occupied in 1967). Dayan compared Israel's condition to that of someone who has to jump into very cold water and swim among ice floes (e.g., Soviet intervention) to reach a safe haven, referring to entering into talks or any arrangement through Jarring.

In his speech, Dayan distinguished between critical objectives and bargaining chips to be used in negotiations, repeatedly emphasizing the urgency of ending the state of warfare and reaching a settlement. His speech meeting with criticism from his party, including Meir.[135] Dayan explained that he was referring to past government actions, such as the decision to accept the Rogers initiative. However, analysts insisted he was speaking of the future. In his memoirs, Dayan admitted that "Even this mistaken analysis contained more than a grain of truth."[136] Dayan continued expressing his opinion at cabinet meetings, and the sense of urgency he projected in these talks starkly contrasted with the approach of the more hardline prime minister and most government members. Meir, having been advised that the new situation on the Suez Canal and the continuing supply of Soviet arms to Egypt had worsened the balance of power, was determined to receive political benefits and military assistance before agreeing to return to the negotiating table.[137] Therefore, Israel agreed to an increased supply of aircraft and other equipment that the United States was in no hurry to provide.

In a television interview in November 1970, Dayan was asked if he had changed his position. The interviewer noted that while Dayan now favored negotiations, he had called on September 6 for suspending talks with Egypt over ceasefire violations. Dayan answered that he now preferred renewing the talks even if the missiles were not withdrawn and that he was not interested in renewing the war.[138] Israel's Foreign Ministry presented Dayan's plan as its own,[139] as if the government had adopted it. But in November 1970, Meir made it clear that "[the proposal] had not been brought before the government and the government has not discussed it."[140] While Dayan viewed his plan as a foundation for a political path for breaking the deadlock, the government opposed it, Meir seeing it as a technical move only regarding military aspects of preparing forces and equipment at the Canal.[141]

In a mid December visit to the United States to meet with President Nixon and senior officials, Dayan told Nixon he lacked the authority to discuss the

---

[135] Boymfeld, *Kfitsa lamayim hakarim*, p. 67.
[136] Dayan, *Avnei derekh*, p. 524.
[137] Cabinet meeting, November 8, 1970, State Archive, in Boymfeld, *Kfitsa lamayim hakarim*, pp. 68, 69.
[138] Ibid., p. 84.
[139] Foreign Ministry/public diplomacy document, November 28, 1970; defense minister requires a new document, State Archive, in ibid., p. 83.
[140] Minutes of Labor Party meeting, November 26, 1970, in ibid., p. 84.
[141] Ibid., p. 85.

political situation with him but felt that if the United States provided for Israel's security needs – especially additional Phantom fighter jets – talks could be renewed.[142] The president reiterated the US commitment to Israel's security, even if it could not always immediately respond to all requests. Dayan somewhat retreated from his partial settlement idea, partly because neither the government nor Meir supported him, and partly because he realized Egypt would not accept his condition for ending the conflict, as Dayan was unwilling to retreat as a precondition to extending the ceasefire.[143]

At this point, Dayan and Meir had different priorities: Dayan, reaching a settlement and replacing the fragile ceasefire to prevent more fighting; and Meir, talking with the United States about ensuring military aid.[144] There seemed to be a role reversal, with Dayan holding a comprehensive political vision, generally a prime minister's task, and Meir viewing the situation through the security prism usually reserved for a defense minister. By the end of December 1970, Dayan's partial-arrangement idea faded out after it became clear that its supporters, Israeli and American, were in the minority.

Why did Dayan, so popular and enjoying a prestigious reputation, fail to realize his initiative? Perhaps it was precisely because he was so admired that the other ministers viewed him as a political threat. They were reluctant to support him, fearing a political plan bearing his name would have brought him more glory and strengthened his chances of succeeding Meir. Politically unable to fight for his independent views, Dayan faithfully followed Meir's instructions, never taking a stand that might appear insubordinate. Thus, when visiting Washington, he stressed that he was there only to discuss security. Indeed, Dayan won Meir's trust and maintained good and well-coordinated working relations.

January 1971 brought another reversal. While all sides were busy preparing for planned talks on a comprehensive settlement, Egypt, using backdoor channels, asked the United States to transmit a proposal largely based on Dayan's plan to Israel – a partial withdrawal and arrangements for the Suez Canal. Israel would withdraw some 40 kilometers, in exchange for which Egypt would reduce its forces in a zone 40 kilometers deep. Afterward, the sides would enter into talks to maintain a six-month to one-year ceasefire.[145]

Sadat, too, realized that something had to be done before the ceasefire's expiration on February 5. In December 1970 and January 1971, he sounded out

---

[142] Minutes of Nixon–Dayan conversation, December 11, 1970, in ibid., pp. 88–89.
[143] Ibid., pp. 91–93.
[144] Telegram from Dinitz [Israel's ambassador to the UN] to Rabin [IDF defense attaché in Washington DC], December 14, 1970. In the telegram, Dinitz noted that Meir was examining the summary of Dayan's visit to the United States. State Archive, in ibid., p. 93.
[145] Foreign Ministry document, January 15, 1971, from Rabin's report on his conversation with Sisco. State Archive; Yitzhak Rabin, *Pinkas sherut* (Hebrew) (published in English as *The Rabin Memoirs*), Tel Aviv: 1979, vol. 2, p. 327.

the Americans about a possible Suez Canal agreement, even giving a speech about his initiative in February. But because of Sadat's inconsistent messages, Israel could not ascertain his seriousness. While Egypt claimed Sadat's initiative was based on Dayan's earlier plan, it differed in some essential respects. Essentially, Dayan's proposal was a partial, stand-alone settlement that was not to be part of a broader agreement. In addition, Dayan demanded far greater security arrangements – a nonaggression agreement rather than just a ceasefire agreement.[146] Sadat, however, presented the partial agreement as an interim stage to be followed (actually, preceded!) by a commitment to peace in exchange for Israeli retreat from all territories occupied in the Six-Day War and acceptance of Palestinian rights. Unlike Dayan's proposal, the Egyptian one was asymmetrical, clearly to Israel's disadvantage.

Despite the gaps between the proposals, there was a reasonable point for starting negotiations. But Dayan again could not advance more than a reluctant, cautious Israeli government response to Egypt's initiative. While interested in a peace agreement, Golda Meir was not prepared to return to the pre-Six-Day War border, which was problematic from a security perspective. Dayan's position was similar: He demanded fundamental changes to Israel's earlier borders and insisted that the Egyptians express support for full peace and direct negotiations. Dayan was willing to withdraw from the Suez Canal and retreat 30 kilometers to the Sinai passes but was firm on ending the state of aggression and would not settle for a temporary ceasefire. He also demanded unlinking the agreement from UN Resolution 242.[147] Dayan felt that Egypt's proposal did not reflect a sincere willingness for peace, and he opposed Egypt's preconditions. On this, he and Meir agreed.

Meir, highly suspicious of Egyptian intentions after their blatant violation of the ceasefire agreement, raised her concern that the agreement would require Israel to repeatedly retreat without Israel's conditions ever being met. Government ministers Galili and Allon and some IDF generals objected to it also. Dayan would eventually tell Sadat that, "Unfortunately, I didn't even manage to convince our army commanders that a Suez Canal open to shipping would be a better defense than a network of fortifications."[148]

At the end of May, the differences between Meir and Dayan sharpened. In talks with Rogers, Meir refused to commit to the precise distance from the canal that Israel was willing to retreat, leaving Dayan doubting whether she had left enough latitude to continue the negotiations.[149]

---

[146] Boymfeld analyzes the differences between Dayan's ideas and Egypt's proposals, in Boymfeld, *Kfitsa lamayim hakarim*, pp. 164–165.

[147] Alignment ministers meeting, February 20, 1971, State Archive; cabinet meeting, February 21, 1971, in Boymfeld, *Kfitsa lamayim hakarim*, p. 226.

[148] Moshe Dayan, *Hala-netsah tokhal herev: Sihot hashalom – reshamim ishi'im* (Hebrew), Tel Aviv: Idanim, 1981, p. 88.

[149] Yosef Harif, "M. Dayan: End of the rope" (Hebrew), *Maariv*, September 14, 1973, in Boymfeld, *Kfitsa lamayim hakarim*, p. 397.

In a June 18, 1971, interview with *Maariv*, Dayan sounded very pessimistic about the likelihood of an interim agreement because of the gulf between the sides, concerned that absent any movement on the political side, war was inevitable.[150] He described the disagreements as involving the nature of the ceasefire, whether permanent (Israel) or temporary (Egypt); whether Egyptian and Soviet forces would be able to cross the canal; and how to link an interim and a permanent comprehensive agreement.

On June 22, Sadat gave a speech declaring 1971 as the "year of decision" for Egypt, the year in which a war would be fought if no political arrangement was reached. The United States tried to jumpstart the talks but failed. On July 23, Sadat reiterated Egypt's demands for a settlement, including significant scope for Egyptian troops to cross the canal and a ceasefire limited to six months only. Later, he again spoke of the "year of decision" to pressure the United States to pressure Israel.[151]

At a government consultation in late August 1971, Dayan proposed trying to reduce the gaps with Sadat and giving him an "excuse he could seize upon."[152] Dayan felt that Sadat was looking for an excuse not to renew the fighting and feverishly sought ideas that would provide Sadat with assets he would be interested in obtaining – for example, broadening the Suez Canal and laying pipelines for infrastructure and energy going from the Gulf of Suez to Alexandria. According to Dayan, the key lay in giving Sadat a reason not to start shooting.[153]

Rabin recalled that, at the end of September 1971, Sisco revealed that he had spoken with Sadat about Israel's willingness to withdraw on the basis of Dayan's proposal. Given Dayan's sterling reputation at the time, the Americans had assumed that Dayan's proposal would eventually be adopted.[154]

On August 19, Dayan gave a talk to the IDF Command and Staff College, "Israel Will Act with Force." In it, he emphasized that the Arabs did not want to make peace with Israel and that peace could not be imposed on them. Furthermore:

> We cannot leave "open options" for the day of peace lest that day recede. Now that Arab states are announcing their willingness to make peace with Israel, they view this as a tactic meant to unseat Israel from the territories it occupied. Sadat's peace offer is not a sign of acceptance, but rather a tool for getting rid of us.[155]

[150] "Defense minister in *Maariv* interview: War might be renewed" (Hebrew), *Maariv*, June 18, 1971.
[151] Sadat speech, July 23, 1971, in Boymfeld, *Kfitsa lamayim hakarim*, p. 490.
[152] Prime minister's bureau document, August 5, 1971, in Boymfeld, *Kfitsa lamayim hakarim*, p. 490.
[153] Ibid.
[154] Rabin, *Pinkas sherut*, vol. 2, p. 352.
[155] Dayan's statements at the Command and Staff College report in *Davar*, August 19, 1971.

In an August 21 interview with the army radio station, Dayan said that the permanent border Israel must strive for need not include an IDF presence at the Suez Canal and that Egypt should accept Israel's presence in Sharm El Sheikh as the permanent border. He noted that Israel must push the "cart" of the political settlement forward as the only alternative to a renewal of fighting but distinguished between pushing for a settlement and conceding: "A political effort – yes. Concession, retreat, flight – no. If we had to choose between deadlock and conceding, deadlock is preferable." With Dayan's pessimism about reaching any sort of settlement clearly growing, he began preparing the public for the possibility of war.[156]

In a September *Haaretz* interview, Dayan again spoke of the need for Israel to enter into negotiations to end the state of war and find a compromise. He repeated that Israel should not return to the 1967 lines but also said the sides must be open to every suggestion. He added that the chances for an agreement then were low, "but I do not think they ought to be brought to an end. If [the talks] are handled properly, something will come of them."[157]

Arguably, Dayan was inconsistent in this period: Although the idea of a partial arrangement at the Suez Canal was his, between August and September 1970, he led the opposition to the Americans' March proposal because it lacked guarantees against Egypt renewing the fighting after the extended ceasefire expired. He therefore saw no reason to withdraw Israel's defense systems from along the Canal. God was in the details.

Despite his public statements reflecting great confidence in Israel's military superiority, Dayan worried about the renewal of the War of Attrition and its effects on Israelis. He was willing to pay a higher price than all the other cabinet ministers, believing that opening the Canal to shipping was a more effective barrier to Egyptian belligerence than the Bar-Lev Line. But in return, he demanded the end of the state of war, to which Sadat would not agree. Dayan's awareness of Sadat's political needs and limited room for maneuver was exceptional among cabinet members. Dayan felt that Israel could and should be flexible and meet Sadat part of the way, which he thought doable without compromising on anything essential. For example, he supported the idea of Israel assisting Egypt with expanding the Canal and constructing fuel tanks and pipelines.

But Dayan found it difficult to advocate his own positions alone against the prime minister and senior cabinet members. He was the target of intense criticism for the positions he had shared with Sisco in May 1971. Both the State Department and Cairo cynically exploited Dayan's position, claiming it reflected an Israeli willingness to withdraw a considerable distance, while hiding Dayan's insistence that Egypt agree to ending the state of war and

---

[156] Boymfeld, *Kfitsa lamayim hakarim*, p. 534.
[157] *Haaretz*, September 19, 1971.

that the United States make a long-term commitment to provide Israel with arms.

This reaction so discouraged Dayan that during Sisco's second visit to Israel in August 1971, Dayan passively said hardly a word, only retracting his support for the April 1971 document, mostly because the United States, exerting pressure on Israel, had stopped sending Phantoms. Dayan continued an indirect dialogue with Egypt through the Israeli media, downplaying his enthusiasm for the US promise, although Meir viewed it as a great achievement.

Dayan, then, remained true to his principles during this period and continued to be an independent thinker whose original ideas drew criticism from his colleagues in the government. Dayan's strong position as defense minister, especially with the prime minister, and his popularity with the public drove his opponents to try to undermine his authority on security issues, in part by enlisting Bar-Lev and General Staff generals to their position that an IDF withdrawal to the passes would pose a severe security risk if hostilities were renewed.[158]

In a speech on August 17, 1972, Dayan said:

> The might of the IDF is a precondition for peace but not a substitute for it. We must strive to renew talks, even if indirect ... first and foremost Egypt, which holds the key to war and peace, in order to reach peace treaties ... For two years, they have been facing us on the western [Egyptian] side of the Suez Canal with more than half a million soldiers. While they aren't unsheathing their swords, they are also not holding out their hand in peace.[159]

Dayan hinted to journalists that the partial settlement was part of a comprehensive peace treaty. His statements were understood by the Israeli media and the State Department as implying that Israel was willing to make far-reaching concessions whenever negotiations began,[160] thus again tossing Sadat a political lifeline to stave off an escalation that might have led to renewed Egyptian shooting.[161]

In an August 1972 conversation with Zuerlein, a US embassy representative, Dayan explained that while he felt the Suez Canal was a good line strategically, he was concerned it was provocative for Egypt and that the situation could not last indefinitely. Still, he added, neither Israel nor Egypt was ready to start talking about a final border. Israel would not withdraw to the 1967 lines, while

---

[158] Boymfeld, *Kfitsa lamayim hakarim*, p. 591.
[159] "Moshe Dayan: We're prepared for peace in stages too" (Hebrew), *Maariv*, August 18, 1972.
[160] Haggai Asher, "Gold–Nixon talks create opportunity for talks and arrangement with Egypt" (Hebrew), *Davar*, December 29, 1971, www.nli.org.il/he/newspapers/dav/1971/12/29/01/article/6.
[161] Editorial in *Haaretz*, August 20, 1972, in Boymfeld, *Kfitsa lamayim hakarim*, p. 808.

Sadat would not cede even a square inch of his soil. Moreover, said Dayan, even a complete Israeli withdrawal would not suffice to lead to a final agreement: Sadat had already vowed to negotiate about Jerusalem and the rights of the Palestinians and would not be able to sign a treaty with Israel merely because it satisfied Egypt's demands. Any attempt to reach a comprehensive Israel–Egypt agreement at this point was doomed to failure.[162]

Dayan suggested that a partial agreement could possibly include paragraphs that would present another deadlock, knowing that would be problematic for Sadat.[163] The State Department saw Dayan's statement as an opportunity to promote interim agreements, although it doubted that the Israelis would adopt this approach. The State Department responded to Zuerlein's report:

> Were Dayan's statements to reflect Israel's official position, they'd have been able to barrel through the logjam over the Suez Canal agreement. But what he said reflects his personal view and we doubt if he'll go as far so to try to persuade his fellow cabinet members to accept it ... His statements reflect his desire to exploit regional developments and provide Sadat with a political alternative to the military one he is liable to choose.[164]

Ultimately, Dayan's initiative failed, and the idea of a partial settlement never got off the ground.

Conclusion

Between the War of Attrition and the Yom Kippur war, many attempts were made to mediate between Israel and Egypt, but they were all basically manifestations of one of two fundamental ideas: one, a comprehensive agreement to include Israel's full withdrawal from all territories occupied in the Six-Day War and realizing the Palestinians' rights (including the right of return into Israeli territory) in exchange for peace and recognition; and two, a possible interim agreement at the Suez Canal, including a significant Israeli withdrawal and the reopening of the Canal to shipping. Sadat adamantly opposed the interim agreement becoming permanent. Israel, which had several times been burned by agreements with Egypt, felt that any agreement was viable only if it was unlinked to other agreements.

Dayan was the only cabinet member who felt that Israel's presence at the Suez Canal did not serve the nation's interests, even displaying empathy for the important role the Canal played for Egypt. He therefore concluded that an interim agreement was good for both nations and would serve as a guarantee against war. Dayan insisted on several components in the agreement: limiting the forces that Egypt could deploy east of the Canal as well as preventing an

---

[162] Zuerlein's report to the State Department, August 21, 971, in ibid., p. 809.
[163] Ibid., p. 811.
[164] Draft of telegram from State Department to Zuerlein, August 8, 1972, in ibid., p. 812.

increased Soviet military presence; and he wanted an end to the state of warfare rather than a limited ceasefire. But as the talks progressed, Dayan also took a more flexible approach, showing willingness to accept some of Egypt's conditions, and he started saying that an interim agreement could be a stage toward an overall peace treaty. Still, the gap between the Israeli government, unwilling to return all of Sinai, and Egypt, demanding a commitment to a full withdrawal as a precondition to negotiation, stood in the way of achieving a comprehensive agreement.

Therefore, the only practical solution from Israel's perspective was an interim arrangement, and therefore a failure in it would have very severe repercussions. Dayan had a smart policy but did not fight hard enough for his ideas within the government or with the Israeli public. Preferring to avoid clashing with Meir, he held his tongue and stopped promoting any more independent initiatives and was even accused of being too compromising. In December 1971, after the Soviet ouster from Egypt, Dayan was even more willing to moderate his positions.

Possibly Dayan's relative weakness was partly due to his position in the government and its internal struggles. Galili and Allon opposed Dayan proposals for a number of reasons: the arrangement itself; the fact that Dayan belonged to a competing political camp; the historic rivalry between Dayan and Allon; and the struggle between them over leadership after Meir.[165]

However, despite the criticism, Dayan still exerted great influence over Meir: She changed her position and, to some extent, moved closer to Dayan's. She valued his political thinking and trusted him, as demonstrated by the fact that, on her two critical trips to Washington, she settled on the positions she would present to the Americans in one-on-one meetings with Dayan. Nonetheless, it is possible there were already fundamental differences of opinion between the two on several issues other than the distance of the withdrawal from the Canal.

Later on, Dayan would have much to regret. He wrote, "If only Golda's government had, in 1971, accepted my proposal to station out forces far from the Suez Canal at the Gidi and Mitleh passes, we may have reached an agreement with Egypt and the Yom Kippur War may have been averted."[166]

On June 4, 1979, after the Israel–Egypt peace agreement was signed, Dayan met with Sadat in Isma'iliya and the two spoke of the proposal Dayan had suggested earlier. Sadat told Dayan, "I know, Moshe, I know. It was genius. I know that Mrs. Meir didn't want it." Dayan responded, "Not just Golda. The entire government rejected the proposal."[167]

---

[165] Ibid., p. 1239.
[166] Dayan, Hala-netsaḥ tokhal ḥerev, p. 88.
[167] Neora Barnoah-Matalon, *Makom tov batsad* (Hebrew), Tel Aviv: Kotarim Publishers, 2009, p. 206.

On December 5, 1973, after the Yom Kippur War, Meir conceded, "I must admit that, several years ago, when the defense minister proposed we agree to withdraw from the Suez Canal so that the Egyptians could open it to shipping and return to its cities, I had no idea what he was talking about. Just withdraw from the canal for no reason?"[168]

Despite all this, no one knows what may have happened "if only." There is no way to prove that an arrangement based on Dayan's proposal would in fact have prevented the 1973 war and led to a sustainable peace. There are good reasons to think that another war would have occurred in any case, though the starting point and date would have been different. However, the years of talks with the Egyptians highlight his original and flexible way of thinking. His early opposition to a partial agreement and his reversal on the issue due to changing geopolitical conditions are typical of many of his decisions. However, this may also be seen as the beginning of Dayan's waning power, politically and personally, reflected in his need for Meir's approval and not insisting on his position even when he felt he was right. This became all the more apparent in the period preceding the Yom Kippur War and through its duration.

---

[168] Braun, *Moshe Dayan bemilhemet yom hakippurim*, p. 16.

8

The God Who Failed

General Muhammad Abdel Ghani al-Gamasy, Chief of Egypt's Armed Forces General Staff Operations Division and Deputy Chief of the Armed Forces General Staff during the 1973 Yom Kippur War and later Egypt's Minister of War, once said, "In the October War, we got our revenge for the 1967 War. It was personal between me and Dayan ... I hated Dayan more than I ever hated Sharon or Bar-Lev."[1]

On October 6, 1973, Judaism's holiest day, Yom Kippur, Israel came under a coordinated Egyptian–Syrian assault, considered among the greatest and most successful strategic military surprise attacks of all time. Israel's recovery after the defeats of the first few days and ultimate victory in the war, despite its terrible opening, are also considered among the most dramatic reversals in military history. The astute Dayan understood the disaster's dimensions perhaps better than anyone around him. It was to Dayan that commanders and soldiers looked in the nation's difficult hours for confidence and hope. But Dayan could not provide them.

After the initial shock of the opening salvos, the Israeli army, buoyed by the soldiers' heroism and self-sacrifice, regrouped within just a few short days. Dayan, too, recovered and regained his powers. He soon became a key player, especially after the most intense battles were over, effectively steering difficult negotiations. However, his immense personal prestige had suffered a mortal blow. The Israeli public, furious at the leadership's perceived hubris before the war and at the high casualties, never forgave him. His role in history appeared to have ended.

To this day, questions about Israel having been taken by surprise and failing to respond adequately in the war's first few days remain unanswered. For example, how did Dayan, with all his experience and wisdom, err regarding both the Egyptians' intentions and their capabilities? Dayan is still blamed for not calling up the reserves in time, for failures to heed intelligence, and for ill-judged responses in the war's first days, followed by an alleged failure of nerve and messages of doom he conveyed to the public. This chapter addresses these questions and offers some possible answers.

---

[1] In an interview with Kenneth Stein, in Kenneth Stein, *Mediniyut amitsa* (Hebrew), Tel Aviv: Maarakhot, 2003, p. 131.

The Yom Kippur War: The Strategic Background

With half a century having passed since the Yom Kippur War, we can now better see the processes that led to the war – undoubtedly Israel's most difficult, excepting the War of Independence – through a broader historical lens.

Israeli faced a strategic quagmire between the 1970 War of Attrition and the 1973 Yom Kippur War. It could either pay very steep costs in human life and resources to attain its political objective of not conceding any territory without satisfactory and commensurate political security; or it could significantly reduce human and other costs while making territorial concessions without adequate security benefits in return. With its ends not congruent with its means for attaining them, Israel either had to adjust its ends to the means available or change the possible means to match the ends.

To understand how Israel confronted this situation and Dayan's role in this, we must revisit the end of the Six-Day War and the War of Attrition to examine the political and military processes and events that brought Israel to this point.

At the end of the Six-Day War – after nineteen years of vulnerability to Egyptian, Syrian, and Jordanian forces abutting its rear and threatening it from higher elevations – Israel finally felt more secure. With Israel's borders pushed to the Suez Canal and Jordan River, and the Golan Heights under its control, Israelis were now living beyond the range of enemy fire for the first time since the country's establishment.

Still, on June 19, 1967, less than two weeks after the war's end, the Israeli government decided it was prepared to return the Sinai Peninsula to Egypt, all of the Golan Heights to Syria, and even most of the land conquered from Jordan, in exchange for peace treaties backed by acceptable security arrangements. The official Arab response to Israel's gains in the war (and to the Israeli proposal, if it was communicated to them) was articulated in the Arab League's decision at the end of the Khartoum summit on September 1, 1967: no peace with Israel, no recognition of Israel, and no negotiations with Israel. Even before the summit, on July 1– less than three weeks after the end of the Six-Day War – small-scale fighting was resumed by the Egyptians, soon followed by the Syrians. This fighting made it clear that despite the Arab armies' recent crushing defeat, Israel's fundamental strategic situation remained unchanged. While secret negotiations were conducted between the Six-Day War and the Yom Kippur War, Arab demands of full territorial withdrawals in exchange for nothing – or, at best, a limited something that would be ensured only after the lands were returned – were unacceptable to Israel and rigidified its positions.

Calling Up the Reserves

With the 1967 Arab defeat only temporarily changing the regional balance of power, Israel had to continue relying on its reservists for its military power and on early intelligence warnings for moving them to the front. However, with call-ups proving costly, Israel had to minimize them as much as possible, delay them to the last moment, and end any war quickly so the reservists could return to productive economic activity. Frequent full-scale call-ups could so damage the Israeli economy that it would be unable to withstand a joint Arab assault. Consequently, Israel had to avoid unnecessary call-ups and ensure that any call-up would so weaken its enemy that a future call-up could be postponed. While the toll of war – certainly when unprepared – is far greater than an unnecessary call-up, the economic costs of frequent call-ups can come close to those of war. Unnecessary call-ups also undermine morale: The public loses trust in the government, possibly even suspecting its motives. A reservist, paying an economic and personal price for call-ups, may be reluctant to appear, fearing an unnecessary call-up. Consequently, even if a call-up reflects a genuine military emergency, many may not come or might postpone coming until certain that "this time it's for real" – either way, not making it to the front in time. Moreover, frequent unnecessary reservist call-ups could harm the stability of Israel's democratic government.

Another key consideration in Israel's national security policy between 1949 and 1967 was the proximity of the civilian rear to the nation's borders. With no strategic depth, Israel could never allow itself to be taken by surprise, its standing army incapable of keeping the enemy from reaching the civilian rear. Israel always preferred to strike first, keeping the fighting as far away from its civilians as possible.

The Six-Day War's political and military outcomes resolved some matters and complicated others regarding the need for the reserves. One complication was Israel's growing dependence on the United States, both for political support and as its almost-sole arms provider, making starting a war without explicit US permission unthinkable. The United States explicitly demanded that Israel not shoot first; thus, any future war would have to be started by the Arab nations. However, since 1967, the new distance of mostly uninhabited land between Israel's fronts and its civilian rear provided some relief. With Israel able to absorb enemy attacks before they reached civilians, the US demand not to fire first was easier to accept.

Nonetheless, the added territory proved a mixed blessing, introducing two new complications in planning for the next war. One was that it now would take many reservists longer to reach the front from their homes, requiring an earlier call-up or letting the regular army handle the fighting on its own at the front, where they were greatly outnumbered by the larger regular Arab armies. The possibility of failure was, ironically, greater than before, and the assumption was that even if the regular soldiers succeeded, Israel's losses would be massive. The second complication was that it now took longer to allocate and move troops from one front to another, meaning it was now more critical than before 1967 that the General Staff correctly decide how to allocate forces.

Because of the enemies' absolute superiority in population size and their dictatorial regimes, the Arab nations could – and did – maintain very large regular armies near the fronts at a relatively high, if imperfect, state of alert. For these armies, the reserves were used for very particular niches, and they could shift from calm to war quite rapidly. Tiny Israel had no such luxury.

In this situation, Egypt and Syria could maneuver Israel into an impossible predicament. Egypt could permanently maintain tens of thousands of fighters (and administrative personnel) and two entire armies along the Suez Canal, prepared to strike at any time, and another army to defend the approach to Cairo. Against this force, Israel had – in the case of a surprise attack – fewer than 1,500 men permanently stationed at the front, a force that could be augmented by at most another 1,000 troops within three hours of an order being issued. The Syrian force, ready to fight on short notice, numbered some 15,000 men against Israel's permanent force of fewer than 1,500, and the weapons gap was similar. Israel would need twenty-four to forty-eight hours to call up the reserves and move them to the Golan Heights, and anywhere from seventy-two hours to seven days to move them to Sinai, depending on how they traveled. Added to this, Egypt and Syria could complete almost all their preparations for war without actually attacking for an extended period of time. While these nations would have paid a certain economic toll, it would have been much lower than the financial and social costs to Israel of calling up and holding its reserves over time.

With Egypt and Syria able to continue threatening war without specifying when, the imbalance of army size and troop availability between the sides enabled Egypt to manipulate Israel, constantly forcing it to decide whether or not to call up the reserves. Israel found itself in an untenable situation, like that of the boy who cried wolf, made worse by Egypt ostensibly negotiating with Israel over a political settlement, leading some Israeli leaders to consider any bellicose declarations all talk and bluster.

In hindsight, these constraints, Israel's dilemma about reservists, and the risks they faced at the moment of truth on October 6, 1973, had clear implications. But that is not how it seemed then. Some Israeli leaders did not fully grasp the impact of the dilemma and the depth of the predicament in which Israel found itself. Others, believing that the regular army could hold out longer at the front, were less concerned about the late mobilization of reserves than were those who considered the regular troops' capacity to withstand an attack more limited.

Shortly before his death, Dayan analyzed Israel's dilemma:

> The three Egyptian armies were a standing army. They were all soldiers. Not teachers, not craftsmen, not engineers . . . For two and a half years of attrition, [the Israeli reservists] spent one month in the army for every month at home, for a total of 172 days per man.

> What should we have done? Called up the entire IDF? How long could this have gone on? A week, two, three? ... And then what? You go home because the factory worker has to work at the factory and the engineer has to work and the teacher has to go back to school, otherwise you'd just be extending the [War of] Attrition ...
>
> Sadat could have waited two weeks, because he knew we didn't have more than two weeks' worth of air, and then he'd postpone the invasion by two weeks, because his army at the Suez Canal only needed a few things: backgammon, to grease [machinery] and check the distilled water of batteries, and fava beans to eat.[2]

When the war broke out, Dayan told the government ministers:

> When a state with fewer than three million Jews wants to hold the lines for years and live a normal life, it holds [the lines] very sparsely, knowing that we live on our reserves and that it takes time to call them up. So, until we get around to doing that, things will be uncomfortable and at time risky, and that's currently the situation at the canal.[3]

One could say that Dayan tried to justify himself in hindsight for his failure to call up the reservists in time. We have no reliable Egyptian sources about the Egyptian leadership's true prewar intentions. Egyptian witnesses published material only after the war to promote their own political agendas, and their work is rife with contradictions, even over Egypt's plan for war on October 6. The Egyptian archives remain closed. Some support for Dayan's claims is provided by Major General Herzl Shafir, Director of the Manpower Directorate during the 1973 war, who later represented Israel at the Geneva Conference, discussing the separation of forces agreement with Egypt in 1975. There, he spoke with Egyptian generals, trying to uncover their intentions on the eve of the war. He was curious as to what would have happened had Israel discovered Egypt's plans and called up its reserves in time: Would Egypt have called off the attack, or would it have gone on the offensive according to plan? Only years later, after the generals had retired from the military and met with Shafir again, did they answer him – even then taking care to emphasize that they were merely speculating, because Sadat made all decisions on his own. The Egyptians felt that the element of surprise was crucial to Egypt's planning, and therefore, had their true intentions been revealed, Egypt would have concluded the exercise as an exercise and not launched an attack.[4]

---

[2] Yizhar Be'er, "Moshe Dayan's last monologue: Antithesis to Israel's first family" (Hebrew), blog: Sacred Cows – Israeli Myths, *Haaretz*, July 30, 2019, www.haaretz.co.il/blogs/israeli myths/BLOG-1.7581303.

[3] Government Meeting, October 6, 1973, 10 p.m., Tel Aviv, in Shimon Golan, *Milhama beyom hakippurim: Kabalat hahahlatot bapikud haelyon bemilhamat yom hakippurim* (Hebrew), Ben Shemen: Maarakhot and Modan, 2013, p. 336.

[4] Herzl Shafir, *Milhemet yom hakippurim: Mabat shoneh* (Hebrew), Ben Shemen: Modan and Maarakhot, 2020, p. 96.

The security challenges Israel faced were obvious to its political and security leaderships. To understand how the security leadership, spearheaded by Dayan, planned on confronting them and to appreciate the trouble the plans ran into, the defensive plans and the arguments about them in the years preceding the war must be examined.

Prewar Defense Plans

After the end of the Six-Day War, the general expectation, including that of the senior IDF command, was that the deployment along the new front lines was only temporary – the territory gained would soon be returned. Over the next few months, it became increasingly clear that Israel would have to hold the new lines over an extended period, whereupon the senior IDF command decided to prepare an orderly defensive plan.

This plan tried to integrate a response to two strategic threats – the continuing attacks of attrition and a full-scale assault – into a unified framework. In the five years preceding the Yom Kippur War, this plan was the subject of professional debates and various updates. Ultimately, the military designed three defensive plans for each front, differing in their scope of reservist call-up should war break out: Sea Sand – with no reservists beyond those already doing routine annual reserve duty; Chalk – partial reserve call-up; and Rock – full reserve call-up. The Southern Command changed these names, deciding on Small Dovecote instead of Sea Sand, and Full Dovecote or Big Dovecote instead of Chalk; Rock remained Rock.

Arguments revolved around the operational concept, especially for the Egyptian front. The range of opinions can be categorized into two basic schools of thought: the rigid defense school versus the flexible defense school. Those favoring a rigid defense on the Egyptian front, first and foremost Major General Yeshayahu Gavish and Major General Avraham Adan, felt that the defensive battle should be conducted along the Suez Canal, creating thirty strongpoints to identify locations from which the Egyptian forces were liable to launch their crossing and alert the tank troops to embark immediately on a counterattack. This defense was based on a counteroffensive rather than on a fixed placement at preselected positions and firing at the approaching enemy until it was stopped in its tracks.[5]

Those championing a flexible defense in the south, led by Major General Israel Tal and Major General Ariel Sharon, who had also opposed constructing strongpoints during the War of Attrition, preferred to allow the Egyptians to cross the canal and to wait for them as they tried to move deeper into Sinai. Warfare dozens of kilometers from the Suez Canal and west of the mountain passes would be more mobile – a manner of warfare the Israelis were better at

---

[5] Shafir, *Milhemet yom hakippurim*, pp. 5, 53–55.

than the Egyptians. In 1969, Sharon was appointed the new commander of the Southern Command, and he pushed for his plans.

The first round of arguments between the two viewpoints ended when Chief of Staff Haim Bar-Lev made his decision: While from a purely military standpoint, a flexible defense was preferable, politically, it did not reflect the government's determination that the enemy be denied any success. Pushing the Egyptians back to their territory with a flexible defense would take two weeks or so, whereas any Egyptian achievements against a rigid defense could be quickly reversed within days. Bar-Lev claimed that Israel's experience showed that the superpowers might impose a ceasefire within days; therefore, under a flexible defense plan, the Egyptians would gain conquered territory, and the IDF would have failed its mission.

On January 1, 1972, David Elazar (Dado) replaced Bar-Lev as Chief of Staff. While he appreciated the advantages of a flexible defense, he ultimately, endorsed plans based on a rigid defense integrated with mobile troops due to political considerations. Nonetheless, arguments continued over the number of strongpoints, so that the final plans were presented and again approved in late April and early May of 1973, during the Blue and White state of alert, when, following intelligence alerts, the IDF called up IDF reserve units and made organizational changes and equipment upgrades to improve its state of readiness.

One of the enduring myths of the Yom Kippur War is that the IDF command thought it was possible to stop the Egyptians and keep them from achieving any territorial gains, no matter how small or temporary. It must be stressed, however, that this was not the prevailing opinion.[6] Dayan didn't agree, either; his conceding "not one inch of land" stance related not to conditions at a war's start but to those at its end. All the exercises and war games assumed that the enemy would make territorial gains, with drills focused on how to repel them. In August 1972, the IDF conducted the Battering Ram exercise, a war game centered on a scenario in which the army had only a two-day early warning of war. In the game, the Israelis quickly reversed Egyptian advances and even crossed the canal. Still, after the exercise

---

[6] Based on minutes of discussions from 1968 on the defense plans, summaries of war games played out under varied scenarios on the Egyptian front, notes taken at presentations of the Southern Command plans, and other discussions during the Blue and White state of alert in April–May 1973. For summaries and partial citations from these deliberations, see Carmit Guy, *Bar-Lev: Biografia* (Hebrew), Tel Aviv: Am Oved, 1998, pp. 174–80, 191–92; Hanoch Bartov, *Dado: 48 shana ve'od 20 yom* (Hebrew), expanded and footnoted editions, Dvir: Kinneret Zmora-Bitan, 2002, vol. 1, pp. 188–191, 210–215, 229–231, 256–257, 263–264, 273–276, 279, 282; Uri Dan, *Besodo shel Ariel Sharon* (Hebrew), Tel Aviv: Yedioth Ahronoth – Hemed Books, 2007, pp. 67–68; Ariel Sharon with David Chanoff, *Warrior: An Autobiography of Ariel Sharon*, New York: Simon and Schuster, 1989, pp. 218–221, 229–231, 237–238, 265, 269–271.

concluded, Chief of Staff Elazar expressed skepticism about how quickly the tables had turned during the war game: "The number of losses, the speed, and the place we reached within such and such number of days ... Personally, I have certain reservations with the scope of the success, the speed of the success, and the ease of the success as it was played out here."[7]

The difference between the political and the tactical "not one inch" was lost on the junior commanders who thought their mission was to repulse the Egyptians before they could set foot on the Israeli side of the Suez Canal.[8] In contrast, the top brass was discussing the question of how far the Egyptians would advance into Sinai before the IDF could launch a counteroffensive to repel them back across the canal.

There is no denying that the upper echelon of the IDF disdained the enemy, despite their advantages. They felt that the Arabs would not try their luck again for years to come, and even if they did, they would be defeated with relative ease. This self-confidence of Israel's top military leadership was fueled primarily by Israel's very clear aerial superiority (despite problems the IAF had in the last months of the War of Attrition with the Egyptian antiaircraft defense, now greatly enhanced by the Soviets both along the Suez and in Syria), even though the IAF's leaders claimed that in the first two or three days, ground troops could not rely on aerial support because the IAF would be busy trying to destroy the enemy's aerial defenses. Dayan later admitted on several occasions that his own confidence came from his underestimation of the enemy and perhaps overestimation of Israel's own power.[9]

The solution was to preemptively strike the enemy's antiaircraft defense system. But even a limited first strike was a political impossibility, although it seems that the senior military leaders had, until the moment of truth, not internalized the understanding that permission for a preemptive strike would be denied. Still, under the unique political and military conditions of the Yom Kippur War, the question of how significant a first strike could have been when the campaign began remains unresolved by experts to this day.

Sadat Prepares a Surprise

A retrospective study of strategic surprises like the Yom Kippur War often raises the question, "How did they not see it coming? It was all right in front of their eyes!" With all the information available, it seems that all that was to put

---

[7] Bartov, *Dado*, vol. 1, p. 230.
[8] Amnon Reshef, *Lo nehdal! Hativa 14 bemilhemet yom hakippurim: Sippuram shel kravot hashiryon ha'akh'zari'im beyoter bahistroiya* (Hebrew), expanded edition, Or Yehuda: Dvir, 2013, pp. 51–55; Immanuel Sekel, *Hasadir yivlom? Kakh huh'metsa hahakh'ra'a besinai bemilhemet yom hakippurim* (Hebrew), Tel Aviv: Maariv Library, 2012, pp. 41–43.
[9] Yaakov Erez and Ilan Kfir, *Sihot im Moshe Dayan* (Hebrew), Ramat Gan: Massada, 1981, p. 107.

the puzzle pieces together correctly. Those who lived through that period and paid the price for the mistake seem the most incredulous.[10]

There are several approaches to studying this surprise. One is a retroactive analysis and reconstruction of the flow of information and the work of intelligence, the knowledge and insights derived from that information, and the decision-makers' lacunae in correctly reading reality that led them – chiefly Golda Meir, Moshe Dayan, and David Elazar – to make key and painful errors in decisions.[11] A different approach examines not information but the leaders' presumptions, based on what can now be seen as faulty assumptions about the enemy's objectives and capabilities.[12] A third perspective examines whether the political echelon, armed with political biases, persuaded the military that no immediate attack was expected.[13] Some, going even further, argue that decision-makers were aware of the impending attack but did nothing, hoping it would result in a favorable political settlement for Israel.[14]

Research shows that intelligence was crucial to both sides of the conflict in terms of operational decisions, presumptions, and political considerations. Sadat, for example, decided to go to war after realizing the United States would not pressure Israel to withdraw from all of the Sinai Peninsula. Consequently, in November 1972, Sadat ordered his generals to prepare for war.[15] Aware of these developments, Dayan acknowledged the possibility of renewed conflict along the Suez Canal to the government on November 26, citing AMAN's intelligence failures in predicting the removal of Soviet "advisors" from Egypt earlier that year. These "advisors" were actually Soviet units that had fought in the last half of the War of Attrition, instructed Egypt's military forces, and, importantly, reinforced Egypt's aerial defense systems. Dayan therefore believed that a renewal of violence was likely.

[10] The Japanese fleet's attack on the US naval base at Pearl Harbor (December 7, 1941), Operation Barbarossa (Nazi Germany's invasion of the USSR, June 1941), and the 9/11 terror attacks on the United States are striking examples of surprises that, in hindsight, appear to have been preventable. See Uri Bar-Yosef, *Mitkefet peta: Manhigout umodi'in bemivhan elyon* (Hebrew), Shoham: Kinneret Zmora Bitan, 2019.
[11] For an example of this approach, see Uri Bar-Yosef, *Hatsofeh shenirdam: Hafta'at yom hakippurim umekoroteha* (Hebrew), Shoham: Zmora Bitan, 2001.
[12] Tsvi Lanir, *Hahafta'a habsisit: Modi'in bemashber* (Hebrew), Tel Aviv: United Kibbutz, and the Center for Strategic Studies, Tel Aviv University, 1983.
[13] Yigal Kipnis, *1973: Haderekh lamilhama* (Hebrew), Or Yehuda: Dvir, 2012.
[14] Michael Bronstein (ed.), *Nitsahon bisvirout nemukha: Amitot al milhemet yom hakippurim* (Hebrew), Ramat Gan: Effi Meltzer, 2017.
[15] Meir Boymfeld, *Kfitsa lamayim hakarim: Hamaga'im hamedini'im bein yisrael, mitsrayim ve'artshot habrit bashanim shekadmu lemilhemet yom hakippurim 1970-1973* (Hebrew), Reut: Effi Meltser Ltd., 2017, p. 824; Uri Bar-Yosef, *H'amalach: Ashraf Marwan, hamossad vhaftat yom hakippurim* (Hebrew), Or Yehuda: Kineret Zmorah Dvir, 2011, p. 188.

In a December 1 government meeting, Dayan predicted, "we must assume that Egypt will renew fire at the canal in early 1973."[16] AMAN Director Eli Zeira differed: "The chances that Egypt will begin a war are not high ... The chances they'll try to cross the canal are close to zero."[17] Dayan responded:

> All of the AMAN Director's rational analyses explain why it is not worth Egypt's while to open fire, but he has no advice to give Egypt on how to secure Sadat's position in Egypt, how to reach a pan-Arab arrangement, how to jumpstart some political activity. In Egypt, an irrational rationale can hold sway, and it may be quite rational in intra-Egyptian terms ... It's not to be expected tomorrow, but it may certainly occur before next spring.[18]

On December 1, 1972, Israel informed the United States that it would retaliate against any Egyptian aggression. Secretary of State Kissinger warned Israel against a preemptive strike.[19] This was not the first such American warning, and it would be a mistake to underestimate how much this caveat influenced Meir's and Dayan's prewar strategy.

In February 1973, Sadat dispatched Hafez Ismail, Egypt's National Security Council Chair, to propose a peace initiative to Kissinger. The proposal involved Israel's full withdrawal from territories seized in the Six-Day War, the creation of a Palestinian state, and granting Palestinians the right to return. In exchange, Egypt would end the state of war but would not sign a peace treaty until negotiations with Jordan, Syria, and the Palestinians were concluded. Sadat hoped the United States would force Israel to accept these conditions, including a full withdrawal and the Palestinian right of return.[20] This was a nonstarter for Israel, who also requested to resume negotiations after the election in October. Sadat, frustrated after the initiative's failure, accelerated Egypt's preparations for war. In April and May 1973, Israel received warnings of possible renewed hostilities in May. Whether Egypt really intended to go to war that May remains unclear.[21]

In April, sources warned of Sadat's disappointment with the political route and his resolve to resume hostilities. Israeli intelligence suggested two potential dates: May 15 and 19. They also learned of an Egyptian plan to cross the Suez Canal with five infantry divisions, isolate the area to be captured, erect a bridgehead, and move armored divisions into Sinai to seize the mountain

---

[16] Political-military consultation, December 1, 1972, in Arie Braun, *Moshe Dayan bemilhemet yom hakippurim* (Hebrew), Tel Aviv: Idanim Publishing, 1993, p. 17.
[17] Ibid., p. 18.
[18] Government meeting, December 3, 1972, in ibid., p. 18.
[19] Kissinger memorandum to the president, December 1, 1972, in Boymfeld, *Kfitsa lamayim hakarim*, p. 833.
[20] Boymfeld, *Kfitsa lamayim hakarim*, p. 905.
[21] Uri Bar-Yosef, *Hatsofeh shenirdam* (Hebrew), Lod: Zmora Bitan, 2001, p. 148.

passes.[22] Historians still argue over Egypt's war strategy: Would conquering a 10-kilometer strip suffice, or would they try to seize control to the mountainous ridge bisecting Sinai 40 kilometers from the canal?[23] Success hinged on a concurrent Syrian attack on the Golan Heights to distract Israel, especially the IAF. Sadat accurately anticipated that the IDF would split its forces between the Syrian front, close to civilian settlements, and the Egyptian front, thus enabling the Egyptian force to establish its bridgehead more easily. However, Syria was kept unaware of Egypt's intentions to ensure cooperation, so that Egypt misled both Israel and its Syrian ally.[24]

Nonetheless, there was no increased activity on the southern front suggesting war preparations. At an April 13 General Staff meeting, AMAN Director Zeira downplayed the threat's severity, while Dayan and Chief of Staff Elazar were more concerned. Dayan found in AMAN's data "implications and hints that very much strengthen the idea of war in terms of [Egypt's] general approach."[25] On April 18, AMAN reiterated that Sadat aimed to unnerve Israel as in the past but was not really preparing for war. Dayan, like Zeira, believed Sadat was taking military steps to strengthen himself politically; unlike Zeira, Dayan thought Sadat really intended to fight. "Sadat will sleep well even if 20,000 of his soldiers are killed," said Dayan. "He'll sacrifice them for the sake of his political goal."[26] By May 1973, Dayan and Elazar developed their own assessment countering AMAN's underestimation of war.[27]

The most important discussion of the probability for war in May occurred on April 18 at a meeting of Prime Minister Meir's closest associates in "Golda's Kitchen Cabinet." Attendees included Meir, Galili, Dayan, Elazar, Zeira, and Mossad Chief Zamir, the handler of Ashraf Marwan, an important intelligence

---

[22] Bar-Yosef, *Hatsofeh shenirdam*, p. 167.
[23] The narrower plan (up to 10 kilometers) is presented in the memoirs of Egypt's then Armed Forces Chief of Staff Lieutenant General Saad El Din Mohamed el-Husseiny el-Shazly, *Hatsiyat hate'ala: Zikhronot haramatkal hamitsri bemilhemet yom hakippurim* (in Hebrew translation), Tel Aviv: Maarakhot, 1987, pp. 19–28, 176. The expanded plan (to the passes) is presented in the memoirs of the Egyptian army's Chief of the Armed Forces General Staff Operations Division Major General Mohamed Abdel Ghani el-Gamasy, *Zikhronot el-Gamasy: Milhemet oktober 1973* (in Hebrew translation), Tel Aviv: Hatsav Publishers, 1994, pp. 120, 213–236. Different parts of Anwar Sadat's memoirs alternately support el-Shazly's and el-Gamasy's approaches: Anwar Sadat, *Sippur hayay* (in Hebrew translation), Jerusalem: Idanim, 1978, pp. 184, 191, 193, 195, 218. For another example of contradictory versions, see Hassan el-Badry, Ta el-Majdoub, and El Din Zahadi, *Milhemet Ramadan: Hasivuv hayisraeli-aravi harevi'i – oktober 1973* (in Hebrew translation), Tel Aviv: HATSAV Translation and Publishing, 1974, pp. 21, 28.
[24] Bar-Yosef, *H'amalach*, p. 191.
[25] Bar Yosef, *Hatsofeh shenirdam*, p. 170.
[26] Israel Tal and Yair Tal, *Prakim lehilhemet yom hakippurim* (Hebrew), Rishon Lezion: Miskal – Publishers Founded by Yedioth Ahronoth and Hemed Bood, 2019, p. 74.
[27] Bar-Yosef, *Hatsofeh shenirdam*, p. 172.

asset, who provided information on Egypt's war preparations, including a potential war in May.[28]

Dayan opened by focusing on the central issue of the probability of war. Zeira believed the Egyptians were not ready and that AMAN would know if and when they were. Zamir, in contrast, felt that Egypt was ready to launch an attack: Antiaircraft missiles now covered the Suez Canal, and bridging materials had been placed nearby. Similarly, Elazar felt that while a reserve call-up wasn't yet necessary, the plans needed to be updated. Dayan's opinion was likewise grim: "If you ask me ... I believe they are heading for war." Dayan felt that the IDF's strength might actually push the other side to decide it had nothing to lose. He added, "If going to war doesn't provide military results, it will cause a change to the political order ... They are counting on the Russians and the Americans and the oil more than on their own commandos." Dayan thought any Egyptian fire would begin along the Suez Canal.[29]

The next day, Elazar announced that the IDF must prepare for a two-front war, the preparations codenamed the Blue and White Alert.

On May 21, Dayan predicted a high chance of war with Egypt and Syria in the latter half of 1973, without Jordan but with help from other Arab nations. Believing that Egypt would use a limited military move for political gain, Dayan exhorted Elazar: "We the government say to the General Staff: 'Gentlemen, please prepare for war ... ' This is what we ask of the General Staff: to be ready by this summer."[30]

Dayan mentioned in his briefings to the IDF commanders a preemptive strike, promising a good excuse, even though it wasn't clear that this was even conceivable politically: "If a provocation is needed, we'll get you that too ... If it emerges that Tel Aviv is about to be bombed, there's no need to wait for it to happen ... As for explaining to the world that we didn't start a war at that time – we'll take care of that."[31]

During the Blue and White Alert, improvements were accelerated in military personnel, infrastructure, and equipment. The IDF received more tanks and weaponry, while roads and strongpoints were strengthened. Despite the alert being lifted on August 12, the IDF's readiness for the October war undoubtedly benefited from these changes.[32] However, there were also shortcomings, such as relocation of ammo depots and other uncompleted tasks, causing some confusion among the units called up when the war began.

The alert also had drawbacks, including high costs, leading to careful consideration of future call-ups[33] and a growing complacency due to the lack of

[28] Bar-Yosef, H'amalach, pp. 202, 210.
[29] Bar-Yosef, Hatsofeh shenirdam, pp. 176–177.
[30] Golan, Milhama beyom hakippurim, p. 106.
[31] Ibid., pp. 67–68.
[32] Bar-Yosef, H'amalach, 209.
[33] Ibid.

immediate conflict. A false sense of security resulted, with Dayan's views shifting from imminent war to a distant threat.

In the same month that the state of alert was canceled, we now know that Syria and Egypt decided to wage war on October 6, secretly strengthening their front lines.[34]

On September 13, disputes on the Syria border escalated due to an air fight that the IAF won, hitting twelve Syrian fighter planes. However, this came with shattering repercussions, resulting in a false sense of security for Israel and enabling the Arab armies to surprise them less than a month later. The Syrians had two operational principles: react to every Israeli action and have the last word, usually meaning firing artillery at IDF positions.[35] Therefore, after the air fight, Syrian reinforcements on the Golan Heights were misunderstood as preparations for a limited retaliation,[36] thus leading to the eventual surprise of the all-out offensive.

In the weeks before the war, Israel's Northern Command, led by Yitzhak Hofi, was concerned about Syria's aggression due to the vulnerability of Israeli towns near the border and the lack of intelligence on Syrian forces.[37] At a September 24 General Staff meeting, Hofi urged prioritizing the Syrian front over Egypt, arguing that while weaker, the Syrians posed a greater threat than Egypt. Dayan felt that a Syrian surprise attack was a more perilous scenario because of the proximity of civilian settlements to the border.[38] Dayan and Elazar, certain that the Syrians could not take the Golan Heights, discussed various scenarios. Elazar foresaw a comprehensive Syrian invasion while Dayan considered a limited Syrian action designed to punish Israel.[39] Dayan's insistence that a response was needed to the Syrian threat probably led to the decision to reinforce the Northern Command.[40] Ironically, Israel's intelligence interpreted Syrian troop reinforcement observed on September 24 as indicating Syria's fear of an Israeli attack.[41]

On September 25, King Hussein of Jordan met with Prime Minister Golda Meir, warning that Syria was preparing a military offensive against Israel. To

---

[34] Golan, *Milhama beyom hakippurim*, pp. 156–157.
[35] A similar reactive pattern still operates in the Middle East: between Israel and Hamas, and between Israel and Hezbollah/Iran.
[36] Operations Division document, September 1973, in Golan, *Milhama beyom hakippurim*, p. 158.
[37] General Staff discussion, September 24, 1973, in Golan, *Milhama beyom hakippurim*, p. 164.
[38] Dayan's statements at General Staff discussion, September 24, 1973, in Golan, *Milhama beyom hakippurim*, p. 165.
[39] Moshe Dayan, *Avnei derekh: Autobiografia* (Hebrew), Jerusalem: Idanim Publishers, 1976, p. 571.
[40] Telephone conversation with Shimon Golan, December 28, 2020.
[41] AMAN Research document, September 1973, in Golan, *Milhama beyom hakippurim*, p. 167.

Meir's question as to whether he thought Syria would go to war on its own, he said that Egypt might join Syria.[42]

Dayan immediately allayed Meir's fears, assuring her that, aware of the situation, he intended to reinforce the northern front the next day. Israeli intelligence noted Hussein's assessment that Syria would go to war only if Egypt also did, but the senior command ranks never gave it proper attention.[43]

On September 26, the eve of the Jewish New Year (Rosh Hashanah), Dayan and Elazar agreed with AMAN's assessment that Egypt would not start a war, and consequently, neither would Syria. While Elazar dismissed Dayan's concerns about Syrian retaliation.[44] Dayan toured the Golan Heights. While worried about massive Syrian reinforcements there, Dayan tried to calm the Israeli public, now alarmed following the escalation there.[45]

Due to the possibility of Syrian action, the outcome of deliberations and Dayan's visit to the Golan Heights resulted in troop reinforcement in the north from September 30. The 77th Battalion was transported to the Golan Heights with additional artillery forces, and antiaircraft companies were deployed. More forces were placed on standby. The total forces placed in the Golan Heights increased significantly, and the IAF was set on alert to attack Syria's missile systems on short notice.[46] As of September 30, Israel's security establishment, including Dayan, felt that war was unlikely but expected increased border activity from Syria.

On September 29, the CIA warned Israel that Syria intended to reclaim the Golan Heights, and Israel learned of Egypt's upcoming military exercise in the Sinai.[47] This information did not alarm AMAN, which rationalized Egypt's troop movements toward the Suez Canal as part of the exercise. The next day, AMAN Director Zeira, supported by his deputy, dismissed the CIA's warning regarding Syria's intentions.[48]

In the days leading up to the war, multiple sources indicated that Egypt and Syria were preparing for war. However, AMAN firmly believed that Egypt and Syria would not initiate war until they held stronger positions, causing AMAN to ignore every sign to the contrary.[49] This set of assumptions would become known after the war as "the conception." AMAN persistently disregarded the

---

[42] From summary of meeting between Meir and Hussein by the Prime Minister's Office Director General Mordechai Gazit, in Arieh Shalev, *Kishalon vehatslaha behatra'a: Ha'arakhat hamodi'in likrat milhemet yom hakippurim* (Hebrew), Tel Aviv: Maarakhot, 2006, pp. 108–112.

[43] Bar-Yosef, *Hatsofeh shenirdam*, pp. 243–246.

[44] Ibid., p. 248; Golan, *Milhama beyom hakippurim*, pp. 173–174.

[45] Bar-Yosef, *Hatsofeh shenirdam*, p. 249.

[46] Golan, *Milhama beyom hakippurim*, p. 180

[47] AMAN Research document, September 1973, in Golan, *Milhama beyom hakippurim*, p. 182.

[48] Brigadier General Arieh Shalev's assessment, in Golan, *Milhama beyom hakippurim*, p. 184.

[49] Bar-Yosef, *H'amalach*, p. 230.

influx of contradictory information, steadfastly adhering to its "conception." For example, on the night of September 30, a warning of imminent war came from inside Egypt, but AMAN did not inform Elazar. Instead, Zeira told Dayan that he believed Egyptian movements were just part of a military exercise.[50]

On October 1, regarding the CIA warning, AMAN repeated its assessment, authorized by Dayan, that Syria would not engage in the Golan without Egypt, and that Egypt was embarking on an exercise that might appear to be war, but added, "Our assessment is that it is just an exercise."[51]

On October 2, a written warning arrived to the effect that Egypt was planning to launch an attack.[52] Despite increasing signs of war preparations, AMAN maintained its opinion that there would be no war.[53] When Dayan and Elazar met, the latter assured Dayan that he and AMAN were convinced that the situation in Egypt was linked to the Egyptian exercise, and Syria was unlikely to attack. Elazar felt the Golan reinforcements were sufficient and assumed the IDF would have early warning if Syria launched a large-scale offensive. Dayan was uncertain about Syria's preparations and the reliability of the warnings on war.[54]

On October 3, the CIA transmitted another assessment indicating Syria's intention to go to war. Dayan called for a comprehensive military-political consultation, saying he "wanted to share responsibility for the issue."[55] In the ensuing meeting, Elazar accepted AMAN's assessment that Egypt and Syria did not plan to wage war together.[56]

On October 4, reports AMAN received of an Egyptian military delegation in Syria did not trigger alarm among decision-makers or cast doubt on "the conception."[57] That night, the leadership consensus remained: There was no danger of a full-scale war. Dayan, although worried about Syria, accepted AMAN's assessment about Egypt.

On the night of October 4–5, Israeli intelligence learned about the sudden and hasty evacuation of Soviet advisors' families from Egypt and Syria, suggesting preparations for war. Information from Ashraf Marwan indicated war was imminent. Aerial photos taken above the Suez Canal that night showed a significant reinforcement of Egyptian troops.

At a meeting on October 5 of Dayan, Elazar, and Zeira, Dayan opened. Reading data on Egyptian and Syrian forces from a piece of

---

[50] General Staff discussion, October 1, 1973, in Golan, *Milhama beyom hakippurim*, p. 192.
[51] AMAN document, October 1973, in Golan, *Milhama beyom hakippurim*, p. 197.
[52] Golan, *Milhama beyom hakippurim*, p. 198.
[53] Bar-Yosef, *H'amalach*, p. 229.
[54] Golan, *Milhama beyom hakippurim*, pp. 202–203.
[55] Braun, *Moshe Dayan bemilhemet yom hakippurim*, p. 51.
[56] From military-political consultation, Tel Aviv, October 3, 1973, IDF Archive, in Golan, *Milhama beyom hakippurim*, pp. 210–211.
[57] Golan, *Milhama beyom hakippurim*, p. 218.

paper, he said: "The numbers alone are enough to give anyone a heart attack." He then turned to the officers in the room, saying: "You don't take the Arabs seriously." AMAN Director Zeira hypothesized that the Soviet evacuation could indicate Arab fear of an Israeli attack following bellicose Israeli rhetoric and the Golan reinforcement.[58] He insisted on his assessment despite the evacuation, and shared Marwan's information with Dayan and Elazar. He mentioned a meeting with Marwan, concluding by saying, "[After the meeting], we'll be wiser."

Dayan, thinking that Egypt's exercises could be a cover for a real attack, accepted his aide Tzvi Tsur's recommendation of communicating to Egypt via the United States that Israel did not want to start a war notwithstanding its knowledge of Egyptian intentions. He delayed in passing the message on, so that it reached Egypt only on October 6 at 1:05 p.m., an hour before the strike was launched.[59] While it is unlikely that an earlier arrival of the message would have made a difference, its delay let to conspiracy theories about Kissinger deliberately delaying it in order to encourage war.[60]

Apparently, during the October 5 meeting, Dayan averred that "special means," referring to Israeli listening devices, surreptitiously placed on Egyptian communications lines for use only if Egypt was about to attack, had in fact been activated. A wary Dayan asked Zeira: "In all this [communications] traffic over the Egyptian lines, is there anything unusual or not?" Although Zeira had reported to Elazar on October 1 that the "special means" had already been activated, Zeira now answered Dayan, "It's absolutely quiet," thus placating Dayan. What neither Dayan nor Elazar knew was that Zeira, without consulting anyone, had decided not to activate the listening devices.[61] After the war, Zeira provided a vague explanation for why he had not activated them: It was difficult, he claimed, to decipher existing information, and therefore he didn't feel there was any need for additional data.[62]

On October 5 at 11:30 a.m., Elazar, meeting with Zeira and government ministers, reassured them that "AMAN's basic assessment that we are not facing a war is the most probable assessment in my opinion ... The enemy's forces bear all the characteristics of a defense." The CIA's answer about the Soviet airlift, received at 8:30 p.m., was also deceptively reassuring about the unlikelihood of war. Despite an accumulation of growing signs of an Egyptian

---

[58] Weekly meeting, October 5, 1973, Defense Minister's Bureau, in Golan, *Milhama beyom hakippurim*, p. 226.
[59] Golan, *Milhama beyom hakippurim*, p. 229.
[60] See the essay on the subject: Rami Rom, Amir Gilat & Rose Mary Sheldon, "The Yom Kippur War, Dr. Kissinger, and the Smoking Gun," *International Journal of Intelligence and Counter Intelligence* 31:2 (2018), pp. 357–373; DOI: 10.1080/08850607.2018.1417526.
[61] Bar-Yosef, *Hatsofeh shenirdam*, p. 302.
[62] Ofer Aderet, "Secret document reveals how AMAN Director misled government about 'special means' in 1973" (Hebrew), *Haaretz*, May 8, 2020.

and Syrian call-up and preparations, AMAN's assessment did not change. Cracks started showing only because of numerous intelligence reports on reinforcements of Egypt's and Syria's front lines.[63]

Historian Shimon Golan outlined Dayan's stance during the critical period of October 4 and 5, during which it was still feasible to mobilize reserves with forty-eight hours' notice per IDF plans:

> [Dayan] raised questions about the basis of AMAN's assessment that ... were left unresolved. On October 5, he didn't protest AMAN's assessment, and confirmed that, militarily, the steps [Elazar] had taken were sufficient. Nonetheless, given the uncertainty about the enemy's [intentions], he decided to add a [political step] to the ... military ones. He advised [Meir] to contact the United States to [learn more about Egyptian intentions] ... He also recommended that ... [if] Egypt and Syria were indeed on the warpath, the United States should inform them that Israel was ... prepared to meet their onslaught, and thus deter them from war ... Another reason for contacting the United States was to ensure that, if war did break out, it would provide Israel with political backing and critical equipment.[64]

Dayan apparently relied on AMAN's assessments and the military's preparations, seeing his task as operating at the political-security level, especially ensuring critical US support in case of war. Dayan also feared creating tension that might deteriorate into war, the 1959 "Night of the Ducks" incident, when an emergency call-up exercise accidentally escalated tensions unnecessarily, resulting in forced General Staff resignations. He aimed to balance between the prospect of war and the fear of an accidental war.

The information that changed the opinion of Israel's decision-makers came from Marwan, who on the night between October 4 and 5 warned of impending war.[65] Meetings took place with between Zamir Marwan in London at midnight October 5 and 6 (Israel time). Marwan had not forgotten past warnings of war that had not materialized, and he was aware that the final decision on going to war was Sadat's alone; having not been by Sadat's side lately made him doubt the reliability of the information he'd forwarded. Responding to Zamir's pressure for certainty, Marwan erupted: "How do I know?! He's crazy! He can go forward, he can say forward, and then go backward."[66]

---

[63] The first cracks are visible in the AMAN Research Document, October 1973, in Golan, *Milhama beyom hakippurim*, p. 245.

[64] Golan, *Milhama beyom hakippurim* p. 248.

[65] *Duah va'adat agranat, helki nosaf* (Hebrew), vol. 1, 1974, in Tal and Tal, *Prakim lehilhemet yom hakippurim*, pp. 174–175.

[66] Bar-Yosef, *H'amalach*, p. 251.

October 6: Prewar Hours

Zamir's message, sent on October 6, indicated that war would start that day "at sundown." It reached Israel at 2:40 a.m., wending its way through the maze of bureaucracy for two hours before eventually reaching Dayan and Elazar between 4 and 4:30 a.m.[67] Another problem, which would have chilling repercussions, was that at some point along its bureaucratic journey, the war's expected commencement was changed from "at sundown," scheduled to begin at 5:20 p.m. that day, to "at 6 p.m.," erasing the original "at sundown." In any case, Marwan's information was incorrect, as the Egyptians and Syrians had decided on 2 p.m., much earlier, to open the attack. These times differences would have fateful results.[68]

Upon receiving the information, Israel's leaders prepared for imminent war. Elazar immediately instructed the IAF to ready for a preliminary strike, expecting readiness by 11 a.m. But Dayan remained doubtful about war:

> The source of the information was trustworthy ... but similar information had been provided in the past and then, when the Arabs didn't attack, the explanation was always that Sadat had changed his mind "at the last minute." This time, too, it was noted that if Sadat learns we have found out about it and the element of surprise has been taken from him, he may cancel or at least delay the time of the attack.[69]

The time available for Israel's leaders to act was less than expected. Nobody knew that the Egyptian defense minister and the Syrian president had decided on the 2 p.m. start.[70] In fact, Dayan had received information from the United States that Egypt and Syria were not about to attack, along with conflicting information from another source later described by Zamir as "not the most reliable."[71]

All the scenarios considered by Israel presumed an early warning of at least twenty-four – perhaps even forty-eight hours – based on various Israeli intelligence sources and CIA input, all suggesting that a warning would come in plenty of time.[72] However, the conditions actually created a perfect storm, and Zeira's "conception" brought Israel to a state that led to Israel entering battle with only its regular, not fully deployed, army. The mobilization of reservists to the front lines in Sinai took between forty-eight and seventy-two hours

---

[67] Tal and Tal, *Prakim lehilhemet yom hakippurim*, p. 176.
[68] Ibid., p. 177; Golan, *Milhama beyom hakippurim*, p. 250.
[69] Dayan, *Avnei derekh*, p. 575.
[70] Bar-Yosef, *H'amalach*, p. 253.
[71] Golan, *Milhama beyom hakippurim*, p. 260.
[72] For more about the United States' flawed assessment, see Ehud Eran, "American Intelligence before the Yom Kippur War: A Failure of Gathering and Assessment" (Hebrew), *Mabat malam: Ktav et le'inyanei modi'in vebitahom mibeit hamercaz lemoreshet hamodi'in* 67 (November 2013), pp. 42–47.

(compared to twelve hours for the Golan Heights), although they arrived in record time.

Israel's great advantage was its air force. Indeed, Elazar's first call was to the IAF commander, who decided to focus on Syria. Due to weather conditions, the IAF would first carry out operation "Headbutt" to destroy Syrian airfields and then implement operation "Dogman" to destroy Syria's surface-to-air missiles. The goal was to establish aerial superiority and support ground troops to quickly halt the Syrian army. The preemptive strike was planned for the afternoon.

On October 6 at 5:50 a.m., Dayan, Elazar, and others discussed two critical issues: a preemptive strike and a general call-up in anticipation of war. Dayan was open to a preemptive strike against Syria even if only Egypt launched an attack but directed that for political reasons such a strike should occur only "with 5 minutes to spare" before the enemy's attack. Dayan was proposing a parallel counteroffensive designed to disrupt the enemy's action as a last-minute response to an imminent enemy attack.[73] He opposed a preemptive strike due to US objections, as Israel relied on US support. There was a heated debate over the scope of the call-up, with Elazar advocating almost a full call-up of the fighting force and Dayan suggesting 20,000–30,000 soldiers, primarily for the northern front, feeling the south had adequate forces. Dayan was thinking defense while Dado was thinking offense. Dayan, assuming a 6 p.m. start of war, saw no significant difference between an immediate call-up and one closer to the war, considering the latter a reasonable risk. He finally agreed to call up two divisions, one for the Golan and one for the south, for the defense, reserving the decision about a third division and the remainder of the reservists if a comprehensive war broke out. He worried that a full call-up could provoke the Arabs to go to war even if they had not planned to. According to a government decision the day before, only Dayan and Meir could jointly decide on a call-up. Unable to reach Meir on the telephone, Dayan decided to wait to meet with Meir and let her decide.[74]

The postwar question was: Why didn't Elazar initiate the limited call-up that had been authorized? Two divisions could have made a significant difference, particularly in the north, which could be reached relatively quickly. Misunderstandings and communication issues often occur under stress, which was the case here. At the postwar Agranat Commission, Dayan claimed he had given Elazar permission to call up two divisions and thought Elazar had begun the process. Elazar, however, believed the proposals needed to be

---

[73] The details of this meeting as described herein are based on the diary of the Chief of Staff's bureau chief, Arieh Shalev, October 6, 1973, and the impressions of the Defense Minister's adjutant, Shlomo Gazit, in Golan, *Milhama beyom hakippurim*, p. 255.

[74] From minutes of conversation between Dayana and Elazar at their October 6, meeting, 6 a.m. See Golan, *Milhama beyom hakippurim*, pp. 254–261.

approved by Meir, and that because preparations had begun, waiting would not be overly damaging.[75] The Agranat Commission blamed Elazar for the delay and recommended his dismissal. Dayan and Elazar both thought they had the go-ahead for the call-up but were waiting for Meir's approval for further action.

In retrospect, the Agranat Commission was harsh on Elazar. Both he and Dayan were responsible for carrying out the instructions, as Dayan himself conceded in his testimony.

On the eve of war, Elazar suggested using unmanned aircraft to take aerial photos of Egyptian preparations. Dayan, worried about escalation, approved, but without the aircraft crossing the border. Elazar wanted to maximize military preparations, preferring a call-up that would either deter the enemy or improve Israel's opening position, while Dayan had to consider diplomatic, social, economic, and internal political factors. Dayan feared a full call-up could trigger war if the Egyptians were bluffing. It was a trap with no exit.

At 7:15 a.m., Elazar held a meeting for updates from which Dayan was absent. Elazar predicted war would start at 6 p.m. and mentioned political opposition to a preemptive strike. He stated a partial call-up had been approved, and there would be a comprehensive call-up at the start of hostilities. He anticipated that the IDF would initially maintain their position under fire, then launch an assault between October 8 and 10.[76] The expectation was for a brief war, resulting either in a decisive Israeli victory or superpower intervention.

Following this, Elazar met with Major General Gonen, the Southern Command commander, to discuss southern preparations, a meeting also marked by misunderstandings regarding the positioning of two of the Command's three tank brigades in the "rear." Gonen believed they were to stay at base camp until war began, while Elazar interpreted "rear" as just behind the forward brigade. There was also confusion about exact deployment times. Zeira joined Elazar and Gonen and informed them that he did not anticipate war; he warned Gonen that advancing the brigades from deep in Sinai to the front line could instigate war and that Gonen should wait until close to 6 p.m. Postwar, Gonen testified that he was not convinced Marwan was a reliable source and therefore doubted that a war was imminent. Regardless, he adjusted his forces' frontline arrival to the specified 6 p.m., with no flexibility. The late departure from base significantly impacted the war: Finally arriving at the front line, the brigades encountered Egyptian infantry

---

[75] *Duah va'adat agranat, din vehshbon helki nosaf: Hanmakot vehashlamot* (Hebrew), vol. 1, July 1, 1974, pp. 36–45, in The Yom Kippur War Center, Agranat Commission Reports, https://kippur-center.org/document-archive/agrant-files/.

[76] Diary of Chief of Staff's bureau chief, October 6, 1973, in Golan, *Milhama beyom hakippurim*, p. 263.

already entrenched on the Israeli side of the canal. The decision to deploy just before the war's expected outbreak profoundly affected the war's opening conditions.[77]

At 8:05 a.m., Dayan, Galili, Allon, Elazar, and Zeira convened at Meir's office to make decisions about the most pressing issues.[78] Raising the question of the call-up and a preemptive strike only around 9 a.m., Zeira, echoing the US position, stated that, despite the offensive deployment by Egypt and Syria, it appeared that Egypt did not necessarily mean war. Dayan reiterated that a preemptive strike was not feasible, but a parallel one immediately preceding or coinciding with the enemy's assault was. He added that an airstrike was possible on Egypt only if the Egyptians carried out a provocation (e.g., launched a single missile or made a "hair-raising" move) or on Syria if Egypt began a war even if Syria did not.[79] Meir accepted Dayan's political consideration and decided against a preemptive strike at that time, authorizing an airstrike against Syria if Egypt initiated war (she actually left the decision for later in the day pending developments). As for the troop call-up, Elazar convinced Meir to call up four divisions and their support troops, amounting to 100,000–120,000 people.[80] Israel Tal, the Deputy Chief of Staff, began the call-up of two divisions at 9:05 a.m., and the call-up of the remaining troops started at 9:25.[81]

The disagreement over a preemptive strike revolved around two interlinked issues: the potential US response and the effectiveness of such a strike given the weather conditions. The cloud cover that day would have limited the IAF's ability to assist ground troops and to effectively destroy Syrian missile batteries.[82] Dayan, in hindsight, explained his opposition to a preemptive strike on the grounds that it would have been ineffective,[83] but, with no contemporaneous confirmation, it seems that the political consideration was paramount.

Elazar supported a preemptive air strike, despite weather conditions making an attack on the missile batteries impossible. Perhaps he overlooked them or was optimistic that they would change.[84] He ambiguously said that if a preemptive strike was not approved, the IAF would attack "simultaneously with the enemy's

---

[77] From Gonen's testimony to the Agranat Commission; Major General Gonen in an interview with the IDF History Department, in Golan, *Milhama beyom hakippurim*, p. 266.
[78] Erez and Kfir, *Sihot im Moshe Dayan*, p. 88.
[79] Tal and Tal, *Prakim lehilhemet yom hakippurim*, p. 181. Israel Tal wrote that Dayan clearly differentiated between a preemptive and a parallel strike.
[80] Diary of Chief of Staff's bureau chief, October 6, 1973, in Golan, *Milhama beyom hakippurim*, p. 274.
[81] Diary of Chief of Staff's bureau chief, in Golan, *Milhama beyom hakippurim*, p. 275.
[82] See Shimon Golan's essay on the topic: Shimon Golan, "In the Shadow of Surprise: The High Command in the Yom Kippur War" (Hebrew), *Maarakhot* 403 (December 2005), pp. 88–97; and Golan, *Milhama beyom hakippurim*, p. 270, footnote 281.
[83] Dayan, *Avnei derekh*, p. 576.
[84] Golan, *Milhama beyom hakippurim*, p. 271, footnote 283.

attack."[85] Elazar was aware, however, that a war was expected at sundown, when an effective aerial attack would not be possible. Dayan eventually pressed for an immediate decision because, to paraphrase, "we're losing precious time."

Meir chose a diplomatic approach, using the US channel to try to avert war by signaling to the enemy that its intentions were known. At 10 a.m., she met with US Ambassador Keating, notifying him that Israel was aware of Syria and Egypt's plan to attack but would not strike first. Keating maintained that the Arab troop formations seemed defensive, to which Meir asked him to convey to Egypt and the Soviets that Israel would not attack but would retaliate if attacked. The ambassador promised to pass the message on to Kissinger, who, he mentioned, was asleep.[86]

Meanwhile, the General Staff discussed war plans. At 11 a.m., they briefed Dayan about the troops' positions along the southern front and anticipated reinforcements by 6 p.m. Still not realizing the gravity of the situation at the Suez Canal,[87] Dayan, referring to the reserve call-up, asked, "What happens if war doesn't break out?" – meaning that he still believed there was a real chance war would not break out and was therefore concerned about what to do with the reservists who may have been called up in vain.

At this point, the military high command was relatively calm. The standing forces of the IDF were supposed to hold the line until October 8 and then transition to offense once all the reservists were in place, with the IAF attacking concurrently with the enemy's assault. Although AMAN kept receiving data indicating the start of a war, it continued to insist that war was not certain.[88]

At noon, the government gathered, and Dayan informed them of a likely outbreak of war that evening, based on Marwan's intelligence. The Egyptians were expected to try and seize Sharm El Sheikh and the Syrians the Golan Heights. Dayan believed the IDF could counter the Egyptian forces but was concerned about the situation in the north, worrying about Syrian forces reaching Israeli civilian settlements in the Golan Heights. He was confident that the IAF patrols in the north could respond to an earlier attack. He emphasized the importance of targeting Syria first to eliminate its threat and to prevent Jordan or Iraq from joining the war.[89]

---

[85] Golan, *Milhama beyom hakippurim*, p. 271.

[86] From telegram sent to Foreign Minister Abba Eban in New York and Israeli Embassy Minister Mordechai Shalev in Washington, in Golan, *Milhama beyom hakippurim*, pp. 276–277.

[87] For more on the topic, see Elazar's testimony to the History Department, in Golan, *Milhama beyom hakippurim*, p. 281, footnote 306.

[88] Summary of information about the state of preparedness of the Arab nations in AMAN Research and MI Air Force documents, October 1973, in Golan, *Milhama beyom hakippurim*, p. 285.

[89] Cabinet meeting, October 6, 1973 (noon), State Archive, in Golan, *Milhama beyom hakippurim*, p. 286.

War Breaks Out and Starts on the Wrong Footing

At the same time, IAF Commander Peled was informed there would be no preemptive strike; at 1 p.m., he ordered the planes to change their munitions and prepare for defense and to assist the ground troops against the attack expected that evening.[90] To attack the enemy's ground forces from the air (Operation Scratch), the hundreds of concrete-penetrating bombs on dozens of planes for attacking Syrian airfields had to be unloaded and replaced with ordinary bombs. The process required many hours and was still incomplete when, shortly before 2 p.m., the first reports came in of Egyptian and Syrian air-force planes taking to the skies. Peled, afraid his planes would be caught on the ground, ordered most planes into the air, with some intercepting enemy aircraft and others dropping the concrete-penetrating bombs at sea and returning for new ones.[91]

The leadership's confidence in the IAF and ground-defense plans was high. It was assumed there would be enough time to call up reserves even if there was a delay, as regular troops could hold the front until reserves arrived. To understand the gaps between expectations and reality during the war, the "Rock" defense plan needs examination.[92]

Under the Rock plan, three armored divisions and four infantry brigades would oppose Egypt's ten divisions and independent brigades and battalions; on the Golan Heights, two full armored divisions and three independent infantry brigades would face Syria's five divisions and several independent infantry brigades; one armored division and four independent infantry brigades would be deployed along the Jordanian border to face the Jordanian army's three divisions. Despite being outnumbered, even with a full mobilization, it was believed that the IDF's qualitative superiority would prevail.

The full defense plan required a regular division, reinforced with some reserves, for defense from the Suez Canal to 30 kilometers inside Sinai. Two other divisions were meant as backup – one each for the Canal's northern and southern sectors. The Sea Sand operation (Small Dovecote) was to be implemented should the reservists not arrive at all, whereupon Israel would be fighting with four regular brigades only. In the Golan Heights, where there

---

[90] Shmuel Gordon, *30 sha'ot be'oktober: Hahlatot goraliyot – heil ha'avir bit'hilat milhemet yom kippur* (Hebrew), Tel Aviv: Maariv Library, 2008, p. 283.

[91] For more on the confusion and turmoil among the squadrons in the early hours of the war, see the book by Yiftah Spektor, an IAF pilot: Yiftah Spektor, *Ram ubarour* (Hebrew), Tel Aviv: Miskal, Yedioth Books, 2008, pp. 238–244.

[92] The first defense order, issued in 1968, was subsequently updated several times. This chapter is based on the version in place when the Yom Kippur War broke out: General Staff/Operations Division/Operations, Rock Master Plan for the Southern Command, March 1971.

were fewer regular troops, reliance on reserves was greater, even for the Chalk (Full Dovecote) plan.[93]

Implementation issues affected the Southern Command ground forces. Only regular troops fought on October 6, as the first reservists needed at least twenty-four hours to begin arriving. Furthermore, two regular brigades were delayed in central Sinai, so when the Egyptian assault started, Israel had only one regular armored brigade and one augmented infantry battalion of reservists. Conversely, on the Golan, Israeli forces had been reinforced to almost Chalk level – five tank battalions and two infantry battalions.

At 1:55 p.m., reports arrived that enemy airplanes were taking off and heading to Israel, and that camouflage nets were being removed from vehicles. The war had started. Within minutes, heavy Syrian and Egyptian artillery attacks were reported. At the Suez Canal, 2,000 artillery barrels targeted the IDF positions, and 240 aircraft bombed them, with nearly 10,500 shells falling on Israel's troops in the first few minutes. On the Israeli side, 460 soldiers manned some 16 strongpoints, backed by 85 tanks only. After fifteen minutes or so, the first wave of 8,000 Egyptian infantry crossed the Suez Canal on rubber rafts, covered by tanks and antitank missile launchers.

On the morning of the 6th, Elazar had informed his generals that war would begin at 6 p.m. As mentioned previously (p. 315), Gonen ordered two of his tank brigades to not arrive at the front till 5 p.m. to avoid provoking the Egyptians into war.[94] When the two tank brigades finally arrived, thousands of Egyptian soldiers armed with antitank rocket launchers were already waiting for them on the Israeli side of the canal.[95]

Gonen had planned to change details in the tactical plan; however, the onset of war interrupted the process, creating confusion as to which plan to implement. Moreover, there was confusion among the mid-ranking and junior officers about whether the Egyptian offensive was a full-scale assault or another limited incursion. Consequently, evacuation of the strongpoints was delayed, and by the time the order came, doing so was nearly impossible.[96] Only a few managed to retreat, with most either killed or captured. Meanwhile, the tank units suffered many losses attempting to assist the strongpoints.

---

[93] The master plan of the Rock Order 73, Operational Order No. 1, June 1973; Rock Order 73, Northern Command, June 20, 1973; Chalk Order 73, Northern Command, June 8, 1973; Sea Sand Order 73, Northern Command, June 11, 1973.

[94] Bar-Yosef, *Hatsofeh shenirdam*, pp. 360–367; Elhanen Oren, *Toldot milhemet yom hakippurim* (Hebrew), Tel Aviv: IDF – History Department, 2013, pp. 100–113; Reshef, *Lo nehdal!*, p. 94.

[95] Reshef, *Lo nehdal!*, pp. 97–153; el-Husseiny el-Shazly, *Hatziyat hate'ala*.

[96] Amir Reuveni (commander of the 68th Battalion during the war), "The 68th Battalion in the Yom Kippur War: The Decision to Evacuate the Strongpoints" (Hebrew), News1/ Mahlaka Rishona, August 15, 2014, www.news1.co.il/Archive/002-D-95197-00.html; Benny Taran (deputy commander of the 198th Battalion), interview with Eado Hecht (undated); Reshef, *Lo nehdal!*, p. 94.

The IDF began deviating from their initial plan following the first salvos. Dado asked if the IAF could carry out the parallel strike on enemy airfields, unaware that earlier, IAF Commander Peled had decided to change the munition configuration of the planes from an offensive to a defensive one, protecting the nation's skies and assisting the ground troops.[97]

At 2:30 p.m., after the Arab attack had begun, Peled responded that no attack on enemy airfields was possible as IAF planes were still in the midst of the munition change.[98] The cancellation of the preemptive or parallel strike on antiaircraft missile systems and airfields would create a critical problem for the IAF's ability to support the ground troops.[99]

Here, it is important to discuss the issue of the IAF's aerial support for ground troops. The IAF had consistently insisted that it could not aid ground troops for the first two to three days of war as it would be busy establishing aerial superiority. Therefore, even a successful preemptive strike in Syria would not enable the IAF to support ground forces on the Golan Heights immediately. The IAF could only provide sporadic attacks. Until nightfall, most IAF planes would be engaged in a preemptive or parallel strike. In addition, after attacking Syria, the IAF would need to handle the southern situation on the Egyptian front. Thus, ground troops wouldn't receive help even with a preemptive strike. A preemptive strike would have been useful in two ways: First, it could have damaged the morale and confidence of the Arab high command; second, after completing the preemptive strike, the IAF could have turned its full attention to assisting the ground troops. The IAF argued that without achieving aerial superiority, any assistance to the ground forces would have only a limited effect and would have cost many planes. But from the perspective of the ground troops, given the ratio of forces on the ground on October 6, a little air assistance in the critical hours was preferable to a lot later on. This point was not considered by the IDF high command, including Dayan. Technically, responsibility for aerial decisions lay with Elazar and former Chief of Staff Bar-Lev. Neither understood the IAF's tactical requirements, and IAF Commander Peled, in reporting his plans, never properly explained their effect on the ground forces.[100]

At 5:25 p.m., Dayan learned that the situation in the Golan Heights was "all right," despite small Syrian local gains. However, on the southern front, the situation was unclear, obscured by the fog of war.[101] After hearing that the southern situation was worse than in the north, Dayan gave instructions to focus aerial efforts there. Given the changing frontline situation, making

---

[97] Gordon, *30 sha'ot be'oktober*, p. 283.
[98] Golan, *Milhama beyom hakippurim*, p. 307.
[99] For more on the chaotic state of the IAF in the first hours of the war, see Gordon, *30 sha'ot be'oktober*, pp. 281–291.
[100] The author wishes to thank Dr. Eado Hecht for his explanations of this point.
[101] Golan, *Milhama beyom hakippurim*, p. 312.

decisions for the next day was challenging. Despite this, at 6 p.m., Dayan reaffirmed focusing aerial forces in the south due to distress calls from southern soldiers about strongpoints falling and heavy attacks.[102] In consultations later that evening, Dayan again described the situation in the north as relatively stable compared to the south, where it was clear that the enemy was crossing into Israeli-held territory in four separate locations; he reiterated the decision to focus aerial efforts on the southern front.[103] Dayan and Elazar agreed on the IAF's southern focus but disagreed on the main mission. Elazar favored destroying the Egyptian antiaircraft missile array, while the Dayan preferred attacking enemy armored troops and pontoon bridges.[104] Peled sided with Elazar, so the IAF planned to attack the Egyptian antiaircraft missile array at 7 a.m. the next day – Operation Tagar (Challenge).[105] Dayan's perspective suggests that he now understood different air-support options and aimed to alter the IAF's original priorities. At this crucial juncture, Dayan preferred immediate, minimal air support to potential future large-scale aid.

At a 10 p.m. cabinet meeting, it was erroneously reported that enemy forces on the Syrian front were halted, whereas Egypt had some successes in the south.[106] It's important to remember that time would elapse between an event occurring and information about it reaching the senior command ranks. Syrian success in breaking through Israel's defensive line in the Golan Heights started around 8 p.m. By 10 p.m., it was clear that there were some Syrian forces deep in the Golan Heights, but the extent of the breach was unclear to the high command until several hours later. In the south, 90,000 Egyptian soldiers had crossed the Canal. Despite losses, optimism prevailed, including from Dayan.

The October 7 Crisis and the October 8 Crash

The IDF General Staff began realizing the extent of Syrian success around 3 a.m. Dayan asked Peled to provide air support for the Northern Command; Peled responded that only one squadron was available, with all the rest focusing on the south as planned.[107]

---

[102] Conversation between Defense Minister and Major General Gonen, October 6, 1973, 7 p.m., Dayan documents file, in Golan, *Milhama beyom hakippurim*, pp. 326–328.
[103] Diary of Defense Minister's adjutant; Chief of Staff's diary; notes by History Department director, in Golan, *Milhama beyom hakipurim*, p. 329.
[104] Diary of Chief of Staff's bureau chief; diary of Defense Minister's adjutant, in Golan, *Milhama beyom hakippurim*, pp. 344–345.
[105] Diary of Chief of Staff's bureau chief, in Golan, *Milhama beyom hakippurim*, p. 345.
[106] Cabinet meetings, Tel Aviv, October 6, 10 p.m., in Golan, *Milhama beyom hakippurim*, p. 335.
[107] Diary of Chief of Staff's bureau chief, in Golan, *Milhama beyom hakippurim*, p. 351.

Figure 8.1 Minister of Defense Moshe Dayan with General Haim Barlev (center) and General Avraham Adan and General Ariel Sharon (head bandaged): Consultation near the Egyptian front. Source: Photo 12/Contributor/Universal Images Group/Getty Images.

At 5 a.m., Dayan met with Elazar, who reported some improvement on the southern front but a troubling situation in the north.[108] Consequently, Elazar ordered the 146th Division, the last ground reserve, located facing Jordan, to the Golan Heights. This proved to one of Elazar's most important decisions of the war, made moments before Dayan reached the same conclusion.[109] This decision was critical, because, unlike the IAF, which could be quickly redirected, sending the 146th north was nearly irreversible if Jordan joined the war or it was suddenly needed in Sinai. Thus, by October 8, the IDF had three armored divisions on each front.

With the fog of war still thick, Dayan, not confined to headquarters like Elazar, decided to follow his pattern of visiting the front to see the situation for himself, telling Peled that the campaign on both fronts now depended on the IAF (Figure 8.1).[110] At the Northern Command at 6:05 a.m., Dayan issued instructions for preparing defense lines and counterattacks focused on destroying the invading forces. Dayan reportedly found the Northern Command personnel,

---

[108] Diary of Defense Minister's adjutant; diary of Chief of Staff's bureau chief, in Golan, *Milhama beyom hakippurim*, pp. 352–354.

[109] Dairy of Chief of Staff's bureau chief, in Golan, *Milhama beyom hakippurim*, p. 360.

[110] Conversation between Defense Minister and IAF commander before the Defense Minister traveled to the Golan Heights; recordings from the booth of the control center, in Golan, *Milhama beyom hakippurim*, p. 352.

including the commander Hofi, exhausted and pessimistic. The situation was so critical that the Jordan River bridges were prepared for demolition in case of a full IDF retreat from the Golan.[111] Hofi told Dayan that the Golan's southern sector was breached, with reinforcements expected only by midday. With the situation dire, Dayan tried unsuccessfully to contact Elazar. Deciding this was not the time to insist on the chain of command, he told Peled, "Unless there are quartets of fighter jets there by noon ... we'll have lost not only the Golan but also the Jordan Valley."[112] Peled responded by dispatching aircraft north (Map 8.1).

Dayan and the IAF are credited with halting Syria's advance on the southern Golan Heights.[113] The truth seems to be somewhat more complicated. Though the IAF certainly had a positive effect, the Syrians' pause was due more to other factors, including Israeli ground resistance, internal uncertainty, and a lack of coordination among their units, all common phenomena of war.

When Dayan learned the IAF would target the northern sector and that the 146th Division was arriving, he thought the Syrians would be stopped; thus, he saw no need to destroy bridges,[114] telling Hofi, "I'm not in love with the idea of blowing up the bridges, because the tanks will be here within the next couple of hours ... We should instruct the commanders to execute counterattacks and establish blocking regions from which they will not retreat."[115]

Postwar, Dayan was criticized for considering a Golan Heights withdrawal[116] and for urging the IAF to divert planes north, thereby disrupting the southern Operation Challenge.[117] However, based on the above timeline, Dayan's decisions were reasonable and justified, and any pressure on Peled, never mentioned by Peled, is simply a matter of speculation. Dayan never mentioned Operation Challenge or the possibility of canceling it. Around 7 a.m., Elazar consulted with Peled about ongoing fighting plans. The IAF was concluding the first phase of Operation Challenge. Despite Dayan's request for immediate Golan Heights attack missions, Elazar wanted a larger action to

---

[111] Notes of Lieutenant Colonel Lavie, in Golan, *Milhama beyom hakippurim*, p. 359.
[112] Braun, *Moshe Dayan bemilhemet yom hakippurim*, p. 93.
[113] Ibid.
[114] Diary of Defense Minister's adjutant, in Golan, *Milhama beyom hakippurim*, p. 360.
[115] Golan, *Milhama beyom hakippurim*, p. 360.
[116] Zeev Schiff, "On the second day, Dayan considered abandoning the Golan" (Hebrew), *Haaretz*, October 10, 2006. In this article, Schiff quotes the diary of the Northern Command's commander. In a conversation with Shimon Golan, a researcher in the History Department, he said that, based on the sources at his disposal, he knows of no such statement or decision on Dayan's part. Personal communication, July 28, 2020.
[117] See Guy, *Bar-Lev*, p. 240; Bar-Yosef, *Hatsofeh shenirdam*, p. 6. Elsewhere, Bar-Yosef claims that Dayan gave the order to scrap "Challenge," even though no notes or testimonies prove he referred to "Challenge"; he only wanted the assistance of a few planes: Uri Bar-Josef and Rose McDermott, "Personal Functioning under Stress: Accountability and Social Support of Israeli leaders in the Yom Kippur War," *Journal of Conflict Resolution* 52:1 (2008), pp. 144–170.

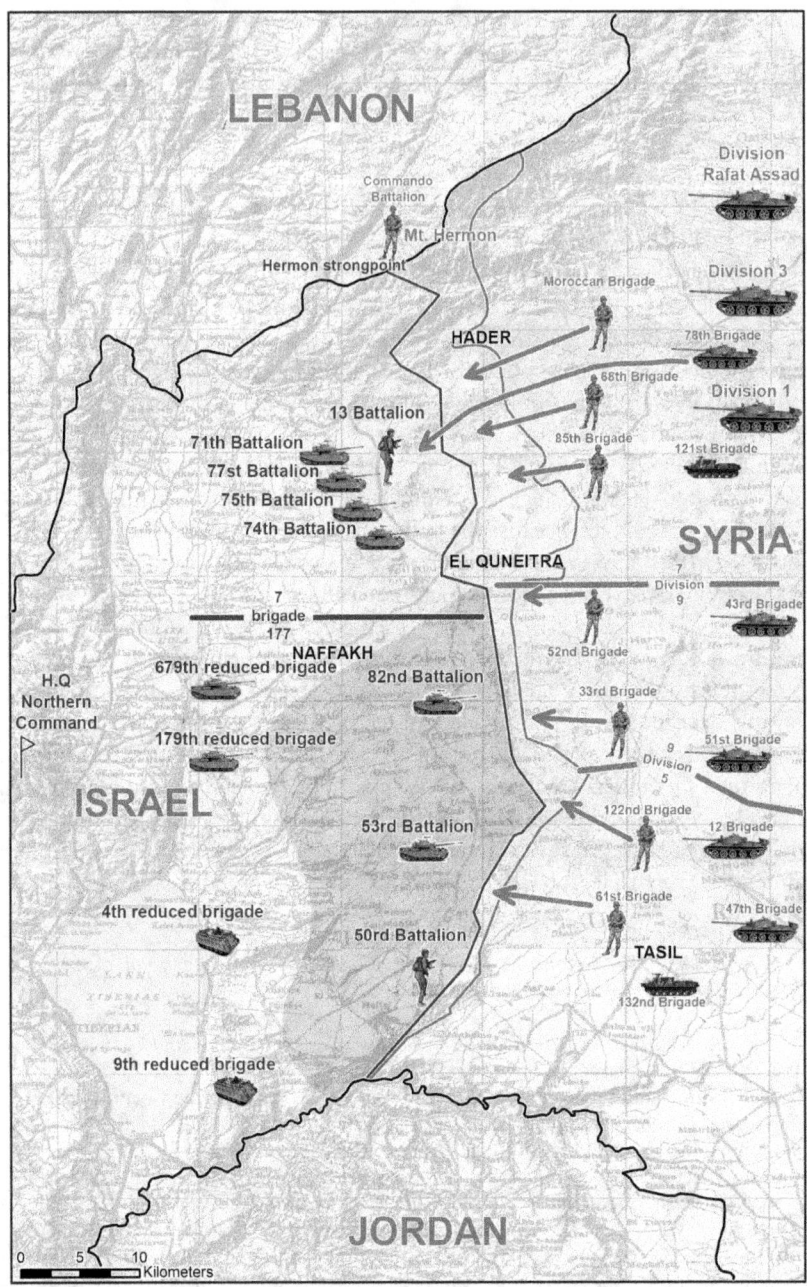

Map 8.1 Yom Kippur War (Oct. 1973): The peak of the Syrian attack on the Golan Heights.

break the Syrian army. Implementing Operation Dogman to attack Syrian antiaircraft missiles in the north meant canceling Operation Challenge in the south. With Dogman needing several hours of preparation, it wouldn't immediately affect the Golan Heights situation. However, under pressure from Elazar, Peled decided to halt Operation Challenge and embark on Operation Dogman by 12 noon.[118] This decision was flawed, an example of a fundamental misunderstanding: Peled explicitly said that Dogman would not stop the Syrian armored troops. Yet he and Elazar decided to focus IAF efforts on Dogman instead of attacking Syrian ground forces advancing in the Golan.

Dayan returned to Tel Aviv from the Northern Command at 8:35 a.m. and shared his findings and actions with Elazar. He believed the IAF would be crucial on both fronts and could halt the Syrian tanks in the Golan Heights. He didn't expect a counteroffensive before October 8.[119] For the south, Dayan advised not to insist on holding fast to the Suez Canal line and strongpoints. "A strongpoint under pressure should be evacuated ... We must not insist forces reach the first-line strongpoints on the canal but rather stabilize the second line."[120] Elazar agreed, already having ordered besieged strongpoints to be abandoned.[121] It was Dayan, accused of abandoning the men in the strongpoints, who received the most criticism for this ostensibly cold-blooded decision. However, this decision was necessary to reduce heavy IDF losses in failed attempts to reach the strongpoints.

Around 9 a.m., Dayan announced he was heading to the Southern Command and asked Elazar to participate in the 10 a.m. cabinet meeting. At 9:25 a.m., reports arrived of Egyptian forces breaching the southern line, urgently requesting air cover. Now the IAF had to split between two fronts, contrary to plans. Elazar redirected the IAF to the south.

Dayan reached the southern front at 11:45 a.m. on October 7 to learn that large Egyptian forces had penetrated several kilometers into Israeli territory and grueling battles were being fought around the strongpoints. At 12:20 p.m., he was informed that Operation Dogman in Syria had failed.[122] By 12:30, Elazar reported that the north was stabilizing with the arrival of reserve tank units, whereas the situation in the south was worsening. Informed that the reserve tank units would begin reaching the southern front in the evening, Dayan instructed the Southern Command to withdraw: "Let us not insist on holding the canal waterline, because the main effort to hold it means a great

---

[118] Recordings from the booth of the control center, in Golan, *Milhama beyom hakippurim*, p. 361.
[119] To clarify: still in the context of defense. There was no talk of an attack to cross the Suez Canal, only to weaken and undermine the Egyptian force that had crossed.
[120] Diary of Defense Minister's adjutant; diary of Chief of Staff's bureau chief, in Golan, *Milhama beyom hakippurim*, p. 368.
[121] Golan, *Milhama beyom hakippurim*.
[122] Recordings from Chief of Staff's office, in Golan, *Milhama beyom hakippurim*, p. 388.

deal of depletion, and the chance of holding it is low."[123] Dayan reportedly told Gonen, "The second thing I insist on is that you establish a new line and not deplete the force on the strongpoints. Talk to Dado about what line – the artillery-road line or some other line." To Gonen's response that it was impossible to hold the artillery-road line, Dayan replied, "My authority is to tell you to hold a line that we can handle, otherwise we'll reach Israel [1967]. Let it be the artillery-road line or the passes. Decide after you see what the IAF can accomplish."[124]

Dayan would later be attacked for this instruction too.[125] However, Dayan's suggestion for a second defensive line matched the General Staff's plan.

Dayan was criticized for claiming the artillery-road line was untenable, a position actually held by Gonen, the local commander, thinking that the reserves would arrive only in the evening. Gonen initially planned to fall back, hoping to hold lateral-road line until the 143rd Division arrived.[126] Those in the room heard the Chief of Staff saying, "The situation is very bad. He [Gonen] has withdrawn to the passes."[127] However, his view changed after Dayan left Southern Command around 1 p.m. Gonen then decided he could

---

[123] Golan, *Milhama beyom hakippurim*, p. 389.

[124] Braun, *Moshe Dayan bemilhemet yom hakippurim*, p. 96. To understand the considerations in these discussions, it is necessary to know the area:

- The artillery-road line was based on the road built parallel to the Canal about 10 km inland behind a chain of low hills, on top of which it was possible to hold good observation positions over the plain leading to the Canal.
- The lateral road was constructed parallel to the Canal about 30 km inland, with several rear camps built along its length. Its major advantage was that Egypt's antiaircraft missiles were incapable of covering any attack from this line without crossing the Canal and redeploying on its east bank, a time-consuming action.
- The passes line: The passes through the mountain chains in the heart of Sinai and through the deep sands of the northern part of the peninsula were about 40 km east of the canal. Passage through these natural barriers – the mountains and the dunes – had been channeled to just a few narrow passes where a small force could stop a much superior force.

The drawback of the lateral road and the line of the passes was the distance to the canal, an area that would require considerable time to regain. The concern was that the IDF would not have time to accomplish this because the superpowers would prevent it by imposing a ceasefire. It is noteworthy that in the discussions about a defense in Sinai in the years before the war, this had been the reason for rejecting Tal and Sharon's proposal to, a priori, plan the fallback to the 30-km line rather than try to stop the Egyptians in battles near the Canal.

[125] Robert Slater, *Warrior Statesman: The Life of Moshe Dayan*, New York: St Martin's Press, 1st ed., 1991, pp. 358–369.

[126] Diary of Chief of Staff's bureau chief; recordings from Chief of Staff's office, in Golan, *Milhama beyom hakippurim*, p. 390.

[127] Recordings from Chief of Staff's office; diary of Chief of Staff's bureau chief, in Golan, *Milhama beyom hakippurim*, p. 390.

hold the artillery-road line, with support from arriving armored units. Gonen added that he was preparing a second line on the lateral road in case he had to fall back.[128] Elazar stressed the need for a solid second defense line rather than depleting the force.[129] Ultimately, Elazar and Dayan reached similar conclusions, their instructions differing because Elazar had received an update before Dayan was informed of Gonen's new assessment.

Historian of the IDF Shimon Golan described the change after 1 p.m. as dramatic:

> Given this information [that reinforcements had arrived] ... the mood of the conversations between the Southern Command commander and the General Staff changed ... Instead of the gloomy reports ... ideas on transitioning to a counteroffensive and even crossing the canal were discussed.[130]

The differing views were reflected in General Staff and government talks that afternoon:

> [Visiting the Southern Command, Dayan] realized the commanders on the ground were sure there was no way to return to the canal waterline and doubted the possibility of stabilizing a line near the artillery-road line. He suggested, instead, stabilizing a line that ... the enemy could not breach ... his visit to the Northern Command in the morning ... had been tough, the commanders pessimistic about ... holding out in the face of the enemy's attack ... He returned to Tel Aviv in the afternoon carrying the burden of the situation on both fronts. By contrast, [Elazar] had not been at the fronts. His impressions were formed [through] telephone conversations ... with the commanders in their command posts and [radio] reports ... rather than via unmediated contact.[131]

Dayan, en route to Tel Aviv by helicopter when the Southern Command's situation assessment changed, was not informed in-flight of this dramatic change of assessment. It is worth noting that Dayan, throughout the war, spent significant time on the ground, often interacting with the IDF commanders in their offices during impromptu visits rather than summoning them to his own. On October 7, Dayan arrived in Tel Aviv at 2:30 p.m. during a discussion between Elazar and his staff officers. Dayan presented a pessimistic assessment, worried that this was an existential war over the land of Israel, he said. Israel's defense doctrine had always stressed a quick decision because of the fundamental asymmetry between the Arab nations and Israel, and Dayan was worried about Israel's ability to sustain

---

[128] Diary of Southern Command's war office, in Golan, *Milhama beyom hakippurim*, p. 394.
[129] Recordings from Chief of Staff's office, in Golan, *Milhama beyom hakippurim*, p. 395.
[130] Golan, *Milhama beyom hakippurim* p. 395, footnote 389. Golan listened to the recordings of the radio communications and could therefore sense the change in the atmosphere.
[131] Ibid., p. 393.

a long campaign. He stressed the need for US aid and for shortening the lines to defend the nation. About the possibility of withdrawing from Sinai, Dayan cautioned that this must be considered, though such a withdrawal was not a foregone conclusion.[132] As for the first-line strongpoints, he advised that troops who could withdraw should do so; the rest would be captured. Regarding the northern front, Dayan said it was necessary to prepare a line that would be held no matter what on the Golan. He also urged preparation for potential conflict with Jordan and with Israel's Arab citizens. After this gloomy assessment, he turned to Elazar, asking him if he disagreed.

Having received updates while Dayan was flying without communications, Elazar agreed operationally but was more optimistic about the northern front's stability and potential counteroffensives at the southern front, where he felt the Egyptian army would be stopped.

Dayan's assessment of the situation was seen as pessimistic, possibly due to his mood after observing difficulties on both fronts. He gave his assessment based on the atmosphere at Southern Command before 1 p.m., while Elazar's report was post-1 p.m., after Dayan had left.[133]

After visiting IDF headquarters, Dayan briefed Meir, leaving Elazar, Major General Tal, Zeira, Major General Rehavam Zeevi (Gandi), Major General Aharon Yariv, and Lieutenant General (res.) Yigael Yadin behind. Zeevi later claimed that Dayan's despair was deeper during his flight back to Tel Aviv, Dayan even alluding to the destruction of the Third Temple (referencing the First and Second Temples in Jerusalem, destroyed by Babylonians in 586 BCE and Romans in 70 CE respectively).[134] But Braun, his aide-de-camp, who was with them, denied hearing Dayan make such statements during that trip.[135] Nevertheless, Dayan admitted, "I don't remember feeling such worry and anxiety at any other point in the past."[136]

After Dayan left, Zeevi defended Dayan's message, telling them, "I don't think that Dayan's situation assessment is pessimistic. I think you're too optimistic. When I came back from the Golan Height, too, I saw overly optimistic [faces]. About Sinai as well." Zeevi explained that Dayan's direct impressions had led him to feel disheartened.[137] Despite proposals for a counteroffensive, Elazar opted to focus on setting up new defensive lines.[138]

---

[132] Recordings in Chief of Staff's office; diary of Chief of Staff's bureau chief; notes of Defense Minister's adjutant, in Golan, *Milhama beyom hakippurim*, p. 407.
[133] Golan, *Milhama beyom hakippurim*, pp. 417–418, footnote 449.
[134] Recordings from Chief of Staff's office, in Golan, *Milhama beyom hakippurim*, p. 411; see also Michael Shahar, *Sichot im Rehavam Ze'evi Ghandi*, Tel Aviv: Yedioth Ahronot, 1992, p. 169.
[135] Braun, *Moshe Dayan bemilhemet yom hakippurim*, p. 98.
[136] Dayan, *Avnei derekh: T'yuta bilti metsunzeret*, p. 61, cited in Golan, *Milhama beyom hakippurim*, p. 411, footnote 432.
[137] Golan, *Milhama beyom hakippurim*, p. 411.
[138] Recordings in Chief of Staff's office, in Golan, *Milhama beyom hakippurim*, p. 412.

At Golda's Kitchen Cabinet meeting, held around 3 p.m., Dayan, still gloomy, again proposed withdrawal to the Sinai passes, believing the Suez Canal line could not be restored – a prediction that proved correct. He also reiterated his fear of Jordan entering the war. Dayan highlighted the discrepancy between earlier optimism and the reality of the Arabs' effective use of antitank and antimissile missiles, neutralizing both the Armored Corps and the IAF.

Despite all this, Dayan believed it was feasible to stabilize a line at the Sinai mountain passes and defend Sharm El Sheikh. He felt a counteroffensive was not advisable, instead suggesting preparation for a prolonged war and potential involvement of more Arab states. Dayan also hedged, conceding, "Perhaps I'm too pessimistic."[139] He was open to a ceasefire but doubted Arab acceptance. Still, he emphasized that "We do not have to initiate a ceasefire, but if one happens, we won't be sorry." Dayan also advised against attacking Syrian infrastructure, saying that a power outage in Syria wouldn't stop a single tank, because "no one dies from [loss of electricity]." He also emphasized preserving Israeli strength for a war of unknown duration. He further believed Israel that could hold the northern front and predicted Jordan would aid Syria rather than open its own front.[140] Dayan was correct on this point as well.

When he concluded his situation assessment, which was rather dismal, Galili asked Elazar to join the meeting to hear his assessment.[141] Galili and the rest of the Kitchen Cabinet, likely stunned by Dayan's dispiriting report, wanted to hear Elazar's opinion.

Elazar presented three southern action plans: withdrawing to the passes; establishing a temporary defensive line near the Canal; or crossing the Suez. He found none ideal and sought to postpone decisions until he could assess the Suez situation personally. Despite recent positive reports, he voiced concerns about the feasibility of the latter two options.[142]

Elazar told the group that he didn't know if Dayan's proposed line was feasible, fearing it could expose the Refidim airbase to artillery fire. Dayan aimed to halt the enemy assault, attack bridges, and stabilize the current line in preparation for a later counteroffensive.[143] Elazar didn't really differ from Dayan but wanted to postpone a decision so that he could travel to the Suez Canal and see the situation for himself, having been somewhat cheered by the most recent reports and Gonen's and Sharon's counteroffensive proposals.

---

[139] Notes of Defense Minister's adjutant, in Golan, *Milhama beyom hakippurim*, p. 415.
[140] Ibid., p. 416.
[141] Golan, *Milhama beyom hakippurim*, p. 417. Golan describes the circumstances of Elazar's invitation to the meeting at Galili's instigation.
[142] The description of the consultation in the Chief of Staff's presence is based on Eli Mizrahi's notes; diary of the Chief of Staff's bureau chief; notes of Defense Minister's adjutant, in Golan, *Milhama beyom hakippurim*, p. 417.
[143] Eli Mizrahi's notes, in Golan, *Milhama beyom hakippurim*, p. 418.

Dayan suggested, "Dado should travel to the southern front, and if he reaches a decision there to attack, I'm for it."[144]

In an afternoon briefing for ex-Chief of Staff Haim Bar-Lev, Dayan reiterated his pessimism about the ongoing war, emphasizing that Israel's forces would diminish while Arab reinforcements increased.[145]

On October 7 at 9 p.m., the government met to discuss the situation. Dayan gave updates about the IDF and enemy losses, and the current situation on the fronts. He pointed out the difficulties the IDF had faced, including the entry of another Syrian division into the Golan and the repair of the Egyptian bridges damaged by the IAF during the night. He reported that the IAF was attacking the bridges and Elazar was exploring counteroffensive options. Meir declared that Israel must not concede territory without negotiations, but that holding a particular line was up to the commanders on the ground.[146]

Elazar reached the Southern Command at 6:45 p.m., following Dayan's recommendation. The commanders there convinced him they could attack. The proposed plan was to destroy Egyptian forces but not return yet to the canal.[147] Elazar agreed that if success was exceptional, they could attempt to cross the canal.[148] Meanwhile, Northern Command too prepared a counterattack. The two attacks were planned for October 8. At 11:42 p.m., Elazar informed Dayan about his decisions for both fronts. He planned offensive action for both, depending on overnight developments and the arrival of troops.[149]

Before starting the assault on October 8, Dayan instructed Elazar to consider what lines the IDF should strive to reach when the UN Security Council decided on a ceasefire. Was it best to form a line beyond the Suez Canal, or to hold the previous line? Dayan was already thinking about the-day-after conditions and was asking Elazar to consider the political significance of the military objectives. Having caught Elazar's optimism, Dayan wanted Elazar to exploit the opportunity to take Port Said and Port Fuad.[150] Elazar had to splash some cold water on Dayan, telling him it was too early to consider such eventualities. "Conceptually ... we're not in disagreement. [But] I have

---

[144] Notes of Defense Minister's adjutant, in Golan, *Milhama beyom hakippurim*, p. 419.
[145] Ibid., p. 423.
[146] Ibid., in Golan, *Milhama beyom hakippurim*, p. 442.
[147] Golan, *Milhama beyom hakippurim*, p. 447.
[148] Notes by Chief of Staff's bureau chief, in Golan, *Milhama beyom hakippurim*, p. 455.
[149] Diary of Chief of Staff's bureau chief, in Golan, *Milhama beyom hakippurim*, p. 446.
[150] Recordings from the Chief of Staff's office; diary of Chief of Staff's bureau chief, in Golan, *Milhama beyom hakippurim*, p. 475. These ports control the northern entrance to the Suez Canal. Dayan wanted to prevent a situation in which the Egyptians held both sides of the canal and then called for a ceasefire. He believed that if Israel seized the ports, it could block the opening to the Mediterranean. However, the axis for reaching the ports is very narrow, meaning a frontal assault was needed. Still, with marshes on one side and the sea controlled by the Israeli Navy, movement along the axis was safe.

a feeling it's too soon."[151] Interestingly, by the time the cabinet met later at 10 a.m., Elazar now supported Dayan and announced his intentions of seizing Port Said when the opportunity arose.[152]

Midday October 8, Elazar began receiving reports of successes in the attacks on both fronts, and a sense of optimism grew.[153] However, reports remained confused and misleading. The fog of battle became near impenetrable after a report was received that an Israeli force of the 162nd Division commanded by Major General Avraham (Bren) Adan had crossed the Suez Canal, a report that was utterly incorrect.[154] In the early afternoon hours, ominous reports of difficulties encountered by the attack in the south came in. However, Elazar's attention that afternoon was on the north. Dayan joined Elazar in his office and suggested a few operational ideas, some of which were accepted.[155] Now Dayan was optimistic about a decision in the north whereas Elazar was uncertain. "I suggest you feel good [about it]," Dayan told Elazar.[156] Dayan wanted to seize strongpoints on the other side of the Canal in the south to serve as bargaining chips should the Security Council impose a ceasefire. "They're occupying a little bit of us, we'll occupy a little bit of them," said Dayan.[157] While Elazar was clearly focused on military achievements, Dayan was already thinking about the political significance after hostilities ended. Within a few hours, it would become clear that both had miscalculated the situation.

That evening, Dayan and Elazar met with the media and presented a hopeful view on transitioning from defense to offense. Elazar's statement at a subsequent press conference would haunt him for years: "We will continue to attack, and we will continue to strike, and we will break their bones. I don't want to commit to how long it will take us."[158]

Soon after midnight between October 8 and 9, Dayan and Elazar arrived at the Southern Command. It was now clear that the October 8 counteroffensive had been a defeat with substantial losses. The meeting at the Southern Command focused on what had gone wrong and future assessments. It was obvious that no canal crossing would happen soon. Summarizing various assessments that had proven incorrect, include the armored corps's and the IAF's abilities, Dayan added, "We have to learn life anew. The Arab nations

[151] Ibid., in Golan, *Milhama beyom hakippurim*, p. 476.
[152] Cabinet meeting, October 8, 1973, 10 a.m.; diary of Chief of Staff's bureau chief, in Golan, *Milhama beyom hakippurim*, p. 481.
[153] Recordings from the Chief of Staff's office, in Golan, *Milhama beyom hakippurim*, p. 489.
[154] Conversation between Major General Zeevi and the Chief of Staff, recordings from the Chief of Staff's office, in Golan, *Milhama beyom hakippurim*, p. 490.
[155] Diary of Chief of Staff's bureau chief; recordings from the Chief of Staff's office, in Golan, *Milhama beyom hakippurim*, p. 501.
[156] Ibid., in Golan, *Milhama beyom hakippurim*, p. 502.
[157] Ibid., in Golan, *Milhama beyom hakippurim*, p. 503.
[158] History Instruction Department, press conference on October 8, 1973, with the Chief of Staff, in Golan, *Milhama beyom hakippurim*, p. 507.

went to war against Israel. They have a lot of power and we have to know there are no magic formulas; things aren't simply going to work out for the best, except by means of a military decision."[159] Dayan now proposed that that the army should focus on the Syrian front first, potentially even bombing Damascus. He suggested that the main effort on October 9 should be in Syria, with the southern front taking a break.

The inevitable question is why the October 8 attack failed. The first reason is that Elazar and Gonen were relying on incorrect intelligence about the Egyptian army's location during planning. Egyptian plans were to advance 8–10 kilometers from the canal by the end of October 7. However, the Egyptians were still arrayed only 3 kilometers away, having encountered fierce IDF resistance and various mishaps. However, Elazar and Gonen, relying on AMAN and Southern Command intelligence, incorrectly believed the Egyptians had reached their intended position, so the Israeli plan attacked empty terrain. Gonen mistakenly thought the lack of resistance meant the Egyptians had fled. Due to this unforeseen development that never was, he decided to transition from attack to pursuit, and to cross the Canal using the Egyptians' own pontoon bridges. The hasty change of direction, Egyptian jamming of Israeli radio communications, and the Egyptians arrayed in good defensive positions rather than retreating resulted in the entire Israeli attack coming down to two separate battalions each attacking an entire Egyptian division and being destroyed. While Adan was ordered to pursue a supposedly retreating enemy, Sharon's division was ordered to abandon its defensive positions and drive quickly south to attack the Egyptian Third Army. Sharon argued that this was irresponsible but finally complied. Halfway south, the division was hurriedly ordered back to find its former positions in Egyptian hands, as Sharon had warned would happen, leading him to lose any respect he had for Gonen and refusing to obey Gonen's orders. This inevitably led to a crisis in the Southern Command. Gonen's eventual dismissal was now a mere formality.[160]

Dead End: From the October 8 Defeat to October 12

On the morning of October 9, the situation worsened suddenly. The IDF had expected to repel the invasion swiftly after the October 7 crisis, but the failure on October 8 caused a rollercoaster of emotions. The unsuccessful counteroffensive

---

[159] Diary of Defense Minister's adjutant; diary of Chief of Staff's bureau chief, in Golan, *Milhama beyom hakippurim*, p. 532.

[160] Based on interview with Dr. Eado Hecht, IDF Command and Staff College, August 2020, Tel Aviv.

on the Egyptian front put the nation in one of the most difficult situations it had known in its twenty-five-year history.

The northern counteroffensive succeeded. On October 10, the Northern Command reported that they controlled the Golan Heights except for Mount Hermon.[161] The decision was made to focus on the Syria and regroup in Sinai. The high command recognized the army's need to reorganize and recharge due to the failure in the south. They feared a UN resolution halting the war at this stage, as well as losing their deterrence, along with the possibility of other nations joining the campaign. The realization that the IDF now lacked options and was unprepared for a long war, as Dayan had feared, was a blow to the high command. They worried that the IDF's omnipotent image was cracking, thus potentially tempting other Arab armies – and possibly even Israel's Arab citizens – to join in the fighting. They also doubted the support of the Europeans, always concerned with Arab oil. Dayan was again proved right, as Western European nations, fearing an oil embargo, did not allow the United States to transfer arms to Israel through them.

Already on October 8, the IDF command was changing its approach, focusing on regrouping and then gradually shifting to focus first on Syria and then Egypt. Some of Dayan's instructions were not to withdraw – "not even an inch" – from the northern front; regarding the south, to clarify what the best line was; and until a defensive line was stabilized, not to engage in any offensive action. Worried about a possible third front with Jordan, Dayan also issued instructions to do everything possible to deter the kingdom from joining the campaign.[162]

Dayan spoke of the need to inform the nation of the truth, even though it would be difficult, warning of a crisis once the truth was known. He raised the possibility of another war of attrition with extended depletion to the point that the IDF would run out of soldiers, making it necessary to enlist and train Israelis below and above recruitment age as well as Jewish volunteers from abroad. Dayan added that if Elazar didn't agree with him about informing the country, it could be discussed in the cabinet, which could decide differently. He noted that the government ministers didn't completely comprehend the severity of the situation. "If everything is clear and there is no argument, we can begin to act in the spirit of what I've said," he concluded.[163]

Although the intelligence services had received information that Egypt intended to conquer only a narrow strip of land to use as political

---

[161] Golan, *Milhama beyom hakippurim*, p. 656.
[162] Dayan in recording from the Chief of Staff's office; diary of Chief of Staff's bureau chief; notes of History Department director, in Golan, *Milhama beyom hakippurim*, p. 539.
[163] Ibid., in Golan, *Milhama beyom hakippurim*, p. 540.

leverage,[164] on October 9 Dayan was worried that war would develop into an intensive war of attrition liable to irreversibly weaken Israel. Perhaps Dayan thought that, despite Egypt's initially limited objectives in the campaign, Egypt and Syria might decide to exploit their vast manpower and matériel advantages and expand the war's objectives, continuing to whittle away at Israel. There is no other way to explain Dayan's concern, especially given that five months previously Dayan described Egypt's war objectives as "leverage for political achievements."[165] "The Arab assumption is not that opening fire will lead to the conquest of Sinai or any significant concrete result," he said on May 15.[166]

Nevertheless, Dayan of October 9 was calmer than Dayan of the October 7 and was more optimistic than some of the people around him. In a briefing provided to Meir shortly after the discussion with Elazar, she asked him how long the IDF could hold the second line in Sinai. Dayan, knowing that the army had already stabilized a line on the Golan Heights and calculating it was possible to do the same on a defensive line at the passes, answered, "Forever."

On October 9, following the failed counteroffensive in the south, it was Elazar who was pessimistic, albeit far less dramatic than Dayan. In a discussion with the high command, Elazar said, "For the IDF, the situation is very bad and difficult."[167] Elazar noted that these conclusions were identical to Dayan's of the preceding day, only Elazar hoped the situation at the Canal could be changed. Operatively, Elazar ordered that Dayan's plan to break Syria first before attacking Egypt be implemented. Elazar accepted Dayan's advice on stabilizing the line in Syria – "Not even an inch back" – and authorized Peled to attack infrastructure targets in Syrian cities in response to Syrian artillery striking Israeli towns and villages.[168]

Dayan proposed exploring all means to remove Syria from the conflict, following encouraging reports indicating Syrian weakening on the Golan Heights. Elazar planned the bombing of strategic targets in Syria, including Damascus, which Dayan authorized. The two of them suggested these steps to Meir in a political-military meeting, with Dayan urging her to bomb Damascus to drive Syria out of the conflict. Meir was worried that bombing Damascus would affect US aid, which had just then entered high gear. "Yesterday, Nixon decided to hand over Phantoms," she said.[169] Finally, they reached a compromise to bomb the

---

[164] Recordings from the Chief of Staff's office, in Golan, *Milhama beyom hakippurim*, p. 520.
[165] General Staff discussion, May 14, 1973, in Golan, *Milhama beyom hakippurim*, p. 33.
[166] Conference of Central Command officers, May 15, 1973, in Golan, *Milhama beyom hakippurim*, p. 34.
[167] Recordings from Chief of Staff's office; diary of Chief of Staff's bureau chief; notes by History Department Director, in Golan, *Milhama beyom hakippurim*, p. 541.
[168] Ibid., in Golan, *Milhama beyom hakippurim*, pp. 542–548.
[169] Political-military consultation, October 9, 1973, 7:30 a.m., in sections cited in the Agranat Commission report; diary of Defense Minister's adjutant; diary of Chief of Staff's bureau chief, in Golan, *Milhama beyom hakippurim*, p. 552.

Syrian General Staff. Afterward, Dayan spoke about the situation on the southern front, explaining that the objective was to stabilize a defensive line along the artillery-road line, provided there was a decision in the north first. Failing that, falling back to the passes was an option. He added, "In the present situation, the artillery-road line should not be evacuated. A second line at the passes should be prepared, but it will be necessary to withdraw there only if the situation grows worse ... Many of our truths have been proven false ... We're facing a new reality and we must prepare to meet it."[170] Elazar said that the IDF had not yet struck with full force and that once it did, it should be possible to cross the Suez Canal, although not before October 10 at night. Dayan made it clear that the objective with Syria was not a ceasefire agreement but to force them to stop the physical fighting.[171] If Syria requested a ceasefire, Egypt would be isolated, making it easier to fight. Dayan and Elazar again applied the strategy they had agreed upon in the morning of October 6: to focus on Syria to try to eliminate it from the fighting.

In the afternoon, positive reports arrived. Dayan received news of successful Damascus attacks, including hits on the Syrian General Staff, air-force command center, and oil and electricity installations.[172]

In a 5 p.m. press conference, Dayan explained Egypt's limited advance into Sinai and expressed faith in Israel's Armored Corps, despite the losses to Egyptian infantry antitank missiles.[173] He and Elazar voiced doubts about Gonen's suitability as the Southern Command leader.[174] Both felt appointing former Chief of Staff Bar-Lev to supervise Gonen was a good idea; neither wanted to dismiss a serving commander in the middle of a war.[175]

On October 9, three IDF divisions held a line near the canal, with the Egyptians deployed along a parallel strip. The Egyptians' attempts to move deeper into Israeli territory were blocked in the evening of October 9. To break the stalemate, Elazar's strategy was to let the Egyptians move past their antiaircraft missile umbrella, giving the IDF a chance to destroy them "Let them break their heads over us," said Elazar.[176] In the north, the IDF regained most territory occupied war, leaving the Syrians, who had taken massive losses,

---

[170] Dayan's statements at the political-military consultation, October 9, 1973, 7:30 a.m., in the Agranat Commission report, in Golan, *Milhama beyom hakippurim*, p. 554.

[171] Dayan's statements at cabinet meeting, October 9, 1973, 10:30 a.m., Prime Minister's bureau in Tel Aviv, in Golan, *Milhama beyom hakippurim*, p. 566.

[172] Recordings from the cell of the control post head at the IAF, in Golan, *Milhama beyom hakippurim*, p. 578.

[173] Defense Minister's meeting with newspaper editors, October 9, 1973, in Golan, *Milhama beyom hakippurim*, p. 584.

[174] Recordings from Chief of Staff's office, in: Golan, *Milhama beyom hakippurim*, p. 598.

[175] Recordings from Chief of Staff's office, in: Golan, *Milhama beyom hakippurim*, pp. 595–602.

[176] Recordings from Chief of Staff's office, in Golan, *Milhama beyom hakippurim*, p. 603.

in control of just a small enclave. After touring the Egyptian front on October 10, Dayan stressed the importance of ending the fight with the IDF on the Egyptian side of the Canal, constantly on the lookout for opportunities to shift troops onto the Egyptian side.[177] Informed by Meir of the Egyptians' lack of interest in a ceasefire, Dayan responded that there was no reason for it, since they had only taken a narrow strip east of the Canal and seemed about to lose Port Said. Dayan asked Meir to try to "get Kissinger to put his [political] stopwatch down," adding, "It would be bad for a ceasefire to be decided on before the IDF repels the enemy forces from the territories they have occupied."[178] Dayan's stance had changed from October 7, when he thought a ceasefire was in Israel's best interest.

At 5 p.m., Dayan met with the Editors' Committee, giving rise to a new myth. An allegedly shattered Dayan spoke about the Third Kingdom being at risk, reportedly making Hannah Zemer, the legendary editor of *Davar*, burst into tears. The truth is that Dayan, who attended the meeting with Peled, reported that the war was difficult, but he was confident that the defensive lines would hold. During the meeting, Dayan did not speak about a Third Temple destruction but comforted Peled, who had just been informed that his son was missing in action after his plane had been downed, saying "Benny, the Third Kingdom is now in your hands." Peled was soon informed that his son had been found alive and well, which is when Zemer burst out crying in relief. Rumors were spreading, and in the public mind, Dayan became firmly associated with a loss of faith in Israel's future.[179]

But in October 10's 7 p.m. conversation, Elazar was gloomy about Israel achieving any significant results beyond what it had already achieved, namely, a stable defense line near the Canal in the vicinity of the artillery road and the expulsion of the Syrians from the Golan Heights. On the phone, he told Bar-Lev, "Were they offering us a ceasefire today – that would be it. I mean, a better outcome than this – I don't see in the near future."[180] To Dayan, he said, "If there is no ceasefire, the most important thing is to make sure the situation doesn't get any worse ... To hold the same line and exhaust them. I don't think I can make [the situation] any better."[181]

---

[177] Dayan during visit to the Southern Command's command room, from diary of Defense Minister's adjutant; diary of Southern Command commander's bureau chief, in Golan, *Milhama beyom hakippurim*, p. 648.

[178] Meeting with the Prime Minister, October 10, 1973, 9:30 a.m., diary of Defense Minister's adjutant, in Golan, *Milhama beyom hakippurim*, p. 639.

[179] For more on this meeting with the editors' committee, see Braun, *Moshe Dayan bemilhemet yom hakippurim*, pp. 136-137, 140-141; Naphtali Lau-Lavie, *Moshe Dayan: A Biography*, London: Valentine Mitchell, 1968, p. 279.

[180] Recordings from the Chief of Staff's office, October 10, 1973, 8 p.m., in Tal and Tal, *Prakim lehilhemet yom hakippurim*, p. 432.

[181] Ibid.

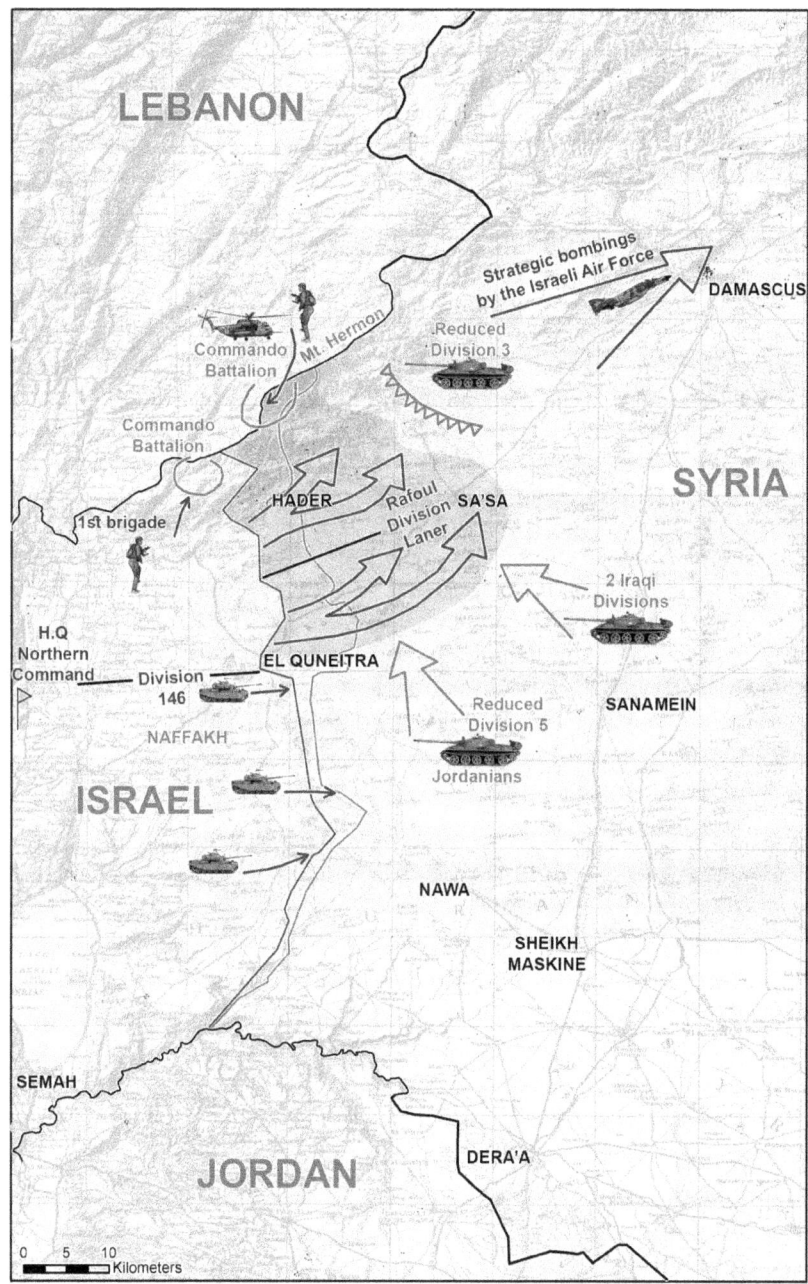

Map 8.2 Yom Kippur War (Oct. 1973): The IDF enclave in Syrian territory.

Dayan rejected Elazar's assessment, convinced Israel could improve its position by capturing Port Said and exhausting the Egyptian army, despite Egypt's taking of the Bar-Lev Line.[182] During the day, Elazar presented various scenarios, reaching an unequivocal conclusion: "The war must be stopped."[183] He felt the right thing to do was to threaten Damascus and perhaps even conquer it, thereby forcing Egypt too to lay down its arms. His deputy, Israel Tal, disagreed, fearing it would only drag Jordan and Iraq deeper into the fight (both countries sent forces to the Golan); Egypt, he said, doesn't care about Syria to begin with. In this, he and Dayan were in agreement.[184]

On October 11, Elazar, lacking creative idea to alter the course of the campaign, considered a major assault on Syria as the only option for restoring Israel's deterrence and the IDF's image. Early that day, IDF forces and the IAF attacked Syria, advancing 10 kilometers deep before facing strong resistance from Syrian, Iraqi, and Jordanian forces. They managed to fire twenty shells at Damascus airport on October 13, creating the impression – at least temporarily – that they were within artillery range of Syria's capital city (Map 8.2). Meanwhile, IDF forces in Sinai regrouped.[185] Reports of a possible ceasefire agreement started coming in, and the possibility of crossing the canal was considered.

On October 12, Elazar predicted that IDF successes would peak by the 14th, after which Israel's position could only worsen. Elazar's decision was influenced by Peled's warning about the air force approaching its red line in terms of functional planes.[186] This, however, was a ploy by Peled to persuade Elazar to order the crossing of the Canal. Instead, it made Elazar more determined to end the war.[187]

---

[182] Ibid.
[183] Recordings from Chief of Staff's office, October 10, 1973, 8:40 p.m., in Tal and Tal, *Prakim lehilhemet yom hakippurim*, p. 435.
[184] Tal and Tal, *Prakim lehilhemet yom hakippurim*, pp. 438–439.
[185] Golan, *Milhama beyom hakippurim*, pp. 724–726.
[186] Discussion with the Defense Minister's participation about the canal crossing, October 12, 1973, 12 noon, diary of Chief of Staff's bureau chief; notes by Defense Minister's adjutant, in: Golan, *Milhama beyom hakippurim*, p. 778.
[187] Tal and Tal, *Prakim lehilhemet yom hakippurim*, p. 864.

9

The Turning Point

A Dead End

On the morning of October 12, Israel faced a predicament. On the one hand, the existential danger had passed, Israel having stabilized the line in Sinai and repelled the Syrian forces on the Golan Heights. On the other hand, in the north, the IDF's advance in Syria had been halted by Iraqi and Jordanian reinforcements, while in the south, Egyptian troops still occupied a strip on the Israeli side of the Canal. Ending the war this way would be considered a defeat for Israel. Moreover, there was no certainty of a ceasefire: Given Egypt and Syria's superior manpower and their Soviet backing and arms, they could continue a long war of attrition that would eventually weaken Israel's position. Israel's leaders sought a ruse or move to force one of them to lay down their arms, allowing the IDF to concentrate on a single enemy. Dayan hoped that the threat of artillery aimed at Damascus would make Syria seek a ceasefire. It did not. Crossing the Canal to reach Egypt's rear was too risky, as the Egyptians could encircle and destroy the Israeli force.

Dayan and Elazar had fundamental disagreements about the next move. Elazar, insistent on achieving a ceasefire by October 14, fearing attrition in men and matériel, wanted to consider crossing the Suez if the political echelon agreed. Dayan supported such a move only if it was absolutely necessary militarily but did not want to link it with a ceasefire, about which only the government could decide. He was clearly marking the boundaries of Elazar's authority: You'll see to the military's successes, and we'll see to the political decisions.

While not certain that crossing the Canal would lead to a ceasefire by October 14, Elazar felt this was the only available option and presented it at a meeting of Meir's Kitchen Cabinet.[1] Elazar and other officers briefed Dayan on the situation. Dayan, concluding that action should be taken quickly, and that Israel should not end the war at the current lines, agreed to bring the plan before the full cabinet.[2]

---

[1] Shimon Golan, *Milhama beyom hakippurim: Kabalat hahahlatot bapikud haelyon bemilhamat yom hakippurim* (Hebrew), Ben Shemen: Maarakhot and Modan, 2013, p. 766.
[2] Recordings from the Chief of Staff's office, in Golan, *Milhama beyom hakippurim*, p. 775.

Discussing the risks inherent in crossing, Dayan expressed doubts about its strategic benefits, given the risks involved. Conceding that he had not fully studied the move, he repeated that it wasn't clear how it could improve Israel's situation. For him, Israel's most pressing challenge was conserving strength for the future, along with the months it would take to integrate and train on the new US weapons being delivered. After reconsidering, Dayan decided against the crossing.

Dayan concluded the debate saying he had to study the subject:

> I want to go there [the southern front] to learn ... If Dado and Bar-Lev [the military] say it will provide a radical solution, I'll vote in favor of it. [But] it's not certain it will be the case, politically speaking. As a military man, I have to study it; as a minister, I trust the army, but I'm not sure it will be possible to translate the military success into a political one.[3]

At that point, Dayan felt a crossing might help relieve the military situation operationally, but it would not change the war's political outcome or, even if operational benefit was possible, it should not be done, given that it might not lead to a ceasefire but, paradoxically, might even extend the fighting with Egypt.[4]

Thus, for Dayan, the situation at the Suez Canal remained unchanged for now.[5]

The Decision to Cross the Canal

The government was still relying on October 11 and 12 reports of significant IDF progress on the Syrian front and preparations for a counterattack on the Egyptian front. It hoped to delay the ceasefire the UN Security Council was now discussing. The United States had announced that diplomatic moves would begin when the Security Council met on the night of October 13–14, Israel time.[6] Israel's major concern was US assistance, specifically, the delivery by US pilots of Phantom airplanes.

The Kitchen Cabinet met on October 12 at 2:30 p.m. due to Peled's warning that the IAF was approaching the red line of 210 aircraft. The main question: Should the IDF wait for the Egyptians to move first or take the initiative? Elazar stressed that a ceasefire should be reached by October 14 and crossing the Canal could be vital in achieving that. Repeating his considerations for and against crossing, Elazar asked for the political echelon's input. Meir reported

---

[3] Golan, *Milhama beyom hakippurim*, p. 778.
[4] Recordings from the Chief of Staff's office, in Golan, *Milhama beyom hakippurim*, p. 781.
[5] A note Dayan passed to the Chief of Staff during the debate, in Golan, *Milhama beyom hakippurim*, p. 780.
[6] Telegram from Dinitz to Gazit, October 12, 1973, in Golan, *Milhama beyom hakippurim*, p. 783.

that the Security Council would discuss this on October 14, but there was no certainty about it leading to a ceasefire, given the uncertainty about the Soviets' influence on Syria and the Arabs' ambitions.

Bar-Lev presented the IDF's alternatives: withdraw to the passes deep in Sinai; hold the current position; or cross the Canal. To Bar-Lev's argument that crossing the Canal could cut off the two Egyptian armies east of the Canal and destabilize their equilibrium, Peled replied that crossing would cause massive damage to the antiaircraft missile batteries on the Egyptian side. Deputy Chief of Staff Israel Tal objected, finding the crossing too risky.

Amid the discussion, two game-changing pieces of news arrived. The first was that the IDF was within firing range of Damascus.[7] The other even more dramatic, albeit much anticipated report,[8] from the Mossad was that the Egyptians were preparing a large-scale offensive aimed at the Sinai mountain passes. The two swords hovering over Israel – a possible Security Council ceasefire and the IAF approaching its red line, both on October 14 – now posed less immediate danger.

Meir explained: "I understand that Tsvika [Mossad Director Tsvi Zamir] has ended this discussion."[9] Everyone realized that they needed to wait for the Egyptian armored divisions to show up, then destroy them and cross the Canal. Dayan suggested telling Kissinger as a ruse that Israel would support a ceasefire, assuming that Egypt would oppose a proposed ceasefire before the Security Council discussion. Thus, Dayan agreed not to the substance of the proposal, but to the process, which would take time that would work to Israel's advantage, and which would make Israel not look like the intransigent side.[10] Dayan was now optimistic about the IDF's ability to overcome the Egyptian forces. The government agreed with Dayan that it was best now to declare that Israel would not oppose a ceasefire and earn much-needed diplomatic points.[11]

The announcement alarmed Kissinger, who mistakenly believed Israeli wanted a ceasefire because it was in deep trouble. But neither he nor Israel's US Ambassador, Simcha Dinitz, nor Foreign Minister Abba Eban, knew that in reality Israel, anticipating a reversal, had expressed its willingness for a ceasefire knowing the other side would refuse.[12]

That same day, October 12, Dayan traveled to the Southern Command headquarters in the evening to assess the situation, telling the senior

---

[7] Military-political consultation, Tel Aviv, October 12, 1973, 2:30 p.m., in Golan, *Milhama beyom hakippurim*, pp. 785-797.

[8] Uri Bar-Yosef, *H'amalach: Ashraf Marwan, hamossad vhaftat yom hakippurim* (Hebrew), Or Yehuda: Kineret Zmorah Dvir, 2011, p. 270.

[9] Military-political consultation, in Golan, *Milhama beyom hakippurim*, p. 792.

[10] Ibid., p. 802.

[11] Ibid., p. 899.

[12] From an interview Henry Kissinger granted historians Uri Bar-Yosef and Ronen Bergman on February 9, 2019, it seems that he never became aware that the Israeli request

commanders that since they were there on the ground, he trusted their judgments and would present their recommendations to the government.[13] Dayan emphasized that there was nothing sacred about any one place: "The desert is yours. Wage war the way you think is right."[14]

Later that night, Dayan reported to the Kitchen Cabinet that he had told the commanders in the south that if they supported the crossing, the government would too. Allon had reservations, so Dayan suggested that Elazar focus his attention on studying a crossing's operational aspects.[15]

On October 13, Israel learned that that President Nixon had instructed Secretary of Defense James Schlesinger to cover Israel's equipment shortages. Schlesinger announced that by midnight, Israel would have ten new Phantoms and that dozens of transport planes would arrive in the country within a few days. Operation Nickel Grass, a US weapons and ammunition airlift to Israel, began late on the night of October 13. Nixon had agreed to it, realizing that arming Israel was the only way to apply pressure on Egypt to agree to a ceasefire,[16] although it would strain US–USSR relations. Kissinger warned the Soviets against intervening; the Soviets told him to warn Israel not to capture Damascus.[17]

On October 13 at 5 p.m., Dayan met to discuss IAF policy and raids into Egyptian territory. Stating that, "We are hemorrhaging," he wanted to focus only on actions supporting the main campaign objectives and forgo those of just tactical value.[18] He thus made an important distinction between high-risk actions of limited tactical value and actions affecting the campaign as a whole. Dayan traveled to the north to study the possibility of another Israeli advance closer to Damascus and found the Israeli troops on the Syrian front exhausted. On October 13, news that Egypt had rejected the ceasefire arrived, confirming Dayan's hunch.[19]

---

he received about not delaying a Security Council resolution was nothing but a ruse on Dayan's part. Kissinger is still convinced that Israel said what it said because it was in trouble. See interview by the Yom Kippur War Center, https://bit.ly/3v6v4Cp.

[13] Notes by the Defense Minister's adjutant, meeting with the Southern Command staff in the situation room, October 12, 1973, 9 p.m., in Golan, *Milhama beyom hakippurim*, p. 812.

[14] Ibid., in Golan, *Milhama beyom hakippurim*, pp. 812-813.

[15] Notes by the Defense Minister's adjutant, October 12, 1973, 11:45 p.m., in Golan, *Milhama beyom hakippurim*, p. 817.

[16] Golan, *Milhama beyom hakippurim*, p. 840, footnote 199.

[17] Telegram from Shalev to Gazit, October 12, 9:20 p.m., in Golan, *Milhama beyom hakippurim*, p. 815; Henry Kissinger, *Crisis: The Anatomy of Two Major Foreign Policy Crises*, Hebrew translation, Jerusalem: Shalem Center, 2014, p. 162.

[18] Discussion about IAF actions, Defense Minister's bureau, the Kirya, October 13, 1973, in Golan, *Milhama beyom hakippurim*, p. 845.

[19] Golan, *Milhama beyom hakippurim*, p. 871.

At 6:30 a.m. on October 14, the Egyptians' armored divisions attacked.[20] During the morning, positive reports began arriving about the battle on the southern front. The cabinet that morning discussed the IDF's defensive successes; they also received good news that the US airlift had started, with fourteen to sixteen Phantoms fighter jets expected to arrive the next day.

Meanwhile in the south, of the approximately 2,000 tanks available to the Egyptian army, around 850 belonging to the reinforced infantry divisions had initially crossed the Canal, of which 300–350 had been destroyed. The Mossad report suggested another 750 tanks, belonging to the armored and mechanized divisions were crossing too – leaving approximately 350 tanks on the west bank of the Canal. In fact, at most perhaps 450 crossed and participated in the attack, so that there were more than 700 tanks left behind on the Egyptian side. The failed attack on October 14 cost the Egyptians about 200 more tanks, so they still had about 800 tanks on the Israeli side of the Canal.

Still, this was the scenario Israel had wanted, as with the major Egyptian force moving to the Israeli bank, the IDF could cross to the relatively sparsely defended Egyptian side.

Dayan missed the cabinet meeting to visit the Southern Command, where Bar-Lev told him, "The Egyptians are coming back to themselves and we're coming back to ourselves."[21] At noon, Dayan and Tal went to Sharon's command room, where Sharon, reporting that a large part of the enemy's force had been destroyed, felt now was the time for a canal crossing. While Tal wanted to wait for the Egyptian army to be drawn deeper into the Sinai Peninsula, Israel decided to start the crossing between October 15 and 16.[22] True to form, Dayan gave the commanders a political overview, explaining that with the Arabs not interested in a ceasefire, there was no choice but to engage in a two-front offensive.[23]

From Sharon's 143rd Division, Dayan continued to the 252nd division headquarters before returning to the Southern Command for updates.[24] In the face of disagreements with his officers over whether the attack on the 14th would be the anticipated large offensive or merely a preliminary strike, Dayan declared: "But none of this really matters. What does matter is that all the commanders are united in thinking that if developments

---

[20] Recordings from Chief of Staff's office; diary of the bureau chief of the Southern Command commander, Major General Gonen, in Golan, *Milhama beyom hakippurim*, p. 860.
[21] Diary of Defense Minister's adjutant; notes of the History Department director, in Golan, *Milhama beyom hakippurim*, p. 867.
[22] Golan, *Milhama beyom hakippurim*, p. 871.
[23] Diary of Defense Minister's adjutant; notes of the History Department director, in Golan, *Milhama beyom hakippurim*, p. 872.
[24] Diary of Defense Minister's adjutant, in Golan, *Milhama beyom hakippurim*, p. 873.

tomorrow are like the developments of today, then the crossing should take place the next night."[25]

Returning to Tel Aviv, Dayan told Elazar at 5 p.m. that regardless of whether the IDF's northern troops were "tired or not," there was no justification for not taking the offense.[26] He told Elazar that, in contrast, the Southern Command was full of fighting spirit and that he was wholeheartedly in favor of crossing the Canal.[27] It seemed that a change for the better was finally happening.

That evening, at 9:00 p.m., the cabinet voted on crossing the Canal. Dayan said that after the IDF seized Egyptian territory, the western bank of the Canal could be left in Israel's hands as a bargaining chip in future political talks. Clearly, Dayan was distinguishing between occupying land for operational ends and holding it for political needs. Dayan stressed the need for compelling Egypt to agree to a ceasefire, especially as Syria had refused. Following the support of Dayan and Elazar, the cabinet voted to authorize the crossing despite the great risks.[28]

Crossing the Canal and Encircling the Third Army

The IDF operation to cross the Suez Canal, Abirey Halev (Knights of the Heart), began in the evening of October 15. Earlier, on the 9th, the 87th Reconnaissance Battalion had identified an open space between the Egyptian Second and Third Armies along the eastern shores of the Great Bitter Lake, providing a pathway to the Canal without engaging in a breakthrough battle.

Dayan and Elazar arrived at the Southern Command shortly before the scheduled 5:45 p.m. crossing to monitor the situation, which was problematic from the start, especially in terms of transporting the necessary matériel. Dayan spoke with Sharon several times, asking him for updates.[29] Sharon's division, along with the Southern Command's engineering forces, were to assist the paratroopers and tanks from the 421st Brigade to cross north of the Great Bitter Lake. On October 16 at 1:30 a.m., the paratroopers reported they were in control of the opposite bank. The tanks started crossing the canal on the rafts and Amphibious Tank Carrier (ATC) Gillois Type I at 6:30 in the morning.

---

[25] Diary of Defense Minister's adjutant; diary of the bureau chief of the Southern Command commander; notes of the History Department director, in Golan, *Milhama beyom hakippurim*, p. 876.

[26] Recordings from Chief of Staff's office, in Golan, *Milhama beyom hakippurim*, p. 879.

[27] Recordings from Chief of Staff's office, in Golan, *Milhama beyom hakippurim*, pp. 879-880.

[28] Cabinet meeting, October 14, 1973, 9 p.m., Prime Minister's bureau in Tel Aviv, in Golan, *Milhama beyom hakippurim*, pp. 891-898.

[29] Notes by Lieutenant Colonel Zohar; diary of Defense Minister's adjutant, in Golan, *Milhama beyom hakippurim*, p. 932.

Meanwhile, in Syria that day, the IDF had successfully confronted a joint Jordanian–Iraqi–Syrian force, destroying sixty tanks, twenty-five of them Jordanian. Dayan asked that the Jordanian participation in the battle not be publicized, assuming, correctly as it turned out, that this would be Jordan's sole contribution to the war effort.[30]

Dayan left the front that night to get an update from Elazar. Dayan distinguished between three issues: (1) opening a corridor to the Canal, noting the difficult topography and suggesting that the IAF and not the paratroopers engage there; (2) stopping enemy attacks on the corridor where a fierce, uncertain battle was still raging; and (3) securing the bridgehead on the Canal's western bank, which Dayan thought possible if a route was secured.[31] Dayan was angry that Meir's earlier Knesset announcement of the IDF having crossed the Canal exposed these troops to danger. The Egyptians had not yet understood what was happening, and he was worried that the situation was still precarious and that they would now need to stop the crossing because the Egyptians would react.[32]

Once alone, Elazar asked Dayan what to do about Sharon, the subject of bitter complaints from Bar-Lev and Gonen. "Right now, nothing," Dayan answered; he then noted media rumors that Elazar wasn't functioning well. Dayan, experienced in media management, suggested that Elazar speak with reporters from the front.[33] Over the next few hours, reports arrived that the 35th Paratrooper Brigade and armored troops had fought a bloody battle at night near the so-called Chinese Farm, while the 162nd Division had continued crossing the Canal.

By October 17, the situation looked less grim when Elazar arrived at Sharon's command center in the morning. The commanders discussed securing the existing bridges and forces, and ways to deliver supplies and further reinforcements to the other side. Dayan and Sharon wanted to move as many tank troops as possible.[34] Dayan crossed the canal on a Gillois ATC to visit the troops at 3 p.m.[35] and reported upon his return at 5:30 p.m. that as of 4 p.m., a bridge was ready for tanks, exhorting them: "Every unused moment is a loss."[36] Dayan saw that an opportunity to break the Egyptian forces had presented itself, as the Israeli forces could advance rapidly south. This was in addition to his having learned that the Egyptian high command was in mayhem and that Sadat had taken control and had ordered troops to launch

[30] Diary of Defense Minister's adjutant, in Golan, *Milhama beyom hakippurim*, p. 940.
[31] Recordings from Chief of Staff's office, in Golan, *Milhama beyom hakippurim*, p. 958.
[32] Recordings from Chief of Staff's office, in Golan, *Milhama beyom hakippurim*, p. 960.
[33] Ibid., p. 961.
[34] Notes by Defense Minister's adjutant, in Golan, *Milhama beyom hakippurim*, pp. 982-983.
[35] Golan, *Milhama beyom hakippurim*, p. 984.
[36] Diary of Defense Minister's adjutant, in Golan, *Milhama beyom hakippurim*, p. 986.

an assault east of the Canal to prevent the Israelis from crossing. The IDF's assessment was that the Egyptian situation would not allow them to carry out such a full-scale attack.[37]

Meeting with Meir at 9:15 p.m., Dayan told her, "I feel that the next two days will be decisive in the war with Egypt and in the war in general."[38] Thus, five days after the Syrian and Egyptian armies shocked Israel unawares, Israel shifted the war into Syria and four days later into Egypt. Now the IDF concentrated its offensive efforts on destroying Egyptian forces in that region.

Meanwhile, the United States and the Soviets tried to renew their ceasefire efforts. On the 17th, it was confirmed that Soviet Prime Minister Alexei Kosygin had arrived in Cairo with a proposal, with the Soviets hoping for a ceasefire that moved the rival forces on the basis of Resolution 242, the 1967 border. Shortly after midnight between the 17th and 18th, Dinitz reported that he had told Kissinger that Dayan, back from a visit to the Suez Canal, wanted Kissinger to know that Israel's situation there was good.[39] On October 18, Dayan received word that more Israeli forces had crossed and advanced along the Canal's western bank. In the morning, he returned to the Southern Command and instructed the commanders to feign an advance on Cairo so that the Egyptians would pull forces back to defend their capital. Rather than moving the 252nd Division, the only division still on the Israeli side of the canal, and weakening the position, he suggested shifting troops from Ras Sudar to the western side, believing there was no threat of an Egyptian assault in that region. He also suggested speaking about the issue with Elazar.[40] At that point, Israel already had 250 or so IDF tanks on the Egyptian side of the canal, the plan being to move another 150, leaving about 250 on the Israeli side facing approximately 650 Egyptian tanks.[41] Now, they needed to decide how far the Israeli troops should penetrate and prepare for the coming ceasefire. Before returning to Tel Aviv, Dayan asked, "Now what? We're at the point where we have to ask ourselves how we end this thing."[42]

At 10 a.m., Dayan and Sharon crossed the canal and met with the paratroopers, and Dayan then traveled to the 162nd Division's command headquarters (Figure 9.1). Dayan later accompanied Sharon to a strategic area that controlled the main road to the canal, named the Chinese Farm. There, he met

---

[37] Diary of the bureau chief of the Southern Command's commander, in Golan, *Milhama beyom hakippurim*, p. 988.

[38] Meeting with Prime Minister, October 17, 1973, Defense Minister's bureau, in Golan, *Milhama beyom hakippurim*, p. 990.

[39] Telegram from Dinitz to Gazit, October 17, 1973, 6:45 p.m., in Golan, *Milhama beyom hakippurim*, p. 1028.

[40] Diary of Defense Minister's adjutant, in Golan, *Milhama beyom hakippurim*, p. 1006.

[41] Debate of heads of directorates, situation assessment, October 18, 1973, in Golan, *Milhama beyom hakippurim*, p. 1012.

[42] Golan, *Milhama beyom hakippurim*, p. 1015.

Figure 9.1 Minister of Defense Moshe Dayan and General Ariel Sharon next to the Suez Canal, October 1973. Source: Bettmann/Contributor/Bettmann/Getty Images.

with Amnon Reshef, the commanding officer of the 14th Brigade, which had fought continuously from the first day of the war. Reshef told Dayan about the fierce battles his brigade had fought in the last several days to ensure access to the bridgehead. Dayan instructed Reshef and the division commander: "You have the mandate to speed ahead. Blow them away! And don't ask anyone, because you have the mandate to push north."[43] Then, Dayan returned to the Southern Command, where he issued further instructions. Still worried about attrition rates, he asked the commanders to do everything to prevent losses. Dayan added that he had issued similar instructions to the division commanders.

When the government met at 9 p.m., Elazar reported on significant enemy losses but noted that the Egyptian army had not reached its breaking point and there was no sign that Egypt wanted a ceasefire. Dayan stressed the IDF's attrition rate and the unknown duration of the fighting. The reports on the political front remained unclear.[44] Kissinger reported that he expected talks would resume about the Soviet ceasefire proposal once Kosygin returned from Cairo and promised that he would stall to gain time.

In the morning of October 19, IDF troops on the Egyptian bank of the canal renewed their momentum. Dayan was pleased that the commands to the 143rd

---

[43] Diary of Defense Minister's adjutant, in Golan, *Milhama beyom hakippurim*, p. 1021.
[44] Cabinet meeting, October 18, 1973, 9 p.m., in Golan, *Milhama beyom hakippurim*, pp. 1032-1034.

Division to move north accorded with his proposal.[45] Dayan gave Elazar suggestions for reducing losses, especially losses resulting from shelling on the Israeli bridges over the Canal. These included preparing several locations for the arrival of supplies in order to disperse the now-concentrated forces and push the enemy's artillery back to reduce its accuracy.[46] He also suggested that the IAF should avoid areas protected by antiaircraft missiles at this stage, not assisting ground troops west of the Canal.[47]

Dayan posed the army's current dilemma: Where next? The options were attacking along the Canal or deeper into Egypt toward Cairo. Dayan thought that the current northward advance along the canal – threatening to encircle the Second Army, threatening Cairo, encircling the Third Army, and controlling the Suez-Cairo Road – met Israel's needs.[48]

Toward a Ceasefire

Dayan then met with Meir at 10 a.m. She told him of the first signs of political pressure to accept a ceasefire, reflecting Israel's improved military position.[49] They deliberated on the optimal lines for the army, for both a ceasefire and a possible resumption of hostilities. Dayan preferred the Canal line, assessing that going into a country of thirty-seven million inhabitants was like "sitting on top of an open fire."[50] He added that the IDF command had accepted his approach of moving the 162nd Division south toward the Suez–Cairo axis, seizing control of the Egyptian bank, and creating a line that could be optimal for a ceasefire when the fighting stopped.[51] Dayan mentioned that he still did not understand why the Bar-Lev Line had failed in the first days or why the 300 tanks were not in position when war broke out.[52] At 2:55 p.m., Dayan instructed the Southern Command that the primary goal was controlling the entire length of the Canal's western side.[53]

That night of October 18–19, the Soviets submitted a draft ceasefire proposal leaving the troops where they were, demanding that Israel immediately retreat

---

[45] Golan, *Milhama beyom hakippurim*, p. 1,041.
[46] Operational discussion, Defense Minister's bureau, the Kirya, October 19, 1973; diary of Chief of Staff's bureau director, in Golan, *Milhama beyom hakippurim*, p. 1042.
[47] Ibid., p. 1044.
[48] Ibid., p. 1045.
[49] Meeting between Defense Minister and Prime Minister October 19, 1973, 10 a.m., in Golan, *Milhama beyom hakippurim*, p. 1050.
[50] Ibid., in Golan, *Milhama beyom hakippurim*, p. 1050.
[51] Ibid., in Golan, *Milhama beyom hakippurim*, p. 1051.
[52] Ibid., in Golan, *Milhama beyom hakippurim*, p. 1052.
[53] Telephone conversation between the Defense Minister and Chief of Staff from the IAF Pit to the Southern Command Center, October 19, 1973, 4:55 p.m.; notes by Gabi Cohen; diary of Defense Minister's adjutant, in Golan, *Milhama beyom hakippurim*, p. 1056.

to the 242 line. Kissinger informed Israel that he would not agree and would stall for time.[54]

On October 20, Kissinger announced he was traveling to Moscow, giving Israel a forty-eight-hour extension.[55] Dayan had again gone to the Southern Command and updated the commanders about the political developments, predicting the war's end by October 23 (which turned out to be fairly accurate). He now wanted them to achieve the already-established goal of seizing control of the full length of the Egyptian side of the Suez Canal within two days.[56]

In the afternoon, after touring three divisions, Dayan reported to Bar-Lev and Gonen that Adan's division had already destroyed fourteen antiaircraft missile batteries. Dayan instructed the 162nd Division to focus on destroying these to enable the IAF to support the ground forces. Moreover, to fire from the Egyptian side of the Canal at the Third Army units on the Israeli side would have political, military, and psychological effects "important for everyone – the Jews, Kissinger, everyone."[57]

In the evening, Dayan authorized limited offensive actions by the Northern Command[58] and attended a cabinet meeting discussing progress in the south, where the IDF had taken an enclave in Egyptian territory 60 kilometers wide and 20–30 kilometers deep. There were signs Egyptian forces were weakening. The government started working on Israel's ceasefire conditions and announced its willingness to discuss its ceasefire terms. Dayan suggested making the ceasefire contingent on Egypt lifting the naval blockade on the Bab al-Mandab Straits controlling Israel's port at Eilat and the entrance to the Red Sea.

Meanwhile, Kissinger reported on a breakthrough in his talks with the Soviets. On October 21, Dayan returned to the south and learned the water supply to the Third Army had been cut off.[59]

Dayan returned to Tel Aviv at 7 p.m. and reported this news to Meir along with updates on battles along the crossing zone and other places. That night, after learning that the Security Council would be meeting soon, Meir then called for an urgent midnight Kitchen Cabinet meeting. Here, Dayan related the political developments and their military implications. Later, Kissinger wrote that Israel should accept the draft of the compromise he had reached

[54] Telegram from Dinitz to Gazit, October 19, 1973, 5:45 a.m., in Golan, *Milhama beyom hakippurim*, p. 1064.
[55] Telegram from Dinitz to Gazit, October 19, 1973, 7:30 a.m., in Golan, *Milhama beyom hakippurim*, p. 1078.
[56] Diary of Defense Minister's adjutant, in Golan, *Milhama beyom hakippurim*, p. 1082.
[57] Diary of the Chief of Staff's bureau chief; diary of Defense Minister's adjutant; notes of Gabi Cohen, in Golan, *Milhama beyom hakippurim*, p. 1084.
[58] Diary of the Deputy Chief of Staff's bureau chief, in Golan, *Milhama beyom hakippurim*, p. 1091.
[59] Telephone conversation between Defense Minister and Deputy Chief of Staff Israel Tal (Talik), October 21, 1973, 10:35 a.m., Defense Minister's bureau, in Golan, *Milhama beyom hakippurim*, p. 1106.

with the Soviets, which did not require an Israeli retreat after the ceasefire's end. The Arabs' reaction remained uncertain.

In the Kitchen Cabinet, Dayan supported the agreement but insisted on certain terms, including a cessation of terrorist activities, a freeze on the military situation, and an interpretation of UN Security Council Resolution 242 favoring Israel.[60] Elazar opposed a break in the fighting now, when Israel had offensive momentum, arguing that a ceasefire would only serve the enemy's interests.[61] The Kitchen Cabinet decided to accept the draft proposal subject to certain terms. Half an hour later, Egypt announced that it, too, was accepting the ceasefire.

Kissinger arrived in Israel on October 22 and met with Meir and senior cabinet members. Elazar then briefed Kissinger, reporting that the IDF had not completed encircling the Third Army but had effectively wiped out Egypt's entire aerial defense system. Kissinger left, amazed with Israel's great achievements militarily and politically, given that the Arabs were now agreeing to direct talks.[62] After Kissinger left, Dayan emphasized that the ceasefire was contingent on the release of Israel's POWs.

At 5 p.m., after Kissinger met with Meir, Dayan, and the military high command, Dayan told Elazar and Peled not to take Port Said, explaining that Meir objected. In fact, Sadat had threatened to fire missiles on Israeli civilian targets if civilian areas in Egypt were attacked. Believing Egypt was capable of carrying out such reprisals, Dayan opposed the conquest of Port Said and the bombing of Egyptian national infrastructure.[63]

The ceasefire was declared on October 22 at 6:52 p.m. Egyptian fire did not cease immediately, and Dayan informed Meir that the IDF would exploit this breach of the ceasefire to advance to the Canal south of the Great Lake to complete the encirclement of the Third Army.[64]

In the Kitchen Cabinet meeting in the morning of October 23, Dayan, keenly aware of the sensitivities of Israel's US ally, reported that he had instructed that the IDF provide security for ships delivering supplies to Israel to reduce the burden on the Americans. Also, he instructed that if Egypt continued to direct fire, the IDF would counterattack, although Israel had to inform the United States in that event.[65] Later that morning, he met with

---

[60] Golan, *Milhama beyom hakippurim*, p. 1129.
[61] Diary of Chief of Staff's bureau chief, in Golan, *Milhama beyom hakippurim*, p. 1130.
[62] Golan, *Milhama beyom hakippurim*, p. 1146.
[63] For more on the effect of the threat to fire missiles at Israeli population centers on the Israeli decision-making process and Dayan's change of decision on the conquest of Port Said, see Shimon Golan, "The Scud That Deterred Israel" (Hebrew), *Maarakhot* 457 (October 2014), pp. 56–61.
[64] Cabinet meeting, October 22, 1973, 10:40 p.m., in Golan, *Milhama beyom hakippurim*, p. 1157.
[65] Telephone conversation with Prime Minister, October 23, 1973, 9 a.m., Defense Minister's bureau, in Golan, *Milhama beyom hakippurim*, p. 1165.

Elazar and others in the military command to discuss the political situation. Dayan believed that because both superpowers were interested in the ceasefire, it would lead to a peace treaty between Israel and Egypt. He ordered the continued encirclement of the Third Egyptian Army, estimating that an agreement between the superpowers would be finalized in about forty-eight hours. He observed that, had Israel fired the first shot in this war, the United States would not have supported it. Finally, he warned that if the POW issue was not settled within seventy-two hours from the beginning of the ceasefire, he would support renewed fighting.[66]

In the afternoon, Dayan again visited the divisions in the south,[67] discussing moves to complete the Third Army's encirclement.[68] He also met with Elazar and briefed him on the upcoming Security Council session, assuring Elazar that this did not worry him, as he believed that until the Security Council reached a resolution, Israel could make further gains,[69] especially since he had received a report that Egypt's situation was very bad. In the evening, Elazar informed Dayan that IDF forces were still advancing on the Egyptian bank of the Canal; he hoped the noose would tighten overnight (Map 9.1).[70]

That night, the United States heavily pressured Israel to return to the October 22 lines. Dayan angrily refused any retreat, demanding that Meir remind Kissinger that the Arabs had started the war, and only after their

---

[66] Operational discussion, Defense Minister's bureau, the Kirya, October 22, 1973; diary of Chief of Staff's bureau chief, in Golan, *Milhama beyom hakippurim*, p. 1169. See also Kissinger's comment on the importance of Israel not having fired the first shot, in Arie Braun, *Moshe Dayan bemilhemet yom hakippurim* (Hebrew), Tel Aviv: Idanim Publishing, 1993, p. 236; and Henry Kissinger, *Years of Upheaval*, Boston, MA: Little, Brown & Company, 1982, p. 477: "It is true that in years past I had expressed my personal view to Ambassador Simcha Dinitz and his predecessor, Yitzhak Rabin, that America's ability to help Israel in any war would be impaired if Israel struck first. But as this crisis approached, the subject of preemption had not been discussed. How could it have been, since Israel had repeatedly told us that there was no danger of war? The morning the war started, Golda had volunteered to Keating that Israel would not preempt. The decision had been her own, without benefit of recent American advice: it confirmed what she had – entirely on her own – asked us to transmit to the Arabs the day before. I remain sure she was right. Had Israel struck first, it would have greatly complicated the prospects of American support. As it was, the majority at the first, early-morning WSAG thought Israel had struck first. Moreover, at that late hour it is doubtful whether preemptive strike would have made much military difference. Moshe Dayan wrote afterwards that the only proposal for preemption before the Cabinet was Chief of Staff David Elazar's scheme to attack the surface-to-air missiles deep inside Syria – a measure that could not have blunted the ground attack that was about to surprise Israel."

[67] Diary of Defense Minister's adjutant, in Golan, *Milhama beyom hakippurim*, pp. 1175-1176.

[68] Diary of Defense Minister's adjutant, in Golan, *Milhama beyom hakippurim*, p. 1177.

[69] Ibid., p. 1181.

[70] Diary of Defense Minister's adjutant; recordings from the Chief of Staff's bureau, in Golan, *Milhama beyom hakippurim*, p. 1190.

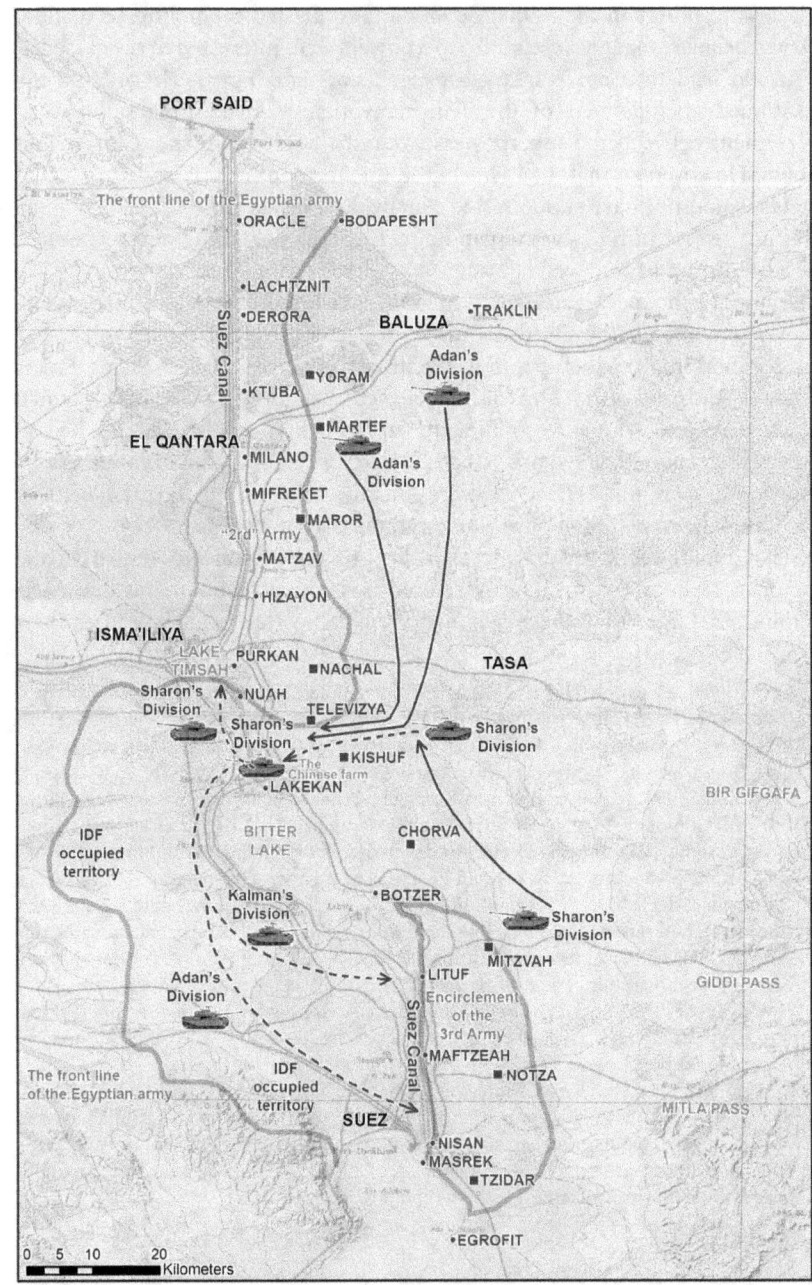

Map 9.1 Yom Kippur War (Oct. 1973): Encirclement of the Egyptian Third Army.

situation deteriorated did they seek a ceasefire, which they were violating. Dayan repeated the need to include the POW exchange in the ceasefire agreement.[71] Later, Dayan and Elazar decided to cut off supplies, including water, to the Third Army. Meeting with Meir at 3:30 a.m., Dayan asked if Kissinger knew that the Third Army was encircled. Meir said he did, adding, "He's very happy about it."[72]

At 5:45 a.m., October 24, Egypt agreed to a ceasefire at 7 a.m. that day. Having flown to the south to see the besieged Third Army, Dayan suggested letting the Egyptians leave unarmed. However, during the day, exchanges of fire continued throughout the front, and the Third Army reportedly tried to break through the siege.[73]

That afternoon, under increasing US pressure to retreat to the October 22 lines, Meir suggested revealing intercepted communications in which Egypt ordered the Third Army commander to continue fighting. Dayan assured her that the IDF was not attacking or advancing and that UN observers were already present. Dayan called Kissinger to update him and invited the US military attaché to the front to see for himself.[74] Later, Israel heard that Sadat had requested that US troops protect them and serve as a buffer between Egypt and Israel. In the afternoon, Dayan refused IAF intervention to help an Israeli force battling in the city of Suez, due to US pressure and Israel's commitment to the ceasefire.[75]

The Israeli leadership believed that the Egyptians viewed the Third Army's surrender or destruction as a defeat, leading them to do everything possible to prevent this and break the siege.[76] Trying to do just that, Egypt lost fifteen planes that day alone. The Third Army, now numbering about 30,000 men, was trapped in a 50-kilometer long and 12-kilometer wide enclave east of the Suez Canal, accessible to Egypt only by water – a route the IDF also controlled.

In a 9:30 p.m. cabinet meeting that evening, Dayan discussed Israel's immediate concerns: UN observers' deployment; the POW exchange; lifting Egypt's Bab al-Mandab blockade; and stabilizing the military lines. He felt that

---

[71] Defense Minister's adjutant, October 24, 1973, 3 a.m., in Golan, *Milhama beyom hakippurim*, p. 1194.
[72] Political-military consultation, Tel Aviv, October 24, 3:30 a.m.; diary of the Chief of Staff's bureau director, in Golan, *Milhama beyom hakippurim*, p. 1195.
[73] Visit to Bren's command center, Defense Minister's bureau, October 24, 9:57 a.m., in Golan, *Milhama beyom hakippurim*, p. 1202.
[74] Political-military consultation, Tel Aviv, October 24, 4 p.m., in Golan, *Milhama beyom hakippurim*, p. 1210.
[75] Defense Minister's conversation with Haim Bar-Lev, October 24, 1973, 5:50 p.m., Defense Minister's bureau, in Golan, *Milhama beyom hakippurim*, p. 1213.
[76] General Staff expanded discussion group, October 24, 1973, 8 p.m., in Golan, *Milhama beyom hakippurim*, pp. 1216-1217.

Israel should encourage Egypt's Third Army to evacuate westward to Egypt.[77] The government therefore ordered the IDF to maintain the calm. On the night of October 24–25, after Egypt appealed to both the United States and the Soviet Union to defend it against "Israel's aggression," the Soviets threatened the United States that it would intercede against Israel unless the United States supported the Soviet formulation of the resolution in the Security Council vote. The notion that both Israel and Egypt retreat was raised, along with demilitarizing the region adjacent to the Canal.[78]

Dayan felt that Israel was in an untenable position. Egypt and Syria could start a war, while Israel was prevented from delivering the *coup de grâce*. Elazar agreed.[79] The United States asked for Israel's military options, including its timeline for destroying the Third Army. The US assessment was that if the Soviets airlifted 4,500 soldiers to Cairo, another four or five days would be needed before they could approach the Third Army, time Israel would have to complete the Third Army's destruction.[80] The United States announced a state of high alert, moving ships and readying airborne divisions.[81] This marked the peak of tension between the superpowers.

Dayan revisited division headquarters of the 162nd and 252nd Divisions and the 460th Brigade early October 25. Concurrently, Kissinger sought to buy time to break the Third Army while also urging Israel to make concessions. For now, Dayan rejected the idea of both armies retreating from the Canal, claiming the time was not right.[82] By the next morning, October 26, Egypt resumed hostilities. Israel sent the IAF in response and received approval to bomb the 4th Division's headquarters.[83]

The arrangement that was being worked out included a UN buffer between the hostile parties. In the course of October 26, consultations continued about the POWs, the Third Army's fate, and lifting the Bab al-Mandab Straits naval blockade against Israel. Dayan suggested potential concessions for a real settlement, such as establishing a demilitarized strip and allowing a Third Army retreat with its weapons.[84] However, he also insisted on tightening the siege without

---

[77] Cabinet meeting, October 24, 1973, 9:30 p.m., Prime Minister's Tel Aviv bureau, in Golan, *Milhama beyom hakippurim*, p. 1222.

[78] Conversation between Chief of Staff and Prime Minister in the presence of Dinitz, diary of Chief of Staff's bureau chief, in Golan, *Milhama beyom hakippurim*, pp. 1225-1226.

[79] Cabinet meeting, October 25, 1973, 6 a.m., Prime Minister's Tel Aviv bureau, in Golan, *Milhama beyom hakippurim*, pp. 1226-1227.

[80] Conversation between Prime Minister and Ambassador Dinitz, October 25, 1973, 9:30 a.m., in Golan, *Milhama beyom hakippurim*, p. 1232.

[81] Ibid., p. 1233.

[82] Telegram from Dinitz to Gazit, October 25, 1973, 5 p.m., in Golan, *Milhama beyom hakippurim*, p. 1241.

[83] Notes of the History Department director, in Golan, *Milhama beyom hakippurim*, p. 1244.

[84] Diary of Chief of Staff's bureau chief, in Golan, *Milhama beyom hakippurim*, p. 1251.

allowing supplies till an agreement was reached.[85] Israel still suspected that Egypt was planning to break through the Third Army's encirclement. Sadat pressured the Americans to help the Third Army in return for lifting the blockade and releasing the POWs.[86] Israel rejected this, demanding a comprehensive arrangement. Kissinger pressured Israel not to destroy the encircled army. Eventually, Israel agreed to resolve the Third Army situation, provided the talks were direct. The United States then issued an ultimatum: If Israel did not allow supplies to reach the Third Army, it would vote against Israel in the Security Council.[87] Israel agreed to allow supplies, and, in return, Egypt agreed to direct talks on the front line. Israel proposed discussing a demilitarized zone on both sides of the Suez Canal with an international force.

This marked the official end of the Yom Kippur War. It was followed by a period in which the separation of forces agreements was hammered out, with continued exchanges of fire.

Separation of Forces on the Southern Front: The Sinai 1 Agreements

Already toward the war's end, Dayan sought an arrangement with Egypt based on his outline for an interim arrangement in 1970.[88] The arrangement and negotiations were complex, aiming to translate military achievement into political gains, complicated even more for Israel by the superpowers' interests, no less important than battlefield reality. To what extent could Israel insist on its interests given the increasing pressure and realize the dividends of winning the war? These and other questions preoccupied Dayan even before the war ended. Dayan, who had initially opposed conquering the Suez Canal in 1967 and had sought an interim agreement in 1971, was now coming full circle with a postwar agreement. Dayan wrote, "I returned to my old plan – the interim agreement. Ever since the Six-Day War, I'd tried to realize it but failed."[89] Dayan advocated a 30-kilometer Israeli retreat, as he had in 1970, in opposition to Elazar and Bar-Lev, who supported a retreat of 10 kilometers from the Canal,[90] and Meir, who initially opposed any withdrawal. She complained to

---

[85] Ibid., p. 1252.
[86] Telegrams from Dinitz to Gazit, October 26, 1973, 6:15 and 6:50 p.m., in Golan, *Milhama beyom hakippurim*, p. 1254.
[87] Telephone conversation of Dinitz with Israel, October 27, 1973, 5:30 a.m., in Golan, *Milhama beyom hakippurim*, p. 1258.
[88] Major Guy Aviad, *Rav aluf Moshe Dayan: Rosh hamateh haclali harevi'i shel tsahal* (Hebrew), booklet published by the IDF Operations Directorate, Doctrine and Training, April 2018, p. 72; Braun, *Moshe Dayan bemilhemet yom hakippurim*, p. 300.
[89] Moshe Dayan, *Avnei derekh: Autobiografia* (Hebrew), Jerusalem: Idanim Publishers, 1976, p. 698.
[90] Israel Tal and Yair Tal, *Prakim lehilhemet yom hakippurim* (Hebrew), Rishon Lezion: Miskal – Publishers Founded by Yedioth Ahronoth and Hemed Bood, 2019, p. 748.

Kissinger that "How is it fair, that having started the war, they're now being rewarded? They start a war but we have to withdraw from their territory?!"[91] Ultimately, Dayan prevailed.

Like Sadat, Dayan was thinking more comprehensively and for the long term and wanted the United States to play a central role in the negotiations and edge out the Soviet Union from the Middle East. In exchange for Israeli concessions at the Canal, which he believed in Israel's best interest, Dayan was trying secure US financial and military postwar support.[92]

Talks with Egypt, both direct between Israeli and Egyptian officers and indirect with US mediation, began on October 28. Syria, however, refused to discuss any agreement.

Meanwhile, Egypt and Syria replenished their armies with Soviet supplies and initiated small-scale firefights and raids on Israeli forces, resulting in a tense situation on the fronts. Israel's leadership had to anticipate either a potential peace or another round of warfare. Dayan wanted to prepare for peace and war simultaneously. During the talks, Dayan took a hardline approach toward any Egyptian violations of the agreement, believing Egypt would exploit any weakness to demand excessive concessions. Dayan's subordinates, especially Israel Tal (Deputy Chief of the IDF General Staff and from November 1 the new commander of Southern Command) and Aharon Yariv (chief of the IDF delegation to the talks), found his dual approach confusing and often voiced their criticism, to which we will return later in the chapter (p. 368).

On October 29, a day after the talks began, Dayan held a meeting to prepare for Meir's upcoming US visit. He emphasized that the priority was the POWs' release. He was open to letting supplies in to the Third Army if Israel would not have to retreat to the October 22 lines. Dayan also raised the possibility of renewed warfare but felt that Israel was well positioned on the west side of the canal and needn't fear such threats. Responding to Tal, still the Deputy Chief of Staff, who opposed any situation leading to renewed fighting, Dayan explained that it was necessary "to get out of their heads the notion that you can make gains by waging war."[93] Dayan insisted on obtaining something concrete from Egypt in exchange for any Israeli concession. On October 31, Dayan traveled to the south. As usual, he started out with an open discussion, telling the commanders he wanted "an exchange of unofficial thoughts." Dayan added that the talks had hit a dead end and that hostilities could soon resume.[94]

---

[91] Kenneth Stein, *Mediniyut amitsa* (Hebrew), Tel Aviv: Maarakhot, 2003, p. 143.
[92] Ibid., p. 146.
[93] Shimon Golan, *Hafradat kohot betsel hahatasha: Kabalat hahahlatot badereg haestrategi bamasa umatann al heskemey hafradat hakohot aharey milhemet yom hakippurim* (Hebrew), Ben Shemen, Maarakhot and Modan, 2019, pp. 20–21.
[94] Arik Command Center, October 31, 1973, IDF Archive; operational discussion, the Kirya, October 31, 1973, Defense Minister's bureau, in Golan, *Hafradat kohot betsel hahatasha*, pp. 22–23.

Tal was appointed commander of the Southern Command on November 1 and met with Egyptian Chief of Staff Mohamed Gamasy, who assured Tal that Egypt now accepted Israel's existence and wanted only to recover its territories. Gamasy proposed an Israeli withdrawal to 30 kilometers from the Canal, leaving a UN force as a buffer.[95] Tal informed Dayan about Egypt's willingness to sign a separate agreement. Dayan decided to announce the transfer of humanitarian aid to the besieged city of Suez at the next meeting, but he also spoke with the southern commanders on November 3 on the prospect of attacking the Third Army due to the possibility of renewed warfare.[96]

On November 4, Elazar told Dayan that most General Staff officers supported more fighting to improve the IDF's position. Dayan disagreed, fearing severe diplomatic repercussions and a Security Council resolution that the United States would not veto.[97] At midnight of November 6–7, Dayan informed the General Staff that Assistant Secretary of State Joseph Sisco's arrival with agreement terms from Egypt. Egypt proposed a peace conference in Geneva, but Dayan was adamant about the POWs' return, refusing to send supplies to Suez before receiving complete POW lists and the lifting of the Bab al-Mandab blockade,[98] which had long troubled Dayan.[99] On November 8, Egypt agreed to submit the POW lists. Dayan explained to the General Staff that providing supplies to the Third Army, unpopular domestically, was necessary due to Israel's dependence on the United States. This dependence led Meir to reject the General Staff's recommendation to resume the fighting.[100]

A Six-Point Agreement on November 12 covered supplies to the Third Army and the POW exchange, made four days later. But a broad divide remained about the separation of forces.

On November 14, Dayan rejected Egypt's demands that the IDF withdraw from the Canal's western bank.[101] Dayan prepared the Israeli delegation, highlighting the disagreement over the separation of forces. Israel wanted reciprocity, whereas Egypt, seeking a return of the Sinai Peninsula to

---

[95] The highlights of the conversation between the Chief of Staff and Gamasy from the database of the IDF History Department, in Golan, *Hafradat kohot betsel hahatasha*, p. 24.

[96] Golan, *Hafradat kohot betsel hahatasha*, p. 26.

[97] Meeting between the Defense Minister and Chief of Staff, November 4, 1973, IDF Archive, in Golan, *Hafradat kohot betsel hahatasha*, pp. 27-28.

[98] Golan, *Hafradat kohot betsel hahatasha*, pp. 29-30.

[99] See chapter about the Six-Day War and Dayan's demand of the Israel Navy to be capable of operating in these straits.

[100] General Staff discussion, November 11, 1973, in Golan, *Hafradat kohot betsel hahatasha*, p. 36.

[101] Meeting between Major General Aharon Yariv and the Defense Minister, November 14, 1973, IDF Archive; report by Major General Aharon Yariv, November 16, 1973, IDF Archive, in Golan, *Hafradat kohot betsel hahatasha*, pp. 47, 51.

Egyptian sovereignty, was demanding to station three divisions on the canal's eastern side.[102] Meeting with the Finnish commander of the UN observer mission to the Middle East, Dayan explained that there was a distinction between a technical separation of forces, a topic that officers could handle, and a comprehensive agreement, requiring discussion in Geneva.[103]

On November 19, the General Staff met with Meir. Elazar predicted potential renewed warfare if the talks failed, while Tal argued against any attack on the Third Army.[104] Dayan was able to weigh up two possible and contradicting scenarios – resuming and conducting hostilities and advancing the talks – at the same time.[105] In the November 19 cabinet meeting, Dayan proposed a long-term interim agreement with concessions to avoid warfare.[106] Nonetheless, Dayan instructed the General Staff to prepare a plan to destroy the Third Army.

Early in December, Dayan visited the United States to discuss Egypt's unbalanced proposals with Kissinger. He proposed that in exchange for withdrawing from the Canal, Israel should get an agreement ensuring the end of hostilities that would be linked to opening the Canal and reconstructing Egyptian cities. Dayan insisted that the United States continue to play an active role, particularly in ensuring freedom of shipping through Bab al-Mandab.[107] Thus, Dayan worked toward an interim agreement while insisting on Israeli compensation.

Dayan now promoted the proposed agreement to the IDF command and laid its groundwork, acknowledging the difficulty of accepting Israeli withdrawal from the Egyptian bank of the Canal and a further retreat from territories in Sinai. Speaking on December 4 with Southern Command officers about Israel's low postwar morale and its strong dependence on the United States, Dayan granted, "I understand that we had an earthquake... But the key to this thing is, to a great extent, in the hands of this elite group [IDF commanders]."[108]

In his next meeting with the Southern Command on December 12, Dayan reported he had gained significant insights from the visit. He stressed the importance of the agreement's first stage, when Egypt would reopen the Canal following Israel's withdrawal, in return for which Israel should get

---

[102] Golan, *Hafradat kohot betsel hahatasha*, p. 59.
[103] Defense Minister's meeting with Gen. Ensio Siilvasvuo, December 3, 1973, IDF Archive, in Golan, *Hafradat kohot betsel hahatasha*, p. 62.
[104] General Staff discussion, November 19, 1973, High Command Secretariat, in Golan, *Hafradat kohot betsel hahatasha*, p. 63.
[105] Golan, *Hafradat kohot betsel hahatasha*, pp. 66–85.
[106] Military-political consultation, Tel Aviv, October 19, 1973, History Department database, in Golan, *Hafradat kohot betsel hahatasha*, p. 66.
[107] Golan, *Hafradat kohot betsel hahatasha*, p. 79.
[108] Defense Minister's meeting with Southern Command division commanders, December 4, 1973, Major General Tal's document, Major General Tal's bureau in Refidim, in Golan, *Hafradat kohot betsel hahatasha*, p. 86.

a peace treaty or a nonaggression pact.[109] He also highlighted a problem unique to Israel, of maintaining the military reserves, a burden on the country's economy and morale.

With efforts also underway to convene a peace conference in Geneva, Kissinger began his shuttle diplomacy with nonstop trips. On December 6, Dayan traveled to Washington for talks about the agreements and US security assistance. A conference in Geneva, convened on December 21 with the United States, Soviet Union, Egypt, Jordan, and Israel (Syria was conspicuously absent) concluded on January 9, 1974, without significant results. The serious differences between the two sides were resolved by Kissinger, who shuttled between the leaders, leading to a bilateral arrangement between Israel and Egypt, rather than a regional one.

In late December, Dayan held discussions about Israel's ideal conditions, assuming that a separation of forces agreement was near. He noted that Egypt's stance had eased somewhat since before the war, suggesting that US assurances about future Israeli territorial concessions explained Egypt's willingness to negotiate now without an Israeli commitment to full withdrawal and its apparent readiness for a partial settlement. He asked the military what was the furthest line to which the IDF could withdraw, what arrangements were needed with the Egyptian forces, and what was needed to allow freedom of shipping in Bab al-Mandab.[110] For Dayan, the critical parameters included Israeli troops being beyond Egypt's artillery range and withdrawal timetables.

On December 31, Meir established a new government following delayed elections for the eighth Knesset. On January 1, the new government approved the separation of forces agreement based on Dayan and Elazar's proposed outline.[111] On January 4, 1974, Dayan met with Kissinger and explained Israel's proposed arrangement. Kissinger thought Egypt might accept it, although he was skeptical about Egypt agreeing to commit itself to nonaggression.[112] The problematic issues of 1971 were resurfacing.

Following another Kissinger visit, the government agreed to the various separation of forces parameters. On January 17, 1974, Dayan explained the details of the agreement to the General Staff, reading important sections and explaining that it would be signed by the Israeli and Egyptian Chiefs of Staff. He conceded

---

[109] Defense Minister's conversation with division commanders, December 12, 1973, Major General Tal's document, Major General Tal's bureau in Refidim, in Golan, *Hafradat kohot betsel hahatasha*. P. 86.

[110] Consultation on withdrawal line, the Kirya, December 29, 1973, Defense Minister's bureau, IDF Archive, in Golan: *Hafradat kohot betsel hahatasha*, pp. 98–99.

[111] Golan, *Hafradat kohot betsel hahatasha*, p. 104.

[112] Telegram from Dinitz to Gazit, summary of conversation between the Defense Minister and Kissinger, January 4, 1974, IDF Archive, in Golan, *Hafradat kohot betsel hahatasha*, p. 105.

Figure 9.2 Minister of Defense Moshe Dayan with US Secretary of State Henry Kissinger, January 1974. Source: PhotoQuest/Contributor/Archive Photos/Getty Images.

that it was less favorable than Israel had hoped, because it was a ceasefire and not an end-of-warfare agreement. The Egyptians, planning to demand more Israeli withdrawals, had included a clause that the agreement was just a stage before a final settlement. Addressing Egypt's shift to relying on the United States even at the expense of Soviet cooperation, Dayan added: "It isn't clear what the United States has promised Egypt, but Israel can depend on the United States." About Kissinger, Dayan said, "If he gets all of this done, then he's an international genius, that Jew. To see him at work, by the way, is a real pleasure" (Figure 9.2).[113]

On January 18, 1974, Israel and Egypt signed a separation of forces agreement at the 101st kilometer on the road to Cairo, entailing an Israeli withdrawal of 20 kilometers from the canal and demilitarizing the evacuated zone. The next day, Dayan expressed his satisfaction with the agreement, reminding everyone that he had been willing to accept a similar arrangement before the war. Dayan thought the agreement a good one because it served both sides' interests and allowed for the reopening of the Suez Canal, the resumption of life in the cities along it, and freedom of shipping through Bab al-Mandab as well as increased US involvement in the region.[114]

---

[113] General Staff discussion, January 17, 1974, IDF Archive, in Golan, *Hafradat kohot betsel hahatasha*, p. 115.

[114] Defense Minister's statements to division officers, January 19, 1974, IDF Archive, in Golan, *Hafradat kohot betsel hahatasha*, pp. 117–118.

Continuation of the Fighting at the Canal and a Crisis with Major General Tal

In order to understand the dispute between Tal on the one hand and Dayan and Elazar on the other, we will now journey back in time to November 1, when Israel Tal was appointed as the Southern Commander. After Tal assumed command of the Southern Command, he clashed with Dayan and Elazar.

With exchanges of fire continuing during the ceasefire talks, Israel's leaders feared that Egypt intended to resume the fighting.[115] Gamasy admitted after the war that Egypt was behind most of the ceasefire violations.[116] In the General Staff meeting on November 19, Dayan and Elazar insisted that the difficult conditions on the front required Israel to act decisively and respond aggressively to every Egyptian aggression. Tal disagreed, arguing that this could drag Israel into a fruitless war.[117] Elazar and Tal had serious differences about the Israeli response. Elazar, rejecting Tal's stance that Israel should contain Egypt's provocations, issued open-fire instructions on November 22, 1973. While the IDF was not to initiate fire, it was to respond aggressively to every Egyptian challenge.[118]

The core disagreement was whether Israel should deter Egyptian aggression, which Dayan and Elazar supported, believing Egypt was trying to test Israel's resolve. Tal, concerned about igniting another war, even hinted that Dayan and Elazar were more concerned with rehabilitating their reputations following the debacle of the war's opening days, especially Dayan.[119] Tal accused Dayan of using his many speeches to manipulate the narrative of the war so he could present his conduct before and during the war in a positive light to the commission of inquiry.[120] Dayan responded sharply that Israel would not start a war.[121] Tensions escalated less than a month after Tal's appointment, when Dayan learned that Tal had shared his differences with Dayan and Elazar with Israel's President Katzir, claiming that he, Tal, supported total restraint, and Dayan and Elazar favored initiating provocations. Dayan reprimanded Tal, limiting him to discussing such matters only with the General Staff, defense minister, and prime minister in closed discussions.[122]

---

[115] Golan, *Hafradat kohot betsel hahatasha*, p. 131.
[116] Stein, *Mediniyut amitsa*, p. 135.
[117] Tal and Tal, *Prakim lehilhemet yom hakippurim*, p. 736.
[118] Operations Directorate, open-fire instructions in the Southern Command sphere, November 22, 1973, History Department database, in Golan, *Hafradat kohot betsel hahatasha*, pp. 131-132.
[119] Tal and Tal, *Prakim lehilhemet yom hakippurim*, p. 766.
[120] Ibid., pp. 757-758.
[121] Ibid., p. 773.
[122] Telephone conversation with General Israel Tal, November 29, 1973, 5:45 p.m., IDF Archive, in Golan, *Hafradat kohot betsel hahatasha*, pp. 137-138.

In early December 1973, prior to the Geneva conference, Elazar anticipated a possible Egyptian attack,[123] leading to an IDF policy change about responding to Egyptian ceasefire violations on December 8. Returning from the United States on December 11, Dayan learned that the Egyptians were firing on IDF forces. Dayan, like Elazar, and backed by Meir, favored shelling Egyptian artillery concentrations and threatening to cut off supplies to the Third Army. Dayan nonetheless cautioned against any deterioration; the IDF needed to react aggressively but without escalating to war.[124]

On December 12, Dayan instructed the Southern Command to respond forcefully to Egyptian fire to prevent a war of attrition (escalation for the sake of deescalation) and to cut off supplies to the Third Army if firing continued. Tal demanded these instructions in writing. Dayan jested: "Talik, nobody has ever mistaken me for an organized Jew."[125] Tal tendered his resignation on December 25, but Dayan refused to accept it.[126]

On December 29, Elazar, dissatisfied with Tal, suggested replacing him. Two days later, Elazar told Dayan that Tal had softened his position on the open-fire policy "as if he had heard us talking." Dayan maintained that the Geneva talks could be undermined if Egypt thought Israel feared escalation.[127] Further disagreements surfaced on January 11, 1974. Dayan, having learned of continued Egyptian fighting, confronted Tal for not cutting supplies to the Third Army. Tal's insistence on a written order infuriated Dayan: "I, Moshe Dayan, Minister of Defense, am telling you, Talik, Commander of the Southern Command! What do I have to do [to get your cooperation]? [Get you] a wax seal?!"[128] This may have been the proverbial straw that broke the camel's back.

On January 16, 1974, Elazar replaced Tal with Major General Adan, considered one of the IDF's most honest and well-respected officers, and a critic of Tal's policy of restraint. Adan harshly criticized Tal, writing that, "it is my assessment that our military activity dropped to its lowest nadir under his command."[129] Disagreeing with Tal's defensive posture and insistence on an

---

[123] Chief of Staff's expanded discussion group, November 4, 1973, History Department's database, in Golan, *Hafradat kohot betsel hahatasha*, p. 134.
[124] Meeting between Chief of Staff and Defense Minister, December 11, 1973, IDF Archive, in Golan, *Hafradat kohot betsel hahatasha*, p. 134.
[125] Defense Minister's conversation with division commanders, December 12, 1973, Major General Tal's documents, Major General Tal's bureau in Refidim, in Golan, *Hafradat kohot betsel hahatasha*, p. 89.
[126] Tal and Tal, *Prakim lehilhemet yom hakippurim*, pp. 785–786.
[127] Telephone conversation between the Defense Minister and Chief of Staff, December 31, 1973, 9 a.m., IDF Archive, in Golan, *Hafradat kohot betsel hahatasha*, p. 138.
[128] Telephone conversation between Defense Minister and General Tal, January 1, 1974, 8:30 a.m., IDF Archive, in Golan, *Hafradat kohot betsel hahatasha*, p. 139.
[129] Avraham Adan (Bren), *Al shtei g'deot hasuez* (Hebrew), Tel Aviv: Yedioth Ahronoth, 1979, p. 318.

early ceasefire,[130] Adan also blamed Tal for his responsibility as deputy chief of staff for the poor execution of Operation Dovecote at the beginning of the war and for continuously opposing Elazar's decisions throughout the war, which deeply disturbed Elazar.[131]

Ceasefire with Syria

The official ceasefire with Syria beginning on October 22 reduced the intensity of fighting but did not stop it – the Syrians continued to bombard Israeli forces with artillery and conduct raids against them. The IDF responded in kind.

Dayan's position was cautious, barring assaults across the lines, convinced that no potential achievement was worth the risk to human life.[132] He believed that Syrians fleeing the border shelling and becoming internal refugees would sufficiently pressure the Syrians.[133]

Politically, the stalemate with Syria broke on February 27, with Syria finally disclosing the list of Israeli POWs and agreeing to discuss a separation of forces. Dayan, dispatched to Washington on March 17,[134] believed that an agreement with Syria would help the negotiations with Egypt. Moreover, Kissinger was pushing Israel to reach a settlement on the north, threatening that failure to do so would damage Israeli–US relations. Before leaving Israel, Dayan wanted to know to what extent was Kissinger's pressure real and how far could Israel withdraw.[135]

Syrians insistence on an IDF retreat from all of the Golan Heights gradually moderated. With Syria having greater artillery power, using the IAF would have escalated the conflict. Finally wanting escalation on April 15, Dayan ordered the IAF "to f**k the Syrians but good."[136]

The eventual arrangement involved some minor adjustments to the Six-Day War lines, reduced Israeli forces in the Golan, civilian resettlement, and the first signed agreement in Israeli–Syrian history. As with the Egyptian agreement, Dayan had to convince senior officers about the Syrian agreement. At a General Staff forum meeting on April 22, Dayan told those complaining about perceived US control that their concerns were justified: Israel depended on the United States for money to buy weapons and for political support that

---

[130] Ibid., p. 319.
[131] Ibid., p. 320.
[132] Discussion about Mount Hermon, the Kirya, April 16, 1974, Defense Minister's Bureau, IDF Archive, in Golan, *Hafradat kohot betsel hahatasha*, p. 148.
[133] Lunch meeting between Defense Minister and Motta Gur, January 28, 1974, IDF Archive, in Golan, *Hafradat kohot betsel hahatasha*, p. 142.
[134] Golan, *Hafradat kohot betsel hahatasha*, p. 155.
[135] Political-military meeting, Jerusalem, March 17, 1974, IDF Archive, in Golan, *Hafradat kohot betsel hahatasha*, p. 156.
[136] Discussion about the Northern Command, the Kirya, April 15, 1974, Defense Minister's Bureau, IDF Archive, in Golan, *Hafradat kohot betsel hahatasha*, p. 147.

Israel so desperately needed. Kissinger's mediation also mattered. Israel, said Dayan, argued that territorial concessions to Syria would prevent Egyptian intervention, reducing the threat of a two-front war.

Dayan's last meeting with the IDF high command as Minister of Defense was on May 30, following Meir's April 11 resignation and the installation of Rabin's new government. Dayan reviewed the challenging talks with Syria, which had already lasted thirty days. While not anticipating an ideal outcome for Israel, he thought it was the best possible, noting that Egypt's and Syria's willingness to negotiate indicated their shift from warfare to diplomacy. However, Dayan incorrectly predicted that the Syrian agreement wouldn't last more than a year; yet due to Syria's interests, the Israel border with Syria was the quietest border it had until the Syrian civil war broke out in 2011. The Golan Heights remain under Israeli rule to this day.

The Israel–Syria agreement was signed in Geneva on May 31, 1974, marking the real end of the Yom Kippur War. This agreement was scrupulously adhered to by both sides till the beginning of the Syrian civil war in 2011; during this period, the Syrian regime permitted occasional Hezbollah operations against Israel via the Golan border, prompting the IDF to undertake retaliatory measures within Syrian territory.

Dayan in the Yom Kippur War: Myths, Failures, and Contributions

The Yom Kippur War was the nadir of Dayan's career. The Agranat Commission, a National Commission of Inquiry set up immediately after the war to investigate the failings that resulted in Israel being caught off guard by its enemies (and therefore dealing only with the prelude to the war and its first days), found Dayan had operated acceptably in the role of defense minister. However, the commission decided not to evaluate his more comprehensive political responsibility for the security establishment and with setting its policies,[137] a decision that caused considerable public outrage. Harsh criticism of Dayan persisted for years, with his wartime functioning closely scrutinized and critiqued.[138] Some claims were correct, but others were either exaggerated

---

[137] See Agranat Commission Report (Hebrew), IDF Archive and the security establishment, www.archives.mod.gov.il/docs/agranat/Pages/default.aspx.

[138] Arguments about Dayan's collapse and loss of judgment appears in a number of works on the war. See Chaim Herzog, *The War of Atonement* (Hebrew), Jerusalem: Edanim Publishers Yediot Aharonot, 1975, pp. 60, 124, 248–249, and a similar view in Zeev Schiff, *Earthquake in October: The Yom-Kippur War* (Hebrew), Tel Aviv: Zmora Bitan, Modan Publishers, 1974, p. 111; Hanoch Bartov, *Daddo: 48 Years and 20 More Days*, vol. 2, Israel: Dvir, 2002, first edition 1978, pp. 425, 508; see also Uri Bar-Joseph, and Amr Yossef, "The Hidden Factors That Turned the Tide: Strategic Decision-Making and Operational Intelligence in the 1973 War," *Journal of Strategic Studies* 37:4 (2014), pp. 584–608, p. 592. Following this crisis and throughout the rest of the war, Meir tended to accept the course of action suggested by the Chief of Staff rather than Dayan. A similar

or simply wrong. The following examines some of the central issues regarding Dayan's functioning in the Yom Kippur War.

The Pre-War Call-up

Dayan's position at the end of September 1973 – that the worries of the Northern Commander leader, Yitzhak Hofi, about the situation on the Syrian border were impossible to ignore – directly led to sending reinforcements to the Golan Heights. While General Staff members were complacent about the north, Dayan's sending reinforcements proved pivotal in preventing a Syrian conquest of the Golan Heights and in limiting their success. While Dayan did not expect a comprehensive war, he anticipated Syrian retaliation after their planes were downed on September 12. Arguably, the Syrians would have seized the Golan Heights had the 7th Brigade elements not been deployed there. Although the reinforced regulars alone could not prevent Syrian gains, they delayed them until the reservists arrived. Admittedly, if Dayan had allowed the call-up of a reserve division to the Golan, the course of the war may have been radically different, allowing reserves to move south instead and the IAF to complete its mission to destroy the Egyptian antiaircraft missiles (Operation Challenge) on October 7.

Dayan's reluctance to send more troops to the Golan was due to his increasing reliance on AMAN Director Zeira, whose earlier assessments that there would be no war each time there had been an alert had proven accurate – until war broke out. On October 6, despite Elazar's conviction that war was imminent, Dayan had to consider other factors, such as US reactions, the economic and psychological impact of a reservist call-up, and the possibility that while a general call-up could deter the other side, it could also be misconstrued as a sign that Israel was embarking on a preemptive strike, triggering an Arab attack.

Consequently, Dayan ruled out a preemptive Israeli strike on the morning of October 6 and agreed to a partial call-up, as a defensive measure that Elazar insisted would stop the enemy at the current lines. Believing in Israel's deterrent power, Dayan and Meir sought to prevent war by transmitting deterrent messages to the other side via the United States while simultaneously deploying troops to the borders. Their conclusions were reasonable but their assumptions flawed: They were overconfident in the regular army's ability to stop the enemy, and they underestimated enemy capabilities, leading to excessive self-confidence at all echelons.[139]

---

description of Dayan is seen in Carmit Guy, *Bar-Lev: Biografia* (Hebrew), Tel Aviv: Am Oved, 1998, pp. 238–239, 246.

[139] See Dayan's statements to Yaakov Erez and Ilan Kfir, *Sihot im Moshe Dayan* (Hebrew), Ramat Gan: Massada, 1981, pp. 107-108.

The economic, social, morale, political, and international costs of a full call-up led to overly cautious decision-making. This inevitably leads to the next question: Had Dayan been certain that war would break out on October 6, would he have made different decisions? With regard to the reservists, the answer is that he would probably have supported Elazar's request for full reserve call-up.

However, launching a preemptive strike was more complex, as the US response was pivotal. And, ultimately, there was no certainty about an Egyptian attack.

"The Third Temple Is At Risk": Did Dayan Collapse on October 7?

The Yom Kippur War was the low point of Dayan's career, with October 7 the worst day of the war, possibly of Dayan's entire professional life. Evaluating his performance requires distinguishing between Dayan's leadership and his decision-making. According to military doctrine, command comprises three major components: generalship, leadership, and management. "Generalship" is defined as "knowing and understanding the art of war and military doctrine ... and knowing ... the proper ways of applying them," and leadership "is seen in the desire to be victorious in battle and it provides the purpose, the direction, and the motivation."[140]

Dayan's leadership may have faltered during the war's first days, but his situation assessments and decisions were realistic and precise, based on the situation assessments he received from the commanders in the field and what he saw for himself. Dayan understood before anyone else that this would be a very different and more difficult war than the Six-Day War.[141]

It should be borne in mind that the first two days of fighting were volatile, with assessments changing almost hourly. The fog of war was thick. The picture was unclear and dynamic. In the evening of October 6, the General Staff remained relatively positive: The troops were holding the lines. But the situation changed radically overnight. Dayan felt that the war room – the "Pit" in the Kirya general headquarters from which the war was directed – was too noisy and "didn't allow for measured thinking."[142] Dayan was the only one in Israel's supreme political or military echelons who traveled to the fronts to hear from the commanders on the ground at both the northern and the southern fronts. At this most difficult point in the war, the commanders were pessimistic and exhausted after a day of difficult fighting. They anticipated a morale boost from Dayan – the man turned legend, who had lifted the spirits of the nation and of IDF commanders on the eve of the Six-Day War and restored self-confidence and the belief in victory, the

---

[140] Basic General Staff Doctrine, *Pikud ushlita* (Hebrew), Ekked, November 2006, pp. 11–12.
[141] Martin van Creveld, *Moshe Dayan*, London: Weidenefeld & Nicolson, 2004, p. 1968.
[142] Dayan, *Avnei derekh*, p. 594.

"god of war."[143] Instead, they met a Dayan whose confidence was shaken, who realized the extent of the military disaster and the repercussions of the mistaken assessment he and his fellow leaders had made. Robert Slater, Dayan's English-language biographer, interviewed two deputy commanders from the southern and northern fronts who gave comparable reports about the strong impact of Dayan's feelings of responsibility and guilt and his recognition of the grave situation, which left a deep imprint on everyone who saw him. Aharon Yariv in Tel Aviv also testified that instead of raising morale, Dayan hurt it.[144] His subordinates expected him to fill them with strength and courage, as Churchill had done after the defeat in France.

Leadership is a subjective matter. People's negative response to Dayan's leadership is what matters. However, Yigael Yadin, noted archeologist and a former Chief of Staff, recalled that: "Dayan never collapsed. Dayan was much more optimistic than I was. Dayan stood with both feet on the ground. But I have one complaint about Dayan: a leader should give off a spirit of hope. To say that we are winning. Dayan never said that."[145]

After the war, many analysts and influential writers, including Haim Herzog, Hanoch Bartov, and Zeev Schiff, criticized Dayan's decisions, accusing him of panic and hysteria and of being unable to reach well-considered decisions. Critics claimed he took reckless actions and proposed irresponsible withdrawals and bombings. However, contemporaneous meeting notes indicate that Dayan usually agreed with field commanders' assessments. When Dayan suggested sending one more reserve division to the north, Elazar informed him he'd already done so and had given the order a few moments prior to the conversation. That these two leaders independently reached the same decisions about one of the most critical situations of the war demonstrates not only that Dayan did not reach an ill-considered decision, but a reasonable, perhaps obvious one.

Dayan intervened substantially only once on the northern front, requesting IAF support against the Syrians on October 7. Unable to contact Elazar, Dayan called Benny Peled to warn him, adding, "Benny, the Third Temple is in danger"[146] to convince him to send planes. Despite numerous claims of Dayan uttering this phrase on numerous occasions, documentary evidence indicates Dayan used it only with Peled on October 7 and in the meeting with the Editors' Committee, consisting of Israeli journalism's leaders of that time, on October 9. Any other occasions remain merely rumor. However, because of the many people claiming to have heard Dayan used that precise expression, it

---

[143] Michael Shahar, *Sichot im Rehavam Ze'evi Ghandi*, Tel Aviv: Yedioth Ahronot, 1992, p. 168.
[144] Robert Slater, *Warrior Statesman: The Life of Moshe Dayan*, New York: St Martin's Press, 1st ed., 1991, pp. 355-356.
[145] Slater, *Warrior Statesman*, p. 370.
[146] Erez and Kfir, *Sihot im Moshe Dayan*, p. 92. Dayan himself told people he said it.

became a catchphrase, accurately reflecting the sense of historic danger felt by Israel's leaders and many members of the public.

Regarding Dayan's decision-making, claims that Dayan's pressure for IAF intervention against the Syrian armored advance indirectly undermined Peled's resolve to complete Operation Challenge in the south are speculative at best.[147] Peled never confirmed this, and it was Elazar who canceled the operation. Furthermore, Moti Hod, IAF Commander during the Six-Day War, supported Dayan's request for IAF assistance, proving that Dayan was not acting on the basis of hysteria, as other senior figures shared his assessment.

Dayan was faulted for seeming to hastily allow retreat on the southern front. Actually, he was granting the Southern Command latitude to establish a line where they saw fit – the most sensible instruction possible, even if it meant a retreat to the mountain passes where it would be possible to establish a virtually impenetrable line. Dayan was giving the Southern Command commander freedom of decision and independence, backing him up, freeing him from the "not a single inch of land" mantra of the IDF command echelon. Later, Dayan, maybe unaware of Gonen's new, more optimistic assessment, presented a very gloomy picture to the stunned officers at Elazar's staff conference and a later Kitchen Cabinet meeting.

Later, Dayan's gloomy assessments were validated by events, including the failure of a premature counterattack and the IDF's failure to return to the Suez Canal line. Dayan's anticipation of a protracted war of attrition led to unrealistic proposals, such as calling up and training adolescents, or bringing volunteers from abroad. But Dayan, thinking ahead, envisioned a situation with the IDF stuck on defensive lines, unable to end the fighting in days or even weeks, and becoming worn down because of the enemy's manpower and matériel advantage. That extreme scenario did not materialize, but Dayan felt that his job at that crucial moment was to consider extreme scenarios and devise unconventional solutions. After the October 8 debacle, and given the developments of October 9 through 12, Elazar and others in the high command began speaking of attrition as the central problem and seeking a ceasefire. At this point, however, the situation reversed itself, and a newly collected Dayan urged Elazar to find a way for Israel to gain the upper hand.

While some claim that Dayan at first opposed crossing the Canal, it is noteworthy that Dayan promised Elazar his support for this move and stood by his promise. On October 12, after a "golden piece of intelligence" arrived from the Mossad about Egypt's intention to launch an attack, Dayan was the one who raised the idea of the ploy of not opposing the

---

[147] See this argument in Uri Bar-Joseph and Rose McDermott, "Personal Functioning under Stress: The Role of Accountability and Social Support in Israeli Leaders in the Yom Kippur War," *Journal of Conflict Resolution* 52:1 (Feb. 2008), pp. 144–170 (p. 156).

Security Council working toward a ceasefire, so that Israel would not stand accused of being the intransigent party. On the 14th, Dayan backed Elazar and pushed for a crossing.

Issues Involving Dayan's "Ministerial Advice"

Dayan's ministerial advice came under criticism for his frequent travels to the front, which many claimed brought despair rather than hope to the commanders, whom he gave many instructions that he defined as "ministerial advice." Critics accused Dayan of avoiding responsibility for his own ideas and hiding behind the phrase "ministerial advice."[148] They considered his visits and his advice equally meaningless.

Reality, however, was somewhat more complicated. While clearly pessimistic on October 7, he later recovered and displayed more confidence during his visits. Major General Adan, whose division crossed the Suez Canal, described his meetings with Dayan: "In the Yom Kippur War, I did not experience him as despairing and beaten. He was with me almost every single day on the halftracks ... During the war, he tended to look ahead ... I don't think he lost his head and I certainly don't think he functioned badly."[149]

Dayan himself explained why he called his instructions "advice," pointing to the sensitivity of a defense minister – a former, highly experienced Chief of Staff – going into the field and finding problems to be addressed, but having to be extremely careful not to disrupt the military chain of command. Therefore, throughout the war, he was very mindful of Elazar's dignity and status and made sure that the operational advice he was offering became directives only after being approved by Elazar and the regional commands.[150] He recalled: "When I come somewhere, I don't issue instructions ... [but] I see myself as authorized to ask the commander why he isn't acting [on it]."[151]

After October 7, Dayan's authority somewhat diminished, as he lost the special status he had enjoyed in the Six-Day War and War of Attrition. In contrast, Elazar projected a great deal of personal strength and stability. Yet Dayan's opinions continued to be very valuable and to influence many decisions, including crossing the Canal, Bar-Lev's appointment, the offensives on both fronts, and the ceasefire's timing.[152] In fact, Dayan's opinion still mattered and was often the determinative one in most of the strategic decisions.[153] As defense

---

[148] Einat Fishbein, "The Legend and the Man" (Hebrew), *Yedioth Ahronoth*, October 8, 2010.
[149] Ibid.
[150] Dayan spoke extensively about his authority in Erez and Kfir, *Sihot im Moshe Dayan*, pp. 74–75, 81–84.
[151] Diary of Defense Minister's adjutant, in Golan, *Milhama beyom hakippurim*, p. 1116.
[152] Interview with Shimon Golan, August 2020.
[153] See chart in Golan, *Milhama beyom hakippurim*, p. 1314.

minister, he also dealt with other significant aspects of the war, such as ensuring US aid. While less dominant than in the past, Dayan did not leave the stage but continued to be an influential leader during most of the war and after it, especially in formulating the ceasefire and separation of forces agreements.

Visits to the Fronts

Dayan's visits to the front were closely connected to the issue of his "ministerial advice." Since the Sinai campaign, being close to the fronts and unfolding events was vital for Dayan, an essential part of his generalship and leadership. As in Israel's other wars, he visited the front almost every day to get a firsthand impression, study events in an unmediated fashion, and learn what the commanders in the field were feeling.[154] Dayan usually went to the various division command centers and, after the Canal was crossed, he followed the troops to the new frontline. He undoubtedly placed himself in danger. Adan related that, at least once, a napalm bomb fell near Dayan, who miraculously escaped injury.[155] Yaakov Amidror, then a young officer, provided other testimony about fire near Dayan: "The helicopters were firing just feet away from us ... He didn't move a muscle."[156]

Dayan explained:

> I visited a front practically every day ... It seemed to me crucial given my role in the war. I could not have known – certainly not understood – what was happening on the fronts, what was possible and what was impossible, only by hearing the Chief of Staff's reports and explanations ... There is no substitute for seeing things from an observation post, looking through binoculars, and touring the frontlines. No command center, no map, no aerial photography can illustrate the situation as well as a direct impression.[157]

Dayan would also complain about the noise in the command centers, which wouldn't let him think, and criticized the military method whereby "a commander is surrounded by staff officers and doesn't have a single moment for quiet contemplation ... I preferred going from one commander to another to meet them face-to-face at the front."[158]

Historian Martin Van Creveld describes a general's need to see the battlefield in person, which enables them to develop insights and absorb information

---

[154] See chart detailing the locations and times of Dayan's and Elazar's field trips, in Golan, *Milhama beyom hakippurim*, pp. 1318-1320.
[155] Adan, *Al shtei g'deot hasuez*, p. 235.
[156] Yaakov Amidror, "Moshe Dayan: Between Strategist and Statesman" (Hebrew), *Iyunim bebitahon leumi* Vol. 5 (November 2003), p. 27.
[157] Dayan, *Avnei derekh*, p. 621.
[158] Ibid.

about the terrain and the enemy at any given moment in a way unattainable from reports from the chain of command. Van Creveld calls this ability the "directed binocular"[159] and describes the Prussian army's General Staff officers as men who served as "directed telescopes," because they were stationed in field units and transmitted reports directly to the Chief of Staff, bypassing the long chain of command.[160]

Dayan's visits to the fronts gave him insights into what was happening there and enabled him to better brief the cabinet about events he had personally witnessed. The visits also gave him opportunities to emphasize important points to commanders. Adan described how, on October 16, the "war council" – Sharon, Adan, Bar-Lev, Elazar, and Dayan – crouched in the desert over a map to plan the next move.[161] The next day, October 17, the canal crossing was delayed, and Dayan turned to Elazar and Bar-Lev insisting that they had to speed things up: "The option you wanted from the government is now in your hands. With every hour that passes, the Egyptians are getting better organized!"[162] Sharon, too, described Dayan, on the spot, spurring on Elazar and Bar-Lev,[163] and recalled that only Dayan, not the Southern Command commander, came to see the situation for himself.[164] Dayan also helped make important military decisions on October 18, seeing that the army could advance north rather than west. Dayan's presence, then, was felt and made a difference.

Through his presence, Dayan also kept commanders abreast of political and other military developments. Dayan, true to the mission command approach, by which commanders make better decisions if they understand the overall state of affairs, always made sure to directly inform commanders of general developments. Adan summarized it well:

> Since October 16, Dayan started visiting our division headquarters each and every day. We welcomed him gladly. We would make coffee for the guest who had made a point of getting to know every person in the command center. Dayan would give me the latest update on the other sectors, express his opinion on the direction I should aim at, but make sure to say these were ministerial opinions and not an attempt to interfere with the commands working their way through the channels of command ... When leaving, he'd say "Tomorrow – same time, different place."

---

[159] Martin Van Creveld, *Command in War*, Cambridge, MA: Harvard University Press, 1985, p. 75.
[160] Van Creveld, *Command in War*, p. 142.
[161] Adan, *Al shtei g'deot hasuez*, p. 218.
[162] Adan, *Al shtei g'deot hasuez*, p. 222.
[163] Ariel Sharon with David Chanoff, *Warrior: An Autobiography of Ariel Sharon*, New York: Simon and Schuster, 1989, p. 328.
[164] Ibid., p. 330.

Dayan's Pessimism at Editors' Committee and Media Appearances

During a period of strict censorship and centralized media, Dayan, unlike Meir and Elazar, believed in truthfully informing the public. Dayan insisted on leading authentically and sought transparency with his colleagues and the public. On October 9, he briefed the Editors' Committee. While now more optimistic, he painted a grim picture of the failures of the first days, which contrasted with the committee members' prior understandings. Consequently, the editors urged Meir to prohibit Dayan from saying such things on television, fearing the public would not be able to bear it. Over time, events from October 7 and 9 October merged, causing confusion and leading the public to believe that Dayan had somehow lost his bearings.

This highlights a case of two contradictory communication approaches: Dayan's honesty policy versus Elazar's preference for painting a rosy picture, creating public optimism. Which approach is preferable is debatable, similar to the medical dilemma of whether to tell a terminally ill patient the truth. Each approach has clear pluses and minuses; neither one is clearly better. Ultimately, the decision depends on the situation and the decision-makers' worldview and values.[165]

The Fall of the First-Line Strongpoints and the POW Question

Dayan received intense criticism over his instructions at the war's outset to halt the efforts to reach the Bar-Lev Line's first-line strongpoints, asking soldiers to evacuate on their own, a violation of a core IDF principle to never abandon any man and of the contract between the ordinary soldiers – the "cannon fodder" – and the commanders. Every IDF soldier going into battle understood that their commanders would do their utmost not to leave them behind. At the war's start, there were some 460 soldiers on the Suez Canal line. Most were killed or captured, with only a few managing to evacuate safely. The desperate calls coming from the surrounded strongpoints became a symbol, which was indelibly imprinted in the public mind, along with photos of the humiliated POWs and the fall of the Bar-Lev Line. Motti Ashkenazi, the commanding officer at the Budapest strongpoint who later led the postwar antigovernment protest, said that while surrounded by the Egyptians, he tried to reassure his men by saying, "Look at Moshe Dayan. He won't abandon us." To Dayan, he said later, "To us, you were God."[166]

Dayan's difficult decision stemmed from a realistic situation assessment. The IDF forces had suffered tremendous losses desperately trying to reach the

---

[165] For more on the difference between Dayan and Elazar in their media approaches, see Golan, *Milhama beyom hakippurim*, p. 562.

[166] Motti Ashkenazi, *Ha'erev beshesh tifrots milhama* (Hebrew), Tel Aviv: United Kibbutz, 2003, p. 173.

strongpoints to evacuate the men. Dayan, identifying attrition as the main problem, had to give this difficult order to prevent more losses that could weaken the new defense line. Leaders sometimes must make difficult, even cruel decisions, and there is no doubt that this particular decision haunted Dayan. After the war, when an unknown woman who had lost a loved one yelled "murderer" at him, he wrote that he felt as if he'd been stabbed in the heart.[167] His first demand in the ceasefire negotiations was for a list of POWs, followed by their safe return as a precondition for further progress. The ceasefire talks with the Syrians also began only after they agreed to give Kissinger the list of the POWs in captivity.

Postwar public pressure resulted in the establishment of a National Commission of Inquiry immediately after the fighting ended. Chaired by Shimon Agranat, President of the Supreme Court, it included Justice Moshe Landau, State Comptroller Yitzchak Nebenzahl, and former Chiefs of Staff Yigael Yadin and Haim Laskov. Beginning its work on November 25, 1973, the Agranat Commission examined the war's prelude and conduct until October 8 but concluded that it lacked authority to decide on the members of the political echelon's future public service, limiting personal decisions to military personnel alone. The members probably expected that the government would resign in face of the mounting public protest.

Dayan, with previous experience testifying before the National Commission of Inquiry into the Lavon Affair, came thoroughly prepared with documentation and accompanied by legal consultant Elyakim Rubinstein. The public criticized Dayan for preparing in advance, unlike others appearing before the committee, and for exercising influence over the choice of commission members in his efforts not to be held responsible for the debacle.

As noted, former commander Motti Ashkenazi spearheaded the public protest. Dayan hosted Ashkenazi at his home to hear his criticism, but the two failed to agree on anything. Dayan found Ashkenazi's assertions "confused and childish" and claimed that Ashkenazi had come mostly to "spout off rather than to listen."[168]

The Agranat Commission held the military echelon, in particular Elazar, Zeira, and Gonen, responsible for the catastrophe, a decision which escalated antigovernment protests and calls for Dayan's and Meir's resignations. Despite the pressure, Dayan continued in his post until Meir's resignation the day after the Agranat Commission report was published on April 10, 1974. Her resignation led to the resignation of the entire government. Dayan remained in his post for another two months or so until the establishment of a new government to complete the separation of forces agreement with Syria.

---

[167] Dayan, *Avnei derekh*, p. 726.
[168] Ibid., p. 728.

As the war progressed, Dayan's image as an omnipotent hero cracked and finally shattered, mirroring the public's perception of the IDF leadership. His reputation in Israel (although not elsewhere in the world) never recovered, and his name – more than that of any other Israeli leader of his era – is associated with the war's failures. His past superstar status, which to a large extent nurtured and reflected the Israeli public's sense of superiority, was also the reason for his attracting the most anger. He had become a public symbol of Israel's arrogant blindness that had led to national disaster. The war took a heavy toll, with more than 2,600 killed (out of a population of only 3.3 million) and 7,000 injured. Israelis, accustomed to rapid victories with minimal losses, now viewed humiliated POWs and enemy flags flying over captured IDF strongpoints on their televisions.

The Israeli public, which had believed in the absolute superiority of its army, was looking for scapegoats to cleanse the national conscience. The Agranat Commission, which avoided any public censure of political figures, and Dayan's postwar refusal to resign or apologize – as his own words, "never explain, never complain" expressed[169] – infuriated the public and made him a despised figure: the essence of everything Israel used to be but no longer was.

And, of course, Dayan had his political rivals. Close associates of Allon, Elazar, Meir, and Galili, and others awaited his downfall, exaggerating stories, spreading rumors about Dayan's "hysteria" and "losing his head," and misinterpreting events.

It is interesting to compare Elazar's and Dayan's postwar public images. Elazar, harshly criticized by the Agranat Commission, eventually became a positive figure in public perception due to his premature death while fighting to clear his name and his portrayal by Hanoch Bartov, a renowned Israeli author.[170] He was described as a lone hero bearing the war's burdens, and his untimely passing in 1976 was perceived to be the result of unfair treatment and a broken heart. Over time, Elazar became a national hero, practically free of any lasting criticism. More recently, Meir's public image has undergone a process of rehabilitation, portraying her as a resolute female leader among men, who steadfastly navigated times of crisis. This transition in perspective has been made possible by the release of new publications and documentaries, with the Hollywood feature film *Golda* (2023), starring British actor Helen Mirren in the lead role, having the most pronounced impact. Many decades later, a more balanced view of the war is required. To military analysts, it seems almost obvious that a clash of huge forces in the desert combined with one on the Golan Heights between tens of thousands of soldiers, thousands of tanks, fighter jets, and artillery barrels would inevitably lead to very heavy losses on both sides (the Arab side suffered approximately 16,000 dead and 35,000

---

[169] Quoted by Dan Margalit, *Ra'iti otam* (Hebrew), Tel Aviv: Zmora-Bitan, 1997, p. 120.

[170] Hanoch Bartov, *Dado: 48 shana ve'od 20 yom* (Hebrew), vol. 1, Israel: Dvir, 1st ed. 1978, expanded edition 2002.

wounded, and 8,700 POWs, with 35,000 besieged soldiers on the verge of surrender had it not been for US intervention).[171]

Military history shows that victories like that of the Six-Day War are rare. The Yom Kippur War, which started with Israel the weakest it had ever been, ended with Israeli battlefield victories, an astounding achievement considering the situation at the war's outset. Despite Israel's security doctrine that it must neutralize any immediate military threat, it does not have the ability to defeat enemy nations to the point of forcing them into an unconditional surrender. The Yom Kippur War was further proof of the limits of Israel's power in this sense. Still, it became clear to the Arabs that they could not defeat Israel in a regular war, leading Egypt to prefer peace and the Syrian border becoming Israel's quietest until the 2011 civil war began. Israel's enemies now choose to fight through proxies, the Yom Kippur War thus marking the end – at least for the time being – of the era of large regular wars during which Israel, fighting five wars in twenty-five years, was under continuous threat of military invasion. For many military experts around the world, Dayan was part of the failure but also part of the success in turning the tides of the war. However, the Israeli public and leadership turned their collective backs on him. He once said, "Other nations would have made this war into an unsurpassed victory. Look what happens to the British at Dunkirk and in Singapore, to the Russians with Barbarossa, and the Americans at Pearl Harbor. At the early stages of war, nations take hits."[172]

Perhaps Dayan's biggest mistake lay in the area in which he had previously been a master – communications. He should have helped the Israeli public, army, and political leadership understand and acknowledge that Israel's strategic reality after the Six-Day War and War of Attrition was poor and could potentially lead to a war tougher than any since 1948. Instead, he allowed himself and the nation to succumb to an illusion of superiority that began with the Six-Day War.

---

[171] Elhanan Oren, *Toldot Milhemet Yom HaKippurim* (Hebrew), Tel Aviv: IDF – History Department, 2013, p. 537.
[172] Erez and Kfir, *Sihot im Moshe Dayan*, p. 108.

10

The Dealmaker

Peace with Egypt

"On Saturday morning, May 21, 1977, Menachem Begin called me to offer me the position of foreign minister in the government he was establishing." With these words, Dayan opened his autobiography. They mark the last chapter in Dayan's political career, in which he played a pivotal role in the peace process with Egypt.[1]

On June 3, 1974, after Golda Meir and her cabinet resigned, Labor Party leader Yitzhak Rabin established a new government, excluding Dayan. Dayan's "victory" in the Agranat Commission had been largely a Pyrrhic one, as his having evaded any condemnation from the commission fueled public wrath against him. He even had to be hastily ushered out through a back door at Bar-Ilan University to avoid being pummeled by bereaved parents.[2] Similarly, the media and politicians, including those from his own party, distanced themselves from him. Publicly, he had reached the end of the road. *Sic transit gloria mundi* (thus passes the glory of the world), Menachem Begin muttered on seeing Dayan sitting by himself in the Knesset cafeteria.[3]

After the Yom Kippur War, Dayan believed that a more significant settlement could emerge between Israel and Egypt than in the past, although not the permanent solution the superpowers insisted upon. He thought that Henry Kissinger was essential for reaching a partial arrangement.[4]

On September 3, 1975, the Rabin government, nearly two years after the war's end, reached an interim arrangement with Egypt, the Sinai 2 Agreement, signed September 4. It demanded a 30-kilometer Israeli withdrawal from the Suez Canal and established both sides' commitment to a peaceful resolution.

---

[1] Moshe Dayan, *Halanetsah tokhal herev* (Hebrew), Jerusalem: Edanim Publishers, Yedioth Aharonot, 1981, p. 17.
[2] Robert Slater, *Warrior Statesman: The Life of Moshe Dayan*, New York: St Martin's Press, 1st ed., 1991, p. 385.
[3] Cited in Arieh Naor's essay, "Levi Eshkol's Ouster from the Defense Ministry and the Six-Day War Outcomes: Anatomy of a Savior Complex" (Hebrew), in Devora Cohen and Moshe Lisk (eds.), *Tsomtei hakhra'ot ufarshiyot mafte'ah beyisrael*, Kiryat Sdeh Boker: The Ben-Gurion Institute for the Study of Israel and Zionism, Ben-Gurion University of the Negev, 2010, pp. 446–488 (p. 485).
[4] Slater, *Warrior Statesman*, p. 386.

An addendum included a US commitment to providing Israel with oil and advanced planes.[5]

This represented the first agreement between Israel and an Arab nation not resulting from a war; rather, it set a precedent for dialogue, trust-building, and increased US involvement at the expense of the USSR. The Suez Canal was rebuilt, and its cities were reconstructed, as Dayan had wanted after the end of the Six-Day War.[6]

Despite this agreement, threats against Israel persisted. On June 27, 1976, a group of Palestinian and German terrorists hijacked an Air France plane and flew it to Entebbe, Uganda, holding the passengers hostage. On July 4, the IDF executed a daring 3,800-kilometer rescue mission – Operation Thunderbolt. Defense Minister Shimon Peres, who still held Dayan in great respect after the Yom Kippur War, wanted Dayan's approval before proceeding. Coming specially to a restaurant where Dayan was dining, Peres told Dayan about the bold plan. Dayan responded that "It's a beauty of a plan!"[7] Dayan cited his trust in the proposed operation's commanders – Benny Peled, in charge of flying the planes to Entebbe, and Yoni Netanyahu, in charge of the raid itself,[8] further evidence of the importance Dayan attributed to leadership – for him, the decisive factor in any plan.

For Dayan, Operation Thunderbolt marked the completion of the transfer of leadership to Prime Minister Rabin, Defense Minister Peres, and Chief of Staff Motta Gur. As defense minister, Dayan had prosecuted the war on PLO-led international terrorism, including the infamous Lod Airport attack in 1972, which killed twenty-four and wounded seventy-one passengers in the hall with gunfire and hand grenades, carried out by three members of the Japanese Red Army on behalf of the Popular Front for the Liberation of Palestine (PFLP). Another infamous attack was the murder of the eleven Israeli athletes at the Munich Olympic Games later that summer by the Palestinian Black September terrorist organization.

On May 8, 1972, a Sabena flight out of Brussels was hijacked by Black September. After landing in Israel, the hijackers threatened to blow up the plane and its ninety passengers if 315 Palestinian terrorists were not released from Israeli prisons. Defense Minister Dayan personally directed the negotiations and helped devise a scheme to deceive the terrorists. The plan had been for fighters from the elite Sayeret Matkal unit to board the plane dressed as mechanics and maintenance men. A Red Cross official, discovering hidden guns beneath their overalls, refused to let them board. Dayan grabbed the

---

[5] Kenneth Stein, *Mediniyut amitsa* (Hebrew), Tel Aviv: Maarakhot, 2003, p. 218.
[6] Ibid., p. 217.
[7] Slater, *Warrior Statesman*, p. 387; Mati Golan, *Peres* (Hebrew), Jerusalem: Schocken, 1982, p. 182.
[8] Yaakov Erez and Ilan Kfir, *Sihot im Moshe Dayan* (Hebrew), Ramat Gan: Massada, 1981, p. 41. Yoni was the older brother of Israel's Prime Minister Benjamin (Bibi) Netanyahu.

walkie-talkie and, addressing the official as if he were a junior officer under his command, barked, "This is Gen. Dayan speaking. I am instructing you to let them pass." The Red Cross official obeyed.[9] The rescue operation, Isotope, is still considered a successful model for handling similar situations.

On May 15, 1974, a terrorist cell entered the town of Maalot in northern Israel where its members proceeded to attack an apartment building, killing civilians, before taking over an elementary school where more than a hundred high-school students and their teachers were staying during a field trip. Some managed to escape, but eighty-five students, two teachers, and two medics were held hostage for the next two days. The army began negotiations with the captors, who were threatening to execute the hostages if their demands to release twenty imprisoned terrorists were not met. Dayan traveled to Maalot to order immediate military action and take the terrorists by surprise. But Motta Gur refused, and Dayan, his standing weakened, capitulated. Dayan crawled up to the windows of the school building and was shocked by the sight of armed terrorists facing dozens of adolescents. He – the lifelong fighter – later told his assistant, Naftali Lau, a Holocaust survivor, that for the first time he understood how Jews during the Holocaust obeyed just a handful of men carrying weapons.[10] By the time Gur authorized a military action in the afternoon, the terrorists were expecting it. Twenty-two students, five civilians, and one soldier were killed, and scores were injured in the botched mission, since known as "the Maalot disaster."[11] Dayan's last firefight, it was a jarring final chord.

Dayan's Return to the Political Arena

Following his inauguration as president of the United States in January 1977, Jimmy Carter and his team – Secretary of State Cyrus Vance and National Security Advisor Zbigniew Brzeziński – played a key role in achieving the ground-breaking Israel–Egypt peace treaty. Perhaps somewhat naive, the energetic Carter dove headfirst into the peace process, focusing on a comprehensive arrangement he thought could be achieved through a conference with all sides led by the two superpowers, the United States and the Soviet Union. Viewing such a conference as a trap in light of Carter's vision of a united and therefore powerful Arab delegation, Rabin and his successor Prime Minister Menachem Begin objected, thus bringing Carter closer to Sadat.[12] Carter, who also demanded Israel's return to the 1967 borders, was

---

[9] From the docudrama *Sabena* by Rani Sa'ar (director), Nati Diner, and Moshe Zonder.
[10] Neora Barnoah-Matalon, *Makom tov batsad* (Hebrew), Tel Aviv: Kotarim Publishers, 2009, p. 226.
[11] For more on the Maalot attack, see Moshe Dayan, *Avnei derekh: Autobiografia* (Hebrew), Jerusalem: Idanim Publishers, 1976, pp. 719–723.
[12] Stein, *Mediniyut amitsa*, p. 228.

the first US president to make the Palestinian issue a priority.[13] After meeting Sadat in April 1977, Carter said he and Sadat had "hit it off extremely well."[14] Sadat courted Carter, understanding that by using the US president, Egypt could regain the Sinai Peninsula. Carter became Egypt's de facto representative vis-à-vis Israel.[15]

This paved the way for Dayan's return to politics after three years in the political and public opinion desert. The scheduled elections were held early – in May instead of autumn 1977 – triggered by a political crisis about desecrating the Jewish Sabbath that led to Rabin's resignation. Dayan aspired to a central role but was not in a position to extract promises from his party.[16] He therefore reached out to Begin, with whom he felt more of a shared ideology than with Labor. Dayan's stance on the key point of the West Bank was a mix of Labor and Likud positions. He opposed the Likud's hoped-for annexation as well as Labor's proposed relinquishment. Uncomfortable with Begin's pompous and dramatic style, so far from his own restrained approach, and unable to accept Begin's refusal to guarantee no West Bank annexation, Dayan did not join Likud.

In April 1977, after Leah and Yitzhak Rabin were discovered to be illegally holding US dollar accounts in Washington, DC,[17] Rabin resigned as Labor's leader, and the much less popular Peres became the Labor Party's candidate. This contributed to the Likud election victory, resulting in the first Likud-led government in the country's history. The idea of Dayan crossing party lines was unthinkable. Begin believed that even Dayan, capable of almost anything, would never contemplate such as move, derided as "political prostitution" by a Knesset member.[18] Begin faced public backlash for the very idea, promising bereaved parents that Dayan would not be appointed a minister in his government.[19]

But Begin very much wanted Dayan, and Dayan had often proved that he could disregard criticism and was loyal only to his own beliefs, not any partisan platform. Dayan agreed to join Begin's government under two conditions, one

---

[13] Ibid., p. 233; William B. Quandt, *Camp David: Peacemaking and Politics* (Brookings, 1986) in Hebrew translation, Jerusalem: Keter, 1988, p. 62.

[14] Stein, *Mediniyut amitsa*, p. 236.

[15] Ibid., p. 237.

[16] Slater, *Warrior Statesman*, p. 389.

[17] At the time, it was illegal for Israeli citizens to hold bank accounts overseas, barring exceptional circumstances; the account in question had been opened while Yitzhak Rabin was the Israeli ambassador to the United States (1968–1973) and, according to procedure, should have been closed once he left that post.

[18] Slater, *Warrior Statesman*, p. 393: "Dayan had asked for expert advice and found that there was ample precedent for keeping his seat. Israel Kargman, the former chairman of the Knesset Finance Committee, called Dayan's defection an act of political prostitution and rank treachery."

[19] Ibid., p. 391.

ideological and one personal: no West Bank annexation, and retaining his Labor party Knesset seat, causing even more party outrage, as Labor accused him of joining the enemy and costing them a Knesset seat.

What did Begin gain? Begin, suffering from a very negative image, was desperate for international legitimacy, which he believed Dayan could deliver. Although aware of Dayan's tarnished image at home, Begin needed Dayan's international heroic status. Begin acknowledged about Dayan that, "He has no second when it comes to speaking and negotiating with world leaders," adding "I want statesmen all over the world to carefully check how they're dressed before the Israeli foreign minister enters their study."[20] Dayan's inclusion in the government provided continuity between two dramatically different governments, reassuring many that Begin had a responsible adult by his side.[21] As Yoel Marcus wrote:

> The match between Dayan and Begin would show itself as the most important factor in jumpstarting the peace process ... It was a miraculous encounter: on the one hand, a man seeking to change his image as "terrorist" and enter history as the one to bring the peace, and, on the other hand, a man seeking to erase the stain of Yom Kippur, understanding that a unique situation required unique solutions and only he was capable of providing them.[22]

Ezer Weizman, Begin's defense minister, like others, suspected that Dayan joined Begin's government to promote his own peace plan, writing:

> When he joined the Begin government, Dayan was seeking to continue where he had left off in 1971. He felt that all sides wanted a settlement. Begin's attitude to Dayan was special: almost from the first moment, Begin's door was open to Dayan in a way it never was to any other member of his government.[23]

Indeed, Dayan, with his acute political instincts, sensed the possibility for peace talks. In an August 1977 lecture, he announced: "My situation assessment is that we are on the brink of a national event of the greatest historic proportions since 1948," adding, "It may be that we have reached valid talks of political content ... and perhaps more than that – an actual peace treaty."[24] Dayan continued that he sensed an opportunity to negotiate peace, with

---

[20] Yoel Marcus, *Camp David: Hapetah leshalom* (Hebrew), Jerusalem: Schocken, 1979, p. 28.

[21] Gerald M. Steinberg and Ziv Rubinovitz, *Menachem Begin and the Israel–Egypt Peace Process: Between Ideology and Political Realism*, Bloomington: Indiana University Press, 2019, pp. 59–60.

[22] Marcus, *Camp David*, p. 30.

[23] Ezer Weizman, *Hakrav al hashalom* (Hebrew), Jerusalem: Idanim, 1981, p. 261.

[24] Elyakim Rubinstein, "Moshe Dayan and the Peace Process" (Hebrew), in *Moshe Dayan: Bein estrateg lemedina'ee*, published in honor of the 22th anniversary of the death of Lieutenant General Moshe Dayan, special issue of *Iyunim bevitahon leumi* 5 (2003), p. 97.

Israel's better position than ever, with land to bargain with. While noting points of agreements with the United States, Dayan acknowledged obstacles, like Jewish settlements across the Green Line, the extent of any future Israeli withdrawal, and the PLO's status.[25] Dayan, skeptical that a comprehensive agreement with all Israel's enemies could be reached, supported an incremental approach and stressed the importance of the US guarantees. He was confident of success with Egypt.[26]

Dayan later wrote that he joined the Begin government as foreign minister in order to "to greatly affect the moves of the Israeli government to attain a peace settlement with our Arab neighbors and the Palestinians,"[27] despite his differences with Begin. Begin wanted Israeli sovereignty over the entire historic land of Israel, while Dayan believed "in an arrangement of coexistence between us and the Arabs living in this region with none imposing sovereignty on the other."[28] Now Dayan was committing to attaining peace. His advisor Elyakim Rubinstein wrote, "In his terms as foreign minister, he would work day and night with urgency and passion, pouring his entire being into the process."[29]

On June 24, Dayan presented Begin with a summary of discussion principles for Carter's upcoming Geneva conference. Dayan proposed a phased agreement, with each stage contingent on the success of the preceding one. Dayan believed the immediate goal should be ending the state of war rather than achieving peace, which would be hard to attain. Dayan suggested that the depth of the retreat would depend on the depth of the peace.[30] About the West Bank, Dayan felt: "This is our ancient homeland; a revival of Israel and return to Zion that would forbid Jews to settle in Judea and Samaria is unthinkable." He insisted on resolving the refugee issue before tackling the Palestinian problem in the territories. Dayan envisaged a form of Palestinian sovereignty with some sort of connection to Jordan.[31] Ultimately, he was confident about reaching a peace arrangement, including about the West Bank.[32]

During August 1977, Dayan sprang into action as foreign minister, secretly meeting Indian and Iranian leaders and King Hussein of Jordan. Realizing that Hussein was insisting on Israel's return to the pre-1967 lines, Dayan understood that he had to focus on the Egyptian peace process.[33]

---

[25] Ibid., p. 100.
[26] Ibid., pp. 97–104.
[27] Moshe Dayan, *Hala-netsah tokhal ḥerev: Sihot hashalom – reshamim ishi'im* (Hebrew), Tel Aviv: Idanim, 1981, p. 18.
[28] Ibid., p. 19.
[29] Elyakim Rubinstein, *Darkei shalom* (Hebrew), Tel Aviv: Defense Ministry Publishing, 1992, p. 12.
[30] Dayan, *Hala-netsah tokhal ḥerev*, p. 24.
[31] Ibid., p. 26.
[32] Steinberg and Rubinovitz, *Menachem Begin and the Israel–Egypt Peace Process*, p. 63.
[33] Ibid., p. 70.

That same month, Secretary of State Vance was encouraged by Sadat's and Dayan's attitudes after returning from talks in Middle East capitals, although there had been no breakthrough. Vance felt that Dayan had moderated Begin's rigidity,[34] Dayan having assured Vance that Sinai and its Jewish settlements would not hinder peace.[35]

After the Jordanian channel closed, attention shifted to Egypt. Dayan suggested renewing communications with Egypt via Morocco, prior intelligence-sharing with Morocco making it a natural conduit.[36] A breakthrough occurred when King Hassan of Morocco invited Dayan to a secret meeting at his palace. There, Dayan sent a message to Egypt about Israel's willingness at the highest echelon of heads of state or foreign ministers. Egypt agreed. Dayan immediate asked Meir Rosen, the Foreign Ministry's legal counsel, to prepare a draft of an Israeli–Egyptian peace agreement. The forty-eight-point draft was then sent to Cairo and Washington.[37]

A meeting between Dayan and Hassan Touhami, deputy head of the Egyptian government, was scheduled for September 16, and the US administration was informed. Dayan was to address the UN Assembly on September 18. Touhami was adamant: Sadat would not shake hands with an Israeli leader as long as there was as much as one single Israeli soldier on Egyptian soil. Dayan responded that that was no way to start a negotiation. Dayan later denied Egyptian claims that they had continued the talks after Dayan promised Touhami all of Sinai. Dayan insisted that he had told Touhami not to rely on full Israeli withdrawal or evacuation of Israeli settlements in Sinai, while assuring him that they could reach a satisfactory arrangement.[38] Regardless, Touhami left believing that Israel would withdraw from Sinai, which he communicated to Sadat. The Egyptians agreed to continue talks, with a second meeting taking place only about two and a half months later. In the interim, Dayan ceaselessly sought ways to bridge their gaps and reach a separate peace agreement with Egypt.[39]

After his initial meeting with Touhami, Dayan proceeded to New York, ostensibly to address the UN, but really to prepare for Carter's Geneva conference, on which the United States remained fixated, naively believing that they could resolve the conflict in one comprehensive conference bringing

---

[34] Quandt, *Camp David*, p. 88.
[35] Steinberg and Rubinovitz, *Menachem Begin and the Israel–Egypt Peace Process*, p. 70.
[36] Ibid., p. 74.
[37] Slater, *Warrior Statesman*, p. 397.
[38] Mohamed Heikal, *Secret Channels: The Inside Story of Arab–Israeli Peace Negotiations*, Harper Collins Publishers, New York, 1996, p. 262; Steinberg and Rubinovitz, *Menachem Begin and the Israel–Egypt Peace Process*, p. 74. Stein claims that he examined all existing sources and found no trace that Dayan promised the Sinai Peninsula to Touhami: Stein, *Mediniyut amitsa*, p. 248.
[39] Quandt, *Camp David*, p. 102.

all the sides together, including the Soviets.⁴⁰ Sadat, wary of Palestinian or Syrian interference and eager to neutralize Soviet influence, sought an alternate route – direct talks with Israel.⁴¹

On September 19, 1977, Dayan and Vance met, followed by a meeting with Carter. The meeting with Vance went well, with Dayan hinting at returning all of Sinai to Egypt, a hint forwarded to Ismail Fahmi, Egypt's foreign minister, on September 21.⁴² However, the meeting with Carter was more confrontational, with a belligerent Carter accusing Israel of being more stubborn than the Arabs. "You put obstacles on the path to peace," a refrain Carter would utter often in the near future.⁴³

Dayan repeated Israel's stance on the legality of Jewish settlements in the West Bank and its refusal to withdraw in a peace settlement. He did propose a compromise to restrict new building to military facilities only, to which Begin immediately objected. Another disagreement with Carter was including an independent PLO-led Palestinian delegation at the Geneva conference, to which Israel was vehemently opposed, fearing it would inevitably to the establishment of a Palestinian state. Dayan was also skeptical about the conference, believing it would hinder Sadat's ability to reach a separate agreement with Israel independently.⁴⁴ The US administration misjudged Sadat's eagerness for talks, impatience with delays, and aversion to Soviet involvement.⁴⁵ Despite tensions, Carter concluded he could work with Dayan. However, Carter was unaware that Dayan was sometimes crossing Begin's rigid policy lines. Dayan, too, was unhappy with the meeting's atmosphere and the US positions raised.⁴⁶ Carter later wrote that he respected Dayan because he wanted to achieve peace and end the occupation, writing that Dayan "even showed some flexibility on the Palestinians," proposing a joint Arab delegation for Geneva's opening session and having PLO leaders later join the Jordanian if they were not well known.⁴⁷

On September 29, Dayan received the US draft to convene a joint US–USSR peace conference no later than December 1977. The draft, made public two days later, mentioned Palestinian inclusion. Despite Israel's reservations with US policy, Dayan decided to influence US policy by gaining US public support. Still a magnet for US Jewry, Dayan spoke in interviews and at Jewish community gatherings, relaying a stark message: "We are being told by Carter and

---

⁴⁰ Stein, *Mediniyut amitsa*, p. 146.
⁴¹ Quandt, *Camp David*, p. 63; Stein, *Mediniyut amitsa*, p. 246.
⁴² Steinberg and Rubinovitz, *Menachem Begin and the Israel–Egypt Peace Process*, p. 76.
⁴³ Slater, *Warrior Statesman*, p. 399.
⁴⁴ Stein, *Mediniyut amitsa*, p. 241.
⁴⁵ Ibid., p. 254.
⁴⁶ Quandt, *Camp David*, p. 105.
⁴⁷ Jimmy Carter, *Keeping Faith: Memoirs of a President*, Fayetteville: University of Arkansas Press, 1995, p. 300.

Vance that if we want peace, we must accept the Arab terms. Maybe there will be peace if we do all that but there will be no Israel. We are not going to accept this."[48] Dayan stressed that Israel would not negotiate with the PLO.

Dayan's PR campaign was successful and pressured the administration,[49] resulting in a Carter–Dayan meeting on October 4. Carter was stunned by Dayan's clout and the intensity of public opposition to his rigid positions on Israel. Dayan, too, was aware of the shift in the balance of power and used his advantage carefully. At first, their exchanges were difficult. Brzeziński later recalled being shocked by Dayan's threat to use public opinion against the world's largest superpower. But during the conversation, Carter became more conciliatory, occasionally asking Dayan what he intended to tell the journalists waiting outside and the audiences across the country in his coast-to-coast campaign to sway public opinion.

Dayan asked if Israel could participate in the Geneva conference without accepting the joint US–Soviet declaration and was told it was possible. William Quandt, then on the National Security Council, wrote that Dayan showed creative imagination on the issue of Palestinian representation.[50] The administration suggested lesser-known PLO representatives in an attempt to obscure their affiliation. Dayan joked, saying that by the time they arrived at the conference they would no longer be unknown, and adding, "Mr. President, I may have only one eye, but I'm not blind." Finally, the United States conceded that Israel would have veto power over Palestinian attendees. The administration insisted on a united Arab delegation, contrary to Israel's preference for separate national delegations. Dayan then asked that Carter create the impression that Israel opposed this condition and hint that it was imposed.[51]

Carter asked Dayan if he would support a withdrawal to the 1967 borders in exchange for peace, reminding Dayan that he had objected to occupying the Golan Heights. Dayan answered that it was impossible to turn back the clock. "No withdrawals?" asked Carter. "That would be an overstatement," Dayan retorted. After disagreements, by the end of the evening, the sides had devised a shared US–Israeli working paper, with US compromises on several key points: Palestinian participation but not as a separate delegation; a united Arab delegation that would later split to negotiate bilaterally; and the West Bank and Gaza Strip to be discussed by Israel, Jordan, and the Palestinians without other nations' involvement.[52]

When they left the room, Dayan deflected journalists' questions, motioning that they should ask Vance. This was a calculated gesture, making Vance's statement a joint declaration, with more validity.[53]

[48] Slater, *Warrior Statesman*, p. 400.
[49] Stein, *Mediniyut amitsa*, p. 259.
[50] Quandt, *Camp David*, p. 115.
[51] Slater, *Warrior Statesman*, p. 400.
[52] Ibid., p. 401.
[53] Ibid., pp. 259–260.

Dayan later learned from Sadat that Syria's president Assad had insisted on a united Arab delegation; Egypt's wishes had been similar to Israel's. In the same conversation, Dayan told Sadat that he tried to stop Carter from inviting the Soviets, warning the administration that Sadat opposed Soviet involvement.[54]

Quandt summarized the long but productive meeting[55] in which Dayan deftly navigated the question of Palestinian attendance between Begin's outright veto and Carter's demands. Regarding a separate peace treaty with Egypt, Dayan introduced an important approach: "It's enough to remove a single wheel from a car to keep it from moving."[56] Removing Egypt, the largest and most powerful Arab nation from the conflict would nearly eliminate the possibility of war.

Begin, however, was displeased by the Palestinian inclusion and was furious that Dayan had presented him with a fait accompli. Carter next wanted a secret meeting between Fahmi and Dayan and was surprised that Fahmi accepted a public meeting but wanted Yasser Arafat present. Obviously, Dayan refused. Meanwhile, the government approved the US–Israeli working paper prepared after Dayan's visit.

Publicly, Dayan cooperated with Carter on the Geneva conference, but he actually focused on a separate agreement with Egypt. Both Israel and Egypt felt Geneva was a trap whose potential damage would outweigh its benefits. They made discreet approaches to each other, avoiding superpower interference.

Sadat was known for bold, dramatic gestures that would completely upend strategic reality and thus create new opportunities for change. He was prepared to take huge risks, albeit calculated and deliberate, and made decisions on the basis of his intuition and unique historical understanding. His historic trip to Jerusalem in November 1977 to speak to the Knesset broke decades-old psychological barriers, forever changing the face of the Middle East.

In 1979, Dayan asked Sadat when and why he had thought of going to Jerusalem. Sadat answered that after meetings with Nicolae Ceaușescu, the Romanian dictator, the Shah of Iran, and Saudi Arabian leaders seeking bold moves, he decided that only a personal trip to Jerusalem would effect a fundamental change.[57]

Sadat recalled that he made the decision to go to Jerusalem only on the plane from Riyadh to Cairo. When Dayan asked the purpose of the meeting with Touhami, Sadat explained to Dayan that, "I sent Touhami to set the stage for the Geneva conference." Sadat felt that Geneva was largely ceremonial and would succeed only if everything was previously agreed upon. Once he decided

---

[54] Dayan, *Hala-netsaḥ tokhal ḥerev*, p. 88.
[55] Quandt, *Camp David*, p. 118.
[56] Ibid., p. 116.
[57] Dayan, *Hala-netsaḥ tokhal ḥerev*, p. 87.

to go to Jerusalem, his mind was made up. On November 9, he announced to the Egyptian parliament his plan to travel to the Knesset in Jerusalem to achieve a peace treaty.

Dayan was initially skeptical about Sadat's sincerity[58] but was convinced when Sadat accepted Begin's invitation to Israel, saying that such a visit would be an event of supreme importance.[59] Interviewed on Israeli radio, Dayan said that if there was any chance of a bilateral Egyptian–Israeli peace treaty being signed, he would support it immediately, before the Geneva conference. Dayan realized that Sadat had abandoned his precondition of Israeli withdrawal from all conquered Egyptian territory, which was a tremendous diplomatic victory for Israel and too good an opportunity to miss. Dayan recognized the immense symbolic importance of Sadat's visit but remained worried about bridging the enormous gaps between the sides.[60]

November 19, 1977, is a day no Israeli alive then will ever forget. On that day, the leader of the largest and most important Arab nation broke the absolute boycott the Arab nations had imposed on Israel since the moment of its establishment.

Dayan was one of the first Israelis Sadat met after he stepped off the plane. "Don't worry, Moshe. It will be all right," said Sadat. It was "as if he had read Dayan's concerned mind that somehow Sadat was intent on tricking the Israelis."[61] Israel was gripped by ecstasy, feeling that that peace had already arrived, with just a few annoying details to be resolved. The truth, of course, was that the road to peace was still long, winding, and full of pitfalls.

In the car from the airport to Jerusalem, Dayan asked his Egyptian counterpart, Boutros Boutros-Ghali, if Egypt would be willing to sign a separate peace treaty with Israel. Boutros-Ghali emphatically answered, "No." Dayan requested that Sadat not mention the PLO in his speech to the Knesset, to which Boutros-Ghali did not respond. But Sadat did indeed avoid mentioning the PLO. According to an Egyptian journalist, the reason was Dayan's request.[62]

On November 20, Dayan and Sadat met for lunch, with Sadat restating his peace conditions and asking if Israel was interested in discussions of substantive matters. After Dayan replied that Sadat's crammed schedule lacked time for serious talks, Sadat agreed that the discussion of essential issues would begin immediately and continue after his return to Egypt so that they could come to Geneva already in agreement.[63] Sadat emphasized that he would not sign a separate agreement with Israel. The meetings with Dayan were always

---

[58] Slater, *Warrior Statesman*, p. 403.
[59] Ibid., p. 403.
[60] Stein, *Mediniyut amitsa*, p. 265.
[61] Slater, *Warrior Statesman*, p. 404.
[62] Heikal, *Secret Channels*, p. 263.
[63] Dayan, *Hala-netsaḥ tokhal ḥerev*, p. 82.

business-like, lacking the personal rapport Sadat enjoyed with Ezer Weizman. Dayan's mention of his three visits to Egypt (in 1956, 1967, and 1973) apparently irritated Sadat, as Dayan symbolized the defeats of 1956 and 1967.[64] Egyptian journalist Mohamed Hassanein Heikal recalled the following anecdote:

> After the visit, a Scandinavian ambassador was reported to have asked Dayan: "I hope you are going to compensate Sadat for the political risks he took?" Dayan replied: "I don't see why we should pay a political price for every event. The guests invited themselves to a party on our territory, and we welcomed them. They brought their own food and drink and music. They should be the ones who thank us because we opened our home for their party."[65]

Whether the story is true or not, it reflects the Egyptian feeling that their leader's bold act wasn't being reciprocated and that Israel felt that Sadat's reception was enough for now.

The climax of the visit was Sadat's speech to the Knesset declaring the end of wars and the opening of negotiations between Israel and Egypt. Sadat enumerated his conditions for peace: the full withdrawal and recognition of the Palestinians' right to a state in the West Bank and Gaza Strip. Begin spoke after Sadat, also speaking of peace but in general terms without any specific commitment.

At dinner, Sadat shared his disappointment with Dayan over Begin's response, but Dayan reassured him that Begin was open to negotiations, which was the most that could be expected at this stage. Exhorting Sadat that perseverance would lead to progress, Dayan assured Sadat that he would not be sorry.[66] After Sadat explained that what he meant by the words "a just peace" was that nations must resolve their differences through talk, not wars, Dayan observed that Egypt was willing to provide "nonbelligerence" but not full peace.[67] Dayan was optimistic about the final outcome but pessimistic about the process. He realized Israel was facing difficult negotiations, but for now he – as he often did – wrote a limerick about this historic visit, ending with the line, "Did it happen or was it just a dream?"[68]

After returning to Egypt, Sadat strove to keep the momentum going and planned a conference in Isma'iliya so that all the nations expected at Geneva could hopefully reach agreements beforehand, arriving in Geneva only for the signing ceremony. Sadat also decided on a preliminary conference for senior officials in Cairo in mid December. In this period, contact with Israeli leaders was conducted through the Touhami–Dayan channel in Morocco. Thus, on

---

[64] Slater, 1991, p. 405.
[65] Heikal, 1996, p. 265.
[66] Dayan, *Hala-netsah tokhal ḥerev*, pp. 84–85.
[67] Steinberg and Rubinovitz, *Menachem Begin and the Israel–Egypt Peace Process*, p. 78.
[68] *Jerusalem Post*, November 13, 1987, in Slater, *Warrior Statesman*, p. 406.

December 2, 1977, in Marrakesh, Dayan offered a territorial withdrawal in Sinai in exchange for demilitarization and preservation of the Israeli settlements. Touhami rejected this, insisting on addressing the Palestinian issue in the context of a comprehensive settlement with all the Arab states. Dayan explored Egypt's willingness to sign a separate peace treaty, but Touhami refused to commit. Dayan left Morocco feeling that the negotiations had hit an impasse and that only US involvement would help advance the process. But Carter was still supporting a comprehensive peace, reflected in his November 30 declaration welcoming the Cairo conference and his hopes for the Geneva conference.[69]

To prepare for Cairo, Begin readied a twenty-one-point plan for Palestinian autonomy in contrast to the US and Egyptian demands for a full withdrawal. Begin's proposal included some of Dayan's ideas, among them establishing an elected Palestinian council, abolishing military rule, and letting the inhabitants choose between Jordanian and Israeli citizenship.[70]

On December 14, the Cairo conference began, doomed from the start, as the other Arab delegations did not come. Sadat continued insisting on a comprehensive settlement, the return of all Palestinian land, and Palestinian self-determination. With such large gaps, Dayan concluded that any agreement with Egypt would entail considerable Israeli concessions.[71]

On December 24, the sides met again in Isma'iliya at the senior leadership level. The unproductive meeting ended with both sides concluding that US involvement was needed. Discouraged, Dayan felt that the chances of the talks succeeding were low. Nonetheless, he started to believe that Sadat was serious about wanting peace.[72] Between January and July, both sides focused their efforts on bringing in the United States as mediator, each trying to win American public opinion and administration support.

In February 1978, Sadat visited the United States, charming the administration, especially Carter, who agreed with Sadat's position that Israel had to withdraw from all occupied land and that the Jewish settlements were an obstacle to peace.[73] Israel was now cornered, negotiating not only with a former enemy but also with its superpower patron, the United States, whose continued backing was critical to Israel's existence. While Carter planned more pressure on Israel over withdrawal, borders, and the settlements,[74] the administration came to realize that Sadat was now seeking a bilateral Israeli–Egyptian agreement.[75]

Despite the difficult situation, Israel retained some bargaining chips, including some choice on land it could agree to relinquish; all Egypt had was words. On

---

[69] Quandt, *Camp David*, p. 135.
[70] Steinberg and Rubinovitz, *Menachem Begin and the Israel–Egypt Peace Process*, p. 104.
[71] Dayan, *Hala-netsaḥ tokhal ḥerev*, p. 96.
[72] Stein, *Mediniyut amitsa*, p. 287.
[73] Dayan, *Hala-netsaḥ tokhal ḥerev*, p. 102.
[74] Quandt, *Camp David*, p. 157.
[75] Ibid., pp. 158–159.

February 8, the day Sadat left the United States, Dayan arrived and, in face of a public now pro-Sadat rather than pro-Israel, including most of US Jewry, Dayan embarked yet again on a coast-to-coast PR campaign to change public opinion. In a February 16 meeting with Carter, Dayan realized that the administration was more aligned with Egypt and viewed Israel as intransigent. Dayan asked Carter two questions: Would Sadat insist that Syria conduct simultaneous talks with Israel, and would Sadat agree to sign an agreement if the Sinai issue were completely resolved and principles about the Palestinians were agreed upon even without Hussein's involvement? Carter answered no to the first question and was uncertain about the second in light of Egypt's mixed signals.[76]

On March 21, 1978, Begin visited Washington at Carter's invitation. Carter's initial attempts to ease Begin's rigid line with a particularly warm reception were unsuccessful, leading Carter to shift his approach and become more critical. The two also lacked any personal chemistry, and Carter viewed Israel as the only obstacle to peace. Indeed, Carter criticized Begin and Israel from the outset.[77] Dayan later wrote: "Carter listened with open impatience to Begin's detailed positions ... He wanted to know what was next."[78] Carter pressed about an Israeli withdrawal from the West Bank.

The second meeting on March 22 witnessed a harsher Carter blaming Israel for the failure to reach a settlement, convinced about whose fault it was. According to Dayan, Carter spoke quietly but with fury, his words falling on Begin "like blows." It was clear that Carter was about to hold Israel responsible for the talks' failure.[79] Dayan then explained Israel's position to Carter, concluding that he considered "the chances for peace not to be so terrible."[80] In his memoirs, Carter noted that he decided to pressure Begin in order to determine if it was worthwhile to continue these talks. Carter again read out to Begin six points of Israeli refusal, which US public opinion immediately turned into "Israel's six noes." Dayan, noted Carter, tried to save the situation through explanations while maintaining loyalty to Begin, but it was clear to everyone that Begin would not budge.[81] William Quandt described Carter as combative; while it's true that Carter had planned on pressuring Begin, his anger reflected his genuine frustration with Israel's prime minister.[82]

Indeed, "Begin left the White House battered and bruised."[83] The administration's PR machine immediately began presenting Israel's stance negatively. Still, Dayan found some positives, including US understanding of Israel's need

[76] Carter, *Keeping Faith*, p. 316.
[77] Ibid., p. 384.
[78] Dayan, *Hala-netsaḥ tokhal ḥerev*, p. 108.
[79] Ibid., p. 110.
[80] Ibid., p. 111.
[81] Carter, *Keeping Faith*, pp. 319–320.
[82] Quandt, *Camp David*, p. 164.
[83] Ezer Weizman, *Lekha shamayim, lekha arets*, Tel Aviv: Maariv Library, 1975, p. 263.

for a permanent West Bank Israeli military presence and their agreement that Egypt, Jordan, and Israel together needed to discuss the Palestinian issue. Summing up the limits of US power in the situation, Dayan said: "The United States is a superpower, but to achieve peace between us and the Arabs, it needs our agreement."[84] However, he also asserted that results could be achieved only through US mediation.[85] Israel needed US mediation even if it was clear that the United States clearly favored the other side.

The Carter administration realized that while Dayan was holding a tough line, he was pragmatic and had a knack for finding creative solutions to seemingly insoluble problems. Dayan was therefore invited back to meet with senior administration officials in April 1978. Dayan repeated Israel's stance: that after a mutually acceptable five-year transition period, the West Bank and Gaza Strip would not automatically become an Arab territory and the sides would have to engage in final-status negotiations. Dayan also raised a new proposal based on the unilateral implementation of self-rule after the five-year period, the end of military rule, and elections. Regarding the Jewish settlements, Dayan repeated his position that Jews should be able to settle anywhere they wished. Dayan expressed his approach to an open, evolving reality: "Let's wait five years . . . A new reality will be created (consequent to the implementation of some sort of self-rule) and then we'll discuss the issue."[86] The Americans, preferring definitive solutions and finding Dayan's more open-ended approach unacceptable, demanded a decision on the situation after the five years. This reflected not only the gap between the sides, but their widely divergent strategies and worldviews. Dayan felt that now all they could do was schedule a future decision about the occupied territories in another five years, whereas Sadat wanted to know what would happen at the end of the five years. In light of the deadlock and US support of Egypt's position, the US administration realized that Dayan's pragmatism, together with the legal creativity of Israel's legal advisor Aharon Barak, "[embody] the most concrete hope for real progress on the Israeli side."[87]

Dayan now lost his patience, claiming that Israel was being treated like a criminal defendant forced to answer never-ending questions from the dock while Egypt was exempt from any demands. When US Ambassador to Israel Sam Lewis came to Dayan in May 1978 with a proposal prepared by the Secretary of State for Dayan's approval, Dayan asked sarcastically where he should sign. Highly displeased with the administration's conduct, Dayan told Lewis he would pass the proposal on to Begin and recommend that he reject it.[88]

---

[84] Dayan, *Hala-netsaḥ tokhal ḥerev*, p. 112.
[85] Ibid., p. 113.
[86] Dayan, *Hala-netsaḥ tokhal ḥerev*, p. 114.
[87] Quandt, *Camp David*, p. 168.
[88] Dayan, *Hala-netsaḥ tokhal ḥerev*, p. 117.

On June 18, Israel's cabinet approved Dayan's proposal, which included agreeing to administrative autonomy in the occupied territories for five years followed by negotiations over their permanent status involving local representatives (not the PLO). The US administration was not pleased with the formulation.

Formal talks were suspended between February and July of 1978, with the Americans trying mediation between the sides to produce at least a joint declaration of principles. After these efforts failed, the Americans decided to reconvene the sides again – this time, in the ancient Leeds Castle in England, hoping the relaxed atmosphere would make the participants more conciliatory participants. The main topic of discussion at the July 17–19 conference attended by foreign ministers and staffs was the Palestinians.

Dayan wrote that he had long before suggested to Vance discussing concrete proposals rather than searching for a formulation of general principles.[89] He also wrote that the Leeds conference was important although difficult, with the Egyptians submitting a very rigid position demanding immediate Israeli withdrawal from the West Bank without any of the security arrangements that they had previously agreed upon. To prevent another deadlock, Dayan spontaneously composed a more flexible Israeli proposal, suggesting Israeli openness to territorial compromise and willingness to discuss the status of the West Bank in another five years.[90]

As Dayan had anticipated, the negotiations were tough, to a large extent a dialogue of the deaf.[91] Eventually, Dayan decided to test the Egyptians by exposing their position on the Palestinian issue. He asked them – hypothetically – whether Egypt would sign a separate about Sinai alone if the other Arab nations abstained from talks. Given your rigid positions, asked Dayan, wouldn't it make sense for us to rescind our offer to withdraw from Sinai?[92] The hemming and hawing clearly indicated that Egypt wanted peace and would probably agree to a separate treaty and even compromises over the Palestinians. Egypt's priorities were securing the return of all of Sinai and massive US support. Initially, the Leeds conference was considered a failure, but in hindsight, one can say that the talks were free and direct[93] and even represented a breakthrough in many ways, especially in that the sides started sitting together and understanding each other. However, Carter, not in attendance, felt no progress had been made.[94]

---

[89] Ibid., p. 119.
[90] Marcus, *Camp David*, p. 74.
[91] Ibid., p. 74.
[92] Weizman, *Lekha shamayim, lekha arets*, p. 310; Marcus, *Camp David*, p. 79.
[93] Harold Sanders in the seminar "An Enduring Peace, Part 3," 13:10 onward: https://youtu.be/oo0fdrvvMig?t=807; Sanders was Assistant Secretary of State for Middle East Affairs from 1978 until 1981 and was active in all stages of the negotiations.
[94] Stein, *Mediniyut amitsa*, pp. 293–294.

To advance negotiations, Dayan suggested to Vance that they begin discussing "ending the occupation" rather than withdrawal,[95] an idea that helped bridge the gap between Egypt's interest in ending the occupation and Israel's proposed self-rule. Vance was positive about the new direction, and Dayan offered practical working proposals to Quandt, proposals that Begin would never approve, such as a ban on Jewish settlement in the West Bank. Afterward, "Quandt thought of Dayan as a man who was trying to solve problems."[96] Then Dayan made Quandt a "personal offer," involving an agreement to discuss West Bank sovereignty at the end of five years of self-rule. Begin was pleased with Dayan's achievements but not with Dayan's liberty in making a "personal offer." Dayan told Begin that they could disagree, but that he needed the freedom to make suggestions, especially those clearly presented as his own and not as official government policy, in order to negotiate.[97] Tension between them over this would only increase as the talks continued.

On July 24, Dayan addressed the Knesset, announcing Israel's readiness to discuss the future of the West Bank and Gaza Strip after five years of self-rule, but its refusal to accept any agreement based on withdrawing to the 1967 borders or transferring land to Arab sovereignty, even with US security guarantees.[98]

On the eve of the Camp David summit, which started on September 4, Dayan held personal meetings with Arab figures and leaders from the West Bank and Gaza Strip to hear their opinions on autonomy. Many, eager to maintain economic ties with Israel, were willing to consider various solutions, including autonomy, but wanted Jordan and the PLO included in any solution. Some supported maintaining the status quo, thinking that, ultimately, the Arab demographic majority west of the Jordan River would determine sovereignty, saying, "Give us Israeli citizenship, and within a decade, the Israeli president will be an Arab." Dayan enjoyed these meetings, telling his advisor, Elyakim Rubinstein, that he still had a good reputation among the Arabs (if not with the Jewish public).[99]

On July 28, Begin met with Assistant Secretary of State Alfred Atherton and agreed in principle to accept Dayan's Leeds principles, which Begin emphasized originally represented Dayan's and not the official government position on the subject.[100]

---

[95] Quandt, *Camp David*, p. 177.
[96] Slater, *Warrior Statesman*, p. 409.
[97] Mordechai Bar-On, *Moshe Dayan: Korot hayav 1915–1981*, Tel Aviv: Am Oved, 2014, pp. 338–339.
[98] Steinberg and Rubinovitz, *Menachem Begin and the Israel–Egypt Peace Process*, p. 129.
[99] Rubinstein, *Darkei shalom*, p. 75.
[100] Steinberg and Rubinovitz, *Menachem Begin and the Israel–Egypt Peace Process*, p. 128.

Camp David

Despite difficult, prolonged negotiations, Dayan's media statements suggested Egypt's readiness for peace. However, nine months after Sadat's visit, deadlocked talks led to American officials scheduling an intensive working summit of the parties with extensive US involvement for September 5–17, 1978. For these talks, Dayan would use all his accrued experience – including his leadership in Acre Prison,[101] the Jordanian talks during the War of Independence, the talks with France and Great Britain before the Sinai Campaign, the agreement ending the War of Attrition, and the Yom Kippur War separation of forces agreements. This would be the test of his life.

Carter's initial Middle East policy was ill articulated and naive, leading Sadat to establish direct communication with Israel without US knowledge. Now, recognizing the stalemate, Carter realized that only a conference like Camp David could break the impasse. Carter carefully planned the conference: Camp David was secluded, the atmosphere relaxed, and the conduct and dress (including windbreakers emblazoned with the "Camp David" logo) informal, all contributing to a relaxed, resort atmosphere. Carter also set some rigid rules: no leaving the camp or media communication; only the White House Press Secretary would have media contact.[102] Before the internet and cellphones, Camp David's setting allowed for a disconnect from the outside world, which the Americans believed would foster dialogue (Figure 10.1).

Camp David's Arcadian setting, a secluded Maryland retreat, provided isolation and opportunities for recreation and informal socializing, creating an unprecedented and amiable atmosphere. Carter oversaw the details of the teams' discussions, determined not to leave until a deal was reached. The stakes were high. Carter made it clear that his personal prestige was on the line.

Dayan had no interest in games or socializing. He could not play ball games because of his limited vision, and he never made a habit of seeking company. He preferred solitary walks along the many paths while thinking quietly, an activity he particularly valued. His walks through the forest enhanced his reputation as a lone wolf.

The absence of the other Arab delegations made Sadat's goal of a comprehensive peace agreement seem unrealistic. Both sides seem to have known the key to success at Camp David: Egypt conceding on its demand for comprehensive peace and a Palestinian settlement and signing a separate treaty; Israel conceding the vast majority if not all of the Sinai Peninsula. Sadat was very confident that Israel would be forced to make major concessions. He trusted Carter to manage the confrontation with Begin on his behalf.[103]

---

[101] See Chapter 1.
[102] Slater, *Warrior Statesman*, p. 410.
[103] Quandt, *Camp David*, p. 182.

Figure 10.1 US President Jimmy Carter tours Gettysburg battlefield with leaders of Israel and Egypt. Source: Consolidated News Pictures/Contributor/Archive Photos/Getty Images.

In the Camp David discussions, Begin's and Dayan's differences in style and in essence became quite obvious. Begin was a formalist, a perfectionist, a jurist who examined every word for all its possible nuances, whereas Dayan was flexible, pragmatic, always looking for solutions to problems. For Begin, declarations and expressions of ideals were of paramount importance, while Dayan strove for practical, realistic, albeit imperfect arrangements. Often, Begin's approach was rigid – "take it or leave it," while Dayan would try to find a way to satisfy both sides. Dayan, having spent more time with Americans than had Begin, knew them better; he understood "American," not merely English. Consequently, the US delegates viewed Dayan as someone with whom they could speak, unlike the rigid formalist Begin. Aharon Barak described Dayan as never giving in to despair and never getting painted into a corner; on the rare occasion he did, he always found an escape.[104]

Brzeziński had a more nuanced view of Dayan:

> Superficially, Dayan seemed like a reasonable man. But he was in some ways more devious than Begin. You knew with Begin more clearly what he wanted ... Dayan was less inclined than Begin to put his cards on the

---

[104] Slater, *Warrior Statesman*, p. 412.

table. There was a strangely elusive quality about Dayan. While I more or less knew what made Begin and Weizman tick, I never had that feeling about Dayan. I always saw him in a fog.

Still, he suggested that "Dayan may have been less inclined to dig in his heels than Begin. One had a feeling that Dayan had an instinctive appreciation of the ambiguities and nuances of the Arabs."[105]

The negotiations were difficult. Dayan described them as "the most decisive, difficult, and unpleasant part in the peace talks with Egypt," adding, "There were times that I kept myself from bursting out only by tightening my fists and biting my tongue."[106] Begin wanted Israel's proposal introduced first; Dayan disagreed, preferring to let Egypt make the first offer to forestall a US compromise proposal, which would likely be unfavorable to Israel. Begin conceded, and Sadat presented his offer to Carter first, which Dayan rejected outright. With Egypt still opposing a separate agreement with Israel, the Americans made their own offer on September 8. On September 10, Carter shared an updated proposal, excluding any reference to the Jewish settlements. But the Americans were disappointed by Israel's refusal of any West Bank compromise. Dayan indicated that Israel would reconsider the US proposal.

A significant point of contention was an evacuation of Sinai, where Israel had thirteen settlements, three airfields, and an oil field providing much of Israel's energy needs. What could compensate Israel for relinquishing all this? Any Sinai evacuation could prove a precedent, with Brzeziński claiming that if Sinai settlements could be evacuated, so too could those in the West Bank.[107]

Carter repeatedly turned to Dayan for help in trying to break through Begin's rock-hard opposition. He considered Dayan an ally also seeking a way out of the deadlock and not wedded to old positions.[108]

Dayan's continuous attempts to understand Sadat were noted by the Americans, who found that he, unlike Begin, was trying to understand the other side. Slater wrote that:

> The Americans found Dayan appealing, and used him to soften up Begin, because none of the other [Israelis] puzzled as much about what Anwar Sadat really wanted. Why had he taken a certain position? And what could Israel do to make him change his position? "Dayan would not ask in front of Begin," noted William Quandt, "but would take an American aside, and ask what's making Sadat tick. Is he serious? Is this a bluff? Is this for domestic consumption?"[109]

---

[105] Interview with Brzeziński, in Slater, *Warrior Statesman*, p. 413.
[106] Dayan, *Hala-netsaḥ tokhal ḥerev*, p. 132.
[107] Interview with Brzeziński, in Slater, *Warrior Statesman*, p. 414.
[108] Carter, *Keeping Faith*, p. 379.
[109] Interview with Quandt, in Slater, *Warrior Statesman*, p. 415.

Assistant Secretary of State Alfred Atherton and the US ambassador to Israel, Sam Lewis, both at Camp David, observed that Dayan had the knack for seeing the problem from the other side's point of view.[110] Lewis said that:

> [he] found it easier to talk to Dayan than to the prime minister "because Begin would lapse into stereotypes, never having conversed with a West Banker or Gazan until late into his prime ministry. Dayan could change position without any sense of personal ego involved. He was very results-oriented." To move Begin with arguments was tough, he only moved when he assessed he had to move. Then ... Begin would find his argument, "whereas you could sell Dayan an argument. He was intellectually engageable in a way that Begin wasn't."[111]

Carter considered Dayan's assessments of the Palestinians' positions reliable, sensing that Dayan understood them.[112] Quandt wrote that Carter and Vance started leaning on Dayan, Weizman, and legal advisor Barak to persuade Begin to compromise (Sadat, in contrast, was more flexible than his advisors).[113]

Carter recalled that on the evening of September 10:

> We finally adjourned, and I asked Dayan to walk back with me to my cottage. He was a competent and level-headed man. I felt that if either he or Weizman were heading the delegation, we would already have reached agreement. I needed Dayan's special assistance at this time, but recognized the necessity of his loyalty to the Prime Minister.[114]

Dayan, wrote Carter, promised him that Begin wanted peace despite the problems:

> We talked quietly about the other issues during these early morning hours ... Day break was approaching, but it was still dark as Dayan turned to leave. He had difficulty seeing the trees between him and the path, and when he walked into one of them, I was reminded of how seriously his eyesight was impaired. My heart went out to him; I considered him a friend and a proper ally. Because Prime Minister Begin trusted his Foreign Minister and relied on him for advice, this discussion was to be an important and fruitful one.[115]

Carter wanted Dayan to get Begin to make concessions, as Sadat had already done. Dayan had suggested to Brzeziński to defer the Jewish settlement issue until other issues were resolved, and Brzeziński agreed. Now Dayan tried to persuade Carter get to Sadat to temporarily retain the Israeli settlements. Sadat

---

[110] Ibid., p. 415.
[111] Interview with Sam Lewis, in Slater, *Warrior Statesman*, p. 415.
[112] Interview with Jimmy Carter, in, *Warrior Statesman*, p. 415.
[113] Quandt, *Camp David*, p. 195.
[114] Carter, *Keeping Faith*, p. 386.
[115] Ibid., p. 387.

adamantly refused, now insisting on deploying Egyptian army units in the West Bank and Gaza Strip during the five-year interim period. At this point, Dayan vehemently disagreed. Carter agreed to Dayan's request that the Americans formulate two positions papers to help clarify the issues, one on Sinai and the other on the West Bank. The US side began to realize that an Israeli–Egyptian agreement over Sinai could be reached, while leaving the West Bank and Gaza Strip issue unresolved temporarily. Carter later wrote: "Later that evening, I met for about two hours with Dayan and Barak ... I found Dayan more hopeful, more determined to succeed even than Weizman, who was ordinarily the optimist. He seemed willing to accept failure, however, rather than consider the removal of all Israeli settlers from the Sinai. I wished that Dayan knew Sadat better."[116]

While Dayan reached understandings with Carter, the other members of the Israeli delegation experienced a sense of failure. On September 12, Begin told them he would wait just another three days for results. Dayan asked for patience, explaining that Carter was preparing a new proposal focusing on Sinai. To apply pressure on the Americans, Dayan told them about the Israeli delegation's pessimism, mentioning to Ambassador Lewis that he was planning on returning to Israel the next day. An appalled Lewis immediately told Carter, and the Americans started moving faster, fearing that the talks could slip through their fingers.[117]

When Begin rejected the US position paper the next day, the Americans immediately worked on another version. Scrutinizing each issue, they realized that the primary obstacle was Israel's Sinai settlements. Carter told Dayan and Barak that Israel must agree to evacuate the settlements in Sinai in order to reach an agreement.[118]

Carter and Weizman pleaded with Sadat to sit with Dayan. But Dayan was skeptical, feeling that Sadat viewed him as a sworn and guileful enemy. Carter advised Dayan to develop trust between the two and not discuss points of disagreement. Dayan then promised to speak with Sadat only about "dates and camels."[119] Sadat was somewhat confounded by the idea of such a meeting. The two leaders had not developed any particular chemistry, and Dayan, unlike Weizman, was distant, making no effort to become liked. For Sadat, Dayan symbolized more than any other Israeli in the delegation Egypt's humiliating defeats of 1956 and 1967. The two men finally met on September 14.

Sadat greeted Dayan graciously but immediately began pressuring Dayan about Israel's Sinai settlements. In his book, Dayan joked, "The dates and camels

---

[116] Ibid., pp. 390–391.
[117] Slater, *Warrior Statesman*, p. 415.
[118] Ibid., p. 416.
[119] Dayan, *Hala-netsaḥ tokhal ḥerev*, p. 159.

have disappeared."[120] Sadat offered Israel full diplomatic relations following Israel's complete withdrawal from Sinai and evacuation of the settlements. Dayan refrained from arguing – he believed that Sadat truly wanted peace. On a personal level, Dayan reported, the two men developed no rapport.[121] Dayan also noted that Sadat had avoided speaking about the West Bank and Gaza Strip, indicating that Sadat would compromise on that issue in exchange for full Sinai withdrawal. Dayan reported to Israel's delegation that Sadat's priority was Sinai, and he would accept minor victories about other issues. Nonetheless, Dayan took a hard line, threatening that Israel would remain in Sinai and continue pumping oil if Sadat insisted on all this (Figure 10.2).

Ibrahim Kamel, Egypt's Foreign Minister in December 1977, succeeding Fahmi, later wrote that meeting Dayan was a turning point for Sadat, leading him to agree to several concessions. They were considered "a complete surrender"[122] by Kamel, who resigned that weekend before the Camp David Accords were signed.

On September 15, Dayan informed Carter that his meeting with Sadat was not successful, leading Carter to fear that the summit was about to fail. Responding to Carter's request, Dayan advised Carter to make a list of the still-unresolved issues so that they could become the starting point for the future.[123] Now Dayan became despondent. This was familiar to the Israelis, but new to Carter, now reliant on Dayan's creative thinking.[124]

Dayan told the Israelis that Carter planned to end the summit on September 17 and would blame Israel for its failure. Dayan used this tactic to pressure the Israeli side,[125] threatening that the talks' failure would be catastrophic for Israel–US relations.[126] Dayan was indifferent to Vance and Brzeziński's idea of a security treaty between Israel and the United States as part of a comprehensive agreement, assuming they were simply trying to get Israel to make further concessions.[127] When Atherton asked him why he had originally supported building settlements in Sinai, Dayan answered that he never thought Egypt would want peace. But now that it was clear Egypt did want peace, Israel had to evacuate them.[128] Begin, however, was still refusing.

The breakthrough came at the crunch time, with Begin spinning the steering wheel at the last second, offering concessions which led to an agreement. In the

---

[120] Ibid., p. 159.
[121] Ibid., pp. 159–160.
[122] Quandt, *Camp David*, p. 208.
[123] Lawrence Wright, *Thirteen Days in September: Carter, Begin, and Sadat at Camp David*, New York: Alfred A. Knopf, 2014, p. 28.
[124] Ibid., p. 256.
[125] Slater, *Warrior Statesman*, p. 417.
[126] Dayan, *Hala-netsaḥ tokhal ḥerev*, p. 145.
[127] Quandt, *Camp David*, p. 211.
[128] Slater, *Warrior Statesman*, p. 418.

Figure 10.2 Israeli Foreign Minister Moshe Dayan (left) and Egyptian President Anwar Al Sadat at Camp David, September 1978. Source: Consolidated News Pictures/Contributor/Archive Photos/Getty Images.

evening of September 16, Begin joined the meeting with Dayan and Barak. Carter recalled having thanked God for that.[129] Begin agreed to bring the Sinai settlements to the Knesset for decision.

Now an unexpected crisis about Jerusalem's status came to a head. This looked like a US trap for Israel. Dayan was furious, telling Carter that the Israeli delegation wouldn't have come to Camp David had it known that this was US policy.[130] He continued irately: "How can you claim that the Western Wall, the Jewish Quarter, Hadassah, the university, Mount of Olives, and Mount Scopus belong to the Jordanian kingdom? Just because the Jordanians conquered them in 1948, destroyed the synagogues, and killed or captured the civilians who were living there?!"[131] Begin unequivocally refused any Jerusalem compromise. Dayan advised the Americans to ease the pressure. However, things became more complicated when they learned that Sadat wanted to fly an Arab flag[132] over Jerusalem's al-Aqsa mosque, the third most important site to Islam built over the remnants of the Jewish temple, the holiest location in the

---

[129] Carter, Keeping Faith, p. 405.
[130] Steinberg and Rubinovitz, *Menachem Begin and the Israel–Egypt Peace Process*, p. 161.
[131] Dayan, *Hala-netsaḥ tokhal ḥerev*, p. 150.
[132] It is not clear which flag Sadat meant, because there is no general Arab flag, only specific flags of the various Arab nations.

world for Jews. Dayan sarcastically quipped: "Maybe Sadat wants an Arab flag above the Knesset building too?";[133] he asked the Americans, "If Jerusalem is not Israel's capital, what is it?"[134] Eventually, a compromise was found involving an exchange of letters that would become part of the agreement, making it clear that Israel objected to any transfer of sovereignty for Jerusalem.

By late afternoon, the agreement was almost complete, the issue of withdrawing to the 1967 borders still contentious. Dayan proposed mentioning this only in the context of any future Israeli–Jordanian talks; he also opposed any freeze on the number of Jewish settlers. Begin and Dayan would not agree to a five-year freeze on settlements in the territories, although Carter believed they had reached an understanding, which Begin denied. Years later, Carter admitted Begin was a decent man; the source of the problem seems to have been a misunderstanding between the sides.[135]

Carter praised Dayan effusively: "I can say that the basic terms of the Camp David accords were hammered out substantially under the influence of Moshe."[136] In contrast, Dayan reserved his esteem for Begin, writing that his leadership was invaluable and that he was involved in every last detail of the talks.[137]

On September 17, 1978, the three leaders signed the Camp David Accords in a solemn ceremony on the White House lawn, thus beginning a tradition of signing peace treaties between Israel and Arab nations with US mediation: the peace treaty with Egypt signed on March 26, 1979; the First Oslo Agreement with the Palestinians signed on August 20, 1993; the Washington Declaration with Jordan signed on October 26, 1994; and, most recently, the normalization agreements with the UAE and Bahrain signed in September and October 2020. At the press conference at Camp David, Dayan said that this peace treaty was the first stage of full peace treaties with the Arab world.[138]

Camp David actually produced two agreements. The first, concerning Sinai, had Israel evacuating all military and civilians from Sinai with the United States compensating them by building two new airbases in the Negev. The Sinai Peninsula would become partially demilitarized, with a US force stationed in a large, fully demilitarized buffer zone, Israel preferring US to UN

---

[133] Slater, *Warrior Statesman*, p. 418.
[134] Steinberg and Rubinovitz, *Menachem Begin and the Israel–Egypt Peace Process*, p. 161: "In a public event in Jerusalem one year later, Dinitz said that Dayan asked a senior US official, 'If Jerusalem is not Israel's capital, what is?' The official replied, 'I don't know.'"
[135] Seminar entitled "An Enduring Peace: 25 Years after the Camp David Accords," Woodrow Wilson Center, 2003, YouTube, in three parts: www.youtube.com/watch?v=5udmemjaZN8&ab_channel=WoodrowWilsonCenter; www.youtube.com/watch?v=j-8aiiAs9Qo&t=1556s&ab_channel=WoodrowWilsonCenter; www.youtube.com/watch?v=oo0fdrvvMig&t=3970s&ab_channel=WoodrowWilsonCenter.
[136] Slater, *Warrior Statesman*, p. 419.
[137] Steinberg and Rubinovitz, *Menachem Begin and the Israel–Egypt Peace Process*, p. 162.
[138] Ibid., p. 171.

forces. Egypt agreed to establish full diplomatic relations with Israel nine months after the IDF withdrawal from Sinai.

The second agreement was a framework for a comprehensive Middle East peace with a focus on an Israeli–Palestinian agreement. Israel would provide full autonomy – more than Begin wanted – to West Bank and Gaza Strip Palestinians for five years. After that, Israel could still demand sovereignty of parts of the territories. In practice, as Aharon Barak observed, the document left the Palestinian issue open. Unlike the clearly defined agreement about Sinai, the second document was vague. Perhaps its strength lay in this.

Begin and Dayan discussed autonomy, but from different perspectives. Begin viewed the West Bank (or Judea and Samaria as Israelis call the area) as an inseparable part of Israel. Appreciating rapid Palestinian population growth and their opposition to becoming Israeli citizens, Begin proposed a political distinction between the inhabitants and the land, allowing Israel to continue settling the area and maintain control while still granting autonomy, the concept Dayan had championed for years: autonomy for the people but not for the land. This formula allowed for progress in the talks. Dayan's autonomy, however, was a far more significant and fundamental idea of autonomy for the Palestinians, leaving only security in Israel's hands.[139]

Elyakim Rubinstein, an Israeli legal advisor, noted that much of the agreement was left in "a constructive fog," the vagueness the best they could do and serving the goal.[140] This approach suited Dayan, who wanted such matters left open for future development.

Signing the Peace Treaty

The Camp David Accords were an astounding achievement, leading to the peace treaty and requiring significant compromises.

On September 27, 1978, the Knesset approved the agreements, including the evacuation from Sinai, by a large majority. Before the vote, Dayan said, "In the next few weeks, each of us will take stock, will think of himself, of his family, of his children. It will be one of the great moments of the state of Israel, of its self-examination, of its assessment of the future."[141] However, a November 5 Arab summit meeting criticized the agreements and censured Egypt for betraying the Arab camp, thus pressuring Egypt.

The expectation was to reach a final peace treaty within three months. However, the next conference, scheduled for October 12 at Blair House in

---

[139] Stein, *Mediniyut amitsa*, p. 276.
[140] Rubinstein, *Darkei shalom*, pp. 104–105.
[141] Slater, *Warrior Statesman*, p. 420.

Washington, revealed that the timeline was unrealistic due to disagreements about wording. Gradually, the agreement with Egypt became more important than any autonomy discussion.[142] The points of contention were: the connection between Israel's Sinai withdrawal and the start of full diplomatic relations; US financial and military commitments to Israel and Egypt; compensation to Israel for evacuating the Sinai airfields; Israel's demand for long-term US oil-supply guarantees; and the date on which Israel's West Bank and Gaza Strip military rule would end.[143]

To speed up negotiations, Carter joined on October 17. Dayan had three concerns: Egypt's still-standing defense commitments to other Arab countries; that the talks with Egypt were linked to the West Bank and Gaza Strip; and Egypt's reluctance to accept normalization. In a gesture to Carter, Dayan suggested an expedited withdrawal to the interim line in Sinai and the return of al-Arish within two rather than nine months. This pleased Carter, who agreed to speak with the Egyptians about speeding normalization and to consider aid to help finance the Sinai withdrawal. Dayan also sought Egyptian flexibility toward Israel's requests.[144] Dayan suggested quietly withdrawing from certain areas, allowing the residents to run their own affairs. He also proposed a population exchange between Israeli settlers in the West Bank and Palestinian refugees. Begin didn't like any of these ideas.[145]

On October 30, Dayan conceded to Vance that Begin's interpretation of self-rule was very narrow.[146] On November 11, 1978, the administration submitted the final draft of the peace treaty. That evening, Vance and Dayan were still hammering out outstanding issues before Vance and Begin met the next day. While Dayan told Vance he was pleased with the treaty, Vance's meeting with Begin did not go well.[147] Begin, feeling that Dayan was too eager to compromise, limited Dayan's authority in the negotiations, despite Dayan's protestations.[148]

In mid December 1978, Vance pressed Israel for further concessions, a period Israel called "Black December." Vance, frustrated by Israel, temporarily halted negotiations.[149] But the US administration soon resumed talks. Further talks were held between Dayan and US and Egyptian leaders in Washington and Brussels, the latter leading to a breakthrough, with the Egyptians finally agreeing not to reopen the agreements and to be satisfied with the letters of interpretation alongside them. In February, Dayan and

---

[142] Stein, *Mediniyut amitsa*, p. 300.
[143] Ibid.
[144] Quandt, *Camp David*, p. 236.
[145] Carter, *Keeping Faith*, pp. 504–505.
[146] Quandt, *Camp David*, p. 239.
[147] Ibid., p. 242.
[148] Dayan, *Hala-netsah tokhal ḥerev*, p. 175.
[149] Quandt, *Camp David*, p. 248.

Egypt's Foreign Minister Mustafa Khalil met to resolve the last disagreements. In February and March, Begin met with Carter; neither meeting was pleasant. The leaders, Begin, Carter, and Sadat, were again needed to get the talks back on track, and meetings among the three were held in March, with Carter traveling to the Middle East to close the remaining gaps.

Tensions between the sides were at an all-time high: Would Carter finally be able to resolve the differences? At a briefing Dayan before Carter's March visit, Dayan explained that the Americans urgently needed a Middle East success now to compensate for the loss of Iran as an ally following the revolution there the preceding month. He stated that "[the Americans] need Egypt and Egypt needs them," and that even if Carter did not achieve a peace treaty, he "will not toss away the Middle East; he won't toss away either Israel or Egypt." Dayan added that the Americans would make aid to Egypt contingent on signing a peace treaty.[150]

Carter reached Cairo on March 8, 1979, and Israel the next day. Vance presented Dayan with Egypt's positions on still-open issues: stationing Egyptian liaison officers between Gaza and Egypt, providing oil from Sinai, and the conflict between Egypt's prior defense treaties with other Arab nations and the peace treaty with Israel. This was critical for Israel, unwilling to find itself in a military conflict with another Arab nation that Egypt would join because of a previous agreement. Although the Israeli cabinet met and approved other concessions, the US administration announced they were not enough. In light of this, Carter's March 12 meeting with the Israeli government was very tense. Carter supported Egypt's demand to deploy liaison officers in Gaza, a major stumbling block. The US proposal that Israel buy oil from Egypt via an intermediary clearly indicated that Egypt intended to maintain its commercial embargo on Israel. The meetings ended that evening with the problems still unresolved.

Around 9 p.m., Dayan, with Weizman's help, persuaded Begin to let him meet with Vance for a last-ditch effort at a solution. Vance described this meeting as the most critical of the entire negotiations process. In his book, Dayan would write that he and Vance had established a relationship based on mutual trust and a common language. Vance did not disagree.[151] Dayan used this meeting to convince Vance to convince Sadat to relinquish his demand for liaison officers in Gaza. Vance agreed in exchange for Israeli flexibility on the oil issue. Dayan

---

[150] From deputy directors general meeting just before Carter's visit, Foreign Ministry, March 7, 1979, State Archive, https://docs.google.com/file/d/0BxpR2lHZaDkHam NnNnJwWmZONVk/edit.

[151] Cyrus Vance, *Hard Choices: Critical Years in America's Foreign Policy*, New York: Simon and Schuster, 1983, p. 249.

assented, but he wanted a US commitment to supply oil to Israel for twenty – not ten – years and an explicit clause that Israel would be able to buy oil directly from Egypt. This clause had important declarative value as a repeal of the boycott on Israel, even if the oil was actually sold via a US company. Vance noted later that when Dayan made these suggestions, he knew that a breakthrough had just taken place.[152]

Vance then called Carter while Dayan called Begin to get their authorization.[153] Vance was on cloud nine. He would write: "When we shook hands at the elevator, I thanked heaven for Dayan and his patience, imagination, and courage."[154] Back at his hotel, Dayan told his wife, "The crisis is over." Carter then traveled to Cairo to present the proposals to Sadat, which Sadat approved immediately. Only then did Begin show the draft of the agreement to his cabinet, which also approved it. On March 20, the Knesset, too, voted in favor of the agreement by a large majority (Figure 10.3).

The peace treaty between Israel and Egypt was signed on March 26, 1979. Dayan, detesting ceremonies, found the speeches uninspiring, as everything had already been said. Vance wrote that the future held many difficult problems regarding self-rule,[155] as Dayan knew too. After the ceremony, the sides prepared for the autonomy talks, which would be followed by the end of Dayan's role in the Begin government.

Dayan was a crucial figure for the United States, serving as a buffer between the administration and Begin, helping to understand the Egyptian side, and generating many creative solutions. Carter viewed him as a friend and an ally, and Vance wrote that he came to admire Dayan greatly, finding him "to be a brilliant, imaginative, and honest man."[156] With Sadat, however, Dayan never developed any closeness. Dayan, an introvert who preferred his own company to that of others, wasn't particularly sociable or friendly, especially in that period. In addition, many of the Egyptians never forgave Dayan, holding him personally responsible for their humiliation in 1956 and 1967. Nonetheless, Sadat and Dayan were able to work together to promote their respective national interests.

Sadat and Dayan also had a shared strategic goal: of weakening the Soviets and ousting them from the region while increasing US involvement there. This shared interest helped overcome obstacles between them. Both sides were in fact conducting negotiations over US regional involvement rather than solely bilateral issues, even if this aspect of the talks was not overt.

---

[152] Ibid., p. 250.
[153] Slater, *Warrior Statesman*, p. 420.
[154] Vance, *Hard Choices*, p. 250.
[155] Ibid., p. 251.
[156] Ibid., p. 197.

Figure 10.3 Israel's Foreign Minister Moshe Dayan, US President Jimmy Carter, and Israel's Prime Minister Menachem Begin. Source: Wally McNamee/Contributor/Corbis Historical/Getty Images.

The End: A Political Last Will and Testament

Ezer Weizman, who left the Begin government some seven months after Dayan, recalled:

> To those around me, I said that it wouldn't take long. Dayan pushed Begin to the wall when he stipulated his joining the government on not applying

Israeli law to Judea and Samaria. Begin does not forget or forgive; when he is pushed to the wall, he remains silent and remembers.[157]

After the peace treaty was signed, Dayan knew that his days in the Begin government were numbered. He saw two main issues threatening Israel's existence: the military conflict with the Arab states on Israel's borders and the conflict with the Palestinians for control of Israel. The peace treaty with Egypt had minimized any possibility of an Arab coalition taking on Israel in battle. Without Egypt, the biggest and strongest Arab nation, such a coalition was not on the table. Syria was weak; Jordan did not want to attack Israel and the forces from Iraq and others could only be reinforcements. The remaining issue then, festering like an open wound, was the Palestinian conflict. Dayan hoped he could play a role in finding a solution to the problem. Even after his ouster from Begin's government, the Palestinian question became Dayan's most pressing preoccupation until his death.

Dayan and Begin disagreed about Judea and Samaria. Dayan opposed both annexation and withdrawal, whereas Begin wanted full Israeli sovereignty over the occupied areas. Begin preferred Interior Minister Yosef Burg, a member of the Mafdal party, whose position was closer to Begin's, to head Israel's negotiating team. Dayan refused to be a member of a team he could not steer according to his own worldview. He waited four months to see how the talks developed. When he realized they would not result in anything concrete, he decided to leave the government.

Dayan developed his own idea for Palestinian autonomy – "unilateral autonomy" – assuming there was no chance for a final agreement with the Palestinians. He sought to devise a reality both sides could accept until they could, at some unknown future time, reach a final political settlement that would be mutually satisfactory. Dayan's plan was to reduce Israeli involvement in the civil administration in terms of running the inhabitants' day-to-day lives and the possibility of shared sovereignty between Israel and Jordan or a situation of no formal sovereignty for some interim period. Zalman Shoval, then Dayan's advisor in the Foreign Ministry, wrote: "As a supremely practical person, Dayan felt that it was better to create an interim situation that would improve life for both sides without determining the final status than to insist on a certain final status that was impossible under existing circumstances."[158] Dayan, opposed to establishing a Palestinian state, thought his plan could prevent it.

Begin did not try to prevent Dayan's resignation. He no longer needed him. Dayan had helped the Begin government achieve worldwide recognition and spearheaded the peace process with Egypt. Now, Menachem Begin, a Nobel Peace Prize recipient, a statesman of international repute himself, borne aloft on a wave of support at home, no longer needed Dayan. Perhaps even the contrary: Dayan was now, to some extent, a liability.

[157] Weizman, *Lekha shamayim, lekha arets*, p. 262.
[158] Zalman Shoval, *Diplomat* (Hebrew), Tel Aviv: Yedioth Ahronoth, 2016, p. 135.

Dayan resigned on October 2, 1979. Begin was well aware that Dayan had mounting reservations about how ministers were speaking about the talks with Egypt, land appropriations, and establishing new Jewish settlements in Palestinian-populated areas.[159] He told Begin, "The talks being held right now are a waste of time ... I don't get to deal with issues that matter to me, and I end up dealing with issues that don't matter to me. I did not join the government to meet with foreign ambassadors and go to cocktail parties."[160] Begin's expression of regret over Dayan's resignation letter seems to have been mere lip service. As the old adage goes, "In politics, there are no friends."[161]

On October 23, Dayan left the government. Now a one-person faction in the Knesset, he sat in the last row next to former extremist Likud members who had left their party after the peace agreement with Egypt. He found no support from Labor due to his perceived political betrayal in joining Begin.

Dayan was also very ill, suffering from cancer and heart problems. He had difficulty speaking and was nearly blind, with his vision in his one eye deteriorating. It seemed that this time, his political career had come to an end.

Acutely aware of his situation, Dayan had no immediate plans for another political move and assumed that these would be his last days in the Knesset; he intended for them to pass quietly. He devoted his time to writing about the peace process; the eventual book, *Halanetsah tokhal herev* (*Shall the Sword Devour Forever*), was published before his death.[162] He also started gathering materials for a book about Jewish heroes from Bar Kochba to Yoni Netanyahu.[163] Still, Dayan was not ready to leave the political arena altogether, because the Palestinian issue and the future of the West Bank continued to preoccupy him. When the year stipulated for talks about future Palestinian autonomy in the peace treaty was over without a concrete settlement on the horizon, Dayan began worrying about the treaty's future. He suggested implementing unilateral autonomy and relying on the Palestinian mayors in the West Bank and Gaza Strip. His proposal was rejected by both the Israeli right and left.[164]

At the start of Dayan's tenure as foreign minister, Zalman Shoval, then a new Likud MK and Dayan supporter, established a forum called Habama (the podium or stage) to serve as a platform for Dayan's "political and social inquir[ies]."[165] Its first conference, on September 10, 1977, had been immensely successful, with Dayan, the keynote speaker, sweeping attendees off their feet and enthusing them with his brilliant analyses and proposals for

---

[159] Bar-On, *Moshe Dayan*, p. 353.
[160] Dayan, *Hala-netsah tokhal ḥerev*, p. 244.
[161] Slater, *Warrior Statesman*, p. 428.
[162] Bar-On, *Moshe Dayan*, p. 353.
[163] Slater, *Warrior Statesman*, p. 437.
[164] Bar-On, *Moshe Dayan*, p. 356.
[165] Shoval, *Diplomat*, p. 136.

action.¹⁶⁶ Habama would invite political figures, academics, and business people to express their opinion, with Dayan always the central axis of the meetings. Here, Dayan could articulate his ideas and reach the public through Habama's press publications. Dayan used this serious and thoughtful forum as a place "to toss around ideas and get responses and feedback" and was grateful for criticism and debate.¹⁶⁷ During the talks with Egypt, the forum had helped Dayan articulate his thoughts and hone his positions on the key issues, including the withdrawal from Sinai and Palestinian autonomy.

At Habama conferences, Dayan addressed many topics, but the center of it all was Israel's relations with the Arabs. Dayan's heaviest worry was Israel's control of a million Arabs, which had already lasted ten years. He felt that military rule over the occupied territories should be abolished and unilateral autonomy implemented. This was a revolutionary position and a departure for Dayan: After the Six-Day War, he had been the one to persuade the Israeli public that it was possible to maintain military rule over civilians (albeit a "soft" or "enlightened" rule). Now, having resigned from Begin's government, he was trying to convince others that such rule was unsustainable.¹⁶⁸

Dayan proposed a unilateral autonomy plan, involving shifting Israel's responsibility and authority for many issues – from education to infrastructure – to the Palestinians, while leaving responsibility and authority for security issues in Israel's hands. His complex plan baffled most of the public, eager for simpler solutions.¹⁶⁹

Dayan's autonomy proposal hinged on four principles. First, rejection of any radical solution of either annexation or withdrawal, separating the issues of sovereignty and the military government, and developing some formula for joint civilian rule that would lead to a gradual process of peaceful coexistence. Second, favoring the cumulative power of partial and pragmatic arrangements over a comprehensive settlement. Third, no Palestinian state, but recognizing the need to address the refugee problem. Last, unilateral autonomy, preventing potentially dangerous agreements over the future of the occupied territories involving another Arab state. Dayan never formulated a fully operational plan, perhaps because he felt it was a project in development. For Dayan, this was the right choice for Israel, because continuing the status quo was only damaging Israel.¹⁷⁰

Dayan distinguished between territories occupied beyond the Green Line, such as the Gaza Strip and Sinai, and the West Bank. Like Begin, he viewed Judea and

---

[166] Ibid., p. 137.
[167] Ibid., p. 138.
[168] From the introduction to the book by Natan Yanai (ed.), *Moshe Dayan al tahalikh hashalom ve'atida shel medinat yisrael: Dvarim biknasey habama leberurim medini'im vehevrati'im (1977–1981)* (Hebrew), Tel Aviv: Defense Ministry Publications, 1988, pp. 7–10.
[169] Shoval, *Diplomat*, p. 150.
[170] Yanai (ed.), *Moshe Dayan al tahalikh hashalom ve'atida shel medinat yisrael*, pp. 7–9.

Samaria as part of the historic homeland of the Jewish people and supported Jewish settlement there. But, unlike the Israeli right, Dayan felt it was necessary to consider the rights of the Palestinian inhabitants. He therefore opposed both annexation and withdrawal and instead supported Israel lifting its military rule while maintaining a security presence. Dayan thought Jewish settlement in the West Bank could eventually lead to peaceful coexistence through shared authority and joint economic development but should be planned and built on state land only. True to his worldview, he saw no reason to define the final arrangement now; instead, the right direction would be found through trial and error.[171] For Dayan, unlike the prevailing opinion, the refugee problem and managing Palestinian civilian life in the territories needed to be addressed before discussing any state-like framework in which the Palestinians could express their national aspirations. Dayan cautioned that establishing a Palestinian state before settling the issue of where the refugees would live would be disastrous for Israel.[172]

Although initially declining to run for the Knesset after Begin announced early elections on June 30, 1981, Dayan formed a new political party – Telem – due to pressure from the Habama forum. Encouraged by favorable opinion polls, Dayan believed he could return to the Knesset as the head of a mid-sized party, with chances for serving as a powerful swing factor. The first polls showed the party getting 21 or even 23 seats of the Knesset's 120.[173] Dayan wrote the party's foreign affairs and security platform, which supported the idea of Palestinian autonomy.

Telem's platform focused on relations with the Arabs. It proposed a five-year interim period, as discussed at Camp David, with Israel military rule there and Jewish settlement on state land only, followed by talks with Jordanian and West Bank representatives. If, after the five-year period, West Bank Arabs refused to negotiate, Israel would impose unilateral autonomy to the extent possible. The Palestinian refugee problem would be resolved by settling the refugees permanently in the country where they currently resided (mostly in the Arab countries surrounding Israel), with Israel playing an active role. Jerusalem would remain Israel's capital with the holy sites administered by the various religions and sects. Israel would also strive for suitable arrangements with Christians and Muslims.[174]

However, Dayan's campaign faltered. On the campaign trail, he looked old and tired, and his rallies were poorly attended. In the end, Telem won only two Knesset seats, leaving it with minimal influence at best. At party headquarters, Dayan spoke, assuming sole responsibility for the outcome.[175]

---

[171] Ibid., p. 11.
[172] Ibid., p. 19.
[173] Shoval, *Diplomat*, p. 148.
[174] Yanai (ed.), *Moshe Dayan al tahalikh hashalom ve'atida shel medinat yisrael*, pp. 283–284.
[175] Shoval, *Diplomat*, p. 151.

Shortly after the election, Dayan's supporters made a last attempt to place Dayan in a position of power, arranging a meeting with Begin and a reluctant Dayan. Dayan tried to convince Begin of the merits of unilateral autonomy, but Begin's response was cutting: "Mr. Dayan, I did not accept your proposal when you were my foreign minister. Why would you expect me to do so now?" A weakened Dayan answered: "If you do not institute autonomy now, you are later destined to establish a Palestinian state with your own two hands." The meeting was obviously over.[176] Thereafter, Dayan's health deteriorated quickly. On October 6, Sadat was assassinated by the Islamic Jihad in Egypt. The same day, Dayan published his last opinion piece for the daily press warning against abandoning the peace treaty after Sadat's death.[177]

On his deathbed, Dayan was visited by several close confidants and friends who had been by his side at different points in his career, sharing his political will with some. Rubinstein recalled that Dayan told him to be extremely vigilant in terms of the peace with Egypt and Israel's relations with the United States.[178] Dayan was worried that the peace with Egypt might be affected by an Islamic revolution after Sadat's death, similar to what had happened in Iran (this happened briefly when the Muslim Brotherhood was elected to govern Egypt from June 2012 till its ouster in July 2013). Dayan's request was to strengthen normalization and peace, and he emphasized the importance of maintaining security arrangements and expanding US involvement.[179]

On October 16, 1981, just ten days after Sadat's assassination, Moshe Dayan, aged sixty-six, died in the hospital of a heart attack after dedicating most of his adult life to the service of his beloved country.

APPENDIX

Dayan and Israel's Nuclear Power

It is generally believed that Israel has nuclear capabilities, having crossed the nuclear threshold around 1966.[180] To date, all Israeli governments have adopted a policy of nuclear ambiguity. Israel's possible nuclear capabilities have resonated powerfully throughout the Middle East and the world. The

---

[176] Ibid., p. 152. Dan Margalit, *Ra'iti otem* (Hebrew), Tel Aviv: Kinneret Zmora Bitan, 1997, p. 114. Shoval noted that Dayan passed away shortly thereafter, and Dayan and Begin never made amends. Nonetheless, Begin's eulogy for Dayan was statesman-like and noble. He compared Dayan to the heroes of the Hebrew bible, such as Joshua, Gideon, Jonathan, and David.

[177] Slater, *Warrior Statesman*, p. 435.

[178] Author's interview with Elyakim Rubinstein, Jerusalem, October 15, 2020.

[179] Rubinstein, *Darkei shalom*, pp. 52–53.

[180] Shlomo Aharonson, *Neshek garini bamizrah hatikhon* (Hebrew), Jerusalem: Academon, 1994, p. 18.

nuclear issue has dramatic ramifications for Israel's and its enemies' strategic decisions. For example, how might the possibility that Israel possessed nuclear power have affected the campaigns with Egypt and Syria in the Yom Kippur War? Is it possible that these nations decided to strive for relatively limited goals assuming that Israel possessed the doomsday weapon? There is no certain answer to these questions.

We can assume that Moshe Dayan, who had a significant influence on important decisions between the 1950s and late 1970s, helped shape this policy.

In the absence of any accessible documentation about Israel's nuclear activity, this overview of the nuclear issue is based mostly on second- and third-hand testimony and various hypotheses, circumstantial evidence, and foreign press publications, which in turn are also derived from sources whose reliability is unclear. Therefore, everything stated on the subject must be evaluated very carefully. However, given the importance and impact of the topic, it should be addressed to the extent possible.

Ben-Gurion reportedly concluded that Israel needed nuclear capabilities as early as the War of Independence. The Jewish people, having lost a third of their entire global population in the Holocaust and with its refugees in Israel now facing menacing threats from Arab enemies, feared annihilation. A nuclear program was also seen as a way to help Israel leap to the forefront of scientific knowledge.[181] Ben-Gurion realized that implementing this would require the help of a nuclear power. However, key figures, such as Defense Minister Pinchas Lavon and Moshe Sharret, opposed the project and feared US disapproval.[182]

Cooperation with France in the early 1950s, spearheaded by Shimon Peres, the young, eager Defense Ministry director general, also included the nuclear program. France's military aid, including nuclear assistance with nuclear arms, apparently influenced Ben-Gurion's decision to join the British–French coalition in the Sinai Campaign. France officially promised to arm Israel with conventional arms but unofficially agreed to help build a nuclear reactor.[183]

In September 1956, Peres secured France's commitment to provide a small nuclear reactor for research purposes. At the Sèvres conference a month later, Peres, according to his own testimony, met with French Prime Minister Guy Mollet and Defense Minister Maurice Bourgès-Maunoury, with Ben-Gurion's knowledge and blessing, and finalized this commitment. By September 1957, France had supplied Israel with a nuclear reactor twice as large as initially promised.[184] The nature of the construction was a closely guarded secret; as far as the public knew, the project involved building a textile manufacturing plant.

---

[181] Avi Shlaim, *The Iron Wall: Israel and the Arab World* (Hebrew), Tel Aviv: Yediot Aharonot, Chemed Books, 2005, p. 181.
[182] Aharonson, *Neshek garini bamizrah hatikhon*, p. 10.
[183] Ibid., p. 14.
[184] Shlaim, *The Iron Wall*, p. 181.

At this early stage, Dayan, while apparently aware of the nuclear program, had no active part in it, expressing neither enthusiasm nor reservations. Although interested in Dayan's thoughts, Ben-Gurion did not ask for a formal IDF opinion, concerned about potential competition for budgets between conventional weapons and the nuclear project.[185] Like many others in the late 1950s, Dayan also doubted the reactor's technological feasibility and distrusted the French. The heads of RAFAEL (Hebrew acronym of "Authority for the Development of Armaments") recalled that when touring the research institute as Chief of Staff, Dayan told them, "You know, I don't believe in all this, but you invited me so I came."[186] Nevertheless, there is evidence that he played a role in convincing the French to provide Israel with the necessary equipment to build the reactor in Dimona in exchange for Israel providing the French with the results of its nuclear research, the French being eager to attain nuclear knowledge that its other Western allies were not eager to share with it.[187] So, while Dayan's position and level of involvement remain uncertain, his strong ties with the French, his loyalty to Ben-Gurion, and his cooperation with Peres make his participation likely, even if, in those years, he was not convinced of the project's value.

In 1962, Dayan, now a government minister, became an enthusiastic supporter of the nuclear program. He, together with Peres, called for a massive investment in it, even at the expense of IDF budgets,[188] believing that nuclear capabilities could stop the conventional arms race, which Israel was destined to lose. Furthermore, every round of war would be more complex and costly than the previous one, and Israel could not afford to lose even a single confrontation. Dayan therefore thought that only nuclear potential could give Israel the deterrence needed to weaken the Arabs' motivation to go to war. Dayan and Peres claimed that in the absence of any superpower guarantee of Israel's security, Israel had to create its own guarantees.[189] Israel Galili and Yigal Allon opposed introducing nuclear weapons into the Middle East, preferring that Israel ensure that it could keep up with its enemies' technological capabilities.[190] Ben-Gurion and Peres, however, wanted nuclear capability at almost any cost.

In 1961, Ben-Gurion promised President Kennedy that US representatives could inspect the Dimona reactor. In the summer of 1962, Kennedy decided to

---

[185] Avner Cohen, *Yisrael vehaptsatsa* (Hebrew), Jerusalem: Schocken, 2000, pp. 93–94.
[186] Michael Karpin, *The Bomb in the Basement: How Israel Went Nuclear and What That Means to the World*, New York: Simon & Schuster Paperbacks, 2006, p. 126.
[187] Karpin, *The Bomb in the Basement*, pp. 90–91.
[188] Aharonson, *Neshek garini bamizrah hatikhon*, p. 291.
[189] Cohen, *Yisrael vehaptsatsa*, pp. 194–195.
[190] Aharonson, *Neshek garini bamizrah hatikhon*, pp. 228–231; Udi Manor, "Shikul da'at infantili: Dayan, Allon, ha'amimut hagarinit vehaviku'ah al mekoma shel yisrael bamerhav" (Hebrew), *Politika: Ktav et yisraeli lemada'ey hamedina veyehasim beynleumi'im* 27 (2018), pp. 76–103 (p. 98).

sell defensive Israel Hawk surface-to-air missiles to Israel, the first US weapons trade with Israel, hoping this would signal a US commitment to Israel's security and discourage Israel's nuclear ambitions.[191] The US administration, worried that Israel's nuclear program would escalate extremism and push the Arabs farther into the Soviet orbit, pressured Ben-Gurion for international inspection of the Dimona reactor. The compromise was Israel's agreement to US supervision.[192]

When Levi Eshkol became prime minister following Ben-Gurion's resignation in 1963, he had to meet his predecessor's commitment to the United States. The project faced both external opposition, including US pressure, and internal resistance from several ministers, including Pinchas Sapir (Israeli Minister of Finance from 1963 to 1968 and from 1969 to 1974), who felt Israel could not afford it.[193] To examine possible methods of action, Eshkol called a meeting of senior personnel to consult with them about it. Dayan's assessment was unequivocal: "The most important thing, security-wise, that could change our balance of power is the finished product out of Dimona. There is no substitute for it, there is no other trick ... as long as there is a chance of reaching it, we have to ... do everything to reach it."[194]

Israel's policy during this period was to develop nuclear potential while avoiding direct confrontation with the United States on the subject and to encourage the Americans to provide conventional weapons. This led to the policy of ambiguity as a response to some of the issues that emerged during that period.[195]

On March 10, 1965, Prime Minister Eshkol promised President Johnson that: "Israel will not be the first to bring nuclear weapons into the Israeli–Arab region."[196] Nonetheless, the United States had its doubts about Israel keeping this obligation. Dayan criticized Eshkol's decision to allow US inspection of Dimona, writing that by agreeing to such inspection, Eshkol had admitted that Israel possessed the nuclear option.[197] However, Eshkol, while allowing inspections to take place, cleverly showed the US inspectors only what he wanted them to see, and they didn't press for more.

By the Six-Day War, Israel had not yet developed a close security relationship with the United States, and the nation had not yet been promised US security aid. In the tense prewar period, an isolated Israel worried that the

---

[191] Aharonson, *Neshek garini bamizrah hatikhon*, p. 211.
[192] Ibid., p. 216.
[193] Ibid., p. 217.
[194] Cohen, *Yisrael vehaptsatsa*, pp. 217–218.
[195] Tamar Rahamivov-Honig, "Amanat ha'isur al neshek garini: Hashlakhoteha al hazira habeynleumit vemashmauyot leyisrael (Hebrew)," MA thesis, University of Haifa, July 2020.
[196] Manor, "Shikul da'at infantili," p. 83.
[197] *Haaretz*, March 26, 1965.

Egyptians' first strike could hit the Dimona reactor. By June 2, following Dayan's appointment as defense minister, cabinet members were leaning toward an Israeli first strike, partially because of two aerial photo sorties the Egyptians had sent over Dimona that the IDF failed to intercept.[198] At the height of the tensions, Peres reportedly suggested a controlled nuclear explosion at an isolated installation that would cause no damage but would demonstrate Israel's capabilities and serve as a deterrent.[199]

After the Six-Day War, the security roles of prime minister and defense minister were redivided. The prime minister remained in charge of nuclear matters but was no longer solely responsible. In practice, many issues were handed off to Tsvi Tsur's management at the Ministry of Defense.[200] Through this division of responsibility, Dayan managed to advance Israel's nuclear program even further than the prime minister wanted, and Israel reportedly crossed the nuclear threshold at some point between 1967 and 1969, becoming a fully-fledged nuclear nation.[201]

A further disagreement emerged between Dayan and Eshkol over whether Israel should openly use its nuclear potential as a deterrent. Dayan apparently advocated for transparency, while Eshkol wanted to continue the policy of ambiguity. Israel's prewar crisis emphasized that Israel could not rely on superpower security guarantees and that it had to manage its security concerns on its own. Dayan, canny about the media, was apparently behind Eshkol's decision to have a member of Israel's Atomic Energy Commission give public media interviews. Dayan likely used these interviews to convey changes he felt Israel had to make in its nuclear strategy, although there is no mention of the issue in any official documents.[202] Dayan may also have sought to increase US involvement in the Middle East given the Soviets' growing influence in the region.

In March 1969, when Golda Meir became prime minister, some measures were taken keep control of Israel's nuclear program solely with the prime minister. To regulate the division of authority between the prime minister and defense minister, a confidential document entitled "The Constitution" was prepared with Meir's and Dayan's permission. The document was confidential, but based on what has been published, an integral part of it clarifies the supremacy the prime minister has on the subject over the Defense Ministry's authority.[203]

---

[198] Cohen, *Yisrael vehaptsatsa*, p. 351.
[199] Shimon Peres, *Battling for Peace: A Memoir*, New York: Random House, 1995, pp. 166–167.
[200] Cohen, *Yisrael vehaptsatsa*, pp. 358–359.
[201] Avner Cohen, *The Worst-Kept Secret: Israel's Bargain with the Bomb*, New York: Columbia University Press, 2010, pp. 174–176.
[202] Cohen, *Yisrael vehaptsatsa*, pp. 359–360.
[203] Cohen, *The Worst-Kept Secret*, pp. 96–97.

At the end of the 1960s, Dayan was concerned about the growing Soviet threat in the region. Understanding that Israel could not face down the superpower alone, Dayan saw nuclear potential as Israel's only plausible deterrent against the Soviets. Israel's decision-makers hoped Israel's nuclear capability would spur the United States to take a more active role in the region or at least try to prevent confrontation between Israel and the Soviet Union.[204]

Israel's nuclear potential possibly helped increase US involvement and ensure its commitment to Israel's security. In the late 1960s, talks aimed at signing the nonproliferation treaty (NPT) were making progress, and Israel had to decide whether to sign. At a meeting with Meir and Israel's security leaders at Dimona, Dayan apparently opposed signing the treaty, emphasizing that Israel's enemies were cruel dictators. According to testimony, immediately after Dayan's remarks, Meir decided not to join the NPT[205] that was signed in 1968 and went into effect in 1970. At this point, the United States preferred that Israel keep its nuclear activities confidential and not adopt open nuclear deterrence. Israel, having promised the United Sates it would not be the first to bring nuclear weapons into the region, also promised not to reveal their existence publicly.[206] Nixon's administration, led by National Security Advisor Henry Kissinger, decided not to oppose its allies, including France, acquiring nuclear capabilities, assuming that, if ever used, nuclear power would be aimed against the Soviet Union. In the Middle East, the US aligned with Israel facing the Soviet client states of Egypt and Syria. Wanting to avoid criticism for not having forced Israel to sign the NPT, the United States halted inspections of the Dimona reactor in 1969, leaving Israel with a nuclear infrastructure without any international inspection routine. However, the United States demanded that Israel never declare its nuclear capabilities out in the open.[207] Thus, political necessity all but dictated Israel's policy of ambiguity.

During Dayan's term, Israel reportedly transitioned from having nuclear potential to producing a small nuclear arsenal. More than any other event, the French embargo on arms sales to Israel after the Six-Day War and the Soviet rush to rearm the Arabs exposed Israel's fragility. Moreover, the War of Attrition placed Israel in direct conflict with the Soviets. Dayan, fearing that Israel might get caught in an extended war of attrition it could never win because of its matériel inferiority, articulated a new formula for Israel's policy he called "the bomb in the basement," meaning manufacturing nuclear

---

[204] Cohen, *Yisrael vehaptsatsa*, pp. 372–373, 392.
[205] Cohen, *The Worst-Kept Secret*, p. 75.
[206] Shlaim, *The Iron Wall*, p. 292.
[207] Aharonson, *Neshek garini bamizrah hatikhon*, p. 24.

weapons without publicly declaring their existence. This avoided international pressure while signaling that Israel had nuclear bomb capabilities.[208]

There is some evidence, based on hearsay, not unequivocal proof, that in the Yom Kippur War, when IDF's battlefield situation seemed disastrous, Dayan, for the first time, raised the possibility of using nuclear weapons.[209] Arnan ("Sinai") Azaryahu, an aide to Minister Israel Galili, provides key evidence of the political-security Kitchen Cabinet meeting that took place at noon on October 7, 1973. Dayan had just returned to Tel Aviv after visiting both fronts, where he heard nerve-wracking reports on Egyptian and Syrian troops surging ahead. At the end of the official meeting, after Elazar had left the room and no more minutes were being taken, Dayan suggested considering a nuclear demonstration of capability to deter the enemy, but not its use on the enemy. Prior to the meeting, Dayan invited the head of the Atomic Energy Commission, Shalhevet Freier, to attend to explain the feasible nuclear options if the need arose. Freier waited outside the conference room to be called to explain the implications. Yigal Allon and Israel Galili objected, saying there was no reason to discuss those questions at the current time. Meir agreed, and the topic was not discussed. This is apparently the only recorded evidence of Dayan referring to nuclear weapons during the war.[210]

According to historian Avner Cohen, Azaryahu's testimony strengthens Israel's image as a mature, responsible state, even in the most difficult hours of the Yom Kippur War. Azaryahu's description provides a much more sober view than that presented in various publications on Israel's willingness to use nuclear weapons in the first days of the Yom Kippur War. For example, according to journalist Michael Karpin, Dayan ordered Israel's warplanes to be fitted with nuclear bombs and missiles with nuclear warheads and even had the IAF provided with specific targets to attack should the situation rise to the level of an existential threat to Israel.[211] Journalist Seymour Hersh described

---

[208] Uri Bar Joseph, "The Hidden Debate: The Formulation of a Nuclear Doctrine in the Middle East," *Journal of Strategic Studies* 5:2 (June 1982), pp. 205–227 (p. 217); Shlaim, *The Iron Wall*, p. 293.

[209] Cohen, *The Worst-Kept Secret*, p. 80.

[210] Ibid., p. 80. The description in Cohen's book erroneously dates the meeting to October 9; the particulars of the description make it clear that the meeting in question occurred on the 7th, at Dayan's low point of the day. By the 9th, Dayan was much more optimistic, and there would have been no reason for him to propose the use of nuclear weapons or even the threat of their use. On that day, Dayan was saying that Israel would be able to dig into its defensive lines and defend them for as long as necessary.

The details of the interview and further discussion about it may be found on Cohen's website at The Avner Cohen Collection: Interview with Arnan Azaryahu, www.wilsoncenter.org/arnan-sini-azaryahu; Avner Cohen, "When Israel Stepped Back from the Brink," *The New York Times*, October 3, 2013; www.nytimes.com/2013/10/04/opinion/when-israel-stepped-back-from-the-brink.html.

[211] Karpin, *The Bomb in the Basement*, p. 324.

a Kitchen Cabinet discussion on October 9 following Israel's failed October 8 counterattack, purportedly attended by Freier, who briefed the ministers. According to Hersh, the nuclear weapons option was raised primarily to pressure the United States to hurry to Israel's side.[212] But the description is quite improbable because on October 9, the immediate existential threat had passed. Ronen Bergman, a journalist from the *New York Times* and the Israeli publication *Yedioth*, penned an article on the nuclear dimension during the 1973 war. In his piece, he argued that in response to an Egyptian threat of deploying ballistic Scud missiles armed with unconventional warheads against Israel, the Israeli government intentionally moved its Jericho missiles in a conspicuous manner, visible to both Soviet and US satellites. This move was aimed at signaling that these global powers should exert pressure on Egypt in order to deescalate the situation. However, Bergman's account suggests that this strategy had an unintended consequence. Rather than deterring further escalation, it exacerbated tensions and led to a nuclear standoff between the superpowers. This was the most critical nuclear escalation since the Cuban Missile Crisis, prompting the United States to announce DEFCON III, its highest nuclear alert level since the Cuban Missile Crisis itself. The crisis only came to an end when the United States imposed a ceasefire on Israel on October 24.[213]

Postwar, Dayan again called for Israel to openly declare itself a nuclear power for several reasons. First, paradoxically, it could help advance a territorial compromise with Egypt and Syria and a process of reconciliation and peace, as Israel would feel safe while the Arabs would know that it was impossible to eradicate it. Second, such a declaration would make it possible to cut defense spending and strengthen the nation's economy. Dayan was very concerned about a conventional arms race, which Israel would never be able to win.[214] Yitzhak Rabin, then prime minister, was convinced that Dayan's proposal was too risky and therefore ordered the continuation of the policy of ambiguity.[215]

Toward the end of his political road, Dayan debated the issue of Israel's nuclear policy in Telem, his political party, arguing that the nuclear option would serve as a safe deterrent umbrella for Israel and help it avoid the conventional arms race and take further risks for peace. The combination of deterrence and a hand stretched out in peace would guarantee the nation's existence.

---

[212] Seymour Hersh, *The Samson Option: Israel's Nuclear Arsenal and American Foreign Policy*, New York: Random House, 1991.
[213] Ronen Bergman and Or Polyakov, "Nuclear Pressure," *Yedioth Aharonot Friday Supplement* no. 3113, September 8, 2023.
[214] Bar Joseph, "The Hidden Debate," p. 217.
[215] Cohen, *The Worst-Kept Secret*, pp. 75, 280, footnote 14.

Dayan's claim seemed justified when, in the aftermath of the Yom Kippur War trauma, and following Dayan's death, Israel built the largest military it ever had.[216] However, the Israeli economy was incapable of sustaining such a large army, and by the mid 1980s, the costs contributed to a period of hyperinflation. The economic recovery plan then included serious defense cutbacks. But Dayan could not have foreseen the tremendous changes of the 1990s and early 2000s: the end of the Cold War; the geopolitical changes in the Middle East; the development of technology; and the revolution in military matters. As a result, Israel no longer faced a coalition of Arab armies. Moreover, the major threats to Israel now come from missile and rockets operated by terrorist organizations aiming at the nation's civilian rear. Moreover, since the 1980s, Israel has been transformed from a poor state to a high-tech superpower with a healthy GDP. While Dayan's concerns then may be outdated today, they could resurface if Iran becomes a nuclear state.

---

[216] Between the Yom Kippur War and the mid 1980s, the IDF's order of battle more than doubled. Source: Dr. Eado Hecht, *Milh'mot yisrael* (Hebrew), IDF Command and Staff College, 2020.

11

The Development of a Strategist

I walked my own path and lived my own life. I knew how to do just two things: to sow, plow, and gather the grain, and, when the cannons roared from the gates at our homes, to fight back. The field of our forefathers shall ye work with the sword hanging above your bed.[1]

Moshe Dayan, July 29, 1980

This book offers two major insights into Moshe Dayan's strategic approach. The first refers to the body of Dayan's strategic work, and the second to how he formulated his strategy. Both are interwoven into Dayan's worldview, forged by his character and experiences. Having started at the bottom as a private and scout, he climbed the ladder to become IDF Chief of Staff and Minister of Defense. Thus, Dayan's personal development included firsthand knowledge of all aspects of war and strategy, from minor tactics to grand strategy. Undoubtedly, his many experiences, ascending to the pinnacle of the military and political ranks, heavily influenced his perspective on strategy development and the strategist's role.

This trajectory is not unique; many Israeli and other generals have followed a similar route, from junior to senior command positions – the traditional trajectory from soldier to general. However, Dayan stood out for simultaneously serving as an officer in an established military organization and acting as a revolutionary guerrilla fighter. Moreover, his deep and nuanced political awareness guided his military actions, as, from very early in his career, he viewed them in a much broader political context.

Unquestionably, with his adventurous spirit, Dayan was one of the few who felt little fear on the battlefield and found his true destiny in the army. As defense minister, he revealed that he preferred the company of soldiers to that of politicians. Soldiers, he said, had special qualities.[2] Anwar Nusseiba,

---

[1] From the poem entitled "At Nightfall," which Moshe Dayan wrote for his three children a few months before his death, in Neora Barnoach-Matalon, *Makom tov batsad* (Hebrew), Tel Aviv: Kotarim Publishers, 2009, opening page of the book.

[2] Moshe Dayan, interview with Llew Gardner, Thames TV, 1972, www.youtube.com/watch?v=FzVrRStVo9k.

a moderate, Cambridge-educated Palestinian leader, noted that what motivated Dayan was his passion for adventure. Nusseiba likened Dayan to British explorers of the Elizabethan era, such as Sir Francis Drake, a state-sanctioned pirate.[3]

Dayan grew up on the seamline between conventional wars between states and revolutionary guerrilla fighting of the twentieth century, including the Great Russian Revolution and the Spanish Civil War. Even as a youth, he was aware of the conflict with the Arabs, which escalated from local confrontations between neighbors over adjacent fields to a national conflict. Figures like Yitzhak Sadeh, the guerrilla fighter who established the Palmach, which, from its inception, operated like a guerrilla outfit, and Orde Wingate, the British officer skilled in antiguerrilla warfare, deeply influenced him. Dayan also received orderly training in conventional warfare during courses in the British army and Haganah training, developing in the dialectic between structured, conventional military knowledge and guerrilla tactics. As a senior officer, he recognized the need for discipline and organization in a large army facing large, established enemy armies, but never abandoned his wild, revolutionary guerrilla fighter conduct, backing commanders who sometimes broke the rules, like Ariel Sharon. Dayan's policy of reprisals and his general security approach applied in the army reflected elements of guerrilla warfare.

Dayan never hid his disdain for the rigidity of traditional European armies. Not having been educated at a military academy and lacking any long-standing military tradition, he found it difficult to understand the ceremonies and customs they preserved. One night during the Camp David negotiations, the delegations were treated to a US Marine show of drills. Dayan, then Israel's defense minister, was familiar with the Marines and greatly admired their fighting prowess, once describing them as "fearless fighters ready to attack, in perfect control of their excellent weapons." Seeing the parade drills flawlessly executed, Dayan expressed aversion to the performance. He explained that, like the others:

> I clapped and appreciated the perfection and precision of the show, but somewhere within me I felt resentful, almost insulted by the use of combat soldiers as marionettes, as if they were chocolate soldiers at the opera. Since the beginning of my service in the army, I've related to shows of order, drills, and parades with feelings that ranged from negativity to hostility.[4]

---

[3] In Moshe Dayan, series of great figures of the Jewish people, Peter Freistadt Center for Film Commemoration of the Great Figures of the Jewish People, Item No. 1843097, www.youtube.com/watch?v=LU01xeeMl8c&ab_channel=IsraelArchives.

[4] Moshe Dayan, *Hala-netsaḥ tokhal ḥerev: Sihot hashalom – reshamim ishi'im* (Hebrew), Tel Aviv: Idanim, 1981, p. 144.

The drills Dayan viewed were remnants of a time when battlefield success hinged on a unit's ability to synchronize individual's actions precisely and efficiently. These drills gained importance in the seventeenth and eighteenth centuries with technological advances in firearms. However, in the twentieth century, parade drills became unnecessary, shifting from the battlefield to the parade grounds only as a symbol of tradition and demonstration of unit discipline. Dayan took issue with this approach, believing that soldiers and their commanders should exhibit their individual capabilities in the battlefield:

> Soldiers are destined for war, and war is not waged in straight lines or rhythmic motions. War is not only the most dangerous event in a person's life ... [but] demands supreme physical and mental effort. Despite the shelling, shooting, and bullets swirling around, you must concentrate ... and see what is happening around you with clear eyes: exploit the folds of the terrain, provide covering fire for your advancing comrades, prepare an ambush for an approaching enemy unit, sharpen your senses to do the right thing at the right time. ... The characteristics and actions required in battle are a distillation of the full individual capacity of every man, not the action of robots moving arms and legs at the touch of a button.[5]

This protest reflects Dayan's view of war as a phenomenon that can be understood only in its local concrete geographical, cultural, and political contexts. The individual fighter, no matter how junior, can have a great impact on the events. This dismissal of rigid, established military patterns is central to revolutionary guerrilla movements. As a former guerrilla fighter and as a general in a formative army, Dayan imparted this thinking to others. Dayan's view of the IDF differed radically from Ben-Gurion's, as evidenced when "the old man" reprimanded Dayan for the 89th Battalion's misconduct during the Lod raid in the War of Independence, deeming it more fitting for unorganized partisans than soldiers. Ben-Gurion wanted an orderly, apolitical army befitting a state, similar to the British army, which he knew and greatly respected. He envisioned an army behaving along the lines much later proposed by the political scientist Samuel Huntington, wherein an army has its own ethos and values differing vastly from those of civilian society. However, Ben-Gurion also recognized that such an army could not fulfill the vast social missions he expected the IDF to undertake after the state's establishment. He needed generals like Dayan to instill a fresh spirit in the army, realizing that this could not be achieved through procedures, handbooks, or parade formations. Dayan, in turn, learned that a large army needs order, discipline, and organization. Thus, in the dialectic between the two, the modern IDF emerged: an established military reflecting Ben-Gurion's vision, yet allowing for individual commanders' expression and some unruliness.

---

[5] Ibid.

In choosing Dayan to lead the IDF because of Dayan's military capabilities and political affinity, Ben-Gurion was responsible for Dayan's central role. Inevitably, the question arises as to what lay behind that intense bond between Ben-Gurion and Dayan. One factor was Dayan's political and personal loyalty to Ben-Gurion. Another is a psychoemotional one: In Dayan, Ben-Gurion saw the personification of the "new Jew" – the farmer-fighter instead of the fearful ghetto resident. Beyond these reasons, the two shared an ideology, putting the state's welfare first, and complemented one another. Ben-Gurion, breaking from socialism and turning to the West, the United States in particular, focused on national independence, cultural revival of the nation in its land, and the state as an organizing principle attracting immigrants and refugees from all over the world.

Ben-Gurion's life's work was building the state and settling the land. Dayan, never identifying with any major twentieth-century ideology, whether socialism, communism, or capitalism, shared this view. Dayan's ultimate commitment, like Ben-Gurion's, was the success of the Zionist undertaking – the revival of an independent Jewish nation in its historic homeland. Mordechai Bar-On said of Dayan, "As long as he lived, he remained true to himself and his fundamental values: love of the land and dedication to the Zionist enterprise. These were the two values to which he devoted his entire life."[6] Even Tom Segev, one of Dayan's harshest critics, agreed that while "he was an extreme pragmatist, he was born into Zionist ideology and clung to it until his dying day, and, like Ben-Gurion, he was willing to pay any price it demanded."[7] Fulfilling the Zionist vision was Dayan's lodestar, and Zionism was the true strategic purpose. As long as his actions served this ultimate purpose, Dayan, beholden to no one path, felt free to choose different ways of operating depending on conditions and circumstances.

Despite Ben-Gurion and Dayan's deep connection, their relationship was not one of equals. Ben-Gurion was the undisputed leader and mentor and helped shape Dayan's political worldview. Still, there was a certain division of labor between them as well. Dayan was the architect, translating Ben-Gurion's vision into concrete military plans. Much like building contractors, bold and resourceful tactical commanders, such as Ariel Sharon, would then help execute these plans. The most striking example of this was the Sinai Campaign, for which Dayan was able to reflect the ageing leader's goals, constraints, and worries in a workable plan and then execute it.[8]

---

[6] Mordechai Bar-On, *Moshe Dayan: Korot hayav 1915–1981*, Tel Aviv: Am Oved, 2014, pp. 358–359.
[7] Tom Segev, *Media bekhol mehir: Sipur hayav shel David Ben-Gurion* (Hebrew), Ben Shemen: Keter, 2018, p. 534.
[8] Brigadier General Dov Tamari used the terminology of vision, architect, and construction engineer to represent political vision, strategy, and tactics in various lectures; Shimon Naveh did so as well in a report: Shimon Naveh, "Operational Art and the IDF: A Critical

Dayan's military and political experiences, including fighting alongside and against the British, his underground activity, and his stint in prison together with Arab gang members and rival underground fighters, vastly expanded his understanding of the connection between fighting, even small-scale, and the broader political context. Zalman Shoval recounts his first meeting with Dayan in 1946. Dayan, rather than sharing war stories, as his youthful listeners sitting around a bonfire with him expected, spoke of the challenges facing the impending Jewish state. Shoval, a future Israeli ambassador to the United States, recognized that Dayan spoke not as a soldier but as a political visionary.[9] Dayan's political aptitude increased during the War of Independence, in which he was tasked with negotiating Jerusalem's ceasefire lines with Jordan and, later, ceasefire lines in general, gaining strategic political experience rather than running large-scale military operations. While this primarily benefited him, it also presented some challenges.

To understand Dayan's approach to strategy, it's crucial to examine his perception of reality, particularly his perceptions regarding the knowledge and nature of reality. The creation process for the two types of strategy – deliberate versus emergent – differs significantly. Deliberate strategy involves top-down planning to create a final, complete product, a type of "strategic good," to be imposed on reality. Conversely, emergent strategy takes a more open approach, assuming a continuously evolving reality. Thus, there is never a final product. The different approaches manifest variations in several dimensions: the level of detail, time frames, goals, and the planners' organizational echelon. Deliberate strategy emphasizes control, striving to implement and realize the original intention, while emergent strategy concentrates on learning, developing new understandings, and adapting the plan to them.[10] Organizational theorist Karl Weick explained that emergent strategy does not reflect a dichotomy between thought and action but involves trial and error, with no defined order in which analysis precedes interaction with the environment. This approach sees the world not as a stable entity existing "somewhere out there," awaiting analysis and reconstruction, but as a constantly emerging reality subject to reinterpretation and updating based on past experience.[11]

Undoubtedly, Dayan's strategic approach was emergent. He viewed life as a continuous, uncontrolled struggle among varied forces, creating a constantly changing reality. Therefore, decisions had to be equally dynamic, although, with Dayan, always guided by the beacon of ensuring Israel's existence and

---

Study of a Command Culture," Center for Strategic and Budgetary Assessment (CSBA), Secretary of Defense, 2007, p. 23.

[9] Zalman Shoval, *Diplomat* (Hebrew), Tel Aviv: Yedioth Ahronoth, 2016, p. 39.

[10] Henry Mintzberg, Bruce Ahlstrand, and Joseph Lampel, *Strategic Safari: The Complete Guide through the Wilds of Strategic Management*, New York: Simon & Shuster, 2005, p. 219.

[11] Ibid., p. 198.

security. Any means for serving that end, whether a certain policy, political party, or ideology, could be abandoned if Dayan felt they no longer served the larger goal.

Dayan's frequent changes of mind led some to view him as inconsistent, believing that leaders should maintain the same fixed ideology and policy, and criticized him for this. Dayan's response, "Only a donkey never changes its mind," became one of his famous quips. Dayan had the rare ability to admit, "I said what I said; the circumstances were different, conditions developed differently than I'd thought, and I'm therefore updating policy."[12] Historian Mordechai Bar-On, Dayan's bureau chief when the latter was Chief of Staff, characterized him as follows:

> One of his most prominent character traits was his rejection of any extreme position, of any subjugation to prearranged, ordered ideologies. He was remarkable in his relentless aspiration to re-examine, without prejudice, the ever-developing and ever-changing reality ... Undoubtedly, he was capable of clever maneuvering but not of pretending or exploiting empty pathos. He would always say what he was thinking and fled falsity as if it were fire ... He had no trouble changing his mind when circumstances turned different[ly] than expected or when he realized he had been mistaken.[13]

Dayan's ability to reach a certain decision and then change it, sometimes by 180 degrees, is key to understanding his unique development and functioning as a strategist, leader, and manager. Drawing on philosopher Isaiah Berlin's categorization of thinkers as hedgehogs and foxes, historian John Lewis Gaddis wrote that strategists must have a strong sense of direction – like the hedgehog – as well as the sensitivity to the changing environment – like the fox.[14] According to historian Michael Oren, Dayan's mind could contain far more than two contradictory ideas at once, and he could shift from impassioned opposition to unhesitating support within hours.[15] This tendency was a magnet for condemnation, as "Fox-like thinking and behavior were considered inferior and illogical."[16] It was considered evidence of a fundamental character flaw in Dayan, despite all evidence that creativity is achieved through intuition, association, and contextual suggestions that do not submit to hedgehog logic.

Raised on classical Russian literature, Dayan had an interest in Hebrew poetry, the Kabbalah, and the *Book of Splendor*, which helped him "fill layers of

---

[12] Shlomo Gazit, "Moshe Dayan vtsh'al" (Hebrew), in Mordechai Bar-On (ed.), *Lenochach gvulot oyevim: tzava ubitachon ba'asor harishon shel medinat Yisrael*, Israel: Efy Meltzer, 2017, pp. 167–178 (p. 168).

[13] Bar-On (ed.), *K'shehatsava hehelif madav*, pp. 358–359.

[14] John Lewis Gaddis, *On Grand Strategy*, United States: Allen Lane, 2018, pp. 19–20.

[15] Michael Oren, *Six Days of War: June 1967 and the Making of the Modern Middle East*, in Hebrew translation, Or Yehuda: Dvir, 2004, pp. 393–394.

[16] Tsvi Lanir, *Pinkas hakis shel hashual: Al hashualim shebanu kehashiva ukhederekh hayim* (Hebrew), Herzliya: Yaniv Books, 2020, p. 11.

thought."[17] Addressing Dayan's interest in Kabbalah, Gershon Hacohen, an IDF major general with a master's degree in philosophy, explained that in the Kabbalah, the *shekhina* ("dwelling" or "settling," generally used to denote God's presence) is dualistic and contradictory: male and female, strict judgment and mercy. Similarly, the hedgehog and the fox suggest opposites: The fox can shatter conventions and judge situations in relation to the concrete context, while the hedgehog represents the polar opposite – the desire for universally valid rules and principles. A systematic and strategic leader must be able to both challenge convention and merge universal principles with context-based action, even if it contradicts those principles.[18]

While Dayan was blessed with the hedgehog's sense of direction, the fox outweighed the hedgehog in his nature. His academic studies in political science and the Middle East at the Hebrew University had little influence on him, because he was skeptical about broad, universal theories. Like a fox, he believed in a fluid reality that required new ways of thinking and different approaches to action for each situation. Therefore, Dayan – the fox – rejected theories that claimed to explain everything, preferring to live with questions rather than insisting on answers and solutions.[19] Like a fox, he often adopted local, partial solutions rather than comprehensive ones.[20] This approach applied to how Dayan dealt with the occupied territories. While he refused to annex them, insisting on the inhabitants' political freedom, he also supported Jewish settlement due to its importance for to Israel's security. In the talks with Egypt, Dayan used what Elyakim Rubinstein called "constructive obfuscation,"[21] suggesting some vague formulation, assuming that over time, things would work themselves out.[22] Unlike proponents of absolute solutions – the right's annexation and the left's withdrawal – Dayan sought local, temporary fixes, which, while imperfect, allowed for some freedom for the Palestinians and security for the Israelis.

The hedgehog also applies general knowledge to individual cases. Dayan, like a fox, always recognized the uniqueness of each situation and depended on in-depth, context-specific intelligence, rather than on an external source, as would the hedgehog.[23] This view, that "effective learning comes from the learner's conceptual context,"[24] guided his actions throughout his career, including developing new practices as a soldier in the British Jewish auxiliary, refusing to act according to the universal defense doctrine during a battalion

---

[17] Shabtai Teveth, *Moshe Dayan: Biografia* (Hebrew), Tel Aviv: Schoken, 1971, p. 415.
[18] Private correspondence between the author and Gershon Hacohen, October 2, 2020.
[19] Lanir, *Pinkas hakis shel hashual*, p. 9.
[20] Ibid., p. 34.
[21] Elyakim Rubinstein, *Darkei shalom* (Hebrew), Tel Aviv: Defense Ministry Publishing, 1992, p. 104.
[22] Telephone interview with Elyakim Rubinstein, August 2020.
[23] Lanir, *Pinkas hakis shel hashual*, p. 23.
[24] Ibid., p. 106.

commander course, and his decision-making during the Sinai Campaign. Despite fighting the same enemy in the Six-Day War, Dayan set a different military objective due to different political and strategic conditions.

Dayan, unlike most but like the fox, perceived reality as a series of rapid changes, which forced him to reevaluate each situation. The fox's approach isn't "you only live once," but rather "every day you live anew; you only die once."[25] This attitude was evident in Dayan's inconsistent instructions to Major General Aharon Yariv during negotiations after the Yom Kippur War. First, Dayan criticized Yariv's painstaking transfer of supplies to the Third Army. "Hurry, hurry," Dayan urged. The next day, Dayan told Yariv to slow down the supply. Yariv, upset, asked, "But why? Yesterday, you told me to hurry!" Looking Yariv in the eye, Dayan answered, "Today is a new day."[26]

Shabtai Teveth, Dayan's biographer, who spent considerable time with Dayan, claimed that his inspiration and originality came "from within, from contexts and circumstance, not from extended study of military doctrines and history."[27] Teveth pointed to Dayan's natural curiosity and creativity, enabling him to learn from every situation and create a frame of reference under changing conditions while seeking a solution whereby he could "test the waters," as he suggested in his well-known speech "Diving into Cold Water" after the War of Attrition, explaining why it was impossible to determine everything ahead of time and necessary to "dive into the cold water."[28] Describing Dayan's way of thinking and operating as creative and artistic more than scientific and technical, Teveth wrote:

> His wants to do things with his own two hands, not by ordering someone else to act, [just as] no painter or musician will give instructions to someone else to create their art ... Like an artist, Dayan changes his mind depending on how his creation is developing. He has no predetermined formula the way a technologist has. Like an artist, he adds and removes colors based on the state of the canvas and his mood and his new flashes of genius.[29]

Kissinger, always acute, considered Dayan the most original, realistic, and poetic leader in Israel,[30] writing:

---

[25] Ibid., p. 22.
[26] Amos Gilboa, *Mar modi'in: Ahreleh, aluf aharon yariv, rosh aman* (Hebrew), Tel Aviv: Miskal, 2013, pp. 641–642.
[27] Teveth, *Moshe Dayan*, p. 415.
[28] Meir Boymfeld, *Kfitsa lamayim hakarim: Hamaga'im hamedini'im bein yisrael, mitsrayim ve'artshot habrit bashanim shekadmu lemilhemet yom hakippurim 1970–1973* (Hebrew), Reut: Effi Meltser, 2017, p. 67.
[29] Teveth, *Moshe Dayan*, p. 415.
[30] In a meeting with Gad Yaakobi in 1987, in Gad Yaakovi, *Pgishot bemaslul hayay* (Hebrew), Jerusalem: Carmel, 2009, p. 91.

Dayan was a singular blend of the old and the new. Among his colleagues, he was unique in the sweep of his imagination, the nimbleness of his intellect, the ability to place Israel in a world context. His hobby was archaeology; this gave him an historical perspective beyond even the long history of his own people. He understood that the experience of catastrophe was not peculiar to Jews, even if destiny seems to have meted it out to them more amply than to most other peoples. He therefore had more understanding, and more tolerance, of the viewpoints of other societies – especially the Arabs' – than was characteristic of most Israeli leaders. He had the intuition of a poet. Sometimes he was able to see so many sides to a question that he lost the single-mindedness essential to all leaders and very marked in his own Prime Minister [Golda Meir].[31]

Dayan's leadership and management approached was shaped by strategic understanding, evidenced in his daily management practices, such as delegating authority, flexible planning, time management, running meetings, and managing teams. The following are several practices that characterized Dayan's management style:

The Pareto principle:[32] Dayan used the Pareto principle, or the 80:20 rule. This rule suggests that 80 percent of system activity originates in 20 percent of active factors, with a single factor responsible for causing 80 percent of the system's issues. Identifying and improving this factor can improve system performance by 80 percent. Regardless of whether he knew about the Pareto principle, he operated in accordance with it, always identifying one pivotal problem and then focusing on fundamentally improving it to effect change. As Chief of Staff, he concentrated on combat leadership and the reprisals, and he later focused on preparing the army for an eventual clash with Egypt. While defense minister, he devoted himself to managing the occupied territories, the War of Attrition, and the long, convoluted war with Egypt, before shifting his attention to Palestinian self-rule. Shlomo Gazit, Chief of Staff's Dayan's first bureau chief, and later AMAN Director, described Dayan's "anti-comb" approach: Unlike a manager who uses a comb, with its many equal-sized teeth to address many different subjects in parallel, Dayan felt that he had a staff to handle the full gamut of issues for which he was responsible: "I . . . choose one, maybe two topics, and focus on those and nothing else . . . There, my work can lead to transformation."[33] Sometimes, feeling that a solution was being found, he would shift his attention, leaving the day-to-day work to his staff. Gazit recalled that Dayan spent three months with the Moshe Kashti, the

---

[31] Henry Kissinger, *Years of Upheaval*, Boston, MA: Little, Brown & Company, 1982, pp. 562–563.
[32] Vilfredo Pareto (1848–1923), an Italian economist and sociologist, formulated this principle, which while not precise, and possibly subject to different ratios, e.g., 70:30, serves as a rule of thumb.
[33] Gazit, "Moshe Dayan vtsh'al," pp. 171–172.

Chief of Staff's financial consultant, drawing up the IDF's 1954 budget. Their work complete, Dayan told Kashti they hopefully wouldn't meet again until September, saying, "You have your business, I have mine." Kashti didn't take Dayan seriously, returning to Dayan's bureau the next morning with a question. Dayan refused to see him and ordered him to leave.[34]

Relying on staff and advisors: To succeed, Dayan surrounded himself with skilled professionals, delegating authority to handle issues for which he was responsible but did not deal with directly. His staff was able to work independently, and all knew how to read Dayan's quickfire, overnight changes of mind and rapid decision-making. He would deliberate a day or two to implement a decision to avoid wasted effort,[35] having conceded to his staff that, "Whatever I mess up in the morning, you'll fix by evening."

Those who worked with Dayan from afar found him cold, distant, and rigid, in contrast to those who worked closely with him, with many of whom Dayan forged close relationships, including his secretary Neora Barnoach-Matalon, Shlomo Gazit, and Mordechai Bar-On, who remained loyal to Dayan for decades. Other key people included Meir Amit, Tsvi Tsur, Mati Niv, and Aryeh Braun; in political and legal affairs, Zalman Shoval, Yosef Chechanover, Gad Yaakobi, Hayim Yisraeli, and Elyakim Rubinstein, all of whom were gifted and independent. They experienced pleasant and mutually respectful and trusting working relationships with Dayan and recall that he encouraged them to disagree with him without fear.

In his last years as defense minister, Dayan often suffered from severe headaches related to his eye injury to and could be impatient with people as a result, although always courteous to his inner circle.[36] Gad Yaakobi, an intimate assistant and later Israel's finance minister and ambassador to the United Nations, described Dayan's attitude to his confidants:

> Dayan provided everyone who worked with him a great deal of freedom, a sense of initiative and independence, but he also made it a point to give guidance. He was unforgiving of those who betrayed his trust. It was therefore easier for self-disciplined, rigorous mavericks to work for him than it was for weak and sloppy people. There were usually no barriers between him and those whose work he appreciated, and he shared with them his deliberations and state of mind.[37]

As Chief of Staff, Dayan kept only a skeleton staff and a modest office with a plain desk covered with a military blanket. He even wouldn't use the air conditioning, to express solidarity with the soldiers in the field.

Dayan also appreciated skilled, independent people, surrounding himself with those who compensated for what he recognized as his weaknesses. He

---

[34] Ibid., p. 172.
[35] Rubinstein, *Darkei shalom*, p. 208.
[36] Ibid., p. 221.
[37] Gad Yaakobi, *Hesed hazman: Pirkey otobiografiya* (Hebrew), Tel Aviv: Miskal, 2002, p. 200.

appointed future Chiefs of Staff Tsvi Tsur, Haim Laskov, and Yitzhak Rabin to positions, recognizing their organizational skills and force buildup expertise, areas with which he had little patience. Despite professional disagreements, Dayan brought Yitzhak Rabin back from England to appoint him Director of Training on the General Staff, a position that suited Rabin. Dayan also trusted Meir Amit to head the army's Operations Directorate to the point that Dayan left Amit to lead the Sinai Campaign while Dayan rushed to the front. Dayan preferred those who were ready to challenge him over sycophants.[38]

Amit described Dayan as "a creative, impatient man who dominated and intimidated everyone he met. He knew what he wanted and demanded that his wishes be fulfilled at once."[39] According to Amit, Dayan projected authority and leadership, was a deep thinker, grasped things quickly, considered the long term, and analyzed situations with astounding clarity while calculating surprising moves, always able to discern what was essential. But Amit conceded that it was not easy to work with Dayan. "He was an impatient person. He abhorred wasting time and always wanted to start at the end, what we'd now call 'the bottom line.' There were only a few he was willing to listen to for long."[40] Amit explained that Dayan's impatience was due to his severe headaches as well as his personality and his critical judgment of some of those around him.

Still, those closest to Dayan found him tolerant and appreciative, empowering his staff and delegating authority. For example, Dayan demanded that his bureau chief Shlomo Gazit, previously responsible for shuffling papers and handling correspondence, would now participate in all discussions and meetings and be responsible for taking the minutes. He told Gazit, "Once the discussion is over, I don't want to hear about it again. You're to distribute the summary." According to Gazit, "This was a revolutionary approach."[41] Dayan would say, "A good commander is tested in two ways: picking the correct priority – what to handle and what to ignore – and picking the right assistants to do the work for him."[42]

Nevertheless, many viewed Dayan as remote and unpredictable, prone to harsh and hurtful responses, and leaving a trail of aggrieved people behind him. Chief of Staff Mordechai Maklef, once Dayan's commander, said of him, "He doesn't fight with others; he just cuts them out of his life."[43]

Time management: Dayan's time-management method differed significantly from the norm. Time is the most highly prized asset of managers, and

---

[38] Barnoach-Matalon, *Makom tov batsad*, p. 248.
[39] Meir Amit, *Rosh berosh: Mabat ishi al eru'im gedolim ufarshiyot ne'elamot* (Hebrew), Or Yehuda: Maariv-Hed Arzi Publications, 1999, pp. 39, 85.
[40] Ibid.
[41] Teveth, *Moshe Dayan*, p. 380.
[42] Barnoach-Matalon, *Makom tov batsad*, p. 248.
[43] Ibid., p. 371.

the professional literature considers "attention management" – a manager's decision to devote time to a particular issue – critical. The schedules of most senior managers, whether a CEO or high-ranking officer, are fully packed and planned months in advance. When the inevitable emergency arises, prior commitments are moved.

Dayan, in contrast, insisted that his calendar be left open. He had two regular weekly appointments: Friday mornings with the defense minister and Sunday middays with the cabinet. One day was set aside for direct meetings with senior commanders, and another for the field visits. Dayan's calendar was otherwise blank and flexible, his schedule filled in mostly day to day.[44] This method of time management meant he had open windows for meetings about urgent issues. Dayan instructed his secretary to leave him a lot of free time to sit by himself and think. This gave him time to reflect and considerable flexibility to respond to new, unanticipated developments, reflecting his view that reality was constantly changing and rigid planning futile. He would often decide to make unexpected, unannounced visits to bases to gain a sense of what was going on, and once a month, he would make planned visits to certain bases together with all IDF General Staff division heads to solve transorganizational issues on the spot.[45]

Dayan would end his day in the early evening. Dayan once explained to Shimon Peres that he had so much free time because: "I have a rule: any piece of paper I don't have time to read by six in the evening, I forget it exists. Whatever I manage by six – great. At six, my desk is clean and problems are all gone."[46]

Dayan valued free time immensely, as shown by his requests for quiet time from his secretary Neora Barnoach-Matalon, when he was Chief of Staff in the 1950s and, twenty years later, when he was at the Foreign Ministry, from Elyakim Rubinstein.[47] Without it, Dayan felt like a fish out of water. His later interest in archeology led him to glue pottery shards together as a type of meditation or mindfulness practice that enabled him to think. He found noise disruptive, making it impossible for him to think, and he criticized the military method whereby "the top-ranking officer of a regional command is surrounded by his staff and doesn't have a second to think in peace and quiet ... Perhaps there is something wrong with me, but until the last day of the war I preferred to skip the regional headquarters and instead meet directly at the command centers on the front."[48] During breaks at the Camp David

---

[44] Interview with Shlomo Gazit, Kfar Saba, Israel, August 20, 2018; interview with Neora Barnoach-Matalon, Dayan's personal assistant, Herzliya, Israel, November 10, 2018.
[45] Barnoach-Matalon, *Makom tov batsad*, pp. 34–35.
[46] Teveth, *Moshe Dayan*, p. 410.
[47] Rubinstein, *Darkei shalom*, p. 208.
[48] Moshe Dayan, *Avnei derekh: Autobiografia* (Hebrew), Jerusalem: Idanim Publishers, 1976, p. 621.

negotiations, he preferred the solitude of walking the surrounding trails so he could think to socializing or playing sports.

Debate management: An inevitable, routine task of a manager or military commander is holding meetings, where people with different roles can exchange information, coordinate action, and, most importantly, make decisions. If meetings are inefficient, the organization pays a steep price in efficiency and effectiveness.

Dayan held two types of meetings. The first were small operational decision meetings that would begin with relatively simple topics, gradually moving on to weightier issues. In the other type of meeting, periodic gatherings of the senior ranks, participants would try to clarify essential strategic questions. Dayan encouraged open discussions, although once a decision was made, he made sure everyone was completely on board with it, down to the last detail.[49]

Minutes from Dayan-led General Staff meetings show a consistent pattern. Dayan set the tone of a free and open discussion. He would first update the General Staff on political developments and listen to military updates before presenting central military dilemmas with clear, targeted questions. These often pertained to an emerging political reality directly affecting military action, political constraints affecting military conduct, or the possible political ramifications of certain military actions.

For example, during the War of Attrition, Dayan often opened meetings with a central dilemma, such as a potential military action that might compel Egypt to hold its fire or what sort of response would lead to Soviet intervention. After listening to each General Staff officer, Dayan would summarize the military actions and their political ramifications, or, in some cases, the significance of a political situation for the army, then ask the General Staff to prepare an appropriate plan to respond to the political scenario. In this way, Dayan was able to integrate political insights into his military thinking. Dayan was apparently aware that he, more than anyone else, could combine a broad political and diplomatic view with the necessary military thinking. He made a point of intervening whenever he felt that a military action would have political consequences, for example, becoming personally involved in choosing and authorizing Egyptian targets during the War of Attrition.[50]

Leadership from the front line: The concept of leadership from the front line often refers to managers who spend time at the point where the actual work is done. The analogy to the military is obvious. Throughout history, many commanders have chosen to spend time with the soldiers at the front,

---

[49] Shlomo Gazit, *Meta'em bemalkodet: 30 shnot mediniyut yisraelir bashtahim* (Hebrew), Tel Aviv: Zmora-Bitan, 1999, pp. 74–75.

[50] Yoav Gelber, *Haz'man hapalestini: Israel, yarden, vehapalestinim 1967–1970* (Hebrew), Hevel Modiin: Dvir, 2018, pp. 460–461.

experiencing the conditions firsthand. This practice boosted morale and provided a better understanding of the full situation.

Dayan believed in experiencing things for himself, unfiltered, so he could form his own, independent judgments. As Chief of Staff, he frequently toured bases and units, often meeting units returning from raids at the border. He was noted for accompanying the troops during most of the Sinai Campaign, receiving heavy criticism for being absent for long stretches from headquarters. In typical dispassionate fashion, Dayan responded that: "Perhaps they're right. But I cannot, or maybe do not want to, do things differently."[51]

As defense minister, Dayan's attitude remained unchanged, as he spent considerable time in West Bank and Gaza towns and villages, speaking with local inhabitants about their concerns, which earned him a great deal of respect and appreciation among them. During this time, the IDF would set ambushes and chase terrorist teams infiltrating from Jordan. Dayan couldn't resist and joined an ambush that intercepted and killed three infiltrators. An armed Dayan got off a few shots but mostly enjoyed the break from routine and being close to the land.[52] As Chief of Staff and as defense minister, he often bypassed bureaucracy to expedite decisions and would not keep to itineraries by the local echelon to support their interests, preferring spontaneity, even changing course midway to pursue his curiosity.[53]

In the Six-Day and Yom Kippur Wars, he often was at the fronts, especially during the latter, when he was at the front every day but one, even reaching brigade command posts on the move, unthinkable today. A few days before the war, he toured the northern front, ordering manpower increases. He always regretted not undertaking a similar tour of the southern front.[54]

There is certainly a merit in unmediated study and proximity to events, and Dayan's decisions were often influenced by his field visits, which enabled him to respond quickly before situations became more complicated. But proximity can impede one's ability to make well-considered decisions, as when Dayan as defense minister would impulsively order severe punitive measures, contrary to his own policy, after witnessing a terror attack.[55]

Attention to detail: Dayan was dismissive of military etiquette and formality and focused on strategy and essential issues, but he was actually quite detail oriented. His secretary Barnoach-Matalon noted his meticulous choice of words when addressing commanders and soldiers. He personally wrote orders and lectures and thoroughly read intelligence updates, reports on army morale,

---

[51] Dayan, *Avnei derekh*, p. 288.
[52] Ibid., p. 536.
[53] Shlomo Gazit, *HaMakel vehagezer: hamemshal hayisraeli beyehuda* (Hebrew), Tel Aviv: Zmorah Bitan, 1985, pp. 125–126.
[54] Barnoach-Matalon, *Makom tov batsad*, p. 211.
[55] Ibid., pp. 125–126.

and soldiers' complaints.[56] Gad Yaakobi described Dayan during his term as defense minister:

> His attitude to any undertaking was serious and exact. He was one of the most meticulous people I ever met, and not just about being on time but also on using data. He always strove for the most concise and cohesive formulations dealing with the heart of the matter, removing the external layers and penetrating to the sometimes-difficult truth.[57]

Learning methods: Today, leaders are expected to be very quick studies, able to respond correctly and in time to changes. Dayan, criticized for his lack of formal education, having never excelled in IDF courses or completed his undergraduate studies, had a more practical approach to learning. He was self-taught and felt that his military career was the result of need rather than of choice. His attitude is captured in Winston Churchill's words, "Personally, I'm always ready to learn, although I don't always like being taught."[58]

Dayan's learning style aligns with the reflective practitioner concept developed by organizational psychologist Donald Schön. Schön explains that learning through reflection involves observing actions to facilitate a process of extended learning. This approach encourages learning through personal experience rather than studying formal knowledge and requires relinquishing well-established ideas and techniques to reach new understandings.[59]

A reflective practitioner relates to unique situations as already-existing realities. Dayan was a problem solver, not a military thinker. His thought development was that of a practitioner, not a philosopher of strategy, and was driven by the challenges faced by Israel, especially the IDF.

His autodidactic approach was manifested in his 1966 visit to Vietnam to understand the war and in his preenlistment preparation prior to the Six-Day War. After a decade away from the military, Dayan, keen on becoming commander of the Southern Command, began wearing a uniform and became reacquainted with the army by traveling among the units to learn about the state of the army after his ten-year absence. As he did in Vietnam, Dayan began these visits at the top, meeting with senior commanders and the High Command headquarters, and systematically working his way down the ranks to the very bottom, from the strategic level to the tactical level that translates the strategy into action. "I wanted to see what the IDF was like, what it can do, what it

---

[56] Barnoach-Matalon, *Makom tov batsad*, pp. 27–28.
[57] Yaakobi, *Hesed hazman*, p. 200.
[58] "Anglophenia: 50 Sir Winston Churchill Quotes to Live By," BBC America, April 9, 2015, at www.bbcamerica.com/blogs/50-churchill-quotes-49128.
[59] Donald A. Schön, *The Reflective Practitioner: How Professionals Think in Action*, New York: Basic Books, 1984, p. 68.

can't... I found a much better IDF. It revived my soul."[60] His confidence in the IDF's capabilities grew during this period, and he was ready for action when he became defense minister in June 1967.

Dayan's Political Principles

Dayan's strategy, although unique, had consistent policy elements or principles.

On key national security issues, Dayan adopted Ben-Gurion's stance of ensuring superpower support for Israel, and very early considering it more beneficial to align with the West in the Cold War, despite the Zionist Labor Movement's socialist roots and popular support for the Soviet Union in many circles. Dayan's awareness of the superpowers' decisive role in the Middle East conflict, lacking when he was Chief of Staff, grew when he became defense minister. Although he was quite worried about possibly confronting the Soviets on the Syrian front during the Six-Day War, he decided to do so in order to gain US support, despite condemnations from many in Israel's intelligence community. In the War of Attrition, Dayan did not hesitate to confront the Soviets but understood the limits of Israel's power, particularly when Soviet intervention became massive. By 1973, his belief in the necessity of US support for Israel became so strong that he refused to authorize a preemptive strike.

During and after the Yom Kippur War, Dayan focused on securing US aid, believing that the key to peace settlements in the Middle East lay with the US administration. Sadat shared this interest, which helped advance the negotiations process with Egypt, as both countries wanted to expand US influence in the region at the expense of the Soviets.[61] Dayan's strategy differed from Weizman's more limited vision of negotiations without US involvement. "From the very first moment," Weizman wrote, "I was unhappy with the involvement of the United States."[62] On nuclear issues, Dayan, like Ben-Gurion, considered nuclear power as Israel's insurance policy against its conventional arms deficiency.

Throughout his career, Dayan grappled with two fundamental aspects of Israel's security doctrine: *basic security* – confronting the threat of comprehensive war by a coalition of Arab states – and *routine security*. To meet both, Israel has always engaged with various forms of deterrence, from denial to punishment. It was primarily Dayan who linked routine and basic security and formulated the principles of responses to threats, understanding that a decisive

---

[60] Yaakov Erez and Ilan Kfir, *Sihot im Moshe Dayan* (Hebrew), Ramat Gan: Massada, 1981, p. 46.
[61] For Dayan's approach to U.S. involvement, see Rubinstein, *Darkei shalom*, p. 222.
[62] Ezer Weizman, *Hakrav al hashalom* (Hebrew), Jerusalem: Idanim, 1981, p. 284.

response to routine security affects deterrence and basic security by demonstrating Israel's resolve. He wrote: "Our victories and defeats in skirmishes along and across the border are of great importance not only because of their effect on routine security but also – perhaps because of – their effect on the Arab assessment of Israel's strength and Israel's belief in its own strength."[63]

Dayan's perspective on the Jewish–Arab conflict evolved from a child's view of a biblical struggle between farmers and herders to a mature youth's recognition of it as a national, ethnic, and religious struggle between two communities over land. Despite the Palestinians' decisive defeat, they continued with an ongoing campaign of guerrilla warfare and terrorism, representing the main threat to routine security. An Arab military coalition, in contrast, represented an immediate existential threat, necessitating basic security measures. Israel's inability to secure a total victory whereby it could dictate its enemies' surrender, given the asymmetry in size, doomed it to continuous warfare, thus giving rise to the unwritten concept of deterrence – early-warning – decision. By the Yom Kippur War, other principles had been added, such as preemptive strikes and preventive war. In 1973, Dayan abandoned the preemptive strike principle, relying on the buffer zones and anticipated US support.

Dayan considered Egypt, the strongest Arab state, as the linchpin of the Arab coalition, believing that neutralizing Egypt could significantly reduce the threat to Israel's basic security. Dayan fought against Egypt in five wars; he focused the IDF's force building to face Egypt and strove for a treaty with Egypt that would change Israel's strategic balance 180 degrees. After Sadat was assassinated and shortly before his own death, Dayan urged Israel to do its utmost to maintain the peace with Egypt, viewing this as vital for Israel's security.

Following the Six-Day War, Israel found itself in control of the West Bank and Gaza Strip with their large Palestinian populations and facing growing Palestinian terrorism from Jordan and Lebanon. The Palestinian conflict once again became central to Israel security considerations. Dayan worked hard to resolve it, taking firm stances against terrorism, yet advocating for an "enlightened" occupation and championed "economic peace" as an incentive for cooperation among the Palestinians to prevent a popular uprising. He rejected the right wing's demand for annexation, understanding the inherent problems, while also supporting Jewish settlement in what he viewed as the Jews' historic homeland. He also believed Israel could not withdraw from the area because of its geostrategic importance. Rubinstein observed: "Dayan doesn't suggest a one-time, constant prescription, but rather a process to consistently examine three fundamental principles: the absence of foreign sovereignty of the western part of the land of Israel, the Jewish right to settlement, and security."[64]

---

[63] Moshe Dayan, "Pe'ulot tsva'iyot biymey shalom" (Hebrew, based on Lieutenant General Moshe Dayan's lecture to officers), *Maarakhot* 118–119 (April 1949), p. 54.
[64] Rubinstein, *Darkei shalom*, p. 222.

Dayan's solution was autonomy, which he tried to promote through the peace treaty with Egypt and later as a key idea of his independent political party. Despite failing, this vision is, ironically, the current de facto status quo, with the Palestinian Authority autonomously controlling parts of the occupied territories and the majority of the West Bank population, while Hamas is the ruler of a de facto state in the Gaza Strip. This imperfect solution seems to be the only viable one at the moment, just as Dayan proposed.

Natan Yanai, a political science professor and a close advisor to Dayan in the late 1980s, differentiated among four stages in Dayan's approach to the Israeli-Arab conflict. In the 1950s, his strategy was one of retaliation, escalation, and deterrence to stabilize borders and build military strength for use in the next round of warfare; this proved itself in 1956 and peaked in 1967. Following the decisive Six-Day War victory, Dayan moved to the second stage of seeking ways to stabilize control of the new territories while simultaneously using them as political bargaining chips. In the third stage, after the War of Attrition, Dayan supported normalization and reducing friction to minimize the conflict, even offering to withdraw from the Suez Canal. In the fourth stage, after the Yom Kippur War, Dayan sought to reach a peace agreement wherever possible, together with other arrangements elsewhere that could serve as foundations for future peace agreements.[65] Each of these strategies coexisted with his overall approach, and in any given period he would show preference for one or the other, depending on circumstances. Dayan believed that Israel could coexist with the Arab world. While Israel, he said, could never put its sword down, "it was obligated to choose not to live by the sword forever."[66]

Accordingly, in his last year, Dayan apparently stressed the importance of building good relations with the United States and preserving the peace with Egypt after Sadat and seeking compromise with the Palestinians without giving up Judea and Samaria but also without annexing them. This approach aimed at reducing the conflict with the Arab world as a whole, even amid the Islamic Revolution in Iran in 1979 and Iran's increasing influence.

Historical Memory and Legacy

It is impossible to avoid acknowledging the tragic dimension of Moshe Dayan. More than any other Israeli leader, he embodied the Zionist ideal of "the new Jew." His incomparable contribution to the IDF's force construction and might of the Jewish people in its own land is indisputable. He symbolized

---

[65] Natan Yanai (ed.), *Moshe Dayan al tahalikh hashalom ve'atida shel medinat yisrael: Dvarim biknasey habama leberurim medini'im vehevrati'im (1977–1981)* (Hebrew), Tel Aviv: Defense Ministry Publications, 1988, pp. 7–8, 14–16.

[66] Yanai (ed.), *Moshe Dayan*, p. 18, where he quotes Moshe Dayan at the September 10, 1977, Habama conference.

the success of the Zionist enterprise. Despite international admiration, he faced controversy and even hatred in his own beloved country.

Field Marshal Mohamed Abdel Ghani el-Gamasy claimed that the Yom Kippur War was a vendetta against Dayan. If so, it succeeded beyond all measure. Dayan's public and historical persona in Israel was never fully rehabilitated after the war, despite his key role in securing peace, and has become even more tarnished with the passage of time.

With his acute vision, Henry Kissinger clearly saw the tragic aspect of Dayan in his later years, likening Dayan's life to that of the biblical figure for whom he was named: Moses, who was only able to see the Promised Land but not allowed to enter it. Dayan never recovered from the Yom Kippur War, and in Kissinger's opinion, Dayan mistakenly failed to assume responsibility for what was perceived as the early debacles, even though the war ultimately ended with impressive achievements for Israel. Kissinger said that only in private conversation was it possible to see Dayan's profound frustration. In contrast to Golda Meir, who had in any case done what she could as prime minister, and unlike David Elazar, who was soon forgotten by the general public, Dayan remained haunted by his unrealized ambitions and his feeling that fateful events would unfold before he had fulfilled his destiny.[67]

The epitome of the tragedy of Dayan's life is his failure to complete his course of leadership and meet the expectations of him by becoming the first native-born prime minister of Israel. Ironically, that honor was achieved by Yitzhak Rabin, who had never appeared to harbor such ambitions and who seems to have recoiled from the political activity required to reach that pinnacle. While Dayan witnessed and contributed to peace with Egypt, perhaps the most important strategic event since Israel declared independence in 1948, Dayan did not live to see an end to the Israeli–Arab conflict, nor even a hint of any resolution to the Palestinian conflict. The first Intifada (1987–1993), the widespread popular uprising in the West Bank and Gaza Strip, broke out six years after his death. Following the Oslo Accords (1993), the PLO returned to the occupied territories and established Palestinian autonomy in the form of the Palestinian Authority. In 2005, Israel withdrew from the Gaza Strip, evacuating civilian settlements and withdrawing its troops. In 2007, the PLO was ousted from the Gaza Strip by the radical organization Hamas, which has been in control of that region ever since. On October 7, 2023, Hamas launched an attack on Israel, resulting in the deaths of approximately 1,200 people in Israel in a single day. In response, the Israeli military invaded Gaza. As of this writing, the conflict is ongoing.

Dayan's life and person are deeply intertwined with the era in which he lived, an era of great changes: he was born during World War I, and the major milestones in his life were World War II, the establishment of Israel, and Israel's wars. Like the nation he defended, everything was in flux, in the process of being established and

---

[67] Kissinger, *Years of Upheaval*, pp. 562–563.

shaped. More than anyone else, Dayan – the man and the life – reflected the soul of his era.

Dayan is commemorated in almost every city in Israel, with street, squares, sites, and military bases named for him. He remains one of the IDF's best Chiefs of Staff, and the Sinai Campaign is studied in military colleges. How, then, does one explain that much of the Israeli public has a negative opinion of him?

There are several reasons. The first is that his refusal to resign after the Yom Kippur War was seen as a way to avoid taking responsibility for the costly mistakes of judgment that had been made. As the Israeli public learned more about the level-headed functioning of David Elazar during the fighting, his image underwent rehabilitation over the years. Similarly, Golda Meir's public image in Israel was also damaged but recently was somewhat rehabilitated through new research, documentaries, and most of all the 2023 Hollywood drama *Golda* starring Helen Mirren. Public rage toward Dayan was further fueled by the perception that only those in uniform paid the price, while the politicians evaded any accountability. Dayan's alleged collusion with Kissinger in planning the war, in addition to other conspiracy theories, further sowed confusion in the public.

The second explanation lies in the psychological realm of projection, whereby people attribute the negative aspects of their own personality to those around them. After the Yom Kippur War, Israeli society underwent a similar process. As a result of the Six-Day War, Israeli society became marked by blindness, arrogance, and a sense of invincibility. In a collective process of projection and distancing itself from guilt following the shock of the Yom Kippur War, Israeli society sought a scapegoat, and Dayan fit the bill perfectly. Dayan, more than anyone else, exemplified the spirit of pride and complacency prevalent before the war in the collective consciousness of Israeli society; he, indeed, personified the spirit of those times. Dayan's laconic veneer, which hid an internal turbulence, was perceived by the public as indifference and cemented his image as cynical, conceited, and insensitive.

Dayan's public image suffered not only due to the Yom Kippur War but also due to changes in Israeli society. Disputes over who bore responsibility for the Yom Kippur War's failures and existing disagreements between the left and the right were amplified by the rise of the spirit of political correctness, and past acts were increasingly judged by present criteria. Thus, Dayan was accused of stealing antiquities from the state, and many have censured his numerous extramarital affairs, although it must be noted that he was never accused of sexual harassment (unlike other contemporaneous generals and politicians), and women who worked for him testified that he treated them with respect. An additional and related explanation is the rise of a cultural and academic elite in Israel that detests the machismo and militarism associated with Israeli society, denouncing it as aggressive, even belligerent. The voice of the New Historians has dominated the public discourse since the 1990s. They have reinterpreted Israeli history, lauding moderates like Moshe Sharett and Levi Eshkol, and have attacked Israel's official policy of the first decades of the nation's existence, a policy of which Dayan was one of the chief architects. His image was also tarnished by the extensively media-covered conflict between Dayan's children and Rachel, Dayan's second wife, over his estate, and the fact that both his sons, Udi and Assi, publicly excoriated Dayan for his failures as a father.

Perhaps a key reason for his negative image lies with his internally contradictory strategic worldview, because of which he was not accepted into the folds of the left or the right, falling right through the cracks. The right never forgave him for opposing annexation and for having given the keys to the Temple Mount to the Muslim Waqf, while the left never forgave him for opposing a Palestinian state in the West Bank and Gaza Strip and for supporting Jewish settlement there. In the political reality of Israel, not belonging definitively to one camp or the other condemns one to a political vacuum without support from anyone and exposed to criticism from everyone. Apparently, most people identify their leaders by clearly defined categories. Thus, Shimon Peres and Yitzhak Rabin are clearly identified with the Zionist left because they strove for a peace settlement that included territorial concessions, whereas Menachem Begin and Benjamin Netanyahu are darlings of the right. Ariel Sharon was a hero to the right until he initiated the disengagement from the Gaza Strip, whereupon he became highly controversial. Dayan was never a member of either camp in a clear, definitive way and was therefore labeled an opportunist.

In his later years, Dayan wrote, "The future of Israel's borders has been closest to my heart since the establishment of the state. What will today's Israel be like?"[68] Despite the pointlessness of any "what if," it is difficult to imagine what Dayan would have thought of Israel now. One may speculate that he would have been awestruck by the demographic, economic, and technological developments that have taken place in Israel in the four decades since his death. He would have been pleased by the special relations that have been forged with the United States and its solid support for Israel; he would have been satisfied that the peace with Egypt has remained stable and that Israel also has peace treaties with Jordan, Bahrain, Morocco, and the UAE; and he would have rejoiced in the normalization agreement with Sudan and the current direct contacts with Saudi Arabia. He approved of the Jewish settlement blocks in Judea and Samaria and would have been pleased that the Palestinians have self-rule. One can assume he would have been disturbed by the protective fence system Israel built between Israel and the occupied territories to defend against terrorist attacks, because he believed in coexistence; by Iran and its nuclear project; and by Hezbollah, Hamas, the radicalization of both Palestinian and

---

[68] Moshe Dayan, *Lihyot et hatanakh* (Hebrew), 1st ed., Jerusalem: Idanim, 1978, 5th ed. published by Yedioth Ahronoth, Tel Aviv, 1986, p. 202.

Israeli society, and the lack of any solution to the conflict on the horizon. However, this is all speculation. Perhaps Dayan, blessed with original analytical skills, would have reached different conclusions about some of these issues.

Today, it is difficult to see senior generals leaving their calendars blank for days on end, spontaneously visiting troops, preferring a modest office with a simple desk covered by an army blanket, and lying in ambush with the rank and file, as did Dayan. It is now also impossible to engage in any of those proscribed acts Dayan then allowed himself in a world less restricted by codes of conducts. The organizational and legal environment in which leaders operate today is much more complicated and rigid on many levels and laden with many more rules and regulations than in Dayan's era. However, adopting Dayan's leadership principles – following a contextualized learning process, applying the 80:20 principle for setting priorities, delegating and empowering, managing time for maximum flexibility, using meetings to generate and test new ideas, and, lastly, striving to be close to the action – can serve as an invaluable blueprint for today's leaders. There is much to learn from Dayan, and today's leaders can take inspiration from his methods.

It is most fitting to conclude this book with the last paragraph of Dayan's book *Living with the Bible*, in which he beautifully expressed his inner conflict between heart and mind, his ability to hold two opposing points of view simultaneously, and above all his love for the land of Israel:

> During the planning stage to devise a proposal for our borders with the Arab states I would spend days with our army commanders reconnoitering the fronts, our minds intent on military and political considerations – separation of Arab and Jewish zones, lines of fortification, observation posts, passable tracks through the desert. But with dusk, in the helicopter on my way home, all these considerations vanished. Beneath me as we flew was a land without division between Arab and Jew; a land strewn with villages and cities, fields and gardens; a land bounded in the east by the river Jordan and in the west by the Great Sea, crowned in the north by the snowy peak of Mount Hermon, sealed in the south by the parched wilderness. One land. The Land of Israel.[69]

---

[69] Moshe Dayan, *Living with the Bible*, New York: William Morrow & Company, 1978, p. 227.

INDEX

Abdullah, King, 48, 85, 86
Abeidat, Abed, 26
Abu Jildah. *See* Dayan, Moshe
Acre Prison, 36, 40, 41, 47, 393
Adan, Avraham (Bren), 331, 332, 349, 362, 369, 370, 371
Agranat Commission, 236, 314, 315, 364, 373, 374
Agranat, Shimon, 373
al-Agassi, Nureddin, 227
al-Assad, Bashar, 8
al-Assad, Hafez, 259, 385
Alexander the Great, 7
Alexandroni Brigade, 56
Alfasi, Shimon, 81
al-Gamasy, Muhammad Abdel Ghani, 296, 357, 361, 437
Algeria, 140, 141, 254
Algerian Revolution, 123
Allon, Yigal, 48, 60, 66, 67, 69, 71, 72, 73, 75, 92, 208, 250, 265, 412, 416
Alpha Program, 121
al-Qassam, Adib, 72
al-Tal, Abdullah, 48, 82, 83–84, 85, 87
Alterman, Natan, 22
AMAN. *See* IDF Military Intelligence; IDF Military Intelligence
Amit, Meir, 101, 133, 134, 148, 157, 176, 177, 192, 209, 239, 429
Andronowitz, Nicholas, 83
Arab Revolt, 110
Arafat, Yasser, 250, 257, 385
Armistice Agreements, 84, 85, 87, 90, 99, 103
armistice talks, 48
Arnan, Avraham, 52
art of strategy, 4

Ashkenazi, Motti, 372, 373
Atherton, Alfred, 392, 396, 398
Atomic Energy Commission, 414
Auftragstaktik. See mission command
Avidan, Shimon, 43, 75, 76, 77
Ayalon, Tsvi, 80, 96, 97
Azaryahu, Arnan (Sinai), 416
Azrieli, David, 41

Baghdad Pact, 138
Balfour Declaration, 21
Barak, Aharon, 394, 396, 401
Bareket, Shaikeh, 206
Barker, Barker, Evelyn Hugh, 37
Barnoach-Matalon, Neora, 100, 126, 233, 428, 430, 432
Bar-On, Mordechai, 104, 116, 152, 174, 178, 243, 422, 424, 428
Bar-On, Uri, 56
Bartov, Hanoch, 367, 374
basic security, 102, 103, 174, 190, 434, 435. *See* routine security
Battle of Stalingrad, 59
Baum, Abraham J., 57–59, 63
Begin, Menachem
  a 21-point plan for Palestinian autonomy, 388
  and Moshe Dayan, 42
  and revolt against Britain, 41
  asking Moshe Dayan to join his government, 379–381
  fighting the IDF, 55
  meetings with President Carter, 389–390
Ben, Aluf, 106
Ben-Ari, Uri, 97, 98, 149, 163, 166, 167

INDEX

Ben-Gurion
  views on the IDF as a military institution, 421
Ben-Gurion, Amos, 53
Ben-Gurion, David
  and Dayan's advancement, 48
  and Nasser, 119
  and the 22nd World Zionist Congress, 43
  criticism of the charge on Lod, 72
  Dayan and mutual influence, 89
  Dayan's political and diplomatic skills, 88
  decision on Dayan as the leader of the IDF, 422
  defense of Jerusalem, 64
  Israel's national security concept, 101
  Jerusalem command, 75, 78
  Rafi Party, 197
  views on nuclear capabilities, 411
  Zionist General Council, 43
Ben-Hur (Cohen), Eliyahu, 78
Bergman, Ronen, 417
Berlin, Isaiah, 18, 424
Bismarck, Otto von, 4
Black September, 258, 377
bomb in the basement policy, 415
Book of Splendor, 424
Bourgès-Maunoury, Maurice, 141, 146, 151, 411
Boutros-Ghali, Boutros, 386
Braun, Arie, 221, 229, 328
Bresner, Amiad, 132, 186
Brezhnev, Leonid, 209
British Mandate, 37, 44
Broida, Alex, 82
Bronfeld, Shaul, 132
Brzeziński, Zbigniew, 378, 384, 394, 395, 396–397, 398
Bull, Odd, 230–232
Burg, Yosef, 406

Cairo conference, 388
Carmel, Moshe, 36, 49, 146
Carter, Jimmy
  and setting up the Camp David Accords, 393
  as new US president, 378–379
  meetings with Dayan, 389

Ceaușescu, Nicolae, 385
Chalk plan, 319
Challe, Maurice, 125, 146, 150, 151, 152, 153, 154
Chechanover, Yosef, 428
Churchill, Winston, 16, 17, 212, 367, 433
Clausewitz, Carl von, 11, 12, 13, 16, 30, 108, 164, 182, 234
Cohen, Avner, 416
Cohen, Mula, 66–67, 74, 75
command of a theater, 159
coup d'œil, 16
Creveld, Martin van, 10, 66, 180, 240, 370
Cuban Missile Crisis, 417
Cyprus, 145, 162

Dado. *See* Elazar, David
Dani Operation, 71
Davar (newspaper), 70
Dayan, Assaf, 41
Dayan, Devorah, 21
Dayan, Moshe
  "Cold Water Speech," 286, 426
  "Israel Will Act with Force" speech, 290
  and ministerial advice, 369
  and some empathy toward the Arabs, 46
  and the 89th Battalion, 48, 49
  armored revolution, 132
  as a *moshavnik*, 40
  as Director of the General Staff Directorate, 131
  guerrilla and counterinsurgency warfare, 34
  IDF's military culture, 171
  irregular warfare, 29
  leadership, 366–367
  Moshe Dayan Network, 40–41
  policy of reprisals, 420
  public perception, 2
Dayan, Rachel, 439
Dayan, Ruth, 28, 40, 82
Dayan, Shmuel, 21
Dayan, Udi, 41, 439
Dayan, Yael, 41
Dayan, Zohar (Zorik), 45

Diffre, Thadée. *See* Eytan, Teddy
Dinitz, Simcha, 341, 346
directed binocular, 371.
    See directed telescopes
directed telescopes, 371. *See* directed binocular
Dixon, Norman, 93
Dori, Yaakov, 29, 30, 31, 36, 43, 47
Drake, Spencer, 420
Dromi, Yosef, 27
Duke of Wellington, 232

Eban, Abba, 192, 208, 209, 210, 211, 229, 341
Eden, Anthony, 144, 155, 157
Eisenhower, Dwight, 78, 92, 137, 160
Elazar, David
    and the 146th Division, 322
    Dayan and fighting Egypt, 321
    ongoing fighting plans, 323
    public image, 374
    strategy for the stalemate, 335
    three southern actions plans, 329
Elron, Ze'ev, 120, 121, 132
Erel, Shlomo, 205, 267–268
escalation dominance, 260
Eshkol, Levi, 261, 266
    and General Staff generals, 204–205
    as the prime minister, 196
    criticism of Dayan's role during the Six-Day War, 194–195
    Dayan, and deterrence, 414
    dispute over Dayan's appointment as defense minister, 206–207
    stuttering speech, 204
    US nuclear inspection, 413
Etzel, 41, 42, 43, 44, 47
Eytan, Teddy, 61

Falk, Avner, 207
Farhoud, 41
Fedayeen, 106, 110, 115, 121, 122, 162, 172, 174
Fefferman, Hillel, 79, 80
Feinerman, Uzi, 226
Ferro, Marc, 16, 17
Fingerspitzengefühl, 16. *See* coup d'œil

First Intifada, 251, 437. *See* Second Intifada
First Oslo Agreement, 400
Fitzgerald, F. Scott, 18
Foreign Affairs, 104
forward command, 178, 180, 183. *See* mission command
Frederick the Great, 16
Freier, Shalhevet, 416, 417
Fuller, John Frederick, 30

Gaddis, John Lewis, 18, 424
Galili, Israel, 42, 44, 329
game theory, 98
Gaulle, Charles de, 209, 266
Gavish, Yeshayahu, 196, 201, 202, 204, 207, 301
Gazit, Shlomo, 126, 128, 158, 176, 177, 180, 183, 248, 427, 428, 429
Geneva Conference, 300, 362, 381, 382, 383, 384, 385, 386, 388
Ginat, Rami, 119
Gladwell, Malcolm, 17
Glinka, Shmuel, 168
Glubb, John Bagot, 60, 104, 140, 143
Golan, Shimon, 312, 327
Gonen, Shmuel, 202, 315, 319, 326–327, 332, 368
grand strategy, 7, 9, 19
Granek, Yaakov, 78
Gray, Colin S., 8, 10, 13, 282
Guderian, Heinz Wilhelm, 71, 180
Gur, Mordechai (Motta), 185, 377, 378

Haaretz, 106, 242, 291
Habama, 407, 408, 409
Habinsky, Nahum, 27
Hacohen, Gershon, 425
Hadassah Hospital, 27, 39, 40
Haganah, 27, 28, 30, 31, 35, 36, 37, 38, 41, 44
Hakel, Muhammad Hassin, 162
Halutz, Dan, 91
Hamas, 190, 260, 436, 437, 439
Hamel, Gary, 15
Hanhana, Wahash, 23
Harari, Yehuda, 116
Harel, Yosef, 57
Harkaby, Yehoshua, 141

INDEX

Harkavi, Yehoshafat, 86
Har-Zion, Meir, 114, 143
Henkin, Yagil, viii, 100, 101, 191
Hezbollah, 190, 254, 259, 260
Hindenburg, Paul von, 181
Hod, Mordechai, 233, 283, 368
Hofi, Yitzhak (Haka), 170, 308, 323, 365
Huntington, Samuel, 421
Hussein, King, 140, 144, 174, 205, 214, 216, 218, 222, 223, 255, 257, 308, 381
Hussein–Nasser agreement, 207
Hut, The, 22

IAF Intelligence Department, 206
IDF Military Intelligence
    assessment of Egypt's surprise attack, 306, 309, 310
    conception, the, 309–310
    King Hussein and President Nasser phone conversation, 216
Irgun, 55–56
Ismail, Hafez, 305
Israel's security doctrine, 104, 375, 434.
    See basic security; routine security

Jabotinsky, Ze'ev, 105
Jarring, Gunnar, 278, 285, 286, 287
Jewish Agency, 31, 37, 40, 41, 43, 44
Jibli, Yitzhak, 129
Johnson, Lyndon B., 204, 206, 209, 239, 413

Kabalan, Ismail, 45
Kabbalah, 424
Kadesh 2, 157, 158–159, 163, 171
Kadesh plan, 149. *See* Kadesh 2
Kamel, Ibrahim, 398
Karpin, Michael, 416
Keightley, Charles, 144
Kennedy, John F., 412
Khartoum summit, 297
Kimmerling, Baruch, 106
Kissinger, Henry
    and the preemptive strike, 305
    on Dayan, 426
    the Soviets and ceasefire, 349
Kitchen Cabinet, 306, 329, 339, 340, 342, 349, 350, 368, 416, 417
Klein, Elhanan, 282

Kochba, Bar, 407
Kollek, Teddy, 57
Kosygin, Alexei, 346, 347

Labor Unity Movement, 42
Landau, Moshe, 373
Laskov, Haim, 142, 179, 184, 186, 192
Lau, Naftali, 378
Lavon Affair, 137, 197, 373
Lavon, Pinchas, 121, 134, 411
Lev, Raphael, 36
Levkov, Haim, 50, 128
Lewis, Sam, 390, 396, 397
Liddell Hart, Basil Henry, 7, 30, 191
Life magazine, 82
Likud Party, 379, 407
Lloyd, Selwyn, 152, 154, 155
Logan, Donald, 152
Ludendorff, Erich, 181
Luttwak, Edward, 10, 116, 143, 159

Maalot disaster, 378
Maarakhot, 66, 73, 74
Mafdal Party, 406
Maklef, Mordechai, 99, 100, 101, 113, 114, 127, 135, 429
mamlachtiut, 42
maneuverist approach, 167
Mao Tse-Tung, 6
Mapai Party, 43, 47, 197
Marcus, David Daniel (Mickey), 56, 57
Marcus, Yoel, 380
Marshall, George, 92
Mart, Zalman, 39, 80
Marwan, Zamir (Ashraf), 306, 310, 311, 312, 315, 317
Mass, Dani, 60
Matkal, Sayeret, 52, 377
McNamara, Robert, 209, 239
Meir, Golda
    and Dayan, 261
    and Dayan's suggestions prior to the Yom Kippur war, 286–288
    and Eshkol's political influence, 284
Mellenthin, Friedrich von, 181
Mem-Gimmel, 36, 38, 40, 47
military strategy, 8
Milley, Mark, 13
Mintzberg, Henry, 14

INDEX

Mirren, Helen, 374
mission command, 13, 71, 180, 181, 371. *See* forward command
Mollet, Guy, 141, 151, 189, 411
Moltke the Elder, Helmuth von, 11–13, 181
Montgomery, Bernard Law, 191, 237, 238
Morris, Benny, 118
moshav, 21, 25, 61, 129
Munich Olympic Games, 377
Muslim Brotherhood, 410

Nahshonim Order, 213
Napoleon, 7, 10, 51, 78, 232
Narkiss, Uzi, 94, 95, 96, 97, 177, 194, 205, 218, 235, 252
Nasser, Gamal Abdul
  and the West, 139–140
  Dayan's assessment of Nasser's policy objectives, 142
Nebenzahl, Yitzchak, 373
Negev Brigade, 55, 75
Nelson, Horatio, 193
Netanyahu, Benjamin, 3, 439
Netanyahu, Yoni, 377, 407
Neville, René, 83
Nevo, Yaakov, 285
New York Times, 238, 417
Night of the Ducks, 312
Nixon, Richard, 259, 287, 334, 342
Notrim, 28
Nusseiba, Anwar, 419

Operation Caucasus, 274
Operation Challenge, 323
Operation Danny, 60, 71
Operation Dogman, 314, 325
Operation Gaza, 106
Operation Headbutt, 314
Operation Iraqi Freedom, 59
Operation Kavkaz, 274
Operation Lulav, 144
Operation Moked (Focus), 213
Operation Musketeer, 144, 146
Operation Nachshon, 16
Operation Nickel Grass, 342
Operation Priha (Blossom), 273
Operation Tagar (Challenge), 321

Operation Tarnegol (Rooster), 160
Operation Thunderbolt, 377
Operation Uvda, 86
Operation Volcano, 107
Operation Yarkon, 122, 123
Operations Branch, 203
Oren, Michael, 5, 18, 424
Oslo Accords, 437

Palestine Liberation Organization, 254, 257, 377, 381, 383, 384, 386, 437
Palestine Post, The, 84
Palestinian National Council, 257
Pareto principle, 427–428
Pasha, Glubb. *See* Glubb, John Bagot
Patton, George, 57, 71, 180, 237
Peled, Benny, 318, 320, 321, 323, 334, 336, 338, 340, 350, 367, 377
Pelly, Claude, 144
Peltz, Yohanan, 53, 55, 61–65, 70
Peres, Shimon
  Dayan and the Operation Thunderbolt, 377
  Israel's nuclear power, 411, 412
  Labor Party's leadership, 379
  map of the Sinai Peninsula, 156
  relationship with France, 123, 124, 139, 141
  St. Germain Conference, 146
personality school, 188. *See* structural school
PFLP. *See* Popular Front for the Liberation of Palestine
Pineau, Christian, 146, 151, 155, 157
PLO. *See* Palestine Liberation Organization
policy of ambiguity, 413, 414, 415, 417
policy of escalation, 281
Popular Front for the Liberation of Palestine, 255, 258, 377
Prahalad, C. K., 15

Qassamiya movement, 24
Quandt, William, 385, 389, 392, 395, 396

Rabi, Uzi, 1
Rabin government, 376

INDEX

Rabin, Yitzhak
  as chief of staff, 196
  as the Training Directorate Director, 130
  Dayan and the ceasefire during the Six-Day War, 216
  first term as prime minister, 376
  military build up prior to the Six-Day War, 208
  Sinai 2 Agreement, 376
  Southern Command, 92–93
Rebel Movement, 43
Red Army, 76, 283
Reshef, Amnon, 347
Riyad, Abdul Manam, 270
Rogers Plan, 272, 276, 278, 279, 287.
  See Rogers, William P.
Rogers, William P., 272, 278, 285
Rommel, Erwin, 9, 10, 38, 41, 71, 180, 237
Rosen, Meir, 382
Rostow, Walt W., 206, 239
Rotberg, Roi, 104
routine security, 100, 102–103, 135, 174, 190, 434, 435. *See* basic security
Rubinstein, Elyakim, 373, 381, 392, 401, 410, 425, 435
Rumsfeld, Donald, 59
Rusk, Dean, 229

sabra, 2
Sadeh, Yitzhak, 52, 53, 56, 61, 68, 71, 420
Saison, 41, 42, 75
Schein, Edgar, 125
Schlesinger, James, 342
Second Intifada, 117. *See* First Intifada
Sereni, Enzo, 41
Shafir, Herzl, 300
Shaham, Mishael, 113
Shaltiel, David, 65, 78, 82
Shapira, Anita, 67, 70
Shapira, Moshe, 228
Sharett, Moshe, 87, 106, 107, 130, 134, 135, 138, 175, 438
Sharon, Ariel
  and merged forces, 116–117
  and terrorists in the Gaza Strip, 247
  commando Unit 101, 113–114
  Gonen, 332
  Mitla Pass, 169–171
  Northern Command, 98–99
  public perception, 439
Shemen, Ben, 61, 64, 69, 74
Shiloah, Reuven, 84
Shimron group, 33
Shimshoni, Jonathan, 109
Shlaim, Avi, 87, 189
Shlonksy, Avraham, 22
Shoval, Zalman, 406, 407, 423, 428
Simhoni, Assaf, 164–166, 171, 172
Simpkin, Richard, 3
Sisco, Joseph, 257, 277, 290, 291
Slater, Robert, 367, 395
Smilansky, Moshe, 23
St. Germain Conference, 146
Stalin, Joseph, 16, 17
Stern Gang. *See* Lehi
strategic depth, 298
strategic intent, 15. *See* Prahalad, C. K.; and Hamel, Gary
structural school, 188.
  See personality school

Tahar, Rashid, 27, 39
Tal, Israel, 71
Telem Party, 409, 417
Teveth, Shabtai, 22, 40, 42, 56, 61, 66, 67, 87, 92, 95, 111, 197, 243, 426
Tolkovsky, Dan, 151
Touhami, Hassan, 382, 385, 387
Tsur, Tsvi, 54, 93, 212, 224, 266, 311, 414, 429

ummah, 23
UN Security Council
  and ceasefire during the Six-Day War, 220, 222, 229
  anti-Egyptian resolutions, 138
  Resolution 242, 279, 286, 289, 346, 350
United Labor Movement, 42
US Marine Corps, 113

Vance, Cyrus, 378, 382, 383, 384, 391, 392, 396, 398, 402–404
Vichy regime, 38

Wallach, Yehuda, 148
Wehrmacht, 59, 148
Weitzman, Ezer, 188
Weizmann, Haim, 31
Wilkinson, Spencer, 181
Wingate, Orde Charles, 32–35, 36, 46, 71, 110, 420
Workers' Party. *See* Mapai Party
World War I, 21, 30, 78, 437
World War II, 35, 43, 58, 95, 124, 180, 210, 437

Yaakobi, Gad, 428, 433
Yadin, Yigal, 43, 75, 78, 88, 92, 96, 98, 99, 135, 206, 214, 328, 373
Yanai, Natan, 436
Yariv, Aharon, 127, 212, 224, 227, 272, 328, 356, 367, 426
Yermiya, Dov, 32

Yiftach Brigade, 50, 66, 68, 72, 74, 75
Yishuv, 38, 41, 43, 44, 110
Yisraeli, Hayim, 428
Young Turks, 42, 47

Zaid, Giora, 45
Zalmanovitch, Boaz, 74
Zeevi, Rehavam, 93, 170, 176, 193, 221, 328
Zeira, Eli, 305, 306, 307, 309, 311, 313, 315, 365, 373
Zemer, Hannah, 336
zero-sum game, 6, 196
Zionism, 1, 21, 422
Zionist Federation, 31
Zionist General Council.
    See Ben-Gurion, David
Zippori, Mordechai, 203
Zorea, Meir, 79, 179, 186

For EU product safety concerns, contact us at Calle de José Abascal, 56–1°,
28003 Madrid, Spain or eugpsr@cambridge.org.